Brutes in Suits

GENDER RELATIONS IN THE AMERICAN EXPERIENCE

Joan E. Cashin and Ronald G. Walters, Series Editors

Brutes in Suits

Male Sensibility in America, 1890–1920

JOHN PETTEGREW

The Johns Hopkins University Press
Baltimore

The Johns Hopkins University Press
2715 North Charles Street
Baltimore, Maryland 21218-4363
www.press.jhu.edu

Library of Congress Cataloging-in-Publication Data
Pettegrew, John, 1959–
Brutes in suits : male sensibility in America, 1890–1920 / John Pettegrew.
p.   cm.
Includes bibliographical references and index.
ISBN-13: 978-0-8018-8603-4 (hardcover : alk. paper)
ISBN-10: 0-8018-8603-1 (hardcover : alk. paper)
1. Sex role—United States—History. 2. Masculinity—United States—History.
I. Title.
HQ1090.3.P49 2007
305.31.—dc22   2006025984

A catalog record for this book is available from the British Library.

For Helen and Nick

CONTENTS

In completing this study, I've come to view masculinity as a type of cultural disease—a contagion that spreads through the communication of ideas as well as through the transference of emotional and cognitive disposition. This pathological model may in some ways resemble post–Civil War elites' assumptions about the origins of male aggressiveness and violence. But, as I describe and criticize in the pages that follow, late nineteenth- and early twentieth-century American thought predominantly represented brutish masculinity as an instinct—an innate, biologically transferred trait of male human beings. Measuring the difference between instinct and contagion is the analytical purpose of *Brutes in Suits*. I understand hypermasculinity to be a self-perpetuated and half-understood sickness, one that debilitates men even as it empowers them over women and other men. Masculinity as contagion helps us see the de-evolutionary impulse as a contingent cultural and psychological accretion rather than some sort of preordained return to a natural or essential state of being. Contagion incorporates a historical sensibility that recognizes the hegemonic power of gender while affirming human capacity for resisting mental habit, social inequality, and patterns of violence. Masculinity is an educative process, I argue, its de-evolutionary variant a matter of learning to be instinctive.

I'm happy to have the opportunity to recognize the many debts I have accrued over the course of this long-term project.

Before beginning my formal study of masculinity, I developed an appreciation for learning, inquiry, and relativism from my parents, Fred Pettegrew and Mary Pettegrew. Grandparents Muriel Pettegrew and Percy Pettegrew shared with me, among many other things, the joys of historical argument and of the Horicon Marsh. Aunt Jean Lindemann and grandmother Lu Spidell generously supported me throughout my education. And, outside of my family, Buzz Berg led me to intellectual history and the Progressive Era while providing a model of a committed college history teacher.

This study began as a Ph.D. dissertation at the University of Wisconsin–Madison, and it is to that institution and my friends, teachers, and colleagues there that I owe the largest debt. The library of the State Historical Society of Wisconsin facilitated my research and writing. Fellow graduate students Jennifer Frost, Mark Koerner, Samantha Langbaum, Andrew Rieser, Landon Storrs, Paul Taillon, and Rafael Vela made early contributions to my understanding of U.S. manhood. Special thanks to Glen Gendzel and Paul Schuck for their good humor, critical intelligence, and high sociability. I also received assistance from a number of faculty members, including Jeanne Boydston, Carl Kaestle, Tom Schaub, Stanley Schultz, Richard Sewell, and David Zonderman.

Before leaving Madison I had the pleasure of meeting two of Wisconsin's most esteemed historians. Several lunches with George Mosse sharpened my understanding of manhood in relationship to nationalism, war, and sexuality. And one of the real high points of my graduate training was to become friends with Merle Curti. His reading of my Turner material and other work, our discussions of pragmatism (which included his personal reminiscences of Dewey), and his constantly probing questions in conversation all proved invaluable to me.

Since my first days in Madison, Hendrik Hartog was a constant source of support and learning. The original idea that underlies this study and was first advanced in my dissertation emerged from discussions with him, and through every step of the dissertation he offered his time, enthusiasm, and considerable historical imagination.

I can't imagine having completed this study without Paul Boyer's extraordinary talents as intellectual historian, editor, and adviser. His teaching and scholarship have been absolutely exemplary, and, since leaving Madison, I have only come to appreciate more his writing, integrity, and friendship.

In beginning the long transition from dissertation to book manuscript, I benefited greatly from a critical and intelligent reading of my work by Elliott Gorn. A summer at Stanford University's Institute for Research on Women and Gender provided a wonderful opportunity for reopening and recalibrating my thoughts on manhood around feminist history and theory; Stanford's Green Library and Special Collections and Archives were extremely helpful in my work on college football. Also important during this middle period was Patrick Miller, whose close attention to my work sharpened my analysis of sports, culture, and masculinity. Carl Degler bestowed very timely guidance in my understanding of Darwinism and gender. And at a crucial point in this study, I benefited from generous readings by David Leverenz and Jim Livingston.

Thanks are due to the Johns Hopkins University Press for sticking with me through the long slog of revision; Bob Brugger's assertive patience and seasoned guidance have been just what I needed; and thanks also to Amanda Slaybaugh for her careful attention to readying the manuscript for production.

I owe a lot to Lehigh University and its overall support over the past several years. Franz and Class of 1968 summer research awards as well as faculty research grants have been very much appreciated. Lehigh's libraries, special collections, and interlibrary loan office have all been crucial to completing this book; Pat Ward, Phil Metzger, Ilhan Citak, and Steve Lichak have been most helpful. Sandy McLaughlin helped me prepare the manuscript and illustrations for final submission. And Christianne Gadd has been great in final preparation of the endnotes.

My colleagues in Lehigh's History Department have provided a comfortable and attentive environment for scholarly work; Steve Cutcliffe's brown bag lunch series has been a wonderful forum for honing my thought and writing. Bill Shade and Tricia Turner provided smart, helpful readings of early chapter drafts. And thanks to Mike Baylor, Gail Cooper, Steve Cutcliffe, Monica Najar, Jim Saeger, John Savage, Bill Scott, Roger Simon, and Jean Soderlund for their questions, suggestions, and general intellectual and collegial support.

Thanks to Alex Levine for sharing both his knowledge of Darwin and his pizza. Adriana Novoa's friendship and historical understanding of masculinity have been crucial to me—her critical reading of the first chapter added almost another year to my work but made the final draft, I think, that much better. And while Seth Moglen charitably abstained from reading one word of this study, our many long discussions about history, gender, culture, and psychoanalysis have undoubtedly added to the book and its author's well-being.

Finally, I owe this study's title and a great deal more to Dawn Keetley—generous and gifted critic, and nearly constant intellectual companion. Thanks. As for Helen Keetley and Nick Pettegrew, you've done more than you know or I could say, and it is for you finally teaching me that there are far more important things than work that I dedicate this book.

Brutes in Suits

The De-Evolutionary Turn in U.S. Masculinity

"My mind-set has shifted from the intellectual to the animal," Timothy McVeigh wrote to his sister in February 1995, two months before bombing the Oklahoma City Federal building: "I want to rip the bastards' heads off."[1] This book locates the modern origins of such thinking in late nineteenth- and early twentieth-century masculinity. The broad spectrum of masculine psychology and self-understanding are not examined here; there is little about friendship, fatherhood, and other benign aspects of male identity. Instead, I focus on the institutional formulation of a particular mind-set, as McVeigh called it, a pathology that bifurcates thinking into realms of reason and instinct and, in turn, leads to a regressive sequence from conscious control to animalistic aggressiveness. Structuring this masculinist psychology has been the zoomorphic attribution of animal traits to masculine thought, emotion, and behavior—an attribution that necessarily entails anthropomorphic reading of animal character. As can be seen in McVeigh's mass-murderous example, the interpretive loop between animal and human male psychology culminates in violence, or at least a predisposition toward brutality. And, yet, de-evolutionary masculinity, I argue, has not been limited to a psychotic few but has been a common denominator among men living in the United States. It certainly can be subdued, tempered, and rejected—out of hand; but reflexive aggressiveness has been a starting point for many men. It has enjoyed normative psychological status.

To some extent my claim of normativity for de-evolutionary psychology goes against the grain of current scholarship on masculinity as a system of competing codes, subject positions, and sexualities.[2] My study does not eschew heterogeneity, however. Multiple masculinities are considered, among other places, in chapter 5 on heterosexuality and the law. Overall, though, I am unorthodoxly interested less in difference than in a masculinist commonality: brutishness and its relationship to violence. While renewing itself as a dominant masculine standard, brutishness hardly achieved universal status among post–Civil War U.S. men. Though a prevalent state of mind, devolution did not engage even the most aggressive of men throughout their waking hours. Best to think of it, I contend, as a disposition that, because of its toxicity, can also be analyzed as a pathology, contagion, or disease—although, as brutishness spread through modern culture, men did not take it on unwittingly or without advantage. Recognizing variant norms of manhood is crucial, but that approach doesn't cover all important historical questions regarding gender and masculinity. De-evolutionary masculinity's racial, class, and ethnic origins in modern America; its effectiveness in homosocial and male-female relations; and its close intellectual ties to human understanding of animal instinct: these matters receive primary attention in the following pages.

Zoomorphism wasn't new to turn-of-the-twentieth-century U.S. masculinity. The history of American manhood includes countless examples of exaggerating one's strength and ferocity through comparisons to wildlife. Backcountry brawlers in the antebellum South, for instance, liked to crow about their beastly fighting prowess, as in the celebrated Mike Fink's tall talk: "I'm half wild horse and half-cock-eyed alligator."[3] What sets post–Civil War masculinity apart is Darwinism and its evolutionary connection between man and beast: humans not only descended from the ape, but they also inherited mental characteristics from animals, traits that informed their behavior through instinct. Darwinism pointed masculinity backward in time. Indeed, de-evolutionary masculinity has been a radically historical enterprise. Set within the broad intellectual context of evolutionary thought, and drawing from Darwinian biology for explanatory metaphor as well as scientific knowledge, the cultural construction of this dominant strain of masculinity worked back constantly to the imagined origins of maleness in its early human and animal forms. As the naturalist novelist Frank Norris wrote about early twentieth-century men's literature, "The great wonder is this unerring groping backward toward the fundamentals, in order to take a renewed grip upon life."[4] What many American men took to be the "fundamentals" of masculinity, and what psychological and behavioral strategies they developed to realize these forms, are also central concerns of this book.

Darwin said an awful lot about masculinity and its origins. In proposing in *The Descent of Man* (1871) that human male and female reproductive roles determined their respective "mental dispositions," Darwin launched the evolutionary psychology of sex difference, a powerful and still active line of sociobiological reasoning that characterizes such traits as feminine nurturing and masculine aggressiveness as inherited and fixed rather than socially constructed and variable.[5] In contrast, I advance a feminist view of masculinity as a mind-set developed through language, habit, and knowledge and therefore remediable through those same cultural forms. As the anthropologist Gayle Rubin has reminded us, the source and cause of masculine domination "form the basis for any assessment of just what would have to be changed in order to achieve a society without gender hierarchy." Her classic second-wave feminist tract "The Traffic in Women" (1975) opens practically: "if innate male aggression and dominance are at the root of female oppression, then the feminist program would logically require either extermination of the offending sex, or else a eugenics project to modify its character." Rubin's ameliorative impulse is edifying, especially in locating masculine domination in the "sex/gender system" and not in instinct.[6] It suggests a certain pragmatic approach to mediating evolutionary psychology and cultural history, one that recognizes the possibility of biological influence on cognitive and emotional differences between the sexes but sees a focus on patriarchy, gender, and the habits of mind that reproduce sexual inequality as more critically productive.

In addition to introducing this study's component parts, what follows here is a brief for drawing a narrow time frame for analyzing de-evolutionary masculinity. Simply put, sociobiology and evolutionary psychology don't place enough value on human agency and recent history. "Why imagine that specific genes for aggression, dominance, or spite have any importance," the paleontologist and evolutionary theorist Stephen Jay Gould wrote in criticism of the position, "when we know that the brain's enormous flexibility permits us to be aggressive or peaceful, dominant or submissive, spiteful or generous?"[7] Masculinity is a contingent habit of mind, I contend, whose turn-of-the-century American proponents self-consciously used Darwinian biology to classify brutishness as an essential and natural male trait. The phrase "brutes in suits" comprises my argument, then, as I render the psychological state of aggressive masculinity not as an animal instinct or an adaptation from the Stone Age but as a modern strategy for power taking.

Darwin and Evolutionary Psychology, Then and Now

"Humans are animals and the mind is evolved."[8] After assenting to these two Darwinian principles, it makes sense for gender historians to consider how patterns of behavioral differences between the sexes may have been oriented in the distant human past. There's no reason to ignore the species' early history. Biology and culture are intertwined strands of the same human time line. (Alternatively, the anthropologist Adam Kuper and historian David Courtwright suggest we understand human history by picturing a three-handed clock. The sweep hand follows the major news-making events of electoral politics, economic cycles, international relations, and the like. The minute hand tracks the longer-term processional changes in society and culture, such as the emergence of industrial capitalism. The hour hand covers the evolution of human beings as a species. To know what time it is we need to locate all three hands.)[9] While it is necessary to distinguish between biology and culture—overdrawn as it is, the nature-nurture argument can be quite edifying in assessing the capacities of each dynamic—the dualism should never be pursued to the point of erasing one component for the sake of the other. Indeed, a coevolutionary theory can be imagined for the history of gender and masculinity: biology—in the form of genetic makeup—and culture—in the form of language, habits, and ideas—are both "informational systems" that work to distinguish and separate male and female thought, emotion, and behavior.[10] Within this framework, the goal would be to compare and contrast the content of slow-changing biologically based sexual differences and the more dynamic social and culturally constructed meanings and institutions formed in relation to that preexistent difference.

A potential contribution to this approach to gender history is the principle of differential "parental investment," evolutionary psychology's recognition that in pursuing reproductive success men first and foremost search for access to women, an effort that involves extensive inter-male competition, which, in turn, rewards traits of daring, cunning, and aggressiveness. In contrast to the male advantage in spreading sperm as widely as possible, women gain nothing by mating with many men—female reproductive success depends instead on extracting time and support from one man.[11] In contrast to women being physically and psychologically built for long-term protective and, in a word, nurturing parental investment, men are built for the "law of battle," Darwin's term for the sexually selecting struggle among men, a biological imperative yielding the male instinct of pugnacity.[12]

In extending Darwin's theory of sexual selection, current evolutionary psychology makes a sweeping historical argument about why early twenty-first-century humans are still working with cave men and women minds. The putative uniformity of cross-cultural differences between men's and women's mental traits can be explained by the proposition that all human beings are born with a cognitive and emotional makeup adapted from the recurring environmental demands during the 2 million years the species spent as Pleistocene-period hunter-gatherers. *Homo sapiens* lived its first 250,000 generations hunting and gathering; in contrast, humans developed agriculture about 400 generations ago and industrial capitalism just over the past dozen or so generations. Psychological design evolves very slowly. The 10,000 years since the scattered appearance of agriculture is a very small stretch in evolutionary terms, about 1 percent of human history. Therefore it is improbable that the human mind evolved complex adaptations during the agricultural period, let alone during industrial or postindustrial society. Having established this schema, evolutionary psychologists use as their favorite example the universally higher levels of male violence and aggression. Pugnacity, anger, and aggressiveness suited the male experience of hunting and war. And, again, this Hobbesian bundle of brutish character traits served men's striving within the inter-male competition of sexual selection. Evolutionary psychologists argue, then, that despite cultural evolution, men have an "evolved motivational mechanism," or an instinct, toward aggression.[13]

Evolutionary psychology is both a promising and deeply flawed enterprise. While providing a time line for measuring the coevolution of biology and culture and how they influence male and female mental traits, evolutionary psychology—even in its most sophisticated, academic forms—has a gigantic blind spot over intervening causal sources of masculine pugnacity, feminine nurturing, and other normative gender traits. It ignores patriarchy, "androcentrism," in Charlotte Perkins Gilman's term, or whatever name we may use to describe long-standing and deliberate combinations of male power.[14] Evolutionary psychology ignores the compromised nature of its own intellectual heritage. Charles Darwin wrote Victorian gender stereotypes into his theory of sexual selection. The implications of this point are profound. Darwinian science has not simply been an autonomous, value-neutral endeavor uncovering the biological sources of sexual difference but an active cultural agent in the ideological formation of gender, including the essentialization of masculine brutishness. Darwin's psychology of sex difference has sparked well over one hundred years of sociobiological thought on violent masculine nature, including that by the principle figures of this book—turn-of-the-twentieth-century elites who enthused over aggressive male instinct—and contemporary evolutionary psychologists who portray man as a combative, self-centered gene maximizer. To place current behavioral science on this masculinist continuum doesn't completely erase its value. But after realizing that masculinity itself has been one elaborate exercise in evolutionary psychology, it does become difficult to figure out whether we should treat its scientific findings as a tool for or subject of historical analysis.

It isn't difficult to find the imbrication of culture with science in Darwin's theory of sexual selection. *Descent of Man* explicitly states that "man has ultimately become superior to woman."[15] That superiority, Darwin reasoned, is most clearly seen in the "intellectual powers of the two sexes." Man achieves "a higher eminence, in whatever he takes up, than can woman—whether requiring deep thought, reason, or imagination, or merely the use of the senses and hands." Darwin continued by making one of his most baldly drawn comparisons: "If two lists were made of the most eminent men and women in poetry, painting, sculpture, music . . . history, science, and philosophy, with half-a-dozen names under each subject, the two lists would not bear comparison."[16] Darwin left no room for recent social causes of this putative disparity. He naturalized gender differences in the distant past. Man's "half-human ancestors" passed on higher male energy levels and a male propensity for striving. Darwin added that masculine "characters would, however, have been preserved or even augmented during the long ages of man's savagery, by the success of the strongest and boldest men, both in the general struggle for life and in their contests for wives; a success which would have ensured their leaving a more numerous progeny than their less favored brethren."[17] Darwinian biology is a historical science, but its application routinely skips over the past 10,000 years or so of human social and political experience.

Darwin achieved this rather monstrous historical omission by programmatically "analogizing" between human and nonhuman animal psychology. In *Descent of Man* he argued that the fact that "sexual selection played a highly important part" in forming "inherent differences in the mental powers" of men and women "is at least probable from the analogy of the lower animals which present other secondary characters." Darwin understood "mental disposition" to be a secondary sexual character; like facial hair, aggressiveness should be seen as a heritable trait of man. "No one disputes that the bull differs in disposition from the cow, the wild-boar from the sow, the stallion from the mare, and, as is well known to the keepers of menageries, the males of the larger apes from the females."[18] In examining sexual selection's "law of battle" among men, Darwin did consider the fact that Australian aborigines, North American Indians, and other "savages" fought wars over women. "But even if we had no evidence on this head," Darwin concluded in very characteristic fashion, "we might feel almost sure, from the analogy of the higher Quadrumana [gorilla], that the law of battle had prevailed during the early stages of [man's] development."[19] And if such a "law" existed in early human history, as Darwinian evolutionary psychology reasons, then it continues to have force among "civilized" men in the form of instinct. In this line of thinking, the content of the instinct—what the innate trait actually feels like, what it motivates an individual man to do—is determined through a largely unrecognized anthropomorphic-zoomorphic loop: in skipping over the species' more recent social history, Darwin necessarily read human subjectivity into nonhuman animal "disposition" and then turned it around and used that brutish mind-set to define man's psychological base.

Frederick Engels criticized Darwin's social construction of natural law in his oft-quoted response to *The Origin of the Species* (1859). "The whole Darwinist teaching of the struggle for existence is simply a transference from society to living nature, of Hobbes' doctrine *bellum omnium contra omnes* [war of all against all] and of the bourgeois-economic doctrine of competition, together with Malthus's theory of population. When this conjurer's trick has been performed (and I question its absolute permissibility," Engels emphasized, "particularly as far as the Malthusian theory is concerned), the same theories are transferred back again from organic nature into history and it is now claimed that their validity as eternal laws of human society has been proved. The puerility of this procedure is so obvious that not a word be said about it."[20] Engels smartly fixed on the function of law within Darwinism, for it is the assumption that a particular phenomenon always occurs under certain conditions that has encouraged evolutionary psychologists to believe that the biological force of instinct breaks through the vicissitudes of human societies and their cultural overlays. As late twentieth-century sociobiologist E. O. Wilson put it in characteristically deterministic terms, all creatures "obey" the "biological principle." With chapter 5 focusing on man-made laws of sexual selection, this book as a whole will expose the fallacy behind evolutionary psychology's biological determinism by examining the intervening masculine habits of aggressive thought and feeling.

In addressing the question of behavioral causation, some early twenty-first-century evolutionary psychologists distinguish between proximate causes, the "how" of behavior, and ultimate causes, the "why" of behavior. "A proximate cause of behavior is the mechanism that pushes behavior buttons in real time," psychologist Steven Pinker writes, "such as the hunger and lust that impel people to eat and have sex. An ultimate cause is the adaptive rationale that led the proximate cause to evolve, such as the need for nutrition and reproduction that gave us the drives of hunger and lust."[21] Under this scheme, "proximate and ultimate causes operate together," evolutionary theorist and legal scholar Owen D. Jones explains, "with all behavior depending on ultimately-shaped proximate mechanisms." Crucially, as Jones adds, ultimate causes shape behavior by way of "heritable predispositions."[22] We'll look at predisposition in the following section, but, generally speaking, this proximate-ultimate cause distinction seems compatible with a coevolutionary approach to masculinity. It leaves intact the explanatory distinction between a socially constructed, temporally specific motivation and an abstract, suprahistorical pattern of human behavior. But like other formulations of evolutionary psychology, the proximate-ultimate model leaves out a vast middle ground of human history, thereby omitting the capacity of large-scale social institutions to pattern individual thought, feelings, and behavior along lines of sexual difference. That is to say, the proximate-ultimate causal model disregards patriarchy and gender.

While most evolutionary psychologists ignore feminism altogether, those few who take it up usually do so in such an awkward and self-serving manner as to betray just how threatening a critical historical view of sexual relations is to the sociobiological enterprise. An egregious example of this latter approach is Steven Pinker's book *The Blank Slate: The Modern Denial of Human Nature* (2002), which, in arguing for innate mental differences between the sexes, misrepresents "gender feminists" (using a binary borrowed from arch conservative Christina Hoff Summers) as politically unhinged ideologues on the radical fringe of the otherwise wholesome liberal project of "equity feminism." Pinker offers no refutation of gender feminists' attention to the institutional structures of masculine domination—a core concern, of course, of the whole social-intellectual movement—and instead dismisses it by way of name calling and guilt by association: focus on the gender system is "allied" with "Marxism, postmodernism, social constructionism, and radical science."[23] Anxiety over analysis of male combinations of power runs all the way through evolutionary psychology. In his textbook on the subject, for instance, leading evolutionary psychologist David M. Buss writes that "Simpleminded views of same-sex conspiracies by one sex defy evolutionary logic."[24] Inattention to the strategies and results of male power taking is reminiscent of earlier sociobiology's untroubled acceptance of masculine dominance, as in Steven Goldberg's work *The Inevitability of Patriarchy* (1973): "The thesis put forward here is that the hormonal renders the social inevitable."[25] Or, as Freud put it succinctly, "anatomy is destiny." Evolutionary psychology's antifeminist bias must be neutralized before a coevolutionary approach to masculinity can be achieved.

That is to say that a coevolutionary approach to masculinity would need to factor in patriarchy as a powerful intermediate cause of psychological differences between the sexes. Patriarchy isolates the historical epoch when men transformed a biologically determined sexual division of labor arising from the demands of female childbearing into a self-perpetuating system of male dominance, manifest in the use and control of violence, the emergence of kinship structures promoting the exchange of women among men, and the invention of private property.[26] The concept of patriarchy points us to the law, the state, the military, and marriage and family, among other deeply structured yet dynamic institutions, to explain sexual-social hierarchies and the mental dispositions that go with them. Well defined by economist Heidi Hartmann as "relations between men, which have a material base, and which, though hierarchical, establish or create interdependence and solidarity among men that enable them to dominate," patriarchy also directs us to male homosociality and the finding that brutes in suits emerge from both a will to power over women and a desperate fear of being humiliated and shamed among other men.[27] Shame is a master emotion of de-evolutionary masculinity, while its avoidance pushes men to fits of seemingly instinctive acts of aggression and violence.

John Dewey, Pierre Bourdieu, and Masculinity as a Habit of Mind

Instinct has been so central to past and present evolutionary psychology because the concept defines an impulse that is, first, universal to humans and, second, biologically inherited; for those committed to a cross-cultural psychology of sex difference, it locates in nature a preexistent motivational force, one that is "followed," as Darwin described instinct, "independently of reason."[28] Not surprisingly, the de-evolutionary turn in normative masculinity paralleled the turn-of-the-twentieth-century rise of instinct theory. The prospect of innate, unlearned, sexually specific behaviors—faculties handed down untrammeled from the species' first days—drove the imagination of men already feeling cornered by feminism, the metropolis, the corporation, and other vicissitudes of modernity. And the putative content of human instincts—male pugnacity and female nurturing—supported patriarchal reassertion. The individual men who cultivated a brutish nature didn't necessarily appreciate the political consequences of their effort; and, yet, the following pages trace an unmistakable affectation and knowingness in their systematic appeals to masculine instinct.

Some turn-of-the-century American intellectuals recognized the conservative sexual politics driving instinct theory. While not altogether rejecting a role for instinct in human psychology, they tended to pay far more attention to the cultural evolution of mental habits and the way that conventions in thought and feeling rooted the sexes in a seemingly natural hierarchy of female subordination. Feminists attacked the shoddy application of evolutionary psychology to the long-standing assumption of higher male intelligence. As Helen Thompson Woolley, author of *Psychological Norms in Men and Women* (1903), put it in 1910: "There is perhaps no field aspiring to be scientific where flagrant personal bias, logic martyred in the cause of supporting a prejudice, unfounded assertions, and even sentimental rot and drivel, have run riot to such an extent as here."[29] Charlotte Perkins Gilman, a leading American feminist intellectual of the time, and an evolutionist through and through, insisted that men had seized upon early human sex differences (primarily female childbearing) to build "androcentric culture," a bulwark of institutions allowing only men to realize their "humanness," her favorite word for a self unencumbered by gender. She used evolutionary analysis to chart women's arrested development and to illustrate the many openings for the sex's future growth. "Now let us shake free," Gilman wrote in her book *The Man-Made World* (1911), "from the androcentric habit of mind."[30]

With Gilman and twentieth-century U.S. feminism setting a critical standard for my study, I focus on the many discourses of masculine self-definition and analysis, most of them anxiously stressing men's primal attributes, but also including a certain progressive treatment of the mind's capacity to perceive its own limitations and to set a course for purposeful growth and amelioration. John Dewey heads this masculine counterintelligence. Although he didn't often write explicitly about masculinity, his work does include profeminist critiques of male excesses, as well as an invaluable theory of the mind's social construction. While not denying human instinct, Dewey relentlessly criticized the feral fantasies of an autonomous individual man.[31] And in leading other pragmatist thinkers, Dewey concentrated on the power of mental habit to shape social psychology and behavior. Indeed, his findings regarding habit and disposition are remarkably compatible with turn-of-the-twenty-first-century theories of gender difference and masculine domination.

Among the male intellectuals who contributed to the contemporary critical consciousness of normative masculinity, William James may have been the most implicated in the idea that instinct determined man's aggressiveness. James centered his discipline-forming text *Principles of Psychology* (1890) on the dynamism of human instinct, what he defined as "the faculty of acting in such a way as to produce certain ends, without foresight of the end, or without previous education in the performance."[32] His latter writings nevertheless exhibit intriguing ambiguity over whether instincts are biologically fixed and immutable or socioculturally selected and transformable. James's essay "The Moral Equivalent of War" (1910) speaks of the species' fundamental affinity for organized violence, death, and destruction: with human "history" an absolute "bath of blood," contemporary "man inherits all the innate pugnacity and all the love of glory of his ancestors." But when he added that "[o]ur ancestors have bred pugnacity into our bone and marrow," it isn't at all clear if James meant that "we inherit the warlike type" in a literal biological sense or if he used instinct as a metaphor for a deeply ingrained human value and practice. James finally attacked militarists for representing war as a "biological . . . necessity," unconstrained by "prudential checks and reasonable criticisms."[33] Like Gilman and Dewey, James thrilled over the sheer malleability of human thought and behavior. In describing philosophy itself as "the habit of always seeing an alternative, of not taking the usual for granted, of making conventionalities fluid again, of imagining foreign states of mind," James also offered an incisive formula for transcending brutish modes of masculinity.[34]

Another valuable assessment of modern masculinity can be found in Thorstein Veblen's treatise *The Theory of the Leisure Class* (1899) and its explication of the "instinct" or "trait" of "exotic ferocity." In pursuing his own version of evolutionary psychology, Veblen focused on the "barbarian" stage of human history (equivalent to the height of the Pleistocene hunter-gatherer period) and the ever-widening differentiation between, on one side, female "drudgery" and the corresponding feminine passivity and, on the other, that "sudden and violent strain" in men, the "inclin[ation] to self-assertion, active emulation, and aggression." At times Veblen loosely labeled this cluster of traits the "predatory instinct," but he carefully distinguished it from the older gender-neutral instincts of workmanship, idle curiosity, and parental care formed during the prebarbarian stage of peaceful "savagery." This is a crucial turn in Veblen's evolutionary psychology, for it places sociable nonviolent characteristics at the lower "generic" level of "human nature"; masculine brutishness is less rooted, an example of what he called an institution—a powerful "habit of thought" that, while usually understood to be stable and final, is really contingent and subject to change. He had no illusion as to the ease with which masculine ferocity could be dissolved. The "habitual bellicose frame of mind" served the material and social interests of those men in the corporate vanguard of industrial capitalism.[35] But Veblen made such amelioration the very goal of his anthropological study of the leisure class: to relativize that which many others considered natural and then to lure readers to the productive values that he understood to be more consistent with basic human impulses.

John Dewey's book *Human Nature and Conduct* (1922) may mark the most thoroughgoing critique of the substantive and causal character of instinct. Two decades earlier, Dewey had ascribed enthusiastically to instinct's power to "pattern" the human mind. In a standard evolutionary psychology move, he concentrated on how "the psychical attitudes and traits of the savage are . . . outgrowths which have entered decisively into further evolution, and as such form an integral part of the framework of present mental organization." Following the sociologist W. I. Thomas's essay "The Gaming Instinct" (1901)—which asserts that "our pleasures and pains, our moments of elation and depression . . . go back for the most part to instincts developed in the struggle for food and rivalry for mates"—Dewey wrote that "we may well speak, and without metaphor, of the hunting psychosis" in the modern human male mind.[36] Dewey's thinking on instinct evolved dramatically by the end of the First World War. Rather than looking to the "genetic significance of savage mind" for "comprehending the structure of present mind," he stressed the affective quality of *habit:* an "acquired predisposition to *ways* or modes of response," in his distinct definition, a "special sensitiveness or accessibility to certain classes of stimuli, standing predilections and aversions, rather than bare recurrence of specific acts."[37] Dewey's conception of habit matters to our approach to masculinity because it situates the most generalized and diffuse psychological propensities not in the biological inheritance of a Stone Age past but in the specific social contexts of the here and now.

To understand masculinity as a habit of mind doesn't require the absolute denial of instinct. Dewey carefully pointed out in *Human Nature and Conduct* that "there are definite, independent, original instincts"; it's just that they are "without effect" until joined with "social habits." He saw instinct as the "practical equivalent" of "impulse." Like bursts of nervous energy, instincts are, in Robert B. Westbrook's paraphrasing of Dewey, "completely plastic"—"a neutral potentiality." As Dewey described, "any impulse may become organized into almost any disposition according to the way it interacts with surroundings." As a type of elemental life force, instincts may in one sense precede structured habits, but, as Dewey emphasized, "The *meaning* of native activities is not native; it is acquired. It depends upon interaction with a matured social medium."[38] Under this conception, instincts prepossess neither causal direction nor gendered content. Masculinity doesn't become masculinity until behavioral impulses meet up with the social divisions between human males and females.

In privileging the determinacy of social habit over that of biological impulse, Dewey wanted *Human Nature and Conduct* to present a sharp alternative to Freud's instinct theory. Freud construed instinct as being full of destructive intent and purpose, constantly threatening the civilized state of human society and culture; as discussed in chapter 4, he thought humans are so quick to make war because "killing an enemy satisfied an instinctual inclination." In contrast, Dewey had high hopes for the liberatory potential of instincts: "Impulses are the pivots upon which the re-organization of activities turn, they are agencies of deviation, for giving new directions to old habits and changing their quality."[39] As Phillip Rieff stated in his penetrating examination of the Austrian psychoanalyst and American philosopher, "Dewey sees the impulses as capable of rescuing a society in which habits in institutional structures (i.e. collective habit) have become petrified and therefore impediments to progress, where Freud sees the instincts as themselves the force which limits progress by threatening a renewal of conflict." For Rieff, "Dewey and Freud meet back-to-back," with their different perspectives producing a great divergence in "ethical vision." Like the evolutionary psychologist that he was, Freud boiled "social results" down to, in Dewey's terms, "psychic causes"; while Dewey, ever hopeful for improving combinations of instinct and context, looked primarily for the social motivations for psychic phenomena.[40]

The psychic phenomena at issue here are the "heritable predispositions" that evolutionary psychologists like Steven Pinker call ultimate biological causes but which Dewey insisted are acquired via social habits. Male predisposition to aggression and violence, while consistent with Stone Age competition for mates and hunting to stay alive, may very well be determined by the masculine habits of concentrating on homosocial differences of race, economic class, physical prowess, and sexuality, for instance; holding property interests in women's sexuality; and pride in country. Dewey pictured habits as mental "channels" of energy. "Every habit creates an unconscious expectation," Dewey wrote, a disposition or, really, a predisposition to behave in a certain way. Dewey made the point explicitly: "We must bear in mind that the word disposition means predisposition, readiness to act overtly in a specific fashion whenever opportunity is presented."[41] To emphasize, then, habits may be considered to be intermediate causes, intervening, socially transmitted prompts to certain behaviors, which, in practical terms, cover up or take over from biologically rooted inclination. Just how much predisposition can one have?

Regardless, Dewey's *Human Nature and Conduct* directs our critical attention to the way that habits of mind slow up adjustment of the self to the social realities of the day. Rather than instinct working as a drag on social psychological progress— "instincts are most readily modifiable through use, most subject to educative direction," Dewey wrote—"it is precisely custom which has the greatest inertia, which is least susceptible of alteration." Habits "restrict" the "reach" of the "intellect" for Dewey: "They are blinders that confine the eyes of the mind to the road ahead."[42] In looking at contemporary American thought, Dewey believed that mental habit had locked men into "an acute[ly] maladjust[ed]" attachment to the notion of an autonomous individual self. He charged in his book *Individualism, Old and New* (1930) that while "individuality" had been "a reality because it corresponded to the conditions" of "the wilderness," it now distracted urban Americans from realizing "that they are sustaining and sustained members of a social whole."[43] The rugged individualism of yesteryear, Dewey pointed out, now only served the interests of corporate capitalism and the Saturday afternoon moviegoer. We'll look closely in chapter 1 at the twentieth-century staying power of frontier individualism. It bears emphasis here that Dewey idealized fluidity in thought, psychology, and identity. Mental habits could never be dropped altogether, but they could be shaped for progress and responsiveness. "In learning habits," Dewey wrote hopefully, "it is possible for man to learn the habit of learning."[44]

Pierre Bourdieu's conception of *habitus* and disposition is so congruent with Dewey's use of the same ideas that it's surprising that the turn-of-the-twenty-first-century French social theorist didn't cite his American predecessor. Like Dewey, Bourdieu defined *habitus* as a culturally "acquired system of generative schemes," dispositions that can be easily mistaken for instinct as they operate beneath the level of consciousness. "Understood as a system of durable and transposable dispositions which, integrating all past experiences, functions at every moment as a matrix of perceptions, appreciations, and actions," *habitus*, for Bourdieu, coheres in and through the body, whose "gestures," "stylistics," and "unconscious 'knowingness'" make up, in the words of Loïc Wacquant, "a repository . . . of incorporated history."[45] Bourdieu's greatest improvement on Dewey's concept was his explicit application of *habitus* and disposition to patriarchy, gender formation, and, in the title of his valuable book, *Masculine Domination* (2001). Bourdieu asked a question in that study which is central to *Brutes in Suits:* "what are the *historical* mechanisms responsible for the *relative dehistoricization* and *eternalization* of the structure of the sexual division and the corresponding principles of division?" To answer that question is to get at what Bourdieu called "the *paradox of doxa*"—the overwhelming respect for arbitrary systems of difference.[46]

Bourdieu contended that the "symbolic violence" of masculine domination—"a gentle violence, imperceptible and invisible even to its victims, exerted for the most part through the purely symbolic channels of communication and cognition"—routinely inverts the cause and effect of sexual difference and gender hierarchy. "It is the visible differences between the female body and the male body," Bourdieu argued, "which, being perceived and constructed according to the practical schemes of the androcentric world view, become the most perfectly indisputable guarantee of meanings and values that are in harmony with the principles of that world view." No necessary relationship or association exists between primary sex characteristics and the meanings they take on under patriarchy. "It is not the phallus (or its absence) which is the basis of that worldview," he continued, "rather it is that worldview which, being organized according to the division into *relational genders,* male and female, can institute the phallus, constituted as the symbol of virility, of the specifically male point of honor, and the difference between biological bodies as objective foundations of the difference between the sexes, in the sense of genders constructed as two hierarchized essences." Bourdieu elaborated: "Far from the necessities of biological reproduction determining the symbolic organization of the sexual division of labor and, ultimately, of the whole natural and social order, it is an arbitrary construction of the male and female body, [and] of its uses and functions. . . . The particular strength of the masculine sociodicy," Bourdieu concluded with a point quite applicable to evolutionary psychology, "comes from the fact that it combines and condenses two operations: *it legitimates a relationship of domination by embedding it in a biological nature that is itself a naturalized social construction.*"[47]

Given the naturalizing power of gender difference, Bourdieu worried about our ability to gain critical distance on that subject of study. We've already seen how indifference to this concern makes up a gigantic blind spot among evolutionary psychologists: their embrace of Darwinian science and its androcentric assumptions regarding sexual selection and the emotions and "mental dispositions" that attach to the sexes place these contemporary behavioral scientists on an ideological continuum with the turn-of-the-twentieth-century hypermasculinist figures whom I take as the subjects of my book. In "try[ing] to understand masculine domination,"

Bourdieu warned, we are "likely to resort to modes of thought that are the products of domination." As a way out of this trap, Bourdieu recommended an anthropological turn: a "detour through an exotic tradition is indispensable in order to break the relationship of deceptive familiarity that binds us to our own tradition."[48] In addition to cultural anthropology, we will rely on reader response literary theory, older-fashion American character studies, extracting epistemology and meaning from social scientific discourse, psychoanalysis, and queer studies. While I have adopted a decidedly eclectic methodology, the book as a whole develops an anthropologically driven ironist perspective on essential masculinity. Making the normal strange—that core anthropological tenet—turns out to be quite feasible when it comes to the violent, zoomorphilogical strain of modern American masculinity.

After combining Bourdieu and Dewey, de-evolutionary masculinity, like other gender formulations, can and should be understood as a habit of mind—a socially generated scheme of perception, feeling, and behavior, absorbed from infancy, and reproduced through psychologically intricate dispositions.[49] Working in tandem with social conventions and institutions, and the ideational and ideological content of language, disposition answers the astonished feminist parent's question about the seemingly automatic adoption of traditional gender roles among unknowing toddlers and even infants. It's not only the blue and pink blankets but the diffused social address to young subjects. Writer Barbara Ehrenreich relates her own experience as a young mother witnessing a waitress cooing over her baby: "Oh isn't she a beautiful princess"; after Ehrenreich told the woman that the child is a boy, the waitress adjusted without missing a beat, "oh a real tough guy huh." Gender difference transmits itself below even that verbal level though. Tone of voice, facial expression, gesture, the way a body is carried, presented, and, in Judith Butler's term, "performed" to others—disposition bears the essences of gender and sexual hierarchy.[50]

"The Caveman within Us" and the Masculinist Culture of Mimicry

With a coevolutionary model of masculinity, one would expect culture to grow out from its biological base, to extend if not break its leash.[51] Whatever the metaphor, because culture is able to evolve faster than biological predisposition—because, as Dewey understood, culture can be guided by intelligence—a certain distance or difference between human thought and biological limitations is expected. What is most notable about normative masculinity in the turn-of-the-twentieth-century United States, though, is that rather than trying to outrun the brutish aspects of early human history, it circled back and embraced predation like never before, breaking down along the way barriers between animal and human, and savagery and civilization that had been so endemic to earlier ideals of white middle-class American manhood.[52]

Connections between human and animal, and man and savage had been made before; but never in the full array that we'll find in modern U.S. thought and culture; and never with such scientific seriousness and psychological specificity. Darwinism, it has been said, transformed late nineteenth-century understanding of man's beastlike nature from metaphor to scientific reality. Crucially, Darwin himself depended immensely on metaphor.[53] He based natural selection on the Hobbesian and Malthusian metaphor of "struggle for existence," while sexual selection sprang from a heterosexual imperative that has men locked in potentially deadly competition with each other over access to impassive women.[54] From these fictions (accounts that do not hold to any direct correspondence with social reality) grew late nineteenth-century evolutionary psychology and the putatively radical differences between the sexes' mental constitutions, with men inheriting pugnacity from their savage progenitors and prehistory's violent demands of heterosexual competition, hunting, and war.

As this evolutionary-psychological story line gained immense appeal among post–Civil War middle- and upper-class white men, the concept of animal-savage instinct would pattern normative masculinity's core mental habit, what I call *devolution:* a thought sequence that first identifies the static, restricting, and ultimately emasculating nature of contemporary consciousness and experience and then moves deliberately backward to what is considered to be an original, unmediated state of mind, with body, behavior, and existence following closely behind. Chapter 1 begins detailing the de-evolutionary origins of modern U.S. masculinity by examining the elaborate cultural reflex against the closed spaces and mass society of the turn-of-the-century metropolis; the nobly savage Indian, the rough-riding cowboy, and, in general, the prospect of reestablishing rugged American individualism all worked as existential lures toward authentic selfhood. De-evolutionary masculinity, I argue, involved *mimicry:* the effort to assume the bodily and psychological form of an archetype, a culturally constructed ideal that paradoxically accrued ideological power through its self-representation as natural and historically essential.

The performative and textual dimensions of masculinist mimicry warrant close attention. Consider Joseph Knowles, who in 1913, amid great fanfare, plunged naked without equipment into the Maine woods to live off the land for two months. With the Boston press covering his endeavor, this "modern cave man" reportedly made fire with two sticks; nourished himself with berries, trout, and venison; and trapped and killed a bear for its fur coat. Having survived the wilderness healthy and whole, Knowles was received by a good part of Maine, Boston, and the country as a hero for successfully shedding the trappings of civilization and living as a "primitive." After evidence emerged that he had actually set himself up in a safe and well-stocked cabin, "a vociferous denial arose in reply," as historian Roderick Nash has written: "quite a few Americans in 1913 apparently wanted to believe in the authenticity of the 'Nature Man.'" Knowles had mimicked savagery's imagined "tooth-and-claw" dictate—Maine fined him $205 for killing a bear out of season—and, in turn, stories of his prowess modeled devolution for, among others, weekend campers, Boy Scouts, and recreational hunters.[55] As discussed in chapter 2, popular literature formularized the joys of hunting and killing in nature's wilds. "Did I feel sorry for what I had done?" a sportsmen asked rhetorically in his 1907 written account of shooting a caribou in Canada. "Well! No, I did not," he continued: "Ten thousand years of superficial and unsatisfying civilization have not altered the fundamental nature of man, and the successful hunter of to-day becomes a primeval savage, remorseless, triumphant, full of a wild, exultant joy, which none but those who have lived in the wilderness" will ever know.[56]

By the early twentieth century, instinct theory rolled off the tongues of amateur and professional evolutionary psychologists alike. The long history of human savagery still influences individual thought, emotion, and behavior, the central message read, oftentimes overpowering or "taking the place of reason and experience," as J. Howard Moore said in his book *Savage Survivals* (1916). "Civilization is only a skin," he contended, using this extremely popular metaphor for depth and surface: "The great core of human nature is barbaric."[57] Academic social scientist William F. Fielding illustrated the idea even more explicitly in his work *The Caveman within Us* (1922). "There is the basic organism which we have inherited, with its engrained impressions, instincts, and emotions that have been picked up during millions of years of struggle with the remorseless forces of nature," Fielding wrote: "And over the mechanism of this wild and ancient heritage there has been thrown, during the past few thousand years, a slight coat of cultural whitewash, which may be called the veneer of civilization." Although he wanted to help his readers "to *visualize*" the "struggle" in their "nature" between "the Caveman and the Socialized Being," Fielding, like his turn-of-the-twenty-first-century evolutionary psychology successors, virtually ignored the latter, describing "social development" as a "surface strata" waiting to be broken through by the hard everlasting core of biological instinct.[58]

Early twentieth-century evolutionary psychologists sharply distinguished male fighting instinct from a nondescript female psychology. "The fighting instinct is weak in women and girls," Moore reasoned, "because it was the men (not the women) who did the fighting and hunting during those vanished ages in which the foundations of human nature were laid." While "[w]omen are the drudges and burden-bearers among savages," he added, "[t]he chronic condition of savage man is one of war." Moore made these observations amid World War I, a conflict that instinct theorists read as a most brutal manifestation of masculine nature. In documenting the power of male fighting instinct, Fielding smartly noted that "the actual expenditures of the U.S. during the fiscal year 1919–1920, for education, research, public health and development, amounted to $59 million, while the expenses of the same period, incident to war, amounted to $3238 million." He concluded: "Fifty five times more of the public funds were used in behalf of the destructive caprices of the Caveman, and in catering to his instincts, than for purposes of education and of adding to our cultural possibilities."[59] Chapter 4 opposes this instinct theory of war by examining how culture has been the most dangerous source of war making through its invention of racial and other differences that trigger deadly group conflict and through its privileging of battle as heroic masculine adventure. It's not male instinct we need to worry about but rather the masculinist culture of *mimicry* that casts fighting, killing, and dying in combat as *essential* male experience.

Suffice it to say here, though, that most World War I–era analysis agreed with commentators like G. T. W. Patrick who argued in his *Popular Science Monthly* article "The Psychology of War" (1915) that, contrary to appearances, all of Europe has not gone "insane"; the massive death and destruction are masculine instinct in action: beneath man's "superior brain, and sometimes perilously near the surface, there lies a vast network of inherited dispositions connecting the man of today with his warlike ancestors." William Lee Howard concurred in his *New York Medical Journal* article "The Psychology of War: Why Peoples and Nations Fight" (1915). Total war is inevitable, he came close to saying, and it would be unhealthy to deny human disposition toward making war: "in spite of religious and ethical movements, peace palaces and rocking chair pacifists, man in nature has not changed from the days of the war clubs and war axes." But a dissenting opinion could be found in the book *The Psychology of War* (1918) by John T. MacCurdy, M.D., who, in observing the war in Europe, took seriously the notion of collective insanity. War, he wrote, results from "a change in the mind of man." Once that transformation happens, MacCurdy emphasized, war in the head takes on the properties of "mental disease." By the early twenty-first century MacCurdy's view has gained ground, at least among nonevolutionary psychologists. "Epidemicity" has become a key word in war studies. It describes the way war spreads through space and time like an infectious disease.[60]

This last metaphor of disease fits my take on normative brutish masculinity as a whole. De-evolutionary masculinity spread in the manner of a contagion, insinuating itself through language and ideas as well as through the less-conscious transference of habits and dispositions. The brutes in suits I keep in focus are mostly white European American elites—those individuals and combinations of men who most benefited from emulating predatory instincts. Such mimicry aggrandized their social power over women and other men. But this masculinist mind-set, like a pathology, clearly crossed lines of sex, class, and race. As discussed in chapters 3 and 4, African Americans looked to athletic and military achievement to prove their manhood and thereby to gain some measure of inclusion in modern American society, even as those institutions segregated blacks from other men and even as African Americans used sports and the armed forces as sites of resistance to racial discrimination. In chapter 5's examination of turn-of-the-century southern lynching, I take up the social construction of race as an incisive counter to evolutionary psychology's understanding of sexual jealousy as the result of a biological motivational mechanism built into the male mind. Fear of the black brute—an archetypical figure arising from white imagination—prompted elites to attempt to control the sexuality of African American men and white women through lynch law.

In researching and writing this book I have developed an episodic approach to modern U.S. masculinity. The chapters are connected in their references to each other and their discussion of the central issues regarding the origins, power, and effects of de-evolutionary masculinity. But, at the same time, my strategy has been to separate late nineteenth- and early twentieth-century thought and culture into somewhat discrete discourses and formulations that, to some extent, can be examined in their own cultural and historiographical terms. Each chapter focuses on a specific post–Civil War *institution:* professional history and its view of American individualism; the hunting and killing genre of popular men's literature; college football; militarism and the emergence of finding pleasure in killing; and heterosexuality and the law. "Institutions," as John Dewey said, "are embodied habits"; they inculcate disposition and structure mimicry.[61] If masculinity involved the process of learning to be instinctive, then institutions bear the specifics of that education. They also reveal the dynamics of power taking. De-evolutionary masculinity, I argue, contains its own critique. The goal is to lay bare the pathological paradox of normative U.S. masculinity: its self-conscious adoption of natural impulse; its affected fear of weakness, femininity, and civilization; and its privileging of collective and individual violence.

I begin this project by looking at how *Americanism* fed de-evolutionary masculinity. The following chapter examines the intellectual passage of the American character trait of rugged individualism from nineteenth-century romantic thought to twentieth-century social psychology and history through Frederick Jackson Turner's 1893 speech and essay "The Significance of the Frontier in American History."

His thesis influenced masculinity in a number of ways, including its historical mapping of an existential crisis of American modernity spurred by perceived spatial loss after the close of the frontier and separation from the open spaces that once made the nation's men free, independent, and strong. Working from Darwinian, Spencerian, and neo-Lamarckian evolutionary theory, Turner intriguingly suggested that modern Americans inherited rugged individualism from their ancestors' pioneer experience. The trait needed exercise, however, and this is where Turner's environmental determinism intersected with contemporary escapist attempts to recapture masculine primitivism, as seen in such broad-based popular cultural developments as the commercial promotion of the Old West, including the dude ranch. Rugged individualism, in short, entailed an elaborate process of mimicry.

CHAPTER ONE

Rugged Individualism

In examining masculinity, we need to consider at least two types of discourses, figures and texts. Ultragendered, outwardly violent hypermasculinity is a core component of this study. And in this realm, no subject deserves more attention than Teddy Roosevelt. Author as well as adventurer, the young Roosevelt's seven-volume study *The Winning of the West* (1885–94) and his man-making magazine articles on his own Dakota hunting and ranching experiences put forward a historical vision of the frontier as a source of rough and rugged American character and manhood. With his "frontier thesis" celebrating Indian subjugation as a necessary and natural step in the advancement of the Anglo-Saxon race, as Richard Slotkin explains, Roosevelt also developed the "regeneration-through-regression" theme—"the passage of a highly civilized man through a revivifying return to the life of an earlier stage" where "the demands of the historical moment foster the emergence and triumph of a distinctive biosocial 'character' or 'type.'"[1] There is great reason to focus on Roosevelt. That TR's dude, hunter, and soldier personae exemplified the brutish turn in American character and masculinity explains his utter ubiquity in this book.

But masculinity also works indirectly and obliquely. It can be found in apparently gender-neutral language and structures of knowledge. And, here, more compelling than Roosevelt is Frederick Jackson Turner. Due to Turner's great absorptive and synthetic powers, his essay "The Significance of the Frontier in American History" (1893) is a virtual compendium of nineteenth-century literary and social scientific convictions—including romantic primitivism, realist attainment of comprehensive factual detail, and high regard for the evolutionary dynamic between organism and environment. In keeping with long-standing conventions of European imagination, Turner tended to cast the North American continent in feminine terms, assuming man as sole agent and actor and all but dissolving women as historical subjects. Turner's frontier thesis is deeply ethnocentric. Even as he urged Americans to turn away from Europe in understanding themselves and their institutions, Turner adopted an east-to-west frame of reference, from European civilization to American savagery, a perspective that marginalized Indian subject positions. Racialist, nation-building violence, for Turner, resulted *naturally* from the westward course of European American expansion. He neither celebrated nor ignored that part of American history. He assumed it. This can be seen in his crucial reading of American character: the core trait of individualism had been modified by ruggedness—a euphemism for exceptional violent capacity.

Turner's work penetrated modern U.S. middle-class consciousness. He popularized the frontier thesis through countless commencement addresses and other public speeches, through numerous articles in middle-brow magazines and journals, and, most effectively, during thirty-five years of college teaching. With research in his University of Wisconsin and Harvard students' class notes, among other material, I attend to the extension of Turner's thesis from one generation to the next. In this regard, we should understand Turner less as the originary source of any one idea—the frontier as crucible for American exceptionalism certainly had its antecedents, for instance—and more as a multivalent figure bridging nineteenth- and twentieth-century naturalist thought, romantic literature and social science, culture and biology, and academic scholarship and popular understandings of the past. With de-evolutionary masculinity resting on a radically historicist sensibility, Turner contributed a distinctly American dimension to the conviction that man's natural state is one of solitude, mobility, and autonomy.

Far more than Roosevelt, Turner engaged the gendered ideology of American individualism. The idea that the West gave rise to solitary, atomistic existence permeates the whole thesis but is most clearly stated in the essay's last, climactic section. "To the frontier the American intellect owes its striking characteristics," Turner wrote:

> That coarseness and strength combined with acuteness and inquisitiveness, that practical, inventive turn of mind, quick to find expedients, that masterful grasp of material things, lacking in the artistic but powerful to effect great ends, that restless, nervous energy, that dominant individualism, working for good and evil, and withal that buoyancy and exuberance which comes with freedom, these are the traits of the frontier, or traits called out elsewhere because of the existence of the frontier.[2]

Turner begged the question of what form individualism would take in postfrontier mass society. One answer would be an urban quest for individuality through mobility of consciousness and differentiation of personality—a countercultural project linked with Turner as well as Nietzsche. At the same time, American men learned to throw themselves out of the city with abandon, turning to the (shrinking yet still existent) open spaces of the West for what they hoped would be rugged man-making experience. Modern U.S. masculinity entailed the city-bound fetishization of the West. With the "roughneck" cowboy as archetype, (sub)urban middle- and upper-class men lit out for dude ranches, where they sought *authentic* masculinity within elaborate cultural productions of the "Old West"—a self-conscious and affected pursuit of real manhood that betrays the whole "brutes in suits" complex.

The limitations of masculinist individualism come into sharp relief when compared to American women's use of individualism as a tool for both pursuing sexual equality and differentiating themselves from men and each other. If, as Nancy Cott has written, pre–World War I U.S. feminism largely amounted to "a movement of consciousness," a collective act of psychic and subjective self-realization, then that movement also managed to avoid the privatist and de-evolutionary impulses of the era's Greenwich Village male intellectuals. At the same time in the West, we find cowgirls cultivating a type of athletic feminism through rodeo competition and other outdoor work and play. As the Daughters of the American Revolution *Madonna of the Trail* statue illustrates (fig. 1.1), western women drew from the pioneer tradition in adapting rugged individualism: portrayed in midstride, the figure is mobile and undoubtedly headed westward; with rifle at her side, she is also deadly; and given her husky stature and determined expression, "Madonna" is self-reliant, although not solitary, as two young children clutch at her dress.

In somewhat complicated fashion, while attending to feminist adoption of individualism, this chapter works from the premise that the discourse of individualism, and the American character studies that have driven it, is largely an ethnocentric idealization of manhood, even though it seldom rejects women outright. "The classic statements of American individualism are best understood as guides to masculine identity," as the historian Linda Kerber has explained: they "have made the implicit assumption that the 'individual' was male. Even when a vaguely generic language was adopted to make it seem that women were included, a careful reading reveals that virtually all commentators—except explicitly feminists ones like [Elizabeth Cady] Stanton—contemplated the self-actualization of men."[3] To emphasize, in analyzing masculinity we need to extract two discourses. One interpellates men as gendered beings, relying on such essentialist descriptors as "real man," "he-man," "manly," and "man's man," while anxiously differentiating masculinity from all things feminine. The other employs such neutered nouns as "self," "citizen," "person," "American," and "individual"; it may concentrate on such seemingly gender-neutral conceptions as human nature, consciousness, and instinct; but, while not explicitly excluding women, its perceptual and historical focus is masculine. Its cultural work mostly augmented the masculinist project of the time. Seldom venturing into the former hypermasculine realm, Turner nevertheless advanced atavistic masculinity through the latter, by integrating American character with primitive rugged individualism.

Finally, Turner's thesis warrants close attention because of its paradigmatic relationship to turn-of-the-twentieth-century Darwinism and evolutionary theory. As with other key figures in this book, it is difficult to measure Turner's exact debt to Darwin himself. The frontier thesis is highly consistent with the work of Jean-Baptiste Lamarck and Herbert Spencer—evolutionary theorists with whom Darwin differed but who nevertheless contributed to common understandings of "Darwinism" (widely used as a synonym for post-1859 evolutionary thought) during Turner's time. Adding to the difficulty is the fact that the most pernicious aspects of Darwin's actual writing—those that have civilization naturally overcoming savagery, for instance, and that may have contributed to Turner's easy ethnic acceptance of American racial violence—in no way originated with Darwin. With roots deep in Western thought, they came together in mid-nineteenth-century racial anthropology and other conservative evolutionary theory to which Darwin and Turner had access.[4] That Darwinism was an especially dynamic and inexact conglomeratic world view at the turn of the twentieth century cannot be overemphasized; but it is still worth drawing the connection while examining Turner because, for the most part, he saw himself as a man of social science, and within his generation that meant coming to terms with Darwinism. The frontier thesis follows the Darwinian principle that variations in the environment create new needs, modify behavior, and shape physical and psychological traits. Turner's description of the exceptionally American derivation of rugged individualism follows Darwin's master theory of natural selection.

This chapter presents a wide-ranging examination of Turner's promotion of rugged individualism in modern U.S. culture. We begin with a close reading of his 1893 thesis, giving special consideration to its evolutionary framework, and its ethnocentric assumptions regarding historical progress and the primitive, de-evolutionary origins of American "intellectual traits." Turner's backward-looking understanding of American character provided a type of epistemological platform for more specific and exaggerated constructions of modern masculine selfhood. These formulations will be considered in turn, including the frontier thesis's congruence with social psychology and that discipline's attention to the effect of the urban environment on American temper. The second half of the chapter surveys postfrontier variations of individualism in early twentieth-century middle-class identity formation: namely, countercultural individuality of pre–World War I Greenwich Village, and rugged individualism as reconstructed in the "Old West." These sections attend to the gendered workings of individualism—how women and men found disparate and similar meanings in the ideal of the autonomous and highly differentiated self.

Frederick Jackson Turner's Frontier Thesis: Origins, Composition, and Meanings

Turner's frontier thesis engages a composite theory of evolution. With Darwin serving as a capstone to his attempt to make history scientific, Turner matches up more substantively with Herbert Spencer, Lewis Henry Morgan, and the amalgam of mid- to late nineteenth-century sociologists, anthropologists, and social psychologists who used evolution to compare the institutional, cultural, and intellectual stages of racial and gendered development. For these Victorian thinkers, psychology was very much an evolutionary science. They believed that biological inheritance determines not only the physiological makeup of a people but also their common mental traits and thought patterns. The idea that culture is carried in the "blood" informed Turner's effort to understand the origins and staying power of rugged individualism. His reconstruction of that "intellectual trait" in turn-of-the-twentieth-century thought depended on a fusion between culture and biology and the emerging concept of human instinct. It turned on a subtle and powerful racialist perspective in which the European pioneer became American through contact with and survival of the savage—read Native American—wilderness: "This perennial rebirth, this fluidity of American life, this expansion westward with its new opportunities, its continuous touch with the simplicity of primitive society, furnish the forces dominating American character."[5]Oftentimes brilliant in locution, the frontier thesis needs picking apart. Only after identifying its terminology, assumptions, and metaphors in other evolutionary thought is it possible to appreciate the contribution Turner made to the extension of individualism into twentieth-century American culture and the place of that mind-set in modern masculinity.

To begin, Turner's formulation of individualism fits closely with the stage theory of Lewis Henry Morgan, a founding figure of American anthropology. Turner read and cited Morgan's book *League of the ho-de-no-sau-nee or Iroquois* (1851), one of the first scholarly ethnographies of Native American Indians. And it is almost certain that Turner knew Morgan's highly influential *Ancient Study; or, Researches in the Lines of Human Progress from Savagery through Barbarism to Civilization* (1877). Morgan's stage theory worked from the concept of intellectual monogenesis—the idea that operations of the mind, as he explained it, "have been uniform in . . . all the races of mankind."[6] Psychic unity did not indicate racial equality but meant only that different peoples followed the same track of mental development. Morgan transfigured cultural difference into hierarchical "ethnical" positions within the "ratio of human progress." While placing African Americans and Native Americans hopelessly behind the superior "Aryan" and "Semitic" races, Morgan relegated Indians to the white nation's past, a historical view that framed Turner's

ethnocentric understanding of American social evolution, including his definition of the frontier as "the meeting point between savagery and civilization."[7] For
Turner, the frontier represented a cultural dynamic as much as a geographic space.
It broke down European manner and thought. Like Morgan, Turner assumed the
ultimate fitness and supremacy of European American civilization as it grew out
from the savage state, even as that same point of savagery provided the origins of
exceptionalist national character and manhood. As middle-class white American
men desperately searched for ways to recover a natural masculine essence, psychic
unity between civilization and savagery set up an easy slide toward de-evolutionary
self-realization.

Perhaps the most fundamental evolutionary reference point for Turner's frontier thesis is the English philosopher Herbert Spencer and his biological view of
social and cultural history. No mean social Darwinist, Turner dodged the sharpest
points of the Spencerian tooth-and-claw ethic. But Spencer's more basic insights
into social evolution organized the founding of American social science, an enterprise in which Turner was integrally involved. Spencer's definition of evolution as
change from a state of indefinite homogeneity to coherent heterogeneity, the accompanying teleological or progressive component in his understanding of social
growth (Spencer's most distinct difference from Darwin), and the conviction that
psychology and institutions make up coequal parts of the organic social whole all
informed Turner's understanding of American democracy and individualism as
well as his very conception of historical study.[8] In his essay "The Significance of
History" (1891), Turner borrowed directly from Spencer in writing "Society is an
organism ever growing." To this, Turner added, "History is the self-consciousness
of this organism." Here we find Turner's early sociological formulation of history,
his turn away from great men and events and toward, as he said in an 1895 lecture, "the great undercurrents of society, that ocean that moves, and changes, and
surges." Turner's primary interest in "the vital forces" that lie beneath institutional
and mental forms repeats the essential evolutionary dynamic that Spencer called
"the persistence of force."[9] It also prefigures Turner's environmental determinism
and his fusion of history, geography, and national character.

Spencer's influence on Turner becomes clearer after recognizing that the philosopher's evolutionary theory advanced the Lamarckian principles that new organs and traits arise in close response to environmental changes and demands
and that those acquired characteristics are passed on to succeeding generations
through sexual reproduction. Lamarckianism, especially in Spencer's hands, accounted for the biological development of national character—the belief that a
race's mental qualities and behavioral habits sprang from the environment itself
and that they could become hereditary, a matter of instinct.[10] Clearly Turner em-

braced the idea of the direct action of the environment; indeed, it leads to one of the most significant statements in his thesis: "to the frontier the American intellect owes its striking characteristics." Personal autonomy, high energy, and physical toughness came from contact with the West, Turner said, and these characteristics then filtered back eastward to influence all of United States culture.

While seldom using the word *instinct,* Turner's reconstruction of individualism advanced the idea that the trait had been inbred in American character. "Long after the frontier period of a particular region of the United States has passed away," Turner wrote in the *Atlantic Monthly* in 1903, "the conception of society, the ideals and aspirations which it produced, persist in the whole of its people." Whether Turner envisioned cultural evolution happening through the automatic biological succession of psychologies, as did Lamarck and Spencer, or if he contemplated the transference mechanism as being the generational passing down of traditions and outlooks through language will be discussed later. The point here is that some of Turner's most inflated and sweeping language engages the then very current concept of the inheritability of acquired characteristics. The frontier had been the "constructive force" over the past four hundred years of national evolution, as he concluded in the *Atlantic;* it is "wrought into the very warp and woof of American life."[11]

One definite social scientific influence on the frontier thesis was the Italian political economist Achille Loria, whose book *Analisa della Proprieta Capitalista* (1889), translated for Turner a year before his 1893 essay, relates closely to the historian's signal application of stage theory to American social evolution. Loria believed that the presence of "free land" marked the initial and determinative stage of social development and that America, with its great geographic expanses and its large metropolises, provided a type of compressed physical record of historical evolution.[12] Turner's intellectual biographers have differed over the exact influence of Loria on the thesis. Turner synthesized many sources into his work. And, as Ray Allen Billington argued, Turner had come to the fundamental conclusions of his thesis before reading Loria.[13] Moreover, free land (whether understood as empty of people or free of rent) does not fully explain his conception of the American frontier; again, Turner thought of it as not only a geographic space but also a particular social environment—one marked by cultural exchange and warfare with "primitive" Indians. Nevertheless, when it came to introducing his masterful evolutionary passage in which he asked the listener-reader to imagine that "The United States lies like a huge page in the history of society," Turner cites Loria by name in the topic sentence, going on to say that "[t]here is much truth" in the economist's understanding that the country "'reveals luminously the course of universal history.'"[14] Loria helped Turner decide to overlay stage theory onto to the horizontal axis of the North American continent. The result is the remarkably compelling image of the social development from savagery to civilization following a left-to-right, west-to-east historical progression.

In fully appreciating the effect of this ideologically loaded passage, we should recognize that Turner placed it after two elaborately composed introductory sections in which he paid close attention to geographic detail and organic process. "The Significance of the Frontier in American History" opens by quoting from the *Extra Census Bulletin No. 2, Distribution of Population According to Density: 1890*: "Up to and including 1880 the country had a frontier of settlement, but at present the unsettled area has been so broken into by isolated bodies of settlement that there can hardly be said to be a frontier line." The *Bulletin* lends factual authority to Turner's great periodizing claim that 1890 "marks the closing of a great historical moment," thereby infusing drama and urgency into the address, while also fusing spatial dimension with temporal consciousness. The first paragraph ends with an essential organizing theme of the thesis: "The existence of an area of free land, its continuous recession, and the advance of American settlement westward explain American development." In the following paragraph Turner seems to have included as many evolutionary terms and images as possible: "vital forces" bring "organs into life," and American forms "adapt themselves"; he used the word "develop" five times, and "growing" and "evolution" twice each.[15] Turner's opening enacts natural movement and change, constant stimulus and response. It lays down an organic historical base from which American institutions and character arise.

In another introductory paragraph, Turner presented a compelling version of the de-evolutionary origins of American character. In contrast to the west-to-east direction of the social evolution passage, this passage begins in the East and recounts "how European life entered the continent, and how America modified and developed that life." The force behind this transformation is the frontier—"the line of most rapid and effective Americanization." As the European "man" goes west, he encounters an environment that Turner portrayed in animated, lifelike terms. "The wilderness masters the colonist. It finds him a European in dress, industries, tools, modes of travel, and thought." As the narrative unfolds, it becomes clear that Turner conflated the wilderness with Native American ways; what he really described is cultural exchange, although without recognizing Indian perspective or agency: the frontier takes the European "from the railroad car and puts him in the birch canoe. It strips off the garments of civilization and arrays him in the hunting shirt and the moccasin. It puts him in the log cabin of the Cherokee and Iroquois and runs an Indian palisade around him."[16] Part of Native American–European contact involves warfare, as Turner acknowledged indirectly: the new European American learns to "shout the war cry and take the scalp in orthodox Indian fashion." Rather than examining the violence historically, Turner closed this passage with evolutionary abstraction: "In short, at the frontier the environment is at first too strong for the man. He must accept the conditions which it furnishes, or perish."[17] The suggestion is that the frontier selects in social-Darwinian fashion those most fit, with physical prowess becoming a leading trait of American character.

In the section immediately preceding the social evolution passage, Turner set down "the stages of frontier advance" with impressive compositional skill. In preparing his thesis, Turner pored over the State Historical Society of Wisconsin Library's growing collection of maps, historical atlases, climatic studies, and census reports. The work paid off. The thesis demonstrates a certain mastery of U.S. geography. It offers a sweeping, comprehensive account of the frontier's movement westward, through the "Atlantic river courses" and "tidewater region," across "the Alleghenies into Kentucky and Tennessee," on to the "Great Lakes" and the "Great Plains," and up to the "Rocky Mountains."[18] The east-to-west descriptive effect in this passage provides the linear context for the subsequent account of social evolution. While using no actual maps in presenting his thesis, Turner prompted the mind's eye into picturing historical development within the geographic frame of the continent.

Imagine, Turner wrote, that "the United States lies like a huge page in the history of society. Line by line," he continued, "as we read from west to east we find the record of social evolution." The story

> begins with the Indian and the hunter; it goes on to tell of the disintegration of savagery by the entrance of the trader, the pathfinder of civilization; we read the annals of the pastoral stage in ranch life, the exploitation of the soil by the raising of unrotated crops of corn and wheat in sparsely settled farming communities; the intensive culture of the dense farm settlement; and finally the manufacturing organization with city and factory system.[19]

Moving from left to right, this text advances a self-satisfying history of national progress—self-satisfying, that is, from a European American perspective. While relatively undemonstrative in his racial views, Turner built dissolution of Native American culture into his ethnocentric account of American development. Late nineteenth-century U.S. social thought produced few more economical statements of the vanishing Indian.[20]

Turner's account of American social evolution also envisions the vanishing individual European American man. Indeed, the west-to-east narrative portends the erasure of male autonomy and identity altogether: beginning with the archetypes of the "hunter" and "pathfinder" placed one step to the east of the Indian, the historical presence of these individual human figures is lost to civilization and the rise of "the manufacturing organization with the city and factory system."[21] A profound antiurban bias emerges from this passage. And within Turner's highly schematic west-east, wilderness-urban historical continuum, the direction is clear for reversing evolution and recapturing a primal autonomous self. No longer ordered by sequential organic growth, moving back from east to west privileges return to a natural state, an originary essence. No longer seen as a historical accomplishment, civilization is something to overcome, a condition from which oneself can be removed. And it is exactly this point that intersected with the turn-of-the-century escapist attempts to recapture primitive masculinity, as seen in such broad-based popular cultural developments as the romanticization of the Wild West and the cowboy's role within it, the back-to-nature movement in literature and art as well as travel and leisure, and the whole modern embrace of the Indian as noble savage and embodiment of an authentic American past. Turner's instructions to return to the frontier for primary American experience read like a remedy for the perceived crisis of masculinity.

That faith in both American progress and primitivism emerged from the same historical vision is a basic argument of this book: a brute in a suit could serve the "civilizing" interests of corporate nation building while privately trying to slip the bonds of modernity through programmatic acts of devolution. Also, within Turner's work we find the idea that primitivism combines with progress through the passing on of savage character traits into the advanced stages of civilization. This brings us back to Lamarck and the inheritance of acquired characteristics. As stated previously, any number of passages in the frontier thesis, as well as in Turner's popularization of it through other speeches and publications, propose that American character had been indelibly marked by the wild and hostile environment of the West. Turner made the point repeatedly in the "Intellectual Traits" section of the thesis, where he draws the closest equation between the frontier environment, the composite traits of rugged individualism, and their carryover into modern American culture. Turner wrote, for instance, that "these traits have, while softening down, persisted as survivals in the place of their origin, even when a higher social organization succeeded."[22] While Turner didn't discuss *how* individualism survived, one explanation would be that the trait moved from one generation to the next through hereditary transmission. And given the acceptance of the inheritability of acquired characteristics among many leading late nineteenth-century evolutionary figures, including Spencer and Darwin, we can speculate at least that Turner well understood that his thesis regarding the staying power of rugged individualism would draw support from neo-Lamarckian thought.

Yet the fact that turn-of-the-twentieth-century biological science would prove Lamarck to be flat wrong about the inheritance of acquired characteristics had little bearing on the acceptance of Turner's point that the frontier had ingrained rugged individualism into modern Americans' psyches.[23] While benefiting from the scientific aura of evolutionary theory, Turner remained strategically vague about specific biological matters.[24] It's as if Turner appreciated that national character could be explained by either the linguistic communication of tradition or the biological maturation of habits into instinct and decided to let the question go unanswered so that he could engage the concepts from both sides.

When it came to describing the carryover of rugged individualism from one generation to the next, Turner relied on a wide variety of corporeal metaphors and similes, as in his 1903 *Atlantic* article speaking of frontier traits being "wrought into the very warp and woof of American life." In the thesis Turner likened the permanence of American intellectual traits to the rocklike presence of topographical formation: "As successive terminal moraines result from successive glaciations, so each frontier leaves its traces behind it, and when it becomes a settled area the region still partakes of the frontier characteristics." This analogy comes right after Turner's introductory de-evolutionary passage on the frontier taking the European "from the railroad car," placing "him in the birch canoe," and teaching him "the war cry." Though disparate, the two images combine to illustrate how character traits became part of the national landscape itself. Turner created a similar, even more compelling rhetorical combination in his key social evolution paragraph. After likening American development from savagery to civilization to "a continental page" to be read "from west to east," Turner wrote that "[p]articularly in eastern States this page is a palimpsest." Within this metaphor, the East exhibited a surface of urban culture and social sophistication, but the primitive traits of the Indian and hunter could still be read through that outer layer.[25] Notably, this remarkable palimpsest image did not appear in the original frontier thesis. Turner added it to later, more widely published versions after further appreciating the power of metaphor in historical description.

In establishing Turner's reliance on metaphor we may go as far as to conclude that he understood biology itself as metaphor. That is to say that he may not have believed that biological knowledge, language, or perspective enjoyed any privileged relationship to material reality, at least not in the realm of social and cultural history. Turner filtered biological vocabulary and evolutionary imagery into his writing far more for descriptive effect than for claiming objective scientific truth. This generalization especially applies to his examination of American intellectual traits. Consider one final example: in elaborating on the de-evolutionary impact of the frontier on European culture and civilization, Turner told his Harvard University class in 1911 that "We should call this atavism in biology." He did *not* say here that the actual historical-psychological happening *was* one of atavism—the involuntary biologically determined reemergence of a recessive characteristic; rather, he urged his students to draw from biology in coming to terms with the cultural dynamic of the American frontier. "The nature of the struggle," he continued, "reduced society to one of individual atoms. This has its direct effect on the character of man. He goes to his end without scruples, leaving out more and more the moral phase and with a certain element of coarseness."[26] It is to this quality of national "coarseness" or "ruggedness" that we now turn, while keeping an eye on the historical methodologies and assumptions Turner employed in promoting American individualism.

It would be a mistake of course to think that Turner's picture of the rugged individualist springing from the Indian-inhabited wilderness was new to American thought. Neither the individualist character type nor focus on its environmental origins began with Turner. Originally a European philosophy based on abstract fictions of man originating in a state of nature, individualism took on a vivified, almost literal meaning as John Locke, Alexis de Tocqueville, and countless other European and American writers found material confirmation of the ideal in what they considered to be the exceptional quality of freedom in the vast open spaces of the new world. Individualism "incarnate," as literary historian Myra Jehlen has smartly called it, dug deep into late eighteenth- and nineteenth-century national consciousness, manifesting itself in, among many other ways, an early popular typology of American manhood: Crevecoeur's "new man," Franklin's woodsman, Jefferson's republican, Cooper's Natty Bumppo, Tocqueville's democrat, Emerson's "Young American," Thoreau's isolation, popular mid-nineteenth-century accounts of Davy Crockett and Daniel Boone, Seth Jones and other frontiersmen of the post–Civil War dime westerns—all these archetypes turned on the mythopoetic formulation of a solitary and self-reliant figure, awash from Europe, reborn in the American wilderness.[27]

What Turner did with the classic definition of individualism incarnate and its corollary typology of the new American man was to help convert it from myth to knowledge and thereby assure its life in modern thought by formalizing its real-time existence in the past and adding an epistemological foundation to his own day's masculine anxiety over its apparent absence. Social science provided the incremental difference between the frontier thesis and the earlier versions of American individualism. Consequently, the modern appeal of Turner's thought— the way the thesis sunk into turn-of-the-century Americans' consciousness—happened less through tapping into the emotional wellspring of the frontier spirit, although he offered up this also, and more through his ability to ground that preexistent belief in historical knowledge. But what exactly was the epistemological basis of Turner's frontier thesis? *What* Turner said about American individualism is integrally caught up in *how* he said it.

While, as we've already seen, Turner's frontier thesis enjoyed only an indirect and rhetorical relationship to evolutionary biology, he nevertheless looked to science in establishing the epistemological foundation for historical scholarship. In 1883, as an undergraduate at the University of Wisconsin, Turner ruminated in his Commonplace Book that since "[s]cience of late years revolutionized zoology, biology, etc. [i]t must now take up recorded history and do the same by it. This," the young Turner added, "I would like to do my little to aid." Eight years later—after graduating from college, working briefly as a journalist in Madison, teaching as an instructor at Wisconsin, earning a Ph.D. in history at the Johns Hopkins University (then the only true doctoral program in the United States), and returning to Wisconsin to continue teaching—Turner's essay "The Significance of History" distinguished the work of professional academic historians from the "romantic literary artists who strive to give to history the coloring and dramatic action of fiction." He urged his colleagues to seek "truthfulness of substance rather than vivacity of style." Alongside his trust in science, though, Turner insisted throughout his career that it is impossible to avoid the subjective side of writing about the past. "Objective history" refers only to "the events themselves," he stated in "The Significance of History"; "man's conception of these events," on the other hand, cannot help but be written "anew" and "with reference to the conditions uppermost in its own time." Understanding the past is never certain or final. "Knowing the truth in history" is a dynamic undertaking, Turner told a classroom of students at Harvard University: "it involves experiment, adjustment, and the process of life."[28] As in so many other parts of his writing, Turner depended on organic metaphor to describe the development of historical understanding.

In mediating the contingency of historical knowledge with his confidence in science, Turner put less stock in the ideal of objectivity—attaining a God's-eye view—than comprehending the details of past experience.[29] This high esteem for *realism* comes through in his reviews of Teddy Roosevelt's and Francis Parkman's histories of the American West. Roosevelt got caught up in viewing westward expansion as a "grandiloquent" story of conquest, Turner pointed out, adding that he "leaned to the romantic side of the story." As for Parkman, he had achieved great "literary beauty" in *The Oregon Trail* (1849) and other works: he "was the greatest painter of historical pictures that this country—perhaps it is not too much to say, that any country—has produced," Turner wrote in tribute. "It was the picturesque story of the American forest that filled his imagination, . . . and this romantic period permitted, nay, demanded, those very qualities of Parkman's mind and style that might have led him astray in other fields." Times had changed, though, and modern historical scholarship needed to distance itself from romanticism and the painting of literary pictures. Pursuant to this goal Turner and other late nineteenth-century professional historians embraced the emergent photographic medium as a new representational model. In 1890, for example, Justin Winsor suggested that historians approximate the credibility and detail of the camera. Just as people believe what they see in a photographic picture, Winsor stated, history gains authority by registering "everything, however trivial." In his Parkman review, Turner sharpened the realist ideal by critically describing his predecessor as a greater "artist than historian," ostensibly separating creativity from accurate examination of the past, even as his own work betrayed this dichotomy by combining rhetorical and imagistic flourish with maplike description of western settlement.[30]

Historical realism worked as a cover for the ideological content of Turner's frontier thesis. The concept of realism explains how Turner could ignore women in western expansion while still claiming a holistic view of that history. The exclusion of women from American historical thought has deep and complex roots; identification of man as sole agent of change runs back to the earliest production of knowledge in the West; and nineteenth-century romanticism favored masculine subjectivity by tending to dissolve female presence into nature itself. Turner did not completely drop this prescientific dimension from his views on the frontier experience. He could be found waxing romantic, for instance, in his 1903 *Atlantic Monthly* article, describing how the "New World" had taken "European men" to "her bosom" and "opened new provinces" in "her most distant domains." The "material treasures" of the continent "furnished to the pioneer" the strength for "hewing out a home, making a school and church, and creating a higher future for his family."[31] But Turner's professionalized realist discourse also proved to be effective in subsuming women. "The Significance of the Frontier in American History" essay simply assumes a male agent. The thesis's masculine pronouns are matched by the adoption of male figures in its fateful stage theory of American social development from savagery to civilization. In Turner's work, realism augmented ideological power by passing off its particularist view as a neutral or generic frame of analysis.

Seeing through Turner's realist rhetoric points to other problems with his thesis, including the fact that, despite his interest in scientific history, he hardly supported the contention that rugged individualism sprang from the frontier.[32] Turner's typologizing of American intellectual traits is based on neither direct evidence of lived social experience—not oral histories, diaries, manuscripts, or other papers of literate pioneers—nor contemporary cultural expressions of that identity, as might be found in books, songs, stories, and folk tales created during frontier settlement. Turner did append a footnote to the individualist characteristic of "restless, nervous energy," although here he only cited other historians' works along with an early nineteenth-century European-authored travelogue, which presumably records the presence of the trait among people living on the American frontier.[33] This reference fits nominally with Turner's standard of historical realism. While at least one person removed from the actual historical subject, the perceived psychology of others has some claim to "known reality" and "real facts"—Turner's key phrases for authentic documentary evidence.[34] But one source is meager support indeed, especially given the boldness of Turner's historical conception of individualism and its particularly rugged American form.

To understand Turner's reconstruction of individualism, we have to go back to how the frontier thesis, under the guise of realist history, resonated with earlier, nonscientific formulations of personal autonomy thriving in American nature. Considerable textual evidence suggests that the romantic primitivist tradition informed Turner's historical understanding of rugged individualism. His Commonplace Book excerpts Benjamin Franklin's proclamation that "The boundless woods of America are sure to afford freedom and subsistence to any man who can bait a hook or pull a trigger." And we know that Turner, as a boy and college student and throughout his academic life, plied himself with heavy doses of Emerson— perhaps the single biggest influence on his thought outside of history and social science. Turner's 1881 Commonplace Book is full of Emersonian aphorisms and fragments, while the latter part of the journal includes a biographical sketch of the sage from Concord.[35]

Personifying the transmutation of nature into intellect, Emerson offered Turner a spiritually laden source of environmental determinism, one that meshed with the historian-to-be's intimate attachment to Wisconsin's forests, lakes, and rivers. "The Young American" (1841)—always a favorite essay of Turner's, as we find him assigning it, for instance, to his Harvard students in 1911—establishes clearly the symbiosis between national environment and character: "The vast majority of the people of this country live by the land, and carry its manners in their manners and opinions." And in seeming response to Emerson's instruction in "History" (1841) to shape the mind with one's senses—"what it does not see, what it does not live, it will not know"—Turner took to recording in his Commonplace Book his own fragmentary perceptions of the natural world: for example, "The surping rivers solemn chant marked by the metronome of the swaying pines." In college Turner favored Lake Mendota (the largest of the lakes surrounding Madison's campus) with special poetic treatment, replete with romantic association of its qualities with feminine beauty. "Thou art lovely, Mendota, and soft at sunset," Turner cooed, when "Blushes steal over thy face." In another journal entry made during the winter of 1883, Turner observed "the cold white ice lay heavy on Mendota's breast, but in the evening came wind from the southern flurry meads and the ice departed. . . . Did you ever see a lake, placid, still?"[36] During this formative stage of his intellectual biography, Turner combined environment and self with a naturalist optics, a configuration of mind-set and feeling from geography that certainly informed the frontier thesis.

Considering Turner's lifelong attention to the American wilderness, it is fitting to characterize him as a naturalist. In fact, historian William Cronon places Turner among Frank Lloyd Wright, John Muir, Aldo Leopold, and other extraordinary Wisconsin artists and writers of the early to mid-twentieth century whose reconceptions of nature stemmed from an intimate self-generated sense of place. Working from this naturalist framework, perhaps Turner's crucial finding that "to the frontier the American intellect owes its most striking characteristics" came from his own thoughts and feelings. Turner said as much. "I did not keep my personal experiences in a watertight compartment away from my studies," he wrote toward the end of his career. "I have poled down the Wisconsin in a dug-out with Indian guides . . . through virgin forest of balsam firs, seeing deer in the river." Turner felt "that I belonged to it all"; "[t]he frontier in that sense," he concluded, "was real to me."[37] Turner's claim to realism becomes more legitimate with the notion that he drew from his own experience in emphasizing the centrality of rugged individualism to American character. Even though he couldn't refer to the source in his scholarly writing, there is an authenticity to first-person perception that fills in the otherwise abstract environmental determinist explanation for American individualism, whether it be of the romanticist state-of-nature variety or from neo-Lamarckian, direct adaptationist evolutionary theory.

Since its early to mid-nineteenth-century emergence in the United States, individualism has proved to be an unusually elastic and composite thought system. Within modern urban culture, individualism begat individuality, personality, and the privileging of self-expression; it spurred the secular quest for artistic creativity, psychic liberation, and subjective potency. Earlier versions of individualism concentrated on economic autonomy and political rights—the cluster of liberal principles of the self later labeled "possessive individualism." In the first and one of the most accomplished analyses of U.S. individualism, Alexis de Tocqueville focused on the acquisitive origins of the ideal, observing in 1840 that after "retain[ing] sufficient education and fortune to satisfy their own wants," Americans believe "[t]hey owe nothing to any man, they expect nothing from any man; they acquire the habit of always considering themselves as standing above, and they are apt to imagine that their whole destiny is in their own hands." Individualism, wrote Tocqueville, "disposes each citizen to isolate himself from the mass of his fellows." Individualism's antisocial ethic corrodes republican virtue and civic consciousness, he emphasized, while its material striving leads to a "strange" nervousness, a "feverish ardor" in the mind and manners of Americans. Tocqueville's study of national character fused "restlessness of temper" to the economic core of American individualism. The combination led to his brilliant caricature of "American man" psychologically unable to enjoy his prosperity because of the felt need to "rush forward" and acquire all the more.[38]

In the frontier thesis, Turner worked from Tocqueville's critique of American individualism. He, too, recognized the "evil" (as well as the "good") of individualism. And, like the French political scientist, Turner highlighted "that restless, nervous energy" among the basic American intellectual traits—both writers combined individualism with high-energy anxious striving. Turner associated nervous energy with westward movement itself and the European American experience of "winning a wilderness": frontier warfare played a much larger role in his formulation of American character than in either Tocqueville's economic determinism or Emerson's poeticized self-reliance. As much as Turner remained caught up in the classic romanticist vision of man isolated in nature, his historical conception of American individualism included rougher-hewn traits best summarized by the word *rugged*. His modification of individualism spoke to the violent capacity and proclivity of European Americans. He described the trait variously as "that coarseness and strength," a condition of being "without scruples," and "stalwart[ness]."[39] But "rugged individualism" stuck. Since the turn of the twentieth century it has been one of the most widely used terms to describe national character overall.

Several sources may have contributed to Turner's understanding of ruggedness, including his own childhood memories. "I have seen a lynched man hanging from a tree as I came home from school in Portage," Turner wrote to Carl Becker, "have played around old Fort Winnebago at its outskirts, have seen the red shirted Irish raftsmen *take* the town when they tied up and came ashore." Prefrontier thesis histories of the American West undoubtedly contributed to Turner's recognition of its violent past. Parkman's work, including *Oregon Trail,* and Roosevelt's *Winning of the West* present the Indian wars as the central heroic events of nation building. While Turner did not look to European American mastery in the same celebratory manner as Parkman and Roosevelt, he certainly recognized that each successive boundary line separating "savagery and civilization" was "won through a series of Indian wars." And he spoke of how the pioneer arriving on the frontier quickly learned to "shou[t] a war cry and tak[e] the scalp in orthodox Indian fashion."[40] Rather than detailing the European American man's warrior ways, though, Turner strategically relied on the rugged individualist typology to subsume the violent traits that he thought distinguished the American from his European ancestry.

Another possible influence on Turner's conception of the ruggedness produced by the frontier is J. Hector St. John de Crevecoeur's *Letters from an American Farmer*

(1782). Striking comparisons can be drawn between their understanding of the way the wilderness imprints itself upon the Europeans who come into contact with it. Equally striking is their common rhetorical approach in geographically locating the origins of American character. In Letter III, "What Is an American?" Crevecoeur created an east-to-west frame of analysis, "trac[ing] our society from sea to our woods" and insisting that "[h]e who would wish to see America in its proper light . . . must visit our extended line of frontiers where the last settlers dwell." What happens there is a type of conversion or reversion experience in which civilization dissolves away and "men are wholly left dependent on their native tempers." The mechanism for this devolution is "the wildness of the neighborhood," Crevecoeur insisted: "there is something in the proximity of the woods, which is very singular. It is with men as it is with the plants and animals that grow and live in the forests; they are entirely different than those that live in the plains." For Crevecoeur the crucial difference is "the perfect state of war" between "back woods settlers" and animal life. "The deer often come to eat their grain, the wolves to destroy their sheep, the bears to kill their hogs, the foxes to catch their poultry. This surrounding hostility," he continued, "immediately puts the gun into their hands; they watch these animals, they kill some; and thus by defending their property, they soon become professed hunters." For Crevecoeur—who, like Turner, idealized the pastoral state of the farmer—hunting and the "eating of wild meat" triggered "degenera[cy]" and a host of character traits that rendered hunters "no better than the carnivorous animals." He found them "ferocious, gloomy and unsociable." They are, Crevecoeur concluded, "our bad people."[41]

Crevecoeur's finding may have contributed to Turner's rugged individualist typology, although the Wisconsin historian never went as far in denigrating the frontiersman and, while he wrote about "the hunter type" who "lived remote from city life," he used the modifier *rugged* to describe Native American influence on European American character.[42] To emphasize, for Turner, ruggedness—that most distinct American adaptation of individualism—arose from fighting and killing Indians. With Native Americans posing a "common danger, demanding united action," the frontier served "as a military training school, keeping alive the power of resistance to aggression, and developing the stalwart and rugged qualities of the frontiersman." Turner would elaborate the point outside of his 1893 text. In his speech and article "The Development of American Society" (1908), Turner said that the frontier "first" represented a "line of fire"—"a stern warfare against the Indian." The Native Americans put up a good fight, he added. "Each chief," Turner wrote, "rallied his tribesmen and strove to make alliances to stem the tide, but only succeeded in making life in the west a peril, a discipline in courage, a training school for a hardy and conquering stock."[43] Sounding not unlike Teddy

Roosevelt here, Turner thus took on the racialist discourse of modern American nationalism.

The 1908 "conquering stock" passage notwithstanding, Turner tended to cover up, though not forget, the martial dimension of European American expansion westward. "Ruggedness" helped him in this effort. The "rugged qualities of the frontiersman," Turner wrote carefully in his 1893 thesis, arose by "keeping alive the power of resistance to aggression." Turner used ruggedness as a euphemism for exceptional capacity for force and violence, and he strategically cloaked that violence in the necessity of overcoming the preexistent belligerence of the "Indian frontier." Turner also concealed frontier warfare by portraying Native America as a built-in part of the environment: settling the West involved clearing forests and its original inhabitants, whom he referred to in his "Development of American Society" text as "nature-people." His very definition of the American frontier—that "meeting point between savagery and civilization"—conflates Native Americans with the wilderness. And the de-evolutionary section of the thesis confuses cultural exchange for geographical determinism. "The wilderness masters the colonist. It takes him from the railroad car and puts him in the birch canoe," he explained, representing this transformation as a natural state rather than the result of acculturation. For Turner, it's worth repeating, the conversion experience leads to "shout[ing] the war cry and tak[ing] the scalp in orthodox Indian fashion."[44] The "Americanization" of European pioneers included deadly savagery, a trait that they took on through close mortal contact with Indians and would carry with them in encounters with themselves as well as other peoples.

Turner usually downplayed violent frontier traits by redescribing them in general positive terms. In the concluding paragraph of his thesis, Turner placed what would become one of his most quoted passages: "He would be a rash prophet who should assert that the expansive character of American life has now entirely ceased. Movement has been its dominant fact, and unless this training has no effect upon a people, the American energy will continually demand a wider field for its exercise." These fateful words have been read to portend everything from the coming of the skyscraper and the metropolis to the Spanish-American War and the long history of twentieth-century U.S. foreign wars. The fruition of American imperialism is difficult to disregard when reading these lines, especially after Turner's construction of national character with the traits of ruggedness and belligerency. Turner understood "American energy" as a naturally expansive impulse, a "restless, nervous energy" selected from the hostile social environment of the frontier and instrumental in dispensing with those peoples who impeded future "movement."[45] Compared to Tocqueville's "feverish" economic man, Turner's rugged individual directed his energies toward human exploit as well as material acquisition. And in his vaguely sociobiological way, Turner suggested that frontier "training" had ingrained ruggedness into American character. Although the frontier was closed and the Indian wars won, rugged individualism would pass into modern American life. It had become a force in itself, independent of its supposed sociogeographic origins.

Turner's Influence on the Social Psychology of the City

Since the late nineteenth century, the concept of individualism has been used to gauge the alienating effects of modernity. While many have tried to maintain the romanticist notion of the sovereign self, sociologists, psychologists, and, following Turner, cultural historians have also reduced individualism to a type of neurological dispensation for the high energy essential to productive exertion and self-reliance. How would this behavioral predisposition stand up to corporate regimentation of work and culture, extensive immigration, and the hyperstimulus of the densely populated metropolis? Historians and social theorists have answered this question differently, to be sure, but individualism and its mental trait of nervous energy provided a common denominator throughout the ensuing analyses: neurologists George Beard and S. Weir Mitchell incorporated individualism into their diagnosis and treatment of neurasthenia; social and evolutionary psychologists have assumed it in their examination of human instincts in modern urban environments; in the United States especially, concern for the preservation of individualism has driven the whole intellectual and cultural back-to-nature movement. Within the perceived crisis of American manhood, individualism, in close combination with virility, has been that which is most likely to be lost to overcivilization and, in its rugged and primitive forms, that which is most feverishly sought through masculinist devolution.

In one sense, Turner crystallized the cultural crisis of masculinity with his present-minded question concerning the fate of American individualism once the frontier conditions that gave it birth had vanished in the wake of modern industrial society. Turner had a flair for the dramatic: "And now, four centuries from the discovery of America," he wrote in the very last sentence of his 1893 thesis, "the frontier has gone, and with its going has closed the first period of American history."[46] His clear historical periodization of American modernity raised the uneasy imagery of a nation of individuals accustomed to rushing forward now having to turn back upon itself in the closed space of the metropolis. But, as we have seen, while raising the specter of a fundamental break with the past, Turner optimistically suggested that frontier traits had become so ingrained in national character that they would find new expression in post-1890 America. He begged the question of what new forms rugged individualism would take. And Turner's biography as well as his work show that back-to-nature escapism and the infusion of individualist energy into urban culture would be two meaningful alternatives.

In assessing the impact of the frontier thesis, it is worth noting that Turner himself shrank routinely from modern urban life. His longing for nature often distracted him from the increasingly demanding indoor ways and responsibilities of a history professor. From Turner's continued pleasure in the wilds while canoeing, camping, and hunting—"Blessed be the woods," he wrote to his fiancée in 1886, "Wish I might never see a city again"; to his notorious difficulty with writing books; to the nearly self-parodying practice, after moving to Harvard, of sleeping in a tent in the backyard of his Cambridge home: the tension between outdoors and inside would disturb Turner throughout his career (fig. 1.2).[47] His early retirement from Harvard in 1924 underlines the point. And his movement westward to Madison and a cottage on a lake, to summer teaching posts in Provo, Utah, and then finally to southern California and a senior research position at the Huntington Library, where friends, beautiful surroundings, and his disposition kept him from completing THE BOOK, suggests a backward arc of his person that uncannily retraces the de-evolutionary sequences in his thesis.

The chances for the post-1890 life of rugged individualism increased with the fact that great expanses of American wilderness still existed. This point went unrecognized in the frontier thesis, although Turner's outdoor ways prove that he understood it at an experiential level. (We "paddled in all nearly 400 miles," Turner enthused over a summer canoeing trip in 1908, "slept in a bed only once during the [month], cut our own trails for part of the route, saw no one but our party of ten for nearly three weeks . . . and in general had a belly taste of the real wilderness.")[48] Because Turner measured modernity geographically—through the frontier's closing—it follows that one would be able to reclaim transitorily the essential past and thus one's essential self by moving outside of civilization and placing himself in those pockets of nature that had eluded social development.

Interestingly, though, while Turner certainly appreciated the need for release from the rigors of the workplace and urban life, he tended to distance himself from the more exaggerated forms of escapism. Turner criticized the sports craze of his time. At Wisconsin he led a major reform movement against the professionalization and brutality of college football. The sport did "have the touch of danger, the call to courage, that meets a response in American character," as Turner said in a 1906 speech before the Wisconsin Alumni Association; but with the obsession of football, he concluded, "human values are put in the wrong perspective."[49] Hanged in effigy by Madison students, Turner grew mindful of the excesses of rugged individualism. Moreover, in answering his own question about how the pioneer spirit would carry into twentieth-century life, he seemed to subordinate physical activity to intellectual and even artistic pursuits.

One can go as far as to say that Turner's attention to the impact of space and movement on national consciousness led to the conception of an especially American source of artistic thought and creativity and an early formulation of the avant-garde or modernist aesthetic that influenced so much twentieth-century art and literature. As he told his Harvard class in 1911, the West had imprinted "great spaces upon the American imagination" and produced "ideals of creativity" in its people; American consciousness had gained "freedom from the dead hand of the past." The leading principle of this new sensibility, Turner added, is the attack on convention for its own sake—a primary impulse in American experience, as a Harvard student wrote in his notes for Turner's class, that is "destructive of the old, insurgent of established customs." Turner pointed to many examples of the pioneer spirit in modern urban culture. The rise of American fiction and "its swinging from the discipline and self-restraint" of earlier American literature attracted his attention. But Turner was drawn most to the cityscape itself. In modern architecture, he wrote in 1924, "the American genius has best expressed itself." In this new "age of aspiration," Turner continued, the "skyscraper comes naturally, hugely, beautifully as its best expression."[50] These comments draw the most compelling parallel between frontier and urban sensibilities: the transposing of western expansiveness onto the vertical plane of the new spatially delimited environment. And these later observations by Turner also reflect a buoyancy and optimism about American life that always distinguished his work and person. He ended his career with almost as much wonder for modern society as he had for America's preindustrial past.

There is a disjuncture, though, between how Turner pursued the implications of the frontier thesis and its influence on American thought and culture as a whole. Turner spent most of his scholarly time on the topic of sectionalism in American history, culminating in the 1925 essay that included an even closer equation between environment and a person's "ideals and psychology." Americans did "not [pass] into a monotonously uniform space," Turner emphasized: "They were pouring their plastic pioneer life into geographic molds." Turner worked his way to a promising theory of regional history. "There is a geography of political habit," he explained, "a geography of opinion, of material interests, of racial stocks, of physical fitness, of social traits, of literature, of the distribution of men of ability, even of religious denominations."[51] But, as Michael Steiner has pointed out, Turner's value as a regionalist historian went largely unappreciated and instead he has been remembered "as the Albert Bierstadt and Buffalo Bill Cody of the historical profession, the intellectual godfather of John Wayne and the Marlboro Man."[52] While all too true, more specific judgments can be made regarding Turner's influence. In particular, two strands of scholarship can be traced. The first is in cultural history. As discussed in this book's essay on sources, a rather direct connection exists between Turner's genealogy of rugged individualism, his question of how that mental trait might evolve in modern America, and subsequent study of the rise of sports and the middle-class "re-orientation" around vigorous masculine activity. This line of scholarship culminates in late twentieth-century men's history, an immediate context for my study.

The second strand is social psychology, whose environmental determinist focus on the modern city's impact on individualism and nervous energy bears striking affinity with Turner's interest in population density and his indefinite belief that pioneer instincts would carry over into postfrontier America. To what extent Turner influenced this discourse remains an open question. Impact can be very hard to measure, especially within an emergent social and behavioral science, one that involved the major European theorists of modernity Ferdinand Tonnies, Georg Simmel, Emile Durkheim, and Max Weber; such American urbanist thinkers as Albion Small, Jane Addams, John Dewey, and W. I. Thomas; and the whole cross-Atlantic rise of academic psychology and sociology. Just the same, resonances of the frontier thesis can be found throughout the twentieth century. A close epistemological congruency existed between Turner's environmentalist approach to American intellectual traits and social psychological concern over the individual's existential, cognitive, and neurological response to the metropolis.

A high point of fear for the individual came in the post–World War II period, when the history of fascist and communist totalitarianism, the military-industrial complex, Madison Avenue psychology, and suburban conformity seemed to threaten human autonomy altogether. "Mass society" was the master social-scientific label for the accumulative forces set against the American individual—that once ebullient self-reliant figure now phlegmatic, no longer directed from within.[53] The frontier thesis shows up in a number of crucial midcentury works, including C. Wright Mills's book *White Collar: The American Middle Classes* (1953), whose damning portrait of modern manhood relies on a very basic Turnerian model of environmental determinism. In contrast to the "independence" attained while "struggling to subdue the vast continent," Mills wrote, twentieth-century man had been gradually overcome by "the levelling influences of modern urban civilization." Man, in Mills's critique, is mauled by society. The effect is described physically: he is "pushed by forces beyond his control" and "pulled into movements he doesn't understand." No longer having the land to "lean upon," Mills concluded, man gives in to "the contents of a mass society that has shaken him . . . and manipulates him to its alien ends."[54] As for middle-class culture, desperate alienation would grow into one of the leading mind-sets for disaffected youth for the rest of the twentieth century. Mills on his motorcycle, Kerouac "on the road," and middle-class youth "dropping out" became emblematic of the countercultural strategies of movement, disconnection, and gaining outsidedness. Within the hypermasculinist version of this complex, weekend treks to the wilderness for chest beating, sweat lodges, and paint ball would follow at the end of the century.

High anxiety over the fate of the individual self also peaked during the late nineteenth and early twentieth centuries, as we have seen, and Turner crystallized understanding of this cultural phenomenon by rooting American psychological autonomy in the nation's geography. One of this period's most provocative restatements of the frontier thesis came in middlebrow literary critic Henry Seidel Canby's 1917 *Yale Review* essay on the contemporary back-to-nature craze. "[M]ore Americans go back to nature for one reason or another annually than any civilized men before them" because, Canby explained, "in our sub-conscious nature is peculiarly active. We react to nature as does no other race." The great outdoors had been imprinted on the American mind: "We are the descendants of pioneers—all of us. And if we have not inherited a memory of pioneering experiences, at least we possess inherited tendencies and desires." There is little choice in the matter, Canby said in substantiating Turner's Lamarckian suggestion that Americans inherited the acquired characteristic of rugged individualism: "It *is* an American trait." The "survival of the pioneer instinct" depended on its regular exercise, because the city's "pavements, electric lights, tight roofs, and artificial heat" routinely weaken the trait. A strict reading of environmental determinism underlay Canby's essay. He spoke repeatedly of "the profound and powerful influence of physical environment upon men."[55] And, in one interpretation of Turner's thesis, he saw the closed space of the modern city as anathema to America's frontier past.

Canby's essay is representative of an antiurban grain running through the vast late nineteenth- and early twentieth-century literature extolling the virtues of nature. The theme certainly comes through in Henry Childs Merwin's *Atlantic Monthly* article "On Being Civilized Too Much"(1897): over and against the "weaken[ing]" effects of the city, man can retain his "primeval impulses" and strength "only by perpetually renewing his contact with Mother earth." In his *Harper's Monthly* essay "Jostling the Simple Life" (1907), E. S. Martin insisted that "country life" is "more favorable" for "the development of individuality than the life of the greater cities." In a 1913 article in the *Atlantic Monthly* (1913), G. S. Dickerson warned of the wholesale "lowering of character" involved in the national "drift to the cities." Unlike "the pioneers of our country," who could depend on the unsettled space of the frontier, twentieth-century Americans have to go out and find their individualism in the remaining pockets of wilderness. It is well worth the effort, Dickerson advised: just as "a big tree, an oak or an elm, standing out in an open field, has a toughness of fibre, a spread of boughs and roundness of shape that are never seen in a tree that stands in the woods," so too with "individuality" and other "great human qualities," which "come to their best in a life of comparative isolation." Dickerson echoed the naturalist John Muir's celebration of "Our National Parks" (1901) and that well-known essay's praise for the "thousands of tired, nerve-shaken, over-civilized people [who] are beginning to find out that going to the mountains is going to hope; that wildness is a necessity; and that mountain parks and reservations are useful not only as fountains of timber and irrigating rivers, but as fountains of life."[56] While making little explicit reference to the frontier thesis, the cultural criticism of Muir, Canby, and these other writers repeats its assumption that the social environment of the city drains individual energy and vitality.

Surprisingly similar to the turn-of-the-century, back-to-nature literature, diagnosis and treatment of neurasthenia—that characteristically American "lack of nerve force," as George M. Beard defined the disease—involved a critique of the modern city and the privileging of isolation in the wilderness. *American Nervousness* (1881), Beard's treatise on neurasthenia, links the malady to the exceptionally high levels of material striving and social mobility in the United States. Dissipation of nervous energy, for Beard, was a flip side to individualism. Put differently, neurasthenia stemmed from exposure to "modern civilization": economic competition, excessive "brain work," rapid communication, and the fast pace and constant noise of the city all contributed to nervous weakness and fatigue.[57] The remedy, especially in the hands of Beard's friend and colleague S. Weir Mitchell, was rest cure: indoor quiet and seclusion for women and outdoor air and activity for men. With such hypermasculinist figures as Teddy Roosevelt, Owen Wister, and Frederic Remington following Dr. Mitchell's advice, the imbrication of neurological science and the cultural imperative to go West and escape from the city is clear.[58]

In addition to the various turn-of-the-century critiques of the city, countercurrents can be found that concentrated on the positive neurological affects that urban environments had on individual psyches. One origin of this discourse was European-American modernity theory, including the German sociologist Georg Simmel's famous essay "The Metropolis and Mental Life" (1903), which describes how "the city sets up a deep contrast with small town and rural life with reference to the sensory foundations of psychic life." What Simmel called the "intensification of nervous stimulation" is exactly the reason why Beard, Mitchell, and American back-to-nature writers advised people to leave the city—the traffic, crowds, and noise sapped individual energy.[59] But others saw urban excitement leading to new sense perceptions, its hyperstimulus producing nothing less than modernist forms of cultural creativity. Turner appreciated this point in his later writing and teaching. And, as surveyed in the next section, the modernist embrace of urban culture became a crucial part of early twentieth-century U.S. counterculture and the gendered use of individuality for middle-class feminism and male rebellion.

In general terms, American sociology founded itself in opposition to the prevailing antiurban belief that the city erased personal autonomy. The very nature of the discipline dictated scrutiny of what Albion Small, the first professor of "sociology" in the United States, called the "the preposterous initial fact of the individual"[60] In 1907 Charles H. Cooley, another leading early sociologist and writing in the Small-edited *American Journal of Sociology*, noted that "[p]sychologists, and even sociologists, are still much infected with the idea that self-consciousness is in some way primary, and antecedent to social consciousness." In the opening pages of his canonical work *Social Organization* (1909), Cooley rejected the proposition: "Self and society are twin born, and we know one as immediately as we know the other, and the notion of a separate and independent ego is an illusion."[61] Diametrically opposed to the frontier thesis's romanticist idea of individualism springing naturally from the wilderness, Cooley, Small, and other early twentieth-century U.S. sociologists not only envisioned the continuing integrity of the individual in urban America but argued that modern society alone produced a dynamic highly differentiated self.

New York University sociologist Robert McDougall advanced this promodernity position in his 1912 article "The Social Basis of Individuality." Writing in the *American Journal of Sociology*, he countered the contemporary "fear" that "the flavor of unique and stimulating personalities will be merged and lost in a multitudinous commonality in which a single social type is incessantly repeated." But instead of the close-quartered urban environment erasing "individual existence," McDougall insisted, "it has everywhere resulted in throwing that existence into greater prominence"; rather than "the distinction between self and society" disappearing, "the points of opposition have steadily increased in number and the distinction in question has grown sharper and clearer." Society, for McDougall, is "the general storehouse of cultural materials and personal attitudes the combinations of which give rise to the individual varieties of self-existence." Not existential solitude but "inner differentiation" from other people around you becomes the individualist end point for McDougall; high population density provides intensive social stimulation and endless points of contrast—the stuff from which personal definition is created.[62]

While McDougall's essay discusses the virtues of modernity within the social theoretical abstractions of the individual's relationship to society, another article in the same volume of the *American Journal of Sociology* speaks positively about the neurological effects of the city. In "The Urban Habit of Mind" (1912), City College of New York sociologist Howard B. Woolston took the neurasthenic premise that city life makes huge demands on an individual's nervous system and turned it around by arguing that those adaptive to the environment reach a new level of sociopsychological evolution. Woolston's "process of urban selection" (or alternatively "nervous selection") works like the frontier in Turner's thesis. For Woolston, the city is harsh: "Men are assailed at every sense by the presence of their neighbors. . . . The crowd sets a pace. The individual must hurry with it or be pushed aside." Those able to keep up develop fortitude and vigor. "The restless current in which we are immersed," Woolston explained, "produces individuals who are alert, active, quick to seek new satisfactions." Part of this payoff comes from actual sensory experience—"the bustle and gaiety, the variety and swift movement of the town"; but, like McDougall, Woolston recognizes that the city's "heightened stimulation" includes a valuable social dimension: "In cities men are obliged to live in close touch with each other, not only physically but intellectually." Individual experience is enriched—"contacts are multiplied and reactions are greatly increased"—as a cosmopolitan ethic of tolerance also emerges. In concluding that "[t]his conscious sharing in a common life is the essence of what we call 'the social mind,'" Woolston split the presumed difference between individual integrity and the modern urban environment.[63]

A faithful application of the frontier thesis in twentieth-century American social thought can be found in John Dewey's *Individualism, Old and New* (1930). Dewey took Turner's environmental determinist account of American character at face value, pointing out that nineteenth-century "[i]ndividuality was a reality because it corresponded to the conditions" of "the wilderness." But modern Americans are "acutely maladjust[ed]," failing to realize "that they are sustaining and sustained members of a social whole" and instead clouding their self-understanding with romanticized representations of the West. "Where is the wilderness which now beckons creative energy and affords untold opportunity to initiative and vigor?" Dewey asked. "The wilderness exists in the movie and the novel; and the children of pioneers, who live in the midst of surroundings artificially made over by machine, enjoy pioneer life idly in the various film." Dewey recognized that the frontier spirit of daring and doing also lived on in corporate boardrooms. A great deal had been lost in the transition. "One cannot imagine a bitterer comment on any professed individualism," Dewey wrote, "than that it subordinates the only creative individuality—that of the mind—to the maintenance of a regime which gives the few an opportunity for being shrewd in the management of monetary business." In rounding out his critique of modern American individualism, Dewey noticed that the ideal had evolved into a practice of cultural rebellion, the "habit of opposing" social conventions. Writing at the end of the 1920s, a decade marked by "pathological" pleasure seeking, "unrest, impatience," and "hurry," Dewey concluded that what had once supported the "heroic" settlement of the continent had become a superficial ethic of expressing one's individuality through distinctions of personality and appearance.[64]

Individualism's drift into modern American culture certainly influenced middle-class gender formations. If de-evolutionary masculinity worked from a radically historicist perspective, then the frontier thesis contributed to that psychology as much as any other single source. It helped establish individualism as a habit of mind as well as an expectation of culture. Throughout the twentieth century the frontier would remain a shorthand reference for the lost dynamism of an earlier age. The novelist Norman Mailer's 1957 invocation of the "frontiersman in the Wild West of American night life" as a model for existentialist rebellion provides an exaggerated case in point. Against the drift of post–World War II "conformity," Mailer recommended hypermobility: "Movement is always to be preferred to inaction. In motion a man has a chance, his body is warm, his instincts are quick, and when the crisis comes . . . he can make it, he can win, he can release a little more energy for himself . . . he can make a little better nervous system."[65] Two generations earlier, young cultural and political radicals in Greenwich Village and other urban centers understood psychic and spatial movement as a key strategy of individualization. For these women and men, individuality and rebellion could have quite different and similar meanings.

Radical Individualism: Masculinist Art, Angst, and Alienation in the City

If individualism is a historical guide to masculine identity, then we need to consider its twentieth-century outgrowth of *individuality,* a diffuse dual-gendered ideal that can be distinguished slightly from individualism by its emphasis on uniqueness over singleness.[66] For those white urban middle-class men and women who could claim to possess some measure of economic security and political autonomy, individuality had become a type of liberationist discourse by the beginning of the century, when high-modernist introspections of bohemian poets, avant-garde artists, and radical essayists combined with pop-psychology self-help literature to form a galaxy of appeals to the intricately imbricated therapeutic and freedom-seeking self. Early twentieth-century urban individuality also incorporated a certain western mania, that is, widespread escapism from the city to dude ranches and other renderings of wild and wide open spaces; while easterners sought and found ruggedness on these vacations, such experience tended to feed back into the differential equation of one's personality rather than add any lasting experiential quality of solitariness. Offering its own distinct geography, pre–World War I Greenwich Village made up one of the purest cultural environments for self-creation. It, too, stressed liberation from middle-class routine, decorum, and convention: seeking new pathways to intense subjectivity, young New York intellectuals provided an American home for Friedrich Nietzsche's project of freeing the individual self by historicizing and negating dominant structures of thought, language, religion, and culture. This heady mix of early existentialism and institutionalized bohemianism produced the prototype for Mailer's urban "frontiersman," a once rarified and then increasingly common variation on American individualism.

Nietzsche's contribution to pre–World War I Greenwich Village and the wider modernist American literary culture can be established easily.[67] Literary and cultural critics of the time widely acknowledged his impact: "it is too late in the day to question the vitality of Nietzsche's thought and influence," *Current Literature* reported in 1908; "and no one responsive to the intellectual currents of our time can deny that his influence is steadily growing."[68] While few agreed on exactly what Nietzsche meant, bohemians did gravitate to him in modeling their own rebellion. Many were simply taken with Nietzsche's biography: the story of the prodigious classics professor leaving his tenured position at Basle to wander in the hills of Italy attracted those in Greenwich Village trying to remove themselves from what they defined as an overbearing and puritanical culture. At the same time, Nietzsche's announcement of the death of God in *Thus Spoke Zarathustra* (1883, published in English in 1892)—his best-known work in the United States—and that book's subsequent positing of the *Übermensch* (superman) as one who could attain a higher humanity through self-generated powers of creativity, inspired young white New York intellectuals' close embrace of the avant-garde artist as a hero of cultural rebellion. Within this mind-set, rebellion could and did become an end in itself. Nietzsche helped set white middle-class American masculinity on a privatistic course.[69]

Prewar Greenwich Village intellectuals latched on to the Nietzschean ethic of filial and cultural impiety, stylizing it into a generational critique of the American middle class and a new program for self-identity. The first part of this formula for rebellion—historicizing and thereby distancing themselves from bourgeois values, expectations, and conventions—stemmed from Nietzsche, Marx, Weber, and Freud and their analytical leveling of the long-standing Anglo-American systems of capitalism, rationalism, psychological autonomy, and moral certainty. In the hands of young New York bohemian writers, this critique tended toward caricature of the "genteel tradition," the "boobosie," "puritanism" (in the most popular Greenwich Village term), or what Van Wyck Brooks described in 1915 as that "dry old Yankee stalk."[70] The second step of self-creation depended on the avant-garde artist archetype and the new qualities of "personality" and "individuality" as markers of successful resistance to, as Randolph Bourne encouraged, the institutional pressures of middle-class conformity. For countercultural American men of the early twentieth century, this combination of iconoclasm and liminality often resulted in self-conscious disconnectedness from matters political and social. This relativist tendency becomes transparent when compared to the feminist rebellion of women in and around prewar Greenwich Village. Recognition, in particular, of the crucial link between individual self-development and the advancement of women as a social group provides clear contrast to the privatism of masculine rebellion.

American feminism has long had a conflicted relationship with the ideals of individualism and individuality. In one vein, personal autonomy and its legal recognition in constitutionally protected rights of property, contract, divorce, voting, and birth control, among many other particulars, has helped drive U.S. feminism for two centuries; Elizabeth Cady Stanton's 1892 existentialist appeal to "The Solitude of the Self" and women's "right to an equal place" remains one of the inspirational high points in the whole social movement; and among pre–World War I feminists, the promise of individuality impelled both historical critique of masculine domination and new models of personal liberation.[71] At the same time, high regard for the sovereign self has generated a long tradition of feminist misgivings, including concern over the adoption of male standards for female development. "Difference feminism" has privileged women's primary if not essential quality of interconnectedness with each other over the atomistic self-seeking impulse perceived to be central to masculinity.[72] Women's historians have criticized, in Elizabeth Fox-Genovese's term, the "radical personalism" cultivated by individualist-minded feminists of the twentieth century. "Life-style" feminism, as the critique goes, intimately connected to the white middle-class, slipped too easily into the consumer ethos of modern American commercial culture.[73]

When compared to masculine formulations of individuality, however, especially the Nietzschean privatism of prewar Greenwich Village, feminist individuality can actually be appreciated for its practical politics. Greenwich Village feminists almost always kept in sight the material subjugation of their person and used rebellion to empower themselves against man-made systems that had routinely inhibited women's development as both individuals and as a social group. The collectivist dimension of feminist rebellion can clearly be seen in the Heterodoxy Club of prewar Greenwich Village. Founded in 1912, and meeting twice a month to discuss a wide range of social and political issues, the club self-consciously institutionalized the feminist principle of continuous negation. No single idea united these women except their interest in opposing conventional forms and the personal freedom it afforded. "The only quality demanded of a member," Elizabeth Gurley Flynn ex-

plained, "was that she should not be orthodox in her opinions. The club was therefore called Heterodoxy." In a 1919 study of the club, Florence Guy Woolston added
that the "Heterodites" followed only one rule: to keep themselves free of rules.
"There is the strongest taboo on taboo," Woolston said ironically but with a point:
"Taboo is injurious to the free development of the mind and spirit."[74] The novelist Edna Kenton, another club member, also focused on women's need to break
rules. Writing in a 1914 issue of the Boston journal *The Delineator,* Kenton defined
feminism as revolt against "customs, counts, and prophets"; it meant a "troop of
departures from the established order of women's lives."[75] As Kenton's comments
suggest, heterodoxy as a concept made an important originary contribution to the
mid-1910s American effort to define modern feminism.

Heterodoxy was manifest, for instance, in the two large feminist meetings at
Cooper Union Hall in February 1914. These mass meetings served as centerpieces
of the prewar Greenwich Village effort to define the feminist agenda. The twelve
speakers in the first meeting, focusing on "What Feminism Means to Me," did
vary in their formulations; but virtually all of them stressed the need for women to
break free from male-created standards of sexual difference. Mary Jenny Howe, the
"chairman" of the event and founder of the Heterodoxy Club, acknowledged that
men were "held in prison by [the] convention[s]" of middle-class society; women,
though, "were confined to one room in the prison and had to watch the men walk
about in the corridors in comparative freedom." Howe added that feminists did
not want to limit the power of men—"we do not put any fence around" them—"but
we insist that they shall not put one around us, either." Heterodite Francis Perkins,
another speaker at Cooper Union, exhorted women to transgression. "Feminism
means revolution," Perkins insisted, "and I am a revolutionist. I believe in revolution as a principle," she concluded: "[i]t does good to everybody."[76] Perkins and
other Heterodites wanted to live by a rule of rebellion.

An essential first step in this feminist imperative of rebellion came through the
strategy of detailing standards of sexual difference as old and destructive: roughly
similar to the male bohemians' historicist approach to middle-class conventions,
prewar feminists isolated and analyzed the interlocking social systems that routinely denied women's independence, intellectually removing themselves from
those structures by consigning them to the past. The most accomplished early
twentieth-century critique of male dominance was advanced by feminist intellectual Charlotte Perkins Gilman. A Heterodite, author of the study *Women and
Economics* (1898), single-handed producer of the feminist journal *The Forerunner*
(1912–19), Gilman drew from the evolutionary social science of Lester Ward to detail the origins and enduring power of patriarchy, or what she called "androcentricism": the broad-based set of social practices, relationships, and institutions that

systematically subordinated women well after the original reasons for sexual distinctions had dissolved. In her *Forerunner* series "Our Androcentric Culture; or, the Man-Made World" (1910), Gilman explained that modern society reduced women to a sexually specific identity or type: "Men are people," while "women being the sex, have their limited point of view, which must be provided for. Men, however, are not restricted." Because culture and not biology underwrote this sexual marking, women could erase it through keen and active historical consciousness. "Now let us shake ourselves free," Gilman proclaimed, "if only for a moment, from the androcentric habit of mind."[77]

What exactly would happen, though, once the conventions of sexual difference were shaken off? For Gilman, the payoff of feminist negation would be the development of "humanness" among women: "The new woman is human first, last and always. Incidentally she is female." In contrast to masculine formulations of countercultural individuality—many of which dissolved into a primitivist idiosyncratic sense of self—Gilman called for a filling up of female personhood toward the generic unmarked status that men already enjoyed. To lose that circumscription as the "Other" to the "absolute human type, the masculine," as Simone De Beauvoir put it in 1949, would be, for Gilman, the crucial feminist step: humanness promised both "free subjectivity" and possession of a full complement of rights, including the vote and control over one's property and person.[78]

Gilman also realized that women would have to liberate themselves in synchronicity with each other; widespread female individuality would result only after women as a social group changed its relation to men. This "paradox," if that is the right word, of achieving individual autonomy through group consciousness and collective purpose can be seen throughout the feminism of prewar Greenwich Village and beyond—Heterodoxy, an oxymoronic "club" of "iconoclasts," is only the most apparent example.[79]

Self-differentiation through social interconnection comes through in perhaps the widest-circulated prewar writing on feminism, a two-part declaration in the April and May 1914 issues of *Good Housekeeping* by the Heterodoxy member and novelist Rose Young. Feminist rebellion, for Young, required collective effort. "*We* have to get rid of the man-made woman," she stated, using Gilman's term, "and abide the coming of women as they present themselves in widely diverging personalities." In addressing "What Is Feminism," Young stressed that while the end points of the movement are not always easy to identify, "[o]ne fact that stands out above all vagaries of prediction and all quivels of language . . . is the feministic insistence upon the development of the individual." For Young, the very act of self-definition could be the most liberating process for women. "'Know yourselves! Be yourselves! Use yourselves!' comes the call." Young continued:

"Oh!" cries the individual, "how I want my life for my very own! Free from the trammels, the cut and dried ways of other people's lives. It isn't necessarily, that I'll steal, or murder, or break the seventh commandment, or do extreme violence to any of the others. But just to live life on my own—just to have my fling!"

Young went on to insist that women's self-knowledge developed through engagement with the larger social sphere. "[A]s individuals," Young wrote in apparent contradistinction to men she knew in Greenwich Village, women "don't really want to escape." She emphasized that "The individual's relation to society is a demandant, irresistible part of the individual: in a word, social relations are implicit in individuality."[80] Dissolution of the individual/society split could not have been clearer.

Even as some prewar feminists read and quoted Nietzsche, they routinely matched cultural rebellion and psychic freedom with all women's entitlement to the full rights and status of an individual.[81] Feminist formulations of individuality paid equal attention to bodily autonomy and intellectual subjectivity. The unity between physical and psychic freedom and between rights consciousness and the development of the inner self can be seen if we go back to the second feminist meeting at Cooper Union in February 1914 and see how it balanced the first discussion's emphasis on cultural rebellion. The second evening the speakers focused on the goal of "Breaking into the Human Race," which would be accomplished through the realization of specific rights: Rheta Childe Dorr and Beatrice Forbes-Robertson-Hale, for instance, talked about woman's right to work and to move into male-dominated professions; Fola La Follette emphasized the right to her own name; and Nina Wilcox Putnam discussed the right to ignore fashions. This last issue concerning freedom of dress is a good example of the tangible, material quality of prewar feminism. In addition to Putnam, Charlotte Perkins Gilman concentrated on *The Dress of Women*, the title of her 1915 book on the subject, as both a locus of feminist negation and a medium of human development. For Gilman, conventions of feminine dress provided perfect illustration of how masculine-based expectations constrained women physically and socially. "Cloth is a social tissue," as Gilman put it simply, a restrictive "social skin."[82] And by shedding conventions of dress, Gilman argued, women would free themselves from prescribed roles of femininity in the process.

One of the most particular prewar discussions of the interrelationship between women's dress and autonomy came from a man, Bliss Carman, a self-described radical thinker, poet, and vagabond. Writing in 1913 in *Harper's Weekly*, Carman discussed the connection between social development and "the physical and personal freeing of women's bodies from the slavery of hampering dress." Carman added that by rebelling against conventional forms of dress, women would also realize fuller spiritual growth. "Corsets are for cripples and clogs for slaves," Carman proclaimed; "emancipated women must have the freedom of unspoiled nature in order fully to evince and radiate the spirit and intelligence that inhabit them; else we are nothing but puppets and mummys, unfair, uncomfortable, and debased." In Carman's formulation, the distinction between the physical and the subjective breaks down. "Oh she must assume her right to a free body," he concluded, "in order adequately to express her freedom of thought and feeling."[83]

In sum, prewar feminists sought subjectivity and personal self-possession, individualistic as those goals are, for women as a social group and for material protection and advancement of one's person. Thus, a potentially atomistic search for personal autonomy supported a social movement toward the collective liberation of a sex. Just as feminism tended to dissolve the difference between the individual and society, it also joined physical liberation with psychic freedom. Along with dress reform, birth control and sexual liberation promised enormous practical advantages for American women, and, at the same time, those victories would enhance female subjectivity—whether measured in Nietzschean units of self-creation or simply the perception of feeling like a more complete human being.

Over and against the prewar feminist unity between individual and society and psychic freedom and group consciousness, leading young male Greenwich Village intellectuals of the time deliberately separated out from their political commitment a privatistic ethic of self-creation. This is the most distinctive masculine element of prewar counterculture. Unlike feminism, male-authored cultural criticism included a regressive element, a romantic primitivist impulse that in its most exaggerated (i.e., Nietzschean) form sought to erase the weight of consciousness itself. Male radicals didn't avoid politics. They committed much of their writing to socialism and labor activism, pacifism, and feminism, to name only a few of the causes of the leftist journals and literary magazines of prewar Greenwich Village and other American bohemias. But whereas feminists coupled subjectivity with progressive politics, male rebels divided the two, oftentimes representing self-exploration and social movement as mutually exclusive. Their separation of "inner experience" from the associational quality of art and language, as John Dewey criticized in 1925, "created a vast and somnambulic egotism out of the fact of subjectivity."[84] Early twentieth-century male rebels pursued a strategy of disconnection, alienation, and discontent—thereby rejecting explicitly the modern conception of the social self.

Prewar male rebels triggered individuality by rejecting the world of their fathers, which began by distancing oneself from the overly acquisitive, morally hypocritical, and spiritually ascetic core of "puritanism," Van Wyck Brooks's term for the outworn values governing contemporary Anglo-Saxon upper-middle-class life. In practical terms, for Brooks and others, this meant avoiding a career in business. Men knew little else but work and economic competition, Brooks wrote in 1917 in the Greenwich Village publication *The Seven Arts:* "They find themselves born into a race that has drained away all its spiritual resources in the struggle to survive"; and even "in the midst of plenty," they still "continue to struggle . . . because life itself no longer possesses any meaning." Against this barren backdrop—a psychology and culture delimited by the "possessive instinct"—Brooks envisioned a world that "calls the poetic faculties into play" and "offers something to the soul." A key component in this secular appeal to heightened subjectivity would be the avant-garde artist, the cultural hero who could offer up new "spiritual conflict and adventure," in Brooks's modernist rendering of masculine romanticism.[85]

In its prewar formulation, art had an aggressive physical quality, accruing, in the minds of New York and Greenwich Village intellectuals (both women and men), a distinctly masculine character. Charlotte Perkins Gilman saw artistic drive as one of the few innate features of masculinity: "Art in the extreme sense"—"that ceaseless urge to expression"—"will perhaps always belong most to men." And as E. A. Randall explained in the magazine *Arena* in 1910, the process of art "has masculine emotions, representing the catabolic militant spirit of man. One must confess," Randall continued, "that the artistic impulse in man is more spontaneous, more widespread and more pronounced, than in woman." This gendered view of art based itself on the male figure of the avant-garde artist, a bold individualist "who risks himself constantly," as Nietzsche explained, who "plays the dangerous game." Early twentieth-century American counterculture also celebrated the inner strength and courage of the modern artist. "These are the great venturers!" as Peter Minuit said in *The Seven Arts* in 1916. "These are the artists who have abandoned dead conventionality, removed smug repetition of other men's thoughts to find themselves. These are men who have discarded representation to creep closer to life, and get something of its naked rhythm into their canvas or into their marble." The avant-garde artist became a hero of American counterculture. "It takes courage to realize yourself, to shape your life as you would. For this is the great adventure," Minuit emphasized, "a man's adventure, to risk all for the sake of his faith, to throw his heart out into battle, and win it back again, or fall."[86]

The heroic figure of the artist grew out of the idea that he not only risks himself for his own freedom but for that of others as well. The avant-garde artist offered up freedom and adventure for those men who could not achieve or afford transcendence on their own. As the art historian Donald Kuspit has written in his study of the modernist artist, people bounded by everyday life have learned to "submit to him, and to that collectivity called created art, in order to realize vicariously [their] own creativity. The artist acts it out for us," and "by identifying with him we imagine we have a unique identity of our own." In other words, the artist imparts subjectivity to those who are, as Bourne understood, tied to their nine-to-five jobs and thereby limited in their scope of experience. The artist is exceptional because he can "be himself in a way that is impossible for other people"; as Kuspit writes, "he is able to experience in a more fundamental, original way than they can." Or as editor of the radical journal *The Masses* Max Eastman said simply in 1914, "We literary and artistic people are experts in experience. Experience is our trade. We receive it vividly and we convey it to others."[87] In this sense, the modern artist assumed something of a practical social role or function in early twentieth-century American culture.

Alongside the early twentieth-century appreciation for the hero-artist's delivery of experience, one finds a relativistic celebration of his ability to destroy (to "apply pick axe and dynamite," as Randolph Bourne described) any *and* all preexistent patterns or ways of understanding the world. The avant-garde artist is by definition a "disturber of the social order," as Alfred Booth Kuttner described in *The Seven Arts* in 1917—he is "the *enfant terrible* of the unconsciousness." Artistic rebellion and cultural iconoclasm became valued in and of themselves. This relativistic element in prewar thought did not go unchallenged. A writer in a 1914 issue of *The Little Review* criticized the incessant, mindless rebellion in a book of poetry by Louis Untermeyer. "A careful perusal of its pages," the critic reproved, "fails to reveal against what it revolts. Mr. Untermeyer manfully girds on his armor and sets forth to war, shouting lustily the while," the writer notes sarcastically. "And why, after all, be particular about having an actual enemy? Life can do duty for that," he concludes. "The revolt is the point."[88] Most other prewar intellectuals and critics, however, found great value in the weightless, disconnected quality of modern art—"an art," as an editorial statement of the Greenwich Village journal *The Quill* described, "whose purpose is flaming beauty and nothing else." Above all else, modern art offered a sense of freedom, the feeling that, as James Oppenheim wrote in *The Seven Arts*, "everything may be tried and every picture is possible experience." In this formulation, art became a totalizing yet transitory realm of existence, a type of virtual reality expressed most fully by Nietzsche, who saw "the world [as] a work of art that gives birth to itself."[89]

Because politics tended to get in the way of those wanting to live life as art, prewar Greenwich Village men commonly detached their "political side," as Max Eastman explained about himself, from the "poet" in him. Eastman confessed in his autobiography that "political emotions did not move me to write poetry. Were they less profound, less organic?" he asked. "Less clear, less wholly myself? I don't know," Eastman continued. "I really don't like politics. I'd like to abolish them altogether." Perhaps the best example of this conscious split between social responsibility and art and self-creation came from Floyd Dell, coeditor of *The Masses* between 1913 and 1920 and a prototype of the Greenwich Village bohemian. In an article entitled "A Psychoanalytic Confession," Dell narrated a conversation between his socialist conscious and his pagan unconscious. His conscious denounces the unconscious for being selfish and depraved, "for speaking utopian nonsense." The unconscious, "which prefers poetry to economics," admits that it is quixotic, but responds to the conscious, "and between us, I think you are too. I think you are a socialist simply because you want a different kind of world, one you can be happy in. You work for the social revolution just as other people work to make a fortune. You want to see your dream come true. But the dream which you want," the unconscious continues, "is my dream, not Lenin's seven million electric light bulbs, but a houseboat and a happy family living in a state of semi-nude savagery!" Finally, Dell's conscious asks the unconscious whether it will help work for socialism. After singing "a silly old war song," the unconscious responds rather indirectly: "I have gone through a long period of barbarism too, you know, and I understand that better than you do. Fighting for the sake of victory! You'd be shocked if you really knew me."[90] Clearly Dell figured he couldn't rely on his psyche's full power for his political work; the split also suggests the more severe problem of the unconscious undoing of well-reasoned formulations of social justice.

The regressive component of masculine counterculture included a certain revelry in social relinquishment. Male artists and intellectuals cultivated desolation. "And so the Hamlets among us, or their modern brothers, the Zarathustras," James Oppenheim wrote in 1917 in *The Seven Arts*, "turn to pessimism for something strong and abiding and absolute in this rainbow welter of optimism. Heroically, they tilt against the windmills," Oppenheim added, "and feel themselves alone, isolated, fragmentary, in a land which refuses to despair."[91] For some men during the prewar period, this alienation turned into downright overwrought angst. Listen, for instance, to Nietzschean theologian George Burnham Foster in a 1914 issue of *The Little Review*: "A profound unrest tortures the heart of modern man. The world, slaughtering the innocents, is meaningless; life, bruised and bewildered, is worthless—such is the melancholy mood of modernity. Today life is a burden to many for whom it was once a joy." For others, self-imposed alienation could pay off in freedom, autonomy, and heightened masculinist power. On the one hand, devotion to rebellion is similar to "a soldier's life," John Temple Graves Jr. commented in 1911 in *The Forum* magazine, "forever breaking camp and on the march, with constant skirmishing and battling, eternal in restlessness and discontent." But it also "has the compensating joy of life in the open," Graves continued, "rioting in motion and color—an everlasting youth that lusts in the great delirium of battle."

Randolph Bourne also spoke of the liberation that alienation provides. It lets "our imagination roam over the world," he wrote in his 1913 essay "Adventure and Life," "and dwell on the infinite variety of scenes and thoughts and feelings and forms of life."[92] For Bourne—arguably the most gifted and wide-ranging writer among the young male intellectuals of the prewar period—constant disconnection and movement would be the key to achieving individuality; while this strategy derived from the modernist psychology of James and Dewey, it also betrays curious resonances with Frederick Jackson Turner and rugged individualism.

Before his trenchant critique of Dewey's support of the United States' entrance into World War I and his own slippage into a Nietzschean "malcontent," before his work on progressive education and the cosmopolitan ideal of "trans-national America," Randolph Bourne published *Youth and Life* (1913), a collection of essays that includes "The Life of Irony," an extremely accomplished conception of democratic consciousness, and, most important for this chapter, "The Dodging of Pressures," a founding document of twentieth-century American counterculture and the modern masculine quest for individuality. Characteristic of Bourne's thought, "Dodging of Pressures" is not uncomplicated in its iconoclasm; the essay warns young Americans against relying on rebellion as an end in itself, for instance; full individuality happens through social relations and not in complete isolation from them. At the same time, "Dodging of Pressures" is emblematic of early twentieth-century masculinist alienation and the correlated social and cultural practice of rejecting established values, habits, and vocations. Through constant movement or, rather, by "keeping the way clear, and the sky above his head," and thereby maintaining the possibility of unfettered movement, a man lays down, in Bourne's twice-used phrase, "the free and open road of his own individuality."[93] Bourne conflated the modernist goals of artful subjectivity and free movement of consciousness with spatial movement and physical travel. In "Dodging of Pressures," the "open road" stands for both a geographical way out of the largely urban-based ties that bind and an ideal psychological context for unencumbered self-creation.

Set against masculine individuality is, in one of Bourne's more memorable passages, "the numbing palsy of conservative ascent which steals over so many brilliant and sincere young men as they are subjected to the influence of prestige and authority in their profession." Bourne emphasized the "insidious" quality of the pressure on middle-class men to pursue a corporate or professional career and, more generally, to "offer themselves up to" that "institutional Moloch" of "family, church, business, society, state." Working without benefit of mid- to late twentieth-century insights into the structuring power of language, Bourne nevertheless appreciated the low-level nearly unnoticeable force of "the voices that whisper continually at [one's] side, 'conform.'" These minutely dispersed points of pressure have a bodily effect on an individual man. "They throw their silky chains over him and draw him in. They press gently but ceaselessly upon him, rubbing away his original roughness, polishing him down, molding him relentlessly." Society, as Bourne concluded, is a "vast conspiracy for carving one into the kind of statue it likes, and then placing it in the most convenient niche it has."[94] Once taken in, middle-class man becomes immobile and, with that, a support for the system itself.

With the "silky chains" of bourgeois existence constantly threatening masculine autonomy, Bourne recommended strategic disconnection from work and social relations by preventing anything or anyone else from determining one's course. Here Bourne's "Dodging of Pressures" jibes with the apolitical poeticist impulses of his Greenwich Village friends Eastman and Dell. "It seems, curiously enough," Bourne explained, "that one can live one's true life and guarantee one's individuality best in this indirect way—not by projecting one's self out upon the world aggressively but by keeping the track clear along which one's true life may run." For this reason, Bourne even suggested fostering the dislike of others; it should "fortify [a man's] soul rather than discourage him."[95] If your personality rubs people the wrong way, Bourne reasoned, you must be doing a good job of bucking convention and thus on your way to individuality.

More controversially, Bourne wanted to split consciousness between the work one needs to do to earn a living and the pursuit of self-fulfillment outside the office. Bourne advocated total rejection of "business or industrial work," but, if that is impossible economically, "it is our bounden duty not to be interested in it or like it." We can avoid the exigencies of a "useless" job "by letting the routine of work lay very lightly on our soul." Anticipating what sociologist David Riesman described several decades later in *The Lonely Crowd* (1950) as the "depersonalization of work," Bourne urged men to "cultivate a disinterestedness and aloofness towards" one's job—a man could thereby "keep from breathing its poisonous atmosphere." But does Bourne's strategy of creating these "two worlds" mark rebellion against or capitulation to the dominant institutions of modern America? As the sociologist Daniel Bell has pointed out in his book *The Cultural Contradictions of Capitalism* (1976), learning how to disassociate oneself from the workaday world diminishes the chance of any type of challenge to corporate hegemony. The corporation is served by both halves of the middle-class masculine self. "On the one hand," Bell writes, "the business corporation wants an individual to work hard, pursue a career, accept delayed gratification—to be in the crude sense an organization man. And yet in its products and advertisements, the corporation promotes pleasure, instant joy, relaxing, and letting go."[96] Neither Bourne nor other pre–World War I Greenwich Village cultural critics saw consumerism as any type of opposition to the powers that be. And yet their belief in private experience as *the* pathway to self-creation fed into the duplicitous therapeutic complex of which Bell speaks. In defining masculine individuality against full social engagement, prewar counter-culture promoted inattention to the basic formulations of political economy and public obligation.

Countercultural masculinity also partook of Turnerian individualism. Even as young Greenwich Village intellectuals tried to distance themselves from the nation's past, they embraced Turner's highly mobile and solitary American self. Bourne, who liked to get away to a Catskill cabin and who looked to the naturalist writer John Burroughs as an exemplary dodger of pressures, spoke of escaping one's "niche," by taking to "the open road, with the spirit always traveling, always criticiz-ing, always learning, always escaping the pressures that threaten its integrity." Male rebels also took a keen interest in the work of Bliss Carman, Richard Hovey, and other early twentieth-century vagabond poets. As Floyd Dell explained in his autobiographical account of his prewar Greenwich Village days, these "homeless but happy poets and artists" appealed to us through their "wanderlust"—that is, "the zest for being somewhere else." Dell added that the hobo poet's isolation makes up a distinctly "masculine" model of rebellion: "Divorced utterly from any form of political idealism," the vagabond leads a life of bravado, independence, and "adventure." Dell found historical continuity between the American frontier and urban counterculture: "your true bohemian was the Last of the Mohicans and the First of the Greenwich Villagers."[97] Both the bohemian and the pioneer chased the promise of individual plenitude—what F. Scott Fitzgerald called the "memory of the fresh, green breast of the new world." Like the heroic frontiersman, modern man "believed," as Fitzgerald said of Gatsby, "in the green light, the orgastic future that year by year recedes before us. It eluded us then," Fitzgerald concluded, "but that's no matter—to-morrow we will run faster, and stretch out our arms farther."[98]

In sum, the masculinist individuality of prewar Greenwich Village involved uniqueness *and* solitude: singularity depended on disconnection from things out-side of the self and a personal practice of never staying in one place long enough to be weighed down by the expectation of others. Such a premium on high psychic and physical mobility compromised constructive social engagement in the public sphere. Young countercultural intellectuals *did* concern themselves with the in-terpersonal work of politics, but this happened, we might say, back at the office, very much apart from the inner dynamic of Nietzschean self-creation. The schizo-phrenic consequences of male rebellion come out in comparison with prewar feminist individuality, which purposefully blended self-development with wom-en's empowerment as a social group. Although they employed similar liberatory discourses, the men and women of prewar Greenwich Village rebelled against two different things. Whereas feminism attacked obstacles to gainful employment and the professions, involuntary domesticity and motherhood, and, generally speaking, the tradition-bound subordination of women to men, male rebellion targeted the white-collar workaday world of corporate America and, very broadly, any institutional structure or social relation that delimited individuality. The Greenwich Village men developed an early critique of the "organization man." Valuable for relativizing the middle-class work ethic and its accompanying moral strictures, masculinist counterculture also faltered in its inattention to how radical intrasubjectivity could actually support the very powers it opposed.

Dudism, Cowgirl Feminism, and the Search for Authenticity in the "Old West"

Concurrent with the early twentieth-century growth of modern urban counterculture came the maturation of the American West as a source for middle- and upper-class individuality. Far from getting over the West, postfrontier Americans obsessed like never before by designating its grandest spaces as parks or reserves and advertising its enduring wildness as a powerful experiential counter to the dull routine of modern life. The multimillion dollar dude ranch industry located its product, as one 1920s brochure said, "at the boundary line between civilization and untouched Nature"—a model of liminality remarkably close to Frederick Jackson Turner's definition of the pre-1890 American frontier. Some turn-of-the-century intellectuals criticized the artificiality of the new "Old West," whose "self-consciousness," in Frank Norris's words, "is a sign, surer than all others, of the decadence of a type, the passing of an epoch." Travel literature played on the historical anxiousness driving Turner's thesis, contending strategically that "The old west is *almost* gone" (emphasis added), as Mary Roberts Rinehart wrote in her 1916 book *Through Glacier Park: Seeing America First with Howard Eaton*. "Now is the time to see it," she continued, before the "real" West is forever lost. The need for the real—Rinehart, for instance, insisted that in the Rocky Mountains "a mile is a real mile" and "the call is a real call"—marks the problem behind this whole modern American cultural epoch: the quest for authentic experience within the mediated and affected context of twentieth-century "Old West."[99]

Encapsulating the whole contrivance of western tourism, the word *dude* underlines the self-doubtfulness involved in building one's individuality upon prepackaged roughing it. *Dudism* describes the mind-set motivating the easterner to set off on a de-evolutionary arc to the West, where, despite local knowledge that a visitor could never achieve real Western identity—that's how the label "dude" came about—the tourist spent time and money exposing himself or herself to rugged environment with the belief that its wildness would rub off on one's person.[100]

That is to say that dudism fed individual self-creation. Working from wide-spread assumptions regarding the regenerative powers of the wilderness, wealthy easterners booked vacations with "the idea," as a 1925 dude ranch brochure advertised, "of gaining perfect health, a vigorous body, and renewed zest for work, a voracious appetite and untroubled sleep—things which come naturally in the keen, clean air of Wyoming's boundless open spaces."[101] Along with restoring and balancing one's nervous energy—as we've seen, a core quality of classic American individualism—the "real" and hardy experience of living on a dude ranch offered invaluable material for self-distinction and uniqueness. For constructing one's individuality the more adventurous and taxing the experience the better. Photographs could be shown and stories told back home that would set dudists apart from their (sub)urban friends and neighbors—late twentieth-century commentators on tourism would call this the "bagging trophy" complex.[102] Within late nineteenth- and twentieth-century dudism, ruggedness denoted a proclivity for riding, camping, and other outdoor activity as much as a capacity for violence. Roughing it in the West turned into a psychological possession, something also carried on one's person, seen on one's skin and dress, and recognized in one's gait, confidence, and energy level. It went to one's disposition.

A significant aspect of dude ranches and the brand of individuality they engendered is the large number of women who sought to fold an element of ruggedness into their person by wearing pants, riding astride, and generally partaking in the virile experience of the "Old West." Coeducational dudism flourished in the early twentieth century, especially among young, white, college-educated New Women eager to individuate themselves for coequal participation in the American middle class. Helping them in this project was the *cowgirl*. The very embodiment of women's masculinization in the West, cowgirls evolved from indigenous ranch workers to a potent symbolic construct for female hardness and autonomy; through competitive rodeo, they also served as a prototype for the American female athlete's early emergence (compared to women in other industrialized countries) into intercollegiate and professional sports. Before analyzing dudism's place in normative masculinity, then, it is worth considering the late nineteenth and early twentieth-century emergence of women's rodeo as an example of rugged individualism in action in the postfrontier United States.

Historians of women's rodeo cast it as feminist in effect if not always in concerted motivation toward sexual equality. "It espouses a sort of cowgirl feminism," Laura Jane Moore has written—"cowgirls as symbols of women resisting standard femininity through a no-nonsense independence and rugged individualism."[103] Indeed, the self-conscious vigor and toughness of rodeo cowgirls illustrate the continuing power of the West to grow not just individualism, but individualism of that rugged American variety. Rodeo cowgirls' competitiveness and grit point to the modern congruence between masculinity and liberal individual feminism, as more and more young white American women broke away from Victorian femininity by embracing male models of physical autonomy, strength, and athleticism. This androgynous turn had its limitations: for all the new women's and western women's strenuosity, little if any facet of violence entered into female self-identities; it was one thing for cowgirls to rope steers and quite another, say, to want to kill Spaniards in Cuba.[104] As men came to understand aggressiveness as essential to masculinity, women looked to adventurous travel, outdoor exercise, dress reform, and sports in their march toward what Charlotte Perkins Gilman described as "humanness."

Along with cowgirls, dude ranches, and the whole rugged culture of the West, a new urban-based standard of feminine beauty pulled turn-of-the-century, middle-class women outdoors and toward greater physical independence. A distinctly athletic ideal of femininity arose from Charles Dana Gibson's influential 1890s magazine illustrations of the American Girl or what would quickly become known as the Gibson Girl. Tall, slim but of solid build, and with a taste for comfortable fitting blouses and skirts, the Gibson Girl served as a feminist prototype for the "new woman." They are a "new" and "noble type," Gilman wrote in 1898 of the Gibson Girl: "Not only do they look differently, they behave differently. The false sentimentality, the false delicacy, the false modesty, the utter falseness of elaborate compliment and servile gallantry which went with the other falsehoods,—all these are disappearing. Women are growing honester, braver, stronger, more healthful and skillful and able and free, more human in all ways." Significantly, Gilman traced these changes to women's post–Civil War entrance into higher education.[105] By the end of the nineteenth century, with western coeducational universities and eastern women's colleges offering physical education and competitive sports to their female students, athletics was both cause and consequence of many college-women's more "pronounced manner," as Vassar College's director of physical training put it.[106] The threat that middle-class women's athleticism posed to traditional gender relations was caught brilliantly in Gibson's 1895 work *The Coming Game: Yale versus Vassar* (fig. 1.3), in which man still carries the ball but also realizes fearfully that he will soon be tackled. The absurdist quality of Gibson's illustration stems from the fact that football, as discussed in chapter 3, has been one of the very few intercollegiate sports that American women have not taken up. Again, modern feminism rejected the most brutal elements of masculinity while generally privileging its physicality.

In focusing on cowgirl feminism, early twentieth-century women writers' interest in rugged individualism seems to be less about devolution than liberation—less
about romantic primitivism than growth into full humanness; otherwise, though,
the period's literature on women in the West tended to follow Turner's understanding of rugged individualism as a mental trait that springs from that region's distinct environment. In her popular 1916 account of a horseback trip with Howard
Eaton through Glacier Park, Mary Roberts Rinehart spoke of the women's growing
vigor and self-confidence as well as their new neural balance: "Women, who had
to be helped into their saddles at the beginning of the trip swung into them easily. Waistbands were looser, eyes were clearer; we were tanned; we were calm with
the large calmness of the great outdoors." And in the 1921 novel *The Dude Wrangler,* Caroline Lockhart developed the "The Girl from Wyoming" as something of
a masculine counterpoint to the initially effete eastern protagonist Wallie. After
first seeing her in the Colonial Hotel, Wallie realizes how different she is from the
other women at the resort and from himself: "She was young and good looking
and wore suitable clothes that fitted her; also, while not aggressive, she had a self-
reliant manner which proclaimed the fact that she was accustomed to looking after
her own interests."[107] Suitably impressed, Wallie follows her to Wyoming, where
he successfully courts her after transforming himself into a rugged individual.

Like their cowboy counterparts, most late nineteenth- and early twentieth-century cowgirls got into rodeo after working with horses and cattle on a western
ranch. Beginning as riding and roping contests among local ranch workers, rodeo
grew into a national and international phenomenon during the 1880s and 1890s
through Buffalo Bill Cody's Wild West shows. Professional contests soon took pre-
cedence over Wild West entertainment among the cowboys and cowgirls themselves, with such rodeos as Cheyenne Frontier Days and the Calgary Stampede
offering large cash prizes and formalizing competition through the development
of separate events.[108] Spectacle begat sport, and women were integral to both. By
1886 Buffalo Bill included "lady riders" in his shows, and by the first years of the
twentieth-century cowgirls had become stars of the major rodeo contests. As historian Mary Lou LeCompte argues, early twentieth-century rodeo "offered great
opportunities for cowgirls"—for western and some eastern white women that is,
as LeCompte "found no record of participation by either African-American women
or Chicanas." As professional athletes, LeCompte continues, rodeo cowgirls "could
and did compete directly against men in steer roping, trick roping, trick riding, and
Roman racing. Rodeo was the first, and perhaps the only, sport in which men and
women truly competed as equals."[109] And as rodeo moved eastward—New York
City's Madison Square Garden, for instance, annually held the largest pre–World
War I contest—cowgirls also provided eastern women with a model of indepen-

dence and physicality, some of whom undoubtedly then went West themselves. Western rugged individualism, just as Turner said it would, continued to loop back into eastern culture.

Stemming from outdoor ranch work, cowgirl feminism took hold through the efforts and personae of a few early rodeo stars. Often described as "America's First Cowgirl," Lucille Mulhall grew up on an Oklahoma ranch, where she soon became an accomplished roper and rider. With her father deciding to capitalize on Mulhall's talents, she took to "rodeo road" with her family in 1900 while just fifteen years old. That same year, Mulhall performed at a Rough Riders Reunion; at Teddy Roosevelt's request, as the story goes, she roped a wolf; in any event, the Colonel, duly impressed, encouraged her to keep traveling the country. Mulhall soon gained national fame for her bronco riding and especially for beating men in steer roping contests. Mulhall also drew attention through her dress: usually a long-sleeved blouse, a long divided skirt, boots, spurs, and a high-crowned Stetson. Long skirts could be dangerous for cowgirls. In 1905, for instance, while trick riding in New York City's Madison Square Garden, Mulhall's skirt got tangled in the stirrup as she reached down to pick up a handkerchief from the ground. Dragged for a considerable distance, she finally freed herself without serious injury.[110] The fact that Mulhall and other early cowgirls didn't wear pants until well into the 1920s speaks to the lasting investment that rodeo women and men had in traditional gender roles, even as the burgeoning sport broke new ground in intersex competition and allowed young European American women to move closer to a masculine form of rugged individualism.

As related in her autobiography, *Rodeo Road: My Life as a Pioneer Cowgirl* (1974), Vera McGinnis's career well illustrates the practical differences that rugged individualism could have on a woman's person and those around her. Born in 1895, she spent her first years on a New Mexico ranch. Her family then moved to Missouri, where McGinnis entered her first riding competition at age thirteen. After graduating from high school, she gravitated to the rodeo and its people. "I liked them—period," McGinnis explained: "They had a straightforward, frank code that suited me right down to the core. And that daredevil, all-in-a-day's work attitude they took about their dangerous performances had me jockeying for a better look see." In a short time, while traveling with her new cowboy star husband Earl, McGinnis started competing and winning on the rodeo circuit, which quickly led to marital problems. Earl tired of the rodeo and wanted to settle down. McGinnis felt "torn between two loves—a home and rodeo"—although, as she wrote, "it didn't occur to me to give up my career to save my marriage." With the next season starting, she went alone: "The rodeo had become a compulsion, I followed blindly without questioning where it would lead." The demands of competition also prompted

McGinnis to shed the restrictive "ladylike " clothing of the early rodeo. First, she "junked the corset for life" (since it "interfere[d] with my agility, to say nothing of my comfort"). Next, McGinnis replaced high boots with tennis shoes, which, she commented, "were safer and easier for jumping off and on horses. But they left the calves of our legs exposed," she continued; "I for one decided they'd have to be exposed! Cowgirls were supposed to be rough anyway." Finally, in 1927, after wanting for years to compete in pants, McGinnis appeared in the Fort Worth Fat Stock Show and Rodeo in a pair of men's white trousers.[111] Rodeo historians generally recognize her to be the first woman to have publicly scrapped the traditional but dangerous long skirt.[112]

Along with the sheer challenge and pleasure she got from the rodeo, the dominant story line in McGinnis's autobiography is her struggle against domesticity. The "dream" of home and family poses an attractive alternative to rodeo's hardships throughout the book. And it ends with McGinnis retiring from the sport in her late thirties and settling down with her second husband on a ranch in the foothills of the Sierras. As a younger woman, though, she made several stands against Earl's attempts to reign her in. A climax came when McGinnis joined Earl and his father after her first rodeo season alone. "Earl seemed glad to have me back," McGinnis remembered, "but he didn't hesitate to hang the work collar on me." Earl expected McGinnis to do all the cooking, cleaning, and laundry, despite her full-time work that fall training and racing horses. One afternoon, after Earl's father wouldn't help her lift a large tub of wash water, McGinnis kicked over the table holding the tub and clothes. "Personally I don't give a damn if this washing ever gets done! Do it yourselves if you want clean clothes," McGinnis yelled. "Why did I ever come back to this spread." Later that day, while ostracized at dinner, she "grabbed the edge of the table and upset its entire contents on the floor and screamed: 'If you gypos want to live in a pig pen I'll help you!'" That day led to the end of her first marriage. McGinnis competed on the circuit throughout the 1920s—a high point of women's rodeo. Single and in increasing demand for her trick riding, McGinnis also worked in Hollywood movies and traveled with Wild West shows to Hawaii, Britain, Europe, and Asia.[113]

McGinnis's *Rodeo Road* advances what might be called *athletic feminism*, the individual pursuit of competitive physical experience and the pleasure and autonomy that such endeavor brings. The concept was not new or specific to cowgirls. As early as 1850, Elizabeth Cady Stanton challenged "man's claim to physical superiority," arguing that "We cannot say what woman might be physically, if the girl were allowed all the freedom of the boy, in romping, swimming, climbing, playing ball."[114] To this core element of individualist feminism, women's rodeo added roughness or, in McGinnis's word, "toughness"—an attitudinal trait arising from the rigors of the circuit. Rodeo took a great toll on McGinnis: her injuries included losing two front teeth; a torn knee ligament; a collapsed lung; and a broken jaw, collarbone, ribs, ankle, hip, and neck. To keep going back to the rodeo points to the power of the sport's "compulsion" for McGinnis and the enormous attention she needed to pay to herself and her body. As an "athlete," McGinnis explained, she wanted to achieve "perfect physical condition."[115] This desire prompted her fight against the double shift of the rodeo and domestic work.

While not calling it athletic feminism, historians of women's rodeo have consistently argued that the sport engendered an experiential, distinctly antitheoretical strain of feminism, affording early twentieth-century cowgirls the individual freedom that other American women only talked about. "[T]he ideas espoused by pre–World War I followers of the feminist movement would surely not have attracted them [early rodeo cowgirls]," as LeCompte has written; "they had already achieved feminist goals such as Crystal Eastman expressed: 'How to arrange the world so that women can be human beings, with a chance to exercise their infinitely varied ways, instead of being described by the accident of their sex to one field of activity, housework and child-raising.'"[116] Historian Joyce Gibson Roach believes cowgirls' liberation happened "some distance in advance of the theoretical feminists." She elaborates: "[W]hen Susan B. Anthony and her hoop-skirted friends were declaring that females, too, were created equal, a woman named Sally Skull was riding and roping and marking her cattle with the Circle S Brand on the western frontier of Texas. Riding astride," Roach concludes by emphasizing the cowgirl's autonomy, "she asked no man's leave and needed no man's escort."[117] Cowgirls' disregard for the feminist movement lasted through the twentieth century. In her study of post–World War II cowgirls, Theresa Jordan writes: "'I'm not a women's libber,' I heard time and time again when I broached the subject of the women's movement. The women's movement is primarily an urban phenomenon," Jordan explains, "and most country women see it as just one more outside interference which—like government regulation or Hollywood interpretations of the West—poorly understands their way of life and hardly relates to it."[118] In contrast, and not unlike Turner's thesis, cowgirls saw their physical autonomy and social independence as something that had arisen naturally through their contact with the wide open spaces of the West, and while meeting the practical demands of ranch work and rodeo competition.

As cowgirl and athletic feminism developed among U.S. women, dudism matured into a hypermasculinized program and mind-set for elite men from the East and other urban centers. Dudism embodied normative masculinity's de-evolutionary turn. It relied on a stark distinction between the built environment of the city and the natural open spaces of the West. As the remaining pockets of wilderness became increasingly fetishized as the "real" and "Old" and "Wild" West, white Anglo-Saxon Protestant middle- and upper-class men bonded with cowboys and dude wranglers, recognizing their "rough" traits as something innate to American character, using the new male network for military and other homosocial privilege, and generally trying to build ruggedness into their person.

Ever present in modern imaginative engagement with the American West has been the drive for authenticity and the correlative doubt of whether authenticity could ever be reached. This doubt over western authenticity has come in two very closely related forms. The first has been about the land itself. "The great free ranges with their barbarous, picturesque and curiously fascinating surroundings," Teddy Roosevelt wrote in 1888, speaking of his own time in South Dakota earlier that decade, "marked a primitive stage of existence, but like the primeval forests they were bowing to the needs of the nation. Those who came later," he added, "would never feel the charm of the life in the West, nor exult in its abounding vigor and its bold restless freedom." Of course, Roosevelt's lament leads to the second concern—that "real manhood" would perish with the environment that gave it birth. As we have seen in relation to Turner's frontier thesis, modern Americans' longing for true wilderness experience and rugged individualist character, and the anxiety that they could really be realized, rather than being satisfied or vanquished once and for all, generated an enormously creative tension in late nineteenth- and early twentieth-century culture, an idiosyncratic product of which was the dude ranch and its self-conscious effort to bolster masculinity through transparently affected and inaccurate representations of the past. A 1923 Burlington Railroad brochure for dude ranches in "'Buffalo Bill' Country Wyoming," for instance, described how a summer rodeo brought in "Daring cowboys from all over the West . . . to compete for the twenty-five thousand dollars in prizes. It is the old days of the West lived over again." The same brochure insisted that the Morris Ranch outside of Cody "is not a mountain lodge, but a real horse and cattle ranch with all the atmosphere and color of the Wild West and the open range."[119] Ranch advertising pushed a culture of authenticity while tacitly recognizing that the actual real thing had indeed passed.

At the developmental center of western ranch tourism was the dude wrangler, the self-appellation of one who transformed his skill in stringing horses and herding cattle into taking care of humans eager to rough it while visiting. Wranglers founded and slowly grew dude ranching during the last fifteen years of the nineteenth century, after the collapse of the free-range cattle industry. The dude business prospered in the early twentieth century, especially in the 1920s, when many large railroads, in response to increasing automobile tourism, started to co-ordinate and promote ranch vacations through western train travel. It worked. By

1930, time on a dude ranch had become common among upper-middle- and upper-class Americans. Daily riding, seemingly close interaction with cowboys and cowgirls, western landscapes, and horseback camping trips made a New England coastal vacation, for instance, absolutely pale in comparison.[120] In her satiric novel *Dude Wrangler* (1921), Caroline Lockhart studied a wealthy eastern vacation set's response to the "Wild West" though the trials and travails of Wallie, an unusually foppish easterner who converts himself in Wyoming into a rugged cowboy and then a dude wrangler. With Wallie's first customers being his old friends from the Colonial Hotel back East, the story culminates in his eye-rolling incredulity over their formulaic shedding of civilization, along with the happy realization that he could easily take their money and become one of the richest men in the state. Wallie and his partner end up finding great amusement in the guests' unembarrassed primitivism. "Underneath my worldly exterior I am a Child of Nature," a dude exclaims while bathing in a river. "I love the simple, the primitive. I would live as a Wild Thing if I could choose my environment."[121] In Lockhart's story the wranglers learn to manufacture such moments for their guests, thus milking dudist devolution for everything it is worth.

Early twentieth-century travel brochures illustrate just how freely dude wranglers and railway advertisers played on popular interest in western adventure. Some wranglers highlighted their ranch's proximity to wilderness. Struthers Burt, a wrangler, regionalist writer, and leading dude ranch publicist of the time, proudly claimed in 1927 that out the "back door" of his Bar B C Ranch at Jackson Hole, Wyoming, "is a country it would take ten years of constant horseback exploration to thoroughly know, whose mountains are for the most part unclimbed and unnamed." The ideal of the western frontier—"with its harmony of wilderness and civilization," as those at Eaton's Ranch, Wolf, Wyoming, put it in 1917—proved to be the most common appeal to prospective dudes. "Far from the madding crowd, in the foothills of the Rockies," as a Wyoming ranch brochure touted in 1922, "lies the Bar E D Ranch, where people go to enjoy the wildness of the West, modified by modern conveniences."[122] In describing contemporary attraction to the West, these dude ranch brochures spoke less and less about the physical qualities of untouched wilderness, as in the Bar B C advertisement just cited, and more about how visitors would find and enjoy remnants of what used to be. "[W]ell within reach are railroad, telegraph, telephone and physician," the Eaton's Ranch brochure assured, yet "everywhere there is the constant reminder of old frontier days." Dude ranches dealt in cultural trappings and historical associations. "In this delightful region," the 1923 Burlington Railroad brochure proclaimed, "which is surrounded with a peculiar romance and interest, associated as it is with Indian battlefields, old-time frontier days, the covered wagon, and the activities of that famous old scout,

'Buffalo Bill,' all the conditions combine to restore jaded minds and bodies to normal health and vigor."[123] Immersion in elaborately constructed memory and artifice rather than in untouched nature determined modern American rugged individuality.

In addition to associating their ranches with the romantic West, wranglers made a concerted effort to change the meaning of the word *dude*. Used since the early 1880s as a term of derision for a man given to unusual fastidiousness over dress, speech, and deportment—an American synonym, that is, for the English *fop* and *dandy*—dude and its effeminate connotation worked perfectly for cowboys and others wanting to identity the inauthentic, would-be westerners from the East. Wranglers, on the other hand, worried that their business would be hurt, tried to water down the word's meaning. "Don't misunderstand the term 'dude,'" a 1924 Burlington Railroad brochure assured. "It's a legitimate hundred per cent American term in Wyoming nomenclature—and means any visitor from 'outside' just as 'savage' means the rancher, his cowboys, and all the rest of his business associates." Telling definition this: despite the interest in diluting dude's meaning, the copywriter divides the visitor from the manly and "savage" local. Or consider Struthers Burt's attempt to neutralize the word in his popular autobiographical work *The Diary of a Dude Wrangler* (1924): "The word has none of the slurring connotations attached to the term tenderfoot. It does not imply ignorance or softness, it simply means some one, usually a person not resident in the country, who hires some one else to guide him or cook for him, or who pays money to stay on a ranch."[124] Burt's insistence on what dude does not mean is quite telling regarding the common usage that he felt obligated to change.

Burt's *Diary of a Dude Wrangler* is particularly helpful in understanding the contrived nature of the dude experience and the wrangler's role in making it seem authentic. Other writers had criticized dudism's fake authenticity. In *Dude Wrangler,* Wallie and his partner found an old, broken-down stagecoach. "They had it repaired and painted red, with yellow wheels that flashed in the sun," Lockhart wrote. "And now, there it stood—the last word in the picturesque discomfort for which dudes were presumed to yearn!" Struthers Burt, however, tended to defend the seriousness and propriety of the dude enterprise. Contrary to what some in New York and Hollywood believe, as Burt contended in 1928, the dude wrangler is not "engaged in 'theatrical imitations of something that has vanished.'" And yet Burt also detailed the duplicitous quality of the wrangler's work. "[I]f you wish to sum up the dude-business in a sentence," Burt said in his *Diary,* "it consists in giving people home-made bedsteads but forty pound mattresses." The wrangler may not be engaged in pure theater, but he is clearly responsible for the meanings the dude experience is supposed to produce. "You must do your best," Burt explained, "even in a place where from fifty to over a hundred people are gathered together, not to destroy the impression of wildness and isolation." The inherent tension in mass solitude drew Burt's closest attention. "[H]ere is the inner secret of it all," Burt concluded in his *Diary:* "the dude-wrangler must do these things—'wrangle' his dudes in all their bewildering complexity—without letting them know it. A salient characteristic of the human mind seems to be a dislike of being herded, with an unconscious desire none the less to have it done; people hate to be directed, but they get excessively angry if they aren't."[125] Wrangling called for no small measure of applied psychology. It required nothing less than routinely providing large groups of visitors with the feeling of rugged individuality.

In turning to the visitors' perspective, we can surmise from the amount of time and money spent, emotion invested, historical associations made, and cultural meanings created, that dudes had a lot to gain from being wrangled. First of all, rugged individuality was pleasurable. When compared to the closed space and hyperstimulus of the modern American metropolis, the open vistas, slower pace, and sheer quiet of the West must have made a palpable psychophysical impression on most dudes. Whether such an effect occurred biologically (through measurable neurological differentiation), through the emotional fulfillment of culturally generated expectations, or by some inseparable combination of the two, that matters less than the fact that wranglers carefully crafted the dude experience in response to a perceived *need* for de-evolutionary release and solitude. As Struthers Burt observed in his social-scientific vein, "The need was this: that in our increasingly complex and noisy life there should be places where people could actually be simple and to some extent indulge primitive and heroic tastes."[126] A second benefit from duding was social status. Early twentieth-century dude ranches helped consolidate WASP upper-class identities with "Christians only" restrictions, reference requests, and a basic interest in serving an elite Eastern clientele. Conjugation between class and access to the wilderness can be seen in ranch advertising. For instance, the 1923 Burlington railroad brochure for Wyoming dude ranches exclaimed how "The country is yet new. The call of the Wild West is insistently audible. The Indians still live nearby—the streams teem with wily trout." And in the next paragraph the brochure proudly proclaimed: "At the dude ranches one finds the sort of people most desirable—business and professional men, artists, and men and women of letters who here have found inspiration for some of their best work."[127] Through dude ranching, utilizing the beauty and grandeur of, say, the Grand Teton Mountains to find oneself, to develop a recognizable quality of individuality, became, quite literally, a distinct upper-class privilege, because others from afar simply didn't have the wherewithal to draw from such an environment.

The power that dude ranches had in determining status can be seen clearly by focusing on male homosocial relations and how eastern elites learned to use western trips to make men out of themselves. Dude ranches oftentimes organized separate horseback and camping trips for boys and young men—expeditions explicitly targeted for the upper classes. After explaining that it only solicits the patronage of boys from "the best Christian families," the Valley Ranch in Wyoming further assured that "a discriminating standard of admission is maintained and the endorsement of friends or former patrons is required before an applicant will be accepted. We reserve the right," the brochure added for good measure, "to decline any application without explanation." The trip itself had also "been carefully planned with the view of returning the party in splendid physical and mental shape for school in the fall." Close contact with the Wyoming Rockies, Yellowstone Park, and other "wild country of America" took care of physical conditioning. As for mental preparation, "a carefully chosen group of college-bred men from the faculties of well-known schools" led the expedition.[128] In the early 1920s the Wyoming Pahaska Tepee Winter School for Boys went as far as staffing "college men selected from eastern schools and colleges who prepare the boys for College Entrance Board examinations held at the school in June."[129] During this time some western ranches became a type of auxiliary prep school for the sons of the upper classes.

In tension with the constant lament that the "Old West" had indeed passed and the cowboy with it, these early twentieth-century horseback trips and western ranches developed the premise that dudes had something to gain from contact with both the land and the men who lived and worked there. The claim that "neither the West nor life in general is as adventurous and authentic as they were in my youth" amounts to a gross "intellectual error," Struthers Burt argued in his 1924 *Diary;* what's more, the fallacy is advanced by those who stand to gain from it— namely, older men who supposedly knew the West in its original state and whose person therefore showed it. "Your uncle, perhaps, or your father, or your grandfather could weave enchantment out of the West, but not you," as Burt described the complex. "It ain't what it used to be," Burt's old-timer friends told him when asked if the cowboy was dead: "They're all Montgomery Ward buckaroos now." With considerable personal and professional investment in proving them wrong, Burt set out in his book to demonstrate that "the thing has not vanished" and that young men of his generation could still define themselves through the West.[130]

Burt's *Diary of a Dude Wrangler* can be read as one long resolute yes to Frederick Jackson Turner's question of whether rugged individualism would continue to exist after the frontier had closed. The book's first chapter, "The Making of a Westerner," recounts Burt's own de-evolutionary arc back from the East and the halls of Princeton and Oxford, where he went to school, to the "immense solitudes" of Wyoming's plains and mountains, where he learned about himself.[131] "Like a great many other Americans I have always had the West in my blood," Burt wrote in classic Turnerian fashion, and, once immersed in that environment, he revered "isolation" in nature while reviling the city. "Crowds," he wrote in one of many antiurban aphorisms, "are enemies of Man and God."[132] Having most likely come across the frontier thesis in his formal education or personal reading, Burt seems to have engaged Turner in the last section of the *Diary,* a brief on the continuing existence of the "Old West"—"spotted" but "permanent"—and of the cowboy—the embodiment of that open and rugged environment. He "cannot die," Burt pointed out, "for the simple reason that there are millions of acres of land that can be used only for grazing purposes, and while such acres exist the cowboy will exist along with them. Moreover," Burt added crucially, "the West is a state of mind, and a state of mind lasts longer than any material circumstance." That the West could survive as a "state of mind"—as an "intellectual trait," in Turner's term—legitimated Burt's work as a purveyor of western culture. "[R]epresenting no passing phase between the frontier and civilization," Burt concluded, the dude wrangler "has a serious and important job"—that of "preserv[ing] a reality."[133] For wranglers and dudes alike, that reality was a psychology, a mind-set, a disposition, an identity stemming from but not wholly dependent on the geographic reality of the West.

In practical terms, by keeping rugged individualism alive, dude wranglers maintained a modern pathway to male homosocial status. Chapter 3 on college football examines the anthropological concept of liminality and the hypermasculine reconfiguration of a player's identity through ritualistic separation from his original social and physical context; suffice it to say here that the dudist experience developed its own material and symbolic forms of disconnection, including the several hundred miles of train or automobile travel to the West, and especially the last stretch of the journey, usually a long and bumpy wagon or coach ride that dramatized the ranch's removedness from civilization. As the Wyoming Bar E D Ranch proudly described the last stage of the trip there, "Four miles of rugged, rolling country effectively cut the ranch off from the main highway and incidentally the prying tourist."[134] Dudes moved closer to the real West and rugged individuality by shedding their city clothes for purely functional outdoor wear. "There is no dressing up," the 1917 Eaton's Ranch brochure advised. "For the men, an Easterner who has made many trips, suggests: A comfortable felt hat, saddle slicker, khaki trousers, two suits of light-weight underwear, two flannel outing shirts, two cotton outing shirts, three pairs durable cotton hose, a pair of high laced boot shoes . . . a pair of heavy woolen bed socks, heavy coat or thick woolen sweater, bathing suit, and heavy leather gloves."[135] As Turner had recognized in the frontier thesis, basic dress made the western man, although dudes substituted "the hunting shirt and moccasin" with the clothing of the cowboy.

Eastern male homosocial status stood to gain most from the dudes' nexus to cowboys, wranglers, and other western men. The dude ranch served as an elaborate site for interregional mingling. "As much as possible we try to get the dudes and the outfit to mix," Struthers Burt described. "It is good for both the Westerner and Easterner to know each other, and once the initial embarrassment is over and the provincialism on both sides dissipated, the Easterner and the Westerner as a rule like each other."[136] But underneath this basic regional exchange could be found an intricate homosocial pecking order in which *dude*—a synonym for *tenderfoot, greenhorn,* and *city slicker*—continued to denote inauthenticity and lowly manhood. On the other end of the homosocial spectrum emerged a new label for the cowboy and ranch worker: *roughneck*. "Some of our outfit"—as Burt recorded in his *Diary,* far from its apologia for the word *dude*—"they call themselves 'roughnecks' in contradistinction to dudes." With this distinction hardly lost on the dudes, their stay often involved trying to develop one's masculinity by crossing over to roughneckedness. "I am eating with the rough-necks (that is the help) and not the other dudes," one college-aged dude exclaimed in a 1920 letter home to his mother. "God help my table manners," he added gleefully, "you will have to begin all over again."[137] Whether through bad table manners, dressing down, or more serious risk taking on horseback or in competition with other men, devolution could not have been more valued among dudes; and within this privileging, the indigenous cowboy or roughneck inspired that regression as much as the great outdoors.

Although *roughneck* predated the dude ranch, it is entirely fitting that the word would be used there to distinguish wannabes from real western men. Signifying a "quarrelsome disposition" along with a general propensity for "rowdiness," *roughneck*'s usage exceeded that of *rugged* in its emphasis on physical prowess and capacity for violence—the final index for real manhood.[138] As always, Teddy Roosevelt's biography well illustrates the point. During his first days in the South Dakota Badlands in the early 1880s, the young Roosevelt, wearing a tailor-made fringed buckskin suit and glasses, stood out as a walking definition of a dude. But that changed after he faced down and reputedly knocked out a loud name-calling "bully" in a ramshackle barroom. "Roosevelt was regarded by the cowboys as a good deal of a joke until after the saloon incident," remembered Frank Greene, a local official of the Northern Pacific railroad. "After that it was different."[139] Of course, Roosevelt would capitalize on his rugged reputation upon the outbreak of the Spanish-American War, when he used Washington connections to form a volunteer cavalry unit dubbed the Rough Riders. Consisting mostly of western cowboys and Ivy League football players—roughnecks all—the Rough Riders epitomized homosocial unification between West and East and, significantly, the North and South. They also demonstrated how turn-of-the-twentieth-century hypermasculinity tended to fix itself on killing.

In conclusion, as a master synthesizer of nineteenth-century European American rugged individualism with Darwinian evolutionary theory and his doctoral training as a social scientist, Frederick Jackson Turner had immense influence on the history profession, social psychology, and, more generally, middlebrow thought. He "had literally recreated American history as a branch of study," a Minneapolis newspaper observed in 1921, "and to be unacquainted with his viewpoint is to misunderstood America."[140] Turner's effect on masculinity, if less obvious, was no less profound. It came in a naturalist approach to American character that incorporated both a biosocial and cultural mechanism for explaining the way the nation's rugged sociogeographic qualities imprinted themselves on an individual's psyche and person. Turner's environmental determinism became all the more compelling with his announcement that the frontier had closed coupled with his prediction that it would continue to have force in modern culture. He thus contributed a distinct spatial orientation to American self-understanding: throughout the twentieth century an extremely close correspondence existed between masculine sense of one's person and place. Turner's originary story of American character had an effective, real-time-and-place presence for modern men and women, pointing the way back to strength, vigor, and dominance not through wistful longing for a distant past but in relocating one's body in the material geographical spaces of the North American landscape. At the same time, however, the atavistic impulse went through a process of despatialization. In addition to being able to get away to dude ranches, for instance, Americans could pick up an increasing number of books of fiction whose narratives took readers back into primal experience of an emotional kind. This development is examined in the next chapter on naturalist literature's power to represent and affect a brutish state of masculine existence.

The enduring appeal of rugged individualism can best be seen in its self-conscious adoption by many modern American women. By the second decade of the twentieth century, the new woman's "impulse of individualism," as novelist Margaret Deland described in 1910, was "manifest to everybody." Deland continued: "She apes the independence of the boys, and often emphasizes it with an affected and ludicrous swagger . . .; but with that independence, she has grasped at the splendid possibility of physical perfection, which implies a resulting mental strength heretofore classed as masculine."[141] Deland's inclusion of the word "heretofore" in that last clause raises an interesting issue: must this broadening of women's options in self-development be seen only as the female embrace of a "masculine mystique"?[142] As suggested earlier, while male-generated individualism has enjoyed tremendous ideological power over the past one hundred plus years, in the hands of the most thoughtful early twentieth-century feminists such as Charlotte Perkins Gilman, the ideal of autonomy and self-differentiation presents one of many avenues toward nongendered humanness.

Proof that early twentieth-century feminism did not uncritically adopt masculinity comes with the fact that, generally speaking, women's self-development rejected violence and aggressiveness. Gilman, for instance, wanted nothing to do with war making—something she cast as antithetical to full humanness. "In warfare *per se*, we find maleness in its absurdist extremes," Gilman warned caustically: "Here is to be studied the whole gamut of basic masculinity, from the initial instinct of combat, through every form of glorious ostentation, with the loudest accompaniment of noise."[143] This point is crucial to my study, which hereinafter examines the distinctly male imbrication of violence, pleasure, and self-fulfillment in naturalist fiction, college football, total war, and heterosexuality. "But you have there the myth of the essential white America," D. H. Lawrence wrote in *Studies in Classic American Literature* (1923). "All the other stuff," he continued, "the love, the democracy, the floundering into lust, is a sort of by-play. The essential American soul is hard, isolate, and a killer. It has never yet melted." Lawrence's well-known observation is paradigmatic of the gendered slant of American character studies—for he was certainly talking about "the white man's mind and soul"—and it also provides a suitable transition to the following consideration of killing in the modern masculine literary imagination.[144]

CHAPTER TWO

Brute Fictions

It's hard to determine what it meant for one of the thousands of men who bought Edgar Rice Burroughs's novel *Tarzan of the Apes* when it came out in 1914 to actually sit down and read through this story of the young Lord Greystoke, the infant son of English aristocrats, who is raised in the African jungle by a family of apes and then, through the deadly combination of animal-like ferocity and human intelligence, becomes "king of the jungle." Always one of the most difficult issues in literary history, readerly reception is all the more challenging with such a fantastic story as *Tarzan*. With chapters entitled "Jungle Battles," "The Forest God," "The Call of the Primitive" and its setting, plot, and lead character so removed from the personal experience of, say, a midwestern white-collar employee or factory worker, *Tarzan* may have become popular through its ability to place a male reader outside his workaday world and into an exotic environment in which a man survives or perishes by virtue of his wits, brute strength, and capacity to hunt and kill.[1] And yet without diary entries or personal letters speaking of such an appeal, the novel's primitivist meanings remain a matter of speculation.

Some measure of historical specificity if not certainty can be achieved, though, by approaching *Tarzan* as a culmination of a popular masculine literary genre. If de-evolutionary masculinity is a habit of mind, then literary texts can be seen as multifaceted incitations to certain psychologies, with plot lines and character development helping to pattern a reader's cognitive and emotional predisposition. With *Tarzan* and what will be defined here as the American genre of hunting and killing, we find a routinization of zoomorphic subjectivity—a calibration of male self-understanding toward man's prehistoric past and, more specifically, toward his animal origins and their staying power in modern consciousness.

One way to start piecing together the meaning of a story is to look at its critical reception. Book reviews can serve as a type of "rehearsal" of the reading process, divulging one person's intellectual and emotional response to the story. And because some critics try to analyze the text in relation to popular literary tastes, reviews can add historical insight into the reading practices of a particular time.[2] Unfortunately, few publications reviewed *Tarzan* upon its 1914 release. The *New*

York Times gave it two hundred words: entitled "With Anthropoid Apes," the review treats the book positively, commenting that Burroughs "has so succeeded in carrying his readers with him, that there are few who will not look forward eagerly to the promised sequel." *The Nation* devoted the same amount of space to *Tarzan*: this critic enjoyed the story as well, remarking on how well Burroughs had managed to assemble so many "elements of mystery and thrill" within "a pale of book covers." Or consider a more recent review written by Gore Vidal in a 1963 issue of *Esquire* magazine. In "*Tarzan* Revisited," Vidal wondered how to account for the fact that "the Tarzan books have sold over twenty-five million copies in fifty six languages." In part, he commented, the series is unambiguously written for men; Vidal had "yet to meet a woman" who "identifi[es]" with the ape man. Male readers, on the other hand, let themselves return to Tarzan's "Eden, where free of clothes and the inhibitions of an oppressive society, a man can achieve in reverie his continuing need . . . to prevail as well as endure." Most responsible for pulling readers in is Burroughs's "gift" for creating "action scenes," Vidal wrote, adding that this is a very difficult task for a novelist of any genre or brow level.[3] Vidal put his finger on what had to be one key to *Tarzan*'s early twentieth-century success: its sequence of action scenes, actually lurid fight scenes, in which the hero kills anything and everything that crosses his path in the jungle—from lions and his fellow great apes to countless native African men.

Another related method of getting at the meaning of a story is to place it within at the institutional history of literary culture during the time of its publication and reception. *Tarzan* was released amid what one literary historian has labeled "the new cult of masculine writing" during the Progressive Era.[4] As many men found more leisure time in late nineteenth- and early twentieth-century industrial urban America, a new class of professional male writers produced a large body of fictional work that can be distinguished as middlebrow in content and form. More complex than the sensational serialized stories found in post–Civil War dime novels and more accessible than the fiction of the antebellum American Renaissance or the early twentieth-century modernists, middlebrow male-authored novels and short stories became leading instruments in defining manhood and creating the psychology of masculinity—until, that is, electronic media, oftentimes working from earlier literary texts, took over that role by midcentury.[5] A 1914 male reader of *Tarzan*, for instance, may very well have imaginatively identified with the character's archetypical prowess. That is not to say that the reader ever expected or even wanted to end up in a loincloth in the African jungle eating the raw flesh of his recent kill; rather, he put himself in Tarzan's "shoes," as it were, transitorily experiencing the high episodic and emotional pitch of a life very different from his own.

We can go as far to say that a key historical *effect* of *Tarzan* and other work in the genre was its *affect* on the reader—convincing him that to turn and embrace purportedly instinctual violence is to express his nature. During a time when natural and social science insisted that humans shared a range of instincts with other animals, masculinist literature drew aggressive emotional states out of the reader, representing them as distinctive to males of the species. For instance, one of the most affective scenes in *Tarzan* comes in the hero's battle with Terkoz, a deranged male ape who has taken the American woman Jane Porter into the jungle and "toward a fate a thousand times worse than death." Sexual selection ensues, as Jane—"her lithe, young form flattened against the trunk of a great tree, her hands tight pressed against her rising and falling bosom, and her eyes wide with mingled horror, fascination, fear, and admiration—watched the primordial ape battle with the primeval man for possession of a woman—for her." Finally, after his "long knife drank deep a dozen times of Terkoz' heart's blood, and the great carcass rolled lifeless upon the ground," Tarzan "did what no red-blooded man needs lessons in doing. He took his woman in his arms and smothered her upturned, panting lips with kisses."[6] We may readily construe that *Tarzan*'s sensationally gendered conjunction of eroticism and violence thrilled many readers of 1914.

The following discussion deepens this interpretive assumption by examining the generic formulation of turn-of-the-century hunting-and-killing literature and its patterned evocation of heightened aggressive and violent emotions. Hence the chapter title "brute fictions." *Brute* works here as a composite label, categorizing literary texts that explicitly connect masculinity to savage preconscious psychologies. Few of the works considered here apply the word in a positive idealistic sense. *Tarzan*, in fact, explicitly uses *brute* in the negative, to distinguish its lead character from the apes: "there was that which had raised him far above his fellows of the jungle—that little spark which spells the whole vast difference between man and brute—Reason."[7] Yet it is the brutish nexus to his "fellow" apes that makes Tarzan such a memorable literary figure—he matches their deadly ferocity while also accomplishing such superhuman feats as teaching himself to read and write and learning high French in a matter of days (fig. 2.1). This combination of animalist privileging and distancing could be found in a myriad of pre-*Tarzan* popular literary texts. By the time that our 1914 reader sat down with Burroughs's novel, he may very well have been quite used to feeling vicariously the pleasures of violence and killing, albeit thinly masked by a spurious sense of his own separation.

Tarzan can be read historically, then, as a classic rendering of the fully established hunting-and-killing genre. In setting up its long sequence of battle scenes filled with graphic descriptions of fighting, blood and guts, and death, the novel places the young protagonist in an environment that strips away any civilized traits he may have inherited from his aristocratic parents. The African jungle rather than the Great West of the North American continent (as found in so many turn-of-the-century masculinist literary works) provides the geographic trigger to Tarzan's primitivism. But the literary effect-affect is the same, as the narrative pushes both the character and the reader into a spiral of brutish consciousness. Actually, the ape-inhabited jungles of Africa allowed Burroughs to make more ambitious observations about the evolutionary increment between beast and man; he conjured "unthinkable vistas of the long dead past when our first shaggy ancestors swung from a swaying bough and dropped lightly upon the soft turf of the first meeting place." More common to the genre are the book's constant contrasts between Tarzan's natural savage ways and those of his overcivilized and effeminate uncle living in England. For instance, Burroughs detailed the ape man's hunting skills and the enjoyment in eating raw animal flesh. After killing and devouring a wild boar, Tarzan "wiped his greasy fingers upon his naked thighs." Meanwhile, "in far-off London another Lord Greystoke . . . sent back his chops to the club's *chef* because they were underdone, and when he had finished his repast he dipped his finger-ends into a silver bowl of scented water and dried them upon a piece of snowy damask." *Tarzan* underscores the stark antiurban theme so central to American hunting-and-killing literature by idealizing the "exultant freedom" of the jungle. "This was life!" Burroughs wrote. "Ah, how he loved it! Civilization held nothing like this in its narrow and circumscribed sphere, hemmed in by restrictions and conventionalities. Even clothes," Burroughs added in suggesting the joys of a suitless brute, "were a hindrance and a nuisance."[8]

In close keeping with the hunting-and-killing genre, Burroughs molded his hero into an archetypical human predator: "A personification, was Tarzan of the Apes, of the primitive man, the hunter, the warrior." To fill in this ideal Burroughs followed any number of plot devices and character developments from earlier masculinist literature. The mortal combat scenes, for instance, often pit Tarzan and his adversary within a primordial circle of onlookers that accentuates the performative nature of battle. Burroughs also laid bare Tarzan's deep drive to take another life. "His desire to kill," as Burroughs repeated throughout the novel, "burned fiercely in his wild breast." And unlike other animals in the jungle, Tarzan's human nature causes him to kill "for the mere pleasure of inflicting suffering and death." Burroughs proved to be most accomplished in eroticizing Tarzan and his many acts of murder and bloodshed. At times Tarzan's prowess is seen from Jane's perspective: "As the great muscles of the man's back and shoulders knotted beneath the tension of his efforts, and the huge biceps and forearm held at bay those mighty tusks, the veil of centuries of civilization and culture was swept from the blurred vision of the Baltimore girl." *Tarzan's* eroticism is not always explicitly heterosexual, though. Burroughs made a considerable effort to account for Tarzan's great athletic stature: "His straight and perfect figure, muscled as the best of the ancient Roman gladiators must have been muscled, and yet with the soft and sinuous curves of a Greek god, told at a glance the wondrous combination of enormous strength and suppleness and speed." Indeed, Burroughs added the minor character William Clayton, a member of Jane's hunting party, to develop a distinct measure of homosocial "admiration" for the ape man's "wondrous instinct" and "immense muscles" as they "leap[ed] into corded knots beneath the silver moonlight."[9] This suggestion of homoeroticism, along with Burrough's arduous attention to Tarzan's immense physical capacity and killer instinct, make the novel a valuable introduction to popular masculinist literature of the turn of the twentieth century.

The American Literary Genre of Hunting and Killing

Since at least the nation's founding, American literature has been taken up with stories about men killing humans and other animals. In fact, after considering the recurrence of such tropes as the heroic hunter, the thrill of the chase, the dramatic showdown between two equally matched enemies, and the psychic pleasures of taking another life, a good argument can be made that enactment of deadly force has been *the* dominant theme in nineteenth- and twentieth-century American writing, especially if we direct our focus to male-authored work.[10] The new national fiction of the late eighteenth- and early nineteenth-century—including Charles Brockden Brown's *Wieland* (1798) and *Edgar Huntly* (1799); Robert Montgomery Bird's *Nick of the Woods* (1837); Cooper's five Leather-Stocking novels (1823–41); Melville's *Moby Dick* (1851), *Pierre* (1852), and *Billy Budd* (1890); most of Poe's fiction; William Gilmore Simms's *Martin Faber* (1833) and *Beauchampe* (1842); and George Lippard's *The Quaker City* (1845)—all turns on the excitement, mystery, and degradation of killing. Add to that the sensational pamphlets of the 1840s about real and fictional murderers, hunting stories in *The American Turf Register and Sporting Magazine* and *Forest and Stream* and other sportsmen's publications, the dime novels beginning in the 1860s, and the Civil War literature and naturalist fiction of the of the late nineteenth century, and it becomes clear that the twentieth century's mass cultural formulations of hyperbolic male stories of crime, hard-boiled detectives, adventure, the western, and war drew from a long-standing literary tradition of violence directed against man, woman, and beast.

The pervasiveness of nineteenth-century imagined violence and its profound effect on twentieth-century popular culture became very evident as the predominant theme of killing grew after the Civil War into a full-blown literary genre of masculine reading and writing. *Genre*, in this context, marks the institutional formalization of a certain literature's production, distribution, and reception. It denotes how content is crystallized through routinization of plot, character development, and subject matter. Although specific meaning remains variable among individual readers, genre sets the parameters for that meaning: it determines what a person comes to expect from a literary work, organizing the occasion for and practice of reading within a matrix of separate cultural referents, intellectual assumptions, and social needs.[11]

An emergent genre depends on a large and distinct readership, which American hunting-and-killing literature found in the sharp late nineteenth-century rise in middle-class male readers—a critical mass possessing the leisure time needed to consume the violent and murderous stories churned out in the ever-increasing number of nationally circulated magazines and best-selling novels.[12] Within these middlebrow forms, deadly force became generic, as did de-evolutionary plot structures underwritten by environmental determinism and culminating in bestial states of preconsciousness and being. In turn, accessible primitive psychologies became central to the hunting-and-killing genre, just as notions of biologically based aggressive emotions and violent instincts gained popular and scientific currency within late nineteenth-century American culture at large.

Above all other writers, Stephen Crane, Theodore Dreiser, Jack London, and Frank Norris—authors making up the American naturalist literary movement—solidified the late nineteenth-century hunting-and-killing genre and the maturation of masculine reading culture. These naturalist novelists managed to combine artistic innovation with middlebrow popularity (all four achieved national prominence during their lifetime), and so their success went far in advancing killing into mainstream masculine imagination. Naturalism's subject matter focuses consistently on violent human conflict. Its plot structures often turn on murderous states of mind. Of course, Crane, in his fictions of war and brutal frontier and urban life, obsessed the machinations of fighting and killing; Dreiser's novel *An American Tragedy* (1925) closely traces homicidal motivation in its male protagonist's bent on self-fulfillment even though it means drowning a woman who threatens his rise, and the author's work overall upholds, as one early twentieth-century critic put it, "the jungle-motive"; London stands as the purest example of the naturalist interest in deadly instinct—*Call of the Wild* (1903), one of the three novels examined in the next section, relies on literal animalist renderings to pull the reader out of civilized sensibility; and Frank Norris's *McTeague* (1899) depicts the title character as a brutish dentist unable to live for long above the surface of his murderous atavistic impulses. As "a specific form," the literary theorist Georg Lukacs wrote, "a genre must be based upon a specific truth of life."[13] If so, the hunting-and-killing genre founded itself on the essential inevitability of deadly confrontation integral to naturalism. It also drew from naturalism its truth of pessimistic determinism: a world view that denies human reason and will and instead fixes on the involuntary movement across an ontological-emotional spectrum—a fatalistic slipping and sliding from civilization to savagery, from sanity to criminal sociopathological compulsion.

Another core component of the hunting-and-killing genre, one that preceded naturalist fiction, is the American hunting literature that has accompanied the sport's development since the turn of the nineteenth century. Superficially, sport hunting and hunting literature don't seem to fit with the genre's dark criminal truth of pessimistic determinism. "The free, self-reliant, adventurous life," as Teddy Roosevelt put it in 1893, "the wild surroundings, the grand beauty of the scenery, the chance to study the ways and habits of the woodland creatures"—these things draw a man to the field, "the finding and killing of the game is after all but a part of the whole." Yet the distinct pleasure derived from killing has been so central to that whole that appeals to hunting as a source of good wholesome nature-loving fun are, as Thorstein Veblen pointed out, suspect if not altogether false: they attempt to mask the sport's less-attractive "impulses of exploit and ferocity." (Outdoor recreation, Veblen went on to say at his sarcastic best, "could be more readily and fully satisfied without the accompaniment of a systematic effort to take the life of those creatures that make up an essential feature of that 'nature' that is beloved by the sportsmen.") Within the social and cultural Darwinian context of post–Civil War America, most hunters saw little need to deny the enjoyment and benefits of chasing and killing wildlife. "It cultivates," as Roosevelt explained in classic form, "that vigorous manliness"—a trait crucial to both individual and national development, he added, thereby alluding to the close nexus and moral blurring between hunting and war. As discussed in chapter 4, late nineteenth- and early twentieth-century formulations of the American soldier would take on athletic dimensions of skill, cunning, and performance—qualities that men cultivated in sport hunting. The relation is quite palpable in Roosevelt's sequence of writings on hunting, his four-volume history of the three hundred years of Indian wars in *The Winning of the West* (1889–96), and his glorified account of his Spanish-American War experience in *The Rough Riders* (1899) and his bragging to his sister, "Did I tell you, I killed a Spaniard with my own hand?"[14] In Roosevelt at least, despite his self-conscious efforts to imbricate sport and killing within a progressive national narrative, hunting does finally disclose its pathology, the savagery beneath the civilization, and the atavism that coexists rather uneasily with claims of a forward-moving masculine trajectory.

Emerging from disparate origins among colonial elites, sport hunting threw off most traces of English aristocratic privilege during its nineteenth-century rise,

constructing itself as an indigenous American pursuit that would naturally flourish through the nation's abundant wildlife and its native masculine affinity for
the wilderness. Hunting traditions among American Indians provided a complex
fertile subtext to the sport's growth: European American men identified with what
they understood to be native noble savagery, even as the United States (led by
those same European American men) proceeded to rid the nation of its indigenous
peoples. Another factor in the nineteenth-century hunting boom was the mass
production of firearms beginning in the 1840s, an industrial process that gave
American men the wherewithal to kill on an unprecedented scale—to shoot, that
is, not only Native Americans and each other in the Civil War, but also animal life
in the fields and forests of the North, South, East, and West. Crossing regional, economic, and ethnic lines, hunting (together with angling) became the most popular
participatory American sport during the last thirty years of the nineteenth century.
Post–Civil War hunting clubs sprung up at an exponential rate: between 1874 and
1878, for instance, they tripled in number to 308.[15] While the sport's iconography
often romanticized the solitary heroic hunter, the social history of hunting flourished homosocially—men enjoyed chasing and killing in groups. So in a practice
as old as Pleistocene hunting-and-gathering societies, and yet newly formulated
for modern American imagination, men separated themselves from women and
kin and set out to experience what they understood to be natural and essential to
their masculine identity.

What made the sport essential to so many nineteenth-century American men
was not just the killing and its surrounding ritual but the thoughts and desires
conceived prior to entering the field, the content of which is approximated in the
vast hunting literature that mediated between the act and the meaning derived
from it, thereby shaping the subjective experience of individual reader-hunters. A
precursor to the meta-discursive imperative of recording and interpreting that has
become so integral to modern sport, description of what it's like to kill animals is
among the oldest themes in American men's literature, with one of the first hunting books being *The Sportsman's Companion; or, An Essay on Shooting* (1783). The
following year John Filson published the first biography of Daniel Boone, *The Discovery, Settlement and Present State of Kentucke* (1784), thus beginning a literary cult
that would produce 130 books on the frontier hero in the nineteenth century alone;
Timothy Flint's best-selling *Biographical Memoir of Daniel Boone, the First Settler of
Kentucky* (1833) went through more than fourteen editions before 1868 and was the
most widely read American biography of the century. Along with the lionization
of Boone and its close equation of American character building with deadly prowess, hunting literature helped transform the tracking and shooting of game into a
popular sport by standardizing its technical vocabulary of guns, dog training, and

accessories; writers venerated indigenous quarry, placing different game within an increasingly elaborate natural history, which, in turn, necessitated an ethical or sportsmanlike code of killing. The emergence of nationally circulated magazines went far in pulling sport hunting together in the nineteenth century. The antebellum *American Turf Register and Sporting Magazine* (founded in 1829), and *Spirit of the Times* (1831) attracted large middle-class readerships with their hunting and travel stories, equipment advertisements, and other sporting content. By the time *Forest and Stream* started reaching readers in 1873, hunting incorporated an impressive body of knowledge and expertise as well as deeply grooved textually created expectations regarding the cultural benefits and personal fulfillment derived from the sport.[16]

As seen in the first issue of *Forest and Stream*, modern sport hunting cast itself within a highly developed context of idyllic rusticity, encouraging reader-hunters to regain premodern virtue by reconnecting with American natural splendor. The illustration heading the magazine's early issues is thick with romanticism (fig. 2.2): two men with rod, gun, dog, and each other—framed by lake and woods filled with trees and brush, Native Americans and fauna—are set in peaceful coexistence with seemingly perfect organic surroundings. A poem on the front page of the first issue testifies to the "young life" and "joyous" beauty of such "scenes in the wondrous forest-land"; these are "wild romantic scenes," the last lines emphasize, "dear to the hunter's and angler's soul."[17] The dubious content of that soul is brought to light, though, by returning to the illustration and recognizing the implied violence signified by the nexus between the Indians and deer—both positioned and paralleled as prey—and the European American hunters. With gun at the ready, these men are far more menacing than peaceful, especially from the perspectives of the human and wild life found in the drawing's periphery. As for the personal character reclaimed by hunters in the wild, the illustration finally says more about potential killing prowess than innocent virtue. Its rustic romanticism (with moose head trophy and all) is a lure to the field (or at least to reading about the field), a stylized cultural adornment to sport hunting's experientially violent base.

The early *Forest and Stream* illustration is also indicative of the escapism that many late nineteenth- and twentieth-century American recreational hunters would come to read into the sport. From this context, the Native American camp to the left of the hunters is less a target than a conduit to a precivilized state, less a source for "regeneration through violence" than regeneration through association with savagery. First printed amid the postbellum Indian Wars, the 1873 illustration hardly exemplifies those fierce and genocidal conflicts; rather, it caricatures the intended consequence of Native American–European American contact: after subduing Indian nations with greater firepower, white Americans could safely romanticize their cultures and commingle them with modern conceptions of rusticity. Consistent with Frederick Jackson Turner's understanding of how the wilderness broke down European custom, thought, and dress, rustic Native Americana worked as a postfrontier cultural solvent on the middle-class hunter who would be eager, as the Wisconsin historian described, to "strip off the garments of civilization." *Forest and Stream* didn't encourage direct masculine identification with Indian hunters. Individual Native Americans are mentioned occasionally as hunting guides and more often as the object of sportlike violence. Otherwise, Indians served as an impassive backdrop to outdoor life, heightening a variegated, distinctly European American impulse of returning to nature.

For American sport hunters, going native also meant removing oneself from the city. Taking that step of remove was a founding trope of both the sport and hunting literature, as release from work and other urban-related pressures became a cultural end in itself. "Throw down your book or your pen," Samuel H. Hammond urged in *Hills, Lakes, and Forest Streams; or, A Tramp in the Chateaugay Woods* (1854), "close your ponderous ledger, cast away your briefs . . . and turn your back on the glare and heat of the city, its eternal jostlings and monotonous noise." Escapism, a lure of sport hunting since its early nineteenth-century beginnings, took on a much more urgent tone by the turn of the next century. The introduction to *Guns, Ammunition and Tackle* (1904), a popular hunting manual of the time, asked the reader: "Are you an invalid? Try camping out, and see if you don't say good-by to all the doctor's stuff. Are you brain weary and tired out from business? Only try it once, and you will never regret and forget it."[18] While not all outdoor sports literature struck this overstated Madison Avenue chord, most did incorporate a crucial therapeutic appeal. *Forest and Stream*—with its hunting stories, illustrations, and advertisements for guns, clothing, equipment, and travel—can be seen as an elaborate institutional manifestation of this therapeutic quest through sport. It urged the consumption and use of products and experience (real or literary) as a healthful riposte to the ennui of modern urban life.

As part of the late nineteenth- and early twentieth-century back-to-nature craze in travel, camping, hunting, and fishing, hunting literature promoted close attention to the regional diversity and beauty of American wilderness. As early as 1876, in only its fourth year of publication, *Forest and Stream* proudly claimed that it had already offered more high-quality writing on North American natural history than any other book, magazine, or journal. With contributors "among the most intelligent of our frontier officers, and of the Canadian and United States Boundary Commissions and Government surveys," the magazine's early issues "cover[ed] the prairies of the west, southwest, and the far west. It includes the mountain ranges of the whole country . . . the everglades of Florida, the interior great lakes, the Dismal Swamp of Virginia, and the prominent points along the entire coast from Labrador to Mexico." Amateur writers added regional color to *Forest and Stream*'s pages through the increasingly popular hunting story. The frontier may have officially closed by 1890, but turn-of-the-century issues of *Forest and Stream* and hunting literature in general attested to the lasting abundance of wildlife in the countless unsettled pockets of the country. "Nowhere on the face of the globe," the introduction to *Guns, Ammunition and Tackle* reads, "are all kinds of conditions so favorable to this nomadic kind of life [i.e., the shooting trip] as they are in most parts of this continent."[19] American exceptionalism gained new currency through modern hunting literature as regionalist writing authenticated the regenerative powers of different local landscapes.

A benign even moralistic grain runs through turn-of-the-twentieth-century hunting literature. Paradoxically, antihunting arguments made up part of this sentiment. Accompanying the sport since its inception—in 1790 Benjamin Rush insisted that hunting "hardens the heart by inflicting unnecessary pain and death upon the animals"—concern for the autonomy and protection of wildlife contributed to the modern conservation movement. A common variation on outright opposition to hunting likened the sport to a childhood phase. "I say give me the man who was in youth a brave, keen hunter, but in whom the student nature steadily grew," a *Forest and Stream* reader wrote in a letter to the editor in 1903, "so that by middle life he can no longer find his joy in smashing those beautiful forms, no matter under what romantic difficulties, but has come to wish them all to live their lives out, that he and all may study, or at least know they are there in their own wild places." (John Muir made a similar point in his famous 1903 rebuke of then President Teddy Roosevelt's love of hunting: "when are you going to get beyond the boyishnss of killing things . . . are you not getting far enough along to leave that off?")[20] And ethical considerations sprang up within sport hunting itself, the "logic" of which marked an interest in ensuring the preservation of its prey's species. As hunting developed into sport, thereby taking on the symbolic qualities of a war or competition between man and beast, certain rules of engagement followed: game must be somewhat free to escape (shooting animals in a zoo is unsporting), fowl should be taken on the wing, and not all weaponry are allowed (electric lights, machine guns, and high explosives make killing too easy). Such formalization of hunting practices augmented the hunter's claim to skillfulness under cover of a rudimentary regard for the hunted.

In nearly seamless coexistence with the ethics of turn-of-the-twentieth-century sport hunting was the psychic regenerative pleasure provided by the actual act of killing animals. Post–Civil War hunters, the anthropologist Matt Cartmill writes, in contrast to the early to mid-nineteenth-century romanticist tradition, "adopted a Nietzschean view of the hunt as therapy for the human sickness, a cleansing participation in the healthy violence of the natural order." While few American hunters read Nietzsche, Cartmill's point that they took up the sport to reconnect to a fundamental precivilized violent existence (no matter how fleeting) is at the heart of this chapter and book. Some hunters came to measure the sporting experience in expressly masculinist de-evolutionary terms. After complaining that "since the days of the cave men our race has gone . . . degenerate," the early twentieth-century California congressman and conservationist William Kent explained that the savagery of hunting offered a corrective: after shooting an animal, "you are a barbarian, and you're glad of it. It's good to be a barbarian, and you know that if you are a barbarian, you are at any rate a man." At times, hunting literature described the sport's violence with lurid realism and candor. "Men are the most destructive animals in the world," Charles L. Paige wrote in a 1903 *Forest and Stream* article. "Much of their energy, reason and execution is devoted to arts that annihilate, destroy and renew, for better or worse," Paige added. "Every civilization in the world's history has been built upon the graves of wild beasts and savages. Civilization itself feeds upon flesh and blood, and under its ponderous tread things good and beautiful are ground to dust with the things otherwise."[21] Hunting literature also privileged killing in subtler ways, embedding it within outdoor travel narratives and representing it as the essential culmination of manly integration with nature. Whether implicit or expressly stated, though, the immediate reward of killing—the revivification of man and nation—became commonplace within modern American hunting literature.

One of the most prolific and successful hunting writers of the time was Theodore Roosevelt, that multitudinous figure who embodied so many of the constituent parts of de-evolutionary U.S. masculinity. Heading west after graduating from Harvard in 1880, Roosevelt bought a ranch in the Dakota Territory, donned an expensive buckskin suit, and otherwise became the quintessential turn-of-the-century dude, unabashedly enrapturing himself with the thrill and savagery of hunting. Upon killing his first buffalo, Roosevelt reportedly did an "Indian war-dance" around the prostrate beast, leaving "nothing in the way of delight unexpressed." In 1887 he cofounded with Henry Cabot Lodge the Boone and Crockett Club, whose well-heeled membership included only those hunters who had collected at least three trophy heads.[22] The club eventually concerned itself with preserving as well as destroying the country's wild life. And, of course, as U.S. president, Roosevelt led national conservation efforts. But Roosevelt never gave up his love of hunting. He did as much as anyone to link the sport with American masculinity.

Hunting Trips of a Ranchman (1885), *Ranch Life and the Hunting Trail* (1888), and

The Wilderness Hunter (1893): Roosevelt's trilogy of hunting books did a great deal of ideological work at the turn of the century, including lionizing Daniel Boone, Davie Crockett, and other Anglo-Saxon hunters cum Indian killers as "the heralds of the oncoming civilization, the pioneers in that conquest of the wilderness which has at last been practically achieved in our own day" (fig. 2.3). And, in league with his close friend Owen Wister, Roosevelt romanticized the contemporary status of the cowboy as of the same supervirile type: "In the place of those heroes of a by-gone age, stands, or rather rides, the bronze and sinewy cowboy, as picturesque and self-reliant, as dashing and resolute as the saturnine Indian fighters whose place he has taken." Although writing in the third person, Roosevelt intended that he be counted among this successor generation: he too had exposed himself to the "American wilderness," which, in a classic formulation of environmental determinism, has "a character distinctly its own"; "the West," Roosevelt continued in anticipation of both Turner and Wister, "seems to put the same stamp" upon those who live and survive in it; "their life forces them to be both daring and adventurous, and the passing over their heads of a few years leaves printed on their faces certain lines which tell of dangers quietly fronted and hardships uncomplainingly endured." Hunting provided another, closely related common denominator between the cattlemen and Roosevelt. With autobiographical hunting stories making up the core of the three books, Roosevelt drew a close equation between the "pleasures" of killing and American manhood. "The chase," Roosevelt wrote in 1893, "is among the best of all national pastimes; it cultivates that vigorous manliness for the lack of which in a nation, as in an individual, the possession of no other qualities can possibly atone."[23]

Roosevelt detailed hunting's manly pleasures in "Hunting the Grizzly" (1899), one of his most accomplished stories. Appearing in *Field and Stream* (the new title of *Forest and Stream*), the article relates four separate encounters and killings of grizzly bears, "the chief of American game." First featuring Roosevelt's solitude in nature and then highlighting the dangerousness of his "foe" and the concomitant excitement and thrill of ending its life, the tales build upon a certain compositional formula, one that can be broken into several more specific parts. Each episode begins with an exact geographic reference point: "the Bitter Root Mountains in Montana," for instance; or "a bleak, wind-swept valley, high among the mountains which form the divide between the head-waters of the Salmon and Clarke's Fork of the Columbia." Next, we find Roosevelt enjoying a moment of repose in camp. "Lying lazily back on the bed of sweet smelling boughs" or "a carpet of soft pine needles," he affords himself romanticist sense impressions: "the evening was still with the silence of primeval desolation"; "I had been lulled to sleep by the stream's splashing murmur, and the loud moaning of the wind along the naked cliffs." Come the morning of the hunt, he "did not linger a moment, but snatched up my rifle, pulled on my fur cap and gloves, and strode off" in search of the grizzly. First sighting of the prey is at the midpoint of each story, with Roosevelt always aggrandizing the "brute" quality and "giant strength" of "the great bear" while dramatizing his own animal-like response: "Then I heard a twig snap; and my blood leaped." Stalk and chase build suspense—"In moccasined feet I trod softly through the soundless woods"—the climax coming with Roosevelt lifting his rifle, taking aim, and shooting the bear. The most colorful point in the narrative is usually the deadly effect of Roosevelt's bullets: "the thick spatter of blood splashes, showing clear on the white snow, betrayed the mortal nature of the wound." The stories end quietly, with Roosevelt simply perceiving the result of his action: "I saw the dark bulk lying motionless in a snow drift."[24] The article then moves on to the next kill.

The fourth and culminating story in "Hunting the Grizzly" is worth looking at closely for its near immortalization of the prey, the bloody realism in which the killing is described, and the heroism Roosevelt derives from his conquest. This episode roughly follows the same narrative formula. It begins by setting the geographic context, the "head waters of the Salmon and Snake [rivers] in Idaho." We then find the hunter "camped in a little open spot, by the side of a small, noisy brook, with crystal water." Roosevelt indulges in naturalist observation: "The place was carpeted with soft, wet green moss, dotted red with kinnikinnic berries, and at its edge, under the trees where the ground was very dry, I threw down the buffalo bed on the mat of sweet-smelling pine needles." He then sets off, "rifle on shoulder, through the frosty gloaming." After walking a short while, "I caught the loom of some large, dark object." Roosevelt is close enough to shoot immediately. Having been hit, the animal "turned his head stiffly towards me; scarlet strings of froth hung from his lips; his eyes burned like embers in the gloom." The drama in this story comes not from the stalk and chase but from the grizzly charging Roosevelt. After being shot again, "the great bear turned with a harsh roar of fury and challenge, blowing the bloody foam from his mouth, so that I saw the gleam of his white fangs." Taking another bullet, "he came steadily on, and in another second was almost upon me." Roosevelt shot yet again, just as the bear's paw "made a vicious side blow at me." For better or worse, though, the grizzly dies: "he lurched forward, leaving a pool of bright blood where his muzzle hit the ground."[25]

Roosevelt ended this fourth story and the whole article by confessing his pride in withstanding the "very dangerous antagonist." The risk to "life" and "limb" made the experience all the more worthwhile because it confirmed his "skill and hardihood" as a hunter. The bear's ferocity—made almost human in words such as "challenge" and "vicious," which imply purpose if not intention—also seemed to legitimate Roosevelt's own violence. All told, he put four bullets into the animal, the damage of which is detailed in morbid specificity: the first "piercing one lung"; the second "shatter[ing] the lower end of his heart, taking out a big nick"; the third "entering his chest" and going "through the cavity of his body"; and the fourth "entering his open mouth, smashing his lower jaw and going into the neck."[26] Given this enthusiasm for gore, Roosevelt's hunting stories and the masculine character developed within them should finally be seen as part and parcel of a post–Spanish-American War speech, "The Strenuous Life" (1899), and his glorification of battle and killing as a way to recover the "great fighting masterful" quality displayed by American men of yesteryear. And while heroic character building through risk and lethal self-fulfillment would become integral to the ideal of the modern U.S. citizen-soldier, the transparent bellicosity of Roosevelt's hunting stories isn't completely representative of the late nineteenth- and early twentieth-century hunting literature overall. The American hunting story—formularized well before Roosevelt's writing—did turn on the psychic rewards of violence and killing; but this payoff tended to be presented more seamlessly than Roosevelt's gore, usually under the guise of the regenerative experience of romantically communing with various and distinct wilderness landscapes.

Part travelogue, part testament to homosocial camaraderie, and part chase-and-kill narrative—the American hunting story had reached maturity by the early post-bellum years, as seen in "Elk Hunting in Nebraska" (1873). Appearing in the first issue of *Forest and Stream*, the story's title is typical, tellingly matching specific prey with geographic place and thus presenting them as something to be experienced together as one. "Elk Hunting in Nebraska" also integrates Native Americans into its description of the hunting landscape. "A bad Indian country is that along the Loup Fork [of the Missouri river], for upon its banks lies the trail which the Sioux follow on their horse-stealing expeditions to the Pawnee village." The unnamed author and his companions "wanted game more than we feared the Indians, and therefore we decided to take the risk." Sport hunting in this region almost always blended with Native American contact and conflict. Around the campfire, "after a delightful supper," the men in this article "spent an hour or two talking over the incidents of the day, and listening to . . . stories of hunts and Indian fights." The narrator defined his close relationship with Lute—"my *guide,* philosopher, and friend"—in terms of their shared experiences: "together we have hunted buffalo on the Republican [river], and antelope on the sand hills; have shot wild turkeys on the Beaver [river], and been chased by a rascally band of Minnecoujas, between the stream and the Republican, and now we are going to hunt elk on the Loup."[27] In memory at least, there is commonality, a type of blurring, between hunting animal prey and fighting Indians.

"Elk Hunting in Nebraska" is driven by the narrator's emotional investment in killing his prey. Lute promises his friend that he will get a shot, but the guide isn't sure "whether you'll kill or not. . . . Not many men around here can say they have killed an elk." Tension builds over the hunter's marksmanship. Having "dreamed of elk for weeks," he "feared a miss" and later "secretly prayed that I may be the one to kill it." The story comes to its climax when Lute suddenly spotted several elk. "In a moment we were all excitement," the author recalled. "Fire arms and knives were examined, and we descended into the bed of the creek, whence the elk had just emerged about a half mile further up." The stalk began, with the hunters "crawl[ing] along, not on our hands and knees, but flat on our faces for some distance." Now a hundred yards from the elk, the moment had come, and the author momentarily shrunk from it. The sight "of an old cow elk" proved "too much for me, and I sank back. . . . Then steadying my nerves for a violent effort, I raised my old Sharpe. Carefully with finger on trigger, I full cocked it, and sighted. . . . and I pulled." In the confusion after the shot the narrator "could see nothing of the one at which I had fired." At that point, having apparently failed, "I felt particularly small." But Lute then found the elk laying in short prairie grass. "We rushed to the spot," the hunter wrote proudly, "and there lay the cow, kicking in her death and agony. My ball had passed through her heart, and she had run about fifty yards before falling. That was for me the supreme moment," he added with complete gratification. The kill had regenerated him, as if the elk had sacrificed its life for his: "As I stood over her, all the trouble and annoyance of the trip; all the worries and cares of every day life were forgotten, and I was absorbed in the proud contemplation of the graceful creature laying before me."[28]

By the turn of the twentieth century the hunting story could be found throughout American sports writing. *Forest and Stream* featured the regional-game combination narrative in virtually every issue: "Hunting Wolves in Wisconsin," "A Deer Hunt in the Adirondacks," "Hunting Coyotes in Death Valley," and countless other stories chronicled local color and sporting challenges while stressing the benefits of antiurban escapism. "[H]e who has lived the active life of the hunter in uninhabited lands," Allan Hendricks proclaimed in an 1897 *Forest and Stream* article, "knows well that in those remote regions there may be found enjoyment that civilization cannot yield him." Hendricks continued formulaically: "it is not alone the enjoyment of the chase that attracts men to the wilderness. The wild, free life untramelled by the conventions of society; the charm of wandering in the regions untouched by hand of man; the open hearty comradeship about the camp fire—all these combine to draw men to the far-off mountains and the plains." Writing in *Forest and Streams* series "The Sportsman Tourist," Hendricks spoke specifically about the virtues of hunting "A Turkey of the Wilderness," something he had done

one "bleak gray morning in late November . . . at the foot of the Kiamichi Mountains in Indian Territory"—"where the telegraph does not reach and mail sacks do not penetrate." Rather than focusing on the specific region, Hendricks keyed on the exceptional rusticity of the fall season and its close relationship to his prey: "When the cool winds of autumn and the crisp frosts of early winter have worked their changes in the summer landscape, when the football player appears upon his battlefields in the pink of condition . . . then it is that the wild turkey gobbler, the monarch of American game birds, roams his native heaths in his most kingly manner."[29] Hendricks's hunting story offers an early example of what would become the ubiquitous yet odd American association between turkey, football, and Thanksgiving.

Like "Elk Hunting in Nebraska," Hendricks's story "A Turkey of the Wilderness" is most notable for describing the gratification derived from ending an animal's life. Fulfillment came in part through the chase and kill. Hendricks waxed rhapsodically about how, after the dogs take the trail of the turkey, "the pulse quickens and every sense and every muscle grows alert at the promise that is wafted down the wind by the sonorous, irregular baying." Apparently overlooking sport hunting's rule of only shooting birds on the wing, he waited to fire until the turkey had landed just a few yards away. "The big bird fell over on its back," Hendricks remembered, "and for a few moments thrashed about vigorously with its strong wings. . . . The last struggle ended as I stood above it," he continued, "and with a feeling of such keen pleasure as I think does not often fall to the hunter's lot, I picked up my first wild turkey." The rest of the article closely links the wildness of the bird in the field to the quality of it on the plate. It's what Hendricks did with his kill that brought him the most pleasure: "Sing if you will the gastronomic virtues of the celery-fed canvasback, the well-cooked woodcock, the fragrant venison steak, or any other dish that may tempt your palate; but of them all there should be granted the highest praise to the wild turkey"—a true "table delicacy." The notion is that one takes in the bird's qualities, or rather the human projection thereof, by eating it. "Nor is it less beautiful in life than it is delicious to the taste," Hendricks concluded, "when the scattered sunrays of its native haunts gleam on its plumage of bronze and green and gold."[30] By shooting, killing, and eating the turkey, the hunter consumed its wildness.

Whether through eating the prey, finding emotional transcendence in its death, or enjoying the "the thrill of the fight with dangerous game" (as Roosevelt described), turn-of-the-century hunting allowed killers to absorb cultural constructions of animal wildness into their own person. Sport hunting did finally lend itself well to a vulgarized Darwinian-Nietzschean world view of might makes right. "The passion for power and the distinguishing superiority incidental to it," as a

Forest and Stream editorial put it in 1903, "seems to be a trait common to mankind, whether savage or civilized." The sport, in its most basic formulation, served as an essential counter to modern urban life: "Healthy, normal men inherit their desire to hunt and to fish," another *Forest and Stream* editorial stated in defense of President Roosevelt's urge to hunt bear while in office, "and years of confinement in the cities away from actual temptation does not prevent the longing for woods and streams that periodically rises in the human breast."[31] Finally, though, and perfectly encapsulating a paradoxical modernity, the so-called primal experience of hunting defined itself through literature. "The dweller or sojourner in the wilderness who most keenly loves and appreciates his wild surroundings," as Roosevelt explained, "is the man who also loves and appreciates the books which tell of them."[32] As a crucial formative component of the American hunting-and-killing genre, autobiographical hunting books and stories plotted masculine de-evolutionary pleasure and gratification through close, intimate, and violent contact with nature. In so doing, it provided a generally unrecognized source for the plots of the adventure story, the western, and other related forms of popular American fiction.

Reading for Plot: *Call of the Wild*, *The Virginian*, and the New Male Readership

What difference does it make if the stories American men read at the turn of the twentieth century are rooted in actual lived experience and presented as such or if they make no pretense to factual representation? Central as it is to Western thought and literature, the distinction between fact and fiction can and should be blurred when examining the hunting-and-killing genre and its effect on American masculinity. (Note this blurring is not in reference to deflating the legendary exaggerations of "true" hunting and fishing stories; nor is it about the fact that virtually every piece of writing blends the real and imagined.) When approaching literature from the readers' perspective, we should acknowledge that the emotional and cognitive impact of a novel may have been very close to that of a hunting narrative. Just as one might have thrilled over the chase-and-kill episode of a hunting story, an adventure novel, for instance, compelled readers to identify with the lead character who, more times than not, found himself in life-and-death confrontations that elicited such feelings as excitement, aggression, and the self-fulfilling pleasure that comes with manifesting physical prowess. This is not to say that the compositional differences between types of writing are unimportant. In developing the premise that fiction became a primary source for masculine self-understanding during the late nineteenth and early twentieth centuries, this section will take into account the distinct creative and narrative properties of the novel in general, as well as analyze the particular appeal of Jack London's *Call of the Wild* (1903) and Owen Wister's *The Virginian* (1902). But historical analysis of the popular masculine novel should recognize the interconnection between it and other literary forms within the hunting-and-killing genre. Together these texts developed plot-driven formulae that directed readers to certain heightened emotive states (sometimes called truths) in keeping with man's supposedly vital relationship to the psychic-experiential rewards of violence and killing.

In arguing that the novel became a primary source of masculine self-understanding, we need to piece together a social-cultural history of the modern American middle-class male readership, examine readers' attraction to fiction, and determine what commercial and institutional developments helped privilege this fairly new creative medium. Omniscient third-person fictitious narratives really only took hold in English in the late eighteenth century. Throughout most of the nineteenth-century, the full-length novel (as opposed to shorter fictional forms such as the dime novel or the magazine story) remained, in the United States at least, a pastime of elites. In contrast, the turn of the twentieth century saw the dramatic rise in the production and consumption of novels. American publishing during this time experienced what has been called "the great fiction boom"—a ten-year period in which the printing of novels expanded at a near exponential rate: in 1894 approximately 700 new novels were issued in the United States; by 1901 that number had grown to over 2,200. And this rapid increase in the release of titles was paralleled by the mass appeal of individual books. By the early twentieth century, the yearly sales of the most popular novels reached well into the hundreds of thousands.[33] The popularity of fiction at the turn of the century is usually explained by the rapid development of a middlebrow American readership. As technological improvements lowered costs of printing, publishers cut the average price of a novel to between a dollar and a dollar and a half—a price well below the cost of literature a generation earlier but still above the dime novels popular among working-class readers in the late nineteenth century. Publishers also developed new ways to get books into the hands of middle-class readers. By the beginning of the twentieth century more books were sold in train-station book stalls and new city bookstores—establishments located downtown near office buildings, department stores, and other places of middle-class employment. In general, publishers started using modern business methods to produce, advertise, promote, and distribute books as they tried to integrate fiction into the burgeoning urban culture of consumption and entertainment.[34]

Newfound interest in literary journalism helped integrate the novel into mainstream middle-class urban culture. According to *Publisher's Weekly*, the 428 literary periodicals published in 1883 had more than doubled to 1,051 by 1893. Also, city newspapers started to run columns on current fiction, and by the end of the century men and women could choose from a vast array of nationally circulated magazines that concentrated on literature. They included the *Atlantic Monthly, Harper's, World's Work, The Nation, The Saturday Evening Post, Century Magazine, McClures, North American Review, The Forum, The Independent, The Bookman, The Chap-Book, The Cosmopolitan, The Critic,* and *Review of Reviews.*[35] As literary sections of magazines and newspapers announced the release of new fiction to readers, publishers spent large sums of money on print advertising with the hope of expanding the boundaries of the consumer's reading experience. Critical reviews of new fiction had a similar impact.[36] Although certainly not taken at face value, reviews did make the most personal appeal to individual interest in fiction—literary criticism became the leading medium connecting readers to texts. Just like middlebrow book and film critics today, turn-of-the-twentieth-century reviewers offered practical advice about whether a title was worth the money and time. A standard review started with a plot summary and then offered the writer's own aesthetic and emotional response to the book. Taken as a whole, this critical literature offers insight into how contemporary readers might have approached a novel and what they hoped or expected to get from it.

The 1895 founding of *The Bookman: A Magazine of Literature and Life* is particularly useful in coming to terms with the rise of American middlebrow fiction and the concomitant emergence of a distinctly masculine reading culture. The monthly magazine, glossy and informal in style, was packed with articles about novelists, books, and the publishing business. Each issue included several columns reviewing new fiction. All the major publishing houses advertised in *The Bookman;* some companies drew up full-page, elaborately illustrated announcements of recent releases. *The Bookman* also created the first American best-sellers list. The editors took sales figures from leading bookstores throughout the United States and compiled a monthly list of the ten most popular novels and thereby connected its readers to a national literary culture. That this culture took on a masculine quality can be seen from the pages of *The Bookman* and its focus on male-authored novels. The magazine's advertisements and reviews adopted a particularist rather than a generic male caste, oftentimes explaining how a book would appeal to masculine sensibilities.

To say that more and more turn-of-the-century middle-class men connected themselves to an increasingly national literary culture—to propose that the cultural concept of the novel took on a masculine quality that had not existed before in the history of American letters—is not to suggest that women's literature and its readership subsided during this time. In the nineteenth century, middle-class popular fiction had largely been a feminine enterprise. Historians have discussed in detail how women in the antebellum period created a literary culture of "sentiment and feeling" separate and distinct from the masculine world of business and competition. And in the late nineteenth and early twentieth centuries, female-authored literature only expanded as women made inroads into the male-dominated publishing business. Kate Chopin, Ellen Glasgow, Edith Wharton, Frances Ellen Watkins Harper, Angelina Grimke, Susan Glaspell, Willa Cather, Charlotte Perkins Gilman, and others created an artistically accomplished body of literature that advanced the feminist movement by supporting women's interest in self-creation.[37] Men, however, began to match women's close relationship to literature. As middle-class men found more leisure time in turn-of-the-century urban America, they developed practices of reading similar to those of women, realizing in the novel what literary theorist Wolfgang Iser has described as "as an operational mode of consciousness that makes inroads into existing versions of the world. In this way," Iser continues, "the fictive becomes an act of boundary crossing which, nonetheless, keeps in view what has been overstepped." Male readers learned that the novel could displace the external world. Displacement happened only temporarily, but during that time a new interior relationship could be forged between the story and the reader, incrementally but indelibly shaping his subjectivity.[38]

This theorizing about the novel's lasting impact is borne out in turn-of-the-twentieth-century literary reviews and criticism. Awareness that the novel had achieved cultural primacy during the time—it can be understood as *the* most effective and affective narrative form before the emergence and eventual dominance of Hollywood and television—empowered authors to deliberately engage and move readers from one way of understanding themselves to the next.

In his 1903 essay "The Responsibilities of the Novelist," Frank Norris stressed the great artistic opportunity that the novel provided: "More than a simple diversion, whiling away a dull evening," it had become "the great expression of modern life"; much like the theater of earlier days, fiction created a "vital interest" in those who experienced it. Readers "take the life history of fictitious characters," Norris wrote, and compare them to their own. The novel functioned, he concluded, as a "tool" or a "vehicle" for "The People."[39] Norris used the fictive tool to explore modern man's darker impulses and pathologies—the destructive lure of capitalism in *The Pit* (1903), for instance, and atavistic aggression and violence in *McTeague* (1899). In the hands of more formulaic writers, the novel brought opportunity to idealize exceptional states of masculinity or, alternatively, to essentialize supposedly normative masculine consciousness and behavior.

As indicated by contemporary reviews, formulaic masculinist novels connected with readers by luring them into close identification with the lead characters. Reviews of Wister's *The Virginian,* for instance, urged male readers to find themselves in the cowboy. A *Saturday Evening Post* critic put it perfectly: "these pages are an open text on the fundamental instincts of American manhood."[40] This may seem baldly stated, but Wister himself understood his purpose in rather straightforward terms of man building. While dedicating the novel to Teddy Roosevelt, he outstripped his close friend in romanticizing the West and postulating how the cowboy's life could remedy eastern degeneracy. In his "To the Reader" comments preceding the novel, Wister fixed on the difference between past and present American manhood. In comparison to the "shapeless state" of men today, Wister wrote, there was a solidity to the cowboy's work ("The cowpuncher's ungoverned hours did not unman him") and overall manner: "Whatever he did, he did with his might." In this lead-in to the novel, Wister asserted that the cowboy still somehow lived on: "His wild kind will be here among us always."[41] The crucial point—and this is what makes popular fiction so instructive of de-evolutionary masculinity—is that a close one-to-one correspondence existed between what the author intended and the meaning and message received by readers. The popular masculine novel is longer and develops its plot lines and characters more than the dime novel and the hunting story; unlike the self-help manual so prevalent at the turn of the century, it necessarily involves the variable reader's imagination; but in contrast to, say, the modernist novel, this literature is uncomplicated, relatively unopen to broad interpretation.

The hunting-and-killing genre, like any genre, can be understood to involve a type of contract between the writer and reader. In exchange for the time spent assembling and experiencing a text, the reader obtains an anticipated emotional and cognitive payoff, an output intentionally arranged by the author's meaning-making selection and combination of literary conventions.[42] Many popular masculinist novels of the turn of the century can be placed within the hunting-and-killing genre by determining the ways in which authors brought readers to preconfigured states of primitivism and imagined brutality via such conventions as wilderness settings, de-evolutionary plots, and heroic characters. In the hunting-and-killing genre, plot becomes the master convention, incorporating both setting and character into its narrative flow. As seen in the classic hunting story, the generic text begins with the narrator's dislocation, his transportation from the civilized, safe, and familiar to a dangerous and challenging natural environment. In a sense, the precise geography of the new setting isn't as important as its function in throwing the subject into deadly confrontations during which he must tap into heretofore unrealized instincts of cunning and aggressiveness. Character works as a consequent and more precise component of plot, developing through rather than surpassing events of the story.[43] As the reader takes on the protagonist's perspective, he gradually identifies with the character's risk taking and eventual triumph. Popular fiction followed this formula set by the hunting story, although the novel gained more cultural currency through its unique capacity for incorporating and manipulating multiple literary conventions.

A master manipulator of literary convention, Jack London became America's first millionaire novelist, publishing more than forty books, which sold an esti-mated 16 million copies. In some ways London saw writing as a workshop indus-try. Setting himself on a one-thousand-word-per-day production schedule, Lon-don's "brainwork" turned him into a hound for formulae—at times he had to buy plots from other writers because of his own "damnable lack of origination." A hack writer? Not really. London's talent lay in using plots to get himself to a point where he could examine and vivify contemporary thoughts and sensibilities—to inter-pret "things which are," as he put it, rather than create "things which might be." He reduced serious complicated ideas into accessible middlebrow form. London's commitment to Marx is well known, as is his exploration in *The Sea Wolf* (1904) of Nietzschean supermanhood; and his embrace of Darwinian determinism in *The Call of the Wild,* among other novels, has earned him a place in the naturalist canon.[44]

The difference between *The Call of the Wild* and other great-outdoor adven-ture stories of the period is London's richness of language, mood, and psychol-ogy; labeling his approach to fiction as "emotional materialis[m]," London filled the subjective experience of his lead character Buck and, in turn, his readers with the stuff of animal instinct. This zoomorphic effect is what makes *The Call of the Wild* central to turn-of-the-century masculinity. In describing Buck's transforma-tion from a civilized house dog to a wild, roving creature, London perfected the de-evolutionary story line, evoking instinctive states of mind by blurring the cognitive difference between animal and human consciousness.

A cultural Darwinist through and through, London contemplated the descent of man in *Before Adam* (1907), a novel that, when read in tandem with *The Call of the Wild,* demonstrates the author's fascination with the intimate "kinship" between animals and humans and its play upon masculinity. Actually, *Before Adam* can be seen as a close precursor to Burroughs's *Tarzan.* It centers on the conscious-ness of an American "city boy" who, rather than being dropped into the jungles of primitive Africa, has increasingly detailed dreams of life in the "Mid-Pleistocene" period. With this de-evolutionary plot line examining the prehistorical transition into humanity, the narrator tries to figure out the source of or reason for his vivid dreams. He first understands that they emanate from a second self. "This other-self of mine is an ancestor," London wrote, "a progenitor of my progenitors in the early line of my race, himself the progeny of a line that long before his time developed fingers and toes and climbed up into trees." Then, at college, the narrator "discovered evolution and psychology," which lead him to see the dreams as freakish "racial memories." London continued: "Evolution was the key. It gave the explanation, gave sanity to the pranks of this atavistic brain of mine that, modern and normal, harked back to a past so remote as to be contemporaneous with the raw beginnings of mankind." At the apex of this epoch the narrator meets his Pleistocene father—"half man, and half ape." The modern man fixes on his progenitor's body and the masculine physical prowess that it brings. "It represented strength," London explained, "strength without beauty; ferocious, primordial strength, made to clutch and grip and rend and destroy." Memories of human origins are not cheerful or peaceful in nature—they are best relegated to the past. But *Before Adam* leaves readers with the clear impression that man is still intimately connected with his primitive beginnings through the "dictate of instinct," what London defined as "merely a habit that is stamped" onto our psyche and heredity.[45]

London's novel *The Call of the Wild* impresses animal instinct onto human consciousness by way of two de-evolutionary literary devices. The first is perspective. Introducing and describing the St. Bernard and Scotch shepherd dog Buck in humanlike terms, the book encourages readers to identify with the creature's experience and feeling. The story begins with Buck enjoying the comfortable surroundings of his master's California estate: "During his four years since his puppyhood he had led the life of a stated aristocrat; he had a fine pride in himself, was even a trifle egotistical, as country gentlemen sometimes become because of their insular situation."[46] Buck possesses the increments of human sensibility, cognition, and motivation—he "decides," "realizes," "knows," "divines," and "wonders."[47] While these mental actions are clearly anthropomorphic—they animate a dog's life with human consciousness—the novel as a whole blurs animal and human identity to the extent that a primary readerly effect is not anthropomorphic but its opposite: animalism or zoomorphism—the infusion of human existence with beastlike behavior and emotion. As the story unwinds, as Buck develops his character through atavistic prowess, the reader's own consciousness is flooded with the sense impressions of a dog, and a rather brutish one at that.

The second literary device leading the reader to primal instinctive emotions is pure plot development. Buck is kidnapped and shipped to the Alaskan Klondike where he is sold into service as a sledge dog—geographic dislocation that initiates the peeling away of his domesticated consciousness. Once in the new environment, "every hour was filled with shock and surprise. He had been suddenly jerked from the heart of civilization and flung into the heart of things primordial," London wrote, apparently following the hunting-and-killing formula. "No lazy, sunkissed life was this, with nothing to do but loaf and be bored. Here was neither peace nor rest, nor a moment's safety. All was confusion and action, and every moment life and limb were in peril. There was imperative need to be constantly alert," London continued, making the point as completely as possible; "for all these dogs and men were not town dogs and men. They were savages all of them, who knew no law but the law of the club and fang." London laid it on thick. Like its title, *The Call of the Wild* is dripping with such social and cultural Darwinian imperatives as "the law of the club and fang"; "the dominant primordial beast was strong in Buck"; or "kill or be killed, eat or be eaten, was the law."[48] The novel is a tribute to "survival of the fittest." Published eleven years before *Tarzan's* veneration of "the savage ape-man," London had perfectly timed his novel with the popularization of de-evolutionary thought. (*Tarzan's* long-term success in print and film suggests that many people never tire of such exaggeration.) He happened to be very good at illustrating primitivism and getting readers to imagine precivilized existence.

As in *Before Adam,* London used heredity and ancestry in *The Call of the Wild* to enliven the primitive origins of both lead character and reader. Once Buck started living in the Klondike wilderness, "memories of heredity gave things he had never seen before a seeming familiarity: the instincts . . . quickened and became alive again"; he "linked the past with the present, and the eternity behind him throbbed through him in a mighty rhythm to which he swayed as the tides and the seasons swayed." At night, Buck "loved to lie near the fire, hind legs crouched under him, fore legs stretched out in front, head raised, and eyes blinking dreamily in the flames." At times he thought of his old home in California or "the good things . . . he would like to eat." Then he started to envision in the place of the cook another man, hairy and "shorter of leg and longer of arm," who "squatted by the fire with head between his legs and slept." Through the dog's imagining, the reader sees not Buck's canine origins but his own early human ancestry. Still further blending takes place between human and animal. When the man awakes, he and Buck venture out into the forest, sharing the same primal sensations and impulses. Both were "alert and vigilant, the pair of them, ears twitching and moving and nostrils quivering, for the man heard and smelled as keenly as Buck." Both are moved to answer "the call of the wild," to turn their backs "upon the fire and the beaten earth around it, and to plunge into the forest, and on and on" until "the last tie to civilization was broken."[49] London left readers to complete the picture of man's rightful place in nature, but, having already established the close zoomorphic parallel, he could rest assured that the vision would be brutish.

In charting Buck's primordial transformation, London first highlighted the dog's newly discovered love of vigorous exercise and then fixed on hunting and the psychic pleasures of killing. After a short while on the trail, Buck "was mastered by the sheer joy of each separate muscle, joint and sinew." He enjoyed "movement" for its own sake, "flying exultantly under the stars and over the face of dead matter that did not move." Buck's reflexes grew razor sharp—"He perceived and determined and responded in the same instant." He took on the strength of an athlete—"His muscles were surcharged with vitality, and snapped into play sharply, like steel springs." Buck's athleticism soon found expression in the "boundless delight" of hunting, and, with that plot development, London examined the allure of killing. *The Call of the Wild* replicates turn-of-the-century hunting stories in finding release and regeneration through killing. Hunting "sounds the deeps" of Buck's "nature," which includes an attraction to the gore of killing—"running the wild things down, the living meat," and deriving pleasure in "kill[ing] with his own teeth and wash[ing] his muzzle to the eyes in warm blood." Amid this "joy" and "blood lust," the book posits transcendence through killing. "There is an ecstasy that marks the summit of life, and beyond which life cannot rise," London proposed. "This ecstasy," he continued, echoing Stephen Crane's *The Red Badge of Courage* (1895), "comes to the soldier, war-mad on a stricken field and refusing quarter; and it came to Buck . . .straining after the food that was alive and that fled swiftly before him." Buck lost himself in chasing and killing. The experience brought "a complete forgetfulness that one is alive."[50] It dissolved the last remnant of civilization: self-consciousness.

Buck's most ecstatic moment comes when he challenged Spitz the husky for the lead position of the sled team. Buck sought the confrontation. "It was inevitable that the clash for leadership should come. Buck wanted it. He wanted it," London emphasized, in yet another essentialist construction, "because it was his nature." One clear night, then, while out on the frozen tundra, Buck attacked Spitz. "The time had come." As the two dogs "circled about, snarling, ears laid back, keenly watchful for the advantage, the scene came back to Buck with a sense of familiarity." Buck "seemed to remember it all—the white woods, and earth, and moonlight, and the thrill of battle." The other sled dogs formed a ring around the two, creating a timeless circle, a natural stage for the combatants. As witnesses to the fight, they stood "silent, their eyes only gleaming and their breaths drifting slowly upward." To Buck and the other dogs "it was nothing new or strange, the sense of old time. It was as though it had always been, the wonted way of things." Finally, while "streaming with blood and panting hard," Buck gets the better of his opponent. Spitz falls and the circle of dogs closes. "Buck stood and looked on, the dominant primordial beast who made his kill and found it good."[51] *The Call of the Wild* doesn't actually end in this climax: Buck goes on, among other things, to fell single-handedly and eat a great bull moose; to avenge the murder of his friend and master John Thornton by slaughtering a group of Yeehat Indians (he became a "Fiend incarnate"—"ripping the throat wide open till the rent jugular spouted a fountain of blood"); and finally to take up the leadership of a wolf pack.[52] Each subsequent episode, however, turns on Buck's transcendence into killing—a transformation most fully imagined in the willful destruction of his equally matched antagonist.

As sensationalist as London's language of "blood-longing" and "war-madness" sounds to the early twenty-first-century ear, contemporary reviewers of *The Call of the Wild* underscored its unsentimental veracity and the author's ability to render something more basic or immediate than fiction. "It is a man's book, through and through," a reviewer commented in the *San Francisco Chronicle*, adding that London's "complete mastery of the material and that unconscious molding of style to thought . . . marks real from make-believe literature." Another reviewer in the *Reader* believed "the power of Jack London lies not alone in his clear-sighted depiction of life, but in his suggestion of the eternal principles that underlie it"—that is, "the appeal (and in Buck's case, the triumph) of barbarian life over civilized life." The book made an impact, literally. "[W]e feel at times the blood lashing in our faces," the critic explained; "it is cruel reading—often relentless reading." That early twentieth-century readers physically experienced this story about a dog is confirmed by a reviewer in *Book News Monthly*, who testified that *The Call of the Wild* "makes one groan in desperate resistance to the savage that is not worlds away, nor in ancestors dead and buried centuries ago, but within us." This writer embraced devolution. One finds a "sublime and pathetic beauty in the way the brute comes out in this noble dog," the critic admitted and, in any case, there is a "deep and underlying truth" in the novel. "The call of the wild is no fiction," the reviewer emphasized: "The things pointed out are the nameless things we feel, and the author shows clearly, unobtrusively that it is 'the old instincts which at stated periods drive men out from the sounding cities to forest and plain to kill things.'" Whether readers should embrace all of London's blood and gore is not mentioned; rather the article ends with sociocultural insight. The savage impulse comes in response to "the trend of the times," the overcivilization "which muzzles and massacres the individual, that touches society with decay and drags men back to the primal forest where their hairy ancestors clung with long arms to trees."[53]

From these reviews it is apparent that *The Call of the Wild* struck a brutish chord among at least some of its many early twentieth-century readers: the blurring of human and animal perspective along with Buck's own joyful immersion in savagery offered "truthfulness" in their resistance to modern consciousness. But what exactly is the source of the story's countercultural sensibility? Is Buck's wildness really a matter of discovering a preexistent natural state? Or is the dog's brutishness something that must itself be learned and affected, no more natural than a mind-set that would get one through, say, a nine-to-five desk job? Literary critic Jonathan Auerbach raises the issue about the novel's construction of the primordial, and it is a valuable point to end on because it confirms this study's overarching argument that hypermasculine violence has been largely determined culturally. *The Call of the Wild* can be read as an elaborate educational experience, a learning process all the more effective because it teaches under the cover of regaining instinct. At times, London himself recognized the paradox. When narrating Buck's transformation in the Alaskan Klondike, for instance, London wrote that "his development (or retrogression) was rapid." It is as if London caught himself after admitting that Buck wasn't coming by his prowess atavistically but rather building it up through self-conscious effort. In another passage, London explained that Buck's pride over his prowess "communicated itself like a contagion to his physical being," suggesting in a different way that the dog's brutishness originated outside himself.[54] This metaphor of disease that manifests violent behavior will be taken up in the examination of Frank Norris's gruesome novel *McTeague*. But first we turn to Owen Wister's heroic tale *The Virginian*, the best-selling novel that did as much as any text to locate American masculinity in the idiosyncratic cowboy of the West, a figure that embodies the brutal yet seemingly purposeful use of force.

The Virginian is often regarded as the seminal novelistic rendering of, not the hunting-and-killing genre, but the western, whose highly stylized narrative conventions, popularized in literature, film, radio, and television, make up a genre in and of itself. Also complicating the propriety of placing *The Virginian* in the hunting-and-killing genre is the archetypal figure, the cowboy hero. While "retrograding to the level of the brute," as the extremely successful author Zane Grey said about masculine character development in the western, the "hard men of the open also climb to the heights of nobility and sacrifice, to a supreme proof of the evolution of man." The Virginian's elevated ethical sense, for instance, may have been lost on London's dog Buck. Despite these reservations, though, it is valuable to include *The Virginian* within the broader-gauged hunting-and-killing genre. The congruities are more compelling than the differences. Wister's novel, like the western overall, should be seen as a most stylized example of a national literature that aggrandizes violent expression within a naturalistic, loosely Darwinian framework. As the label indicates, the western roots itself in a distinct geographical context, thereby exemplifying the hunting-and-killing genre's reliance on place or, more specifically, change in place to trip characters' emotions, motivations, and behaviors into new forms. Within popular American literature the West—the "Wild West"—erases prior consciousness. It initiates "the fleeting trance-like transformation back to the savage," as Grey elaborated in his 1924 article on the psychological impact of the desert and the wilderness. "The wide, open spaces, the lonely hills, the desolate, rocky wastes, the shifting sands and painted steppes, the stark naked canyons—all these places," Grey concluded, "with their loneliness and silence and solitude awake the instincts of the primitive age of man."[55] And, of course, the western fulfills the genre's killing component. Virtually all plot lines lead to deadly confrontation, as in *The Virginian's* righteous lynching of cattle rustlers and the melodramatic shoot-out between the unnamed hero and Trampas the villain.

As part of the hunting-and-killing genre, Wister's novel takes readers to these climactically violent episodes through exaggerated masculine consciousness or, more specifically, through two intertwined masculinist perspectives. The first is that of the narrator, a thinly veiled autobiographical character from the East. Raised in upper-class Philadelphia and educated at Harvard, Wister had followed the advice of family friend S. Weir Mitchell to seek neurasthenic rest cure by taking an extended hunting trip to Wyoming in 1886, a year after his close friend Teddy Roosevelt had done the same in South Dakota. Like Roosevelt, Wister fortified himself by holding his own in work and play among the young native-born ranch hands. His man-making transformation happened through homosocial acceptance as well as close contact with the rugged western wilderness. "[R]emembering my Eastern helplessness in the year" of my arrival, Wister wrote of *The Virginian's* narrator, "I enjoyed thinking how I had come to be trusted" among the cowboys. "The man who could do this"—set off alone on a several day hunting trip—"was scarce any longer a 'tenderfoot.'" And, again like Roosevelt, Wister decided to memorialize his experience in published text, although (after writing some magazine articles like the *Harper's Monthly* 1895 piece "The Evolution of the Cow-Puncher") he decided to do so through fiction. The novel allowed him to dramatize at length the sharp contrast he found, and for which he had desperately looked, between eastern decadence and western exhilaration. "I instantly preferred this Rocky Mountain place," the narrator comments in the beginning of *The Virginian*. "More of death it undoubtedly saw, but less of vice, than did its New York equivalents."[56] Within the novel and the maturing myth of the West, this caveat of death in no way discouraged those contemplating their own metamorphosis; rather, it provided the requisite weightiness and intrigue of an imagined life outside the gray predictability of the metropolis.

The narrator's personal story line, however, proceeds without great incidence of violence against human or beast. Even though he had gone West for hunting, the narrator relates little of his exploits, save shooting with the Virginian "young sage chickens" for dinner. Within this fictional work, violence comes in far more dramatic man-on-man confrontations—deadly conflicts to which the narrator only bears witness. His own western experience centers on romantic integration with nature, a process Wister described with some artistic flair.

The novel's opening scene places the narrator and the reader on a railroad car pulling into Medicine Bow, Wyoming. After spending a night in town, he separates himself from "the commercial travellers" and sets off with the Virginian across country on horseback to his friend's ranch: "And in a moment we were in the clean plains, with the prairie-dogs and the pale herds of antelope. The great, still air bathed us, pure as water and as strong as wine; the sunlight flooded the world." Upon arriving at the ranch, the narrator wants to lose his old self, loathing any artifact of civilization: "merely the sight of the newspaper half-crowded into my pocket had been a displeasing reminder of the railway, and cities, and affairs." A climactic and fulfilling episode comes when the narrator travels alone to meet up with the Virginian: "[T]o leave behind all noise and mechanisms, and set out at ease, slowly, with one packhorse, into the wilderness, made me feel that the ancient earth was indeed my mother, and that I had found her again after being lost among houses, customs, and restraints." He stops on the trail to rest for the night and describes how "[t]he great level around me lay cooled and freed of dust by the wet weather, and full of sweet airs. Far in front the foot-hills rose through the rain, indefinite and mystic." The man embraces his solitude. He "wanted no speech with anyone, nor to be with human beings at all. I was steeped in a revery as of the primal earth; even thoughts themselves had almost ceased motion. To lie down with wild animals," the narrator concludes in pure de-evolutionary if not bestial fashion, "would have made my waking dream complete."[57] Nature has done its therapeutic work.

The other masculinist perspective is that of the Virginian himself, a closely drawn character who eventually eclipses the narrator's point of view and pulls the reader's consciousness toward, to repeat the words of a *Saturday Evening Post* reviewer, "the fundamental instincts of American manhood."[58] Wister created enormous attraction to the cowboy hero. He did so compositionally, blending or intertwining the two characters through narrative. The nameless narrator begins the story in the first person, but after meeting the Virginian he often describes the action in the third person. In a sense, the traveler from the East and the Virginian and, ideally, the reader become one: except for a few instances, the narrator is no longer an active agent in the story; he focuses on the actions of the Virginian as if they are his own. With the narrator's dissolution, the reader could come to see everything through the eyes of the Virginian and thereby identify with his exploits and adventures as well as his person.

To argue that the narrator (and through him the reader) is both attracted to and identifies with the Virginian is to fly in the face of a basic distinction in psychoanalytic literary theory between desire and identification. Is it not impossible to *be* someone one wants—or to want someone with whose identity one has merged? Desire between two humans is thought to require a distance between subject and object—a border between them rather than their blurring. Within homosocial relations, however, this distinction breaks down, as *The Virginian* illustrates remark-ably.[59] The narrator both wants to be and wants the cowboy. His emulation involves an exaggerated attraction to the cowboy as a type—those "lusty horsemen ridden from the heat of the sun, and the wet of the storm"; those "wild and manly forms," in whose "flesh our natural passions ran tumultuous."[60] And the narrator's desir-ous identification is consummated in the perfection of that type, the Virginian.

The element of desire is revealed in the homoeroticism the Virginian gener-ates in the narrator and, by implication, in male readers. Wister's manipulation of perspective pays off here. Before the narrator blends into the Virginian, he has oc-casion to admire the cowboy from a distance. A hybrid homosexual-homosocial at-traction results—an attraction predicated on the separateness of the two characters but nevertheless formed in anticipation of at least subjective intertwinement. The narrator first sees the Virginian from inside his train car. He presses his face up against "the looking glass of our Pullman" and gazes out to a corral where a num-ber of cowboys are trying to rope a wild pony. Each fails until the Virginian steps up and, with the "undulations of a tiger, smooth and easy, as if his muscles flowed beneath his skin," effortlessly completes the task. From that point on the narra-tor is hooked. He doesn't miss a chance to detail his attraction to the "slim young giant, more beautiful than pictures." At an early point he describes the allure of the Virginian's cowboy suit—"the fringed leathern chaperreros, the cartridge belt, the flannel shirt, the knotted scarf at the neck, these things . . . worn by this man now standing at the door, seemed to radiate romance." But it is his overall physical presence, irreducible to one trait, that produces the narrator's sexual excitement: "In his eye, in his face, in his step, in the whole man, there dominated something potent to be felt." As to feeling his potency, the narrator displaces his desire onto an imaginary female figure, thus channeling it into a homosocially and heterosexu-ally sanctioned form: in an opening sequence, for instance, when the Virginian is needling another man for getting married, the narrator confesses disjointedly, "Had I been the bride, I should have taken the giant, dust and all"; and, later, in re-sponding to the Virginian's intense gaze, he realizes again, "Had I been a woman, it would have made me his to do what he pleased with on the spot."[61] These sexual fantasies fade as the two characters become friends, and as the narrator's point of view folds into the Virginian's; but that homosocial identification is accommo-dated, made more fluid, by a preexistent homoerotic attraction.

Adding to the Virginian's attractiveness is his ability to handle other men—both verbally and, if need be, through physical force. The Virginian is, first and foremost, a man among men. He has a "genius" for the intricate and dangerous relations among cowboys on and off the job—a pure homosocial world of rank, confrontation, and alliances built on such standards as skill in handling horse and cattle, bravery, physical and emotional strength, native intelligence, honor, and capacity to overcome and kill another man. Each one of these traits is manifest in the Virginian. Made foreman of the Sunk Creek ranch by Judge Henry, he ultimately assures his homosocial veneration in what would become the classic showdown, shoot-out scene with Trampas. Wister was obsessed with homosociality in *The Virginian*. After stepping off the train in Medicine Bow, the narrator presents a veritable sociological study of masculine conversation, competition for female affection, and the conventions of barrooms, poker games, and boardinghouses. He quickly learns to swallow his own eastern class distinctions: upon meeting the Virginian the narrator reflexively speaks freely and patronizingly, only to be put down through his guide's "veiled and skillful sarcasm," while still respectfully addressing the traveler as "Seh."[62] The narrator appreciates the Virginian's verbal acuity as well as his love of practical joking and outwitting others through humor, indirection, and guile. The bet with his friend Steve that he could trick a drummer into giving up the only vacant bed in the boardinghouse exemplifies the ease with which he masters other men. The Virginian, who despised the less-than-masculine commercial drummers, could have simply commandeered the bed. But gamesmanship is more fun. So after crawling into bed with the salesman and warning him to keep clear of his violent Indian-killing dreams, the Virginian starts thrashing about in pretended sleep. The episode ends with his would-be bunkmate bolting out the door in fear and the other cowboys riotously laughing in homosocial approval.

The narrator's keen powers of homosocial observation also focus on the initial confrontation between the Virginian and Trampas and the wildly varying meaning of the epithet "You son of a bitch." The first person to say it to the Virginian is his friend Steve. This takes the narrator by surprise. He "expected that the man would be struck down" for using "a term of the heaviest insult." But Steve says it while "grinning" at the Virginian "affectionately," and therefore his friend does nothing except smile back. "Evidently he had meant no harm by it," the narrator notes, "and evidently no offence had been taken. Used thus, the language was plainly complimentary." The second time it is spoken comes later the same day in a poker game after the stranger Trampas had already addressed the Virginian gruffly while dealing the cards. As the other players at the table drop out of the hand, Trampas turns to the Virginian and says, "Your bet, you son of a bitch." In response, "[t]he Virginian's pistol came out, and his hand lay on the table, holding it unaimed. And with a voice as gentle as ever, the voice that sounded almost like a caress . . . he issued his orders to Trampas:—'When you call me that, *smile!*'" From this astounding exchange, the narrator understands that context and inflection determine the meaning of words. The narrator also learns that the Virginian will kill another man, and risk his own life, over a matter of respect. He confronts Trampas not so much in defense of his mother's good name but over the stranger's brusque and aggressive manner. It marks a tear in the homosocial fabric. As soon as Trampas uttered those words, a "silence, like a stroke, fell on the large room. All men present, as if by some magnetic current had become aware of this crisis." Trampas let the challenge pass, but, as the narrator recognizes, "[a] public back-down is an unfinished thing." The Virginian had rung "the bell of death" and, after the two cultivate throughout the story a keen hatred for each other, it would be answered in a gunfight in the streets of Medicine Bow.[63]

The Virginian's most compelling trait is his purposeful use of physical force. For all his practical joking, the Virginian is deadly, and this very combination of good naturedness and violence helps explain as much as anything the character's success as a popular literary figure and eventual matinee idol. Wister carefully composed his hero: born and raised in the South, the Virginian brought traditions of manners and honor to the West, where that region's ruggedness forged him into a moralistic killer. The Virginian acts violently only when a point of principle is involved. After the rancher Balaam cruelly maims one of his own horses, for instance, "the Virginian hurled him to the ground, lifted and hurled him again, lifted him and beat his face and struck his jaw" with "sledge-hammer blows of justice." The proposition that in the West justice is meted out physically and extralegally is driven home in the lynching episode in which the Virginian must oversee the execution of Steve and another man for falling in with Trampas to steal horse and cattle. Putting "iron on another man's calf" is a capital offense among the territory's ranchers and cowboys, and the Virginian, head of the vigilantes, sees the job through even though Steve is his best friend. Later, when Molly the schoolmarm and the Virginian's wife-to-be objects to his actions, Judge Henry steps in and maintains that, in contrast to "burning Southern Negroes in public," "hanging Wyoming cattle-thieves in private" is a proper and necessary "*assertion* of the law" where there otherwise is none. The conversation ends with Molly quieted yet unconvinced—"It is all so terrible to me"—and this result, the narrator suggests, is about the best the Virginian could hope for.[64] From Vermont, Molly would never accept the savage nature of frontier justice. What's more, being a woman, she is not supposed to understand or be a part of it. While the lynching is ostensibly about protecting private property, the Virginian understands it as a natural response to men who had gone bad. Eliminating "miscreants" maintains homosocial order, and Molly has no role in that process except to stay outside of it.

This same homosocial dynamic can be found at work in the epic showdown between the Virginian and Trampas. Within this climactic episode, Molly's resistance to her fiancé's fighting and killing works to intensify the homosocial imperative of standing up for oneself. After Trampas slanders the Virginian and tells him to get out of town before sundown, it is inevitable that they will settle things in a shoot-out. Molly begs the Virginian to leave town, insisting that "there's something better than shedding blood in cold blood" (fig. 2.4). But the Virginian explains to her that the situation had become a matter of honor. To back down would mean that "I could not hold up my head again among enemies or friends." After public ridicule, the Virginian would be expected to protect his reputation. "It had come to the point where there was no way out, save only the ancient, eternal way between man and man," the narrator says. "It is only the Great Mediocrity that goes to the law in these personal matters." In a last desperate attempt to make the Virginian change his mind, Molly threatens that "If you do this, there can be no to-morrow for you and me." With these words he turns ashen white, for he dearly loves Molly; but the Virginian has made up his mind and says good-bye to her. So the two men meet each other face-to-face on the street and, after Trampas draws and fires his gun, grazing the sleeve of his enemy's arm, the hero shoots him dead. The Virginian shows no emotion. After confirming his enemy's demise, he returns to Molly and says "Yu have to know it . . . I have killed Trampas." Molly replies joyfully, "Oh, thank God!"[65] The two get married the next day and, it must be added, live happily ever after.

With Trampas and the Virginian facing each other, the other cowboys and townspeople form that timeless circle of mortal combat from the safety of Medicine Bow's ramshackle stores, barrooms, and boardinghouses. They bear witness to the fight and kill, though, reminding the reader that the Virginian risks life and love for the sake of their high regard. Having wholly internalized standards of honor, he explains to Molly that he must meet Trampas to keep his self-respect. "Can't yu' see how it must be about a man?" he asks her. "What men say about my nature is not just merely an outside thing. For the fact that I let 'em keep on sayin' it is a proof I don't value my nature enough to shield it from their slander and give them their punishment." He would not be shamed. And that the Virginian understood the matter as one between men—"There's cert'nly a right smart o' difference between men and women," he tells Molly, "men's quarrels were not for women's ears"—further solidifies the fact that he must ignore her wishes and step outside to meet Trampas.[66] A large part of the Virginian's literary appeal, and this is not an uncomplicated character, is his homosocial fidelity. He follows not the law administered by courts but the higher unwritten law among men. He's a man's man, an archetype that the reader or movie goer could hardly resist idolizing and/or falling in love with. In addition to his handling of other men and keen adherence to homosocial code, the Virginian is physically attractive, even alluring—his body, dress, and person give pause to both woman and man.

Just how deeply well intentioned the Virginian's violence is raises another issue altogether. Within the ethos of the western, Trampas certainly has it coming—he would become known in the movies as a classic American villain, black hat and all. But it is this very ethos that need scrutinizing. A man's mother being unmarried when she bore him had little material consequence in the late nineteenth-century West, and yet the Virginian "rings the bell of death" over being called a "son-of-a-bitch." He uses the slander as a pretense for gaining power over Trampas—the only man in Medicine Bow who doesn't recognize it in the Virginian. With this point in mind, the Virginian's motivation in his showdown with Trampas looks quite similar to that of Buck's fight to the death with Spitz: they both involve an impulse toward preeminence. That the Virginian doesn't outwardly share Buck's revelry in the atavistic pleasures of killing speaks more to the cowboy's (and Wister's) immersion in the ideological code of masculine honor. Within male homosocial relations, honor serves as a cover, a mask for a predisposition toward violence, a reversion to force in deciding matters of self-worth and status. Thus, with the Virginian's high-mindedness deflated, Wister's novel and indeed the western story overall fit more neatly within the hunting-and-killing genre.

Irony, Atavism, and Other Variations on the De-Evolutionary Theme

As turn-of-the-century popular fiction celebrated the cowboy hero and the redemptive powers of the West, another line of literature developed a more discriminating take on these ideals, reminding readers that the frontier had vanished and laying bare the violence underneath its romanticization. In a 1902 article entitled "The Frontier Gone at Last," Frank Norris spoke of how the West had "become conscious of itself, acts the part for the Eastern visitor; and this self-consciousness is a sign, surer than all others, of the decadence of a type, the passing of an epoch."[67] The continued embrace of a life since past presented more highbrow writers like Norris with an uncommon opportunity to play with the tropes and story lines holding together modern American collective consciousness. Norris's novel *McTeague* is set primarily in San Francisco, but the title character, who grew up in a mining region of the California Sierra Nevada mountains, returns to his home after brutally killing his wife Trina. Chased by a posse into the Death Valley desert, McTeague confronts his mortal enemy Marcus in what seems like another rendition of a classic showdown. The book ends in death, although in totally atypical form: just before he takes his last breath, Marcus handcuffs himself to McTeague, betraying how their hatred for each other has done them both in; without water, McTeague looks around "stupidly" at the "distant horizon" and then at the "half-dead canary" that he had inexplicably brought with him to the desert.[68] Another most incisive parody can be found in Stephen Crane's short story "The Blue Hotel" (1899), a purely ironic work that does nothing less than deconstruct the whole mythos surrounding the West's transformative and self-fulfilling powers. It also brilliantly exposes the insidious, compulsively violent nature of homosocial relations, even or especially among men who insist they are civilized.

Crane constructed this minor literary masterpiece around the Turnerian environmentally determinist focus on what happens when a man travels from the East and is taken from a train car and dropped within a new less-developed western environment. The story begins with a train pulling into Fort Romper, Nebraska, where Pat Scully, proprietor of the light-blue-colored Palace Hotel, induces three men to stay at his establishment. One man is a "a tall bronzed cowboy"—not terribly smart but apparently well intentioned or at least not openly hostile. The second is "a little, silent man from the East," Mr. Blanc, whose impassive knowing character insinuates him as a stand in for Crane and the omniscient narrative voice. The third figure is "the Swede," a light-haired "shaky and quick-eyed" man from New York City, where he had worked as a tailor for ten years. Upon arriving at the hotel, the Swede acts nervous and agitated. "He resembled a badly frightened man," the narration explains, although the other men in the story at first simply scratch their heads in bemusement. Their confusion only increases at dinner when, as the Swede's "eyes continued to rove from man to man," he comments with a forced wink and laugh "that some of these Western communities were very dangerous." Later in the day, Johnnie (Scully's son), the cowboy, the Easterner, and the Swede sit down to a card game. The game proceeds, with the cowboy violently "board-whacking" his winning cards, until the Swede suddenly says to Johnnie: "I suppose there have been a good many men killed in this room." As the other men insist they don't know what he is talking about, the Swede springs up from his chair and shouts, "I don't want to fight!" While nobody else moves, the Swede backs himself into a corner of the room, his hands out in front of his chest. He then quavers: "Gentlemen, I suppose I am going to be killed before I can leave this house! I suppose I am going to be killed before I can leave this house!"[69] As Scully reenters the hotel and asks what is going on after seeing the Swede's "tragic attitude," the other men look at each other in utter stupefaction.

Slowly the other men come to think that the Swede is paranoid about western savagery. While Scully takes the Swede upstairs to reassure him of Fort Romper's peacefulness—"Why, man, we're goin' to have a line of ilictric streetcars in this town next spring"—the cowboy and Johnnie turn to the Easterner for his opinion. After hemming and hawing he ventures that the Swede is "clear frightened out of his boots." Johnnie and the cowboy respond indignantly, "What at?" believing the hotel and town to be perfectly safe. "It seems to me," the Easterner explains, "this man has been reading dime novels, and he thinks he's right out in the middle of it—the shootin' and stabbin' and all." The cowboy is further scandalized: "But . . . this ain't Wyoming, ner none of them places. This is Nebrasker." Johnnie agrees: "Yes . . . an' why don't he wait until he gits *out West*?" The Easterner laughs at their assumption that a real West still exists: "It isn't different there even—not in these days." Apparently the cowboy and Johnnie don't understand the Easterner's point that the Swede's fear is based on what's in his head and not where he is. The Easterner doesn't press the point, instead summarizing simply that the Swede "thinks he's right in the middle of hell."[70]

For his own part, the Swede's person adapts to his perception of danger. He devolves into the type of man who he thinks can survive the West. Upon returning downstairs, the Swede takes on a boisterous manner: he displays a "grandeur of confidence"; orders others in "a bullying voice"; and "talk[s] arrogantly, profanely, angrily." At supper the Swede "seemed to have suddenly grown taller." He "domineered the whole feast"—looking "brutally disdainful, into every face" and giving the meal "the appearance of a cruel bacchanal." Afterward, the Swede insists on another game of cards. "Scully gently deprecated the plan at first, but the Swede turned a wolfish glare upon him." So Johnnie, the cowboy, and the Easterner sit down with the Swede, who quickly "adopts" the manly "fashion of board-whacking" his cards. The game continues until the Swede looks up from the table and suddenly says to Johnnie, "You are cheatin'!" A short silence is followed by a scuffle until the others separate "the two warriors." After Johnnie denies cheating and the Swede insists that he had, the accused says, "We must fight." The Swede turns into a "demoniac," roaring "Yes, fight! I'll show you what kind of man I am! I'll show you who you want to fight!" With the challenge accepted, all the men go outside into a blinding snowstorm, finding a small section of grass on "the sheltered side of the hotel." After Scully assures the Swede that he won't have to fight all of them, Johnnie and the Swede face each other with their fists up, "ey[ing] each other in a calm that had the elements of leonine cruelty in it."[71] The other men look on in excited anticipation.

The ensuing fight scene says as much about those watching as it does about the combatants. As Johnnie and the Swede "crash together like bullocks," the cowboy is quickly overtaken by emotion. "Suddenly a holocaust of warlike desire caught the cowboy, and he bolted forward with the speed of a bronco." While Scully holds him back, he remains entranced: his face "contorted like one of those agony masks in museums," the cowboy yells "Go it, Johnnie! Go it! Kill him! Kill him!" Eventually Scully and even the Easterner join the cowboy in rooting for Johnnie, "bursting into a cheer that was like a chorus of triumphant soldiery." But the Swede is too "heavy" for Johnnie, whose face he beats into a "bloody, pulpy" mess. After Scully announces that "Johnnie is whipped," the whole group returns to the warmth of the hotel, with each man exhausted by the fight. The Swede gathers his belongings and, before leaving, "guffaw[s] victoriously" and then mimics the cowboy: "'Kill him! Kill him! Kill him'" Scully is also subject to this jeering and, once the Swede walks out the door, he and the cowboy lapse into a spasm of violent half-intelligible passion. "I'd loike to take that Swede," Scully wails in brogue, "and hould him down on a shtone flure and bate 'im to a jelly wid a shtick!" The cowboy joins him, groaning sympathetically.

> "I'd like to git him by the neck and ha-ammer him"—he brought his hand down on a chair with a noise like a pistol shot—"hammer that there Dutchman until he couldn't tell himself from a dead coyote!"
>
> "I'd bate 'im until he—"
>
> "I'd show *him* some things—"
>
> And then together they raised a yearning, fanatic cry: "Oh-o-oh! If only we could—"
>
> "Yes!"
>
> "Yes!"
>
> "And then I'd—"
>
> "O-o-oh!"[72]

The cowboy and Scully drift off in an ecstasy of imagined fantastic erotic violence.

The story ends with the Swede walking from the Palace Hotel through the snowstorm to a saloon with "an indomitable red light" burning in front. Upon entering, he "smil[es] fraternally" at the barkeeper and orders a whiskey. After being asked about his beat up face, the Swede starts bragging about "thump[ing] the soul out of a man down here at Scully's hotel." This catches the attention of four men sitting at a nearby table—the district attorney, two local businessmen, and a prominent socially respected gambler. The Swede calls out amiably for them to have a drink with him. They politely but firmly say no. Dissatisfied, the Swede approaches the table. Insisting they drink together, the Swede "by chance" puts his hand upon the gambler's shoulder. After an increasingly antagonistic exchange between the two men, the Swede grabs "the gambler frenziedly at the throat," dragging him out of his chair. With that the gambler pulls out a long-blade knife: "It shot forward, and a human body, this citadel of virtue, wisdom, power, was pierced as easily as if it had been a melon. The Swede fell with a cry of supreme astonishment." Dead, the Swede's eyes had set upon a sign on top of the bar's cash machine: "This registers your amount of purchase." The last scene is an epilogue: months after the killing, the Easterner and the cowboy discuss the Swede's demise. "It's funny, ain't it?" the cowboy comments. "If he hadn't said Johnnie was cheatin' he'd be alive this minute. He was an awful fool." The Easterner is incensed: "You're a fool! . . . You're a bigger jackass than the Swede by a million majority. Now let me tell you one thing. Let me tell you something. Listen. Johnnie *was* cheating." The cowboy is dumbfounded. "I saw him," the Easterner continues. "And I refused to stand up and be a man." The Easterner concludes that all five of them—"you, I , Johnnie, old Scully, and that fool of an unfortunate gambler"—are all to blame. "We, five of us, have collaborated in the murder of this Swede." The story ends with the cowboy, "injured and rebellious," asking blankly: "Well, I didn't do anythin', did I?"[73]

"The Blue Hotel" sets in motion an ironic interpretive spiral, a sequence of readings that undermines any single straightforward explanation for the Swede's murder. One common reading is that the Swede's initially unreasonable fear of being killed works as a self-fulfilling prophecy: his frightened accusatory state agitates others into behavior outside their dispositions; the Swede gets what he deserves, as confirmed by the saloon's sign, "This registers your amount of purchase."[74] But, as the Easterner points out, the Swede has help. Scully pulls him into the Palace Hotel where a group of men act, by their own standards, deficiently: Johnnie cheats at cards and then lies about it; the cowboy is too slow or self-interested (he is Johnnie's partner) to recognize what is going on, eventually backing the person at fault; Scully does the same, and he had more reason to know the character of his son, of whom he is contemptuous and critical before the fight; and the Easterner, not wanting to get involved, fails to step forward in support of the Swede, even when he knows that the others respect his word. The Swede is the only one who closely follows homosocial rules of honor; he calls Johnnie on cheating and then doesn't back down when challenged to a fight.

Yet, if not for the Swede's overwrought behavior, he would have lived through the night. Where does his excitement come from? He starts fearing for his life only after entering the hotel and getting to know the others. He may see something deep within the men, individually and as a group, that warrants his alarm. Or perhaps, as the Easterner suggests, the Swede simply confuses facts of life in Fort Romper for the sensationalist fiction of western dime novels. Crane's story smartly divulges the western myth's circularity of fact and fiction, expectation and experience. That the Swede may have carried violence with him from the East illustrates the point of this book's chapter: the hunting-and-killing genre shapes a man's emotions—as in the Swede moving down the cognitive scale from reason to ferocity—and that reading such material also affects behavior, as in his Palace Hotel bluster and suicidal aggression in the saloon.

An overarching question presented in "The Blue Hotel" is whether the Swede is paranoid or, more generally, if everyday homosocial relations are indeed peaceful and to be trusted. Again, the story denies any lasting answer about whether the Swede is delusional. What it does make clear is the thinness of good homosocial intentions. The same men who insisted that the Swede is crazy for thinking Fort Romper dangerous are pathologically violent toward him a short while later. And the fact that the gambler, "a thieving card player" with a deadly vicious streak, enjoyed such high regard among the town's prominent men says a great deal about the makeup of that homosocial community. Still, it is hard to have much sympathy for the Swede. For someone who suspects the worst among Fort Romper's men, he carries himself rather recklessly among them. The Swede isn't too smart. Misreading the colored signs denoting that the blue hotel could be safe and the red-lighted saloon lethal, the Swede lets his guard down exactly when he is in the greatest danger and thus the man originally wary in the extreme falls "with a cry of supreme astonishment."

Alternatively, perhaps the Swede knows exactly what he is getting into, for another unanswered question in the story is why the Swede leaves New York and goes West in the first place. Whatever explanations there are for the Swede's demise, for which he is most likely partly to blame and partly the victim of others, the story brilliantly enacts the Turnerian paradigm: compelled West, the easterner vanishes amid that environment's homicidal process of natural selection. Still more incisively, however, "The Blue Hotel" suggests that such a paradigm—celebrated by Turner and countless others as a regenerative good, as the collective experience driving American national identity—is in fact a self-destructive de-evolutionary nightmare. In this interpretation, the Swede's trajectory looks very much like a death wish. And it is fostered by dime novels and other fiction, bred in the literate world of civilization.

Like Crane's story "The Blue Hotel," Norris's novel *McTeague* develops a critical distance on devolution. These two texts, more than any others in the American naturalist canon, disassemble romantic primitive individualism. Self-destruction rather than self-fulfillment awaits the Swede and McTeague; they are both thrown into plot lines ending in fatal violent pathology. And the two stories similarly suggest that this sickness is a contagion, a disease unspecific to their lead characters. Norris's most ironic moment comes in his account of the great anticipation everyone in McTeague's San Francisco neighborhood has for a fight between two dogs who "hate each other just like humans." When finally let loose to fight, though, their "snarling and barking" dissolve into mutual indifference. They sniff about and, then, "with all the dignity of monarchs," walk off in different directions. The bloodthirsty crowd surrounding them is outraged by the dogs' unexpected "humanity." Marcus, the owner of one of the dogs, has a shamed fit, promising to take his "nasty, mangy cur" and "cut him in two with the whip."[75] Norris imputed to the dogs a level of "humanity" woefully lacking in his human characters. Even more ironically, Norris divulged how humans project onto beasts a ferocity that they create while coming to understand themselves in relation to other animals.

McTeague is an extremely gruesome novel.[76] Animalistic impulse, male-on-male violence, spousal abuse, and grisly murder mark Norris's effort to break down the line of pretension separating beast from man, and savagery from civilization. To that end, *McTeague* diverges from "The Blue Hotel" by closely studying the psychological movement between these two ontological poles. Unlike Crane's Swede, whose state of mind is seldom known, McTeague's thoughts and feelings are presented in near-clinical detail. What emerges from Norris's work is a typology of the *brute*, a keyword used in close combination with carefully constructed narratives in which McTeague reverts back to a lower human state, a criminally degraded condition. The result is a version of primal return radically divergent from the regenerative ideal expressed in the work of London and Wister. Norris saw through that fiction. In its place, he bought into social Darwinism and its criminal anthropological variants. As a prime example of American naturalist literature, *McTeague* examines the grievous absence of human volition and, because of that vacuum, the easy slippage into atavism. It can be read as a literary brief on the social and bioemotional forces driving a man down to violence and self-destruction.

Norris wrote the first draft of *McTeague* in 1894–95, at the height of an intensely formative period in his short work life (he died in 1902), when he had absorbed both the naturalist fiction of Emile Zola and Darwinian science and theory. Darwinism came in typically eclectic form. While at the University of California at Berkeley from 1890 to 1894, Norris took a course from the popular geology and zoology professor Joseph LeConte, whose major work *Evolution: Its Nature, Its Evidences, and Its Relations to Religious Thought* (1888; revised edition 1891) stresses that "man alone is possessed of two natures—a lower, in common with animals, and a higher, peculiar to himself." LeConte's understanding of human history as an ongoing struggle between these two forces—"The whole meaning of sin is in the humiliating bondage of the higher to the lower"—provided Norris with a general evolutionary template for his stories of individual degradation and loss. As documented by his short stories and novels from this period, Norris also took in Cesare Lombroso's criminal anthropology, although it may very well have come through the summary of that thought in Havelock Ellis's treatise *The Criminal* (1891) and Max Nordau's best selling book *Degeneration* (1892). Norris's broad reading in contemporary fiction at Berkeley and then at Harvard in 1895 only added to his growing obsession with the origins of mental instability and violent crime. Zola's elaborate works examining the impact of heredity and environment on his characters dispossessed of reason and will ("beings powerfully dominated by their nerves and their blood") greatly influenced Norris's fiction.[77] Of equal importance during Norris's first stage of writing was Robert Louis Stevenson's romantic tale *Dr. Jekyll and Mr. Hyde* (1886) and its dramatization of the conflict between "those provinces of good and ill which divide and compound man's dual nature." Norris followed Stevenson in creating plots that would formalize, make literal, this split in human consciousness. Stevenson used elixirs and transfiguration to separate and distinguish Mr. Hyde's "extraneous evil" from his "upright twin," whereas Norris relied on contemporary understanding of atavism and disease to detail sociopsychological impulses toward violence and self-destruction.[78]

Two short stories from 1897 illustrate Norris's method of bifurcating his characters' consciousness. The first, "A Case for Lombroso," proves his familiarity with the Italian physician and psychologist; it shows, as directly as any work, how he drew from science-based typologies for his own literary purposes. The story is about a beautiful young woman of "purest Spanish blood" and her uncontrollable love of a finely bred recent Harvard graduate who, despite his original indifference, pursues her because of her social standing. She, as Norris pointed out from the story's beginning, is a lost cause. In foreshadowing her downfall, Norris made clear reference to Nordau's point about the high incidence of degeneration among the overpurified upper class: "Her race was almost exhausted, its vitality low, and its temperament refined to the evaporation point. To-day . . . [she] might have been called a degenerate." The man's outcome is less certain. He admits his ill intentions to her, but it makes no difference. And thus begins his fall. Knowing "that she would take anything from him . . . made the man a brute." Needing to torment her, he cannot break the relationship off: "It became for him a pleasure—a morbid, unnatural, evil pleasure for him to hurt and humiliate her."[79] The affair ruins them both. The second story, "A Reversion to Type," is a short study of Lombrosian atavism in which Schuster, a San Francisco department store employee leading a terribly "commonplace" existence, suddenly ("like the . . . abrupt development of a latent mania") launches into a spree of drinking, sex, and crime. Schuster bolts to the Sierra Nevada mountains, where he kills a man for his gun. Returning to the city, he takes up his old life as if nothing had happened. The story ends tellingly, with the narrator finding out that, while Schuster's father led a peaceful life as a hotel barber, his grandfather had done time at San Quentin for highway robbery. With Lombroso having identified heredity as a key source for the reappearance of a criminal trait, Norris followed this medical tenet by showing how, in his words, "inherited tendencies" could come alive in apparently the most normal of men.[80]

These short stories on degeneration can be seen as apprenticeship sketches that Norris made while revising his first two novels, *McTeague* and *Vandover and the Brute,* both of which elaborate the atavistic figure of the brute within the lurid urban environment of fin de siècle San Francisco. A great deal of Norris's talent as a writer lay in his ability to present, as one contemporary critic put it, the "sensory reality" of city scenes—the teeming Polk Street neighborhood in *McTeague* (subtitled *A Story of San Francisco*), for instance; and *Vandover's* (subtitled *A Study of Life and Manners in an American City at the End of the Nineteenth Century*) demimonde "resorts," oyster houses, Turkish baths, and "disreputable houses." Norris "knew how to present persons as if they had air on all sides of them," a *Boston Herald* reviewer wrote in 1914 after *Vandover* was published posthumously, "streets as if they could be walked upon, even an entire city, San Francisco, as an organism with a life and visage peculiarly its own."[81] Like Crane's portrayal of New York's Rum Alley in *Maggie: A Girl of the Streets* (1893) and Dreiser's Chicago in *Sister Carrie* (1900), Norris's fiction develops an intimate deterministic relationship between the tactile sights, smells, sounds, and colors of the American metropolis and its characters' material wants, sensual impulses, and moral depravity. For Norris and other naturalist writers, urban culture did not necessarily breed effete overcivilized men in need of escape to the rugged wilderness; the city could create and sustain its own de-evolutionary types, although these figures display demented violent traits that are often covered up in the romantic primitive individualist literature of the turn of the century.

   Vandover and the Brute, as its title suggests, represents Norris's most didactic effort to uncover the brute in man. Vandover and the brute are one and the same, his person "divided itself" in two: first, "there was himself, the real Vandover of every day, the same familiar Vandover that looked back at him from his mirror," the Harvard graduate and talented aspiring artist; and, second, there "was the wolf, the beast, whatever the creature that lived in his flesh, and that struggled with him now, striving to gain ascendency, to absorb Vandover into his own hideous identity." Throughout the novel Norris struggled to render the lower form within Vandover. A literal zoomorphic dimension can be found: with Vandover, at his lowest moments, crawling around on all fours, naked, howling like a wolf, some critics argue that Norris's protagonist suffers from lycanthropy. Alternatively, Donald Pizer believes that Vandover is struck by general paralysis of the insane; details of his "illness" conform to contemporary medical texts' description of that disease. So often, though, Norris relied on the compellingly murky traits of the *brute* to fill in Vandover's psychological profile. "Far down there in the darkest, lowest places," Norris wrote in initiating Vandover's loss of moral control, "he had seen the brute, squat, deformed, hideous; he had seen it crawling to and fro dimly, through a dark shadow he had heard it growling, chafing at the least restraint, restless to be free." Vandover's de-evolutionary slide is consistently linked to licentiousness.

"All at once . . . [he] rushed into a career of dissipation," Norris wrote in describing Vandover's final turn away from his art and any semblance of a respectable life, "consumed with the desire of vice, the perverse, blind, and reckless desire of the male. Drunkenness, sensuality, gambling, debauchery, he knew them all."[82] A broken pitiable derelict by the end of the novel, Vandover's masculine profligacy is at once cause and manifestation of his spiral into brutishness.

That male desire triggers Vandover's "fall" raises again the question of whether his brutishness represents a fall at all. Like the canine character Buck in *Call of the Wild*, Vandover's devolution is less a matter of being taken over by a preexistent force than building up that condition through self-conscious pleasure seeking. A 1914 *New York Times* review of Norris's novel makes a similar point about the "growth" of Vandover's animalism. "There have been many tales told of multiple personalities which sleep in us," the writer began, "of which probably the most gripping is Stevenson's famous romance. But all such stories have one fundamental weakness," the reviewer continued: "they are stories of fatality, not of cause and effect. The manifestations of multiple personality bear no relation to the man's voluntary inward life, which is all of him that really matters." *Vandover* is quite different in its insinuation of purposefulness, the *Times* critic concluded. It "is a story of growth, of evolution." Most men cultivate qualities of gentility and good intention. Not Vandover though. "Where these are lacking, something else grows, something invariably ugly, melancholy, and finally destructive—the brute in man."[83] The novel suggests that Vandover and other men who exhibit such masculine depravity are well aware of their predation even though that behavior is often cast as the product of involuntary pathology.

Norris's most accomplished study of the brute can be found in *McTeague*, a complex psychological and episodical study of the title character's slide into atavistic criminality and murder. McTeague is different from Vandover. A brute from the beginning, McTeague is able to cover his true nature as long as he is well fed and otherwise materially comfortable. In the first chapter the reader learns that McTeague, a bulky self-taught dentist, came from the Sierra Nevada mountains, where he worked for his father in the ore mines. McTeague inherited his father's rough crude nature. While "[f]or thirteen days of each fortnight his father was a steady, hard-working shift boss of the mine," Norris wrote, "[e]very other Sunday he became an irresponsible animal, a beast, a brute, crazy with alcohol." McTeague exhibits certain Lombrosian stigmata: a "great square-cut" and "angular" head; a "salient" jaw, "like that of a carnivora"; and "enormous" red hands, "as hard as wooden mallets, strong as vises." He pulls his patients' teeth with his "bare hands."[84]

Despite these degenerate traits, there is also a certain "everyman" quality to McTeague. We meet him on a Sunday afternoon relaxing in his Polk Street "Dental Parlors." Having just taken an early dinner, McTeague is laying back in his operating chair, drinking beer, and smoking a pipe. He is, in Norris's memorable description, perfectly content: "crop-full, stupid, and warm." Norris also tried to make McTeague ethnically and racially normative. With blond hair, the white Anglo-American McTeague seems like other modern urban men enjoying their day off work. This impression changes as McTeague devolves. But at first it is possible to identify with him. Norris imputes a certain affection for him: "there was nothing vicious about the man. Altogether he suggested the draught horse, immensely strong, stupid, docile, obedient."[85] Our 1914 reader of *Tarzan* may have found something of himself in McTeague.

Norris's inspiration for *McTeague* came from an October 1893 San Francisco murder case in which Patrick Collins killed his wife Sarah Collins for not handing over her wages. It was a particularly grisly crime. Stabbed some thirty-five times about the face, neck, chest, and arms, the victim managed to drag herself out to the street from her place of work (a local kindergarten) and ask a bystander for help who then pulled out the knife still protruding from her neck. Before being announced dead at a nearby hospital, Sarah Collins identified her husband as the assailant. Arrested the same day while praying in a Catholic church, Patrick Collins became the focus of intense scrutiny by the two major San Francisco newspapers, the *Chronicle* and the *Examiner*, which quickly made the murder a cause célèbre. The Collins murder and its coverage clearly influenced *McTeague*'s plot about a man who kills his increasingly miserly wife while she is working at a San Francisco kindergarten. Norris's development of McTeague's person also bears close resemblance to the newspapers' study of Collins, especially their immediate use of the label "brute." Furthermore, both newspapers drew loosely from evolutionary thought and criminal anthropology in declaring confidently that he "is a type." Collins "is not a rarity by any means," the *Examiner* insisted; "his counterparts are numerous enough."[86] Norris's novel can be read as a continuation of this contemporary typological impulse; *McTeague* is an imaginative yet fact-based rendering of masculine degradation and violence.

The most interesting account of Collins came in the *Examiner* four days after the murder. After briefly speaking with him in jail, the reporter began the article with the headline "HE WAS BORN FOR THE ROPE" and then the sentence "If a good many of Patrick Collins' ancestors did not die on the scaffold then either they escaped their desert or there is nothing in heredity." Collins's physical traits and general demeanor confirm his criminally atavistic character, the reporter explained: "Seeing him you can understand that murder is as natural to such a man when his temper is up as hot speech is to the anger of the civilized." The reporter continued in Lombrosian fashion, emphasizing that Collins "was made an animal by nature to start with." His face "is broad" and "brutish," for instance, the jaw "heavy and cruel"—a description similar to McTeague's "great square-cut" head and "salient" jaw. The reporter then shifted to a more psychological or anthropological perspective, asking the reader to "realize" Collins's "wrongs as he realized them before he avenged them." To begin with, his wife "was earning what appeared to him a comfortable living," and yet she deserted him. "True," the reporter elaborated, "he drank whenever he could get drink, and when in liquor was liable to be rough with the old woman, but then every good fellow, every man who is a man, has his little weaknesses." They didn't give her reason to refuse him. "What did the woman mean by treating him as if he were dirt under her feet! By the lord, he'd see whether she'd give him money or not. . . . He would bring her to her senses or know the reason why."[87] After recounting the murder the article ends by venturing that Collins may have actually felt some remorse for his actions. Did Norris read this *Examiner* article? While it cannot be proved, this semi-ironic journalistic effort to humanize Collins the brute may have launched Norris's personalized typology of McTeague.

Norris expanded the journalistic profile of Collins by not only exaggerating the Lombrosian stigmata in McTeague but also deepening his character's psychology to include the powerful factor of instinct. At first McTeague is only concerned with innocent creature comforts—"to eat, to smoke, to sleep, and to play upon his concertina." The plot thickens when Trina, a young attractive woman and McTeague's future wife, comes to him for dental work. "With her the feminine element suddenly entered his little world." And with this new stimulus, "The male virile desire in him tardily awakened, aroused itself, strong and brutal." So begins another episode of Norris's epic conflict between animal impulse and conscious control. Finally McTeague couldn't check his desire. "It was resistless, untrained, a thing not to be held in leash an instant." Trina returns to McTeague for further dental work and, in a key moment early in the story, he uses ether to knock her out so that he can extract a tooth. "Suddenly the animal in the man stirred and woke; the evil instincts that in him were so close to the surface leaped to life, shouting and clamoring." At the same time, "a certain second self, another, better McTeague rose with the brute." But it proves no match. While "she lay there, unconscious and helpless, and very pretty," McTeague "leaned over and kissed her, grossly, full on the mouth." In explaining McTeague's motivation for this assault, Norris relied again on the force of instinct lying directly "[b]elow the fine fabric of all that was good in him." As to why or how McTeague's instincts are "evil," Norris turned to criminal anthropological understanding of atavism: "The vices and sins of his father and of his father's father, to the third and fourth and five hundredth generation, tainted him. The evil of an entire race flowed in his veins." Apparently, within

Norris's biological schema, McTeague is unusually susceptible to the "foul stream of hereditary evil"—that is the definition of an atavist.[88] Again, however, Norris also suggested that others inhabiting McTeague's world are not necessarily free of the same corruption.

As McTeague and Trina fall into a romantic relationship, Norris stressed that brute instinct could be an attraction for both man and woman. To begin with, McTeague is turned off by Trina's eventual receptivity to his advances. "The instant that Trina gave up, the instant she allowed him to kiss her, he thought less of her. She was not so desirable after all." For McTeague, the pleasure is in the taking. Similarly, Trina is inexplicably drawn to his brutishness. "Why did she feel the desire, the necessity of being conquered by a superior strength? Why did it please her? Why had it suddenly thrilled her from head to foot with a quick, terrifying gust of passion . . .?" After marrying, McTeague and Trina settle into a less passionate yet content life: she finds an "equilibrium of calmness and placid quietude," and he "relapse[s] to his wonted stolidity." But things change quickly. Marcus, McTeague's friend and rival, exposes the dentist for practicing without having earned a degree. McTeague loses his patients and the marriage unravels. Trina becomes downright "niggardly." She had earlier won five thousand dollars in a lottery but refuses to go into her savings. McTeague starts drinking whiskey, which rouses the animal in him. "It was not only the alcohol" though: "it was idleness and a general throwing off of the good influence his wife had over him in the days of their prosperity." McTeague begins to box her ears and bite the tips of her fingers. But, in keeping with Norris's conception of sexual instinct, Trina enjoys the abuse: "in some strange, inexplicable way this brutality made Trina all the more affectionate; aroused in her a morbid, unwholesome love of submission, a strange, unnatural pleasure in yielding, in surrendering herself to the will of an irresistible, virile power."[89] Violence is a natural component of heterosexuality, then, or at least in Norris's demented version of it.

Violence, for Norris, is also a built-in component of homosocial relations. McTeague and Marcus are "intimate friend[s]" at the beginning of the novel. "They took a great pleasure in each other's company, but silently and with reservation, having the masculine horror of any demonstration of friendship." Their closeness, though, eventually leads to mutual and competing interests, beginning with Trina's affections. Trina and Marcus had been going together, but, after McTeague sheepishly admits his interest in her, Marcus accedes, magnanimously telling his friend "I'll give her up to you, old man." Marcus does not so easily forgo Trina's five thousand dollars, however. (Norris's characters are far more driven by money than sex. It is in part why McTeague kills Trina. And, along with Norris's anti-Semitic character Zerkow, Trina is sick with gold lust, at times making a type of love with her lottery winnings: "She would plunge her small fingers into the pile with little murmurs of affection, her long narrow eyes half closed and shining, her breath coming in long sighs.")[90] On a run of bad luck, Marcus confronts McTeague in a tavern, drunkenly demanding the money and, after McTeague says it isn't his to give, flinging a jack knife at and just missing his former friend's head. Marcus's resentment festers. His crippling retributive blow comes in reporting to City Hall that McTeague isn't qualified to practice dentistry. Having lost his livelihood, McTeague takes to brutishness, falling into an instinctual stupor that leads to Trina's murder, the stealing of her money, and the vow to kill Marcus if they cross paths again. The novel ends in the desert with Marcus and McTeague, dead and dying, pathetically chained together by handcuffs and their hateful attraction to each other.

Another climactic scene of homosocial violence comes on a Sunday afternoon when McTeague and Trina and her family along with Marcus and his new girlfriend go to a park for a picnic. The "day was very jolly" until an impromptu shooting match "awakened a spirit of rivalry in the men" and "the rest of the afternoon was passed in athletic exercises between them." With the women arranged "on the slope of the grass, their hats and gloves laid aside," the men are "[a]roused by the little feminine cries of wonder and the clapping of their ungloved palms." They begin to "show off," especially McTeague, whose "crude untutored brute force, was a matter of wonder for the entire party." With this, "Marcus's gore rose within him," and, once a wrestling tournament had been organized and he and McTeague end up facing each other for the championship, it became only a matter of time until the two come to blows. After McTeague wins with ease, Marcus's girlfriend exclaims "Ain't Doctor McTeague just that strong!" Marcus is shamed. "[T]he hate he still bore his old-time 'pal' and the impotent wrath of his own powerlessness were suddenly unleashed." While still in each other's grasp, Marcus bites through the lobe of McTeague's ear. Upon seeing "a sudden flash of bright-red blood," the dentist loses control. He jumps to his feet, letting out "an echo from the jungle," a "hideous yelling of a hurt beast." At the same time, "The brute that in McTeague lay so close to the surface leaped instantly to life, monstrous, not to be resisted." He "became another man," filled with "an evil mania, the drunkenness of passion, the exalted and perverted fury of the Berserker, blind and deaf, a thing insensate." Searching for new ways to describe his character's brutishness, Norris had McTeague pick Marcus up by the wrist and pull him off his feet "as a hammer-thrower swings his hammer."[91] McTeague lets go and Marcus crashes to the ground "like a bundle of clothes" and with his arm badly broken. The picnic scene ends with Marcus's girlfriend, as witness to the savagery, giggling and then laughing in hysterics.

In creating a typology of the brute, *McTeague* clearly implicates homosocial competition and heterosexual desire as interpersonal sources for animal-like human instinct. Even though McTeague is branded the criminal, Norris spread brutal compulsion among the novel's characters far and wide. Marcus is especially vicious. He, too, could have been criminalized if his knife had found its mark in McTeague. Moreover, despite Norris's repeated use of the word, McTeague is hardly an *evil* figure, even at his lowest most primitive point of descent. He doesn't have the presence of mind to formulate malice. Compared to Stevenson's character Mr. Hyde, whose very reason for being is to enact violent transgression, McTeague inhabits a world of stimulus and response. *McTeague* is as much a novel of behaviorist psychology as criminal pathology. Insisting, in his one semi-self-conscious refrain, "You can't make small of me," McTeague lashes out furiously after feeling that he had taken enough from his wife Trina and best friend Marcus, among others. McTeague is a common type of man governed by purposeful instinct, one who becomes a criminal more through chance and social circumstance than by possessing a distinct character trait. In turn, the close reader of Norris's novel is left to wonder if he too is subject to the same forces that drive McTeague to brutality.

This chapter argues that hunting-and-killing literature had an affective impact on turn-of-the-century male readers. Its intensely masculine perspectives engaged men personally and emotionally. Its de-evolutionary narratives established purportedly natural and necessary states of aggression and predation in lead characters and readers alike. Character development worked as a culminating component of plot in these texts: after identifying with a story's protagonist, readers found themselves within a highly episodic masculinist psyche and, in turn, followed its inevitably downward spiral toward primordial instinct. Lead characters and their readerly appeal do vary within the hunting-and-killing genre. Not all are idealistically prescriptive. McTeague, for instance, is stupid and dense—hardly the stuff of emulation; and, yet, an assumptive quality can be uncovered in the man's criminal brutality; his emotional makeup is mostly indistinct from the novel's other characters. In contrast, the Virginian is purely archetypical, a heroic man among the rough-and-ready cowboys of the West. Underneath his honorific character, though, is an impulse toward homosocial preeminence maintained through deadly force. So too with Buck in *Call of the Wild*, the anthropomorphically drawn canine character whose absolute revelry in killing triggered a sharp animalistic response in readers' imaginations. Transcendence through death and destruction is also the central theme of American sport hunting stories. In its strong antiurbanism, deep-rooted animalism, and exuberant pleasure in killing, hunting literature helped found the plot lines and tropes of popular masculinist fiction as a whole.

What's more, in blurring the line between the experiences of reading about killing animals and actually doing it, sport hunting stories raise the vexing issue about the relationship between an individual reader's interior imaginative world and his behavior outside of the literary text.

After considering the ubiquity of violent instinct in turn-of-the-century hunting-and-killing literature, it would seem that our 1914 reader of *Tarzan* may have been less than shocked with that novel's rendering of predation and bloodletting. That is not to say he would have been bored. *Tarzan's* gory tale of "the son of an English lord and an English lady nursed at the breast of . . . the great ape" who then goes on to enjoy the "whole mad carnival of rage" and death in the African jungle certainly offered more than enough excitement to keep most readers' attention.[92] The point is that *Tarzan* owes its popularity to its close keeping with popular masculine fiction's atavistic formula. Just how structured and matter-of-fact the de-evolutionary scale had become by the early twentieth century can be seen by briefly revisiting Zane Grey's 1924 definition of "what took place in my mind" during his time in the desert wilderness. "During these lonely hours I was mostly as civilized man," Grey recognized, but he also routinely experienced "trance-like transformation[s] back to the savage." He registered surprise over the reality of this primordial stage: "I could bring back for a brief instant the sensitory state of the progenitors of the human race." Science helped Grey locate the cause of his metamorphosis. "Nature developed man according to the biological facts of evolution," he reasoned. "Therefore all the instincts of the ages have been his heritage." But he concerned himself more with the quintessential savage experience: "When I had a gun in my hands and was hunting meat to eat, why was the chase so thrilling, exciting, driving the hot blood in gusts over my body?" He had been "able to revert to the animal," Grey answered his own question, concluding with an exaggerated plea for modern culture to somehow preserve the possibility for future devolution: "Harness the cave-man—yes! . . . but do not kill him. Something of the wild and primitive should forever remain instinctive in the human race."[93]

That the desert triggered Grey's primordial emotional state suggests that men needed contact with geography rather than books for devolution. By the time of Frederick Jackson Turner's frontier thesis and the whole modern back-to-nature craze, however, wilderness itself had taken on a textual quality that blurred the distinction between reality and artifice. Grey and others still appreciated the experiential difference between, say, hunting in the Rocky Mountains and reading about it. But, at the same time, premodern experience and cognition could be readily transformed from field to page, as Grey himself thoroughly understood. In pursuing this despatialized dimension of devolution, we now turn to American college football, a new cultural form that developed striking affinities with popular masculine literature in its elaborate textual appeal to savage sensibilities. For both player and fan, football's effect was its emotional affect. To include turn-of-the-century college football within the rubric of brute fiction is not to overlook the game's astonishingly dangerous and deadly nature—it is, rather, a means of casting the blood sport's violence as culturally constructed and contingent. In examining a phenomenon still so prevalent in the early twenty-first century, the following discussion draws from anthropological methods that facilitate an ironic critical distance. Anthropology helps the historian make the familiar strange.

CHAPTER THREE

College Football

If ever there was a good time for an anthropologist from outer space to drop down and take a reading of modern U.S. masculinity, it would have been at a college football game between Stanford University and the University of California at Berkeley played in 1896 in San Francisco's Central Park. More than twelve thousand people came together to watch two squads of large, heavily padded men face each other and try to push an oblong ball through the other team and over its goal at the opposite end of the field.[1] The violent crunching and grunting sounds produced by the clash at the line of scrimmage may very well have drawn the anthropologist's attention, as would have the impassioned cheering of each team's supporters located in separate sections of the grandstands. The Stanford fans' cardinal red clothes, flags, and banners and Berkeley's colors of blue and gold would have suggested the student bodies' extremely close identification with their teams playing below—a point confirmed by the radically divergent response to Stanford winning the game 20–0. As Berkeley fans "saw defeat at hand," reported the *San Francisco Chronicle,* "there was a hush, a cessation of yells from the blue and gold"; in sharp contrast, "the Stanford bleachers rose to the occasion and gave out a cry of victory, that swept grief, despair and gloom flying before it." It was, the *Chronicle* continued, "the climax of a scene of the wildest sort," with one "delighted young gentleman arrayed in a Sunday suit and irreproachable linen, lay[ing] down in the dirt and [rolling] over a dozen times in ecstasy."[2] For the visiting anthropologist, this scene alone would have been worth the trip, as it betrays a type of deep-seated emotional investment usually reserved for religion. Overall, the highly ritualized event centering on extreme physical exertion and risk taking by the young men on the field of play would have given the alien social scientist more than enough material from which to gain understanding of masculinity at that particular time and place.

Imagining an extraterrestrial anthropologist at the Stanford-Berkeley Big Game is a way to demonstrate by exaggeration the analytical goal of creating a perspective free from prior knowledge of or contact with the event at hand. The anthropological ideal of outsidedness can be useful to the historian considering a topic central to his or her own culture and experience. Of course, this form of historical objectivity can never be realized in full; affected unfamiliarity is the best one can do, an ironic distance that can lead to close observation and fresh insight. To be sure, ironic analysis isn't exclusive to the anthropologist or cultural historian. The *Chronicle* reporter exhibited a good measure of it while covering the Stanford-California game. As the "collegians invaded the field, carried away the heroes, marched about cheering and hollering and hugged each other in excess of joy," the reporter noticed that the Stanford fans focused most of their attention on the team captain, Charles Fickert; in honoring him "there was placed about his shoulders a wreath of olive leaves and everybody shouted and red flags waved, and the homage of a crowd had been paid to the man who led his team to victory." The *Chronicle* reporter—at this point at least, clearly separated emotionally from those around him—found added meaning in the celebratory scene: "That wreath, by the way, showed that brawn, and not brain, is the fin de siècle fashion. The laurel was so big that it fell to his waist—a tribute to his muscle."[3]

As trenchant as the *Chronicle* reporter's reading of Stanford's celebration is, academic anthropology offers specific methodologies for breaking down a football game into distinct dynamics and then tracing the deep structural ties between the sport and de-evolutionary masculinity at the turn of the century. That is the goal of this chapter. After surveying the rise of American football through Thorstein Veblen's understanding of the sport as the self-conscious expression by male elites of the "predatory instinct," we focus on the birth and growth of one program, that of Stanford University, and the way it conferred manly identity to the new institution. Understanding football as cultural performance is central to my analysis, and Victor Turner's work on liminality leads to tracking how Stanford's student body separated out its largest, most muscle-bound men to represent the school in the Big Game against Berkeley. Reading that game as a cultural or literary text is Clifford Geertz's signal contribution to examining football. Sport and literature are alike, one may construe from Geertz's words, in how they both "bring a particular cast of mind out into the world where men can look at it"—both speak in a "vocabulary of sentiment" that "educates" those engaged with the text.[4] Consistent with this book as a whole, anthropology focuses our attention on the psychological content of football and how the form of its play incited the supposedly natural masculine emotion of pugnacity or, as Veblen put it, "the bellicose frame of mind."[5] Anthropology is extremely valuable in helping the historian speak about the cultural creation of habits of thought and feeling. And because anthropology also attends to the relationship between modern culture and early primate and hunting-gathering history, it provides a good context from which to consider the sociobiological issue of whether football reflects preexistent biologically determined impulses toward aggression or if the game creates those feelings through the vivid and dramatic enactment of war.

Football was integral to turn-of-the-century U.S. society and culture, as proved not only by its extremely rapid rise during the post–Civil War years but also by the widespread contemporary discussion of it as having, for better or worse, a special relationship to modern American character. From George Santayana and Charles Francis Adams, who championed football's expression of Anglo-American martial superiority, to Frederick Jackson Turner and E. L. Godkin, who believed its brutality too dominant in American college life, to Walter Camp, who celebrated it for, among many other things, teaching obedience and organizational skills beneficial for business and military success, analysis of the sport transcended the specifics of actual play and ran to its evocation of, in David Reisman's and Reuel Denney's phrase, a distinct "style of life."[6] If so, that style was purely masculine. Football's requirement for such bulk and muscle mass, along with its close association with war, has kept women from playing the sport for well over one hundred years. Football constructed a tightly wound homosocial universe that, rather than excluding women altogether, subordinated them to a spectatorial role, which, in turn, heightened the martial heroic element of the sport. Like the ideal of the citizen-soldier, football demanded from its players a performative combination of aggression and sacrifice, the ability to both inflict and endure pain. And, as rendered in Douglas Tilden's statue on the University of California's campus (fig. 3.1), football displayed male-to-male affection and desire—homoeroticism unthreateningly exhibited within the high-risk drama of an unusually brutal blood sport.[7]

The rapid growth of Stanford's football program in the early to mid-1890s provides a condensed version of the way many other American universities devoted their resources to building champion teams. Stanford's accelerated effort was due to deliberate overcompensation for being founded as a coeducational institution as well as its natural rivalry with the older fully established University of California at Berkeley across the bay. For many years, the Big Game was virtually the only game for Stanford; it played athletic club and high school teams as warm ups for Berkeley. Stanford football is also compelling because for two years in the early 1890s it drew Walter Camp to Palo Alto to serve as coach for the preparation and play of the Thanksgiving Day Big Game. In effect, it had been anointed by the "father of football"—a gift from "mother Yale" who inspired Stanford's student body to take the game all the more seriously. Listen to the student newspaper sending off the football team to the Big Game of 1894. In the contest that follows, an editor wrote, "the hopes and desires of a score a thousand sympathizers are to be realized or disappointed. All the patriotism in the University is centered on the outcome of the game," he continued, "and any misfortune to the team is a misfortune to all. Our heroes are the football heroes, and their success is ours as is their defeat. Captain Downing! The University supremacy is in your keeping."[8] Stanford invested a tremendous amount of time, energy, and emotion in football. After considering the origins of U.S. football via Thorstein Veblen's study *The Theory of the Leisure Class* (1899), we look closely at how Stanford University—with all its good-willed interest in joining the national obsession with the sport—underwrote one of the most brutal and gender-polarizing pursuits in American culture.

Thorstein Veblen and the Rise of "Exotic Ferocity" in American College Football

"The culture bestowed in football gives a product of exotic ferocity": with that utterance Thorstein Veblen made a major inroad into critically understanding the American college sport by naming the belligerent mind-set it evoked in player and fan alike. The modifier *exotic* is open to interpretation: Veblen may have been referring to the look of the 1890s players' long hair, padded uniforms, and gladiatorial headgear; he may also have been buttressing his own anthropological perspective, trying to denaturalize the game by separating his readers from easy acceptance of its form and content. Far more explicit is *ferocity*, by which Veblen meant an aggressive violent "habit of mind" originating in the "early barbarian stage" of human history when men started to "invidiously distinguish" themselves from women and other men through hunting, warfare, and the possession of women. A "modern survival of prowess," football served the "leisure class" by keeping a fine active edge on its capacity for material "exploit." It also dramatized "temperamental" and "physiological" differences between the sexes during a time when women were challenging male predominance in business, higher education, and other masculine mainstays in the public sphere. Linked to deeply rooted masculine "instincts" toward brutality and predation, football's "exotic ferocity," as Veblen saw it, nevertheless took on an intentional and affected quality in the minds and bodies of late nineteenth-century male elites.[9]

Veblen's genealogy of exotic ferocity is in some ways similar to late twentieth- and early twenty-first-century evolutionary psychology's sociobiological explication of masculine violence. Both return to the 2 million years of the Pleistocene hunter-gatherer period (or Veblen's "barbarian" stage) and the ever-widening differentiation between female drudgery and the corresponding feminine sociopsychological passivity and, in Veblen's words, that "sudden and violent strain" in men, the "inclin[ation] to self-assertion, active emulation, and aggression." As pointed out in this book's introduction, it is important to realize that Veblen differentiated aggressive predisposition from older gender-neutral "instincts" of sociability, workman-

ship, and care. Compared to current sociobiology, which has masculine aggression hard-wired into the brain as an "evolved motivational mechanism," Veblen
saw the "habit of judging facts and events from the point of view of the fight" as a
historically contingent trait and therefore subject to opposing values and ready for
change.[10]

Over and against understanding masculine ferocity as biologically determined,
then, Veblen explained the continued presence of that "archaic trait" among modern men through a nascent theory of cultural evolution—an approach to which
mid- to late twentieth-century anthropologists such as Victor Turner and Clifford
Geertz would add much detail and sophistication. Within this scheme, football can
be seen as a distinct cultural accretion, an elaborate institutional form that makes
unusually creative and compelling appeals to brutishness. Compared to evolutionary psychology, which would have football as an unremarkable superstructural
expression of the cross-cultural biological base of masculine aggression, Veblen
criticized the sport as diametrically opposed to the peaceful instincts of primitive
savagery and, even more tellingly, as an unnecessary aping of latter-day predatory
conventions. Football amounts to "a one-sided return to barbarism or to the *fe-
rae natura*—a rehabilitation and accentuation of those feral traits which make for
damage and desolation, without a corresponding development of the traits that
would serve the individual's self-preservation and fullness of life in a ferine environment." The game, in other words, is a distortion through and through. Veblen
cast football as a type of evolutionary problem or mistake: while misrepresenting
what it took to be its biosocial origins, the sport—rightfully understood as an increment of cultural evolution—set its enthusiasts in an "essentially unstable" and
"narrowly self-regarding habit of mind." Football, Veblen concluded in one his
most trenchant statements on the subject, to "a peculiar degree marks an arrested
development of man's moral nature."[11]

Veblen's characterization of football as a cultural distortion invites attention to
the deliberate self-serving nature of the sport's deployment: it raises such questions as how the actual play of the game subordinated women through its hypermasculinist structures and symbols, and how the ritual and publicity surrounding
college football contributed to the institutional luster of American universities like
Stanford. Veblen knew football players and fans to be self-aware in their revelry
of the sport's dramatic violence and the corresponding idealization of "the manly
spirit" as it attached to a school's team and student body. He saw football as a staged
performance. A "large element of make believe" can be found "in all sporting activity," Veblen wrote, and football is most typical in this regard: "there is almost
invariably present a good share of rant and swagger and ostensible mystification—
features that mark the histrionic features of these [the sport's] employments."

Football's theatrical "reversion to prowess" is unusually effective in building "college spirit," Veblen added crucially; it evokes a type of martial heroic celebration of the team's exploits, which in turn produces patriotic devotion to one's university—"our expression of unity," as one Stanford student described in 1900, "the binding together of all our little differences in the heat of a common purpose."[12] What emerges from Veblen's evolutionary study is understanding American college football as an elaborate corporate enterprise that instills two key attributes in those men preparing for the business class: its enactments of "exotic ferocity" hone the essential competitive streak of predation while the game also stresses the sacrifice of individual interest and identity for the good of a larger whole; my argument is that Stanford, not unlike other universities, produced real live brutes in suits—middle- and upper-class organization men, who, when the situation called for it, could also tap into the cultivated trait of predation.

Veblen's evolutionary analysis of football can be deepened by looking at the sport's change over time and in place, starting with its medieval English origins as a daylong competition that involved whole towns of men to its nineteenth-century institutionalization into London Football Association rules ("soccer") and Rugby Union rules, and then focusing on the post–Civil War founding of the American college game as a *cultural adaptation* to the social environment of the United States. David Riesman and Reuel Denney used this framework in their important 1951 essay on the sport, a study that helped establish the insight that Americans built into football rules and strategies a distinct dimension of "procedural rationalization" and managerial efficiency that fit "their industrial folkways," including Frederick Winslow Taylor's simultaneous time-motion studies.[13] Fifty years later, one can speak of historiographical agreement on the unusual corporate nature of American football, a synthesis formed in large part around the figure Walter Camp: Yale University player, captain, and coach and business executive of the New Haven Clock Company, who, in his writing, rule making, and overall governance of the late nineteenth- and early twentieth-century collegiate sport, transformed it into a technocratic training ground for a new generation of the country's business elite, in part through American football's unusual penchant for hierarchizing authority and decision making during the game, with coaches assuming increasing power over the team's play.[14]

North American football's most direct roots go back to eleventh-century England where the men of two nearby villages would place a cow's bladder midway between them and try to kick it along the countryside and roads to the opposing town center. This obviously territorial competition had additional martial connotations, including the fact that its participants tried routinely to hurt each other. It came to be known as "Dane's Head," named in celebration of the expulsion of the Danes from Great Britain and in reference to the myth that the first contest used for a ball the excavated head of a vanquished foreign soldier. By the 1600s football was played throughout Great Britain, with one of the most celebrated contests waged by the men of Chester on Shrove Tuesday in commemoration of their ancestors forming a wedge and pushing the Roman garrison out of the city in 217. Before taking hold in the nation's universities and public schools, where it was formalized into the two separate games of rugby and (what North Americans call) soccer, the folk game of English football had a riotous quality that included substantial free-form gouging, biting, and kicking of each other.[15] In support of his 1906 decision to terminate football in favor of rugby, Stanford University president David Starr Jordan cited the following sixteenth-century description by Phil Stubbs of the English game; Jordan introduced the passage in his memoirs with apparent reference to Veblen (who taught under him at Stanford), "Certain characteristics of the American sport may perhaps be atavistic reversions!" Jordan continued:

> For as concerning footeball playing I protest unto you that it maie rather bee called a friedlie kinde of fight than a plaie or recreation; a bloudie and murtherying practise than a fellowlie sporte or pastyme. For doeth not everyone lye in waight for his Adversarie, seekying to overthrow hym and to picke hym on the nose, though it bee uppon harde stones, in ditch or dale, in valley or hill? In what place so ever it bee he careth not, so he may have hym downe: And he that can serve the moste of this fashion, he is counted the onlie fellowe, and who but he? So that by his meanes sometymes their neckes are broken, sometymes their backes, sometymes their legges, sometymes their armes, sometymes the noses gush out with bloud, sometime their eyes start out; and sometymes they are hurt in one place, someymes in an other. But who so ever escapeth awaie the best, goeth not scotfree, but is either sore wounded and bruzed, or els scapeth every harlie. And no marvaile for they have sleightes to meet one betwixt two, to dash hym against the harte with their elbowes, to hitte hym under the shortte ribbes with their griped fists, and with their knees to catch hym upon the hip, and to picke hym on his necke, with an hundred such murtherying devices: And hereof groweth envie, malice, rancour, cholour, hatred, displeasure, enmitie, and what not els? And sometyme fightyin, braulyng, contention, quarrell pickying, murther, homicide, and great effusion of bloud, as experience daily teacheth.[16]

While Stubbs may have exaggerated these contests' dangers—historians of early football don't account for such deadliness—it is clear that, from an early point on, the game built in a distinct measure of extracurricular fighting.

Football certainly maintained this English attribute of homosocial violence in its early U.S. form. More peaceful casual ball kicking games could be found in seventeenth- and eighteenth-century America, but football did not achieve any type of continual expression until the turn of the nineteenth century, when men of Harvard and Yale and other eastern universities adopted it as an intramural hazing ritual "played" between the freshmen and sophomore classes. A Harvard class poem from the 1840s catches the spirit and tactics of the competition:

> The Delta can tell of the deeds we've done,
> The fierce fought fields we've lost and won
> The shins we've cracked
> And noses we've whacked,
> The eyes we've blacked, and all in fun.[17]

For all practical purposes, football rush provided a pretense for collegians to beat each other into submission, or at least to enforce the seniority-based status system of the university through low-level, less-than-completely-serious violence. In many American universities rushing continued well into the late nineteenth and early twentieth centuries.[18] At Stanford, though, student leaders downplayed it, charging that interclass rush detracted from common cause against Berkeley.

Initial post–Civil War intercollegiate contests followed the rules of soccer, but largely between the mid-1870s and the late 1880s English football developed into a highly organized and exceptionally violent sport, when Harvard, Yale, and Princeton and a few other elite eastern universities selected rugby's combined running and kicking game and then proceeded to modify it into what is now called American football.[19] The sport evolved by way of a sequence of rule changes made by the Intercollegiate Football Association, founded in 1876, and informally led by Walter Camp, who sought to routinize what he saw as the chaotic nature of rugby. Drawing immediate attention was rugby's scrum, whereby teammates lock arms, butt up against the opposing side, and try to kick the ball backward to a waiting runner. This method of putting the ball into play involved, as Camp described, "too much luck and chance as to where or when it came out, and what man favored by Dame Fortune would get it."[20] The ensuing 1880 modification called for possession of the ball by one side and play beginning with a man kicking (it would later be changed to "snapping") the ball back to the "quarter-back." Two years later the association provided that a team could keep the ball as long as it continued to gain five yards in three "downs." Set plays and signal calling followed shortly thereafter, and, in turn, an elaborate division of labor arose with several designated positions on both the line and in the backfield. Taken together, these new rules and tactics placed an unusual premium on intricate synchronization between a team's players. At the same time, American football's distinct offensive-defensive configuration set over a static line of scrimmage clarified the martial symbolism long present in the English game. And American delimitation of field action between the timed snap of the ball and the tackling of the ball carrier led to the routinization of increasingly large and fast players smashing violently against each other in short bursts of complete exertion and force.

Of all the rule changes passed by the Intercollegiate Football Association, perhaps its 1887 decision to permit tackling below the waist did the most to raise the new sport's level of violence. Camp correctly believed that low tackling would shift power to the defense by adding to its ability to stop open-field running. But tackling below the waist, along with gradual legalization of interference ahead of the ball carrier, also led to mass plays, including the infamous flying wedge and other dangerous mobile blocking formations designed to smash through awaiting defenses.[21] These mass-momentum plays resulted in so many injuries that they were abolished in the mid-1890s. Low tackling has remained an integral part of American football, however, marking one of the game's sharpest differences from rugby. Rather than using one's hands and arms to pull down the ball carrier by his shoulders or torso, as in rugby, tacklers in American football lead with their head and shoulders, oftentimes launching themselves off the ground and, from a horizontal missile-like position, colliding with the runner under tremendous force of impact. Needless to say, the low-tackling adaptation dramatically expanded the likelihood and range of injury. While the ball carrier's legs and knees, among other body parts, became extremely vulnerable, the tackler also placed himself at great risk, as concussions to the head and spine became a major cause of death and serious injury in late nineteenth-century American football.

College football evolved into an exceptionally violent sport through its brutal combination of high-speed running plays and full-body tackling, as well as the expansion of the slugging, kicking, and gouging that had always accompanied English football. Play organized over a static line of scrimmage presented routine opportunity for extralegal mugging. Official rules did forbid such assault. The Intercollegiate Football Association rules of 1893, for instance, provided that "A player shall be disqualified for unnecessary roughness, hacking or striking with the closed fist." But, in practice, this prohibition seems to have been rarely enforced. In the 1893 game between Stanford and the Reliance Club, for instance, constant ear cuffing and neck twisting sparked a full-fledged fistfight; players suffered swollen eyes and broken noses, and yet no one was ejected. In another example, the New York City Police superintendent threatened to shut down the 1894 Princeton-Yale game played in Manhattan if it grew into a "brutal prize fight" like the Harvard-Yale slugfest the week before.[22] Clearly the referees of a contest did little to stop the violence. The 1905 Pennsylvania-Swarthmore game precipitated the most sustained effort to reform football: in the contest, Swarthmore star lineman Bob Maxwell sustained a deliberate attack lasting almost the whole game, until he finally staggered off the field, his face a "bloody wreck." After a photograph of the mangled Maxwell appeared in a number of newspapers, President Roosevelt called Camp and other leading football officials to the White House to work toward ending the game's rough play.[23]

As testament to the sport's brutal nature, American football had been opposed by a host of public figures since its inception. Reaching a peak in the early 1900s and with university presidents and faculty, muckraking journalists, and U.S. presidents leading the way, the push to abolish or, alternatively, to reform college football can be seen as one of the more coherent efforts of the Progressive Era. But like the broader reform movement, the effectiveness of those attempts to clean up football remains difficult to gauge. Decisions to terminate certain programs or contests succeeded on a piecemeal basis. In 1893, for instance, President Grover Cleveland shut down the Army-Navy contest after the hospitalization of twenty-four midshipmen.[24] And in 1906 Stanford, among several other universities that year, decided to end football and switch to the less-violent rugby game. Rugby involves far more running and open play, as Stanford's President Jordan explained his support of the change, compared to football's "mimic battle, a game of plunging and pushing." He continued: "Modern football is not only to be decried because of the dangers it offers in the way of bodily injury, but because of its brutalizing effect on the morals"; "all the energy and power that can be thrown against the human form, directly interfering with the passage of the man carrying the ball, is fairly hurled to the point of attack"; "there is but one sentiment in the minds of that entire team, and that is to beat down by force a single member of the opposing team."[25] Jordan had readily accepted football's brutality in the early to mid-1890s, when he appreciated what the sport and its "sentiment" could do for masculinizing Stanford's student body and public image. Ten years later, with the university's reputation relatively secure, Jordan apparently felt that football's excesses outweighed its benefits. Stanford started playing football again in 1919.

The more ambitious attempts to make football a safer game proved to be unsuccessful, however: just as some historians argue that Progressive Era trust busting and graduated income tax, among other measures, ensured the long life of the corporate-capitalist complex, one could say that the leading football officials' efforts to improve the sport's image by smoothing out its most jagged edges only worked to solidify the game's violent core dynamic of high-speed collision. The 1894 abolition of the flying wedge and other mass-momentum plays did little more than add speed and excitement to a game that had run the risk of getting bogged down in constant interlocking offensive and defensive lines. So too with the Roosevelt inspired reform of 1905. The following year the newly formed National Collegiate Athletic Association legalized the forward pass to break up the collisions and slugging at the line of scrimmage. Yet, this significant rule change, one that further separated American football from rugby, seems only to have increased the game's brutality. (One football historian has thirty players killed in 1909 alone.)[26] The forward pass would end up producing the hardest hits and most dangerous tackling in twentieth-century college and professional football, as defensive backs, following the textbook method of tackling, leveled a helmeted head and padded shoulders into the back or rib cage of an opponent just catching a pass.

The violent hegemonic effect of football reform can also be seen in the uniforms that the American game adopted in the late nineteenth century. Beginning in the late 1880s, players donned a padded canvas jacket over their jersey; loose fitting knickerbockers were replaced by specially made football pants with heavy padding in the hips and knees; next came such accessories as shin guards, elbow pads, head harnesses, mouthpieces, and the exotic nose guard or "nose beak" (fig. 3.2). By the 1890s players and commentators commonly referred to this equipment as armor, and the easy use of that word points to the brutalizing effect of this particular adaptation to the English game.[27] Ostensibly designed for the humane purpose of protecting players from injury, it actually helped make permanent the severest traits of the American sport. As one boxing expert said of football's late nineteenth-century unparalleled violence, "the very makeup of the players"—their "leather head cases, ear, eye, nose and mouth protectors," the fact that "their whole bodies were thoroughly padded"—proves "that each and every one of them expects to be injured."[28] Rather than prohibiting low tackling, for instance, American football tried to soften the increasingly heavy blows, perhaps allowing a player to make it through to the next down. Also crucial in reinforcing football's head-on, feet-off-the-ground hitting, head gear (eventually the full-fledged helmet) worked offensively, as a weapon, as much as for protection; similarly, padded shoulders, hips, and knees encouraged players to launch themselves into the air and to otherwise generate the hardest impact.

By the time that Stanford founded its team in the early 1890s, then, American football could clearly be seen as an "exotically ferocious" sport. Veblen's tag caught the gladiatorial look and feel of the game during that decade, a time when rule changes and armored equipment encouraged a type of daring in line play and full-body tackling that in turn produced countless serious injuries and numerous deaths. Exactly how many "casualties" occurred—another key word in turn-of-the-century football commentary—is difficult to say since partisans on both sides of the issue exaggerated the sport's safety and danger. In 1893, amid a sharp rise in the game's condemnation, Walter Camp surveyed coaches and former players about their football injuries and current mental and physical health. But in the ensuing publication, *Football Facts and Figures* (1894), Camp excluded the most critical responses; the report concluded that football produced only a few minor injuries, no more serious than in other sports such as rowing.[29] On the other side of the equation, many late nineteenth-century journalists sensationalized football's brutality, as in this oft-quoted German newspaper account of an 1893 contest:

> The football tournament between Harvard and Yale, recently held in America, had terrible results. It turned into an awful butchery. Of twenty two participants seven were so severely injured that they had to be carried from the field in a dying condition. One player had his back broken, another lost an eye, and a third lost a leg. Both teams appeared upon the field with a crown of ambulances, surgeons, and nurses. Many ladies fainted at the awful cries of the injured players. The indignation of the spectators was powerful, but they were so terrorized that they were afraid to leave the field.[30]

The injuries mentioned here simply did not happen, nor does any other record of the game mention anyone fainting. At the same time, big games between rivals could be extremely violent. The 1894 Harvard-Yale contest produced several accounts of brutal play and, as reported in the *Harvard Crimson,* a "remarkable . . . number of casualties." The *New York Times* described it as "a game in which an unusual amount of bad blood was shown. . . . Charles Brewer of the Harvard team had his leg broken," as the paper listed the players injured in action, "Wrightenton had a collarbone broken and Hallowell goes back to Cambridge with a broken nose. As for Yale, there was rumor abroad in the night that Murphy, Yale's massive tackle, had died in the Springfield Hospital but it turned out to be merely a contusion of the brain." The *Crimson* reported, though, that the teams' doctors said that accounts "of the injuries of the men were greatly exaggerated"; Murphy had made it back to New Haven the same evening of the game and could be seen sitting "in an easy chair engaged in study" and speaking of playing against Princeton the following Saturday.[31]

Despite the uncertainty over the number and severity of college football casualties during the 1890s, it remains clear that the sport's popular appeal depended in large measure on its violence, both real and symbolic. Journalistic exaggeration of the game's brutality was an expression of widespread interest in locating brawn, danger, and even death on the football field. This is what Veblen meant by the predatory "culture bestowed in football": he saw its "exotic ferocity" as a "habit of mind," an artificial construct that could be changed through self-conscious interest in other more sociable values. But even Veblen didn't fully appreciate football's deep and distinct roots in American history and culture, including the late nineteenth-century college game's intricate overlap with the then emerging romantic memory of the Civil War. As universities dedicated new stadiums to soldiers killed in action, as students wrote "fight songs" to the tunes of Blue and Gray marching songs, and as southern schools adopted team names and uniforms explicitly venerating the Confederacy, football fans in both the North and the South experienced intercollegiate contests through the historical prism of war, conflating line play with hand-to-hand combat, athletic achievement with battle prowess, and physical sacrifice with martial heroism.[32]

These meanings and their contribution to the turn-of-the-century reconstruction of the American citizen-soldier are examined in the last part of this chapter but, first, we consider more closely how football's elaborate color, pageantry, and play came to dramatize a distinctly brutish ideal of manhood. Like no other sport in the United States, college football glorified masculine size, strength, and capacity for violence. By the 1890s the physical demands of playing football selected only the largest most sturdy men: "The violent exercise of football," as Walter Camp wrote with Lorin Deland in one of the few concessions he ever made regarding the American game, "is too great a strain upon many young men who attempt to play it."[33] As American universities placed more and more prestige on football, individual schools increased their efforts to build superior male bodies and to synchronize them off and on the field. A military-corporatist organizational model took hold, with mounting excitement, drama, and import invested in contests between two equally matched squads. Thus we come to Stanford's football team, its rivalry with the University of California, and the anthropologist Victor Turner, whose work on ritual and cultural performance provides another valuable crossover for the historical study of American football.

Victor Turner, Stanford Football, and Hypermasculine Liminal Subjects

Victor Turner's anthropological perspective, specifically his concepts of liminality and *communitas*, provides a methodology for understanding a football game as an elaborate "social drama" that bestows new levels of status by separating itself from structured time and enacting a set of rituals recognized as integral to the sport. Liminality refers to the specific ritualistic process by which, in this case, football players are distinguished as symbolically potent "threshold" subjects whose prowess on the field will determine their alma mater's power and prestige. *Communitas* is the performative context in which liminality happens. Turner believed that liminality operates in combination with the temporary dissolution of "normative social structure." Those party to this "anti-structure"—say the thousands of fans at a football game—momentarily transcend "politico-legal-economic" differentiations to form a "communion of equal individuals."[34] While a football *communitas* bears witness to the play—thereby adding spectatorial weight to the outcome of the contest—it also, following Turner, has a creative extrafunctional effect. The myths, symbols, and rituals emanating from a liminal-*communitas* dynamic create "a set of templates or models" that achieve nothing less than the "reclassification of reality and man's relationship to society, nature, and culture."[35] Turner spoke of social drama's "subjunctive mood": a group psychology that expresses supposition, possibility, and desire.[36] Through Turner, a college football game such as the one between Stanford and California in 1896 can be seen as a culturally productive disconnection from social form and custom, a supercharged event that says less about the way things are than how they could be.[37]

Around the edges of Turner's work one finds further insight into the socio-psychological state of *communitas* and its presence in football. Turner's interest in social drama emerged from his mid-twentieth-century fieldwork among the Ndembu of Zambia. With his first publications focusing on Ndembu mediation of group conflict and transitions of power through high ritual, Turner's later writing ventured into modern Western society and its different genres of cultural performance, sport among them. In *From Ritual to Theatre: The Human Seriousness of Play* (1982), Turner marveled over the "pure potentiality" of cultural performance, "when everything, as it were, trembles in the balance. (Like the trembling quarterback with all the 'options' but with the very solid future moving menacingly towards him!)" He also turned to the early flow theory of psychologist Mihaly Csikszentmihalyi to speculate about the cognitive qualities of *communitas* and its production of ideal mental states of "total involvement" when consciousness of time dissolves away and when "action follows action according to an internal logic."[38] Understanding *communitas* as a collective of intense enraptured attention adds dimension to the emotional history of early Stanford football fan culture. It contextualizes an 1899 declaration of a Stanford student, for instance, that the Big Game against California "stirs us so powerfully" because it is a time when "Life is not measured by hours, but by *living*."[39] Recognizing this condition of total yet willful experiential absorption suggested by Turner's *communitas* fits well with Clifford Geertz's more precise approach to an athletic contest as a cultural text that creates emotion for cognitive ends.

The core application of Turner to football is liminality. In looking closely at Stanford's emotional investment in its team—in getting at the how, why, and what of a student being so powerfully moved by a football game—the historian would do well to focus on the ritual that cut the contest off from ordinary time and place. Turner's concept of liminality isolates the process by which a sporting event elevates itself into the dramatic and even sacred realm. It concentrates on the transformative effect of athletic competition. A liminal subject is without identity—"neither here nor there," in Turner's well-known phrase, "betwixt and between" positions.⁴⁰ But rite of passage wholly assumes that a new position *will* be realized, definitely. This promise of determination goes far to explain the excitement over the Big Game between Stanford and California. It also accounts for the enraptured attention to the football players: exceptional in physical size and athletic ability, they symbolized their university's masculine aspiration, status, and prestige.

With both individual and corporate transitions in mind, Turner identified three stages of rituals associated with passage from one state or identity to another: the first phase "comprises symbolic behavior signifying the detachment . . . from an earlier fixed point in the social structure"—that is, "separation from anteced-ent mundane life"; the second is the liminal period in which the ritual subject's characteristics and status are distinctly indeterminate; and the final stage brings "reaggregation to the daily world"—the subject "is in a relatively stable state once more" within his or her original social context.⁴¹ In applying these three phases to college football, the team's players are the ritual subjects. The athletes' detach-ment from the student body happens, initially, in identifying what men are strong, big, and tough enough to hold up in the sport and, then, in the days preceding the contest, in literally leaving the campus (as Stanford's team did the week before the Big Game) and secluding themselves in rest and preparation for the competi-tion ahead; the playing of the game between equally matched teams is the liminal phase in which the identity of the opponents as winner or loser, superior or in-ferior, is suspended until the final whistle; reaggregation proceeds with the team returning to campus after the game and then with the subject's identity as a player dissolving after the season.

It is crucial to recognize that liminality in football involves the simultaneous passage of two closely related subjects, the individual and the institutional, and thus codetermination in two overlapping realms, physical prowess and corporate status. What moves and changes is both the prowess of the players, whose mascu-linity is achieved through rigorous physical training and ranked through competi-tion, *and* the status of the university in whose name the men play as surrogates or symbol bearers. Late nineteenth-century football, in particular, served as a ve-hicle for establishing pride in alma mater through ritualistic masculine display.⁴² The products of that display—hypermasculinity, the vanquishing of an equally matched opponent through combat over territory—folded into the corporate con-stitution of the university. It paid to produce brutes in suits; homosocial cohesion, identity, and prestige all hung in the balance.

Liminality in football directs the historian back to the organization of the uni-versity as a whole. At Stanford one finds the evolution of a sophisticated corporate structure and mind-set, a program geared to building school spirit and privileging devotion to the university as a good in itself. "The student who is so absorbed in his books that he has no time for various interests of the University," Stanford's student newspaper reminded its readers in September of 1896, is "failing to do his duty here. It should be the pride of the student to know that he is giving something of himself to add to the fair name of his alma mater."[43] Within this corporate context, football can be seen as a pretense for organizing a student body into essential roles for the university's success.

At Stanford, a coeducational institution since its 1891 founding, the prescription of duties included an intricate system of gender roles, so intricate that *three* rather than two separate identities emerged. Femininity was expected among the 65 women of the 461 students in the university's first class; the ideal amounted to a subsidiary position, especially within Stanford's football culture.[44] Something of a split occurred in the gender of Stanford's men. A man would be considered masculine if he acted heterosexually and otherwise appeared and behaved normatively. But from this base came the hypermasculine football player, a (perceived to be) radical departure from the other men in terms of the size and strength and toughness he would have to amass to make it through the season. The university expended a great deal of effort to find its biggest men, implore them to service on the team, and then train them for the Big Game against California. That these select few would determine Stanford's rank through their performance on the field helped assure a separate gendered identity.

In short, with its most masculine men leading the way, Stanford looked to its football team to secure legitimacy for the new school. Stanford longed for respect from Harvard and Yale and the other old private universities of the East, while the University of California at Berkeley became its most immediate reference point. The two schools played their first football game within six months of Stanford's opening. And a half year later, by the fall of 1892, both universities extolled "the tradition" of their "great rivalry." They expended extraordinary effort in building up their teams for what would quickly become known as the Big Game. And through its early success on the field, Stanford could claim that it had achieved parity with or superiority over California. The *San Francisco Examiner* put it clearly after Stanford's 20–0 victory in the Big Game of 1896: "This defeat is by far the most crushing that the State University has ever experienced, and proves conclusively either that the system of education there is at fault or that the material to select from is inferior to that of the rival institution."[45] This conflation of institutional status with the "material to select from"—that is, the masculinity of the school's student body—can also be found at the heart of Stanford fans' emotional embrace of their football team. The same Stanford student of 1899 quoted previously asked rhetorically why he should be stirred "so powerfully" by "[t]his thing of forcing an air-filled pigskin sphere over some yards of earth? . . . Abstractly, why should we, when this sphere goes to the north, weep with bitterness, and why, when it flies south, weep in ecstasy?" His answer divulges identification with the corporate commitment to Stanford football: "During the flight of a single hour this Thanksgiving Day we are to live all that we have spent months building for; we are to know, as nearly as anything save war may tell, of the comparative material fitness of our men."[46] With the added sacramental dimension of a Thanksgiving Day game, homosocial status derived through hypermasculinity had unusually strong resonance among the young university's student body.

While perhaps more pronounced at Stanford than some other universities, the effort to gain prestige and national recognition through football could be found throughout late nineteenth-century American higher education. By the time Stanford and California had played their first game in the spring of 1892, ardent rivalries had already formed among such eastern schools as Harvard, Yale, and Princeton; Army and Navy, and Lehigh and Lafayette. Several upper midwestern state land grant universities had also established strong football programs. By the turn of the century, Michigan, Minnesota, and Wisconsin, along with the newly founded University of Chicago (and its renowned coach Alonzo Stagg) would challenge Harvard, Princeton, and Yale for supremacy in the sport.[47] College football took hold in the South in the late 1880s and early 1890s. As southern university administrators hired experienced coaches from the Northeast, students, alumni, and other boosters increasingly touted football as a requisite condition to their alma maters' modern prominence. Intrastate rivalries quickly sprung up between Wake Forest and Trinity (later Duke), Texas and Texas A&M, Georgia and Georgia Tech, Louisiana State and Tulane, and Alabama and what would become Auburn.[48] Regional conferences formed in the mid-1890s and a decade later the best southern teams could claim to be competitive with the strongest in the country.

Football also spread to many African American and American Indian schools where students and educators appreciated what the sport might do for racial and institutional acceptance. The Carlisle Indian Industrial School's football team drew national attention in the 1890s and beyond for its competitiveness against eastern powers as well as its unusually good sportsmanship even after blatantly unfair calls by referees cost it a number of games. The Carlisle Indians saw football as a source for both acculturation and new expression of traditional warrior ideals of strength and bravery. In beating Army two of three times in the 1890s, the Indians, according to a Carlisle historian, "play[ed] football as if they were possessed."[49] In general terms, African Americans also understood sport as an opportunity for, in Patrick B. Miller's phrase, "muscular assimilation."[50] As an editorial in the Howard University student newspaper put it in 1924: "Athletics is the universal language.

By and through it we hope to foster a better and more fundamental spirit between the races in America and so to destroy prejudices; to learn and to be taught; to facilitate a universal brotherhood."[51] Well before this time, though, in the 1890s, Howard, Lincoln, Fisk, Tuskegee Institute, Atlanta University, and other black institutions had started football programs and their own intercollegiate rivalries. Racial integration on the football field came extremely slowly. A few exceptionally talented African Americans played for northern college teams in the 1890s, but it wouldn't be until the 1930s that southern white teams agreed to play northern teams with a black player, and it took a few decades more before those southern schools would open themselves to African American students and athletes. Still, for African American colleges, the game of football, with its rich symbolism of coordinated masculinity, provided a medium for social mobility. Wiley College, to take one example, proudly introduced football in 1901, just "as it is played at Yale and other Eastern colleges."[52]

At Stanford football was integral to the university from the beginning. Former California governor, U.S. senator, and "big four" partner in the Central Pacific Railroad, Leland Stanford spent $17 million to build the university on several hundred acres of his horse farm some thirty-five miles south of San Francisco. With David Starr Jordan (a Cornell trained zoologist and former president of Indiana University) hired as the new university's first president and with fifteen faculty members in place, instruction began at Stanford in October 1891 for the first class of 461 students. By November the Student Athletic Association had been formed, and by early December daily football practice had begun.[53] "Football fever" quickly set in, as the student literary journal the *Sequoia* reported. "We have many promising men," the journal enthused, "and it only remains for us to organize and get down to good steady work to bring out a team which the University may well be proud."[54] The excitement, color, and pageantry surrounding Stanford football sprang up immediately. When Stanford played its first game against a team from the Berkeley Gymnasium in San Jose in early February 1892, two hundred cardinal-red-clad students with tin horns traveled by train to root their men on. As the *Sequoia* reported, "The station at San Jose fairly rang with ''Rah! 'Rah! 'Rah! 'Rah! 'Rah! 'Rah! 'Rah! Stanford!' when the train stopped"; it added that the "half dozen co-eds who braved the elements deserve special mention for their courage and patriotic spirit."[55] Stanford's first game against California took place on Saturday, 19 March 1892, in San Francisco. For the trip students chartered five train cars, which they decorated profusely with red bunting. "Then with band, tin horns, and other noise-producing implements," as the *Sequoia* recorded, "almost the whole University, students and faculty, proceeded gaily to the city. Equally enthusiastic crowds came from across the Bay, and the city seemed to blossom out with lavish display of blue and gold and cardinal." In total, eight thousand people watched Stanford win 14–10.[56] The tradition had begun.

Football fever at Stanford set in amid a broad university commitment to athletics. As part of the original faculty, a physical director and his two assistants offered athletic courses that could be taken for credit. The first Stanford class enjoyed the use of a thirteen-and-half-acre athletic field, a quarter-mile running track, six tennis courts, and two gymnasiums—Roble for the women and Encina for the men. While both housed baths, dressing rooms, lockers, and other facilities expected in a modern gymnasium, Encina had more extensive equipment: a large indoor running track, a pulley and ring system, weights, chest developers, six hydraulic rowing machines—"everything," a writer for the *Sequoia* proclaimed, "that is necessary for the perfect and ready development of every muscle in the human body."[57] Writers for Stanford student publications tended to implore their fellow students to physical exercise, usually set within a high-minded almost philosophical appeal to self-fulfillment through sport. "Mind or Muscle?" a highly emblematic *Sequoia* editorial published during the first year, instructs that "in the model university of today the gymnasium stands side by side with the library and laboratory" and that therefore the reader should "take an inventory of your own physical and mental stock in trade" (you will "find yourself sadly deficient") and routinely develop "physical power" and "strength and agility" as well as intelligence. The *Sequoia*'s answer, so representative of late nineteenth-century physical culture, was to forge a balance between brain and brawn—although, as always, it spoke far more about muscle than mind.[58]

From the beginning, football was paramount among Stanford sports and student activities. During the spring term, after the football season, baseball received a fair amount of attention from students; but nothing like the football craze, which transcended Stanford's everyday interest in athletics and physical culture. In 1893 David Starr Jordan, while backing football financially, championed the sport for building "brotherhood and loyalty." He also spoke of football's regenerative powers: "Football is action. It is genuine. It makes for decision of character. It is an antidote to the maladies of dilettantism and pessimism which are said to afflict the end of the century." Jordan and others appreciated that football could build Stanford's "prestige," as the student newspaper, the *Daily Palo Alto*, said in September 1893; in rallying support for the team, it reminded readers of "the glory to be attained by a great intercollegiate victory, where 20,000 spectators will sound our praises if we are victorious." Football gave definition to the university. It carried historical weight and even bore moral authority. "This year's football team, probably more than any other in the history of Stanford athletics, has been a direct force in University life," a *Sequoia* editorial proclaimed in 1899. "The influence of the team may, without any sentimentality, be said to have been profoundly moral. One thing is certain," it concluded: "the manly spirit of all associated with this year's team has spread like a contagion until, as a result, every fellow on the quad walks straighter and works harder."[59] In a word, football had a *spiritual* effect on the young university.

Indeed, students most often used the words "Stanford Spirit" to describe and motivate further support of the football program and the school overall. School spirit amounted to a belief system—a type of "patriotism" in small, a word used interchangeably with Stanford Spirit—that subordinated the individual to a larger corporate whole. "It is our expression of unity," as a student explained in 1900, "the binding together of all our little differences in the heat of a common purpose." He emphasized that Stanford Spirit manifested itself most fully at "the football game on Thanksgiving Day." The student went on to describe the *communitas*-like psychology of the Big Game. "We all know how it is: for awhile there are no longer any inequalities in the Cardinal," he said, and then added in a very compelling phrase, "but only one red living fact." Ideally, the game-time dissolution of ego into school spirit would stay with the students: "This conscious unity of the moment should be so branded in the being of every Stanford man that it will never again give place to anything else. Our victory must make of us every one a thorough-bred,—the true Stanford Stock." And the promise of this transformation, he concluded, should push each student to vocal support of the Stanford eleven: "So grip your red flag tightly, drop all your excessive dignity, and Y-E-L-L!!"[60]

In addition to stirring up school spirit, the football program also reached down and ordered Stanford social life, forging, among other things, a conservative template for university gender relations. Variously called "co-eds," "girlies," and "angels," Stanford's first women students inhabited an extremely "liminal" state, as Carroll Smith-Rosenberg has described the New Woman college student of the late nineteenth century. Betwixt and between feminine gentility and feminist androgyne, Stanford women found themselves in a coeducational environment that on one side, in Smith-Rosenberg's words, "threatened the very principle of gender polarity" and, on the other, encouraged traditional patriarchal forces.[61] Leland Stanford, for instance, stressed that college should contribute to a woman's preparation for motherhood. "We have provided in the articles of endowment," Stanford said in a speech to the student body and faculty in 1891, "that the education of the sexes shall be equal—deeming it of special importance that those who are to be mothers of the future generation shall be fitted to mold and direct the infantile mind at its most critical period."[62] And, in the broadest terms, football worked retrogressively, subordinating women to a spectatorial role as it found new ways to exaggerate masculine traits of superior size, strength, and aggression.

Conversely, Stanford's physical culture outside of football tended to equalize gender relations among the students. With their own gymnasium and tennis courts, Stanford's first women understood sport to be a powerful source of feminine pride. "Don't think for an instant the young women of Roble Hall [the women's dormitory] are less enthusiastic over athletics than the boys, for it is not so," one Stanford woman wrote in the *Sequoia* in December 1891; she also reported the organization of the university's first tennis tournament: "we are all very anxious to get into practice because there is to be given to our champion a beautiful silver-mounted racket. Happy girl who wins it!" And her article concluded by challenging Stanford men: "we look forward to our champion successfully competing with the champion of Encina Hall [the men's dormitory]." By 1893 the Women's Athletic Association had been founded. Over the next ten to fifteen years it supported a number of athletic clubs, including archery, cycling, boating, tennis, and equestrian. And eventually the association folded into Stanford's Athletic Department, which finally funded and oversaw women's intercollegiate athletic competition.[63] Given Stanford women's success in tennis, basketball, track and field, and other sports since the mid-twentieth century, the early years of physical culture created a long-standing legacy of raising women's university and public profile through athletic accomplishment and thereby blurring gender differences.

Stanford football countered the gender neutralizing effect of women's athletics with a vengeance. Unlike its English predecessor, the rough and violent play of American football kept women from playing the sport. Indeed, while women would compete in intercollegiate soccer by the 1960s and 1970s, football never became an NCAA female sport at Stanford or anywhere else—it is about the only major sport, along with wrestling, of which this is true. Football didn't completely exclude women though. At the end of the nineteenth century it developed an unusually prominent place for women in the stands (unusual compared to English football, for instance, and baseball), where their Victorian feminine attire and cheering added a distinctly heterosexual charge to the game.[64] Psychologist and Clark University President G. Stanley Hall contended in 1900 that football's enactment of martial conflict accounted for women's attraction to the sport. "Military prowess has a strange fascination for the weaker sex, perhaps ultimately and biologically because it demonstrates the power to protect and defend. Power," Hall emphasized, "has played a great role in sexual attraction," and football produces a surplus.[65] Hall's brief comments demonstrate all too well how college football could have been seen and enjoyed for its reestablishment of a natural sexual order during a time when young middle-class women otherwise pushed the bounds of traditional, circumscribed gender roles.

Issues of agency and causation arise here. While many Stanford women may have willingly accepted the retrogressive gender roles of football—the game's romantic martial heroism *was* new and dramatic—it is also clear that their male counterparts helped cultivate a proper place for the "co-eds" within the sport. The last weeks of practice before the Big Game drew large numbers of Stanford students, including many women as early as the fall of 1892.[66] During these practice sessions, though, emergent custom largely segregated women from men. One student in 1895 reported being "green with envy because I was not a boy, and, therefore, could not walk around the field and see what the men did when they worked away from the grand stand."[67] Within college football's increasingly gendered fan culture, Stanford men played up the feminine contributions women made to the practices and games. For example, in the days preceding the Big Game of 1893, a male writer in the *Daily Palo Alto* documented the great stir created in a practice by "the applause given to the players by the young ladies. In one instance in particular," he described, "there was a half suppressed murmur of excitement from the young ladies side. The 'oh oh's' had a soft musical ring immensely pleasing to the ear and in marked contrast to the vociferous salutes of 'Jack's' squad of hooters."[68] And while on display during the Big Game against California, Stanford students' gender differences separated even farther through middle-class conventions of dress and public comportment, at least before the contest ended. With the men in a long-coated dark suit and a high stiff collar and tie with a top hat, and the women in a light-colored full-length dress, hat, and gloves, the Thanksgiving Day affair manifested genteel formality. We are ladies and gentlemen, their appearance seemed to say: Stanford's experiment in coeducation had not altered the basic heterosexual identities of its young men and women.

Given the dictates of late nineteenth-century American masculinity, non-football-playing Stanford men tried to distinguish themselves from the women fans. Formal dress functioned in this way, but more blatant efforts can be found, including the *Sequoia*'s 1897 illustrated ditty "To the Rooting Co-Ed" (fig. 3.3). The intent of the line "You're nothin' more than a woman, an' a woman's a woman born" is unmistakable, although, while wanting to put the female fan in her place, the author also urged her to support the team (that is a purpose of the whole page), thereby acknowledging her importance to the cause: "An' you must yell like bloody 'ell / For we've got to win the groun'." The song repeats this dualism of condescending dependency in the last two lines: it is honorific—"'Ats off to the dame who 'elps at the game"—while underlining that "she's only a woman born!" The author's affected lower-class Irish or cockney brogue may speak to his self-consciousness over the felt need to put Stanford women down—the parenthetical note "With apologies" betrays a certain awkwardness. The song's rough masculine voice permitted the writer to air his apparent unease over Stanford women's public presence in an aggressive demeaning manner while, at the same time, couching that response in an ironic less-than-serious tone.

As Stanford's fall term began, and as the student body started organizing itself toward beating California on Thanksgiving Day, the first order of business was to identify the most fit men for the team. Did those men not chosen feel uneasy over this separation process? Maybe not. To begin with, football was extremely dangerous and otherwise physically taxing and time consuming; some men may have preferred to stay on the sidelines and let others risk life and limb for Stanford's good name; football's whole superpublic ritualistic artifice allowed for close injury-free identification with a team's success. Moreover, the emergence of the third gender of hypermasculinity didn't necessarily make the nonplayers effeminate. Even though Stanford students would draw stark comparisons between the football star and the limp-wristed weakling, a middle ground of gentlemanly manhood could be inhabited, provided one met the minimum requirements of sound body and heterosexual identity.

Yet heterosexual relations may have been the area in which the non–football player would lose the most ground. Homosocial status and female desire privileged athletic and especially football prowess, as seen in the 1897 *Sequoia* short story "The Difference." This male-authored piece tells of a first-year Stanford woman's initial visit to a football practice, where she recognizes a "college friend. An esthetic Greek he had been in her eyes until now, an immaculately groomed, proper young man, a shining example of Nineteenth Century culture." But as she continues to watch him play, "something else" becomes apparent. He devolves before her eyes: "She saw the dirt and sweat that streaked his face and hands and neck that were coarsely red. . . . She saw him turn over, digging his hands, and knees and toes into the soft dirt. She saw the beast." Rather than being repulsed by this brutish display, she is enthralled: after he scores a touchdown, "[s]he leaps to her feet, waving her parasol and . . . arms. She cries aloud his name." For the author, the woman's emotional response marks her own transformation: "She is no longer a Freshman. She is an enthusiast."[69] Also, though, "the difference" in the once "proper young man" brings a type of feminine adoration that he would not have otherwise received; the story worked as a recruiting tool, reminding male readers of the benefits of risking one's neck for Stanford.

The heterosexual benefit of hypermasculinity is made more explicit in a poem of 1899 entitled "A Hero." Written by a Stanford woman, it draws a sharp contrast between the football player and the man on the sidelines. On the one hand she sees "My hero, tall and strong": "Out into the mud and wet he goes . . . Under his jersey the muscle shows, / And, Samson-like, his dark hair grows / Delightfully thick and long." On the other hand she is "[b]other[ed]" by "these boys with their dapper ties! / Who come and compel me to turn my eyes / Away from a nobler sight." She persists in focusing on the man on the field, however, "strain[ing] my eyes for his every run," and noting that "[o]ut from his feet the black mud flies," and that "[h]is jacket is far from white." And after practice the woman's thoughts, feelings, and "appreciation" are with her hero, even as she "stroll[s] back with a soft-tongued chap / Whose muscles I know aren't worth a rap, / And whose hair is an imitation."[70] Feminine physical attraction to football players, in tandem with derision toward the nonplaying "chaps," would not have been lost on Stanford men deciding whether or not to try out for the team.

Amid the development of hypermasculinity at Stanford, what is perhaps most impressive is the early institutional commitment to building football players, including the effort that the student publications made to recruit the best "material" for the team. The widespread use of the word "material" at Stanford to describe the bulk of a man or a group of men betrays the impersonal corporatist imperative of mustering the university football team. Because Stanford had just been founded in 1891, the editors of the *Daily Palo Alto* observed in 1894, and because "few of our students enter from preparatory schools where football is played," it is all the more "necessary to find and develop our own material. Men of the right physique, men who may never have seen a scrimmage, must be interested in the game and got into training" (fig. 3.4). The opening issue of the *Daily Palo Alto*—first page, second paragraph—rallied Stanford men to the cause of football. "No heavy athletic assessments are made here as there are in other colleges," the editors said encouragingly in September 1892, so "[e]very man who has in him one spark of college patriotism" should consider playing. Two months later, the student newspaper had grown a bit more discriminating, charging that "[e]very large, muscular man should begin training at once" and adding that "we see plenty of such men in the quadrangle"; but it invoked the same masculine duty to alma mater: "A man's loyalty to his college should be sufficient to induce him to daily hard work." The following fall, in September, not nearly enough men had turned out for practice. "This state of affairs must not be allowed to last," the paper exhorted. The editors then took an extra step and claimed that "Everyone of whatever class, is duty bound to investigate the athletic possibilities of every man in the University and to do his best to see that scores of men appear in the field daily."[71] According to the *Daily Palo Alto*, every Stanford student could be held responsible to team and school.

By early October, after the practice games had selected twenty-five men or so as candidates for the team, training began in earnest. The regimen included weight lifting in Encina gymnasium, long-distance running, and daily scrimmaging. The *Sequoia* boasted that "the circumstances here are the best of any institution in the United States for good systematic training. With the men altogether in one hall," the editors continued, "with an able physical director, with a climate which permits outdoor exercise the year round, with the flower of the youth of the Pacific Slope to pick from, all that is needed to produce the best athletic teams in the United States is the will to take advantage of the opportunity." It was during the midfall training period that the football players split apart from the rest of the Stanford student body. This separation happened socially, as the students started looking to them to represent the university as a whole—"MEN FROM WHOM WE EXPECT GREAT THINGS," read a *Daily Palo Alto* headline in fall of 1893. The players' liminality also had a physical, "material" dimension. "Three months of it [playing football] can easily add twenty pounds to a man's physique," a *Sequoia* off-season editorial claimed in 1892. (This unabashed recruiting effort also maintained that football could add "10 percent to his examination marks and 50 percent to his manly self-respect and ability to use his common sense.")[72] And as Walter Camp and Lorin Deland contended in their book *Football* (1896), it must be kept "constantly in mind the great difference in strength and endurance between a person undergoing a course of football train-ing and one of the same size, age, and weight who is not accustomed to vigorous exercise." So certain of this difference, the authors quantified it "by the ratio of 3 ½ to 1."[73] How they came by this number is unknown, but the point remains: the per-ception grew that, while in training, the football players quite literally transcended the student body.

Adding dramatically to the social and physical separation from the rest of the Stanford students was the football players' formal pledge in October to stay in training. "I as a candidate for the Leland Stanford Junior University football team," the pledge read, "do hereby promise to conform to the following training rules: 1) to abstain absolutely from the use of all alcoholic drinks and tobacco; 2) to retire regularly no later than 10:30; 3) not to rise before 6 a.m.; 4) to abstain from eating between meals; and 5) to obey implicitly and regularly the call of coach, captain, or manager for cross-country running, gymnasium practice, and field practice."[74] After the players signed this promise, the *Daily Palo Alto* published it in full, fol-lowed by each man's name. The commitment was made publicly. And while the pledge's particulars may not seem so onerous (how difficult could it have been not to get up before six in the morning?), the symbolism couldn't have been stronger in denoting sacrifice for the university.

With even greater symbolic effect, Walter Camp's fall visits to Stanford and his coaching of the team in the Big Games of 1892, 1894, and 1895 boosted the young football program immeasurably. "The father of football," as the *Daily Palo Alto* referred to Camp, bestowed a level of legitimacy not only to Stanford's team but to the sport on the Pacific Coast overall. "The annual intercollegiate contest between Berkeley and Stanford will become a permanent fixture," the student newspaper said in anticipation of Camp's first visit, "and before long so much interest will be centered on the outcome of this game, that it will be eagerly awaited . . . with a zeal strongly akin to that manifested in the Harvard-Yale-Princeton contests." At Stanford, Camp's arrival, approximately a month before the Big Game, focused the university's energy and attention toward beating California—"Enthusiasm is going up to a white heat," the *Daily Palo Alto* reported in November 1892.[75] As Camp inspired the team to more rigorous training and scrimmages, he also imparted technical expertise at a time when Stanford men still needed to learn the game. During the first months of football at Stanford, in preparation for the first game against California in March 1892, the players taught themselves the sport through Camp's book *American Football* (1891)—one team member supposedly read it five times, while taking thorough notes.[76] Publicly, Camp occasionally criticized Stanford's play, especially the team's high tackling "at the heads and shoulders"; "the second eleven in any of the big colleges in the east would run through such tackling."[77] But Camp largely understood his role to be one of quiet behind-the-scenes instruction and support. Although the record in the three Big Games that Camp coached was modest (Stanford won once and tied twice), merely his presence in Palo Alto gave Stanford the recognition that it so desired.

With Camp (or another Yale man) on campus as visiting coach, and the Big Game a month away, the Stanford student body started preparing more fervently for Thanksgiving Day. Hundreds of cardinal flags needed ordering; cheers had to be composed, learned, and practiced with the band; travel plans, hotel reservations, and postgame entertainment had to be arranged. Central to this preparation was the heightened public scrutiny of the team during its daily intrasquad scrimmages. The *Daily Palo Alto* led the way with an array of criticism: "lack of vim and vigor"; too much talking back to the captain; too little "team play"; the need for "quick starting" off the line of scrimmage; "too much time is taken up before the ball is passed"; no "appreciation of the value of sleep."[78] As with Camp, the newspaper editors concentrated on tackling. "Aspirants for the football team must—simply must—learn the philosophy of low tackling," the *Daily Palo Alto* implored in 1892; "the closer a man is to the ground the more force he can bring to bear in the direction of the enemy's goal"; "shun the high tackle, for as long as you tackle high, remember you are no football player." This pre–Big Game commentary involved greater authority over the team. "Every muscle of [each player's] body should be placed in the best possible condition," the *Sequoia* stressed before the March 1892 game against Berkeley. And in the fall of that same year, after Camp had arrived for the first time, the *Daily Palo Alto* pointed out that "all the best coaches in the country will count for nothing unless the players by their constant practice, training and unity in action demonstrate their determination to win. . . . Remember," the editors said heavily, "only a few weeks intervene between now and the great contest of the year."[79] The players served not themselves but the university.

With this assumption came a distinct readiness on the part of the student commentators for the players to incur physical hardship and danger for the sake of Stanford. Non-football-playing students applauded the practice games that exhibited the most "recklessness," a trait "characteristic of football." While downplaying sacrifice—a *Sequoia* editorial from 1893 casually spoke of how "scarcely a game [is] played that some player is not placed hors du combat"—this commentary encouraged risk taking. "The playing in the practice games has been fast and furious," the *Sequoia* enthused, "and characterized by a roughness which a year ago would hardly have been conceived. Ample padding, shin-guards, and nose protectors have made this possible."[80] In an extraordinary *Sequoia* article, published a week before the fall 1892 Big Game, the unnamed author ridiculed the "football player" for being "sad and dejected" after a hypothetical loss to Berkeley. Apparently, the writer first intended to put the player in his place: "The professor and he have had a little misunderstanding as to what constitutes university work. The university no longer smiles upon him as it did before he played the deciding game. He no longer eats at the inviting training table where the morsels used to give him muscle. He must return, take off his royal football clothes and take a back seat." Next came shame: "He has caused his university much chagrin. He deserves to be scowled at. He should have played better football. Let him droop his head in shame." And finally the author demonstrated an exaggerated callousness toward the injuries stemming from college football:

> Skin will soon grow over his nose and face again. His black eye will turn green and then he can see as well as ever. His hair-part and Samsonian locks meet with a sad, sad fate. He needs not limp around with a broken leg for the broken leg did not win glory for the university. If he has such good lungs what did he get the wind knocked out of him for, and call forth a useless scream from the ladies. His deeds be upon his head. He has failed. Let students steer clear of him.[81]

This article is strange and anomalous in its negative sarcastic tone and yet it shows the purpose of much of the student writing on football. The closer Stanford got to the Big Game, the more the student body monitored the team, infusing (by whatever means necessary) a sense of duty and sacrifice along the way.

Not only the football players owed a duty to Stanford. In readying the university for the Big Game, student leaders stressed the importance of fan support. "Every student who has the college interest at heart should turn out at practice games each evening now as regularly as do the players themselves," the *Daily Palo Alto* urged; "nothing so encourages a player, new or old, as the presence of a large number of college mates watching the practice." Students found roughly similar pressure placed on them as on the players: "Without any hesitation, it can be said that the man who shirks his duty on the bleachers ought to be put in the class with the man who shirks his duty on the field." As an ultimate type of pressure, the *Daily Palo Alto* reminded its readers in 1894 that "at Princeton, Harvard, and Yale systematic cheering is considered as an equal factor with the team in winning a game, and consequently great attention is paid to the proper training of students in the matter of cheering at the right time." The student publications editors and organizers paid great attention to the content of the cheers, their timing, and delivery. "Our manner of giving the yell was, and is yet, ineffective in two ways," the *Sequoia* criticized in 1893: "shrill tones are used instead of deep chest tones, and only small groups yell in unison." The belief arose that fans had a direct connection to the play of the game and that they could thereby influence the Stanford eleven by the volume and quality of their cheers. "No man has a right to wear the cardinal who is too dignified to give the yell," as the *Sequoia* put it in 1897, "and the student who does not give it stronger if we are being forced back than he did when we were working towards a touchdown lacks the Stanford spirit."[82]

In conjunction with increasing support at the practice games, students started holding rallies in Encina gymnasium and the college chapel during which they would practice songs and yells and generally prepare themselves for the game against Berkeley. A week or two before the Big Game, students capped off these rallies with a larger university-wide "mass meeting." In the 1895 meeting, for instance, the student body listened to short speeches by President Jordan, Coach Camp, several faculty members, the student body president, the team captain, and a few other players. It culminated in spontaneous cheering and the serpentine dance in which male nonplayer students formed a long chain and wove through the crowd to the sound of raucous student singing.[83] A clear purpose of these large rallies was to heighten Stanford spirit by establishing a close emotional connection between the students and the team and to emphasize that both would determine the outcome of the game. "With the enthusiasm of the side lines," the team captain said in 1895, "we do not see how we should not beat Berkeley." But, of course, these large rallies featured the team. With the players standing apart from the rest of the student body, the mass meeting dramatized the team's responsibility in the game ahead. Through their cheering and dancing, the students paid tribute to the team—they meant to inspire it to greater effort. "We have come to look upon the rally as a telling force in the preparation of our players," a *Sequoia* editor wrote in

1894, "and to believe that the psychological influence we exert upon the players, by our reception of them as they enter the assembly, and by our enthusiasm in the yells and serpentine will materially aid our heroes of the pig skin in their struggles against the Blue and Gold."[84] Indeed, in keeping with this insight, the mass meeting should be seen as a key component in the ritualistic transformation of the players into surrogates for the university, figures expected to sacrifice themselves for the greater good of Stanford's glory.

In 1894 Camp started a Big Game tradition that ritualistically separated the players from the Stanford student body: a week before the contest he took the team to a health resort in the coastal mountain foothills where they could practice and rest in solitude. A certain environmental determinism can be detected in the reasoning behind the retreat. "While our men are getting the benefit of exhilarating mountain breezes and rustic scenery," the *Daily Palo Alto* commented, "the Berkeley footballers are filling their lungs with that smoky slop which in San Francisco they call 'the air.'" The paper added that "already the fellows have lost all signs of logginess, and are in the finest of spirits and condition."[85] The time in the mountains was also rich with symbolic meaning. Anthropologists have noted that rites of passage include detachment from the profane activity of everyday life; separation is meant to avoid "pollution"—"an impure ritual state," as William Arens writes—"as the result of contact with contaminating acts or situations."[86] The mundane responsibilities of course work and attending lectures, routine social relations with other Stanford students, including the potential sexual distraction by the women—these were the things that Camp wanted his team to be free of before the game. In 1894 he insisted that students keep from attending practices in the hills.[87] After some students showed up anyway, Camp moved the retreat the following year to a site one mile farther up into the mountains. The clear intent was for the team to no longer be seen until its entrance on the football field in San Francisco on Thanksgiving Day.

Back at "the farm," Stanford students made final preparations for the game, including distribution of cardinal flags. The days leading up to the Big Game brought great attention to Stanford's color—after the team itself, the most symbolic manifestation of the university. "Cardinal, we believe, is the most beautiful shade of red," the *Daily Palo Alto* stated proudly just before the 1892 Big Game. Between crimson and scarlet, it "is a strong, striking beautiful color," the paper continued: "Too much cannot be said to impress upon Stanford supporters the effect of a great, blazing mass of bright, unvarying cardinal in flags, banners, ribbons, and whatever way the color can be displayed at the game."[88] Each year, in the last issue before the game, the student newspaper profiled the starting eleven for Stanford. In tribute to the university's "material," this information included the results of the final team weigh in at Encina gymnasium, where each player "was stripped" in front of the others, as the paper described, and placed on the scale. The *Daily Palo Alto* reported both the individual and aggregate results. In 1892, for instance, "the combined weight is 2465 lbs. And the average weight is 164 ½ lbs."[89] Finally, the paper also posted on its front page a tribute to the team before the game. "OFF FOR THE BATTLE FIELD," the headline read in 1893. "The finest football eleven that Stanford has ever had will leave for the city today on the flyer, there to take a well earned rest before the mighty struggle on Thanksgiving."[90]

Stanford's fixation on the Big Game is demonstrated by the fact that Thanksgiving lost virtually all meaning for the students except as a sacred occasion for establishing the university's prominence on the football field. "This Thanksgiving day is the most important of the year to us of Stanford," a *Sequoia* editorial stated in 1897: "We are thankful to be alive and able to get to the game and we do not care what else happens so long as the team wins."[91] Even after the game, the students paid little attention to the older Thanksgiving traditions of visiting family and turkey dinner; in the evening, the students attended a vaudeville show at a downtown San Francisco theater. With the Thanksgiving football tradition having started in the East, Stanford and Berkeley developed this exceptional American mix of sport and holiday with a fervor that bordered on the religious.[92] As a bizarre illustration, consider the front cover of the *Sequoia*'s 1895 Thanksgiving issue (fig. 3.5). With football in arm and radiance beaming from his youthful head, the liminal Stanford player emits an aura of the sacred. As he is led out to the field by two fully plumaged cock turkeys, a distinct parallel can be drawn between the birds and the football player. Both can be seen as a sacrament of the Thanksgiving Day Big Game. And, given his gladiatorial pose and the martial context of college football overall, the player appears to be the subject of physical sacrifice to the game. Players' risk of serious injury came to mean very little to the Stanford student body. Or, conversely, it meant everything. The very possibility of blood and broken bones added to the dramatic weight of the event. Sacrifice underlined the importance of that for which the teams played or fought.

Focus on the 1896 Big Game further demonstrates the fetishistic devotion to Stanford football. "The University has opened," the *Daily Palo Alto* reported in early September, "and football is, as usual, the all absorbing topic around the campus"; prospects looked especially good: "Never before have we had so many strong, well-built men from whom to choose our eleven"; and as a boon to this year's "material," the newspaper added, "the freshman class has quite a number of large husky-looking men who are likely to amount to something on the football field." Adding to the optimism over the 1896 season was the September arrival of the new coach, recent Yale graduate and former football team captain Harry Cross.

Handpicked as Camp's successor, Cross's presence on campus "put new life into football matters," the *Daily Palo Alto* reported. The first day he appeared at practice, the paper noted that "the players went at things with a vim and dash" that had yet to be seen that season.[93] As early as the end of September, large numbers of students were gathering each night to watch the scrimmages.

As in other years, the approach of the 1896 Big Game saw the football players grow closer together, and apart from the student body. By late October, all the players had signed the five-point training pledge. And come November the university directed all its hopes, aspirations, and scrutiny toward the football team. The *Daily Palo Alto* stressed "the last two weeks of work before the big game—weeks that in the past have counted so much for Stanford in putting the finishing touches on the team. From now on," the paper urged, "every effort will be directed towards bringing the men to such form that every individual movement shall have its effect in strengthening the team as a whole, until the eleven men shall lose their identity as individuals and each shall become but a part of a larger whole." Nine days before the Big Game the student body held a rally for the team in the university chapel. With attendance "required" by the student newspaper, the specific purpose of the meeting was "to 'send off' the football men" before their retreat to the foothills. After "lusty 'rooters' bellowed for the team in a way that exceeded all previous records," Coach Harry Cross addressed the students, calling for full support of the team. "At Yale," Cross said, "the team knows all year that the student body is behind it. Tomorrow when the men leave," he directed, trying to develop as close a bond as possible, "each one of you wants to go to every man who is a friend or even an acquaintance and tell him that you believe in him and that you are with him."[94] The next morning the team left for Congress Springs, a mountain resort even farther from Palo Alto than the retreat the year before.

While receiving word from Congress Springs that "the air is clean and bracing . . . and the place is eminently fitted for bringing athletes into perfect condition," the Stanford students readied themselves for the Big Game by practicing songs and yells and holding one last rally before leaving for San Francisco. As the university band practiced daily, students printed and distributed songbooks. Two days before the game students read in the *Daily Palo Alto* that "the team will aggregate in weight 1918 pounds, an average of 174 lbs."[95] And the following day the students held their rally in Encina auditorium after realizing that the chapel would be too small for the crowd. The rally began with the cardinal-clad students trying out the college yell in a new shorter cadence, "Rah, rah, rah, Stanford!," and then practicing, with the band's accompaniment, the Civil War songs "When Johnnie Comes Marching Home," "Marching through Georgia," and other football fight songs. The rally reached a fevered pitch after the band struck up "The Honeymoon

March" and the men took the Indian clubs off the gymnasium walls and marched through the auditorium yelling and shouting and keeping time with the music by striking the floor with their sticks. A former football candidate who had been in Congress Springs then spoke briefly. After reporting that team is "in splendid form," he was picked up and carried through the crowd of students.[96]

The next morning a fifteen-car train adorned with cardinal banners and wreaths left Palo Alto at 8:30 to take the Stanford fans to San Francisco for the Big Game. After attending a short musical reception given by Stanford's band in the lobby of the city's Palace Hotel, the students made their way to Central Park, which by 1:30 was filled with, in the words of a *San Francisco Examiner* reporter, "a jam of humanity." To the reporter's eye, the Stanford fans in the north section of the bleachers made up a "solid block of crimson." Then came "the boom of drum and blare of brass" announcing Stanford's band. "[H]eaded by two banner-bearers and a drum major ablaze with color," the forty-man band wore cardinal gowns and mortar boards and played a "Stanford air" while marching to its designated section in the stands. "Their entrance was startling, bright and illuminative," the *Examiner* reporter wrote. With California's fans and band also in place, twelve thousand people awaited the two teams. "At 2:30," the reporter continued, "the braying of the rival bands was silenced by a roar of voices. From under the side line fence far down the field the figure of first one and then another and another shocky-haired, cardinal-clad athlete bobbed into view." The *San Francisco Chronicle* reporter described the same scene: "presently came a quick movement over there, a scattering of the crowd, a flash of crimson sweaters and the joy and pride of Stanford were out on the field in a bunch. All the north side bleachers were on fire in a moment," he continued, "and for two or three minutes they alternatively yelled and cheered at the men who were about to battle for their colors." The California team generated a similar response from the Berkeley section of the stands and, then, the play began.[97]

Within five years of the university's founding, Stanford had created a devotion to its football team perhaps unsurpassed by any other school in the country. This effort had a purpose: as a new institution, Stanford considered football a surefire way to establish its prestige among elite private universities and especially with the University of California across San Francisco Bay; college football's expansive cultural space and exaggerated masculine form provided a unique means for demonstrating Stanford's corporate integrity, student loyalty, and manly toughness of character. Accordingly, Stanford sought and built unusually strong and large men for the football field. ("STANFORD'S SUPERIOR WEIGHT AND STRENGTH DEFEATED BERKELEY," read an *Examiner* headline after the 1896 Big Game.)[98] Stanford's football players can be seen, following Victor Turner, as "liminal subjects," symbolically laden figures whose ritualistic separation from the other students added dramatic effect to their performance in competition. The football team's hypermasculinity also tended to subordinate the rest of Stanford's student body into a gendered mass of supportive fans. While subordinate to the team, nonplaying Stanford students, like other college fans, nevertheless shaped the game through their response to the play on the field. It is to this topic that we now turn. Via Clifford Geertz's methodology of reading a sporting event as a cultural text, we piece together the historical meaning of the 1896 Big Game as well as that of late nineteenth-century college football overall.

Clifford Geertz at the Big Game: "Thick Description" of Football as the Cultural Equivalent of War

For more than thirty years now, historians have found Clifford Geertz's work enormously practical for its elegant explication of culture and for its careful commitment to the interpretive role of the social scientist.[99] Ethnography, for Geertz, first involves attention to the "flow of social discourse"—the enactment of symbolic behavior—and then the attempt to "rescue the 'said' of such discourse from its perishing occasions and fix it in perusable terms." Most valuable to historians, Geertz has provided strategies for isolating the *conceptual content* of culture. Central to this project, and so important to cultural and intellectual historians in particular, has been his focus on the *meaning* of human action—the discursive, cognitive, and emotional increments through which "individuals define their world, express their feelings and make their judgments."[100] In terms of the cultural history of college football and its meaning, Geertz points to the substantive interplay between the action on the field and the fans' ideational response and consequent contribution back to both the game before them and to the culture surrounding the sport at large. Through this methodology, late nineteenth-century college football's obsessive violence and martial metaphor can be seen as a historically specific gloss on the game rather than a benign expression of an inalterable masculine drive toward aggression and war.

Geertz is useful in working through a long-standing sociobiological issue in sports scholarship: has violent sport such as college football served as a type of catharsis or safety valve for innate masculine aggression, diverting it from ultimate expression in war; or, as the so-called cultural pattern theory holds, has football overlapped with martial values, stirring and even creating added interest in war? Although he didn't directly address this question, Geertz's investment in culture and its power in substantiating human emotions and actions does support the view that aggression is built up through football. Geertz centered his practice of cultural anthropology on a textual model of edification. A Balinese cockfight, for instance, along with other cultural performances, should be understood as popular art forms, "generat[ing] and regenerat[ing] the very subjectivity they pretend only to display. Quartets, still lifes, and cockfights are not merely reflections of a pre-existing sensibility analogically represented," Geertz continued; "they are positive agents in the creation and maintenance of such a sensibility."[101] This emphasis on the edificatory agency of culture doesn't necessarily preclude the existence of an earlier biological origin of aggressive feelings (although, as I understand him, Geertz did not acknowledge a noncultural source of emotion). One could tenta-tively accept the catharsis theory's assumption and evolutionary psychology's argu-ment that male aggression is biologically rooted while still believing that football strengthens rather than dissipates that source of pugnacious emotion through its increasingly attractive and ritualized cultural appeals.

Late nineteenth-century college football, in other words, amounted to a cultural equivalent of war. It didn't serve as a substitute for war, as William James used the term "equivalent." Rather, football dramatized war. It conditioned and excited Americans toward war's constituent parts of willful violence and physical sacrifice. Geertz's approach to culture as text guides the historian toward interpreting exactly how this close association between sport and war came to be.

"Thick Description: Toward an Interpretive Theory of Culture" (1973) is one of Geertz's two essays that, when brought together, provide a most effective bridge be-tween anthropology and history. "Thick Description" features Geertz's best known definition of culture: "Believing with Max Weber that man is an animal suspended in webs of significance he himself has spun, I take culture to be those webs, and the analysis of it to be therefore not an experimental science in search of law but an interpretive one in search of meaning." In appropriating this understanding of cul-ture as humanly woven "webs of significance," the historian comes to the meaning of a symbolic act by "uncover[ing] the conceptual structures" that inform it. For Geertz, culture is not so much "a power, something to which social events, behav-iors, institutions, or processes can be causally attributed; it is a context, something within which they can be intelligibly—that is, thickly—described." Thick descrip-tion involves "sorting out the structures of signification," charting the deep layers of meaning.[102] It is necessarily a historical process because the strata of meaning and signification emerge from the past and transcend the cultural text at hand, running to such broad and basic concerns as what assumptions, values, and tenets have held the subjects' world together. As historian Ronald Walters has described, "The achievement of thick description comes when a close reading of particular bits of human behavior—sheep theft, cockfighting, feasts, bazaars—unmasks the nature of a larger society and culture."[103] To read a late nineteenth-century college football game closely is to discover just how emotionally attracted many Americans were to the idea of war, with the romantic memory of the Civil War generating an especially compelling context for taking in the violent and sacrificial play on the field. The Civil War provided key referential strands of meaning for college football; it bestowed historical detail to the overarching metaphor of sport as battle.

Geertz's essay "Deep Play: Notes on the Balinese Cockfight"(1973) offers the cultural historian more specific ethnographic strategies, including the distinct idea of interpreting a sporting event as a literary text.[104] The reason for this analytical move is that both sport and literature are "imaginative works," Geertz wrote, created not just for play or diversion but as meta-commentary on the subjects' own existence. "An image, fiction, a model, a metaphor, the cockfight is a means of expression; its function is neither to assuage social passions nor to heighten them . . . but, in a medium of feathers, blood, crowds, and money, to display them." For Geertz, a sporting contest is an unusually complex text, one that brings out a depth of meaning in a contained space and period of time. He called such a happening a "paradigmatic human event": an experience that speaks less to what actually "happens than the kind of thing that would happen if, as is not the case, life were art and could be as freely shaped by styles of feeling as *Macbeth* and *David Copperfield* are." He continued: "Enacted and re-enacted, so far without end, the cockfight enables the Balinese, as, read and reread, *Macbeth* enables us, to see a dimension of his own subjectivity."[105] So too with late nineteenth-century college football. An individual contest, like the Stanford-Berkeley Big Game, spoke volumes about the emotional composition of the game's fans and players, their corporately organized drive toward competition, and their impassioned embrace of violence.

One method of analyzing a sporting event as a piece of literature is, as Geertz described, to "read over the shoulders" of those to whom the text belongs. This step requires some understanding of the text's "sustained symbolic structures" of action—that is, attention to *how* the particular text speaks to its audience.[106] Reading a football game as a literary text could be understood in a literal structuralist sense. To the person in the stands, the four corners of the field resemble the page of a book; out-of-bounds lines contain the play, as do a set of rules that are enforced by referees through the assessment of penalties. Football also organizes itself temporally. A clock determines the length of the contest, and the action of the game is divided into plays, each with a distinct beginning and end. It could be said that these parameters of the game work like rules of grammar, making the experience of football recognizable and understandable for the spectator through the repetition and ritual of play. And, as the literary historian Michael Oriard has pointed out, to use Geertz's model of the literary text "for football actually confirms a sense of the game expressed" by fans and the press at least as far back as the early twentieth century. For instance, in the book *Football and How to Watch It* (1922), the sportswriter Heywood Broun noted "the striking resemblance" between a football game and popular literature. "To be sure," Broun wrote, "every football play is in a sense a short narrative. First come the signals of the quarterback. That is the preliminary exposition. Then the plot thickens, action becomes intense and a climax is reached whereby the mood of tragedy or comedy is established."[107] The implication is that by visualizing the play on the field, by trying to imagine what a fan saw and experienced from the stands, the cultural historian can piece together the story of the game and then construe how its narrative structure (much like the generic hunting-and-killing literature discussed in the preceding chapter) led to such master meanings as victory and defeat and revelry in the struggle, sacrifice, pain, and glory of competition.

To interpret a sporting event as a literary text, Geertz wrote, "is to bring out a feature of it that treating it as a rite or pastime, the two most obvious alternatives, would tend to obscure: its use of emotions for cognitive ends."[108] This crucial insight leads to a final methodological step: in determining what meaning the fans derived from football, shift focus from the play on the field to the fans' emotive responses, which in turn can be read as texts that reveal the conceptual content of the game. For the Big Game of 1896, San Francisco newspaper accounts provide invaluable documentation of audience behavior, including complete text of the fans' elaborate cheers supporting their teams. The Stanford cheers reveal the students' deep emotional investment in the team, as well as the added belligerent meanings they overlaid on to the sport. Many took cheering very seriously. "Cheering is the life of the team," a *Daily Palo Alto* editorial stated in 1892; "they [the players] cannot play ball without it and that which it expresses, the enthusiasm and the psychic, moral support of the university. We are to play this game and if we do our duty there are eleven men who will take that ball over for a touchdown."[109] Indeed, football songs and cheers demonstrate just how much the fans influenced the character of the sport, especially at this critical point in its evolution.

In working from newspaper accounts of the 1896 Stanford-Berkeley game, the first and most awe-inspiring fact of the event was its sheer scale, energy, and spectacle. "12,000 people watching every move of two groups of athletes hurling themselves one against the other," the *San Francisco Examiner* reporter wrote; "a great, huge patch of flaring, flaunting cardinal, waving masses of yellow and dull blue; noise from all sides and at all times marked the opening of the sixth intercollegiate football game between the University of California and the Leland Stanford University." The game itself proved to be very one-sided. "We were beaten, and beaten fairly," said A. W. Ransome, captain of the California squad: "The trouble was that our line was too weak and the lads from Palo Alto having once found that they could break through, tossed all other tactics to the winds." With the outcome of the game decided early on, once the umpire yelled "time," the Stanford fans exploded in celebration. The *Examiner* reporter continued writing in sense impression: "A howling, marching crowd of cardinal-bedecked students, headed by sixty crimson-gowned and capped musicians, wildly enthusiastic Stanford men carrying high on shoulder their laurel-crowned heroes of the football arena, a blast of tin horns heard loud above the blare of instruments of reed and brass, a field overrun with men old and young excited almost to frenzy, a drooping of banners of blue and gold under the crush of crimson . . . "The scene ended with a fistfight breaking out between half a dozen California and Stanford men. Apparently the Stanford fans had torn down and started parading with the large canvas scoreboard declaring their team's 20–0 victory. The Berkeley men took the canvas from them and ripped it in shreds. The ensuing fight betrayed the competitive violence underlying the color and pageantry of the day.[110]

The brutality of the play and the fans' interest in it certainly comes out in the newspaper coverage of the game. The Stanford and Berkeley teams played a clean game, which nevertheless included a number of injuries or "accidents," as the *San Francisco Chronicle* called them. In the second half, for instance, Stanford's halfback Searight was tackled "so hard," as the *Chronicle* reporter noted, "that his scalp was cut for three inches across the top of the head, but with blood streaming down his face he played it out and played it well." Earlier, Berkeley's quarterback Kennedy broke his nose. A California song leader shouted to his rooters, "Say fellers, poor old Kennedy's nose is broke." A coed sympathizer responded, "Let's give him three cheers with the yell at the end." They did so "with a will," the *Chronicle* reporter documented: "'Give him another rally,' yelled Gooding, as Kennedy was led off the field. They screamed themselves hoarse." Interestingly, when Haskell ran out to replace Kennedy, Berkeley fans made several remarks about the substitute being a "daisy" and about whether he could do any damage to the other team. This virility taunting could be seen to be quite functional here, serving as a type of challenge to Haskell to play his hardest. Indeed, he was reported to have played with exceptional aggression.[111]

A sampling of the Big Game cheers and songs underline the fighting spirit of the day. Both the Stanford and Berkeley student bodies formed football song committees that published and circulated the new selections of 1896. Berkeley's prize football song of that year first paid tribute to the game being played on Thanksgiving Day:

> The turkey gobbler struts abroad
> In festival array,

But lies full low upon the board
> When comes Thanksgiving Day,
And though a red and fussy force
> May puff as turkeys do,
We'll eat their cardinal Cranberry-sauce
> And gobble Stanford too![112]

By far the most memorable utterance of the day was Stanford's Axe cheer. Written by freshman Will Irwin, and included in the student songbook, the cheer would be transformed in a few years into a material symbol of the Stanford-California rivalry and the aggression underlying it. In verse form, the Axe tradition was first sounded in the second half of the 1896 Big Game after a fifteen-yard gain by Stanford's quarterback. In seemingly spontaneous unison, according to the *Chronicle* reporter, the Stanford section rang out with

Give 'em the Axe, the Axe, the Axe,
Give 'em the Axe, the Axe, the Axe,
Give 'em the Axe,
Give 'em the Axe,
Give 'em the Axe—
> Where?
Right in the neck, the neck, the neck,
Right in the neck, the neck, the neck,
Right in the neck,
Right in the neck,
Right in the neck—
There.[113]

Vivid in its imagery, and unambiguous in its meaning, the Axe cheer became the mainstay of Stanford cheers for football games against Berkeley.

The Axe tradition evolved considerably in the spring of 1899 when Stanford students decided to vivify the cheer by producing an actual axe for games against Berkeley. The occasion for this development was an unusually intense baseball series against California. Between the first and second games, students located a lumberman's broadaxe shaped like a tomahawk and proceeded to paint a large Stanford "S" in cardinal red on its fifteen-inch blade. The night before the second game students held a pep rally, heretofore unprecedented for baseball, during which the new axe was carried out and sharpened on a grindstone amid bursts of wild applause. Next came a blue and gold effigy of a California man. A student laid its head on a block and chopped if off to the accompaniment of the Axe cheer. After brief speeches by coaches and players an Indian war dance ended the rally. The intense and violent symbolism of the Axe tradition increased dramatically during that second baseball game in San Francisco when, after Stanford students brought the totem to the contest and brandished it in front of the California stands, several Berkeley men overpowered the Stanford student carrying the axe out of the park after the game. Several fights and a wild chase through the streets of San Francisco ensued, until California finally won the battle and carried the prize axe on a ferry across the Bay and to the Berkeley campus. Over the next few decades Stanford students made a number of unsuccessful raids on the California campus to recover the axe (it had been hidden in a bank vault). They finally succeeded in 1930, though, and eventually, similar to other football rivalries throughout the country, the winner of the Big Game took possession of the axe for the following year.[114]

Together the original axe cheer and the materialization of it as a totem to college supremacy offer yet another window into the violent martial meaning emanating from the Stanford-California Big Game rivalry and turn-of-the-twentieth-century college football overall. "Every people loves its own form of violence," commented Geertz. And if "the cockfight is the Balinese reflection on theirs: on its look, its uses, its force, its fascination," so too with football and American violence. Compared to the Balinese cockfight, which expresses group status conflict through individuated nonhuman competition—as Geertz described, "a wing-beating, head-thrusting, leg-kicking explosion of animal fury"—American football kept aggression in its original human form, elevating it to a large corporate scale that quite obviously mimicked and otherwise referenced war.[115] In the late nineteenth and early twentieth centuries these references were oftentimes made to the material culture and romantic memory of the Civil War. Not so much at Stanford though. Students did sing "When Johnnie Comes Marching Home" at the rally before the 1896 Big Game. But, for the most part, because of the Pacific Coast's distance from the main theaters of the Civil War, Stanford football's martial metaphors emerged either generically or in rough allusion to the Indian wars. Indeed, the Axe tradition can be interpreted within this historical context. In gradually taking on the nickname "Indians" at the turn of the century (it became official in 1930 and remained so until 1972) and in adopting axe chopping as a dominant symbol of violence against Berkeley, not to mention the baseball rally's enactment of cutting off the head of the blue and gold California effigy (the colors of federal troops in the postbellum Indian wars), Stanford embraced the perceived savagery of Native American warriors to aggrandize its own hypermasculine affectations.[116]

The overlap between U.S. football and war has been widely recognized. (The comedian George Carlin's 1970s comparison of football to baseball and the words and emotions suffusing the two sports is still one of the most trenchant summaries of football's martial character: "baseball is played . . . in a park. . . . Football is played on a gridiron, in a stadium, sometimes called Soldier Field or War Memorial Stadium." "[I]n baseball the object is to go home," whereas "in football the object is for the quarterback, otherwise known as the field general, to be on target with his aerial assault, riddling the defense by hitting his receivers with deadly accuracy in spite of the blitz, even if he has to use the shotgun. With short bullet passes and long bombs, he marches his troops to enemy territory, balancing this aerial assault with a sustained ground attack that punches holes in the forward wall of the enemy's defensive line." During a baseball game fans enjoy "a kind of picnic feeling," whereas "in football, during the game in the stands, you can be sure that at least twenty-seven times you were perfectly capable of taking the life of a fellow human being.")[117] The relationship between war and football can be detailed further than overlap or conflation though. The two have informed each other in different ways. The following chapter discusses how sport has contributed competitive athletic standards of performance for U.S. soldiers since the late nineteenth century. Here the focus is on what war has given to football—namely a certain moral and cultural readiness for sacrifice and violence. To thickly describe turn-of-the-century college football, then, is to turn toward the historically deep layers of martial meaning in the game.

A primary aspect of war in American football was the understanding of the sport as a less deadly expression of preexistently natural biological impulses toward combat.[118] The catharsis theory of football did not originate in mid-twentieth-century sports psychology or sociology but in turn-of-the-century commentary on and general appreciation for the new game. One of the most highbrow accounts of catharsis in football came in the Harvard philosopher George Santayana's 1894 essay "Philosophy on the Bleachers." A Harvard football fan, Santayana found the beginnings of sport as release for "pent-up energy" in antiquity: "It was not the utility of athletics for war that supported the Greek games; on the contrary, the games arose from the comparative freedom from war, and the consequent liberation of martial energy from the stimulus of necessity, and the expression of it in beautiful and spectacular forms." Santayana did not look to sport as just a functional safety valve though. "The relation of athletics to war is intimate," Santayana analogized, "like that of drama to life"; and he saw football as an unusually "well-conceived contest," portraying "all the primitive virtues and fundamental gifts of man."[119] In a more practical vein, football's greatest publicist, Walter Camp, did speak explicitly of the sport as a "safety valve" for "superabundant vitality"—it provides a "new systematic outlet for the animal spirits in young men." In a December 1892 talk to Stanford's student body, he explained in detail how "barbarism" among Yale men before the Civil War—for example, hazing, vandalism, and routine fighting with New Haven's firemen—had gone down dramatically since football drained off their "surplus energy."[120]

Catharsis theory applied to spectators as well as to players. At Stanford, Camp spoke of an innate human attraction to violence: "We may not be like the man who 'If two dogs beneath his window fight, He'll close his Bible to enjoy the sight,' but we all admire contests which call into play these qualities."[121] The most developed discussion "of the psychological laws of identification and catharsis" and how one "benefit[s] mentally, physically, and morally by spectator participation in his favorite sport" is the psychologist's A. A. Brill's 1929 *North American Review* essay "The Why of the Fan." Brill drew from Freudian drive theory in substantiating the masculine need to "absent himself" from "his house" and "wife" and, through watching football, boxing, or baseball, "let off the accumulated steam of ancient instinct." The linchpin of Brill's championing of spectator sports is the assumption that modern men still have within them "what psychoanalysis calls 'the aggressive component.'" He reasoned from an evolutionary biosocial perspective: "The life of man in America or in any of the industrialized countries today, laboring on the farm, in the factory, in the office, is not the natural life of man. He is still an animal formed for battle and conquest, for blows and strokes and swiftness, for triumph and applause." Given man's war-making nature, according to catharsis theory, it is surprising that Brill thought that spectatorship would satisfy that "primary instinct." He was quite clear on this point though: "Vigorous physical activity is by no means an invariably sound prescription for the man whose normal occupation is sedentary or inactive, and indeed it may be distinctly dangerous." Brill's highly emblematic essay prescribes another version of the brute in a suit: every man needs some "substitute for the old struggle of tooth and claw," but most should do it vicariously for fear of overexertion.[122]

Along with catharsis theory, the Civil War—its historical fact and its superabundant cultural resonance in late nineteenth- and early twentieth-century America—added considerable martial meaning to college football. The most explicit allusions arose in the South, where pride in winning football teams came to parallel Lost Cause pride in Confederate military prowess.[123] In honor of its state's fallen heroes, the University of Virginia chose silver gray and cardinal red for its football team's uniforms. And Louisiana State University adopted the team name the Fighting Tigers in reference to the Donaldsville Cannoneers, the New Orleans Zouaves, and other parts of the state's distinguished Civil War fighting unit, the Louisiana Tigers.[124] Northeastern and midwestern university football traditions also imbricated themselves with the Civil War. Stadiums were dedicated to northern war dead. Fight songs evoked the bravery and prowess of Union troops. During the very first intercollegiate football game, the 1869 Princeton-Rutgers contest, Princeton fans based the school's soon-to-be-famous war whoop—"Hurrah! Hurrah! Hurrah! Tiger! Siss! Boom! Ah!"—on a New York Seventh Regiment cheer heard a few years earlier as the soldiers passed through Princeton on their way to battle.[125] Decades later, in the early 1930s, and in the most formal reference to the Civil War, Montgomery, Alabama, promoters founded the Blue-Gray football game, an annual contest between squads of northern and southern college all-stars.

In addition to these direct references, the Civil War provided a generalized context for the growth of college football. Consider, for example, the historical overlap between the Civil War and football at the University of Wisconsin at Madison's Camp Randall. Named after Alexander Randall, Wisconsin's first Civil War governor, the camp served as a place for mustering recruits in the early years of the war—some 70,000 of the state's 91,000 troops were quartered and drilled there. And, then, shortly after Appomattox, it became the site of a war memorial to and cemetery for Civil War soldiers. In 1895 Wisconsin's legislature turned over part of the former military camp to the state university, which immediately started using the space for its extremely popular intercollegiate football games. With Camp Randall Stadium completed in 1921, the university played its home football games throughout the twentieth century in the shadow of the Civil War memorial.[126] The nexus between football and war tightened at Wisconsin in 1956 when the university erected Camp Randall Memorial Building for indoor football practice as well as military drill. Founded in memory of Wisconsin's Civil War veterans, the Cold War dedication ceremony bespoke of the continued "obligation," as the president of the Wisconsin Veteran's Council put it, "that a free democratic nation expects of all its citizens"; University of Wisconsin president Edwin B. Fred declared the building "a fitting monument to the memory of heroes of the past and to the preparation of heroes of the future"—a grim dedication after considering that war heroes are usually those men who make the supreme sacrifice; and, finally, a member of the University Board of Regents underlined the expectation "that those who strengthen their bodies and learn the rudiments of national defense in this place will carry on our hallowed traditions. For the traditions which have grown and flourished in these grounds have come to us through thousands of soldiers and athletes who have known Camp Randall as a symbol of struggle, fair play, and courage."[127] The connection between football and battle couldn't have been closer.

Another association between the Civil War and Wisconsin football can be found in the university's well-known fight song "On Wisconsin." Written and first sung in 1909, "On Wisconsin" doesn't specifically reference the Civil War; although, when sung at Camp Randall, that connection must have been made; the words seem to address the state's troops as well as the university football team:

On, Wisconsin! On, Wisconsin!
    Plunge right through that line!
Run the ball round Minnesota
    A touchdown sure this time.
On, Wisconsin! On, Wisconsin!
    Fight for her sake
Fight, fellows, fight!
    And we will win this game.[128]

The song took on added martial meaning during World War I, when many American regiments used it as a marching song. The 32nd Division of Michigan and Wisconsin soldiers sang "On Wisconsin" into battle at Chateau-Thierry, France. A *Milwaukee Journal* newspaper article later recounted how the song's "'rip 'em up' spirit" urged the midwesterners "on to their goal": the Americans "hammered the enemy back to the banks of the Vesle, then would not stop, but pressed tenaciously on until they had driven the amazed German from his stronghold on the opposite shore."[129] Whether deliberate or not, the writer—his imagination filled with the "On Wisconsin" fight song—vividly recorded the battle scene via the excitement of football.

The lyrics of "On Wisconsin" point to a central all-important component of the way Civil War memory infused warlike sentiments into late nineteenth- and early twentieth-century college football: as written and iconographic material on Civil War battles pervaded American popular culture during this time, football's dominant brutal imagery of two mobile differently colored lines of men smashing against each other evoked the excitement and danger of "hand-to-hand combat"— in Patrick B. Miller's words, "the rush of life-threatening violence."[130] The actual sound of football only added to the effect. "Slap!" is how a *New York Times* reporter described the Yale-Princeton game of 1895: "Two masses of humanity would come together with a sound like the crackling of bones of a tasty hot bird between the teeth of some hungry giant." The article is worth quoting at length for its comically realistic account of line play's destruction:

> Legs and arms and heads and feet would be apparently inextricably intermingled, until it looked as if not even the fondest mother would be able to sort out the right parts of her only son. The whistle of the referee would blow sharply, and the lot of legs and arms and hands and heads would sort themselves out once more, and there would be something like the sixteen or eighteen of the boys that seemed to be human beings once more, with all the members of their bodies intact.
>
> The rest of the men that had been in the collision lay prone on the field and Drs. Josh Hartwell and Boviard would rush on the field, followed by assistants with pack-

ages and sticking plaster, buckets of water, and the cases of surgical instruments. A big gap in someone's head would be patched together with plaster, another man's leg would be pulled back until it assumed its normal shape, sprained wrists would be bandaged, and wrenched ankles bound up. Then the crowd would yell itself hoarse with the rival cries of the colleges, possibly because no one had been killed outright.

Sharply the whistle of the referee would ring out its orders and then another human cyclone would be set in motion, and possibilities of carnage can be suggested by the merry cries of "Eat 'em up, Princeton!" and "Kill 'em in their tracks, Yale!"[131]

By stripping the game of its heroic qualities, this article illustrates just how absurd the level of violence could be in college football and just how much the fans enjoyed it. But the *New York Times* account is exceptional in its ironic criticism of the game's violent smashing and crashing over the line of scrimmage—most sports reporters found high drama in football's recurring collision of men. For instance, a *San Francisco Chronicle* dispatch paid tribute to the martially heroic scene during the last minutes of the Harvard-Princeton game of 1896: "in the dim twilight," after the two teams had struggled "for two hours back and forth across the white-lined gridiron," the "battle lines stood shoulder to shoulder in midfield, a swaying mass of struggling muscle."[132]

Newspaper coverage of the 1896 Big Game highlighted this combatlike quality of football's line play, as in Stanford coach Harry Cross's comment that California lost because it could not break through the "stone wall of red" that always "opposed them." The lead *San Francisco Examiner* account of the game begins with the brutal sound at the line of scrimmage: "From the side lines one could almost hear the crunch of flesh and bones when the heavy Stanford men went headlong into the Berkeley line." The reporter used the same scene to capture poetically the vivid flashes of color on the field: "Crashing into the Berkeley line, the heavy men of Stanford went through like a ray of crimson sunset piercing a cloud of blue." Evocation of battle was the writer's central impression and interest, and he relied on Stanford's dominant size and strength for his narrative's master metaphor of war: "down the field the wedge of crimson slowly, steadily, unmercifully battered its way. Try as hard as they would Berkeley could not stand up against the beating, hammering, driving rushes." With its headlines reading "HOW THE WEDGE OF CARDINAL WAS DRIVEN THROUGH THE BLUE AND GOLD, Berkeley Was Helpless against the Battering of Stanford's Giants and Could Not Score," the *Examiner* article—as well as the game itself (for the reporter could be seen to have documented the scene as much as creatively imagined it)—melodramatized the contest through allusions to the *gravitas* of war.[133]

Martial movement across the line of scrimmage is also a dominant theme in turn-of-the-century football cheers and fight songs. "On Wisconsin" is quintessential in this regard—"On, Wisconsin! On, Wisconsin! / Plunge right through that line!"—but battle line imagery appeared in earlier football songs. At the Harvard-Yale game of 1894, for instance, Harvard supporters sang these lyrics to "John Brown's Body":

> Old John Harvard is a smiling on you now
> Show Yale your mettle boys, and through the centre plow
> If the Eli cannot play, just show the Eli how
> For this is Harvard's Day.

Yale fans replied to the tune of "Marching thro' Georgia":

> Harvard men from Boston always come with hearts that quail
> When they see the blue upon the sons of Eli Yale
> When they strike our line their tricks will be of no avail
> Down with the Crimson forever[134]

That these late nineteenth-century Harvard and Yale men—many of them grandsons of Civil War veterans or, in any case, conscious of the war's legacy of courage and sacrifice—sang these songs to Union marching airs added to the already momentous quality of their football rivalry.

While the Stanford-California rivalry didn't have the same regional association with the Civil War, turn-of-the-century Stanford football songs nevertheless concentrated on line play and its visual and physical similarities to battle. Examples abound, including the 1901 song "The Stanford Line":

> Like coursers at our captain's call,
> They speed, they charge, they rush the ball,
> Our line, our line, our Stanford line,
> And Berkeley to defeat consign.

The beginning of the chorus rings like the captain's command to his troops:

> Steady, forward, Stanford line!
> Staunch and manly, naught resign,
> Firm as the headland rock in calm or gale,
> Though every foe with might and main assail.

A verse from a 1900 fight song has the same unambiguous charge:

> Buck till their line is broken.
> Rush when the play is on.

Stop them! Hold them! Block them!!
  Fight till the game is won.

As does a Stanford "yell" from 1902:

Tear 'em up! Tear 'em up!
Tear 'em up! Any way to get 'em up!
Stanford! Stanford!
Hit that line! Hit that line!
Hit that line! Hard![135]

This type of short staccato yell would become ubiquitous in twentieth-century college football cheering—as in "hit that line harder, harder" and "push 'em on back, push 'em on back, way back"—and it is critical to understand that its origins lie in the overlap between the sport and war.

The most elaborate Stanford expression addressing the intimacy between football and war is Bristow Adams's 1897 poem "From the Side-lines," a vivid account of a game as seen through the prism of battle. The poem's beginning and end insist that "This is no game, but war": football's play is "Fierce, strong and deep"; demanding "brute force and mighty brawn." Keenly conflating the players' experiences with sense impressions from the stands, the poem enacts the identification process between fan and team, fixing on the violent drama on the field. One sequence tells of a player set "back alone" to receive a kick, "[s]tanding with muscles tense," catching the ball, an opposing player "start[ing] now to meet him there!" where they are "[t]ogether thrown!" The next line suggests a certain fascination with the result of the collision: "Breathless and deathlike! See how still one lies!" The thrill of the hard hitting continues as the players get up and are "[a]t them again so soon!—was that a groan?" The narrator's team moves the ball down the field:

We hear their panting, hoarse and dry and deep?,
See reek of flesh, smell sweat, command we hear!
A waiting, straining space, then in a heap
All fall, and falling get another cheer
Again? They never tire! Now, side by side
Two dart from out of the mass; fierce eddies rage
About them as they run.
Those that have tried
To stop him with the ball, vain combat wage.

The crowd erupts as a touchdown is scored: "The ground beneath us shakes. Men, mad with joy, unite in joyful noise." After celebratory transcendence, the narrator returns to his central impression, "And yet you say 'a game!' Not game, but war," suggesting that only something as grand and dangerous as war could evoke such emotion.[136]

Finally, the thickest description of war's presence in turn-of-the-century football runs to the deep structure of sacrifice in the game and how it reinforced other impetuses (vernacular and official) toward a man risking his life for a cause greater than himself. The self-sacrificial theme is the most peculiar aspect of American college football. Balinese cockfighting also makes blood sacrifices, but, from a human perspective, it smartly locates the suffering and death in the chicken; football placed its violent, smashing competition on the bodies of young men, wrapping the dangerous play in the language of masculine honor and patriotic duty. The next chapter on the late nineteenth- and early twentieth-century reformulation of the American citizen-soldier examines how the institutional imbrication between sport and war cast a new athletic dimension on battle and killing. Here we need to understand that the emergence of college football gained power and meaning through its close identification with a broader culture of death and sacrifice emanating from the Civil War. Within this context the notion that the Thanksgiving Day Big Game, for instance, involved a distinct partially recognized element of human sacrifice doesn't seem so farfetched.

A vivid example of sacrificial citizen-soldiership within late nineteenth- and early twentieth-century college football is the consecration of university playing fields to the memory of American war dead. In *Lincoln at Gettysburg* (1992), Garry Wills describes a Victorian-era "culture of death" within which leaders during the Civil War insisted that "the place of the dead must be made a school for the living."[137] The ethic extended into the turn of the century through a number of channels, including the practice of veterans giving Memorial Day speeches at Civil War cemeteries. Instilling a sense of duty in young American men who may otherwise have felt disconnected from their country's past was also pursued through football stadium dedications, as at Harvard's Soldier's Field, completed in 1890, and donated by Boston Brahmin and Union veteran Henry L. Higginson.

In his dedication speech before Harvard faculty and students, Higginson explained that in making the gift he wanted the grounds to be "marked with a stone bearing the names of some dear friends,—alumni of the University, and noble gentlemen,—who gave freely and eagerly all that they had or hoped for, to their country and to their fellow men in the hour of great need—the war of 1861 to 1865 in defence of the Republic." After speaking of their "courage in marching and fighting," he asked "what do the lives of our friends teach us?" Higginson answered: "Surely the beauty and holiness of . . . utter, unselfish, thoughtful devotion to the right cause, to our country, to mankind." He concluded on this same duty-bound note: "my chief hope in regard to" Soldier's Field is "that it will help to make you full-grown, well-developed men . . . and that it will remind you of the reason for living, and of your own duties as men and citizens of the Republic."[138] Thus consecrated, Soldier's Field became a superliminal space. While holding status-determining intercollegiate football games, the stadium also created a transitory space between past, present, and future: its newly hallowed ground invoked the memory of dead Civil War heroes, infusing the play on the field with the magnitude of their sacrifice, and strongly signifying that such sacrifice would be expected from young men in the wars to come.

Dedication of football fields to American war dead reached a high point after World War I. Both Stanford and the University of California completed new stadiums in 1921. Actually, Stanford didn't explicitly dedicate its Athletic Stadium to American soldiers, instead drawing upon football's more generalized association with war as well as the symbolically homicidal impulses toward its rival across the bay. The university held a ground-breaking ceremony in June 1921, when the entire student body first gathered in Assembly Hall and then marched to the new stadium; the Stanford band led the procession, followed by the ROTC unit, and then the students. Alumni, administrators, and student leaders gave short speeches, including one by a university trustee and chairman of the stadium committee, who invoked a sense of school spirit through the always-effective martial metaphor: "We are erecting a battlefield which must be defended by Stanford men." The captain of the football team followed, promising that the stadium would bring a renewed effort on the field: "Our blood is just as red as in the days of old and we will give you all we have." Finally, the student yell leader introduced a new cheer for the 1921 Big Game, to be played at Stanford; meant to replace the Axe cheer, it had the same unsubtly violent and morbid message for Berkeley:

DIG, dig-dig; dig-dig; dig-dig.

DIG, dig-dig; dig-dig; dig-dig.

Dig 'em a grave, a grave, a grave,

Dig 'em a grave, a grave, a grave

Dig 'em a grave, dig 'em a grave, dig 'em a grave,
   Where?

Under the sod, the sod, the sod,

Under the sod, the sod, the sod,

Under the sod, down by the Quad, under the sod,
   There![139]

In August 1921 the University of California completed its Memorial Stadium, officially dedicated to those "Californians who gave their lives in the World War to vindicate the principle of peace and justice in the world." General John J. Pershing wrote a letter—read at the dedication ceremony—in tribute to the Californians' military sacrifice: "The memory of their deeds will never perish. The dash and spirit which enabled them to achieve are powers that can be sustained only so long as vigorous health and enlightened patriotism avail. The stadium," Pershing concluded, deliberately connecting military service to the lessons of football, "will stand as a lasting memorial to your gallant sons and serve to nurture the sources from which they drew their strength."[140]

In sum, the educative impulse in stadium consecrations had a dual effect on U.S. war making and college football. With high-minded homosocial elites sanctifying military duty, the dedications worked to buttress the state's effort to motivate young men to fight and kill and die in what would become a long sequence of late nineteenth- and twentieth-century foreign wars. Alongside military functionalism, athletic field commemorations deepened and historicized the warrior mentality within football itself. The deliberate congruency between sport and war made football's risk of injury and death seem all the more natural and necessary. As seen in *Out of the Game* (fig. 3.6), an illustration reproduced in an 1891 issue of *Harper's Weekly*, physical sacrifice became one of the most idealized aspects of football. Not everyone liked the sport's violence. Its brutality had been denounced since the game's inception. But to enjoy football still meant recognizing and, at some level, accepting its obvious structural violence. The *New York Times* reported that those hurt in 1894 Yale-Princeton game "were injured unavoidably in the rough collisions that no rules can abolish. When one man, or several men, running at full speed, must be stopped by other men, bruises and cuts are sure to develop."[141] Many reveled in the spectacle of football's bone-crushing play, as divulged in the fans' ecstatic behavior at big college games. And many supported the game's brutality by rationalizing that the danger was somehow worth it.

Among many commentators, football's rationalization process took on a formal quid-pro-quo logic: serious injury and death should be tolerated and even encouraged because the play of football served a higher end. The expressed good of football did vary, although everyone stressed a social end extending past the individual self. In 1904, for instance, Harvard English professor Bliss Perry noted that "the amateur football game, for all its brutalities, has taught a young scholar a finer lesson than his classroom has taught him, namely to risk his neck for his college." In a related vein, many writers praised football for its close correspondence to the necessity of military sacrifice. As early as 1889, in an *Atlantic Monthly* article entitled "The Athletic Problems in Education," N. S. Shaler spoke of the "masterful quality" that "obtain[s] in a game of football." One "learns to take considerable risks of bodily pain without hesitation, and to combine his action with that of his mates,"

Shaler wrote; "[i]n no other form of activity can we, during times of peace, hope to give as valuable training to youth as is afforded by this sport."[142] A similar, although more baldly stated calculation came from Henry Curtis in the 1904 issue of the *American Physical Education Review:* "What does it matter if a leg is broken now and then? It is worth a dozen broken legs if you can teach your boy to be a hero and a patriot." And on the eve of American entrance into World War I, we find Amherst College's physical educator Raymond G. Gettell praising football for its simulation of "physical combat" and evocation of "primitive lust for battle." At the same time, though, football also "satisfies the higher and distinctly civilized interest in organization, cooperation, and the skilled interrelation of individual effort directed to a common purpose. It typifies," Gettell concluded, "the highest achievement in its unusual emphasis on discipline and obedience, on the subordination of the individual to authority and law."[143] Willingness to endure and inflict pain and injury is crucial to the citizen-soldier, in other words, and football taught both parts like no other activity outside of war itself.

The idea that college football educates young men toward sacrifice is also argued in one of the most influential turn-of-the-century publications on the sport, *Football* (1896), by Walter Camp and Lorin F. Deland. The book draws an immediate parallel between football and war in the preface's assertion that the game "calls out . . . the qualities which make the soldier"—namely "physical bravery" and "instant obedience."[144] Throughout *Football* Camp and Deland stressed "the lesson of obedience. The world has never underestimated the value of a military or naval training in teaching implicit, unquestioned obedience and a fine sense of readiness to accept discipline." They then made the connection to sport. "Football demands obedience. . . . The biting sarcasm of the coaches must be borne without a thought of rebellion; the unmerited blame must be accepted without even an excuse; every order must be instantly and unquestionably obeyed." The last chapter of the book makes an explicit "comparison between war and football" by enumerating their common "moral agents"—what they define as the mental traits that make up an effective soldier or football player. In addition to leadership qualities in the captain and quarterback and the mastery of strategy and tactics, these "moral factors" include emotional commitment requisite to football—"the spirit which is infused into the players by a realization of the issue" such as "the prestige of the team, or the college which the team represents."[145] Camp and Deland did not mention willingly suffering injury or death but, then again, neither did recruitment material for the armed forces. The combination of bravery and obedience necessarily meant physical sacrifice, however. In football, as in war, sacrifice is paradigmatic of the homosocial and heterosocial expectations placed on individual men.

With the Camp and Deland book in mind, football could be understood as a moral as well as a cultural equivalent of war: the sport creatively reinforced the martial precept of individual sacrifice for a greater corporate good. Whether William James would have called it moral isn't clear. He had road and bridge building in mind more so than the blood and guts of college football. At the same time, though, he wanted most to find a new, less-destructive expression of man's "innate pugnacity." It isn't going to go away, James told his fellow pacifists, especially when the only proposed alternative is "a world of clerks and teachers, of co-education and zo-oph-ily, of 'consumer's leagues' and 'associated charities,' of industrialism unlimited, and feminism unabashed. No scorn, no hardness, no valor anymore!" Along with his Harvard colleague Santayana, James put forward a most sophisticated version of catharsis theory. He did distance himself from militarists' easy acceptance of war as biologically determined; and he suggested that war could be seen as a "tran-sitory phenomenon in social evolution"; but, like Thorstein Veblen, James had no illusions about rooting out warlike characteristics—the fighting spirit had been "selected" naturally. "Dead men tell no tales," James wrote: if there ever were in-herently peaceful peoples, they had all been killed off; "our ancestors have bred pugnacity into our bone and marrow, and thousands of years of peace won't breed it out of us."[146] From this view of human evolution, channeling aggression and vio-lence onto the football field—as if it could really be done—may have struck James as an ingenious stroke of social-psychological engineering. The wrinkle is that college football, unlike James's proposed army of good workers, evolved in close tandem with and not in substitute of war.

Emerging in the postbellum America, college football embodied the nation's deep obsession with war. If, as James said, "the popular imagination fairly fattens on the thought of war," then football's smashing crashing line play, brutal tack-ling, and spectacular color and ritual would feed American lust for battle until it burst at the seams during the Spanish-American War and the U.S. entrance into World War I, among other examples.[147] Anthropology helps the historian examine how football's constituent parts intensified, in Veblen's term, the predatory habit of mind. Victor Turner's work on liminality leads to a closer understanding of why a turn-of-the-century university corporately organized itself to field a team of the largest, strongest, and most synchronized hypermasculine men—it served as a surrogate, whose success or failure on the gridiron established the school's intercollegiate social status. Stanford's administration made a competitive invest-ment to enhance institutional prestige. In turn, football fans invested themselves emotionally in the play on the field. Clifford Geertz's strategy of reading a sport-ing event as a literary text points to the conceptual content of the fans' response and contribution to the game. The bloodthirsty football songs, cheers, and yells leave little doubt as to football's effectiveness in interweaving itself with and thus strengthening turn-of-the-century martial spirit.

College football had a retrogressive effect on American gender relations. Like no other sport, football's emphasis on strength and body mass cordoned off women from the prestige of athletic participation. Instead, women took on an unusually prominent place in the stands, where their feminine presence supercharged the already hypermasculine play on the field. That football's conservative gender dynamic reached outside of the gridiron and the university is suggested by its deep structural ties to war making. Together, football and the military can be seen as a strategic counter to feminism and, more generally, to women's increasing participation in the public spheres of politics, labor, education, physical culture, and business. Football had an ideological impact on turn-of-the-century U.S. society. It helped to achieve nothing less than the reestablishment of the classic republican ideal of the citizen-soldier and its assumption of masculine capacity for killing as well as its imperative of physical sacrifice. It is to citizen-soldiership that we now turn: its emergence from public memory of the Civil War; its remedy for an apparently oversafe and ultracommercialized society; and its modern formulation of the age-old impulse to take another human life.

Figure 1.1. Madonna of the Trail by August Leinbach, Vandalia, Illinois.
1927. One of twelve memorials commissioned by the Daughters of the
American Revolution commemorating the spirit of pioneer women.
Courtesy of Frank Brusca.

Figure 1.2. Frederick Jackson Turner on a Sierra Club hiking trail with his daughter Dorothy. 1904. Courtesy of Wilbur R. Jacobs.

Figure 1.3. The Coming Game: Yale versus Vassar by Charles Dana Gibson, originally printed in *Life* magazine. 1895. Courtesy of Lehigh University Library.

Figure 2.1. Facsimile of the *Tarzan of the Apes* frontispiece. 1914. Courtesy of Lehigh University Library.

Terms, Five Dollars a Year. Ten Cents a Copy.

NEW YORK, THURSDAY, AUGUST 21, 1873.

Volume 1. Number 2. 103 Fulton Street.

Figure 2.2. Masthead illustration in the first issues of *Forest and Stream* magazine. 1873. Courtesy of Lehigh University Library.

Figure 2.3. Drawing of Theodore Roosevelt in hunting costume, by Henry Sandham. Frontispiece from Theodore Roosevelt's book *Hunting Trips of a Ranchman.* 1885. Courtesy of Lehigh University Library.

Figure 2.4. "For my sake," she begged him, "for my sake." Illustration from original edition of Owen Wister's novel *The Virginian.* 1902. Courtesy of Lehigh University Library.

Figure 3.1. Football Players by Douglas Tilden at the University of California–Berkeley. 1893. Courtesy of Glen Gendzel.

Figure 3.2. Illustration from *The New York Journal and Advertiser* previewing games between Yale and Princeton and Harvard and Penn. 1897. Courtesy of Lehigh University Library.

Figure 3.3. "To the Rooting Co-Ed." Illustration and poem from *The Sequoia*. November 1897. Courtesy of Stanford University Special Collections and Archives.

Figure 3.4. Candidate for football honors: "I think I'll make a pretty speedy end, don't you?" Captain: "Yes; from your looks you ought to make a pretty speedy end, but it will be a very sad one. About how would you like the telegram to your folks worded?" Illustration from *The Sequoia*. October 1896. Courtesy of Stanford University Special Collections and Archives.

Figure 3.5. Cover illustration of special Big Game issue of *The Sequoia*. November 1895. Courtesy of Stanford University Special Collections and Archives.

Figure 3.6. Out of the Game by W. A. Rogers, originally printed in *Harper's Weekly.*
23 October 1891. Courtesy of Lehigh University Library.

Figure 4.1. Illustration of Union Civil War soldier from *Century's Battles and Leaders of the Civil War.* 1884. Courtesy of Lehigh University Library.

Figure 4.2. Hobey Baker, captain of the Princeton University football team. 1913. Courtesy of John D. Davies.

Figure 4.3. Hobey Baker, World War I pilot, American Aerial Squadron. 1918. Courtesy of John D. Davies.

ATHLETES MAKE BEST FIGHTERS

That's why we know that the big lot of Taylor Athletic Equipment sent to the troops is in good hands. In one order alone we were awarded the following in competition with all other makes

59,760	Taylor League Base Balls
500	Taylor Basket Balls
1,200	Taylor Foot Balls
3,500	Taylor Baseball Gloves
780	Taylor Base Mitts
1,500	Taylor Bladders

Here's the glad hand, boys, and I wish with all my heart I were there with you. If I can do anything for you let me know. Alex Taylor

ALEX. TAYLOR & Co., Inc.,
Military Athletic Outfitters,
26 East 42nd Street,   New York.

Figure 4.4. Advertisement from *Stars and Stripes*. November 1918. Courtesy of the U.S. Army Military History Institute.

MEN OF ACTION

JOIN THE MARINE CORPS

Marines fight on land or sea and they are always called
first when the war trumpets blow.

For Fighting---Join the Marines

RECRUITING STATION
1317 Pacific Avenue, Tacoma, Wash.

Figure 4.5. United States Marines Corps recruiting poster. Circa 1912. Courtesy of the United States Marines Corps.

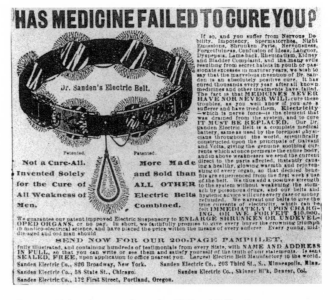

Figure 5.1. Advertisement from the *National Police Gazette.* September 1893. Courtesy of Lehigh University Library.

Figure 5.2. Advertisement from *Physical Culture* magazine. 1899.
Courtesy of Lehigh University Library.

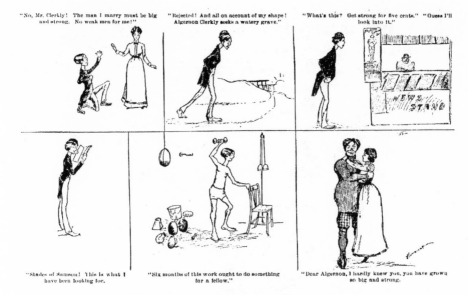

Figure 5.3. Editorial cartoon from *Physical Culture* magazine. August 1900. Courtesy of Lehigh University Library.

Figure 5.4. Charles Atlas's "Insult That Made a Man Out of 'Mac'" advertisement. Circa 1950. Courtesy of Lehigh University Library.

Figure E.1. Matt Groening's *Life in Hell* cartoon originally printed in the *Onion.* 1991. Courtesy of Matt Groening.

CHAPTER FOUR

War in the Head

In an open-letter response to Albert Einstein's questions, Why do humans make war and what can be done to avoid it? Sigmund Freud began by positing that "it is so easy to make men enthusiastic about a war" because "killing an enemy satisfied an instinctual inclination." Written in 1932, Freud's widely published letter presents a succinct application of psychoanalytic instinct theory to war. Freud thought that all humans house two primary instincts: eros and aggression—drives toward life and death. The relaxing of concern for self-preservation in combat—courage under fire, in other words—may be attributed to a "death instinct"—what Freud defined as the impulse "to reduce life to its original condition of inanimate matter." Humans have far more prolifically turned that drive "to destruction in the external world," however; this phenomenon, Freud explained, is the "biological" source of "the countless cruelties in our history," including, most notably, war. "There is no use in trying to get rid of man's aggressive inclinations," Freud believed; but, he assured Einstein, it is "easy for us to find a formula for indirect methods of combating war." He put great stock in culture. "For incalculable ages mankind has been passing through a process of evolution of culture," Freud thought, "[t]he psychical modifications" of which "are striking and unambiguous. They consist in a progressive displacement of instinctual aims and a restriction of instinctual impulses." So the "one thing we can say" about the subject, he concluded, is that "whatever fosters the growth of culture works at the same time against war."[1]

Contrary to Freud's ameliorative view of culture, this chapter argues that the most immediate and effective sources of human motivation to war come not from biologically derived instincts but from culturally evolved incitements to aggress against others. War in the head—the psychological propensity to fight and kill in battle—is temporally based and therefore more contingent and complicated than Freud understood. After finding pleasure in the experience of fighting and killing, humans have represented those feelings publicly for younger generations to absorb, emulate, and desire. In the modern United States, patriotic speeches, recruitment posters, battle songs and poems, regimental histories, soldier memoirs, novels, newspaper articles, movies, and Web sites have created a large field of powerful emotional appeals to war. Many American men have gotten around that field, but it has required concerted effort, while others haven't wanted to try. Freud was right in looking to culture to curtail war—what other possibility is there?—but he had a dangerous blind spot over the enormous cultural privileging of war. William James had no such problem. He too recognized a human instinct for aggression, but James paid more attention to a people's prideful and self-perpetuating attachment to their war making. Turn-of-the-twentieth-century Americans, in particular, understood the Civil War to be a national treasure: "Those ancestors, those efforts, those memories and legends, are the most ideal part of what we now own together, a sacred spiritual possession worth more than all the blood poured out." James further realized that the bloodletting itself had a psychological hold on the country. "The plain truth," he commented in 1910, "is that people want war." They want war not only for its heroes and social cohesion but for the thing itself—war's spectacle, violence, and destruction. Far from being turned off by the horror of war, James wrote incisively, "The horror makes the thrill."[2]

In touting the power of culture to subdue war, Freud emphasized that "Anything that encourages the growth of emotional ties between men must operate against war."[3] In this comment he may very well have meant such values of love, tolerance, and forgiveness that tend to mitigate human difference and conflict; but, again, his thoughts are oblivious to the culturally created appeal of war: it is exactly "the emotional ties between men" that have most effectively eternalized war. The masculine imperative to fight has been deeply rooted in male homosocial institutions. The veteran organization the Grand Army of the Republic (GAR) and its Confederate counterpart inculcated military service in the post–Civil War United States, for instance, extending standards of honor, sacrifice, and manhood to new generations of American men. Homosociality has also worked informally, through emotional as well as institutional bonds, through vernacular as well as statist obligations. Homosociality has promoted wartime violence as a common pleasure among men. In his book *The Things Men Fight For* (1916), H. H. Powers, a Stanford University economics professor who heard William James speak in Palo Alto about war, fully described that shared interest among young American men in joining battle:

> We have not only learned to feel that we must fight, but we have learned to like to fight. The sufferings of war are terrible, but they are borne willingly, even gladly, as the athlete or the ascetic bears his self imposed hardships, for the sake of compensations which are a very real part of character. The sense of achievement—never more real than in overcoming the enemy—the recognition of our fellows, most potent of all social incentives, these and other compensations war has made its own. The pacifist

who is inclined to stake his case on the suffering caused by war, should first try commiserating a football team on its bruises and broken bones.[4]

The interpellative power of the masculine bond can exceed that of the state, a point well made in "The Volunteer," a World War I poem by Robert Service. "My country calls? Well, let it call," a reluctant warrior says to his friend Bill. "Them politicians with their greasy ways; / Them empire-grabbers—fight for 'em? No fear!" But what about duty to your country? "My Country? Mine? I likes their cheek. Me mud-bespattered by the cars they drive, / Wot makes my measly thirty bob a week, / And sweats red blood to keep myself alive!" The narrator quickly succumbs, though, to the draw of other men: "Ay, wot the 'ell's the use of all this talk? / To-day some boys in blue was passin me, / And some of 'em they ad no legs to walk, / And some of 'em had no eyes to see. / And—well, I couldn't look 'em in the face, / And so I'm goin', goin'. . . to face the music with the bunch out there." Bill doesn't see it the same way: "A fool you say! Maybe you're right. / I'll 'ave no peace unless I fight. / I've ceased to think; I only know / I've gotta go, Bill, gotta go."[5]

For generations upon generations, across borders, races, and cultures, war in the head has been one of the most active aspects of masculine thought and consciousness. In terms of science and technology, men have devoted immeasurable creativity to finding new ways to kill each other in more wholesale fashion.[6] And one's personal capacity in war makes up the most self-reflexive of masculine discourses. In philosophical treatise and popular thought alike, it fixes on human nature and man's nexus to both god and beast. Literature and film have structured excitement over killing and questions of courage into the very foundation of masculine imagination. For many twentieth- and early twenty-first-century American boys and men, combat has enjoyed a cinematic power or appeal within one's dream life and stream of consciousness. Modern war stories, especially those of recent American wars, tend to drop the romanticism of earlier literature. Many routinely tell tale of war's atrocities and the protagonist's ultimate disillusionment. Yet young men have continued to rush into war. As Samuel Hynes and many others have noted: "Every generation, it seems, must learn its own lessons from its own war, because every war is different and is fought by different ignorant men."[7] A willful ignorance toward war has plagued U.S. culture since Appomattox. This seemingly deliberate forgetting of war's degradation and destruction is a focus of what follows here. We'll concentrate on how adventure, killing, and man making have predominated war in the head, thus leading new generations of American men backward to a pathologically homicidal and suicidal condition.

Examination of modern U.S. war in the head begins with the Civil War and its layers of historical memory. After drawing out the distinction between biological and cultural inheritance of the acquired characteristic of fighting spirit, we consider how turn-of-the-twentieth-century Memorial Day speeches and popular literature constructed the American citizen-soldier, a pliant figure at once appreciative of his patriotic duty to country and interested in experiencing the danger and excitement of war. Desire for war came together in the Spanish-American War of 1898. A short conflict, the war against Spain was extremely consequential in synchronizing the military, media, and plutocracy with the cause of glorious and deadly American manhood. As combat grew more and more mechanized and suicidal, American culture continued to equate war with the challenges and reward of sport; this phenomenon took on a new hegemonic cast in World War I, when the U.S. military used the action of football and baseball in particular to motivate troops to fight. An arc can be traced throughout this modern American psychology of war: as fewer men thought of dying for their country, martial heroism evolved into a relatively transparent expression of aggressiveness, a culturally transferred impulse "to finally know what it feels like to kill a man," as a Persian Gulf War marine put it.[8] This homicidal trait, I argue, is best understood as a type of contagion, a pathology that originated, not in biological instinct, but in the vicissitudes of time and place and from the power and desire of men in groups who lead each other on to new acts of death and destruction.

Civil War Memory, Blood Sacrifice, and Modern American Fighting Spirit

In ending slavery and preserving national union, the Civil War also achieved an unprecedented degree of human violence, death, and destruction; Antietam, Gettysburg, Cold Harbor, among nearly countless other battles, forged a certain intimacy among American men with fighting, killing, and dying in total war.[9] Within the terms of late nineteenth-century evolutionary theory, and twentieth-century popular thought, American manhood had acquired the characteristic of fighting spirit, a trait that then passed itself on biologically to later generations of men who would be eager to exercise it in their country's future wars. Variations in attitude toward military service certainly existed, especially along modern America's many racial, class, and ethnic lines. Martial spirit also transcended those divides, though, drawing in such large numbers of men from different social groups that capacity for fighting came to be seen by many as a national character trait, a masculine quality to be realized by hyphenated-American immigrants as well as Anglo-Saxon elites. Along with the popular Darwinian notion of a male-specific instinct of pugnacity, fighting spirit as a cross-cultural American ethnic trait effectively joined personal concern over proving one's manhood with the foreign-war-making interests of the United States. American military might depended on masculine eagerness for battle. Government pulled men into service—some of them kicking and screaming—but many other men saw the nation-state as a benevolent sponsor for fulfilling their preexistent interest in experiencing war and shedding blood.

In appreciating the formative power of the Civil War, we need to be precise regarding the transference of fighting spirit from one generation to the next. The neo-Lamarckian notion that postbellum American men biologically inherited the trait from their Civil War ancestors—while highly influential in turn-of-the-twentieth-century thought—has no scientific basis in material fact: acquired characteristics do not pass genetically. Rather, the acquired characteristic of passion and capacity for war descended through culture. The cult of dead Confederate and Union soldiers, intergenerational storytelling of veterans, a massive Civil War literary genre, widespread production of popular and official historical memory of the conflict: these cultural forms and processes had tremendous effect on American attitudes toward battle, including the calibration of masculine psychologies toward committing the violence of modern warfare. In contradistinction to sociobiological focus on the Pleistocene hunter-gatherer origins of male bloodlust, this chapter draws a radically narrower time frame in arguing that American pleasure in killing emerged from the Civil War and the late nineteenth-century masculinist embrace of that conflict as inspiration and instruction toward finding personal gratification through state-sponsored murder.

The Civil War marks a major turning point in the emotional history of American men. Before the war, one finds fewer expressions of American soldiers taking pleasure in killing the enemy. Indian killing had been caught up in European American spiritual regeneration since the seventeenth century, yet that violence seldom elicited such joyful testimony to the "exciting," "anxious," and "exultant" feelings aroused in battle that we find in Union and Confederate soldiers' letters and diaries. In his valuable book on why men fought in the Civil War, James M. McPherson explains that the pitched hatred and vengefulness of that conflict impelled soldiers to unequivocal bloodlust. "[W]e [should] take horses, burn houses, and commit every depredation possible upon the men of the North," a Confederate sergeant wrote upon entering Pennsylvania in 1863; "I certainly love to kill the base usurping vandals." A Confederate artillery officer described how much he "enjoyed the sights of hundreds of dead Yankees" at Fredericksburg. "Saw much of the work I had done in the way of severed limbs, decapitated bodies, and mutilated remains of all kinds," he continued: "Doing my soul good." And a Union soldier under Sherman wrote that "No man ever looked forward to any event with more joy than did our boys to have a chance to meet the sons of the mother of traitors, 'South Carolina.'"[10] In the decades following the Civil War, such "love" of killing would contribute to the growing masculine obsession over countering ordinary civilian life with wartime "adventure": a keyword within the sport hunting discourse analyzed in chapter 2, it worked within this related context as a powerful euphemism for killing and risk of death.

A related development in the late nineteenth-century emotional history of American masculinity was affection for the United States, a bond that promoted a willingness to die for one's country. Given the Civil War's violence, its extraordinary number of casualties—360,000 Union soldiers killed and 258,000 dead Confederates—why did so many American men go so enthusiastically to the wars that followed?[11] First, they didn't fully know or want to know what awaited them. With popular historical memory of the Civil War fixed on the scale and excitement of battle, a significant number of men marched off thinking about action and adventure, eager to test themselves against what they took to be eternal masculine standards of fighting prowess and courage under fire. Second, and in tension with the romantic forgetting of war's hell, American men did appreciate the danger involved, with many feeling, though, that they owed the country their life. Early memory of the Civil War stressed that the causes of freedom and union were worth the tremendous loss of life. Postwar politicians, Grand Army of the Republic (GAR) officials, and other homosocial elites converted bodily sacrifice into a first tenet of an American man's responsibility to the state. In addition to civic duty, and perhaps gratitude for the chance to fight and kill, a man's feelings toward the United States could include emotions of love and devotion.

Patriotism spread itself unevenly in late nineteenth-century America, but spread it did, and in large part through the spiritual force of the Civil War, with the conflict's violence and sacrifice imagined as redemptive acts and the soldiers cast literally as saviors of the nation. Immortalized by Lincoln at Gettysburg—"we've come to dedicate a portion of that field as a final resting place for those who here gave their lives that their nation might live"—the Civil War bore a new organic relationship between an American and the United States, between the concept of individual sacrifice and the well-being of the body politic.[12] Organic nationalism didn't always run very deep. In peacetime, late nineteenth- and early twentieth-century Americans usually acknowledged it, if at all, within the civil religious rituals of Memorial Day, the Fourth of July, and the like. Wartime was a different matter. Then it proved to be highly functional in getting men to the front. Once there, nationalist patriotic spirit dissolved away with the shock of battle, as most acts of heroic sacrifice came from the closest homosocial bonds, dying for one's comrades in arms and avoiding the shame of showing oneself to be less than a man.

To emphasize, dying for one's country must be seen as a product of cultural evolution. Bodily sacrifice in war doesn't make sense from a biological perspective. Darwin listed pugnacity, not a drive toward death, as a basic human instinct. More recently, the biological synthesis has recognized within natural selection the dynamic of "inclusive fitness": altruism, in this theory, arises from an organism's willingness to substitute its own survival for that of its relatives or others with close genetic relatedness.[13] Inclusive fitness could not be said to be an inherited genetic impetus for heroic sacrifice in war, however, because nationality is a culturally constructed category. The same goes for race and ethnicity.

That's not to say that American men didn't go to war for nation or race, but that such motivation materialized through recent historical forces conveyed culturally, as in memory of the Civil War, rather than through some Stone Age masculine instinct for sacrifice, death, and destruction—or even the instinct for family survival. This point underlines the contingency of war making. Furthermore, as appeals to wartime sacrifice emerge from a specific historical context, they usually reproduce the social and political interests of those making them, as in the racialized "Anglo-Saxon" patriotism of the late nineteenth-century United States. Finally, to grasp the cultural determination of sacrifice is to recognize a multiplicity of reasons why men would be willing to die in war. An African American man volunteering in 1898 to fight the Spanish in Cuba may very well have loved his country far less than most nonblack U.S. soldiers; instead, his service may have arisen out of another emotion altogether—hope that killing and dying could somehow be exchanged for greater freedom and equality for himself, his family, and people. This was a legacy of the Civil War. But as African Americans struggled desperately to keep emancipation at the center of national memory of the Civil War, much of white America embraced sectional reunification, forgetting the central racial cause that divided the North and South for the sake of a new nationalist spirit that would set the United States on an imperialist course of foreign wars through the late nineteenth, twentieth, and early twenty first centuries.[14]

Without universal patriotism, modern American nationalism developed the coercive power to mobilize a heterogeneous male population to war. This the United States accomplished constitutionally during the early twentieth century, with the Civil War's draft providing the framework for the state's hold over its citizenry. Military duty had been uncertain in the United States since the Revolutionary War. Decades of peace and the rise of liberal individualism all but eliminated military obligation from late eighteenth and early nineteenth-century definitions of citizenship. By 1828 Noah Webster's dictionary mentioned only the rights, not the duties of citizenship: "In the U.S. [a citizen] is a person . . . who has the privilege of exercising the elective franchise or the qualifications which entitle him to vote for rulers." But the crisis of secession brought duty back into the equation. As the historian James Whiteclay Chambers II explains, Congress adopted legislation during the war that deprived alien declarants of their political rights if they refused to be conscripted into the Union army, and this link between civil rights and military responsibility became the basis for postbellum legal formulations of masculine citizenship. The critical juncture came with U.S. entrance into World War I and the institution of the selective service. In affirming the constitutionality of the draft, the United States Supreme Court held in 1916 that "it may not be doubted that the very conception of just government and its duty to the citizen includes the reciprocal obligation of the citizen to render military service in case of need to compel it." American men must uphold, as the Court concluded, the "supreme and noble duty of contributing to the defense and honor of the nation."[15] Thus, the classic republican model of citizenship—including its male-only imperative to fight, empowerment to kill, and obligation to bodily sacrifice—would take hold in the United States and flourish throughout the twentieth century.

Post–Civil War masculine citizenship also came together outside of official legal rulings—the obligation to fight constructed itself through homosocial norms, practices, and expectations as well as through the law. In fact, as we consider war in the head—defined, in part, as the mind-sets that take men to battle—the distinction between law and tradition blurs. In the post–Civil War period, they informed masculine conceptions of duty in tandem: both made gender-specific appeals to American men to recognize their natural role of citizen-soldier. "There has been too much talk of rights and too little talk of duty," said Memorial Day speaker J. Sloat Fassett at Gettysburg in 1910: "There is no right without a corresponding duty." Late nineteenth- and early twentieth-century Memorial Day speakers explicitly opposed the possessive individualism of the day by reviving the country's tradition of sacrifice. The man who becomes a soldier "from a sense of duty," as the former Confederate John Sharp Williams stated in a 1904 Memorial Day address in Memphis, fills "the very highest possible measure of manhood."[16] Such tributes to service offer some of the clearest examples of antiliberal, republican thought in modern American political culture.

Initiated in 1868 as a rite of mourning for the dead, Memorial Day proved to be highly instrumental in defining a new tradition of military service through a generational transference of responsibility from veterans to young American men untouched by war. As a crucial part of this dynamic, Memorial Day speakers added to the weight of the past by routinely invoking the moral authority of the dead. As early as 1875, former Union officer William Crosby warned his audience in San Francisco that a new generation of Americans "is rising to whom the war is mere history." In response, Crosby tried to transform Civil War sacrifice into lessons for the living. "The dead have left us their fame as a sacred charge," he emphasized. "We must keep it bright. By the survivors the departed will be judged. We must show by our lives that the spirit which led them into the fire was the spirit of loyalty." Appeals to manhood usually accompanied these generational admonitions. In 1880 T. F. Lang urged a Memorial Day audience in Baltimore to include memory of Civil War military service in the "new models of manhood." Lang continued: "In honoring thus our dead Comrades, we strive to keep alive the hope that those footsteps we are now guiding will ever be as ready to march to their country's assistance in her hour of emergency." The question is, as Lang concluded his speech, "Will you do it boys?"[17] Homosocial authority could not have been more deliberately deployed.

In urging devotion to the United States, Memorial Day speakers often invoked the nationalist imperative of overcoming sectional division. Reunification proved to be an especially productive theme during the Spanish-American War. On 30 May 1898, one month into the war, Senator John M. Thurston of Nebraska addressed a gathering at Arlington National Cemetery: "What an inspiring sight to see those who once fought against each other now rallying under one flag," Thurston proclaimed, "exalting and rejoicing that the azure field of the union banner holds in equal honor every star of statehood, and singing together the rearranged music of the Union—'Yankee Doodle' and 'Dixie'—the favorite airs." While looking back to the Civil War, Memorial Day speakers tended to rationalize the conflict's death and destruction as the necessary result of political difference, in no way reflective of hatred or animosity between the men who fought and killed each other. By the early twentieth century, these claims bordered on the absurd: "Between the brave soldiers of the North and South," former Confederate General William Ruffin Cox told his Richmond audience in 1911, "there was never any personal antagonism during this long and bloody struggle." And with "the cause of estrangement being resolved," Cox continued, it is "recognized that we are all Americans; and when she needs our services, it matters not from what section the call may come."[18] This ideologically driven formulation read a certain homosocial unity into the Civil War experience. Forged by the ultraviolence that men of the North and South had wrought against each other, "bravery," among other features of martial prowess, would be recognized as a character trait of American soldiers—past, present, and future.

As the *American* soldier evolved into a social or ethnic type, Memorial Day speakers embellished national battle prowess, describing it as superior physical and psychological fighting capacity bred in the Civil War (fig. 4.1). The worthy-foe concept animated many speeches: "The soldiers of our late war were 'American soldiers' in warfare," T. F. Lang emphasized in Baltimore in 1880, "each combated, respected and admired the prowess of his opponents." Southern speakers came to recognize the bravery and ferocity among American men, although usually after paying tribute to the "private soldier of the Confederacy," as Joseph R. Lamar did before a large Memorial Day gathering in Augusta, Georgia, in 1902. Those who fought against the Confederates, Lamar exclaimed, "must feel that it is their supremest triumph that they overcame such foes,—for no louder paean can be heralded for the victor than to those able to defeat those of his own race, exhibiting such qualities of heroic manhood as the Southern soldier of 1860–65." Even Lamar folded the southern martial tradition into national character: "I think the day has come in which we, whether from the North or South, may begin to view our war as the treasury of American manhood." And, for Lamar, the Civil War's distinctive feature—the feature that made "American manhood" such a treasure—was the magnitude of its violence: "The ascending mountain of our war's superiority over all others lifts its cliff-like head at Cold Harbor, where occurred the most stupendous and appalling loss of any battle on earth." Lamar went on to detail the rate of killing in that battle with what can only be described as pride: "In the space of eight minutes, ten thousand Federal soldiers lay dead or wounded before the Confederate fire; 20 to the second, 1,200 to the minute."[19]

Along with Lamar, many other Memorial Day speakers drew from the Civil War's violence in building up the contemporary archetype of the American soldier. "The war was costly," Union veteran Thomas Chambers Richmond reminded his Madison, Wisconsin, audience in 1902, "but the results are worth the price." The Civil War "gave us the American soldier," Richmond emphasized, "brave in the hour of battle" and, overall, "the highest type of fighting man the world has yet produced." One year later, President Theodore Roosevelt made a similar claim about American character in his Memorial Day address at Antietam: "In the long run in the Civil War the thing that the average American had was the fighting edge; he had within him, the spirit which spurred him on through toil and danger, fatigue and hardship, to the goal of splendid ultimate hardship."[20] For the young men listening to Roosevelt or Richmond, for those who read the speeches in published form, the lesson from the Civil War was clear: that conflict had created a powerful legacy of American fighting spirit, a tradition that could and would be invoked in wars to come. Older men, especially veterans, could demand that an American recognize his inheritance. Coupled with the legal responsibility of a male citizen, the archetype of the American soldier provided an effective source of military obligation. It cultivated that other dimension of a man's emotional orientation toward war: along with duty to and love of country, one could be moved to fight out of excited anticipation of the act itself.

This compulsion toward fighting comes through in perhaps the best-known and most quoted Memorial Day address, "The Soldier's Faith," an 1895 speech delivered before a large gathering at Harvard University by Oliver Wendell Holmes

Jr. Chief justice of the Massachusetts Supreme Court, Union veteran, and future justice of the U.S. Supreme Court, Holmes urged his audience to embrace war, not for any larger cause it might effect, but for the man-making experience it gives off. Belief in battle for its own sake, Holmes insisted, is a matter of "faith," something to be taken as a personal pledge:

> That the joy of life is living, is to put out all one's powers as far as they will go; that the measure of power is obstacles overcome; to ride boldly at what is in front of you, be it fence or enemy; to pray, not for comfort but for combat; to keep the soldier's faith against the doubts of civil life, more besetting and harder to overcome than all the misgivings of the battle-field, and to remember that duty is not to be proved in the evil day, but then to be obeyed unquestioningly; to love glory more than temptations of wallowing ease, but to know one's final judge and only rival is oneself.

Holmes struck a deeply privatistic chord in this speech. While evoking the excitement of combat, he said nothing of the country for which the action would be undertaken. Wounded three times in battle, including a bullet through his chest at Ball's Bluff and being left for dead behind the lines at Antietam, Holmes was decimated by the war, physically and spiritually, as his belief in God and commitment to ending slavery and all other transcendent causes disintegrated in warfare. What remained, or rather what emerged as Holmes gave voice to his war, was a dark and relativistic ethos, one that had the individual soldier offer himself up to the carnage of battle:

> I do not know what is true. I do not know the meaning of the universe. But in the midst of doubt, in the collapse of creeds, there is one thing I do not doubt, and that is that the faith is true and adorable which leads a soldier to throw away his life in obedience to a blindly accepted duty, in a cause which he little understands, in a plan or campaign of which he has no notion, under tactics which he does not see the use.

Holmes understood that sacrifice and killing underlie the romance of war: "Force, mitigated as far as good manners, is the *ultima ratio*." Holmes liked to reduce martial heroism to its basic elements of violence and aggression. If "life is war," Holmes believed, "the part of man is to be strong."[21]

Holmes put forward a decidedly secular view of war and the individual, devoid of the civil religious overtones usually prominent in Memorial Day addresses. In fact, the press censured Holmes's 1895 Harvard speech for its irresponsibility and inattention to the cause and purpose of the Civil War.[22] When addressing the issue of "why men should fight?" some speakers explicitly rejected any value-free, war-for-war's sake conception of military service. John Sharp Williams seemed to have Holmes and Roosevelt in mind during his 1904 Memorial Day speech at the

Lyceum Theater in Memphis. "No matter how bright the uniform, how loud 'the shouting of captains,' how splendid the deeds of valor, how inspiring the clangor of fife and drums," Williams declared, "there is nothing more disgusting, nothing more detestable, and nothing more in the history of the world has been so dangerous and destructive as the puerile thirst for military fame and the schoolboy love for 'glory' and a strenuous life." The ideals behind fighting matter greatly, Williams insisted; only when bravery "is thrown upon the side of the right . . . is it worthy of your praise and your reverence." Three decades earlier, well before the turn-of-the-century height of masculinist revelry in combat as blood sport, William Crosby made sure that his San Francisco Memorial Day audience appreciated that Civil War soldiers "were not moved by the sudden heat, by the love of excitement, of the lust of conquest; but by love of country."[23] As Crosby's admonition suggests, though, and as we know from Holmes, postwar American culture did generate apolitical attraction to warfare. Few at the turn of the century matched Holmes's near-Nietzschean indifference to the cause behind power. But Holmes was representative and influential in his embrace of war as an end in itself. His speech bears an intellectual relationship to modern American popular culture of war—the keen vernacular interest in military history and the soldier's experience in battle.

Pitched interest in combat experience is most evident in the great corpus of late nineteenth- and early twentieth-century Civil War literature—the novels, short stories, plays, magazine and newspaper articles, and hundreds of regiment histories and memoirs written by foot soldiers and generals alike. Leading this literary outpouring was Ulysses S. Grant's personal memoirs (1885–86) and "The Battles and Leaders of the Civil War" series, published in *Century* magazine between 1884 and 1887 and reproduced in volume form in 1887. Increasing *Century*'s monthly circulation from 127,000 to 225,000, the enormously popular series offered more than a thousand pages of stories and pictures—a "composite history," as Civil War historian Bruce Catton commented in remembering his boyhood attraction to it, such as "no war had ever had before." The magazine's editors shot for the real war. They ignored the "political questions," as associate editor Robert Underwood Johnson described, for the sake of "telling it like it was." *Century* gave its readers what they wanted. The series came at the right "psychological moment," Johnson believed; "the air," as another editor explained, was "infectious with the whole war idea."[24]

Veterans' written accounts of battlefields and campfires, of troop movements and artillery fire, certainly spread attraction to the spectacle of war; as did the photographs and drawings: in recalling neighbors visiting his home to look at his family's copy of "Battles and Leaders," Catton thought that the pictures drew more attention than the stories. "For the first time," Catton wrote, "a nation that had fought a great war could visualize its experience. It could see what it had done."[25] Anticipating the allure that moving pictures of war would have in twentieth-century film, the series' carefully drawn illustrations recreated "Union Lines in Front of Kennesaw Mountain," "The Steamboat 'Chattanooga,'" "Spottsylvania Courthouse and Tavern," and other exciting sites and places of the Civil War; the drawings could even produce narratives of danger and destruction, such as "Sherman's Troops Destroying a Railroad," "An Incident at Cold Harbor," and "Going into Action under Fire." And with every page, in picture form or written text, readers took in the homosocial world of the military, the solidarity of comrades in arms, and the increasingly close identification of real manhood with war making.

With the *Century* series, and Catton's recollection of its reception, we can see how the Civil War became romanticized in late nineteenth-century historical memory. Again, Catton focused on the drawings. Despite the intent of capturing the real war, these illustrations could not represent its horrors. Drawings of dead soldiers appeared in "Battles and Leaders," but, as Catton said, "people who die in these pictures almost always do so without the hideous grotesqueries violent death strews across the field"—instead "they are, somehow, the honored dead." Something once "recalled with dread and bitterness passed into romance," he continued; the transformation "bemused" the veterans: "witness the old gentlemen who came to our house to look at these pictures, translating the reality that they knew all too well into the fiction in which imagination led old men's memories down shady lanes." And for the young men paging through the series, the romance of war became the reality, thereby easing the burden of citizenship and the prospect of military service. Without seeing the brutality of combat, Catton concluded, men were far more likely to seek out the adventure, high risk, and "desperate action" of war.[26]

The allure of battle, a central strand of meaning running through late nineteenth- and early twentieth-century memory of the Civil War, found expression in the memoirs of the Union and Confederate soldiers themselves. Published mostly between the early 1880s and the early 1900s, these books documented the excitement of combat, and sometimes its destruction.[27] In *Detailed Minutiae of a Soldier's Life* (1882), for instance, Confederate veteran Carlton McCarthy described the anticipation of confronting the enemy. A "typical" soldier of the Army of Northern Virginia, McCarthy wrote, "weary and worn, recognizing the signs of approaching battle, did quicken his lagging steps and cry out for joy at the prospect." The sheer spectacle of killing also comes through in these memoirs. Samuel Byers, a former major in General William Tecumseh Sherman's staff, described his experience at Jackson, Mississippi, in 1863:

On the edge of a low ridge we saw a solid wall of men in gray, their muskets at their shoulders blazing into our faces and their batteries of artillery roaring as if it were the end of the world. Bravely they stood there. They seemed little over a hundred yards away. There was charging further by our line. We halted, and for over an hour we loaded our guns and killed each other as fast as we could.

While most of the veterans detailed their memories of battle, few went as far as privileging the actual experience of killing the enemy. Compared to the extemporaneous letters and diaries written during the war, representation of killing in the memoirs is vague, imprecise, and sometimes accompanied by feelings of sorrow and regret.[28]

But if pleasure in killing can rarely be found in the memoirs, many veterans did write of the emotional gratification of battle experience. Some former soldiers described the all-consuming quality of combat—"the elimination of all personality amidst the quickened activity and excitement of the action," as one Union officer put it. The Union veteran B. F. Scribner's account of his feelings during the Battle of Chickamauga stands out for its psychological detail. With the "enemy pressing me on both fronts," Scribner wrote in *How Soldiers Were Made* (1887), "all things appeared to be rushing by me in horizontal lines, all parallel to each other. The missiles of the enemy whistling and whirling by," he continued, "seemed to draw the elements into the same lines of motion, sound, light and air uniting the rush!" Scribner also described battle as the opportunity to fulfill one's manhood. After recounting the Union victory at Chickamauga, he proclaimed:

There is nothing that produces upon a man so profound an impression as a great battle; nothing which so stirs and tests the soul within him; which so expands and strains the functions of sensation and so awakens all the possibilities of nature! There is nothing which so lifts him out of himself; so exalts him to the regions of the heroism and self-sacrifice; nothing which so surcharges him and permeates his receptive faculties, and so employs all the powers of his mind and body as a great battle![29]

Such exultation. The man-making power of war is the most prevalent theme in the Civil War memoirs. Few writers reached Scribner's rhetorical heights, but virtually everyone structured their accounts on the deep and abiding pride of withstanding the extreme conditions of battle.

In so privileging war, the authors did not hold back in representing the brutal results of battle. In comparison to the *Century* series, the memoirs tend to be more realistic in their recollection of the Civil War's death and suffering. Echoing General Sherman's "War is Hell" utterance of 1880, the memoirs provide detailed accounts of the "terribly wounded," explosions causing "entrails flying in all direction," the "bushels of dead," "rivers" of "running blood," and countless other "ghastly spectacles": "Dante himself never conjured anything so horrible as the reality before us," Samuel Byers said in recollecting "the hundreds of the half-decayed corpses" he saw after Grant's victory at Jackson; "some were grinning skeletons, some were headless, some armless, some had their clothes torn away, and some were mangled by dogs and wolves." One of the most gruesome experiences recounted in the memoirs was the not uncommon happening of a soldier going to sleep on a battlefield among his comrades, only to wake up and discover that the men on either side of him had died overnight.[30] Civil War veterans had been in intimate contact with death and did not hesitate to relate it to their readers. Just how many readers the memoirs attracted is hard to say. Although, given the number of memoirs, we can surmise that they had an accumulative effect on turn-of-the-century war in the head, one that integrated the hell-like realities of battle with masculinist excitement over combat.

In measuring the emotional development of post–Civil War soldiering, Stephen Crane's novel *The Red Badge of Courage* (1895) must be taken into full account, for no other work in American literature presents a more detailed psychological study of a man's compulsion to battle, at once crystallizing the standard theme of war as a rite of manhood and also exposing that masculine imperative's pathological self-destructive workings. Crane's account of two days in the life and head of a young Union volunteer at the Battle of Chancellorsville is "free from any suspicion of ideality," as an early *New York Times* review stated: it "def[ies] every tradition of martial glory." The book shows heroism to be at one with suicide; courage, rather than an inner-masculine quality, derives homosocially and manifests by delirium; and running from the enemy, rather than a cowardly aberration, is privileged as the only natural thing to do. The antiwar content in *The Red Badge of Courage* offended some turn-of-the-century readers; one Union veteran, for instance, criticized the novel as "a vicious satire upon American soldiers and American armies." At the same time, many veterans praised the book for its realism. "Certainly anyone who spent so much as a week or two in camp thirty years ago," former Union officer Thomas Wentworth Higginson wrote in 1895, "must be struck with the extraordinary freshness and vigor of the book." Or, as one Union veteran simply put it, "he was with me at Antietam."[31] That a young man born six years after the Civil War and who had never seen combat could write with such authenticity makes *The Red Badge of Courage* one of the great feats in modern U.S. literary history. And that the novel has enjoyed such staying power—Henry Fleming's story has been carried mentally into battle from Kettle Hill to Baghdad—suggests its important contribution to the steady willingness of American men to fight, kill, and die in war.

The novel's authenticity came in part through its vivid approximation of seeing violent death for the first time, close up and on grand scale, through "ghastly" sense impressions enveloped in excited appreciation of war's homicidal force. Approaching his first battle, Henry likened war to "the grinding of an immense and terrible machine. Its complexities and powers, its grim processes fascinated him. He must go and see it produce corpses." And, once joining battle, it is the corpses Henry fixed upon. He picked out the action of men being indiscriminately leveled by war: "punched by bullets," soldiers dropped "like bundles"; one "grunted suddenly as if he had been struck by a club in the stomach." He was most taken by the display of motionless bodies: "They lay twisted in fantastic contortions. Arms were bent and heads were turned in incredible ways. It seemed that the dead men must have fallen from some great height to get into such positions. They looked to be dumped out upon the ground from the sky." When Civil War veterans praised the authenticity of *The Red Badge of Courage*, they didn't mean necessarily that they had made the same observations during battle. Rather, their tribute spoke to the believability of the character's "thought images." Turn-of-the-century readers found an immediacy to the Henry's subjectivity—a psychological reality stimulated by the "grotesque agonies" of men meeting death in war.[32]

Crane placed his two closest studies of death in the novel's episodic middle section, just after Henry ran from battle and right before he turned back to rejoin his regiment and the fighting. Wandering aimlessly through thickets and branches, he came to "a place where the high, arching boughs made a chapel." Henry entered. Cast by "a religious half-light," he halted "horror-stricken" after coming to face-to-face with a dead man, his eyes "staring at the youth," their color "changed to the dull hue to be seen on the side of a dead fish." The corpse's "mouth was open. Its red had changed to an appalling yellow." Little ants ran busily over the face's gray skin, one "trundling some sort of a bundle along the upper lip." Henry fled once again, "pursued" by the image of "the black ants swarming greedily upon the gray face and venturing horribly near to the eyes."[33] As so often pointed out about Crane's writing, *The Red Badge of Courage* uses color to enliven the reader's sense impressions, and to no greater affect than in its faces of death. The novel's most memorable death scene comes shortly thereafter, when Henry stumbled upon a road filled with the wounded, "a blood-stained crowd streaming to the rear." Taking in many of the individuals within this "steady current of the maimed," Henry was most struck by one who "had the gray seal of death already upon his face. His lips were curled in hard lines and his teeth were clinched." Henry saw the man "stalk[ing] like the specter of a soldier, his eyes burning with the power of a stare into the unknown." He turned out to be Jim Conklin, a hometown friend of Henry's and part of his regiment. With a battery of horses and wagons racing toward them, Henry helped "the spectral soldier" off to the side, upon which Jim started running into the fields, his friend following closely behind. After some time, Henry "saw him stop and stand motionless," as if "he was waiting with patience for something that he had come to meet." The dying man's "chest began to heave" violently, like "an animal was within and was kicking and tumbling furiously to be free." Henry sunk "wailing to the ground." Finally, the figure "began to swing forward, slow and straight, in the manner of a falling tree. A swift muscular contortion made the left shoulder strike the ground first." The body bounced upon hitting the earth. Having watched the spectacle, "spellbound," Henry "now sprang to his feet and, going closer, gazed upon the pastelike face. The mouth was open and teeth showed in a laugh. As the flap of the blue jacket fell away from the body, he could see that the side looked as if it had been chewed by wolves." This long episode ends with Henry's impressions exploding into emotion: "The youth turned, with sudden, livid rage, toward the battlefield. He shook his fist. He seemed about to deliver a philippic. 'Hell——'"[34] Driven by rage, enlivened by the horror of death, Henry turned back to battle, now ready to fight.

In writing *The Red Badge of Courage*, Crane set out to "subjectify" battle—that is, to isolate and give full perspective to the thoughts and emotions of an individual soldier in combat. Crane had read through the *Century* "Battles and Leaders" series. He found the articles flat and without feeling: "I wonder that *some* of these fellows don't tell how they *felt* in those scraps. They spout eternally of what they *did* but they are as emotionless as rocks."[35] In sharp contrast, Crane developed the character of Henry Fleming, who served as a type of psychological barometer, his mind and behavior indexing the emotional response to battle. Crane structured that response around the common concern of courage and its determination of manhood. Crane introduced Henry as "an unknown quantity"—"he knew nothing of himself" in battle. The question preoccupied him throughout the narrative. At an early point "he lay on his bunk pondering upon it," trying "to mathematically prove to himself that he would not run from a battle." But it wasn't a matter of conviction: "He could not sit still and with a mental slate and pencil derive an answer." Henry "finally concluded that the only way to prove himself was to go into the blaze, and then figuratively watch his legs to discover their merits and faults." He ran away the first time, but on the second day he stayed in the line of fire and actually led a foolhardy charge that brought fleeting respect to himself and his regiment. "By this struggle he had overcome obstacles which he had admitted to be mountains. They had fallen like paper peaks, and he was now what he called a hero." Henry finally knew himself: "With this conviction came a store of assurance. He felt a quiet manhood, nonassertive but of sturdy and strong blood. . . . He was a man."[36] In one respect, Henry's character followed a rather conservative or traditional story line of man making through trial by fire.

In other ways, though, Crane undermined the idea that war presents a straight-forward test of manhood. To begin with, he showed Henry's flight from battle as a perfectly natural response. Battle produced a supremely hostile physical environment: "the war atmosphere" caused in Henry "a blistering sweat" and "a sensation that his eyeballs were about to crack like hot stones." Henry quickly evolved from a volunteer eager to "experience the ecstasy of excitement" to one who sees war as an elaborate conspiracy set against his person. War was a prison, a monstrous human thing determined by the "iron laws of tradition . . . on four sides." Henry was trapped. He found himself "in a moving box."[37] So he ran away—fleeing out of an elemental sense of fear and self-preservation. And he did so without shame or self-recrimination, his decision to run quickly confirmed by nature: after Henry threw a pine cone at a squirrel, it "immediately, upon recognizing danger," took "to its legs without ado"; it didn't "stand stolidly baring his furry belly to the missile, and die with an upward glance to the heavens." Accepting fear and flight as natural, Henry disbelieved those who felt and did otherwise. He couldn't abide the soldiers who fight "with nothing but eagerness in their faces. It was often that he suspected them to be liars."[38] No wonder some veterans took offense.

Crane's smartest criticism of war and manhood involves the self-inflicted nature of Henry's red badge of courage. Much like his short story "The Blue Hotel," as discussed in chapter 2, Crane's Civil War novel exposes the self-destructive consequences of man making. The youth got his head wound not in mortal combat with the enemy but from another Union soldier running from battle; when Henry tried to stop him to ask for direction, the man crushed his counterpart's head with his rifle butt. Ironically, the resulting wound distinguished Henry, upon returning to his regiment, as a brave, battle-hardened soldier. Men hurt and kill *themselves,* says Crane's story, not only in dividing up into sides and fighting each other over material differences, but also as a consequence of their frantic psychological need for acceptance and rank among men on their own side. Far more than any geopolitical factor—such words as "North," "South," "Union," and "America" cannot be found in the novel—Henry finally fought out of a desperate homosocial desire for respect from the men in his regiment. Earlier questions about what happened to him the first day of battle when he ran "had been knife thrusts to him"—the shame such attention brought "multiplied" Henry's "capacity for self-hatred." And after joining the fighting, his fiercest rage came not from his hatred of the enemy but the hatred of a Union officer whom Henry overheard call him and his regiment "mule drivers."[39] More than anything else, vengeance of that blow motivated him toward courage, risk taking, and heroism.

The second half of *The Red Badge of Courage* reads like a type of emotional how-to manual for war. Henry rejoined his regiment in the thirteenth chapter of the twenty-five-chapter novel, whereupon he matched his initial fear of battle with selfless, oftentimes mindless, bravery. Like the Civil War memoirs, the novel finds pleasure in combat. Compare, for instance, Carlton McCarthy's description of how a typical Confederate soldier "did quicken his lagging step and cry out for joy at the prospect" of fighting, to Henry's "subtle flashings of joy" during battle.[40] The supremely self-conscious Henry also registered the apparent erasure of his self while in furious combat. Henry seemed to lift up and out of his bodily senses. "The youth was not conscious that he was erect upon his feet," Crane wrote. "He did not know the direction of the ground." Henry's disembodiment brought fullness and clarity of vision. Like Emerson's eyeball in the sky, Henry felt "that he saw everything. Each blade of the green grass was bold and clear," Crane continued. "He thought that he was aware of every change in the thin, transparent vapor that floated idly in sheets."[41] As his sketch of transcendence shows, Crane finally did idealize one thing about war: the psychology of fighting.

Losing oneself in combat unfolds within a de-evolutionary framework in Crane's book. At the beginning of the story, while pondering how he'd hold up in battle, Henry understood that war could reduce men to an animal state: "The youth had been taught that a man became another thing in battle." He told himself, though, that those days were over. "Men were better, or more timid," as Crane put it for Henry: "Secular and religious education had effaced the throat-grappling instinct, or else firm finance had held in check the passions." But it is just that brutish instinct that Henry cultivated in the second day of fighting. With the enemy relentlessly pressing his regiment, "he began to fume with rage and exasperation." As an unspoken warning to the enemy as well as a source of self-assurance, Henry imagined transformation: "It was not well to drive men into final corners; at those moments they could all develop teeth and claws." In the following fire fight Henry did become something quite different from himself. Described variously as "a war devil," "a barbarian," "a beast," Crane made Henry's de-evolutionary turn clear. With his regiment ordered to charge, Henry, along with his friend and his lieutenant, stood up amid enemy fire and yelled "'Come on! Come on!' They danced and gyrated," Crane described sharply, "like tortured savages."[42] In one of the purest de-evolutionary figures analyzed in *Brutes in Suits,* Crane's Henry took a knowing step into savagery, one that brought him power and good fortune.

At the base of Henry's devolution lay considerable capacity for destruction. With "red rage" and "wild hate" filling his emotional field, Henry "dream[ed] of abominable cruelties" for his "relentless foe." And, yet, within this hyperdescriptive novel, there is very little attention to the actual act of killing. The most explicit passage comes in the fire fight before the charge: "If he aimed at some changing form through the smoke, he pulled his trigger with a fierce grunt, as if he were dealing a blow of the fist with all his strength." Amid the fury of battle, Henry's enemy remained formless and faceless. During the charge, Henry's most aggressive act, he transfixed on his own flag—"a creation of beauty and invulnerability."[43] Henry didn't act upon the enemy soldiers. Like the Civil War memoirs, killing goes unimagined and unremembered. Unlike the memoirs, however, Crane's book covers self-destruction in extravagant detail. The novel enacts Freud's death instinct, as Henry repeatedly directed his destructiveness inward, toward himself.

That is to say that Henry embraced his own death. He idealized the performative possibilities of being struck down in battle; and, I think, he came to recognize sacrificial death as the essence of war. On the first day of battle, while returning to the front, Henry came upon a column of soldiers marching hurriedly toward the enemy. Their great certitude "seemed to the forlorn young man to be something much finer than stout fighting." Henry "wondered what those men had eaten that they could be in such haste to force their way to grim chances of death. As he watched his envy grew until he thought that he wished to change lives with one of them. He would have liked to have used a tremendous force, he said, throw off himself and become a better." Henry then seized upon a new kind of thought image: "Swift pictures of himself, apart, yet in himself, came to him—a blue desperate figure leading lurid charges with one knee forward and broken blade high—a blue, determined figure standing before a crimson and steel assault, getting calmly killed on a high place before the eyes of all." Henry loved what he saw. He imagined "his dead body" exciting a "magnificent pathos" on the battlefield. "These thoughts uplifted him," Crane wrote: "For a few moments he was sublime."[44] Indeed, this exalted state and its recurrence added a great deal toward Henry's psychological reorientation toward battle.

In other words, Henry absorbed the suicidal dimension of war into his person. He had already come to understand the mechanistic nature of war's violence. Throughout battle, Henry's "regiment bled extravagantly," leaving a "coherent trail of bodies" in its wake. Earlier on, in a panic over battle fast approaching, Henry told himself that he never wanted to be there in the first place: "He had been dragged by the merciless government. And now they were taking him out to be slaughtered."[45] As we have seen, though, after first running from battle, Henry started to fantasize the drama of his heroic death. And this transformation to suicide completed itself after Henry and his friend overheard the officer first call their regiment "mule drivers" and then order it to attack because it was expendable. As the regiment readied itself for the charge, Henry "shot a quick, inquiring glance at his friend. The latter returned to him the same manner of look. They were the only ones who possessed an inner knowledge"—an inner knowledge, that is, of their impending sacrifice. "It was an ironical secret. Still, they saw no hesitation in each other's faces, and they nodded a mute and unprotesting assent when a shaggy man near them said in a meek voice: 'We'll git swallowed.'"[46] Henry offered himself up to be slain. Of course, he returned from the charge alive, and a hero. But that heroism depended on Henry's acceptance and even desire of his own death.

Why did Henry want death? Theorists of self-sacrifice have said that suicidal submission stems from a desire for attachment to a sacred ideal or an omnipotent object. In Freudian terms, it's an expression of love for the "primal father" that, within the realm of war, manifests in such nationalist abstractions as France, China, and the United States.[47] But we know that Henry didn't have a patriotic thought in his overactive head. No, if love of the Father motivated Henry, that emotion seized upon a more immediate homosocial entity—namely, military authority in the form of the officers and the collective sentiment of his regiment. Henry's rage over the "mule driver" slight betrayed a deep level of complex emotions: "Some arrows of scorn that had buried themselves in his heart had generated strange and unspeakable hatred. It was clear to him that his final and absolute revenge was to be achieved by his dead body lying, torn and gluttering, upon the field." Another point of irony from Crane: by doing exactly what the officer expected of him—offering himself to die in battle—Henry somehow thought he would gain his "great and salt reproach."[48] Henry would show him. When considering the same-sex bonds within the military, clearly we should attend not only to the smother-the-grenade loyalty to one's comrades in arms but also to the less direct but equally powerful affection for authority.

In sum, *The Red Badge of Courage* added considerable psychological dimension to late nineteenth-century American fascination with war. Henry Fleming's initial compulsion to see and become a part of war's essential processes, his "wild battle madness" once he gives into the violence and destruction, his purposeful self-dissolution into the otherworldliness of the fighting, all added to a widespread cultural interest in the authentic experience of battle: "'Whoop-a-dadee,' said a man," in Crane's novel, "'here we are! Everybody fightin'. Blood an' destruction.'" Henry's devolution came to rest on an apparent death instinct—a "delirium," as Crane described it, "heedless and blind to the odds. It is a temporary but sublime absence of selfishness." Unmotivated by patriotism, Henry's recklessness while in this sacrificial frame of mind nevertheless served larger ends. "He himself felt the daring spirit of a savage, religion-mad," Crane wrote. "He was capable of profound sacrifices, a tremendous death." Henry's lieutenant certainly saw its power: "By heavens, if I had ten thousand wild cats like you I could tear th' stomach outa this war in less'n a week!" As for Henry, after coming out of the "land of strange, squalling upheavals," he found himself in an uncharacteristically impassive state. Having "rid himself" of a contagion—"the red sickness of battle"—Henry looked forward "to tranquil skies, fresh meadows, cool brooks—an existence of soft and eternal peace."[49] With these concluding words, Crane added one last complication. While glad to be out of his brutish condition, Henry's impending peacetime life seemed like death itself, peaceful yet devoid of real life, purpose, or meaning.

Of Rough Riders, Blood Brothers, and Roosevelt the Berserker

In 1898, at the height of national tribute to Civil War sacrifice and battle, the United States fought Spanish forces in Cuba, Puerto Rico, and the Philippines in what amounted to, first, a crucial early step in American imperialism, and, second, the purest example of masculinist compulsion toward war the country has ever seen. Martial spirit alone did not send the United States to war. Globalization of American corporate capitalism, the willful power of political and economic elites, humanitarian interest in helping Cubans free themselves from colonial rule: these factors, among others, need to be included when accounting for the country's turn-of-the-century war making. The modern American state's penchant for foreign wars, I argue though, benefited from (and to some extent depended on) the late nineteenth-century crystallization of the warrior ideal. In every American war effort, we find a close equation between men wanting to experience the extreme danger and violence of battle and the capacity of the state to make war.

A large number of American men jumped at the chance to fight the Spanish in 1898. With only 28,000 regular troops before the war, the army needed to raise a volunteer force of 200,000 men. It easily did so, refusing more than 50 percent of the applicants, and creating, among many other regiments, the soon-to-be celebrated First U.S. Volunteer Cavalry, or, the Rough Riders.[50] As American troops gathered in Tampa, Florida, for the invasion of Cuba, the volunteer regiments nearly fought each other over space aboard the small number of transport ships. Such enthusiasm for war making continued the legacy of the American soldier produced by the Civil War. While swift U.S. victory over the Spanish provided historical basis for the country's military prowess, the cascade of newspaper and magazine articles, photographs, and illustrations from battle, and then the popular histories of the war and soldier memoirs documented American exuberance over and capacity for spilling blood. The war was an extremely self-referential moment for American manhood. As young men from across the country came together to venture overseas, they spent considerable time and effort describing who they were, how they compared to each other, and, once they bonded, how they compared to the enemy. Such self-definition through male bonding can be found in Spanish-American War songs, stories, and typologies—texts that fix upon the pleasure, fulfillment, and primacy of fighting, killing, and dying in battle.

To come to closer terms with the 1898 volunteers' war in the head, Klaus Theweleit's study of the post–World War I protofascist Freikorps may be helpful for its psychoanalytic insights into "the passionate celebration of violence" as a particular result of male bonding. For Theweleit, the Freikorps' desire for perpetual war began with hatred of women—primarily their bodies and sexuality—a misogyny stemming from pre-Oedipal fear of dissolution. In support of this interpretation, Theweleit draws from 250 Freikorps' novels and memoirs from the 1920s, literature that routinely couples the pleasures of war with the figurative and literal destruction of womanhood. In comparison to these Freikorps' writings, Rough Rider memoirs, letters, and songs are downright benign toward women. But, at the same time, Rough Riders and other Spanish-American War volunteers clearly reveled in their separation from the world of women and the masculine camaraderie that flowed from that detachment. The American volunteers and the Freikorps both experienced what Theweleit describes as "the transformation of eros" to affection for each other and, in turn, a highly pitched reverence for what they do together—namely, the widespread commission of violence. For Theweleit, this blood brotherhood made up the psychological center of German fascism.[51] Given the American volunteers' celebration of killing and dying, so too with U.S. militarism and imperialism during the United States war with Spain.

In comparing U.S. soldiers during the Spanish-American War with the Freikorps, I'm less concerned with the fascist label than with drawing out the similarities in the two groups' willful exuberance for fighting. "We marched onto the battlefields of the postwar world just as we had gone into battle on the Western front," a young soldier in the famous Earhardt Brigade of the Freikorps explained—"singing, reckless, and filled with the joy of adventure as we marched to the attack." Each key word and phrase in this statement applies neatly to the Rough Riders and other American regiments during the 1898 war. American troops went to the war *singing*—as documented in soldiers' memoirs, as well as by the hundreds of battle songs published during and after the war. Testament to esprit de corps, singing may also be examined for how it shaped the meaning of war for the soldiers—the lyrics of Spanish-American War songs are dripping with commitment to bloodletting and sacrifice. By any measure, American soldiers fought the Spanish with unusual *recklessness*. War correspondents recorded independently the odd indifference many of the troops had toward Spanish bullets—eager to demonstrate their mettle, many responded not only proudly but cheerfully after being shot. Working as the primary motivation for American volunteers, *joy of adventure* should be understood as a euphemism for "looking for a fight" and love of violence—as in Brook Adams's comment to Teddy Roosevelt weeks before the war: "You are an adventurer, and you have but one thing to sell—your sword." The American volunteers and regulars *marched to the attack.* "The troop-machine produces the front *before reaching it,*" as Theweleit describes the Freikorps: "It *is* the front: War is the condition of its being."[52] This holds true for the American troops. Defining themselves as natural-born fighters, the U.S. forces during the Spanish-American War can be seen as a moving front of violence, with many soldiers fearing only that the war would end before they got there.

On top of Theweleit's psychoanalytic model of male violence, attention needs to be paid to a powerful generational dynamic in the late nineteenth-century United States that also pushed many young men toward war. " Over all of us in 1898," as Carl Sandburg remembered, "was the shadow of the Civil War and the men who fought it to the end." Civil War memory cultivated an archetype of the American soldier, a legacy of toughness and virility that transcended the earlier divisions of North and South, Yankee and Rebel. And the war against Spain, of course, provided perfect occasion for exercising American fighting prowess and the nation's manhood overall. The racial and ethnic identity of that manhood continued to matter. U.S. militarism during the war included both overt appeals to Anglo-Saxon virility (along with several variants) and a covert assumption of the archetypical soldier's whiteness; at the same time, though, political and military elites identified the American soldier less through race than through combativeness—a trait that virtually all minorities could prove in battle. As Senator Albert Jeremiah Beveridge said in a 1900 speech, war against the Spanish and the possible annexation of the Philippines has brought "opportunity for all the glorious young manhood of the republic—the most virile, ambitious, impatient, militant manhood the world has ever seen."[53] Even Teddy Roosevelt's celebration of American manhood had a superficially inclusive dimension during war. At first he praised African American regulars' bravery during the Battle of San Juan, although he forgot that point in later accounts of the Cuban campaign. Roosevelt proudly spoke of the Rough Riders' "equal" treatment of Indian troopers—he welcomed their characteristic "wildness" as a contributing force to his regiment's ferocity.[54]

"This is going to be a short war, and I am going to get everything I can out of it": in his absolute anxiousness for fulfilling himself through fighting and killing the Spanish, Teddy Roosevelt, more than any other example in my study, symbolized American hypermasculinity and its reflexively violent narcissistic core. His role in founding and leading the Rough Riders made up the apex of his masculinist development from sickly child to Harvard boxer, Western hunter and cowboy, New York City police commissioner, and through to the president and the great white hunter in Africa. Rarely one for subtlety, Roosevelt uttered some of the purest, most transparent statements regarding the personal allure of battle: he found pleasure, for instance, in "coming face to face with the Spaniard" and fighting "the issue out with bullet, butt, and bayonet in a deadly personal encounter"; he believed that "All men who feel any power of joy in battle, know what it is like when the wolf rises in the heart"; and he bragged about his martial prowess in a letter home to his sister—"Did I tell you, I killed a Spaniard with my own hand?" Through the Spanish-American War, Roosevelt became a caricature of himself and the youthful exuberance for battle. "Oh, but we have had a bully fight!" he exclaimed to a crowd upon the Rough Riders' return to the United States. And earlier, upon receiving battle orders for the Rough Riders to ship to Cuba, Roosevelt did his Indian war-dance before the troops, the same hand-on-hip, hat-waving-in-the-air dance he had perfected during his large-game hunting out West.[55]

Given his intense need for battle, the American charge up San Juan Hill may have been an authentic instance of self-realization for Roosevelt. He called it "the great day of my life." After the early skirmish of Las Guasimas—in which Roosevelt felt bewildered by the confusion of battle and after which Stephen Crane and others accused him of leading troops into ambush—the Rough Riders and the Tenth Cavalry, an African American regiment of regulars, among other units, approached the principal Spanish fortification on San Juan ridge. Initially pinned down by enemy fire, the American troops received the order to charge. "I [instantly] sprang on my horse," Roosevelt recounted in *The Rough Riders* (1900), "and then my 'crowded hour' began." By his account and others, Roosevelt found himself during the charge; although perhaps it would be more accurate to say he "lost himself" in the moment. Some close to him during the battle used the word *berserker* (which *Oxford English Dictionary* defines as an "ancient Norse warrior of great strength and courage who fought with frenzied rage in battle") to depict his figure starting up San Juan Hill, as in Rough Rider Tom Hall's account: "Colonel Roosevelt was in a fine Berserker rage." For himself, Roosevelt remembered the "delighted faces" and "joyous excitement" of the men joining him in the charge. With the Americans nearing the hilltop, a few remaining Spanish fled from a hut, upon which Roosevelt drew a revolver salvaged from the *Maine,* fired, and dropped one "neatly as a jackrabbit." Roosevelt biographer Edmund Morris describes how, that evening after the battle, while standing over trenches of enemy corpses, the Colonel exulted to Rough Rider and family friend Bob Ferguson, "Look at all these damned Spanish dead!" In a letter to Roosevelt's second wife, Ferguson tried to explain what the battle had meant to her husband: "No hunting trip so far has ever equaled it in Theodore's eyes. . . . It makes up for the omissions of many past years . . . T. was just reveling in victory and gore."[56]

Roosevelt's base revelry in the blood and guts of war would radiate out into American culture in a myriad of forms and texts. A Roosevelt persona formed around photographs of him in uniform, copies of his speeches, stories of his exploits, and several biographies celebrating him as "an American ideal."[57] With his political star rising, Roosevelt cultivated this attention with characteristic hubris and energy. In April 1899 he stood before a large audience at the Chicago Hamilton Club and delivered one of his most famous and widely circulated speeches. In "The Strenuous Life," Roosevelt urged Americans to live life like war. Only the martial ideal could counteract the "spirit of gain and greed which recognizes in capitalism the be-all and end-all of national life." It would order social relations by returning woman to her role as "housewife, the helpmeet of the homemaker, the wise and fearless mother of many healthy children," and by restoring in American man the "great fighting masterful qualities" that had been nearly lost to "over-civilization." Here his Rough Rider persona added greatly to his spoken words. The large crowd received him "wildly," as the *Chicago Daily Tribune* reported: "Frequently he was forced to stop [speaking], while the 3,000 men and women rose and cheered . . . till the golden arches of the auditorium shook." As he warned that "weakness is the greatest of crimes," and as he championed the "mighty lift that thrills 'stern men with empires in their brains,'" American hypermasculinity became one with national expansion and war.[58]

Before winning the New York governorship, Roosevelt wrote his war memoir *The Rough Riders:* first serialized in *Scribner's,* it would become his best-selling book to date, one of the most widely read contemporary accounts of the campaign against the Spanish, and an extremely effective typology of the American as fighter. Since his hunting and cowboy days in the Dakota Territory, he had wanted to lead "harum-scarum roughriders" into battle and, with President McKinley's decision to go to war, Roosevelt pursued a commission in a volunteer regiment with dogged purpose. Finally, Secretary of War Russell Alger offered him the command of a regiment, although he chose second in command, with his friend, Dr. Leonard Wood, army surgeon and Medal of Honor winner in fighting the Apaches, leading the First Volunteer Cavalry unit, which was nevertheless dubbed "Roosevelt's Rough Riders."[59] Most of the regiment's troopers "came from the Four Territories," Roosevelt explained, "that is, from the lands that have been most recently won over to white civilization" through the Indian Wars. "Frontier conditions" had molded these men into exceptionally tough and ready fighters, he continued: "In all the world there could be no better material for soldiers than that afforded by these grim hunters of the mountains, these wild rough riders of the plains." Roosevelt drew out their qualities in his profile of Wood, whose engagement with the Apaches had given him "extraordinary physical strength and endurance" and "robust and hardy qualities of body and mind." Wood's temperament characterized the Rough Riders: "He was by nature a soldier of the highest type, and like most natural soldiers, he was, of course, born with a keen longing for adventure." Roosevelt added, without trace of irony, "though, an excellent doctor, what he really desired was the chance to lead men into some kind of hazard."[60]

The Rough Riders came together in Roosevelt's self-image. With men from the territories filling the first 780 openings in the regiment, Roosevelt then accepted 220 additional volunteers from mostly Ivy League universities and city athletic clubs, thus establishing in the troops that East-West, urban-frontier axis so central to his own person. Southerners joined the regiment, but in *The Rough Riders* Roosevelt downplayed their Civil War heritage, concentrating instead on how the easterners "possessed precisely the same temper" of the other recruits and "in whose veins the blood stirred with the same impulse which once sent the Vikings overseas." In documenting the easterners' fighting spirit, or at least the requisite quality of hardiness, Roosevelt championed their athletic prowess, as in his description of recruit Dudley Dean as "perhaps the best quarterback who ever played on a Harvard eleven." Roosevelt concluded his typology of the Rough Riders on the same characteristic he underlined in Wood: "wherever they came from, and whatever their social position," the troops shared "a thirst for adventure. They were to a man," he repeated, "born adventurers," hereby emphasizing what he most valued in himself—masculine compulsion for risk taking and capacity for taking human life.[61]

Roosevelt's regard for the Rough Riders' ability as fighters involved homoerotic attention to their physical person. Similar to his friend Owen Wister's attraction to the cowboy, Roosevelt was particularly drawn to the rugged western troopers. "They were a splendid set of men," Roosevelt wrote of the cowboy-soldiers from Arizona, New Mexico, and Texas, "tall and sinewy, with resolute, weather-beaten faces, and eyes that looked a man straight in the face without flinching." He also paid close attention to Captain Allyn Capron, a Brooklyn native, eight-year regular army veteran, and "on the whole," in Roosevelt's words, "the best soldier in the regiment." He continued: Capron "was the fifth in descent from father to son who had served in the army of the U.S., and in body and mind alike he was fitted to play his part to perfection. Tall and lithe, a remarkable boxer and walker, a first-class rider and shot, with yellow hair and piercing blue eyes, he looked like what he was, the archetype of the fighting man." Clearly Roosevelt had found his Viking warrior. In a later *Rough Rider* passage, Roosevelt returned to Capron, along with Sergeant Hamilton Fish—"two better representatives of the American soldier, there were not in the whole army." Roosevelt wrote with near abashment: "As we stood around the flickering blaze that night I caught myself admiring the splendid bodily vigor of Capron and Fish—the captain and the sergeant. Their frames seemed of steel, to withstand all fatigue; they were flushed with health; in their eyes shone high resolve and fiery desire." Other Rough Riders shared Roosevelt's physical attraction to the fighting man. "Ah, yes," Trooper Edwin Tyler recalled in his memoir *Santiago Campaign* (1898), "here comes another squadron, headed by Major Dunn, whose fair hair and ruddy complexion shimmer in the sunlight, betraying the manly beauty that women dream about."[62] Not unlike the intense homicidal culture of turn-of-the-century college football, the Rough Riders and other units in the Spanish-American War expressed same-sex attraction and even desire.

In accompanying Roosevelt and the Rough Riders to Cuba, a small army of correspondents promulgated the archetype of the American fighter. Among the most accomplished writers, Stephen Crane, Richard Harding Davis, and Edward Marshall covered the war for the large-circulation jingoist New York newspapers. Of these three men, Crane was the least demonstrative about the Americans' prowess. He felt ambivalently about Roosevelt. One would like to think that he saw through the bluster surrounding the campaign. And, yet, he held little back in his dispatch on the charge up San Juan Hill. It was, Crane wrote, "the best moment of anybody's life."[63] Crane did maintain some distance on American patriotism though. As in *The Red Badge of Courage*, his Cuban dispatches are far more concerned with how the human animal thrives on battle than any distinctive American strain of the species.

Not so with Richard Harding Davis, who did as much as any writer to venerate the American soldier in the U.S. war with Spain and to personify national fighting spirit in Roosevelt. In his book *The Cuban and Porto Rican Campaigns* (1899), Davis influentially named Roosevelt the "most conspicuous man" in the San Juan charge, he "made you feel like you wanted to cheer." Davis further chronicled "the eager spirit" of the Rough Riders in battle. At the end of his chapter on "The Battle of San Juan," Davis related the Spanish impression of the Americans' courage under fire. "And so, when instead of retreating on each volley," Davis wrote, "the Rough Riders rushed at them, cheering and filling the hot air with wild cowboy yells, the dismayed enemy retreated upon Santiago, where he announced he had been attacked by the entire American Army." Davis underscored American ferocity with well-crafted hearsay: "One of the residents of Santiago asked one of the soldiers if those Americans fought well. 'Well!' he replied, 'they tried to catch us with their hands!'"[64] Other writers used this strategy of capitalizing on foreign testimony to American combativeness. In his chronicle *The Fight for Santiago* (1899), Stephen Bonsal quotes a Spanish soldier before Las Guasimas: "'The Americans have great cannon but they have not stout hearts'"; after what he saw at the skirmish, Bonsal contends, the Spaniard reformulated his opinion: "The Americans have no cannon, but, before God, what a stomach they have for a fight." And Edwin

Marshall's book *The Story of the Rough Riders* (1899) begins with an English war correspondent's opinion of the "American soldier": "It would be madness to back the English, German, or French fighting machines against men like those in the First Volunteer Cavalry."[65] The rest of Marshall's book details the qualities of those men.

Indeed, Marshall's *Story of the Rough Riders* is one long exercise in reputation building. It focuses on the manhood of the eastern volunteers—the "dude warriors," the "dandy troopers," the "gilded gang," as Marshall recalled several prewar epithets. "The comic paragraphers had a great deal of fun over the enlistment of these men," Marshall noted, but they "stopped saying funny things when the petted ones of fortune, later, stood up like the real men they were and took, without whimpering, their doses of steel medicine on the battlefields of Cuba." Marshall played up the camaraderie between the Rough Rider dudes and cowboys. "Oil and water are not farther removed than were the everyday natures of these two groups of men," he wrote; yet war or, more precisely, their attraction to war brought them together: "instantly they fraternized, and from that moment—through the hardships of it all, through the blood and death and fever of it all—these men were brothers." Having himself been shot through the spine and nearly left for dead at Las Guasimas, Marshall paid special attention to what he took to be the picturesquely heroic deaths of the Rough Riders in the field. More routinely, he documented the warrior pedigrees of the eastern troopers. "Woodbury Kane was a polo player of note, and a hard rider on the hunting field," Marshall wrote matter-of-factly. "He came of a fighting family; played football at Harvard. Craig Wadsworth was one of the 'fighting Genesee Wadsworths,' whose name had always been among the foremost in the annals of the country in war." This eastern fighting tradition, Marshall's book says in sum, combined with the naturally rough-and-ready cowboy volunteers, amounted to a remarkably deadly military unit. It speaks of the Americans "cheerfully kill[ing]" the Spanish at San Juan.[66]

As further evidence of the Rough Riders' feelings for battle, Marshall reported that "There was not a man in the whole regiment who did not voice in his heart that cry which he shouted from his lips":

> Rough, tough, we're the stuff,
> We want to fight, and we can't
> get enough,
> Whoo-pee.[67]

Marshall wrote little else about these words. How and under what circumstance they were spoken, cried, or sung is difficult to document. So too with the scores of other cheers, songs, and poems from the Spanish-American War. Culled from contemporary newspaper coverage as well as regimental histories and soldiers' memoirs, this turn-of-the-century war verse nevertheless helps fill in American war in the head and the hope for self-gratification through killing and dying in battle. The congressional publication of *Reminiscences and Thrilling Stories of the War by Returned Heroes Containing Vivid Accounts of Personal Experiences by Officers and Men* (1899) is an especially rich source of Spanish-American War songs and poems. Like the "Rough, tough, we're the stuff" cheer, much of this material self-identifies the fighting spirit of the men singing it. More distinct tropes include exultation over bloodletting and the coincident bonds of violent brotherhood.

Considerable extratextual evidence suggests that the most popular song among American troops was a variation of "Hot Time in the Old Town Tonight." A minstrel song written in 1886, "Hot Time"'s original lyrics involve a religious meeting—"When you hear that the preaching does begin / Bend down low to drive away your sin"—and then a visit to a brothel—"There'll be girls for ev'ry body: In that good, good old town"—with each verse ending in the refrain: "There'll be a hot time in the old town tonight, my baby." The song was widely and liberally adapted by the Rough Riders and other Spanish-American War regiments. "Grigsby's Cowboys"—a Dakota volunteer regiment—sang the following while headed south toward Cuba:

> Come along and get you ready, and bring your good old gun,
> For the cowboys are a comin, and there's going to be some fun.
> They are comin on their broncos, and they are comin mighty quick,
> And when they meet those Spaniards, well won't they make 'em sick.

The first chorus includes the lines:

> When they hear those cowboys comin, with Grigsby at their head,
> Well won't they give 'em sin;
> Oh, Yes!, They will give them h-l, and then they'll rub it in,
> There'll be a hot time in Cuba that night, My Baby![68]

Typical of Spanish-American War lyrics' proclamations of group virility and prowess, the song is most provocative in its excited anticipation of the night and the promise of hotness. "Hot Time"'s association between sex and violence, the interplay between doing up the town and shooting up the Spanish, reflected and prompted American troopers' attraction to war.

While proclaiming a particular unit's fighting prowess, a good deal of Spanish-American War verse demystifies killing in battle, as in the "Cowboy's Battle Song": "With our pistols by our side, / We are ready for a ride, / Shouting the voice of western cowboys." It continues: "We're a band of wild an woolly cowboys." And ends bluntly: "We will round the Spanish in, / While this little song we sing; / Death to the Spaniard by the Cowboy."[69] And the poem "The Reg'lar Army Man" couldn't be plainer:

> He's kinder rough and maybe tough,
> The Reg'lar Army man;
> The rarin', tarin',
> Sometimes swearin',
> Reg'lar Army man.
> The millin', drillin',
> Made for killin',
> Reg'lar Army man.[70]

Among the many songs of the Rough Riders, "The Ballad of Teddy's Terrors" touts their desire for violence. "Now Teddy's Sunday School wus movin' on its way / A-seekin' in its peaceful style some Dagos fer to slay; . . . Fer when this gentle regiment had heard the bullets fly, / They had a violent hankerin' to make them Spaniards die." In this song at least, fulfillment of that desire rested with Roosevelt himself: "Then Teddy seen [the Spanish] runnin', and he gives a monstrous bawl, / And grabbed a red-hot rifle where a guy had let it fall, / And fixin' of his spectacles more firmly on his face, / he started to assassinate them all around the place."[71] Along with its jocular tone, this account's straightforwardness betrays the comfort level American volunteers had toward killing. It points to a new expectation of finding pleasure in wartime violence.

Compared to Civil War songs and popular poems, for instance, the turn-of-the-twentieth-century war verse indulges in violence, fantasizing about killing before the fact and celebrating it afterward. As discussed earlier, the massive violence of the Civil War did evoke utterances of stark bloodlust, but record of such statements comes from soldiers' private letters and diaries written spontaneously to the violence itself. The Civil War published verse is tamer: "'Tis my delight to March and Fight / Like a New York volunteer" are among the most explicitly violent words in song, as is the line from the Confederate song "Riding a Raid": "We are all three thousand sabres and not a dull blade."[72] This verse anticipates the Spanish-American War songs' virile self-referentiality. But it doesn't begin to match the latter's pure aggression, as in this song from southwestern volunteers printed in April 1898 in the *Santa Fe New Mexican*:

> We sigh for the field of carnage, the blood-red stream of war;
> We long for the noise of conflict that is borne on winds afar;
> We are tired of this inaction, while the wild and restless sea
> Seems to implore . . . , that we make a people free.[73]

While the stated objective of freeing a people both hearkens back to the Civil War and portends U.S. imperialism, this song's blood and carnage help mark a turning point in the emotional history of American soldiering: a love of war for war's sake; a yearning for adventure as an antidote to peace and quiet; and the use of a heroic cause as a rationalization for or a pretense to the primary motivation toward violent action. These features certainly existed before the Spanish-American War, but never in such transparent, unabashed form.

Most of all, the turn-of-the-century war verse marks a psychological readiness for killing in battle. Compare the Confederate song's declaration, "We are all three thousand sabres and not a dull blade" to the Spanish-American war song "From the Ranks" and the eager specificity of its action: "The proud flesh of Spain must the sabre cut feel, / Their canker spot taste of our bayonet steel / May the flash of the rifle, the boom of the gun, / Be the herald of victory soon to be won."[74] And consider the athletic furiousness of "The Cavalry Charge":

> Resistless and reckless
> Of aught may betide,
> Like demons, not mortals,
> The wild troopers ride.
> Cut right! And cut left!
> For parry who needs?
> The bayonets shiver
> Like wind-shattered reeds! . . .
> Triumphant, remorseless,
> Unerring as death,
> No sabre that's stainless
> Returns to its sheath.
> The wounds that are dealt
> By that murderous steel
> Will never yield case
> For the surgeons to heal.
> Hurrah! They are broken—
> Hurrah! Boys, they fly—
> None linger save those
> Who but linger to die.[75]

As in this song's blood-stained saber and the New Mexican song's "blood-red stream of war," a number of other Spanish-American War songs fixate on bloodletting and its dramatic imagery. "Our Soldier's Song," for example, speaks of "Hearing the hum of bullets! / Eager to charge the foe! / Biding the call to battle, / Where crimson heart streams flow!"[76] The flow of blood also appears routinely in another crucial theme of the Spanish-American War verse: the American soldier dying in battle.

In fact, a preponderance of this fin-de-siècle war verse concerns itself with death. In her study of the popular literature of the Civil War, Alice Fahs writes that the songs and poetry from that earlier conflict tended to "single out" the "soldier's thoughts at the moment of death." She explains that "a sentimental insistence on the importance of sympathy and individual suffering" worked to counter the Civil War's increasingly mechanized and anonymous slaughter. Such sentimentalism can be found in some Spanish-American War songs and poems. If sentimentalism furnishes personalized, "tender," and "emotive" death, as Fahs says, then the poem "After the Battle" fills the bill. It begins with a soldier coming upon a gravely wounded officer: "Brave Captain! Can thou speak? / What is it thou dost see! / A wondrous glory lingers on thy face, / . . . Knowest thou place? / The place?" the dying man answers: "'Tis San Juan comrade. / Is the battle over? / The victory—the victory—is it won? / My wound is mortal; I know I cannot recover— / The battle for me is done!" But after hearing of victory, the Captain faces death proudly and bravely. "After the Battle" ends in Christian pathos, sentiment so common in Civil War poetry about death: "The revile calls! Be strong my soul, and peaceful; / The Eternal City bursts upon my sight! / The ringing air with ravishing melody is full— / I've won the fight!"[77] Spanish-American War verse provided a range of emotional responses to dying in battle—some of it tenderhearted; some of it hard-edged and masculinist, rough and virile to the end; most of it fixed on a bleeding soldier's body, a corporeal sacrifice to cause, country, and brothers in arms.

"The Wounded Soldier"—one of the bloodiest poems from the Spanish-American War—presents a decidedly sober view of death and sacrifice. "[L]ay me down in the hollow," a mortally wounded officer tells his men, where "we are out of the strife. / By heaven! The foeman may track me in blood, / For this hole in my breast is outpouring a flood." The poem proceeds episodically. After being asked if he wants a doctor, he responds "No! No surgeon for me; he can give me no aid / The surgeon I want is a pick-axe and a spade." He then notices one of his men grief-stricken: "What, Morris, a tear? Why shame on you, man! / I thought you a hero; but since you began / To whimper and cry, like a girl in her teens"—so much for tenderheartedness —"By George! I don't know what the devil it means." The officer tries to cut off further emotion by recalling the fighting: "And, boys, that you love me I certainly know, But wasn't it grand, When they [the Spanish] came down that hill over the sloughing sand? / But we stood—did we not—like immovable rock, / Unheeding their balls and repelling their shock." Recounting the excitement of battle, the officer underlines the drama of American death and sacrifice, rather than killing and conquest: "Did you mind the loud cry, when, as turning to fly, / Our men sprang upon them, determined to die? / Oh, wasn't it grand?" he exclaims, seeking confirmation of his own sacrificial heroism. Otherwise, the poem ends unsentimentally: "God help the poor wretches who fell in the fight; No time was there given for prayers or for flight. / They fell by the score, in the crash, hand to hand, / And they mingled their blood with the sloughing sand." The dying man's last moments are consumed by blood over prayer: "Great heavens! This bullet hole gapes like a grave . . . Great God, how I bleed! / Our father in heaven—boys, tell me the rest, / While I stanch the blood from the hole in my breast."[78]

Were American troopers really "determined to die" in battle? "The Wounded Soldier" may exhibit poetic license in celebrating deadly sacrifice, but one should consider that the U.S. war against the Spanish may very well have been the high point in American willingness to take a bullet. It's difficult to generalize about such suicidal impulses, but too many accounts speak of soldiers responding to being shot with indifference and even gratitude to pass it off as pure hyperbole. "Hit? Yes, I wuz hit, but then / So wuz lots of other men," the narrator says in "The Coward." As the poem's title suggests, the soldier is less than enthusiastic about being under fire; he comes around, though, succumbing to expectations of sticking your neck out: "In the din I seemed to hear / Mother, sayin', 'Willie, stan' / An' take your bullet like a man.'"[79] In a different vein, Teddy Roosevelt remembered that when "one of our men would crumple up" from being shot, "[i]n no case did the man make any outcry," he "seem[ed] to take it as a matter of course; at the outside, making only such a remark as, 'Well, I got it that time.'" Edward Marshall reported that after Roosevelt was slightly wounded in the hand from tree bark shattered by a bullet, he started "waving his hand proudly in the air so that the men who were near enough to him could see the blood, and shouted: 'I've got it, boys! I've got it!'" Other Rough Riders, according to Marshall, "were glad of their wounds"—they accepted them "cheerfully."[80] An extraordinary passage from Marshall's *Story of the Rough Riders* speaks of what he saw and felt among the wounded, the dying, and the dead at Las Guasimas: nothing has ever "impress[ed] me as did the silent patience, the quiet, calm endurance, with which those men—heroes all—accepted their suffering, and nothing has ever seemed grander to me, more beautiful, or more sublime, than the deaths of some of them." Somewhat self-conscious about his lionization of these fated soldiers, Marshall nevertheless found a noble manliness in their demise:

> Rough men they were, who had come out of the West to fight, but if a church organ had been pealing on that hillside, if softened lights had been falling on those faces, through stained-glass windows, devoutly patterned, if the robes and insignia of the

most solemn and holy of all the rites of all the churches had surrounded them, I could not have been more impressed than I was then when I looked down into the rusty swaying grass of that Cuban hillside, and saw the dirty, sweaty-faces, the rough and rugged clinched fists, the ragged uniforms on our American soldiers—dying.[81]

To quote Marshall at length is not to imply that his emotional investment in dying in battle corresponded exactly with that of the soldiers themselves. One can only imagine the wide range of actual last thoughts and feelings among the poor men cut down in the Cuban grass. But, at the same time, Marshall's testament to the Las Guasimas dead, along with scores of songs and poems praising such sacrifice, gives us an idea of the powerful homosocial motivation at work among the young volunteers. "Yes, let me like a soldier fall / Upon some open plain," rhapsodizes a Spanish-American War poem. "This breast expanding for the ball, / To blot out every stain; / Brave, manly hearts confer my doom, / That gentler ones may tell, / Howe 'er forgot, unknown my tomb, / I like a soldier fell."[82] If we attribute any ideological power to such war verse, then a determination to die in battle does not seem that farfetched.

The ideology of sacrifice grew more effective when coupled with patriotism. Marshall held nothing back on this score either, writing that "the men who died" at Las Guasimas "exulted because it was their proud privilege to be the first in the United States army, during this war, to perish for their country."[83] And a great deal of Spanish-American War verse connected sacrifice with country, as in "Dirge of the Drums": "Dead! Dead! Dead, dead, dead! / To the muffled beat of the lone retreat / And speeding lead, / Lay the hero low to his well-earned rest, / In the land he loved, on her mother breast, / While the sunlight dies in the darkening West— / Dead! Dead! Dead!" Most of the patriotic songs and poems struck a far less solemn note in their imaginings of death in battle. "The Young American," for instance, announces that the subject, "Dauntless in the battle-plain," is "Ready at the country's need / For her glorious cause to bleed!" Moved by love of country, the narrator is content to leave his life to fate: "Happy if celestial favor / Smile upon the high endeavor; / Happy if it be thy call / In the holy cause to fall." The message in "It is Great for Our Country to Die" couldn't be clearer:

Oh! It is great for our country to die, where ranks are contending:
Bright is the wreath of our fame; glory awaits us for aye—
Glory that never is dim, shining on with light never ending—
Glory that shall never face, never, oh! Never away.
Oh! Then, how great for our country to die, in the front rank to perish,
Firm with our breast to the foe, victory's shout in our ear!

Long they our statues shall crown, in songs our memory cherish;
We shall look forth from our heaven, pleased the sweet music to hear.

This patriotic-sacrificial verse can be seen as a turn-of-the-century variation on sentimentalism, with the nation becoming the object of religious devotion and the American flag a sacrament. "O, wrap the flag around me, boys," began a Spanish-American War song by the same title, "to die were far more sweet, / With freedom's starry emblem, boys, to be my winding sheet. / In life I loved to see it wave, and follow where it led, / And now my eyes grow dim, my hands would clasp its last bright shed." Being buried with the flag assured the soldier a certain spiritual life after death: "But though my body moulders, boys, my spirit will be free, / And every comrade's honor, boys, will still be dear to me. / There in the thick and bloody fight never let your ardor lag, / For I'll be there still hovering near, above the dear old flag." The same theme can be found in "Tell My Mother I Die Happy." The narrator—who will "die happy" because he knows "our foes" are "flying"—tells his "comrades" to "Wrap the starry flag around me, / I would press its folds once more; / Let the cold earth be my pillow, And the stars and stripes my shroud; / Soon, oh, soon, I shall be marching / Amid the heavenly crowd."[84] In these poems of dying for country, the soldier takes on a redemptive Christ-like quality—far more exulted in death than in life.

Turn-of-the-century patriotic war songs and poems pay considerable attention to the life of the nation, its history, and how the past would embolden it against its foes. After asking "what worse than horrid war?" and answering "vile and ignominious peace, / Bought with the price of honor," the poem "War" invokes American history to support fighting the Spanish: "Two strokes sublime Columbia's hand / Hath dealt in war—one stroke to save / From foreign sway our native land— One stroke to free the negro slave. / Now, once again the great sword awes / The despot—flames o'er land and sea— / A volunteer in Cuba's cause; / Spain falls, and Cuba rises, free!"

One of the most popular themes within this patriotic verse is post–Civil War national reunion. "We are All Yankees Now," for instance, recalls how "Once our nation was divided, / And was rent by cruel strife. / Then the Johnnies and the Yankees / Threatened long to take its life." But what didn't tear the country asunder only made it stronger: "Let us shout for the Union, / To the Stars and Stripes we'll bow, No party lines divide us, / For we're all Yankees now." The poem ends on an ominous imperialist note: "With our millions all united, / And with freedom's flag unfurled, / Backed by patriotic freemen, / Uncle Sam can rule the world."[85]

Like the Memorial Day addresses from the post–Civil War period, many poems translated "the romance of re-union" into martial spirit among the late nineteenth-century generation of young American men. Two months before U.S. forces invaded Cuba, in April 1898, *Harper's Weekly* published "The Call," assuring readers that in mobilizing for war, "'Tis a nation answering here." It continues: "From the North, from the South, from East, from West, / Hear the thrill of the rumbling drum? / Under one flag they march along, With their voices swelling a single song, / Here they come, they come, they come!" The ranks swell all the more from a nation united after bloody civil war:

> The Past sweeps out and the Present comes, / A present that all have wrought / And the sons of these sires, at the same camp fires / Cheer one flag where their fathers fought! / Yes, we know of the graves on the Southern hills / That are filled with the Blue and the Gray, / We know how they fought and they died, / We honor them both side by side, / And they're brothers again today, / Brothers again—thank God on high! / (Here's a hand-clasp all around). / The sons of one race now take their place / On one common and holy ground.[86]

Memory of the Civil War also set a standard of risk and adventure, a motivation toward action not lost in turn-of-the-century verse. The poem "Before Santiago" asks rhetorically, "Who cries that the days of daring are those that are faded far, / That never a light burns planet-bright to be hailed as the hero's star? / Let the deeds of the dead be laureled, the brave of the elder years / But a song, we say, for the men of today who have proved themselves their peers!" To emphasize, from the Civil War came a tradition of fighting spirit as a national character trait, a central theme throughout the belligerent, self-referential Spanish-American War verse, especially that celebrating the Rough Riders: "Cow punchers, some of them / Blue stockings, some of them / Born heroes, all of them, / Teddy in front: / Not theirs to be denied, / Victors where 'er betide, / Swelldom's e'lasting pride, / Oh, the Rough riders." As seen in this short poem, "Charge of the Terrors," eastern elites drew closely from martial heroism in affirming their masculinity—a source of considerable self-doubt at the turn-of-the-century.[87]

Indeed, a series of war poems deals specifically with dudism (as defined in chapter 1, an eastern fop pretending to be a real man) and overcoming it through killing and dying in battle. "The Dudes before Santiago," a poem published in a July 1898 issue of the *Chicago Daily Tribune*, documents the initial uncertainty over upper-class WASP capacity for war: "They scoffed when we lined up with Teddy, / They said we were dudes and all that; / They imagined that 'Cholly' and 'Fweddie' / Would faint at the drop of a hat!" In this poem at least, real manhood comes through risk taking or, more flatly, a willingness to be killed:

But let them look there in the ditches,
Blood-stained by the swells in the van,
And know that a chap may have riches
And still be a man!
They said that we'd wilt under fire,
And run if the foeman said, 'Boo!'
But a fellow may have a rich sire
And still be a patriot, too!
Look there where we met twice our number,
Where the lifeblood of dudes drenched the earth!
The swells who be in their last slumber
Prove what we are worth!

Similarly, the poem "The Yankee Dude'll Do" registers initial doubt over "Cholly's" masculinity, focusing on elite enthusiasm for the softer sports as a sure sign of effeminacy: "When Cholly swung his golf stick on the links, / Or knocked the tennis ball across the net, / With his bangs done up in cunning little kinks— / When he wore the tallest collar he could get, / Oh, it was the fashion then / To impale him on the pen— / To regard him as a being made of putty through and through." War, however, changes everything, or at least it presents that opportunity: "But his racquet's laid away, / He is roughing it today, / And heroically proving that the Yankee dude'll do." The poem goes on to celebrate the dudes' bravery:

How they hurled themselves against the angry foe,
In the jungle and the trenches on the hill!
When the word charge was given,
every dude was on the go—
He was there to die, to capture or to kill!
Oh, he struck his level, when
Men were called upon again
To preserve the ancient glory of the old red, white and blue!
He has thrown his spats away,
He is wearing spurs today,
And the world will please take notice that the Yankee dude will do.

Having exchanged racket for gun, spats for spurs, and perhaps life for death, the "dude" (the word had now become a term of playful affection) redeemed himself within the homosocial order of man-making virility.[88]

As suggested in "The Yankee Dude'll Do," a critical theme within late nineteenth-century nationalism was ethnic regeneration through violence. Historians have written extensively about how Spanish-American War jingoists sold U.S. imperialism as a vital return to Anglo-Saxon heritage.[89] In his 1898 article on "The War with Spain, and After," for example, Walter Hines Page urged readers of the *Atlantic Monthly* to not "be content with peaceful industry" but rather match "the adventurous spirit of our Anglo-Saxon forefathers" through foreign expansion. Culminating in Roosevelt's "Strenuous Life" speech, the ideological complex of aggressive Anglo-American manhood and nationhood also appears in popular war songs and poetry. "The Anglo-American Race"—in addition to characteristically confusing cultural nationality or ethnicity with biological race—underlines the historical ties between Britain and the United States: "We are one in the bonds of progression, / In the power to toil and fight, / We are one in our loathing of wrong, / For liberty, honor, and right. . . . Hurrah! Hurrah! For the Union Jack / When joined with the Stripes and Stars!" More pointed in imperialist design, "The Saxons" explicitly connects past conquest with future power: "We sing the fame of Saxon name, / And the spell of its world-wide power, / Of its triumphs vast in the glorious past, / And the might of the rising hour; / And our bosoms glow, for we proudly know / With the flag of right unfurled, / That the strength and skill of the Saxon will / Is bound to rule the world." Within the post–Civil War context of national reunification ("The Saxon" acclaims that "the wound is healed and the friendship sealed"), the appeal to Anglo-American tradition did contribute to martial spirit during the new war against Spain.[90] But—and this is a distinctive and decisive feature of U.S. nationalism—Anglo-Saxonism coexisted with racial and ethnic inclusivity within some aspects of military culture. Far from perfect or benign, this inclusivity was nevertheless real. United States' foreign war making depended on it.

In the Spanish-American War, and in building and exercising its military might since that time, the United States depended on cross-cultural masculine interest in fighting. For example, the large number of Polish American volunteers in the war against Spain believed that military service would provide an inroad into their new homeland's civic life. Along with assimilation, as Matthew Frye Jacobson has pointed out, these men understood their eagerness to fight to be in keeping with their Polish heritage. "It was with certain masculinist bravado," Jacobson writes, "that volunteers under the banner 'The Poles are Ready' crowded into a Chicago recruiting station emboldened by the song, 'Fight, brothers though a hundred will fall I will feel not defeat, / Glory will be your legacy, and so march to Cuba!'"[91] Generally speaking, this dual motivation of the Polish American volunteers exemplified the mind-set of various hyphenated-American soldiers, including Anglo-Americans. That is to say, both sides of the hyphen pointed men to war: the left side invoked a particularist, ethnically or racially determined tradition of battle readiness; the right side, while increasingly particularist itself after Civil War memory crystallized martial spirit as a national character trait, also marked a collective identity for U.S. soldiers. In short, the United States cultivated a democratic feature in its sanction of violence. Hegemonic in nature, loaded with exceptions of race, class, age, sex, and sexuality, inclusive martial nationalism came into full view during the Spanish-American War.

The democratic grain in U.S. war making appears in Spanish-American War verse, but nowhere more fully than in an untitled poem in Thomas Handford's book *Theodore Roosevelt: The Pride of the Rough Riders, an Ideal American* (1899). Heading a chapter on the "Romance of the Rough Riders—Gathering of the Clans," the poem begins with the common theme of the dude and the cowboy dissolving their differences through war: "Broadcloth, buckskin, coats of blue or tan, / Strip it off for action, and beneath you'll find a man, / The boy that bucked the center and the lad that roped the steer / Chums in fighting fellowship—charging with a cheer." The poem is typical in evoking blood—"The shimmering blade of the bayonet / Is red in the downing sun; / 'Twill burn with a rudder crimson yet / Or ever the work is done"—in documenting pleasure in battle—"Kentucky fought with a grim delight / And Texas with his soul"—and in celebrating troopers' mettle—"If the wounded sobbed it was not for pain, / But that they could fight no more." It is also inventive in identifying hyphenated-American soldiers in Cuba: "Hark to the swell of the Rebel yell, / The bugle calm and clear, / The 'uh-luh-luh-loo' of the tameless Sioux / And the roar of the Saxon cheer!" It continues and concludes in this inclusive vein:

> The Baresark [*sic*] awoke in the Teuton folk;
> The Roman was born anew;
> The pride of the blood of the Macabee
> Revived in the fighting Jew;
> While up on the right, like a storm at night,
> Rilled with the riving flame,
> Their eyes ashine, in a steadfast line,
> The negro troopers came.
> Sons of the Past!—her best and last—
> At Freedom's bugle call,
> The Races sweep to the conquered keep
> The flag that shelters all. . . .
> When we trust our weal to the clashing steel,
> The Land call forth her own;
> Then it's Ho! For the men of heart and brain,

And blood and brawn and bone!
Broadcloth, buckskin, garb of blue or tan,—
Rip it with a bullet and beneath you'll find a man,
Ebon-featured, swarthy volunteer,
Chums in fighting—fellowship—charging with a cheer.[92]

U.S. nationalism's particularist and collectivist dimensions work in close accord in this poem. Beginning with the reawakening of specific ethnic and racial martial traditions, it culminates in what unites the soldiers—namely, country, as represented by the "flag that shelters all," and the "blood and brawn and bone" and fighting spirit of American manhood.

In highlighting the "Ebon-featured regular," this poem also raises one of the most critical aspects of U.S. nationalism: African Americans' historic military service and sacrifice for a country that has systematically and violently degraded their race. With the late nineteenth and early twentieth centuries marking a nadir in U.S. race relations, many African Americans certainly argued against such patriotic support. But, on balance, the other side carried more sway, especially after war began. The Emancipation Proclamation of 1863 and subsequent enlistment in the Union army generated an extremely close association in black thought between fighting and freedom—a legacy, as Frederick Douglass described in 1883, of rising "in one bound, from social degradation to the plain of common equality with all varieties of men." George Washington Williams, Civil War veteran and author of *History of the Negro Troops in the War of Rebellion* (1888), also spoke about soldiering in the heightened terms of liberation. In recalling his own feelings during the war, Williams described "the glory of military exaltation" and "the brilliant aggressiveness of a free soldier." Black memory of the Civil War translated into widespread support of the Spanish-American War and World War I. Even W. E. B. Du Bois, who later had grave doubts about black participation in foreign wars, supported the cause in 1917: "Our country is at war," Du Bois wrote in the *Crisis*: "If this is *our* country, then this is *our* war. We must fight it with every ounce of blood and treasure."[93]

African American troops made a major contribution to the U.S. war against Spain. Again, many opposed it and the subsequent imperialist war against the Philippines: the *Afro-American Sentinel* asked in July 1898, "Does it not appear ludicrous for the United States government to be waging war in the interest of humanity and to bring a cessation of Spanish outrages in Cuba, when it has such a [dismal] record at home?"; two months earlier the *Iowa State Bystander* pointed out similarly that "More than 500 colored men and women have been murdered by the white American people in the past 25 years and now they . . . have the audacity to talk about the cruelty of Spain toward the Cubans."[94] At the same time, though, other black newspapers supported the war and foreign expansion; the *Colored American*, for instance, urged its readers to back the country in the same "true blue" way the race had "from Bunker Hill on." While thousands of African American men tried in vain to join the U.S. volunteers, the army turned immediately to four black regiments of regulars: with years of experience fighting the Indian wars, the Ninth and Tenth Cavalry and Twenty-fourth and Twenty-fifth Infantry stood among the country's elite units. Once in Cuba, the black regulars, though formally segregated, fought alongside of and intermixed with white troops, including the Rough Riders. In fact, popular histories of the war had the Tenth Cavalry rescuing Roosevelt and his men from ambush at Las Guasimas. By all accounts, the African American troops fought effectively and oftentimes heroically, earning five Congressional Medals of Honor in the Cuban campaign. The war extended the African American martial tradition into a new generation. The "coolness and bravery that characterized our fathers in the '60s," a black sergeant wrote proudly from Cuba, "have been handed down to their sons of the 90s."[95] The war against Spain also transitorily brought the troops into the fold of Americanism.

Several tributes to African American soldiering circulated widely through the black press and spontaneous histories of the war. Most famously, Roosevelt's farewell speech to the Rough Riders, reprinted throughout the country, acknowledged the common cause and effort between his men and the Ninth and Tenth Cavalry: "The Spaniards called them 'Smoked Yankees,' but we found them to be an excellent brand of Yankees. I am sure that I speak the sentiments of officers and men in the assemblage when I say that between you and the cavalry regiments there exists a tie which we trust will never be broken."[96] Some statements took on a concessionary tone, as in this oft-quoted comment about Las Guasimas from a writer in the *Washington Post*: "If it had not been for the Negro cavalry, the Rough Riders would have been exterminated. I'm not a negro lover. My father fought with Mosby's Rangers and I was born in the South, but the Negroes saved that fight." John Pershing , a U.S. Army lieutenant during the war, described a new sense of national unity among soldiers in Cuba. "White regiments, black regiments, regulars, and Rough Riders, representing the young manhood of the North and South," Pershing recounted proudly, "fought shoulder to shoulder, unmindful of race or color, unmindful of whether commanded by an ex-Confederate or not, and mindful only of their common duty as Americans."[97]

A good number of the tributes to black troops exalted their quality of character. In his book *The Cuban and Porto Rican Campaigns*, for instance, Richard Harding Davis recognized that "the negro soldiers established themselves as fighting men" in the battle of San Juan Hill. "They certainly can fight like the devil and they don't care for bullets any more than they do for the leaves that shower down upon them," commented a veteran from New Mexico: "Now I know what they are made of." Speaking at the Peace Jubilee in Chicago in October 1898, General Nelson A. Miles pointed out that in the war the "white race was accompanied by the gallantry of the black. . . . It's a glorious fact," Miles emphasized, "that sacrifice, bravery, and fortitude" in Cuba "were not confined to any race."[98]

The idea of "sacrifice, bravery, and fortitude" unconfined by race—so beneficial to U.S. nationalism—emerges from the Spanish-American War verse devoted to the black regulars. "White and Black," for instance, a poem published in *Reminiscences and Thrilling Stories of the War*, recognizes African American loyal service against the Indians ("the murdering hostiles") in "the wild and arid West." Consequently, the Indian Wars earned African Americans a leading role against the Spanish: "They do the black race justice; / They're eager for the fray, / And in the reeking Cuban swamps / They yet may save the day— / Firm hands to sight the rifle, / Spite the color of their skin. / Though his head be white—our eagle / Has black feathers in his wing." A popular poem, "The Negro Soldier," published in both *Reminiscences and Thrilling Stories* and *Under Fire with the Tenth U.S. Cavalry* (1899), roughly parallels the man-making verse about eastern dude volunteers. Like the poems already discussed, the narrator speaks in the assumptive voice of real American manhood: "We used to think the Negro didn't count for very much— / Light-fingered in the melon patch, and chicken yard, and such; . . . But we've got to reconstruct our views on color, more or less, / Now we know about the Tenth at Las Guasimas!" The poem emphasizes the soldiers' strength of character under fire: "When a rain of shot was falling, with a song upon his lips, / In the horror where such gallant lives went out in death's eclipse, / Face to face with Spanish bullets, on the slope of San Juan, / The negro soldier showed himself another type of man." Similarly, in crude verse and word choice, "The Rough Rider 'Remarks,'" published in *Under Fire with the Tenth Cavalry*, relates the change of mind of a Texan trooper who, before Cuba, "never had no use for a nigger." Fighting alongside the black regulars made a difference though:

> Up the hill through bramble and briar,
> Leaving killed and wounded there in the brush,
> They pushed straight ahead in the face of fire,
> Then lined up true for the final rush;
> Straight in front was the barb-wire fence;
> Over they went it, hellity split;
> You should have seen the greasers git from thence;
> I swear, I reckon they're running yit, . . .

Right in the nastiest part of the mess;
I swear, when it comes to a stand-up fight,
Or to stay by a comrade in distress,
You bet your sweet life them darkies is white!

After paying the African Americans what he considers to be an ultimate compliment, the Texan Rough Rider betrays his compassion toward a wounded black regular: "Here's a darkie now with an artery cut; / Say, doc, can't you put a compress on? / There ain't no time to be foolin about, / If you do the cuss will surely be gone." In this remarkable poem, the narrator drops that most racist epithet: speaking with the surgeon, he says "I'll grip that hole / And stop the blood as long as I can, / A nigger? Who says it? Blast my soul / If that darky ain't a *man!*"[99] The ultimate compliment—seeing the dying African American soldier as a man—the Texan tries to prove the battlefield's power to dissolve bigotry and, at the risk of hyperbole, to create blood brotherhood.

It is not too much to say that any individual transformations that occurred on Cuban battlefields made extremely little difference to race relations in the late nineteenth and early twentieth-century United States. With several white civilian attacks on African American troops and the Wilmington, North Carolina, massacre occurring in late 1898, intense racial violence and apartheid-like segregation continued during the Spanish-American War and beyond. Any hope among African Americans that military service would bring the race meaningful improvement in voting and other civil rights would not be realized for another half century. Appreciation of black military capacity would dramatically decrease until the Vietnam War, beginning with whites deliberately downplaying African American contribution to U.S. victory over Spain. Most hurtful to turn-of-the-century African American soldiers was Roosevelt's April 1899 article in *Scribner's Magazine* (included as a chapter in his subsequent book *The Rough Riders*), which spoke of the black regulars' "peculia[r] dependenc[e] upon their white officers." In his account of the Battle of San Juan Hill, Roosevelt self-aggrandizingly told of how he, upon seeing black infantrymen "drift to the rear," pulled his revolver and told them that he would shoot anyone who did not stop. "This was the end of the trouble," Roosevelt wrote in remembering his authority, the soldiers "flashed their white teeth at one another, and broke into broad grins." The black press denounced the passage as "a malicious slander," while veterans recalled the incident, adding critically that Roosevelt had later apologized after learning that the soldiers had been ordered to the rear for supplies.[100]

Although the tributes to black soldiering did not last very long past the end of the war against Spain, the ideological formulation that heroic masculine character rather than race determined true American identity would be used effectively throughout the twentieth century to mobilize an increasingly heterogeneous U.S. citizenry to foreign war. The color of a man's blood, not of his skin, defined the American patriot: "For it is to you I am speaking," General Enoch Crowder said in rallying support during World War I, "you, the strong, sturdy, red-blooded sons of adventure and freedom and justice." Or, in a closely related vein, what really matters is having the right spirit. As President Roosevelt told a Memorial Day gathering at Antietam in 1903, "In the long run in the Civil War the thing that the average American had was the fighting edge; he had within him," Roosevelt insisted, "the spirit which spurred him on through toil and danger, fatigue and hardship, to the goal of splendid ultimate hardship."[101] Abstractions all, fighting spirit, red-bloodedness, and strong character showing "sacrifice, bravery, and fortitude," could be invoked by political and military elites cross-generationally, diverting attention from the costs of war, the material conditions, and human consequences of national expansion.

William James made this argument in opposing U.S. forces in the Philippines and the consequent "attempt to turn a concrete political issue into an abstract emotional comparison between two types of personal character, one strong and manly, the other cowardly and weak." James directed his attack toward that "arch abstractionist" of American character, Teddy Roosevelt. Days after reading Roosevelt's "Strenuous Life" speech of 1899, James wrote a letter to the editor of the *Boston Evening Transcript* in which he put forward one of the most stinging critiques of the Colonel's person. "Although in middle life, and in a situation of responsibility concrete enough, he is still mentally in the Sturm and Drang period of early adolescence," James said of his former Harvard student: "he treats human affairs . . . from the sole point of the organic excitement and difficulty they may bring, gushes over war as the ideal condition of human society, for the manly strenuousness which it involves, and treats peace as a condition of blubberlike and swollen ignobility, fit only for huckstering weaklings, dueling in gray twilight and heedless of the higher life."[102] In recognizing the close correspondence in turn-of-the-century U.S. political culture between conceptions of character and nationalism, James found an inroad into American imperialism, although he knew that it would take far more than critical letters to change this habit of mind.

For our purposes, national character traits and typologies of soldiering go to the motivation of American men to fight, kill, and die in battle. Heroic war stories and blood-soaked songs and poems set expectations for future violence and bravery—murderous and sacrificial standards enforced institutionally by a homosocially organized military. American soldiers were not always recognized internationally as exceptionally ferocious; in World War II, German, Japanese, and So-viet troops achieved higher renown. The point is that U.S. war making, in all its prevalence, occurred in part because of individual soldiers' interest in fulfilling what they thought it meant to be an American man. And this is why the Spanish-American War and the Rough Riders merit close attention: that "splendid little war" and "Roosevelt's terrors," drawing from Civil War memory, gave materiality and tradition to national fighting spirit. Tom Hall got it right in his book *The Fun and Fighting of the Rough Riders* (1899): "To recapitulate: the Rough Rider was a regiment. He is now a type. Should we have to go to war again he will be an army. Every type of war machine," the West Point graduate, novelist, and Rough Rider quartermaster noted, "has had a beginning. The originals of most of the types have been lost in antiquity. Will this be the case with the Rough Riders of the Santiago campaign?" Hall asked further: When someone of a "future age searches the ruins of Washington for information concerning the Universal War will he learn that Roosevelt's Regiment of Rough Riders was the germ of a great fighting power?"[103] Whether that regiment will be indirectly responsible for national decimation is yet uncertain; but it clearly helped set the United States on an imperialist course, strategically developing a modern American warrior class.

War as Sport for Doughboys, Golden Boys, and Slackers

Modern American war in the head evolved in close tandem with masculine sports culture. Both war and sport bred heroism—less a romantic ideal of chivalry in the twentieth-century United States than a practical cross-cultural model for hardy aggressive manhood, a highly gendered standard of risk taking and performance. Equating war with sport has been hegemonic. Homosocially cultivated and reinforced through the military, school, team, and state, seeing war as sport has blurred the suicidal danger and homicidal violence of mechanized battle. War as sport is hardly new—the association can be traced back to antiquity—but by the First World War it had become elaborately ordinary, institutionally diffused in the U.S. military's interpellation of the nation's men and enlivened by the astounding popularity of American professional, college, high school, and recreational sport. Concentration on the athleticism of warfare has helped build the U.S. warrior class of Americans, those who volunteer each generation to fight and kill in the Marines and other military branches' special combat forces. War as sport has also been used as a motivator for less enthusiastic recruits. Focus on the World War I American military newspaper the *Stars and Stripes* shows how sports molded the doughboy in his attitude and participation in the Allied cause. In this instance, war as sport involved a comparison between the physical skills developed in sports and those needed for combat. At the same time, *Stars and Stripes* drew from sports in fashioning a certain wartime psychology, an emotional commitment to fighting best summed up by the word *spirit*. Together the physical and psychological aspects of war as sport infused a distinct element of *play* into the American military effort—a quality in stark contrast to the mass death and destruction of the First World War itself.

A great deal has been written about World War I's relationship to masculine consciousness, motivation, and imagination. Malcolm Cowley remembered the "thirst for abstract danger" among the American college men who volunteered to fight and serve in the ambulance corps; he also chronicled the ensuing literary generation's alienation and disillusionment that resulted, in part, from the war's horror and empty promise. And in studying the common soldiers of the American Expeditionary Force (AEF), David M. Kennedy has emphasized the surprising level of interest in knighthood and the medieval romantic tale, especially as interpreted by Sir Walter Scott. "[A]t the level of popular culture," Kennedy has contended, in "the mind-set of the great mass of doughboys, Scott's influence was prodigious—and lasting." Chivalry and knight errantry did provide an active model of martial spirit in early twentieth-century American culture, but, in examining U.S. soldiers' motivation during the First World War, we need to attend more closely to the contemporary historical archetype of the American fighting man, as it emerged from Civil War memory and the Spanish-American War. "[T]he valor of the fathers is not dead," a September 1918 article in *Stars and Stripes* declared; "the spirit of service, of sacrifice, of absolute unselfishness in the face of death lives and moves and permeates the America of today at war."[104] To shift focus from medieval knighthood to modern American fighting spirit leads to the significance of a more banal or deflated heroism in the head of the doughboy—that is, a relatively unromanticized orientation to performance in battle, one in which sport would have a metaphorical and animating role.

This point is sharpened by the fact that the cavalry, the closest nineteenth-century incarnation of knighthood, played a smaller and smaller part in U.S. military operations and, consequently, in the minds of American soldiers. The war of 1898 was a turning point. Cavalry certainly figured prominently in the planning of the Cuban campaign. But the Ninth and Tenth Cavalry regiments, the Rough Riders, and virtually the whole U.S. force fought on their feet. And while some Spanish-American War verse reveled in the prospect of attacking on horseback—"The Cavalry Charge," for instance, pictured how the "The wild troopers ride. / Cut right! And cut left!"—the leading accounts of battle celebrated the grit and determination of troopers running at the enemy while under heavy fire.[105]

Football, not fencing, polo, or rodeo, became the key athletic reference point during the Spanish-American War. "[T]he same spirit that once sent these men down a white-washed field against their opponents' rush-line," Richard Harding Davis heralded the Rough Rider football players, "was the spirit that sent" them "through the high hot grass at Guasimas, not shouting, as their friends the cowboys did, but each with his mouth tightly shut, with his eyes on the ball, and moving in obedience with the captain's orders."[106] It's difficult to imagine a psychology more conducive to the suicidal dimension of modern ground war. And, as Davis's fascinating description demonstrates, football modeled that spirit for American men. The practical nature of the association between soldiering and football warrants emphasis. As discussed in the preceding chapter, late nineteenth-century college football drew from war to add drama and meaning to its game. "This is no game, but war," implored an 1897 Stanford football poem. A year later, the Spanish-American War drained the university's football team, as some of the former-player volunteers no doubt inverted the relationship, approaching battle as a deadly game.

Even before the war against Spain, Americans turned to football while trying to imagine combat. Most notably, Stephen Crane recalled Syracuse University football for *The Red Badge of Courage*. He drew impressionistically from the game in setting battle scenes: "A dark battle line lay upon a sunstruck clearing that gleamed orange color. A flag fluttered." Following the geometrics of football, Crane wrote of how a firing "line lurched straight for a moment. Then the right wing swung forward . . . Afterward the center careened to the front until the regiment was a wedge-shaped mass." And most explicitly, Crane had "the youth" charge at the enemy "as toward a goal." Henry "ran like a madman to reach the woods before a bullet could discover him. He ducked his head low, like a football player."[107] Think of how many American troopers, doughboys, GIs, marines, and special forces carried that scene in their head while attacking the soldiers of Spain, Germany, Japan, Korea, Vietnam, or Iraq.

That football or any other type of game could resonate with men caught in the mechanized horror of World War I tends to substantiate masculine pathology. U.S. forces didn't see the worst of trench warfare, a killing process that leading military historian John Keegan has likened to the Nazi death camp Treblinka: "long lines of young men, shoddily uniformed, heavily burdened, numbered about their necks, plodding across a featureless landscape to their own extermination inside the barbed wire." The less-than-glorious quality of "The Great War" was not lost on Americans, though. In a 1918 *Atlantic Monthly* article, Harvard dean of students L. B. R. Briggs expressed his surprise over college athletes' enthusiasm for a war "in which the part played by romance . . . seems unprecedentedly small. An athlete would be expected to accept, out of hand, the sporting challenge of old-fashioned warfare," Briggs recognized—"to lead mad cavalry charges, to match himself like a knight of old with every newcomer as man against man; but the call of this war is a call . . . to the unrelieved horror of the machine-gun and the gas-bomb." How could sport work within this environment? One tentative answer is to remember the militaristic origins of football and, more specifically, its territorial premium on gaining ground. With this motivation in mind, English soldiers' habit of kicking a soccer ball toward the German line while attacking makes some sort of "sense."[108] Referencing football might be seen as a semi-ironic connection to play amid complete danger—an anomaly that nevertheless worked to push soldiers forward over deadly ground. Some of the associations with sport during the First World War seem pure and complete. As mentioned in chapter 3, the 32nd Division of the AEF, among other U.S. troops, sang the football fight song "On Wisconsin"—"plunge right through that line"—while marching into battle at Chateau-Thierry, France.

At the same time that ground fighting reached new levels in mass brutality, World War I ushered in one of the most exalted forms of killing that humans have ever created: air war. By the Second World War, air forces had achieved a strategic and enormously destructive place in military operations; dropping incendiary and atom bombs, pilots could kill hundreds of thousands of people in a single mission. But killing power during the First World War was usually limited to one other person, the enemy pilot. Individual combat between two equally matched warriors drew raptured attention from cheering armies in the trenches below and from scores of commentators who found in it a distinctly antimodernist allure. In a London newspaper, for instance, H. G. Wells touted aerial combat as "the most splendid fighting in the world." Wells wrote in 1918: "One talks and reads of the heroic age and how the world has degenerated. But indeed this is the heroic age, suddenly come again. No legendary feats of the past, no battle with dragons or monstrous beasts, no quest or feat that man has hitherto attempted can compare with this adventure in terror, danger, and splendor." A number of other writers made specific references to the medieval tradition. Cecil Lewis, an English World War I pilot and author, described the attraction to fighting in the air: "To be alone, to have your life in your own hands, to use your own skill, single-handed, against the enemy. It was like the lists of the Middle Ages, the only sphere in modern warfare where a man saw his adversary and faced him in mortal combat, the only sphere where there was still chivalry and honour."[109] World War I pilots had found a less-catastrophic variation or equivalent of war. For at least this one peculiar moment, as twentieth-century military technology and industry pushed the human species to the point of self-extinction, the World War I airplane with machine gun restored proportionality, gallantry, and competition to killing.

The romance of Scott's knight-errantry flourished in air war, as did the values of sport. The Ivy League made a particular contribution among American fliers.

Many of them had been athletes at one of those Eastern schools before following the challenge of aerial combat to Europe. "Aviation" attracted these men, as Harvard's dean Briggs explained, because it had become the "supreme test of sportsmanship in life and death."[110] Counterposed to the democratic drudgery and random death on the ground, aviation was a gentleman's war, an ultimate expression of patrician martial virtue and a form of fighting that rewarded the quick reflexes and daring of the athlete. Add to that the rarified, performative quality of dueling in the air—the fighting had little effect on any major battle or the outcome of the war—and its overlap with sport seems nearly complete.

The perfect archetype of the Ivy League athlete-flier was one Hobart Amory Hare "Hobey" Baker. Born in 1892 in mainline Philadelphia, an athletic prodigy at St. Paul's School in Concord, New Hampshire, Hobey Baker grew into a living legend at Princeton University, where he starred in hockey and captained the football team. With wavy blond hair, game-winning scores, and the self-effacing modesty of the classic sportsman, Baker was the idol of a college generation and the inspiration for F. Scott Fitzgerald's golden-boy character Allenby in *This Side of Paradise* (1920). After graduating from college and working at Morgan Bank on Wall Street, he went to France in 1917 to join the famed Lafayette Escadrille. Baker eventually became commander of the 141st American Pursuit Group, a squadron with its planes painted orange and black and decorated with the Princeton tiger pawing a Bosche helmet. In 1918, days after the armistice and with his discharge papers in hand, Baker insisted on testing a newly overhauled plane. The Spad single seater's motor failed upon takeoff and Baker fell to his death. U.S. newspapers closely covered the tragic crash, exaggerating Baker's downed-plane count from three to as many as fourteen, and generally memorializing his bravery, skill, and beauty. The Hobey Baker legend flourished with the man's death—his life a touchstone for American athletic heroism. Those most committed to him and that ideal have believed that Baker actually committed suicide with his last flight; they couldn't imagine that he would have wanted to live in a humdrum workaday world, one without danger and chance for gallant achievement.[111]

Along with the utterly romantic arc of his short life, the most compelling aspect of the Hobey Baker legend is the self-conscious continuity between his athletic career and service in war (figs. 4.2, 4.3). He wanted no part of Wall Street. "I realize that my life is finished," the twenty-two-year old Baker stated shortly after starting at the bank. "No matter how long I live, I will never equal the excitement of playing on the football fields." He was wrong of course. Training in France with his friend Eddie Rickenbacker, Baker couldn't spend enough time in the air. Aerial combat exhilarated him. And he recognized how it tapped the same qualities as sport. "You handle your machine instinctively," Baker told a Princeton friend, "just as you dodge instinctively when running with the ball in the open field." Just as pointedly, Baker explicitly likened killing to the action of sport. "I think I wounded the observer but my plane had too damn much speed on and I had to turn off to keep from running into him," Baker described in a failed attempt to shoot down a German plane: "It was just like missing a goal when you had gotten past the defense and have only the goal keeper to stop you."[112] Fighter pilots in World War I and beyond have routinely kept score of kills, and with Baker's comments we find an example of sport metaphor diverting attention from the human cost of battle.

The phenomenon of sport being used to cover up the mass homicide of war can be found throughout the World War I American newspaper the *Stars and Stripes*. Founded for AEF soldiers—the newspaper "should speak the thoughts of the new American Army," as General John J. Pershing wrote in its first issue—the publication's enlisted editorial staff proudly touted its independence from military oversight.[113] And yet, subject to a board of control at General Headquarters, the editors understood that they would have to carry "a certain amount of 'must-go' stuff" from officials above. "But it has got to be handled with extreme care to avoid its being too obvious," an internal editorial memo reads; "small doses of propaganda" are necessary, the staff recognized, although they must be inserted in such a way as to not make the "reader suspicious." Assiduously avoiding the hard sell of war, the editors cultivated a "lively" tone—a "slightly irreverent, plainly spoken" address to its doughboy readership. It worked. The *Stars and Stripes* enjoyed nearly universal popularity among American soldiers. Receiving a constant flow of their poems and letters, the weekly gained the trust of AEF troops—they believed, as Pershing had wanted, that "It is your paper."[114] As the newspaper did reflect (albeit selectively) the feelings of individual soldiers, the level of trust it engendered thereby opened the door to considerable editorial encouragement toward war.

The *Stars and Stripes* largely concerned itself with the morale of American troops. Writing for a heterogeneous army fighting a foreign war in conditions alien to romantic memories of past wars, the newspaper's staff proved to be imaginative in helping to maintain cohesion and consent among those men facing such harshness and danger. One strategy had the *Stars and Stripes* addressing head-on the charge that "only the gallant chasse pilots darting lonely across the perilous skies had inherited the glory that used to be." This August 1918 editorial entitled "Man Power" echoes Crane's *Red Badge of Courage* in admirably summarizing the central criticism against modern war: "They said that the day of the individual in war was done, that the age of the hero was over, that in the struggle of the twentieth century only multitudinous masses counted or could be discerned in the conflict, that, on the battlefields of the world, the opposing armies were but giant machines with each human an infinitesimal, inconsiderable cog." In response, the editorial tries to develop continuity with the past: "war today calls for—and receives—as much individual initiative, as shining a personal courage as ever the marveling world saw at Thermopylae, at Balaklava, at Missionary Ridge." It also reflexively relies on the ideal of heroic manhood: "every hour" we "see some man no one ever heard of before reveal a blazing display of high valor that lights up like some most potent flare against the black night of war."[115] In retrospect, the effectiveness of the direct approach is doubtful, since, at least in this instance, the case against war seems more detailed and convincing than the response. Far stronger, undoubtedly, was the newspaper's predominant strategy of cloaking the action and emotion of war in the language of sport.

World War I *Stars and Stripes* editors put considerable stock into doughboys' orientation to sports. In building its readership, the newspaper covered U.S. professional and college sports for its first five months, from February to July 1918. The publication then shut down its sports page in an effort to gain closer if not exclusive control over the soldiers' interests and emotions attached to sports. The *Stars and Stripes* wanted to narrow its readers' circle of homosocial reference points, highlighting the prowess of American men in war abroad over those playing a finally inconsequential game at home. In devoting considerable space to the army's awarding of different service medals, the newspaper helped create new heroes whose bravery modeled sacrifice and fighting spirit for other soldiers. At the same time, the *Stars and Stripes* appropriated the idiom of sport. Headlines announcing troop movements, battles, and Allied victories struck a vernacular tone of masculine sport, as in "Americans Make First Raids into German Trenches" and "Two Black Yanks Smear 24 Huns."[116] More commonly, headlines explicitly transformed the news of modern war into the phraseology of American sport. Examples abound: "Big League Season Opens in Two Hemispheres"; "Huns Hit .ooo against Lorraine Hurlers"; "Allies Ahead in Big Extra Inning Battle"; "Kaiser Calls Bench Warmers into Play"; "Wet Grounds Delay Play in Picarly"; "Yanks Nip Hun Rally in Belleau Woods"; "Franco-Yank Rally Routs Hun Twirlers." The *Stars and Stripes* editors obviously tried to meld war with sport. In doing so, the newspaper projected a light-hearted and jocular air toward the war, one perhaps meant to ease the tensions of AEF soldiers anticipating battle. The newspapers' sports culture also pushed unity and performance, qualities of great necessity for winning the war.

During the spring of 1918, the newspaper's crackdown on sports at home focused on "slackers"—professional athletes who avoided military service.[117] Criticism first came in a March editorial entitled "Heroes in Wartime" which explains that the *Stars and Stripes* had earlier covered a New Orleans boxing match between Frank Moran and Fred Fulton because of interest among its readers. The editors didn't want anyone to "suppose," though, that "we have the slightest disposition to make heroes of this pair. To our notion," the article continues, "the proper belt for a fighting man to wear in war time is of the regulation canvas web or fair leather—not green silk." The article concludes flatly: "a trained athlete, particularly one who has had the opportunity to lay away a tidy fortune at fighting, owes it to his country to do something in return." It adds in good measure that "an athlete with an extraordinary reach of Fulton should be a mighty hand with a bayonet." Two months later the newspaper took another shot at slacker boxers, ridiculing Fulton and "Mr. J. Willard" as "our most celebrated pacifists—pardon us, the typewriter slipped, of course we mean pugilists." Quoting a statement by the boxers' trainers that the "champs were never in better physical condition," the editorial presses sarcastically: "So, having that worry off their minds, we can expect to see Jess and Fred with the A.E.F. 'Most any day now.'"[118] The slacker issue ended in the *Stars and Stripes* in July when the newspaper dropped its sports page. That month a parting editorial entitled "Sport for Who's [*sic*] Sake?" commented forlornly that "we can only shout 'Bravo' in a faint and unconvincing voice when we learn that Ty Cobb" and others will consider enlisting after the current season ends. The athletes didn't have the right priorities.[119]

Explaining the newspaper's decision to end the sports page fell upon Lieutenant Grantland Rice, a young staff member who would later become one of the most accomplished sports writers of his generation. Sober-minded in tone, Rice maintained that "the glorified, the commercialized, the spectatorial sport of the past has been burnt out by gun fire." Rice did first draw the close equation between war and sport: "This paper realizes the great aid sport has given in the past in developing physical stamina and enduring morale among thousands of those now making up the nation's Army." In itemizing athletics' martial function, Rice rather off-handedly called war a "game," a theme common among *Stars and Stripes* writers: "It was sport that first taught our men to play the game, to play it out, to play it hard. It was sport," he continued, "that brought out the value of team play, of long, hard training and the knack of thinking quickly at a vital point in the contest." But sport "has passed on and out," Rice wrote matter-of-factly about what the newspaper was really prescribing: "Its leading stars are either in the iron harness of war—or forgotten—until Germany is beaten." In a core statement of the *Stars and Stripes'* policy, Rice urged that "There is no place left for the Cobbs, the Ruths, the Johnsons, the Willards and the Fultons in the ease and safety of home when the Ryans, the Smiths, the Larsens, the Bernsteins and others are charging machine guns and plugging along through shrapnel or grinding out 12-hour details, 200 miles in the rear. Back home," Rice conceded, "the sight of a high fly drifting into the late sun may still have its thrill for a few. But over here the all absorbing factors are shrapnel, high explosives, machine gun bullets, trench digging, stable cleaning, nursing . . . "[120] While Rice's rather bleak exchange of athletics for war may not have inspired too many readers, the article does mark the seriousness with which the newspaper treated American soldiers' attachment to sport.

In October 1918, amid the American college football season, the *Stars and Stripes* once again urged AEF soldiers to keep their eye on the ball in Europe. Extending the reasoning in Rice's article on eliminating the sports page, an editorial entitled "Canning the Rah-Rah" first recognizes that sport had initially helped the cause by teaching men devotion to something outside of themselves: "College spirit is a fine thing, and the way in which it was fostered helped to build up in the men now in the Army and Navy that intense spirit of group loyalty without which no Army or Navy could hope to succeed." Now, however, with its work done, college spirit had to be dropped or at least put into sharp perspective. "[A]s some of our readers may have noticed," the editorial continued in a characteristically caustic tone, "there is a large, healthy, vigorous and rather absorbing war going on not very far from here, and the chances are that in the years to come a man will prefer to be known as one of those who busted the Hindenburg line than as the man who set fire to dear old Prexy's woodshed or brought the cow into morning chapel." Grow up, the editorial urges, let the war change you from boys to men: "It is high time that all of us, the young ones particularly, left our frat pins in our bedding rolls, our sheepskins and pass words in our trunks and forget them."[121]

At the same time though that the *Stars and Stripes* insisted on seriousness toward the war, it also cast the fighting of that war in terms of sport. In promoting association between the two, the newspaper made liberal use of the word *game* and the notion that battle is no more or less than sport in different form. Indicative of this strategy is the August 1918 staff-written poem "The Old Game and the New":

> This game is not the game they knew
> Before they faced the guns;
> The game that called for tackle drives,
> Or cracking in the runs;
> The game they played on friendly sod
> Beneath a friendly sky,
> To poke a double down the line,
> Or snag the winning fly.

In contrast to the Germans—a war-loving, "goose-stepping" people with an urge "to turn the rivers red"—the poem portrays Americans as peaceful by nature.

> Until the time came and they knew,
> And with no backward glance,

Their long lines gathered for the test
Upon the fields of France;
And with the same old "hit 'er out,"
Through German steel and flame,
They held the slogan of their youth—
"Heads up—and play the game."
A new game? Yes, but still a game
For those who had the heart
To crack a line or spill an end
Along the sportive mart:
And so the slogan born of old,
Shall be their final aim—
"Come on, show me something, kid;
Heads up—and play the game!"

As seen in this poem, the *Stars and Stripes* made reference to specific sports, be-lieving that the action and skill of a game would carry over into fighting. Track and field drew some attention, although adaptations would have to be made; a February 1918 article called for AEF units to hold their own "track meets of military events"; such competition would "uncover real Hun killers."[122] Overall, though, the news-paper centered its war as sport project on the two most popular American team sports—football and baseball.

With football's main action of advancing across hostile ground so similar to the action of infantry, the *Stars and Stripes* didn't always need to name the sport while using it to motivate AEF troops. The figure in the July 1918 sporting goods adver-tisement "Athletes Make the Best Fighters" (fig. 4.4) could be seen to be running hurdles, but it also references a football player leaping over a tackler with ball in hand. The August 1918 poem "Over the Top," written by an AEF sergeant, details the paradigmatic action of World War I ground combat: "The other day when we went over, / Over the top and up the hill, / We rushed through a field of wheat and clover, / Where German guns did their best to kill." The poem mentions neither football nor any other sport. Its imagery, however, along with its homosocial atten-tion and feeling, clearly parallels the narrative of a football drive: "It was great to see the boys go through—/ The Boche barrage got one or two—But no man fal-tered in his steady gait, / And each man kept in touch with his mate."[123] Breaking through the line, determination in the face of violent opposition, the necessity of teamwork: charging in combat and the play of football melded in World War I.

The *Stars and Stripes* did connect with football by name. An untitled winter 1919 poem, for instance, alluding to "Shades of Spaulding, Walter Camp," speaks excitedly about football in wartime: "Who would have thought two years ago / That we'd have pigskin days in France!" It's unclear whether this poem refers literally to the fact of soldiers playing pickup games of football behind the lines—the army and the *Stars and Stripes* encouraged such play, especially during Thanksgiving 1918—or if its reference is figurative, an elaboration on the similarity between the sport and combat. Either way, though, the poem substantiates the presence of football in World War I soldiers' identity and experience: "But when the fighting doughboy came / He brought his shifts and forward pass, / And he can drop-kick just the same / As when he played on Yankee grass." A March 1918 editorial "The Real Thrill" more transparently used football to assuage doughboy fear over battle, the "actual entrance to the trenches," which "is, oddly enough," the *Stars and Stripes* added in all seriousness, "not nearly as inspiring as that first glimpse from afar." Going into battle creates "a sensation much like that just before you go into a football game—the same nervous tension, the same doubts about whether you will be able to hold your bit of the line." The only real difference "is that the Boches are shooting at you." With this you realize, the editorial continues, "the game is on! All you have to do now is to watch your opponent and keep your ears open for the quarterback's signals." For those readers still a bit uncertain, the newspaper spelled out how football could emotionally guide the soldier through combat: "Remember how it used to be in football games?—Once you mixed into a scrimmage and got roughed up a bit your dander was up and all stage fright was forgotten. And so it is in this game of war."[124] Again, some examples of World War I as sport are pure.

The *Stars and Stripes* also drew liberally from baseball to inspire American soldiers to fight. In a February 1918 issue, the newspaper published the staff-written poem "World Series Opened—Batter Up!" It makes a clean switch from baseball to war, animating battle with the particulars of the sport: "He's tossed the horsehide far away to plug the hand grenade; / What matter if on muddy grounds this game of war is played? / He'll last through extra innings and he'll hit as well as pitch; / Hit smoking Texas Leaguers'll make the Fritzies seek the ditch!" The *Stars and Stripes* also featured major league players who, in sharp contrast to Cobb and other slackers, had left the game at home to fight in Europe. For instance, in August 1918 it ran an interview with the Boston Braves catcher Hank Gowdy, now on the front lines: "We are going to see this one through to a finish till the winning run goes over in the ninth, but after that I don't mind admitting I'll be ready to change the gas mask for the catcher's mask and take my chance against Walter Johnson's fast one rather than one of the fast one's from Fritz."[125] Although Gowdy's name may be lost to early twenty-first-century baseball fans, as the Most Valuable Player in the 1914 World Series and the first major league player to enlist in the army for World War I, he was perfect for the morale and motivation of doughboy troops.

An extraordinary aspect of the First World War as baseball is the way in which *Stars and Stripes* editors and others converted the play of the supposedly pastoral game into the stuff of deadly action. A March 1918 editorial detailed how baseball benefited fighting. After citing the oft-repeated remark that the Battle of Waterloo was won on the playing fields of Eton, the newspapers stated that "[s]imilarly it may be said in time that the battle of _____ was won upon the diamonds of . . . America." Baseball instills "self-reliance." It makes "for quick thinking and quick and sound judgements. It develops speed, endurance, strength of arms and backs and legs—in short, all the physical attributes of the really effective soldier." By the same token, "it will be very bad for the Boche to face an army of baseball-trained, grenade and bomb-tossers; and, in playing with the Boche, spiking, too, is perfectly within the rules!" The most transparent example of trying to extract killing from baseball came in a short *Stars and Stripes* article of February 1918 entitled "A Fighter's Game," which reported the rationale a New York assemblyman gave in support of a bill proposing Sunday games. It's the Sabbath, the politician reasoned, but baseball serves another all-important end: winning the war. "Our soldiers in France are the best bomb throwers among the Allies," the newspaper quoted the assemblyman. "Why? Because of their baseball training. I think we should do everything to encourage a game which makes good soldiers of our young men."[126]

With such wholesome enthusiasm for war as baseball or football, doughboys may very well have found it easier to accept and participate in the violence of battle. Sport masked the homicide of war, including the possibility of one's own death. The sports metaphor did promote score keeping, as in totaling the number of dead "Huns"; although body counting tended to ignore the enemy's humanity, instead rewarding the killing prowess of individual units and soldiers. Within the pages of the *Stars and Stripes*, World War I became its own blood sport. The newspaper didn't always have to reference actual sports to convey the challenge, pleasure, and self-fulfillment of battle. In August 1918, for example, the *Stars and Stripes* reported that "[t]he fighting worth of a good many American units was being tested" in "savage engagements" in the "Battle for Sergy." The combat featured "hand to hand fighting in the streets of a battered town," the newspaper continued, dramatically detailing the brutal action: "Infantrymen fighting with machine guns, rifles and bayonets, slogging with the butts of their guns, fighting in the raw with the great weapon that the Ordinance Department cannot issue—the clenched and angry fist."[127] Having created a performative martial culture that drew meaning from sport, the *Stars and Stripes'* favorite stories documented American fighting spirit, doughboys' physical and psychological capacity for killing.

Along with "fighting in the raw," American martial spirit obsessed the deadly use of a range of weaponry. "With bayonet and shot and shell, We will give the

Kaiser hell" a short *Stars and Stripes* poem reads; "Jab 'em, jab 'em / Shoot and stab 'em; U.S.A." Despite the high technology of twentieth-century warfare, the U.S. military built up soldiers' bloodlust by emphasizing the bayonet. Needless to say, the *Stars and Stripes* supported the effort. In an early World War I issue, for instance, the newspaper's front page included a snippet from its "Doughboy's Dictionary": "Bayonet"—"A long, sharp pointed object whose only satisfactory resting place is the midriff of a hun." Guns, in all their variation, also drew considerable attention. With a pistol "in each hand," the newspaper started an article on the "Wild West Stuff" of Corporal Browne "along the Vesle," the soldier yelled, "Say, boys, tell the wife for me that I was one game guy!" Browne then "went out after the Boches. He got them, too—four of them and a perfectly good machine gun."[128] Wanting to make killing attractive and psychologically undisturbing, the *Stars and Stripes* cast weapons as tools for eliminating a contemptible, nicknamed enemy, something that could be done with the same unflinching dispatch one would have in defeating a less-than-worthwhile athletic opponent.

Enthusiasm for killing also manifest through the most deadly of World War I weaponry: the machine gun. Given its power, attachment to the machine gun isn't surprising. "One had only to see the thing being demonstrated to realize that the force of such a deluge of fire, directed by just one man, could sweep away whole units with nonchalant ease," historian John Ellis has written about the machine gun's effectiveness during the First World War: "Cavalry or infantry, officer or soldier, coward or hero, all could be bowled over like rats before a hosepipe."[129] The *Stars and Stripes* celebrated the weapon in the same lighthearted vernacular tone in which it covered other modes of killing. Consider "The Machine Gun Song," a staff-written ditty printed in November 1918: "We've come from old New England to blast the bloomin' Huns, / We have sailed afar across the sea; / We will drive the Boche before us with our baby beauty guns / To the heart of the Rhine countree!" The song continues:

> Oh, machine guns, machine guns
> They're the things to rake the kaiser aft and fore!
> May they never jam on us
> Until we've gone and won this gosh darn war!
> Oh, machine guns are the handy things to drive the Fritzy out
> When he hides back of bags of sand
> And machine guns are the dandy thing to put the Hun to rout
> If he tries to regain his hand.
> So we just keep the clips a comin', and we give her all the juice
> As we speed along our glorious way

And Von Hindenburg and Ludendorff will beat it like the deuce
When the little old rattlers start to play!*¹³⁰*

Another lyrical tribute to "The Machine Gun" (1918) adopts the perspective of the weapon itself: "Anywhere and everywhere, / It's me the soldiers love, / Underneath a parapet / Or periscoped above; / Backing up the barrage fire, / And always wanting more; / Chewing up a dozen disks / To blast an army corps." The song's excited last lines zero in on the machine gun's ferocity: "Crackling, splitting, demon-like, / Heat-riven through and through, / Fussy, mussy Lewis gun, / Three heroes for a crew!"[131]

World War I machine gun verse sings from the perspective of the shooter, not from the victim's point of view. This isn't too surprising. The *Stars and Stripes* and other publications wanted to motivate men forward in battle; poetry documenting suicidal charges against enemy machine guns would not have been printed. Yet to make three soldiers sitting behind a large piece of machinery—mowing down nearly countless men—the stuff of heroism betrays the pathology of modern war. It also suggests the deception of war as sport. For all its vernacular tone, the *Stars and Stripes* had a propagandistic mission, and so it seized upon the popularity of American sport in urging sacrifice and aggressive bodily action. Since the Civil War, however, American war as sport has also enjoyed a more organic homosocial existence. The *Stars and Stripes* used the idea because the newspaper's editors knew that it would sell. American men's attraction to war as sport finally speaks to their attraction to war. As we'll see, mid- to late twentieth-century U.S. soldiers and marines would continue to associate war with sport, although many started to drop that mask altogether and more purely avow pleasure in killing.

Postscript: Marine Corps Spirit and the U.S. Warrior Class, 1941–2003

This chapter has argued that martial fervor in the United States stems from war in the head, a culturally transmitted psychology that, given its destructive nature, may best be understood as a disease. Pathological enthusiasm for wartime killing has spread via appeals to fighting spirit as an American character trait; through love of country and the tradition of killing and dying for it; through masculine attraction to the adventure, risk, and action of battle. Military history, public memory, written memoirs, novels, short stories, songs, and popular poetry have aggrandized war as a heroic masculine pursuit, cultivating loyalty and sacrifice, aggressiveness and battle madness, and other emotions suited for fighting. Family, school, state, and sport, among a myriad of interlocking institutions, also prepared young American men for war. The military would adapt its lure into service throughout the twentieth century, relying on patriotic duty and the draft in times of large-scale war while featuring job training and "be[ing] all that you can be" in the all-volunteer army. The U.S. Marine Corps has been more constant in its recruiting. Always "looking for a few good men," the Marine Corps has sold itself as an elite fighting unit, unabashedly embracing, as one corps sniper described it during the Persian Gulf War, "the art of killing."[132] The pathological strain of war in the head has flourished in the Marines. Leading war memoirs document the transmission of a killer psychology through Marine Corps "spirit," a battle-ready, bloodthirsty mind-set purposefully passed on from one generation to the next. Recent Marine memoirs attest to the pull of martial culture in the United States, including the power of Hollywood films to eroticize destruction and killing. This literature, as accomplished as any American war literature, examines the madness of modern war. Although, true to form, it also casts wartime experience as essential to one's masculinity.

In attracting young men who want to experience combat, the Marine Corps has greatly contributed to the United States' ability to maintain a warrior class, a force ready, willing, and able for invasion and battle. World War I escalated the Marines into prominence in the Battle of Belleau Wood, France, where fierce American attacks cost the Marines more than 4,700 troops and earned the corps German tribute and the lasting sobriquet "devil dogs" (*Teufelhunden*). Since Belleau Wood, wrote Craig Cameron in his valuable book on the Marines as "American Samurai," the idea "of battle as a test of cultural mettle and institutional reputation figured prominently" in the corps planning and self-understanding. Under the leadership of John A. Lejeune, commandant from 1920 to 1929, the Marines carefully consolidated its elite, "first to fight" reputation through sophisticated public relations and intense interservice lobbying for leading roles in foreign actions. Internally, the Marines cultivated its warrior tradition, in part, starting in 1921, through its famed annual birthday message that celebrates "the eternal spirit which has so animated our corps from generation to generation." Marine spirit, the message implores, must "continu[e] to flourish," so we "will be found equal to every emergency in the future as they have in the past, and the men of our Nation will regard us as worthy successors to the long line of illustrious men who have served." Passed on by veterans and institutional culture, corps spirit would have a palpable, material effect on young marines. "Spirit counts about as much as fighting ability in this war," a lieutenant wrote from Saipan during World War II, "and that is why the marines never fail to take any position, stronghold, or island they invade"[133] (fig. 4.5). Devotion to fellow marines made up corps spirit, World War II veteran E. B. Sledge has said in his memoir, as did a "stark realism" toward battle and killing.[134]

The title of Sledge's book *With the Old Breed: At Peleliu and Okinawa* (1981) refers to the generational presence and corps "tradition" that he felt while training and then fighting the Japanese in the Pacific. His unit, the 5th Regiment, 1st Marine Division, had "a link through time" to Belleau Wood; and, during his first landing and combat, Sledge received guidance from Guadalcanal veterans. One could argue that "with the old breed" also refers to the transference of the aggressiveness and savagery—the fighting spirit—that has distinguished the Marine Corps' interservice identity. A haunting grain runs through the memoir, as Sledge acclimates to "the ferocious fighting" and "the horror of war in the Pacific." During the first day in battle at Peleliu, Sledge stares incredulously at marines' taking souvenirs off of dead Japanese soldiers. "Would I become this casual and calloused about enemy dead?" Sledge asked. "I wondered," he continued: "Would the war dehumanize me so that I, too, could 'field strip' enemy dead with such nonchalance? The time soon came when it didn't bother me a bit." In trying to explain "the incredible cruelty that decent men could commit," Sledge, like Freud and so many other commentators on war, speaks of the relinquishment of humanity and civilization during the heat of battle.[135] Sledge continually relies on the word *brute* and its variations to describe a base, "primitive" form of human nature that, when uncovered, causes such horrors. But as the phrase "with the old breed" suggests, and as this book *Brutes in Suits* claims throughout, the violence men commit may not be so much the result of tenets of love, charity, and humanity having been wiped clean by a particular environment than aggressiveness, hatred, and malice having been positively learned through culture and its penchant for representing these emotions and attendant behaviors as natural, the stuff of culture's opposite, biology.

Motivated "by a deep feeling of uneasiness that the war might end before I could get overseas into combat," Sledge enlisted in the Marines, and went through recruit training at Camp Eliot in San Diego, where he was told upon graduation that "you are a member of the world's finest fighting outfit, and so be worthy of it." The ensuing infantry training taught Sledge how to kill Japanese. "Don't hesitate to fight the Japs dirty," the instructor said: "Most Americans, from the time they are kids, are taught not to hit below the belt. It's not sportsmanlike. Well, nobody has taught the Japs that, and war ain't sport." Having been shipped to the South Pacific, Sledge and his unit "suffered through an increasing number of weapons and equipment inspections, work parties, and petty clean-up details around the camp." With the new marines disgusted "with our existence," an "old salt" commented philosophically: "Don't let it get you down, boys. It's just part of the USMC plan for keeping the troops in fighting shape." He explained: "If they get us mad enough, they figure we'll take it out on the Nips when we hit this beach coming up." The veteran marine concluded, with emphasis: "They want us to be mean, mad, and malicious." It made sense to the new recruits. And Sledge concluded his chapter on "Preparation for Combat" affirming the corps' logic. "I doubt seriously whether I could have coped with the psychological and physical shock and stress encountered on Peleliu and Okinawa had it been otherwise," Sledge wrote. "The Japanese fought to win. It was a savage, brutal, inhumane, exhausting, and dirty business. Our commanders knew that if we were to win and survive, we must be trained realistically for it whether we like it or not."[136]

Peleliu and Okinawa proved to be shocking indeed. One of the most valuable aspects of *With the Old Breed* is Sledge's penetratingly honest account of his utter fear before island landings and while under artillery fire. He also realized in combat the sacrificial dynamic of war: "Slowly the reality of it all formed in my mind: we were expendable."[137] Corps training and tradition paid off though. Sledge stayed on the firing line, not expecting to come out of battle alive, but slowly moving forward anyway, fighting and killing Japanese. Keen "hatred" of the Japanese sustained Sledge and his fellow Marine infantrymen. This emotion appears throughout the memoir, although Sledge doesn't exactly explain the source of the hatred: Pearl Harbor and the motivation of revenge appears nowhere in the book; American dehumanization of the Japanese through racist stereotyping isn't nearly as sharp as in other stories of the Pacific war; the most distinct statement about the enemy is its relentless, suicidal, close-quarter fighting. It's as if Sledge's hatred sprang from his need to face and kill such a "fanatical" enemy, a character trait not unlike that on which marines prided themselves.

American marines and Japanese soldiers made the "savagery" of the Pacific War together. "I had quickly developed a feeling of strong personal hate for that machine gunner who had nearly blasted my head off my shoulders," Sledge wrote of an encounter with a Japanese soldier in a Peleliu bunker. "My terror subsided into a cold, homicidal rage and a vengeful desire to get even." From such fury and fear came the barbarity—"the new, ghastly, macabre facet in the kaleidoscope of the unreal"—that Sledge documented so fully: a hand-to-hand fight in which the marine killed the enemy with a stiff forefinger through the eye socket; a marine with his kabar knife taking out the gold-filled teeth of an alive Japanese soldier; a butchered marine corpse with the dead man's penis cut off and stuffed in his mouth; a marine idly throwing coral pebbles into a rain-filled open skull of a dead Japanese machine gunner. "War is brutish, inglorious, and a terrible waste," as Sledge concluded. "Combat leaves an indelible mark on those who are forced to endure it," he added and thus suggested how the horror of war is transferred from one generation to the next. "The only redeeming factors were my comrades' incredible bravery and their devotion to each other."[138] The memoir ends, then, in prideful memory and with a guilty conscience.

The Marines' heroic, first-to-fight reputation rose sharply after World War II. Producing such war-film classics as *Guadalcanal Diary* (1943) and *The Sands of Iwo Jima* (1949), Hollywood—often drawing from real combat footage—glorified corps' fighting spirit like never before; no government-generated recruiting commercial could be as effective, for instance, as paying audiences watching John Wayne as Sergeant Striker order his rifle squad to "saddle up" and attack the "nips" on Iwo Jima and then seeing them—with flame thrower, rifle, and machine gun in hand—do just that. Meanwhile Cold War dictates of containing communism furnished a virtually constant need for mobile firepower, an expertise that the Marines further developed by adding helicopter assault tactics to their amphibious capability. The 1st Marine Division spearheaded the amphibious invasion of Inchon during the Korean War, a conflict that cost 26,043 corps casualties. During the early 1960s and the lead-up to the Vietnam War, the Marine Corps, protecting its reputation, pressed for a more active role in Southeast Asia. The Marines got what it wanted. During the Vietnam War, from 1965 to 1971, 794,000 Americans would serve as Marines, 120,000 more than in World War II.[139]

From the mass of American marines fighting and serving in Southeast Asia, several extraordinary war memoirs emerged, and none more heartfelt or tragic than Ron Kovic's *Born on the Fourth of July* (1976). Encapsulating the disaster of U.S. intervention in Vietnam, Kovic's story begins with the author as a happy young athletic kid, loving the New York Yankees and hating communists, spending his Saturday afternoons at the movies in a Levittown shopping center theater where he saw, among other war films, *The Sands of Iwo Jima*. "[W]e sat glued to our seats," Kovic remembered: "And they showed the men raising the flag on Iwo Jima with the marines hymn still playing, and [we] cried in our seats." He continued: "after the movies all the guys would go down to Sally's Woods—Pete and Kenny and Bobbie and me, with plastic battery-operated machine guns, cap pistols, and sticks. We turned the woods into a battlefield. We set ambushes, then led gallant attacks, storming over the top, bayoneting and shooting anyone who got in our way. Then we'd walk out of the woods like the heroes we knew we would become when we were men." Marine recruiters visited Kovic's high school his senior year and, after graduating, he quit his job at an A&P supermarket and joined the corps. The Vietnam War didn't go well for Kovic: during a nighttime fire fight he accidentally shot and killed another marine; in attacking a village, his unit confusedly killed and wounded Vietnamese children, women, and old men; and, finally, Kovic was critically wounded in combat. Paralyzed from the waist down, he suffered through attempted rehabilitation and became an activist against the war. Haunted by the destruction of war, Kovic also felt betrayed by the American promise of martial heroism. "I have given it for democracy," Kovic speaks of his penis and manhood: "It is gone and numb, lost somewhere out there by the river where the artillery is screaming in. Oh God, Oh God I want it back. I gave it for the whole country, I gave it for every one of them. I gave my dead dick for John Wayne and Howdy Doody."[140]

Along with feelings of loss and defilement, marine memoirs from the Vietnam War include a quite different emotional register: pleasure, even rapture, in killing. We've already come across positive feelings over killing from earlier American wars—Civil War soldiers' vengeful bloodlust; Roosevelt the berserker; the explicit likening of World War I combat to the fun and action of sport; World War II marines' satisfaction over killing Japanese, as in one machine gunner at Peleliu commenting that he liked to see enemy corpses "stacked up like cordwood. Then you get the feeling you've done something."[141] But something different emerges from the Vietnam War literature. Some Americans fighting that war got off on killing. And they've made a point of saying so. Philip Caputo's memoir *A Rumor of War* (1977) testifies any number of times to the pleasure of fighting. "Anyone who fought in Vietnam, if he is honest about himself, will have to admit he enjoyed the compelling attractiveness of combat," Caputo wrote in the book's introduction: "I could not deny the grip the war had on me, nor the fact that it had been an experience as fascinating as it was repulsive, as exhilarating as it was sad, as tender as it was cruel."[142] The rest of Caputo's psychologically attuned memoir can be read as an inquiry into this phenomenon. Decimated by Vietnam, active in the antiwar movement, Caputo set out to uncover how and why a man could love something so hateful and destructive.

Caputo first looked to his motivation for enlisting in the Marines. Vietnam had "interest[ed]" him "as a place where I might find a bit of dangerous adventure"; also in a traditional vein, he "needed to prove something—my courage, my toughness, my manhood"; Caputo added that he and other volunteers had "been seduced into uniform by Kennedy's challenge to 'ask what you can do for your country' and by the missionary idealism he had awakened in us." In a more ruminative vein, Caputo remembered joining the Marines because "I was sick of the safe, suburban existence I had known most of my life." As a teenager his only break from that environment was in nearby county forest preserves where, finding "flint savage arrowheads in the muddy creek bank," Caputo envisioned the frontier: "I would dream of that savage, heroic time and wish that I had lived then, before America became a land of salesmen and shopping centers." He wanted ruggedness. "Having known nothing but security, comfort, and peace," Caputo explained, "I hungered for danger, challenges, and violence." Given this desire, Caputo may have ultimately judged "the descent" into war in Vietnam as good and fulfilling. "There was nothing familiar out where we were, no churches, no police, no laws, no newspapers," Caputo wrote: "It was the dawn of creation in the Indochina brush, an ethical as well as a geographical wilderness. Out there, lacking restraints, sanctioned to kill, confronted by a hostile country and a relentless enemy, we sank into a brutish state."[143] Caputo finally blamed devolution for the "malice" of the Vietnam War. A virtue of his memoir is that he showed himself complicit in the crimes of that war by wanting primitive release in the first place.

Caputo traced his desire for combat to many sources. Contributing to his youthful interest in adventure, violence, and hardship, Hollywood had raised his expectations of finding drama and meaning through fighting. "I wanted the romance of war, bayonet charges, and desperate battles against impossible odds," Caputo wrote of his feelings going into Vietnam: "I wanted the sort of thing I had seen in *Guadalcanal Diary* and *Retreat, Hell!* and a score of other movies." Once in combat, Caputo experienced repeatedly the "sensation of watching myself in a movie."[144] This phenomenon, inexplicable to Caputo himself, suggests the performative aspect of fighting, especially when entered into with a head full of cinematic killings and close-ups of courage under fire. Used to viewing John Wayne blow away several Japanese soldiers with one burst from a machine gun, Caputo flipped into spectatorial mode when engaging in similar action-packed homicidal behavior.

Lieutenant Caputo had been taught to want to kill in Marine officer training at Quantico, Virginia—a process of "intense indoctrination," as he described it, "which seemed to borrow from Communist brainwashing techniques." Even though he understood its coercive intent, there's little reason to think that the training had no psychological effect on Caputo, given how closely it fit with the pleasure he felt while actually killing Viet Cong. Over several generations the Marines had developed a regimen calculated to ingrain what Caputo's instructor called the "spirit of aggressiveness" in its recruits. Like Sledge before him, Caputo realized that the Marines wanted to "whip us into a vicious mood"—an emotional state that could then be tapped during combat. Pugil stick fights played a crucial role in this regard: "The pugil stick," Caputo explained, "a thick, wooden staff, padded at each end, was supposed to instill 'the spirit of the bayonet'; that is, the savage fury necessary to ram cold steel into another man's guts." Caputo remembered the words of the "bloodthirsty instructor" during the contests: "Parry that one, now slash, SLASH! Vertical butt stroke. C'mon, kill the sonuvabitch, kill im." Before meals Caputo and other trainees had to chant slogans: "Sir, the United States Marines; since 1775, the most invincible fighting force in the history of man. Gung ho! Gung ho! Gung ho! Pray for war!'" In Japan before deployment to Vietnam, Caputo took a class in counterinsurgency taught by a thick necked sergeant whose pedagogy included ordering the marines to chant in unison: "Ambushes are murder, murder is fun."[145]A straightforward one-to-one correspondence between Marine training's incitement to bloodlust and an individual's feelings in combat may not have been achieved, but this conditioning made the enjoyment of killing more likely—like Hollywood, it set up emotional gratification and self-fulfillment through violence.

In describing his attraction to war, Caputo continually likens the feeling to sexual desire. Phallic weaponry, penetration in killing and sexual intercourse, instinctual drive to fight and copulate: the interrelationship between wartime violence and sex has been routinely evoked by soldier and scholar alike.[146] For Caputo, always trying to detail the "emotional pleasures" of combat, sex came closest to describing his yearning—"a tension almost sexual in its intensity"—for engaging the enemy. Before his first action in Vietnam, he watched a fire fight from afar, longing to be a part of it: "More than anything, I wanted to be out there with them. Contact: that event for which so many of us lusted. And I knew then that something in me was drawn to war." Caputo remembered feeling "happy" when finally entering battle. Combat produced a "manic ecstasy of contact. Weeks of bottled up tensions would be released in a few minutes of orgiastic violence." Caputo also compared getting off on war to drug use. His "senses quickened" in battle. He experienced "an acuity of consciousness at once pleasurable and excruciating. It was something like the elevated state of awareness induced by drugs. And it could be just as addictive." But for Caputo and others, sexual desire best captured their deep, "painful" yearning for bloodshed. In explaining his disappointment over Iraqi troops in the Gulf War surrendering "too fast to kill a lot of them," a Marine captain said: "If you've ever got close to a girl hoping to get and you didn't, it was about the same."[147]

The moral of Caputo's memoir, a fundamental truth that he unfolds through his own gradual degradation, is that getting off on war is at one with the inherent evil of war. *Rumor of War* documents "a psychopathic violence in men of seemingly normal impulses," a destructive madness arising from the military itself, as in the Marine Corps commandant simply telling Caputo and other newly arrived infantry that "You men are here to kill VC." Such "tactical operations" meant brutal search-and-destroy missions and ghastly indifference to the enemy dead, evidenced by Caputo being ordered to dig up four mangled Viet Cong bodies to display to a visiting general. First signs of Caputo's madness emerged in the heat of battle. After his platoon had won a fire fight across a narrow river, Caputo wanted to cross "in the worst way. I wanted to level the village and kill the rest of the Viet Cong in close combat. I wanted to tear their guts out with bayonets." Unable to forge the river, Caputo settled for having "enjoyed the killing" that they did achieve. "I had never experienced anything like it before," he wrote, recalling his unit's fire coming together against the Viet Cong: "When the line wheeled and charged across the clearing, the enemy bullets whining past them, . . . an ache as profound as the ache of orgasm passed through me."[148] Caputo later "lost control" of himself and his platoon. This "ugliest" of "sights"—"the sudden disintegration of my platoon from a group of disciplined soldiers into an incendiary mob"—burned down the village of Ha Na, an act Caputo described as an "emotional necessity," "a catharsis," "a purging of months of fear, frustration, and tension." Finally, under "Operation Long Lance," motivated by headquarters' demand for more and more bodies and his captain's promise to the marines of an extra beer ration for every dead Viet Cong, Caputo allowed the killing of civilians, a murderous climax to the young lieutenant's fall into savagery.[149]

A Rumor of War discloses Caputo's guilt and shame for his actions, a conscience suggesting that his homicidal madness stemmed from something other than a Freudian drive toward destruction. Although it doesn't address the nature-nurture issue head on, Caputo's memoir works as a brief for the cultural construction of an "instinct" to make war. The one time Caputo used the word *instinct*, he did so in an ambiguous and telling manner: his unit had killed civilians, in part, out of "the brutal instincts acquired in the war"—that is, out of the emotions and behaviors that they had learned from the Vietnam War, itself a historically determined cultural creation. Caputo spoke routinely of yearning for action and adventure and then, in country, of relieving a tension, a nervous fervor for making contact with the enemy. But from whence did these feelings come? He devoted so much of his memoir to the transference of Marine Corps spirit through officer training and the "rules of engagement" with the enemy. Caputo even linked his young male restlessness to culture and the power of the American frontier myth and Hollywood war films. And, finally, another great truth arises from *A Rumor of War*. Early on during his tour of duty, Caputo wondered why a marine in his unit cut the ears off of a dead Viet Cong soldier. An old veteran sergeant responded: "Before you leave here, sir, you're going to learn that one of the most brutal things in the world is your average nineteen-year-old American boy."[150] Shaped by a hypermasculine culture obsessed with violence, the "raw material" the corps had to work with made it easy to instill Marine fighting spirit.

The cultural sources of brutality for American men would only multiply in the post–Vietnam War era. It's historical commonplace to note, first, the fall of national confidence and manhood in the aftermath of military failure in Vietnam and, second, the overcompensatory remasculinization of American culture in the late 1970s and 1980s. During Ronald Reagan's administration, the United States created an astounding array of pop-cultural appeals to fighting and killing: *First*

Blood (1982), its Rambo sequels, and other Vietnam veteran action movies; warrior pulp fiction and graphic novels; *Soldier of Fortune: The Journal of Professional Adventurers*, founded in 1975, and reaching thirty-five-thousand subscribers by the mid-1980s; a sharp increase in sales of military weapons and the flourishing of a recreational sniping subculture; Reagan's own seamless integration of war films into his Cold Warrior persona; and the 1981 invention of the National Survival Game or paint ball. By 1987, paint ball attracted more than fifty thousand Americans every weekend—a central appeal being its nexus to combat, "the dark side of the game," as one player described. In early 1991, with the Cold War over, and Saddam Hussein's troops in Kuwait, President George Bush ordered a large-scale U.S. attack of Iraqi forces. The ensuing victory over a retreating enemy "kicked the Vietnam syndrome once and for all," Bush proclaimed, as the nation looked on through television, fascinated and regenerated by the Nintendo-like quality of the action and the apparent cleanness of smart bombs and other high-tech weaponry.[151]

Jarhead (2003), Anthony Swofford's impressive Marine memoir from this first U.S. war against Iraq, visualizes the fighting in Kuwait as anything but clean in intent, execution, or result. His own mind's eye is darkened by, among other things, a self-diagnosed sick desire to kill Iraqi soldiers. Swofford served in the Gulf War as a Marine sniper, and the scope from his long-range rifle conveys the anticipated pleasure and power of "one shot, one kill." Set in a hide close to an Iraqi-controlled airstrip, in the last day of the war, Swofford "spent half an hour hopping from head to head with my crosshairs, yelling, *Bang, bang, you're a dead fucking Iraqi.*" Like Caputo's memoir, *Jarhead* psychoanalyzes Marine fighting and killing spirit. More so than the books by Caputo and Sledge, *Jarhead* is didactic in nature: Swofford tries to set himself, or his memoir rather, against the culture and history of American war making. Released months before the start of the second Iraq War, *Jarhead* is awfully prescient in its warning of "warfare's waste." The book's last lines read: "Sorry, we must say to the mothers whose sons will die horribly. This will never end. Sorry."[152]

Swofford's memoir opens fantastically. It's August 1990, and his unit just heard "the news of imminent war" against Iraq, prompting the men to "march in platoon formation to the base barber and get fresh high and tight haircuts." They then "send a few guys downtown to rent all of the war movies they can get their hands on," Swofford relates. "They also buy a hell of a lot of beer," he continues: "For three days we sit in our rec room and drink all of the beer and watch all of those damn movies, and we yell *Semper fi* and we head-butt and beat the crap out of each other and we get off on various visions of carnage and violence and deceit, the raping and killing and pillaging." Remembering how they rewound the films back to their favorite, most brutal parts, Swofford stands back from the scene to comment on the role of vision in the social psychology of Marine violence. "There is talk that many Vietnam films are antiwar," he observes; actually, though, they "are all pro-war, no matter what the supposed message, what Kubrick or Coppola or Stone intended." (Really? *Apocalypse Now* [1979] maybe; *Platoon* [1986] certainly; but *Full Metal Jacket* [1987], a pro-war film?—with its murder-suicide ending of recruit training; its deconstruction of warfare—an unseen Vietnamese woman sniper wipes out the better part of a platoon; its tired and misspoken rendering of war as sport: "Why don't you jump on the team and come in for the big win?") Swofford explains that "the magic brutality of the films celebrates the terrible and despicable beauty of [the marines'] fighting skill." The bursts of graphic violence mattered most to Swofford and his fellow marines: "Filmic images of death and carnage are pornography for the military man; with film you are stroking his cock, tickling his balls with the pink feather of history, getting him ready for his real First Fuck." Having made his point, Swofford flips back into jarhead mode, recalling his own excitement: "Now is my time to step into the newest combat zone. And as a young man raised on the films of the Vietnam War, I want ammunition and alcohol and dope, I want to screw some whores and kill some Iraqi mother fuckers."[153]

Unlike Caputo, Swofford didn't join the corps out of a preexistent yearning for adventure and combat; he learned that desire in Marine training, from (in one of the book's best phrases) "being birthed through the bloody canal of boot camp." Marine Corps culture undid Swofford. It wiped clean his earlier person and the tools he had to understand that self. "The language we own is not ours," Swofford recalls being in the thick of it, "it is not a private language, but derived from Marine Corps history and lore and tactics." He illustrates:

> Marine Corps birthday? 10 November 1775, the Marine Corps is older than the United States of America. Birthplace? Tun Tavern, Philadelphia, a gang of drunks with long rifles and big balls. Tarawa? Bloodiest battle of World War II. Dan Daly? He killed thirty seven Chinese by hand during the Boxer rebellion. Deadliest weapon on earth? The marine and his rifle. You want to win your war? Tell it to the Marines! When you are a part of that thing, you speak like it.

You also think and behave like it. Swofford vividly recounts the de-evolutionary arc to his early days in the corps. Having agreed to play the bugle for taps and reveille, Swofford is rebuked by a staff sergeant, who tells him he's completely wrong for the job: "Swofford, you are a goddamn Marine Corps grunt. You are the most savage, the meanest, the crudest, the most unforgiving creature in God's cruel kingdom. You are a killer, not a goddamn bugle player." And, again, the generational force of Marine culture proves effective. Out in the Kuwaiti desert, targeting Iraqi soldiers, Swofford ruminates over his deadliness. "The enemy are caught in an unfortunate catch-22, in that I care for them as men and fellow unfortunates as long as they are not within riflesight or they're busy keeping dead," Swofford thinks fairly; "but as soon as I see them living," he continues, "I want to perform some of the despicable acts I've learned over the prior few years, such as trigger killing them from one thousand yards distant, or gouging their hearts with my sharp bayonet."[154] Swofford's insight actually came several years after the fact, while writing about fighting for the United States. Swofford may have felt some inkling about the absurdity of war while in its midst, but, at the time, as he relates in *Jarhead*, his emotions were usually quite basic: first, fear during initial contact with the enemy—he repeatedly wet his pants during artillery barrages; and, second, a sharp desire to kill someone.

The quest to "finally know what it feels like to kill a man" runs throughout *Jarhead*—it's the main attraction in "The Vietnam War Film Fest" opening the book, Swofford obsesses it during the Gulf War, and it haunts him afterward. Swofford's assignment to a Surveillance and Target Acquisition Platoon as a sniper crystallizes his homicidal desire. Sniping bestows high technique to combat as well as an unusual intimacy to the act of killing itself. A sniper can supposedly see the expression on the person's face when the bullet hits. Swofford and his fellow snipers fantasize about "pink mist," the effect of a perfect head shot. "I've spent many hours of my life imagining what my bullets will do to the enemy," the author acknowledges. On the last day of the Gulf War Swofford targets three Iraqi soldiers on a rise in the desert. "I could, within two or three seconds, produce fatal injuries to all three of the men. This thought excites me," Swofford writes, adding plainly: "I want to kill one or all of them." But the fire call doesn't come. It never comes for Swofford. And that brings aching disappointment and dissatisfaction. Swofford had expected to kill from the beginning. While enlisting he decided to be a rifleman, to which the recruiter affirmed: "You'll be a fine killer." Killing is synonymous with being a Marine, Swofford emphasizes at the end of the memoir: "To be a marine, a true marine, you must kill." Considering himself less of a marine and a man for not having killed an Iraqi soldier is part of the "wreck" in his head, a madness that remains well after the war and his leaving the military. Swofford appreciates the sickness of that thought and tries to "dismantle" the wreck. He finally realizes that it cannot be done: "It took years for you to understand that the most complex and dangerous conflicts, the most harrowing operations, and the most deadly wars, occur in the head."[155] But producing *Jarhead* may subdue the madness, Swofford suggests, and it might also warn others about the danger that lay ahead.

Swofford's memoir is an antiwar protest. Realizing that *Jarhead* may at points along the way provoke the same fascination with war as, say, *Full Metal Jacket*, Swofford issues a "complaint" at the book's end, pulling his criticisms together, and insisting that, because he served his country, he is "entitled to speak" and we are obliged to listen. "*I belonged to a fucked situation*," is how Swofford sums up "the bad news about the way war is fought and why, and by whom and for whom." Of course, exhibit one is Marine spirit and its manifestation of murderous violence in his own mind. That same mind also cultivates a conscience, though, and Swofford isn't shy about showing it in the book's last pages. As part of Task Force Grizzly, Swofford marches into Kuwait, past charred Iraqi vehicles and hundreds of dead enemy soldiers. "This is war, I think. I'm walking through what my father and his father walked through—the epic results of American bombing, American might. The filth is on my boots," Swofford comments ominously: "If colonialism weren't so out of style, I'm sure we'd take over the entire Middle East, not only to safe-guard the oil reserves, but to take the oil reserves. *We are here to announce that you no longer own your country, thank you for your cooperation, more details will follow.*"[156] Swofford understands that American power depends on grunts like him who are eager to kill and destroy. That's why his closing hopefulness over the fact that he didn't kill has such seditious potential. What would happen to American empire if Swofford's conscience spread the same way that fighting spirit has in previous generations?

Judging from the United States' 2002 war against Afghanistan and its second war against Iraq, Swofford's conscience has a long way to go, although there are signs that some American troops do share his doubts and despair. Such reserva-tions haven't affected U.S. killing power, much of which is accomplished through aerial bombing, where American casualties are limited at the cost of foreign ci-vilian lives. "Ethics seemed to be a matter of distance and technology," as Philip Caputo described such structured violence during the Vietnam War: "You could never go wrong if you killed people at a long range with sophisticated weapons."[157] U.S. aggression following September 11, 2001, though, has also relied on a war-rior class for its ground invasions. And, here, unsurprisingly, the Marines have led the way. In an extraordinary pair of articles on 29 March 2003, the *New York Times* provided new documentation of Marine enthusiasm for war and killing. A *Times* reporter accompanying a Marine regiment fighting its way to Baghdad in the early days of the war spoke with two sharpshooters after a long fire fight. "We had a great day," said one of the marines: "We killed a lot of people." Yes, "we dropped a few civilians," he added in apparent response to the reporter's question about it, "but what do you do." He then referred specifically to killing an Iraqi woman in his line of fire. "I'm sorry," the marine said, "but the chick got in the way." In stark contrast to marine ease over killing, other American infantry have expressed re-morse for their actions. Another *Times* reporter embedded with an Army infantry regiment talked with Sergeant Mark N. Redmond about the combat he had just been through. Never expecting or wanting to be on the front line, Redmond felt troubled after killing the enemy. "When I go home, people will want to treat me like a hero," he said, "but I'm not. I'm a Christian man," he continued, reminding us that there are long-standing thought systems consistent with Swofford's con-science: "I mean, I have my wife and kids to go back home to. I don't want them to think I'm a killer."[158]

CHAPTER FIVE

Laws of Sexual Selection

This chapter on masculinity and sexual violence is predicated on two uses of the word *law.* The first includes the laws passed by legislatures and interpreted by judges—the rules, codes, penalties, and procedures enacted by the state and accepted, contested, and developed by society as a whole. The second conceptualization, as defined in the *Oxford English Dictionary,* is "expressible by the statement that a particular phenomenon always occurs if certain conditions be present."[1] Such covering *laws of nature*—gravity, for instance, and thermodynamics—have most commonly arisen in the physical sciences. Under the influence of Darwinian biology, however, the human sciences have tried to produce their own natural laws. Darwin himself relied on law to establish the fundamental truth of natural selection, sexual selection, and his belief in the emotional affinity between human beings and other animals. He described instincts, for example, as manifestations of "one general law, leading to the advancement of all organic beings, namely, multiply, vary, let the strongest live and the weakest die."[2] This tendency to convert Darwinian narratives into natural law has been extended in evolutionary psychology's recent attention to male sexual jealousy and aggressiveness. Following Darwin's reference to inter-male competition within sexual selection as the "law of battle," evolutionary psychologists posit a fixed and uniform reflex toward violence when a man's reproductive access to women is challenged.[3] They argue, in short, that the natural law of aggressive masculine instinct causes spousal homicides and other acts of sexual violence. In contrast, I contend that the proprietary feelings that men have toward women stem more directly from law in its first meaning: the legal institution of marriage and the common-law support of man's possessory rights over women make up an intervening intermediate cause of the violence in question.

In pursuing the notion of innate masculine aggressiveness, evolutionary psychologists have joined evolutionary biologists in developing Darwin's theory of sexual selection and the apparent logic of male reproductive striving. Compared to the demands of women's nine-month parental investment during gestation and then the years of nursing, protection, and care, men need to invest little time for reproductive success, just that entailed in competition for female contact and then for mating itself. Evolutionary psychology's focus on sexual selection has produced dubious work, including Randy Thornhill and Craig T. Palmer's book *A Natural History of Rape: Biological Bases of Sexual Coercion* (2000), which argues that rape has been evolutionarily selected as a mating strategy for men.[4] More sophisticated studies in social science can be found, however. Most relevant here is anthropologists Martin Daly and Margo Wilson's book *Homicide* (1988). In trying to explain the high incidence of male spousal murder, Wilson and Daly reason that different roles in propagating the species cause men and women to evolve qualitatively different proprietary feelings toward their mates: women, responsible for sustaining the newborn, are more concerned with allocation of their mate's resources and attention, whereas men, not wanting to expend energy without paternity certainty, are more intensely concerned with sexual infidelity per se.[5] This explanation of sexual jealousy is one of evolutionary psychologists' favorite examples of the biological influence on male and female emotions. And, as illustrated by the title of David M. Buss's book *Dangerous Passion: Why Jealousy Is as Necessary as Love and Sex* (2000), the sexual infidelity and jealousy theme has been a leading source of evolutionary psychology's impressive attainment of a nonacademic readership and its high-profile coverage in the media.[6]

Evolutionary psychology's popular appeal comes from its facile emplotment of heterosexual drama onto the human brain. Daly and Wilson write of human beings' "evolved motivational mechanisms" that are "designed to expend the organism's very life in the pursuit of genetic posterity."[7] Their reasoning is circular: Daly and Wilson use the fact that male sexual jealousy is the leading cause of spousal homicide across cultures to prove the existence of the evolved motivational mechanism built to increase male paternity certainty; they document this biopsychological predisposition with police records showing the high incidence of male spousal violence and Anglo-American case law that to some extent excuses that behavior. Daly and Wilson consider no other explanation. They see jealousy simply as a functional outcome of a preexistent and fixed drive to reproduce. Men are fitness maximizers and their emotions prove it. More broadly, evolutionary psychologists say little if anything about how human sexuality has evolved via pleasure seeking as well as reproductive striving. What happens to reproductive striving when, with the improvement of birth control, more and more women and men consider pregnancy an unintended consequence of sexual relations?

Most critically, evolutionary psychology routinely ignores feminism and one of its core convictions that at an early point in human history men started to combine with each other to control women's labor and sexuality. What Darwin took to be the natural law of sexual selection, the feminist anthropologist Gayle Rubin described in 1975 as the "traffic in women": a suprabiological sexual economy in which females become a resource, a type of "currency" among men. "[I]f it is women who are being transacted," Rubin explained, "then it is the men who give and take them who are linked, the woman being the conduit of a relationship rather than a partner to it."[8] This chapter examines a few key man-made laws that govern the traffic in women, including the Anglo-American heat-of-passion defense, a legal doctrine that relies on de-evolutionary psychology to partially excuse homicide: finding his wife in an adulterous relation, the *reasonable man*—one bearing the standard issue cognitive and emotional architecture of a human male—could not help but kill. The heat-of-passion defense recognizes the emotional impact of masculine provocation—a man's public transgression of another man's interests. Provocation doctrine strongly supports my intermediate cause theory of violent sexual jealousy. Even if that emotion can be traced back to early human history and male reproductive strategies, sexual jealousy is always triggered and mediated by a far more recent social factor such as homosocial status and honor. In first turning to lynch law in the post-Reconstruction South, we'll see that evolutionary psychology's interest in an innate motivational mechanism toward violence is further undermined by the fact that the socially constructed category of race triggers pathological jealousy and homicidal rage.

Race, Lynch Law, and the Manly Provocation

One of evolutionary psychology's biggest blind spots with regard to sexual selection is the role of men grouping. The problem goes directly back to Darwin's assumption that sexual competition among men happens at the individual level, "paralleling" the struggle between antler-smashing stags and fiercely pecking humming birds. Like Darwin, turn-of-the-twenty-first-century evolutionary psychologists say little about human beings' supremely social nature. They say very little about the species' sexual violence and the emotions that accompany it arising from transgression of historically specific laws, practices, and alliances rather than from a timeless imperative of one-on-one battle. In emphasizing the social determinism of human sexual selection, this section concentrates on the role of interracial masculine relations in the white lynching of black men over the alleged rape of white women in the post-Reconstruction South. A small fraction of these lynchings actually involved charges of rape and those cases that did were almost always without foundation, as Ida B. Wells clearly showed in the 1890s; but, at the same time, white southern men *did* genuinely fear African American male sexuality, especially after seeing it through their own highly racist construction of the hypersexual black brute, a de-evolutionary archetype whose bestial nature threatened white men's sexual prowess and, with that, their control of women's sexuality and racial supremacy overall. Within this pathological context of the southern rape complex, the very possibility of sexual relations between black men and white women routinely provoked white men into fits of anxiety, jealousy, anger, and, finally, calculated homicidal frenzy. The self-described "savagery" of white lynch mobs tended to mirror the imagined brutality of the black beast rapist, as the ritualized torture, mutilation, and murder of thousands of black men exceeded every other form of violence in the postbellum United States.

In pursuing heterosexual relations, men have grouped in two primary ways. First, men have grouped together as a gender, deliberately setting themselves against female interests, effecting patriarchy, and establishing traffics in women—suprabiological sexual economies in which females become a resource, a type of "currency" among males. Second, men, as a macro group, as a homosocial unit, have formed intricate systems of subgroups and alliances, a function of which has been the assignment of status and power among themselves, including relative positions within inter-male competition for women. Dominance orders among men have followed age, education, wealth, physical prowess, and a host of other factors. Homosocial rank has been realized through general and diffuse formulations of difference, most of which can be found in society at large. Economic-social class has been a key homosocial determinant of an individual man's place in heterosexual pecking orders. Traditionally, class background and material well-being have helped establish patterns of courtship and marriage. By the turn of the twentieth century, though, economic privilege could bring added leverage over male competitors as spending and consuming power became more consequential within the burgeoning heterosexual dating cultures of modern urban America. As discussed in this chapter's last section, during this time heterosexuality itself became a more active homosocial measurement, as the newly explicit dichotomization of it from homosexuality provided the opportunity and necessity to develop manliness via one's exclusive sexual desire for women. And, finally, among the homosocial criteria for status within heterosexual relations, race has been unusually determinant through formal miscegenation laws, strict conventions prohibiting interracial dating and marriage, and extralegal policing and punishment of those crossing the socially constructed lines of ethnicity, nationality, and color.

The late nineteenth- and early twentieth-century U.S. South provides an unusually transparent example of a concerted effort by one group of men to take power from another. With lynch law as its most deadly weapon, the white supremacy campaign encompassed political disenfranchisement of black men, attacks against successful African American businesses and other economic warfare, racial massacres by white paramilitary groups, and the entrenchment of a rigid caste system supported by legal segregation and the threat and use of violence against anyone opposing it. There was nothing subtle about the effort. With slavery's paternalism a thing of the past, southern whites of all classes treated blacks with ever increasing bitterness, hatred, and prejudice. Fueling this systematic hostility was what historian Joel Williams has labeled "radical racism," a somewhat new formulation centered on the idea that African Americans, "freed from the restraining influences of slavery, were rapidly 'retrogressing' toward their natural state of bestiality." Based in contemporary evolutionary thought and aroused by a supposed crisis of black men attempting to rape white women, radical racism fully supported the late 1880s onslaught of southern lynching, a practice that speaks to the inhumanity of the killers rather than that of their victims.[9]

Before the 1880s, lynching (the illegal execution of a person usually accused of a serious crime) had largely been a product of the United States' western frontier and its lack of a formal legal system; but, with the end of Reconstruction, lynch law grew into a monstrous phenomenon of the South, where the number of killings far outstripped those in other regions and where the murders themselves often became public spectacles, horrific performances emboldening the power politics of white supremacy. African American men suffered the most, by far: between 1880 and 1930, approximately 3,945 people were lynched in the South; of those victims, 3,220 were black and 70 of those were women; on average, then, southern lynch mobs killed 63 black men per year for fifty years.[10] By the early 1890s, some of these lynchings replaced hanging with torture, castration, and burning the victim alive. Lynching took on the ritual and meaning of human sacrifice. Southern newspapers often announced lynchings ahead of time with breathless anticipation. Trains were chartered, families gathered, an excited, celebratory atmosphere inspirited the crowd. Following mutilation and death, whites proudly took ears, fingers, and other parts of the victim's remains as trophies of the ghastly event.

Clearly southern spectacle lynching was a highly symbolic practice, paradigmatic of post-Reconstruction white redemption, and explicitly intended to thwart African American contact with white women. Sometimes lynch mobs verbalized the point with notes pinned to the victim's body. "Our mothers, wives, and sisters," read one such note from a 1882 South Carolina lynching, "shall be protected, even with our lives."[11] Finally, though, lynching needed little explanation. One didn't have to witness a lynching for the violence to have its intended effect. The writer Richard Wright described growing up in the 1920s rural South:

> The things that influenced my conduct as a Negro did not have to happen to me directly; I needed but to hear of them to feel their full effects in the deepest layers of my consciousness. Indeed, the white brutality that I had not seen was a more effective control of my behavior than that which I knew. The actual experience would have let

me see the realistic outlines of what was happening, but as long as it remained terrible and yet remote, something whose horror and blood might descend upon me at
any moment, I was compelled to give my whole imagination over to it.[12]

Lynching worked as law. In spreading fear of "horror and blood" dropping down
upon you for the merest of transgressions, or alleged transgressions, lynching
helped set strict standards of social behavior and racial interaction, violations
of which would be met with "swift justice." Lynching wasn't a perfect deterrent.
Along with the fear and intimidation, African Americans met lynch law with violent opposition. But few if any laws are completely effective. And in consolidating
its legal status and function in the late nineteenth-century South, lynching enjoyed
the tacit acceptance of police forces and court systems as well as the imprimatur
of the white press. After the lynching of Reeves Smith, a black man accused of attempting to rape a white woman in DeSoto Parish, Louisiana, in 1886, the editors
of the *DeSoto Democrat* wrote: "As we have said before, 'the will of people is the law
of the land,' and all such monsters should be disposed of in a summary manner."[13]
Public assurance of the dominant group's conviction to police African American
sexuality, legitimating such control via popular support or "will," the radical-racist
assumption of a subhuman black aggressor: the DeSoto newspaper's editors crystallized here the legalistic essence of white-on-black southern lynching.

   Overall, the white press—"the malicious and untruthful white press," as Ida B.
Wells called it in *Southern Horrors* (1892)—played a major role in building lynch
law into the region's civil society. In collusion with law enforcement's failure to arrest and prosecute the lynchers, local white newspapers protected the murderers
through the transparent fiction of pretending not to know their identity. African
American bishop Henry McNeal Turner described the absurdity in 1893: newspapers "can advance what [lynchers] are going to do, how and when it was done, how
the rope broke, how many balls entered the Negro's body, how loud he prayed,
how piteously he begged, what he said, how long he was left hanging, how many
composed the mob, the number that were masked, whether they were prominent
citizens or not, how the fire was built that burnt the raper, how the Negro was tied,
how he was thrown into the fire, and the whole transaction; but still the fiendish
work was done by a set of 'unknown men.'" Indeed, white newspapers' tag line
"at the hands of persons unknown" exemplified the white community's perpetu-
ation of the crime by neither stepping forward with incriminating evidence nor
shouting from the rooftops just how barbarous a practice lynching is. Instead, as
Wells emphasized, the white press, having covered up past murders, impelled new
lynchings by, first, publishing "libelous" articles falsely accusing black men of raping white women; second, elaborately appealing to white men to act in the name of

women's honor; and, third, seizing upon the "brute passion of the Negro" as reason for decisive violent action. Wells's analysis of "the red record," among the most accomplished muckraking in American letters, shows how white newspapers built up "mob spirit" rather than just reporting it after the fact.[14]

To chart the deliberate construction of white outrage over an alleged sexual violation does not deny the felt reality of the passions that drove a lynch mob toward violence. "White women were the forbidden fruit, the untouchable property, the ultimate symbol of white male property," as historian Jacquelyn Dowd Hall has written; and the mere suggestion of African American advance on that property interest could trip, in her insightful phrase, an "emotional circuit" to killing. In pinpointing the motivation to lynching, though, we need to go back not just to the emotion but also to the provocation of the emotion.[15] And, here, the racial source of the provocation to lynching undermines the notion of sexual violence's biological determination. That is to say that southern lynch mobs formed not so much from some universal male motivation to keep another man from a mutually desired woman but from fear of and hostility toward African American male sexuality—a homosocial pathology historically specific to the post-Reconstruction South.[16] White men, in one sense, wanted to be provoked. Black defiance of social-sexual boundaries confirmed their world view, and some men had the presence of mind to use tale of transgression to tighten racial bonds across class lines. In Charles Chesnutt's novel *Marrow of Tradition* (1901), a fictionalized account of the Wilmington, North Carolina, racial massacre of 1898, a number of white town leaders discuss how they should respond to a black newspaper editorial claiming that white women voluntarily entered into sexual relations with black men. "One of our conditions is violated by this article," editor of the local white Democratic newspaper Major Carteret says, "our women [are] made the subject of offensive comment. We must make known our disapproval." Captain McBane, a lower-class figure wanting to drive blacks from town, added excitedly: "I say lynch the nigger, break up the press, and burn down the newspaper office."[17]

The Wilmington racial massacre has served as a type of set piece for proving the violent extent to which the white supremacy campaign would go to reclaim political control of the late nineteenth-century South. In the beginning of 1898, the majority-black city of Wilmington, North Carolina, seemed to enjoy some measure of racial harmony, as whites frequented African American businesses and black and white men worked together in running the municipal government. That year, however, saw the culmination of the white Democratic Party's effort to rid the state of the coalition of black Republicans and white Populists—the "Fusionists," who had been in power for the past four years. In Wilmington, supported by the Democratic press, Colonel Alfred Moore Waddell stepped forward to rally white workingmen and elites alike to "end Negro domination." A lawyer, former congressman, and Confederate veteran, Waddell addressed a large crowd the night before the crucial November county election: "Go to the polls tomorrow, and if you find a negro out voting, tell him to leave the polls, and if he refuses, kill him." Despite the ensuing Democratic victory, Fusionists still held key municipal positions. So on 10 November, Waddell led state militiamen, Redshirt terrorists, recent veterans of the Spanish-American War, doctors, lawyers, and other professionals through the streets of Wilmington. Armed with repeating rifles and rapid fire guns, the force of hundreds of white men first stopped at the city's only black newspaper, where they burned the offices nearly to the ground. They next marched into a predominantly black section of the city, killing at least ten African American men and forcing women and children to seek protection in the swamps outside the city. The insurgents then forced the mayor and ten aldermen to resign. Colonel Waddell became the new mayor, as some fourteen hundred blacks left the city over the next month. "We have taken a city," a white minister rejoiced to his congregation: "To God be the praise."[18]

Propelling the Wilmington massacre and coup was the strategic white response to Alexander Manly's August 1898 article in the *Wilmington Record,* the first target of Waddell's 10 November mob. As editor of the *Record,* Manly had opposed the white supremacy campaign of 1898 from its beginning, especially the Democratic newspaper's smear tactics depicting black men as fiendish brutes and rapists. On 18 August he published a rejoinder to the white rape complex, boldly stating that black men did indeed pose a threat—not to white women, though, but to white men who wanted exclusive control over women they considered to be their own. Manly emphasized the fact that white women, as white men had long feared, could and did find black men attractive. Manly's editorial stepped over the line. It clearly broke the unwritten law that black men didn't even speak of white women in a romantic or sexual way. It was, in short, a provocation: a deliberate, transgressive act that tempted violent response. And respond white Wilmingtonians did, although not immediately. As white Wilmington newspapers decried "the slander," white town leaders seized upon an "effective" long-term "use for this article," as Chestnutt's fictionalized conspirators finally decided: "we'll print the editorial, with suitable comment, scatter it broadcast throughout the state, fire the Southern heart, [and] organize the white people on the color line."[19] The insurgents had found an opening and intended to exploit it as fully as possible.

Staunch white response to black provocation over interracial sex was not new to the post-Reconstruction South. In 1887 Jesse Duke, a leading citizen in Montgomery, Alabama's black community, penned a sharp editorial in his newspaper the *Herald* after witnessing a particularly brutal lynching. Writing in a state of "impassioned indignation at the repeated and increasing lynching of my race," as he later explained, Duke gave the lie to the black rape of white women: "There is a secret to this thing, and we greatly suspect it is the growing appreciation of white Juliets for colored Romeos." Montgomery's whites acted swiftly, passing several denunciations of Duke as a "scoundrel," a "vile and dangerous character" who had "crossed the limit of toleration." They gave him eight hours to leave town. Having already fled, Duke sent a formal apology to a white Montgomery newspaper disclaiming any intention to defame southern white women. He and his family would never again live in Alabama.[20] Ida B. Wells's better known 1892 editorial in her *Memphis Free Speech* received harsher response. After a white mob lynched three close friends of hers, Wells wrote threateningly: "Nobody in this section of the country believes the old thread bare lie that Negro men rape white women. If Southern men are not careful, they will over-reach themselves and public sentiment will have a reaction; a conclusion will then be reached which will be very damaging to the moral reputation of their women." Outraged Memphis whites responded quickly. One white paper exclaimed that "Patience under some circumstances is not a virtue. If the negroes themselves do not apply the remedy without delay," the editorial continued while mistaken over Wells's sex, "it will be the duty of those whom he has attacked to tie the wretch who utters these calumnies to a stake at the intersection of Main and Madison Sts., brand him in the forehead with a hot iron and perform upon him a surgical operation with a pair of tailor's shears."[21] But Wells had already gone to New York City, as whites settled for destroying the *Free Speech*'s presses.

In some ways the Manly provocation set itself apart from these earlier incidents. Manly offered no retraction or apology. He stayed in Wilmington for months after publishing the editorial, sometimes barricading himself in his newspaper office, where groups of black men stood guard after rumors of whites amassing to burn the building and kill Manly. Graduate of the Hampton Institute, former deputy register of deeds, and editor of the only black daily in North Carolina, Manly's prominence among Wilmington's African American middle class helps explain his reluctance to leave the city as well as his initial boldness in opposing white supremacy. That the light-skinned Caucasian-featured Manly was acknowledged to have been a grandson of Charles Manly, the last Whig governor of North Carolina, and one of his slave women, made Manly the younger all the more disposed to challenge the double standard of white paranoia over black rape and white right of access to black women.[22]

Manly wrote his August 1898 editorial in response to the *Wilmington Messenger*'s reprinting of a year-old speech by the white supremacist Rebecca Latimer Felton. From Manly's perspective, Felton's loathsome call for more lynching of black men was a provocation itself. Her speech, originally given as the keynote address at a Georgia farmers' convention, actually criticized white men for failing to provide for and protect poor rural women. Southern "manhood" had rapidly declined since the war, Felton charged, trying to shame white men into action; along with the degradation of poverty, back-breaking labor, and social isolation, "lustful black brutes" increasingly threatened women's "virtue." Something had to be done. If, she concluded infamously, "it needs lynching to protect woman's dearest possession from the ravening human beasts—then I say, lynch, a thousand times a week, if necessary."[23] Joel Williamson has wondered how Manly could have printed his editorial: "One is appalled by his lack of awareness, by the cavalier, almost careless manner in which he published such an essay."[24] The answer lays in Felton's inflammatory words. Even within the context of turn-of-the-century radical racism, Felton's urging of lynching as a positive good crossed a line. We don't know if Manly penned his article in the white heat of anger. Jack Thorne's novel *Hanover* (1901), a barely fictionalized account of the Wilmington massacre, has Manly exclaiming "Narrow-souled fool!" over Felton's speech and throwing the newspaper to the floor before writing his editorial.[25] In any event, unworried about upsetting whites, uninterested in playing the obsequious African American, Manly responded with great desire to set the record straight.

"You leave your goods out of doors and then complain because they are taken away": so reads Manly's provocation of white men. He held little back. "We suggest that the whites guard their women more closely," Manly continued, "thus giving no opportunity for the human fiend, be he white or black." This last phrase regarding the racial makeup of the aggressor was Manly's primary point. He agreed with Felton that rural women could fall prey to the "assaulter." But black women as well as white women suffered from unwanted cross-race sexual advance: "If the papers and speakers of the other race would condemn the commission of the crime and not try to make it appear that the negroes were the only criminals, they would find their strongest allies in the intelligent negroes themselves; and together would root the evil out of both races." Manly's second point, the one that drew so much fire, was that black men attracted white women. White men "are careless of their conduct toward" white women, Manly wrote, "and our experience among poor white people in the country teaches us that the women of that race are not any more particular in the matter of clandestine meetings with colored men than are the white men with colored women." Manly went even further, apparently speaking from his own experience: "Every negro lynched is called 'a big, burly black brute,' when in fact many of those who have thus been dealt with had white men for their fathers, and are not only not 'black' and 'burly' but were sufficiently attractive for girls of culture and refinement to fall in love with them, as is well known to all." He ended the article, though, by criticizing whites' double standard: "Tell your men that it is no worse for a black man to be intimate with a white woman than for a white man to be intimate with a colored woman. You set yourselves down as a lot of carping hypocrites," Manly concluded his editorial: "in fact you cry aloud for the virtue of your women, when you seek to destroy the morality of ours. Don't ever think that your women will remain pure while you are debauching ours."[26]

First to respond in print, the *Wilmington Messenger* carefully constructed Manly's article as an "outrage." The Democratic daily defined it as "the most infernal, slanderous lying article that ever appeared in a North Carolina newspaper"—a "dirty defamation" that has "naturally aroused the indignation and wrath of the white people of this community." The reputation of poor white women drew the most concern from the *Messenger* because, as the paper reasoned, "the intent of [Manly's] teaching is to justify the black brutes who commit rape at the expense of the character of every white woman of the south whose condition is poor as to this world's goods." Behind this concern lay a certain Democratic solicitude of poor white political support. "[T]he assumption of poor white women's purity," as the historian Glenda Gilmore has argued, "would become an integral part of an exchange for poor men's votes. If their men put race over class at the polling place, the Democrats promised, poor white women could be boosted up to the pedestal." This strategy is clearly manifest in the *Messenger.* Five days after the Manly piece, it featured on the first page an excerpt of the editorial from the *Daily Record*—"the organ of the Republican-Populist Fusionist political crowd. This is the way your new friends regard yourself and families," the *Messenger* wrote in preface to Manly's words. "Every white man in the state," it continued, "having any regard for the purity of his mother, sisters and daughters must take this matter into consideration and determine that hence forward he will act as a White man should."[27] The *Messenger* ran this boxed excerpt and commentary throughout the late summer and fall lead up to the election and massacre.

This same anti-Fusionist theme comes through in "A Word from the Slandered Sex," an open letter the *Messenger* published on its first page from the "many ladies" in Wilmington's poor white Dry Pond neighborhood. We "desire to thank you most cordially," the letter to the editors began, "for the brave words and outspoken manner in which you have hurled back the insinuations and aspersions of the negro whose slander upon the white women of North Carolina has called for the much vehement indignation from one end of the state to the other." After pledging to boycott any business that continued to advertise in Manly's newspaper, the women addressed the political loyalties of "the white men of our acquaintance." Any one of you, the letter states sharply, "who may be led into voting for other than the white supremacy ticket at the forthcoming election need never expect respect and recognition from any woman in the Dry Pond section."[28] Without the vote themselves, these women used their social-sexual nexus to push the Dry Pond men in the direction they were probably already going. This section of Wilmington produced the Redshirts, the paramilitary group that intimidated blacks during election day and contributed to the killing the day after.

With the editor of the *Raleigh News and Observer* reprinting 300,000 copies of Manly's editorial and distributing them throughout North Carolina, the Wilmington provocation became a cause célèbre for the state's white Democratic newspapers, as many of their own editorials on the matter made their way back into the *Messenger*. Together the newspapers fanned the flames. Most of the commentary focused on how Manly's slander against white women "is," as the *Monroe Journal* wrote, "the logical result of fusion rule in North Carolina." The *Charlotte News* spoke apocalyptically: "This picture of the dark shadow that is coming over our state like a black cloud is no dream. It is a bold and brutal reality. When the only colored daily newspaper in the state defends and condones the most awful of crimes, we have a glimpse of what we may expect if such rule is perpetuated." The discussion among the state's white newspapers produced another theme, though: why had this outrage gone unpunished? The *Goldsboro Argus,* for instance, commented ten days after Manly's editorial that "we have not heard other than that the negro editor is still living and plying his venomous vocation in that community. The *Argus* is not given to incendiary language," it continued disingenuously, "but we know whereof we speak when we say that the black fiend who penned those lines and published them to the world could not do so in Goldsboro and live till the ink got dry; and we don't' think we do violence to the manner of white men who constitute the community when we say this."[29] No, it was the "manner" of Wilmington's white men that would be increasingly questioned as long as Manly remained in town alive.

Wilmington's white men, or at least those running the *Messenger,* seemed secure in their masculinity, however. Outside criticism continued. "In the name of Heaven," the *Raleigh Post* wrote sharply, "of what can these white men be made?" And the *Goldsboro Argus* asked "What are the white men of Wilmington thinking of to allow the slanderer and his vile publication to live for an hour in their midst?" For that paper, Manly's life had become a matter of state honor: "[N]eedless to say, the editor of the *Record* would not live an hour in one of the cities of Virginia or South Carolina, and surely the people of North Carolina are not behind those of her sister states on the north and south of her." Tellingly, the *Messenger* responded directly to these charges: "While the white men of Wilmington are no more deficient in manly courage than the people in other towns, they have good reasons to be more considerate and less impulsive than other towns under a like provocation would be." Wilmington's whites had grander plans than the lynching of one black man: "We are persuaded that now it is wise and better to be careful to avoid open violence for up-to-date the advantage is altogether with the democrats. If the people were to open now upon the blacks and kill a few thousands, as would surely be the case if war were to begin, it would to a very great extent excite sympathy for the negroes."[30] White Wilmington's initial forbearance, if that's what it can be called, served them well: while the November election and coup returned political control to the whites, the racial massacre allowed the city's men to prove their "manly courage." Meanwhile, the *Messenger*'s handling of this particular masculinity issue betrays the deliberateness with which the eventual violence occurred. In choosing to publish the other city newspaper's challenges to white Wilmington's capacity to punish Manly, the *Messenger* kept the provocation alive, feeding an emotional current that could then be tapped at the most opportune moment.

Wilmington's white supremacy campaign grew to a fevered pitch through two large Democratic rallies in October 1898. The first came together seventy-five miles up the Cape Fear River in Fayetteville, where the leading white supremacist in the country, Senator Ben Tillman of South Carolina, spoke to a rain-soaked crowd of thousands. With the *Messenger* having promoted the event as "the grand white man's rally and basket picnic," and with the railway reducing its rate to Fayetteville for the day, some eighty-two Wilmingtonians made the weekday trip, including members of the local United Confederate Veterans camp and the Wilmington Brass Band. Despite the torrential downpour, the day proved to be, as the *Messenger* reported, "glorious." Introduced as "the liberator of South Carolina," Tillman spoke for over an hour and a half, first taking note of the impressive number of Redshirts in the audience and then focusing on the need to overthrow Fusionist rule. Toward the end of his speech Tillman turned to the Manly provocation. He saw "around him very beautiful girls," who "reminded him to say such articles as that written by the negro editor in Wilmington was an insult to the women of North Carolina." Never one for mincing words, Tillman then asked "Why didn't you kill that nigger editor who wrote that? Send him to South Carolina," he continued, "and let him publish any such offensive stuff and he would be killed. While I was governor and was canvassing the state, I said openly in a speech that I would lynch any negro that outraged a white woman and I still say that." Tillman closed the address by further contrasting North Carolina to his state's white supremacy: "When we were under bayonets [during Reconstruction] we never did submit to negro rule." In words ready made for white Wilmington, Tillman told the crowd that "Your right arm is off. You must get it back."[31]

Emboldened by Tillman, Wilmington's Democrats organized a large political rally at the city's opera house on the night of 24 October. This rally marked the first reported appearance of Wilmington Redshirts, who, sixty strong, marched through the downtown before joining, the *Messenger* documented, a "pack[ed] house" with the city's "leading ladies" and gentlemen. The interclass white crowd had come to hear "North Carolina's most finished orator, the Hon. Alfred M Waddell." Focusing on the need to maintain "the absolute supremacy of the white people," Waddell played on his audience's greatest fear, invoking the "ultimate ambition" of blacks and the "unspeakable crime which has so often within the past year or two been committed in the southern states and which even the awful retribution visited upon it has scarcely served to check." Having raised the issue of sexual competition, Waddell turned to the Manly outrage: "Who would have believed five years ago that it would ever be possible for a negro newspaper editor to dare to publish such an article as appeared in this city two or three months ago, or that if he did so dare that he would not have been lynched?" Wilmington's white men "are afflicted with an excess of the virtue of forbearance which, beyond a certain point, ceases to be a virtue at all and becomes a want of self-respect." Action must be taken, Waddell continued, explicitly linking the Manly provocation to Fusionist rule. "I understand he is here still," Waddell said pointedly, "and doubtless if the white men fail in their duty again on the 8th of November they will be regaled with more of the same sort of literature." Putting an even finer edge on the matter, he added that Manly "was only educating his race up to what will be demanded as a right after awhile, if things go on at the present rate of progress." By this early point in his long "sizzling talk," Waddell had captured his audience's attention and imagination.[32] He made the most of it.

Further exciting their emotions, Waddell masterfully appealed to the audience's sense of state pride and, with that, to the white men of Wilmington's masculinity. The "true sons" of North Carolina, Waddell said in building to the speech's climax, have already started to move against Fusionist rule: they "have put on their armor, and the thunder of their tread, as shoulder to shoulder they come marching to her rescue, fills all the air, and thrills the patriot's heart." Waddell challenged the men in his audience to action. "It would be an insult to your manhood to ask if you are marching with them. The men of the Cape Fear, whatever else may be said of them," he continued in alluding to outside newspaper criticism, "have never been recreant to duty when they heard from their good old mother a cry for help, and they will not be now—now when her honor is in the dust, and when the appealing voices of her dead sons, whose spirits walk disturbed among us, seem to be borne to our ears on every breeze. No we are not degenerates. We hear, and we are ready."[33] With the heroic dead calling and, Waddell might have added, watching, how could Wilmington's white men refuse?

Waddell hadn't finished. He implored Wilmingtonians to rise above daily material concerns and embrace the higher ideal of racial destiny. "My heart instinctively leaps out to the man who, in the crisis, talks and acts, not like the wretch who fears he will lose a dollar, or a customer," Waddell criticized, "but like an Anglo-Saxon, who, stirred by the proud consciousness that he belongs to a race that dominates half the earth and is destined to dominate the whole of it, feels that he is the sovereign and the master on the soil which he treads and dares all who question it to put it to the test." Waddell then detailed Wilmington's martial tradition. "We are the sons of men who won the first victory of the American Revolution at Monroe's Creek Bridge," he started, "who stormed at midnight the rocky face of Stony Point, who stained with bleeding feet the snows at Valley Forge, who swept the field at Germantown, and only left the service of their country when its independent sovereignty was secured." More importantly, Waddell continued, through the Civil War, "We are the brothers of the men who wrote with their swords from Bethel to Bentonsville, the most heroic chapter in American annals; and we ourselves are men who, inspired by these memories, intend to preserve, at the cost of our lives, if necessary, the heritage that is ours." He had finally reached the speech's climax. "We maintained it against overwhelming armies of men of our own race. Shall we surrender it to a ragged rabble of negroes led by a handful of white cowards who at the first sound of conflict will seek to hide themselves from the righteous vengeance which they will not escape? No!," Waddell stormed. "Let them understand once and for all that we will have no more of the intolerable conditions under which we live. We are resolved to change them if," he concluded, in the most quoted phrase of the address, "we have to choke the current of the Cape Fear with carcasses."[34]

Waddell's directive to kill if necessary to retake the city pushed Wilmington's whites toward the early November massacre, while the masculine need to answer the Manly provocation supplied the emotional spark for the violence. The emotional current was palpable. "Colonel Waddell's speech electrified his hearers," the *Messenger* reported the day after the opera house rally: when he "closed his grand address the audience rose to its feet applauding and cheeringly [sic] wildly and all who could reach the speaker wrang his hands and thanked him for his brave and inspiring words." As the city's white elites conspired behind the scenes, and as certain "businessmen" saw fit to purchase a Colt rapid-firing gun, the Redshirts held a parade through town on 2 November, culminating in a rally and barbecue at Wilmington's Hilton Park. With Redshirts and other working-class whites patrolling the city streets on election day, the Democrats won all the city, county, and legislative offices, except for those of the mayor and eleven aldermen, which were decided on odd years. So the next day, 9 November 1898, more than one thousand white men gathered in the city's courthouse, where Waddell, called upon to speak, "judg[ed] from the feeling manifested [that] the pot needed no more fuel to set it boiling." Nevertheless, Waddell read aloud eight resolutions, written by a committee of town leaders, which began with the declaration that white Wilmingtonians "will never again be ruled by men of African origin" and ended with the order that "the paper known as the 'Record' cease to be published, and that its editor be banished from the community." A shout came from the crowd: "Fumigate the city with The Record." Others called to lynch Manly, whereupon someone yelled "He's gone now," to which John Bellamy, the Democratic congressman-elect, replied that the city had "been rid of the vilest slanderer in North Carolina."[35] The following day more than two thousand white men took to the streets of Wilmington. Armed with repeating rifles and other modern weaponry, the mob burned Manly's offices, killed at least ten African Americans, drove out hundreds more, and took over the mayor and aldermen positions.

What happened in Wilmington during the summer and fall of 1898? The tremendous loss of African American life, property, and power resulted from both the strategic workings of the Democrat's white supremacy campaign and, as one white participant put it, the "paroxysm of passion" flowing from Manly's August editorial. Not merely a pretense for political power taking, the Manly provocation went to the heart of interracial sexual competition, triggering a provision of lynch law that called for violent response to black disrespect toward white women. Without legitimating such violence, we might further consider the psychological composition of the southern rape complex and the pressures on white men to follow its dictates. Just after his momentous opera house address, Waddell received a letter from Rebecca Cameron, a relative who hadn't heard his talk. "We have been amazed, confounded and bitterly ashamed of the acquiescence, and quiescence of the men of North Carolina at the existing conditions," Cameron stated flatly: "and more than once we have asked wonderingly: where are the white men and their shotguns?" She continued: "I asked an ex-confederate Major if the election went against us to beg the white men to get out their shotguns and empty them into the hearts of all the decent white women in the state." Feeling "ashamed of the manhood of North Carolina," Cameron ended her letter forcefully and presciently: "It has reached the point where bloodletting is needed . . . and when [it] commences let it be thorough! Solomon says: 'there is a time to kill,' that time seems to have come so get to work."[36] Along with this standard expression of southern honor culture, when it came time to oppose the "black brute rapist," white men found themselves subject to their own deep-seated sexual desires and fears.

In other words, the ritualized and brutal lynchings of black men can be read as manifestations of the sexual war in the white men's head. It's long been argued that white men's caricature of the "sexually aggressive Negro," as historian Winthrop Jordan wrote in 1968, spoke to "their own passion for Negro women," which "was not fully acceptable to society or self and hence not readily admissible. Sexual desires could be effectively denied," Jordan explained, "and the accompanying anxiety and guilt in some measure assuaged, however, by imputing them to others. It is not we, but others, who are guilty. It is not we who lust, but they." Projection of white sexual desires onto African American men involved a certain obsession with the black phallus and its mythic endowment—a point borne out, as some writers have contended, by increasing incidents of castration in lynchings. Anxiety over imagined black sexual superiority could help explain such atrocity, as could feelings of envy and desire. "Even as they castrated the black men," literary historian Trudier Harris has said of turn-of-the twentieth-century southern lynchings, "there was a suggestion of fondling, of envious caress"; the white man's "actions suggest that, subconsciously, he craves the very thing he is forced to destroy. Yet he destroys it as an indication of the political (sexual) power he has and takes it unto himself in the form of souvenirs as an indication of the kind of power he would like."[37] War in the head, indeed. At the hands of this pathology, African Americans suffered terribly, as radical racism also locked white men into a repressive, tremulous, and self-brutalizing sexuality.

Perhaps the most psychoanalytically astute interpretation of lynching's effect on southern white sexuality is James Baldwin's story "Going to Meet the Man" (1964). A psychological profile of Jesse, a deputy sheriff in a southern town split apart by civil rights demonstrations, the story establishes the incapacitating cycle of desire, violence, and sex in the memory and libido of a white man raised under lynch law. "Going to Meet the Man" takes place in Jesse's mind. He lay in bed late one summer night unable to become aroused for sex with his wife Grace. "He moaned" with frustration, "want[ing] to let whatever was in him out; but it wouldn't come out." Part of the problem is that "he could not ask her to do just a little thing for him, just to help him out, just for a little while, the way he could ask a nigger girl to do it." His mind drifts to "the image of a black girl," but to no avail, the excitement too distant. Jesse is also exhausted from his work and the encounter that day with a leader of the black demonstrators.[38]

He decides to recount the episode aloud to Grace who is slowly falling asleep. After the black man had been beaten and thrown in jail by other police officers, Jesse "put" an electric prod to him, ordering him to make the others "stop that singing." At this point in telling the story, Jesse recognizes a "peculiar excitement which refused to be released." He recalls the prisoner "roll[ing] around in his dirt and water and blood," as Jesse continued to use the prod under the man's arm and then on his testicles. "[T]he singing went on," though, so Jesse kicked the man "flush on the jaw." With this vicious and rapelike attack, and with the man apparently losing consciousness, Jesse "felt very close to a very peculiar, particular joy; something deep in him and deep in his memory was stirred, but whatever was in his memory eluded him." Jesse turned and "walked to the cell door," at which point the man called from the floor: "White man." Jesse "stopped. For some reason, he grabbed his privates." The black man asked, "You remember Old Julia?" referring to his grandmother, whom Jesse had known before joining the police. "My grandmother's name was Mrs. Julia Blossom," the man said, his mouth filled with blood: "*Mrs.* Julia Blossom. You going to call our women by their right names yet.—And those kids ain't going to stop singing. We going to keep on singing until every one of you miserable white mothers go stark raving out of your minds." Jesse wanted to beat him more—"pick him up and pistol whip him until [his] head burst open like a water melon." Instead Jesse "felt an icy fear rise in him." He yelled as loud as he could: "You lucky we *pump* some white blood into you every once in awhile—your women! Here's what I got for all the black bitches in the world—!" Jesse was very unsteady on his feet: "to his bewilderment, his horror, beneath his own fingers, he felt himself violently stiffen—with no warning at all; he dropped his hands and he stared at the [man] and he left the cell."[39]

From this raw rendering of the violent, unstable pathology of radical racist sexuality, Baldwin dug deeper for its sources, leaving Jesse as a victim of southern masculinity, tragically unprotected from the pornography of lynching. Jesse's mind drifts back further to his father and the other "[m]en much older than he, who had been responsible for law and order much longer than he," and how these "models" of his used to enjoy the confidence and respect of the whole community. Jesse is now back to his childhood, around age eight, driving home from an outing with his parents and wondering why he hadn't seen for two days his black playmate Otis. Earlier that day a stream of cars had driven to his house. "[W]ith everyone looking excited and shining," a woman told Jesse's father that "They got him." After tying up the dog, the boy and his parents piled into their car, with Jesse asking, "Where are we going? Are we going on a picnic?" His father replied: "That's right . . . You won't ever forget *this* picnic—!" Jesse remembers a short drive, getting out of the car, smoke from a fire, and a mob of "laughing and cursing" people in front of him. "His father reached down suddenly and sat Jesse on his shoulders." He slowly made out the naked black figure chained above the fire. "The head went back, the mouth wide open, blood bubbling from the mouth; the veins of the neck jumped out; Jesse clung to his father's neck in terror as the cry rolled over the crowd." He turned to his mother. "Her eyes were very bright, her mouth was open: she was more beautiful than he had ever seen her." The young Jesse then began "to feel a joy he had never felt before. He watched the hanging gleaming body, the most beautiful and terrible object he had ever seen till then." Suddenly, "brighter than the fire," a knife appeared in the hands of a man in front, "one of this father's friends." Smiling, the man approached the barely living man and reached up. He

> took the nigger's privates in his hand, one hand, still smiling, as though he were weighing them. In the cradle of the one white hand, the nigger's privates seemed as remote as meat being weighed in the scales; but seemed heavier, too, much heavier, and Jesse felt his scrotum tighten; and huge, much bigger than his father's, flaccid, hairless, the largest thing he had ever seen till then, and the blackest. The white hand stretched them, cradled them, caressed them. Then the dying man's eyes looked straight into Jesse's eyes—it could not have been as long as a second, but it seemed longer than a year. Then Jesse screamed, and the crowd screamed as the knife flashed, first up, then down, cutting the dreadful thing away, and the blood came roaring down.

With the black body drenched in kerosene and lit into "a sheet of flame," Jesse's father set the boy on the ground. "At that moment Jesse loved his father more than he had ever loved him. He felt," as Baldwin wrote in driving the point home, "that his father had carried him through a mighty test, had revealed to him a great secret which would be the key to his life forever." And so it was for Baldwin's character. After the lynching, Jesse couldn't think of his former friend Otis without feeling sick. For Jesse the white deputy sheriff, a "soldier fighting a war," he had learned his violent ways during the sublime moment of his life. And that violence ineluctably tied itself to Jesse's sexuality. Back in bed with Grace, Jesse "thought of the knife and grabbed himself and stroked himself and a terrible sound, something between a high laugh and a howl, came out of him and dragged his sleeping wife up on one elbow." The story ends with Jesse sexually excited, "crying and laughing," taking Grace in his arms, and whispering "Come on, sugar, I'm going to do you like a nigger . . . come on, sugar, and love me just like you'd love a nigger." Jesse's "peculiar excitement" finally gets out. Triggered by castration of the black phallus, sexual pleasure for Jesse ends in envy and desire for the same he thing he wants to destroy.[40]

For Baldwin, white sexuality and violence are deeply and absurdly patterned by race. Socially inherited perceptions of racial difference teach white and black children to hate each other, Baldwin's story demonstrates, and they intricately formulate sexual desire: driving home from the lynching, Jesse lay between his parents, his head in his mother's lap; his father—with memory of the castration and killing fresh in mind and black "singing com[ing] from far away, across the dark fields"—lets Jesse's mother know that they'll have sex upon reaching home; Jesse's long day ends, then, with him still in the car, a blanket half over his face, his teeth "gritted" while listening to his mother's "moaning," the bed "rocking," and "his father's breathing . . . fill[ing] the world."[41] Baldwin understood that whites didn't only project their buried passions onto African American sexuality but that they in turn learned from that whole misconception, absorbing it back into their conscious self-image and letting it inform their behavior. This process of *mirroring* can also be found in the self-described savagery of late nineteenth- and early twentieth-century white lynch mobs. Provoked by what they feared to be the sexual aggression of the crazed "black brute," the "monstrous beast," groups of white men cultivated the instinctive "savagery" and "frenzy," as Ben Tillman described the mind-set, needed to put down the perceived African American threat. Contemporary critics of lynching saw the psychological similarities between the white supremacist caricature of the black rapist and the vaunted murderousness of the white mob. In an unusually effective response to Rebecca Latimer Felton's "lynch a thousand black men" speech—the same address to which Manly replied—an editorial in the *Boston Transcript* commented smartly: "When it comes to declaring who are the wild beasts of Georgia society, the black man would not get all the votes."[42]

Psychological mirroring—lynch mobs' mimicking of "black bestiality"—provides a good point of contrast to the way whites legitimated homicide through the idea of uncontrollable instinct and emotion. As we've seen in Wilmington, community outrage and the subsequent mob's emotional state became favorite topics for white southern newspapers. Explanations for lynching differed slightly. An editor for the *Atlanta Constitution* wrote in 1898 that white mob violence constituted a "spontaneous outburst of emotions long felt and long smothered and those emotions are based on love—love for the home and wife and children, love and respect for wives and daughters and mothers." Other commentators relied on the faux-biological concept of blood temperature. "In the veins of the southern man there boils hot blood," a spokesperson for the Georgia Women's Federation stated in 1897, "and when the honor and purity of his home is invaded, personal vengeance he will have." Fitting closely with the spontaneity argument, this formulation of murder involuntarily flowing from uninterrupted "heat of passion" also paralleled the formal legal excuse of a husband who killed his wife or paramour after finding them in sexual contact. "It would be as easy to check the rise and fall of the ocean's tide," as the *Newnan (Ga.) Herald and Advertiser* put it somewhat differently in 1899, "as to stem the wrath of Southern men when the sacredness of our firesides and the virtue of our women are ruthlessly trodden under foot."[43] Overall, white southerners saw the extralegal killing of black rapists as a law of nature—an immutable reflexive response.

The first decade of the twentieth century produced more elaborate psychological examinations of lynch mobs. The Kentucky-born, Harvard natural scientist Nathan Shaler's book *Neighbor: The Natural History of Human Contacts* (1904), in part a confirmation of the southern rape complex, attends to the "ancient devil of the mob" and how quickly it develops "a spirit of association": acting in close unison, mob members all have "a kind of pinched, staring look" on their faces, "which reminds one of people who are hypnotized." But "the most singular part of the process which develops the mob," Shaler wrote, "is that it leads to the immediate overthrow of all those sympathies which characterize the isolated and independently acting men, bringing them, for the time, into the state of the primitive brutes." Temporarily losing their cultural inheritance, the "people associated in passionate action constitute a new kind of human being, one that has a primitive animal nature, if so to term it be not injustice to the brutes." In close agreement with Shaler, Dean Richmond Babbitt, contemplating "The Psychology of the Lynching Mob" (1904) in the political journal *Arena,* said that "fundamental" to lynching is "that a mob has a mind of its own, which is not the aggregate of mental acts of its individual members, but is a new mental entity, a new mind, a different mind, both in kind and in degree, from the particular minds of the members of the mob." Babbitt then zeroed in on the "bestial" quality of mob action, behavior influenced by "the unconscious, the region of the instinct, the place of primitive, of racial, of hereditary powers, the first elements, so to say, of our being."[44] Both Babbitt and Shaler understood the lynch mob to be a de-evolutionary entity, shorn of civilization, unusually free from the mediating effects of individual conscience and consciousness. Neither of these writers recognized, at least in print, the psychological and ontological similarities between the lynch mob and white supremacists' image of the black rapist.

In defending southern lynching, Ben Tillman painted a vivid picture of white devolution, often drawing sharp yet unrecognized parallels between the mental states of the "black fiend" and the white avenger. As Stephen Kantrowitz has shown in his valuable biography of Tillman, the man patterned his whole political career on the "fearsome" alternative of white supremacy or a "racial struggle to the death." After using violence to help overthrow South Carolina's Republican government in 1876–77 and to consolidate Democratic power in his state where he was governor from 1890–94, "Pitchfork Ben" went national, serving in the U.S. Senate from 1894 to 1918, and speaking throughout the country about the absolute necessity for whites to defend the race with their lives.[45] By 1900 Tillman had packaged his message in the same evolutionary thought and instinct theory as Shaler and Babbitt, although he concentrated on the emotional state of the individual more than that of the mob. Also, Tillman unsurprisingly racialized the ferocity of the aggrieved killer: "If you scratch the white man too deep, you will find the same savage whose ancestry used to roam wild in Britain when the Danes and Saxons first crossed over." And nothing raised an Anglo-Saxon man's "anger and frenzy" as much as word that a "daughter had been ravished"; all values other than racial purity, "all semblance" of being a "Christian human being," dropped away from his person. Only racial instinct remained. On the floor of the U.S. Senate in 1907 Tillman spoke of the South's free-roaming black brutes, their "breasts pulsating with the desire to sate their passions upon white maidens and wives." Once that passion is satisfied, as Tillman described, and the "blighted and brutalized" woman tells her husband, father, or brother what happened, "Our brains reel under the staggering blow and hot blood surges to the heart." Our own passion takes over, Tillman stressed: "We revert to the original savage."[46] The reversion would apparently last until the white men's violent passion had been sated.

To the extent that Tillman and other white supremacists tried to justify lynch law, then, they relied on a combination of popular de-evolutionary thought—the white savage lurking beneath the civilized Christian—and the heat-of-passion defense—a common-law doctrine based on a mechanistic view of emotions precluding reasoned judgment and impelling action. Within the context of southern lynching, both devolution and heat of passion began with the threat of the black brute rapist—a type of self-provocation really, because that figure grew out of white imagination. "Consider the provocation," wrote Atticus Haygood, a leading moderate in turn-of-the-century southern race relations: "sane men who are righteous" will concentrate on the "ruined woman," far worse off than "the brutish man who dies by the slow fire of torture." The North Carolina newspaper editor Clarence H. Poe's *Atlantic Monthly* article "Lynching: A Southern View" (1904) argues that mob justice is only legitimate in response to black-on-white rape. "Here and only here," Poe stated in one of the most succinct rationalizations of lynch law, "could the furious mob spirit break through the resisting wall of law and order." In more lurid terms, Ben Tillman, again on the floor of the U.S. Senate in 1907, explained lynch law's abandonment of due process. With southern white women "in a state of siege," Tillman asked rhetorically, should "the demon" get "the right to have a fair trial and be punished in the regular course of justice? So far as I am concerned," Tillman said in justifying murder, "he has put himself outside the pale of the law, human and divine." At the same time that the rape charge jettisons the black man outside of legal protection, the white man loses control of himself, involuntarily yet self-servingly compelled to use deadly force. "Civilization peels off us" Tillman continued, thus excusing the inhumanity that follows: "we revert to the impulses to 'kill! Kill! Kill!'"[47]

The formal heat-of-passion defense, to which we now turn, depends on both of the phenomena Tillman described in rationalizing southern lynching: the severe moral culpability of the victim and the uncontrollable emotional state of the killer(s). As seen in Wilmington in 1898, sexually motivated violence against blacks may have been driven by genuine feelings of fear, anger, and jealousy; but, at the same time, those emotions and their violent deployment could be manipulated by white leaders with the larger picture of interracial social and sexual relations in mind. For some time, fraudulent rape charges worked extremely well in white supremacists' war against African American equality. Lynching did decline after the early twentieth century, in part because of blacks' increasing willingness to resist forcefully. As Ida B. Wells instructed in 1892: "The only times an Afro-American who was assaulted got away has been when he had a gun and used it in self-defense." The Wilmington massacre itself produced Josh Green, Charles W. Chestnutt's *Marrow of Tradition* character, who, after seeing whites whip his mother, dedicated his life to militancy. "Come along, boys!," he says in rallying other blacks to fight: "Dese gentlemen may have somethin' ter live fer; but ez fer my pa't, I'd rather be a dead nigger any day dan a live dog!"[48] Other responses to southern white men's sexual warfare would emerge—one thinks of James Baldwin's nonviolent black activist sending his white oppressor into a fearful frenzy from his jail cell floor.[49] Playing by the white man's rules has been a more common response, however. At the turn of the twentieth century, as Alexander Manly well understood, this meant both exposing African Americans to overwhelming force and hitting psychologically insecure white men right where they hurt most.

Marriage, Cultural Defense in *The People v. Chen*, and the Heat-of-Passion Defense in Texas

Of all the man-made laws of sexual selection, few have been more embedded in U.S. patriarchy than the heat-of-passion defense. For centuries it has supported male possession of women by discounting masculine violence within marriage by reducing the charge from murder to manslaughter when a husband kills his wife's lover after finding them having sex. The defense turns on a de-evolutionary understanding of human (that is, masculine) nature: direct confirmation of sexual infidelity sends the husband into blind rage. Anglo-American common law has defined heat of passion thus: an emotional state set apart from "cool reflection," as 1902 Texas jury instructions depicted it, a state of mind lacking the malice aforethought necessary for a murder conviction.[50] Feminist legal scholars argue that the killer's loss of self-control is a masculinist fiction: like spousal battery, heat-of-passion homicide divulges a husband's intent to dominate his wife and marriage and to punish invasion of that property interest.[51] A cornerstone of provocation doctrine, the heat-of-passion defense extends the homosocial license that men police their own affairs. Under this view, the husband's loss of reason and judgment is clearly a legal pretense for partially excusing the defendant's deadly response to a serious affront. What's more, as heat-of-passion case law developed, nineteenth-century U.S. courts started to rule that an angry cuckolded husband's inability to control his actions would be excused when an "ordinary" or "reasonable man" would also have lost such control—thus, paradoxically, making a man's temporary insanity in the face of adultery an "ordinary" or "reasonable" response.[52] The heat-of-passion defense, in other words, has been based on the culturally determined propriety of a man "flipping out." Rather than tacitly accepting such anger and violence as part of human nature, this section will analyze heat of passion as a contingent emotional configuration arising from the male-centered law of marriage.

If, as argued throughout this book, masculine disposition has developed in large part through social institutions, then marriage has greatly increased male capacity for a wide range of emotions—from love, desire, and commitment to jealousy, shame, and anger. As this latter clump of feelings leads to marital violence and murder charges, lawyers, judges, and juries have paid close attention to its possible clouding of criminal intent. To emphasize, the heat-of-passion defense has never been totally exculpatory; moral blame and usually a prison term accompany manslaughter convictions. But, at the same time, in recognizing the authenticity of a husband's anger over his wife's adultery and in significantly discounting the punishment for an ensuing killing, manslaughter law has helped build up a man's expectation to possess a woman through the institution of marriage. In formal terms, a man realized this expectation through *coverture,* a common-law doctrine delineating the legal disabilities of a *feme covert,* a married woman, whose "very being or legal existence," in William Blackstone's mid-eighteenth-century words, is "incorporated or consolidated into that of the husband: under whose wing, protection, and cover" she lives. In exchange for supporting his wife, coverture granted the husband rights to her labor, property, and sexuality. The marital rape exemption, "domestic chastisement"(moderate physical punishment) and "alienation of affections"(a civil action against a paramour) all supported a man's vested property rights in his wife.[53] Those rights also included defense of his possession. Indeed, as provocation doctrine developed alongside coverture, Anglo-American courts likened adultery to physical assault and trespass. The law expected a man to protect his property against others, with anger and violence understandable parts of that undertaking.

The law of coverture is no longer intact in the United States. A century and a half of marital reform has rid the institution of some of its most pernicious tenets; today, most of the legal rights and responsibilities of wife and husband are, in theory, gender neutral. Amid this change, however, the heat-of-passion defense has gone virtually untouched. While the "reasonable man" standard is now the "reasonable person" test, manslaughter law, in practice, benefits far more male than female defendants. By the early 1980s, a number of states had adopted the Model Penal Code revision of heat-of-passion doctrine, although, as legal scholar Victoria Nourse points out, its results may be more "illiberal" and "perverse" than those of the common law, allowing juries to return a manslaughter verdict, for instance, in the case of a man who killed his fiancée after she danced with another man.[54]

In reform and common-law jurisdictions alike, heat of passion remains a doctrine that is intricately configured from masculine perspective and psychology. In addition to supporting a man's possessive feelings over his wife, the defense's privileging of anger and supposed loss of control tends to divert attention from the cuckold's less virile emotions of jealousy and shame. Upon close scrutiny, the defense's premise that the husband acted involuntarily upon discovering his wife and paramour *in flagrante delicto* (in the very act) and before a cooling off period is little more than a sham. Courts never pay attention to whether there was any psychophysical manifestation of rage—the defendant's rapid heart beats, for example, trembling lips, or shallow breathing.[55] In the end, the heat-of-passion defense invokes a naturalist, de-evolutionary psychology of going out of one's mind in an effort to cover up the law's calculated concern with a husband's expectation of spousal loyalty and sexual security.

The heat-of-passion defense's patriarchal function and purpose become clearer when the doctrine is compared to the late twentieth-century "cultural defense": a legal argument made by recent immigrants to the United States that their criminal behavior should be excused because, in following accepted customs and values of the home country, it lacked the requisite *mens rea* or guilty mind. Invoked in a wide range of cases, from child molestation to politically motivated suicide, the cultural defense's most controversial use can be found in murder trials involving responses to spousal infidelity.[56] And here the case of *New York v. Dong Lu Chen* (1989) is paradigmatic. A year after Dong Lu Chen immigrated from China with his family, he killed his wife, Jian Wan Chen, by smashing her head in with a claw hammer after she admitted to having sex with other men. At trial his defense introduced expert anthropological testimony that in China a wife's infidelity casts great humiliation and shame on the husband. Under the threat of harsh social sanction, Chen was "driven to violence," or so the argument went. The judge bought it. In a nonjury trial, Brooklyn Supreme Court Justice Edward Pincus, having found no criminal intent to murder, convicted Chen of second-degree manslaughter, sentencing him to just five years' probation. Amid the ensuing protest by various feminist groups, Pincus supported his decision by likening Chen's state of mind during the killing to temporary insanity: "I was convinced that what happened at that time was because he had become temporarily, totally deranged." Chen "was the product of his culture," Pincus added in explaining that his reasoning wouldn't apply to a native-born American. "[B]orn in China, raised in China," Chen "took all his Chinese culture with him" to the United States. Chinese culture "made him crack more easily," Pincus concluded: "That was the factor, the cracking factor."[57]

What makes *Chen* so important to our discussion is how it shows heat of passion to be a dominant cultural defense rather than an accommodation to an instinctive emotional response to sexual betrayal. While neither the lawyers nor the judge in *Chen* mentioned heat of passion, the case clearly followed provocation doctrine's principle that word of his wife's infidelity causes a husband to lose control of his actions. Chen's "cracking" equaled uncontrollable anger under the heat-of-passion defense. Pincus may have accepted Chen's explanation, as legal scholars Daina Chiu and James J. Sing have argued, not so much out of respect for cultural difference but because of his behavior's resonance in U.S. law and culture. At the same time, though, the court worked insidiously from "a neutral and unquestioned backdrop," as Leti Volpp has written, "fetishiz[ing]" the difference between gender relations in China and the United States and thereby ignoring the gory fact of American sexual violence and the law's implication in that long-standing and ongoing cross-sexual crime.[58] The expert anthropological testimony and defense argument regarding the influence of socially constructed pressures on Chen to act violently can actually be read as a transparent accounting of Anglo-American heat-of-passion doctrine.

According to Judge Pincus, the case turned on anthropologist Burton Pasternak's "very cogent, forceful testimony" regarding Chen's mental state during the crime. Professor of anthropology at Hunter College, Pasternak stressed from the beginning "the ability of the Chinese community to define values and define appropriate behavior." Given this level of conformity, and given the "enormous stain" a wife's adultery casts upon a man's "person," "family," "ancestors," and "progeny," Pasternak testified, a "normal Chinese" under similar circumstances as Chen would have responded in the same violent way. Along with this extraordinary statement, Pasternak spoke of the Chinese imperative of salvaging one's masculinity: "It's a terrible shame if he lets it slide. What kind of man is that?" Throughout his testimony Pasternak magnified the power of Chinese pressure to respond violently to spousal infidelity by comparing it to the way "we take this thing normally in the course of an event." Pasternak had "no doubt" that a Chinese man faced with the same circumstances as Chen would have "react[ed] in a much more volatile, violent way . . . than someone from our society." When pressed on this generalization during cross examination, Pasternak conceded that "it's difficult to say what an average American is, but most of us are familiar with divorce. Most of us know something about adultery." He ended the line of questioning with another gross generalization: "We become inured to this. They are not inured to this."[59]

From one perspective, Pasternak made sense in contrasting Chinese attitudes toward adultery and divorce with those of the United States. Marital exits probably had become far more common in the late twentieth-century United States than in rural or urban China during that time. "We are at two extremes," Pasternak asserted: Americans have a "certain common awareness of the frequency of divorce and the frequency of adultery. It doesn't take us that much by surprise." His thinking had major gaps, however. While sexual infidelity in the United States may not have been "surprising" in the abstract—that is, many Americans may have become "inured" to it as a social fact—adultery often remained quite startling and disturbing to individuals first learning of their spouse's betrayal. The high level of spousal violence and homicide in the United States attests to that. In comparing marriage and violence in the two societies, Pasternak dichotomized Chinese culture and a liberal, cosmopolitan West but ignored the violent conservatism of the U.S. gender relations as well as the country's complex social and sexual diversity.[60]

In short, the problem was with Pasternak's single, narrow perspective. When the prosecuting attorney asked him "What would you consider your average American?" Pasternak answered "I think you are looking at your average American."[61] He quickly retreated from that statement, but, on the whole, Pasternak's testimony projected his open-minded, relativistic view of adultery onto all Americans. Against this anthropological understanding of the vagaries of sexual desire, Chen's jealousy, anger, and violence appeared benignly traditional or even primitive. It fulfilled the requirements of the cultural defense. As Leti Volpp has said in criticizing the doctrine: "One is left with an image of a spoonful of cultural diversity from immigrants ladled into a flat, neutral base."[62] But that base of U.S. law and culture has not been neutral, of course, especially in regard to marital infidelity.

What would Pasternak have found if he had been asked to compare Chinese law and custom to Anglo-American provocation doctrine and the heat-of-passion defense? What would he have found while comparing the social pressure of a Chinese cuckold to act violently with the past one hundred years of such pressure in, say, Texas? To answer these questions, we must first acknowledge that the Chinese dictate of shame avoidance ("It's a terrible shame" if a husband lets the provocation of adultery "slide"—"What kind of man is that?") hasn't been such a foreign proposition in Texas or, for that matter, New York City. The key is to conceive of common-law provocation doctrine itself as a distinct yet widespread cultural defense, born in early modern England and adopted throughout the late nineteenth-century United States. By that time Texas had paradigmatically created a bulwark of legal allowances for a husband's deadly response to spousal infidelity. Not to be outdone by Chinese custom—*Chen* said almost nothing about the country's law on the matter—Texas statutes and case law made up an elaborate patriarchal accommodation to a husband's property interests in his wife and his correspondent autonomy within homosocial relations.

Heat of passion as a mitigating defense in the criminal law of homicide can be traced back to the sixteenth-century code of honor among English men and that system's sanctioning of violent retaliation to a personal affront. Early modern honor theorists distinguished this homosocial canon of common courtesy, civility, and respect from "acquired" honor—differential reward for exceptional achievement in war or other public service. In contrast to acquired honor, "natural" honor tended to be recognized only in its breach: deserving proper regard from others, a man was expected to retaliate angrily upon serious affront. And in concert with this natural honor code, English common law started to excuse partially homicidal response to specific categories of provocation; they included aggravated assault, witnessing a friend or relative being attacked, illegal arrest, mutual combat, and catching a man in the act of adultery with his wife. Among these categories, though, adultery became paramount. "When a man is taken in adultery with another man's wife," the court ruled in *Regina v. Mawridge* (1707), "if the husband shall stab the adulterer, or knock out his brains, this is bare manslaughter: for jealousy is the rage of the man, and adultery is the highest invasion of property." The court insisted that "a man cannot receive a higher provocation."[63] Blackstone solidified the law in the 1760s: "if a man takes another in the act of adultery with his wife, and kills him directly upon the spot," it is the "lowest degree" of manslaughter. "Therefore in such a case," he illustrated, "the court directed the burning in the hand to be gently inflicted, because there could not be a greater provocation."[64] By the end of the eighteenth century, common law had developed a type of pity for the cuckolded killer. Already suffering the greatest of affronts, the shamed husband was honor bound to retaliate forcefully; and if that response ended in homicide, the court should discount the penalty, given the defendant's high anxiety and pressure to act.

Rather than recognizing such a homicide as an honor killing and building the mitigation around the homosocial pressure to respond, common-law provocation doctrine rested the excuse in the defendant's state of mind during the crime, relying increasingly on a mechanistic conception of emotion that equated anger with loss of self-control. Starting in the eighteenth century, as Jeremy Horder has pointed out, English judges, lawyers, and commentators adapted a series of interchangeable metaphors in depicting the temporary derangement of an individual beset by anger. Whether a defendant had been transported outside of consciousness—as in being "beside oneself," or subject to an "ungoverned storm" of anger, or "thrown off balance" by a provocation, or pushed to the "boiling point," the legal meaning remained the same: a man acting in the heat of passion should not be held to the same standard of culpability as one in complete control of himself. Early manslaughter case law concentrated on the timing of the retaliation. While paying little attention to the defendant's actual psychological state, courts reasoned that a fleeting mindlessness took hold of a man upon provocation and that a killing committed before a "cooling period" should therefore be mitigated.[65]

The provocation doctrine's loss-of-self-control phenomenon certainly carried over into nineteenth-century U.S. law and, more specifically, the American heat-of-passion defense for cuckolded killers. Like its English progenitor, American case law masked the role of male honor in pushing shamed husbands to violence with an unexamined naturalist psychology of reflexive irrationality. In *Maher v. People* (1862), the first American decision to use the "reasonable man" standard for determining sufficient provocation, the Michigan Supreme Court referred to the defendant's attempt to kill his wife's seducer as an act following "the nature of man and the law of the human mind." Recognize here that the reasoning behind *Maher* resembles the logic of *Chen*'s "cracking factor": a normal man under similar circumstances would experience the same uncontrollable impulse to violence. Unlike *Chen*'s cultural defense, though, the mid-nineteenth-century heat-of-passion defense located that impulse in a species-wide male instinct. "It is a true test of manslaughter that the homicide be committed in a sudden transport of passion," the Michigan court held in drawing from a familiar metaphor. In further keeping with English provocation doctrine, however, the *Maher* court didn't care about the defendant's actual capacity for deliberation or reflection. Instead it looked to the victim's provocation: "In determining whether the provocation is sufficient or reasonable, ordinary human nature, or the average of men recognized as men of fair average mind and disposition, should be taken as the standard."[66] With adultery clearly meeting that standard, *Maher* filled in the de-evolutionary loss of judgment on the way to excusing the homicide.

Loss of self-control also played a crucial role in the "unwritten law" cases of the mid-nineteenth century. A cuckolded killer and his lawyer had more options at trial than pushing for manslaughter. Acquittal was a distinct possibility. Extralegal acknowledgment that the victim had it coming, unwritten law was a "not guilty" verdict after defense attorneys had argued to the all-male juries of the time that the defendant's disgrace and dishonor compelled vengeance.[67] Unwritten law acquittals amounted to homosocially motivated jury nullifications. "Apparently unworried about any risk that they would be held in contempt of court," as Hendrik Hartog has explained, "[t]he defense lawyers pressed the jury to ignore what they knew the judge was going to say in his final instructions on the law of the case." He concludes that "the lawyers worked to empower the jury as a community of husbands and men."[68] While the unwritten law was more transparent about the husband's honor than the heat-of-passion defense, lawyers pursuing acquittal tended to plead their client's temporary insanity, as seen in the highly publicized 1859 murder trial of Congressman Daniel Sickles. After learning of his wife's adultery, Sickles had shot her libertine U.S. district attorney Philip Barton Key in Lafayette Park across the street from the White House. Sickles's lawyers contended that he had been overtaken by an "irresistible impulse"—a natural "instinct" spurred by "jealousy."[69] At the same time, they urged the jury to acknowledge the propriety of Sickles's actions—he had a right to protect his property. Despite the argument's incongruity—Sickles had a right to go insane—it worked. The jury acquitted Sickles. And his defense strategy became a model in murder trials of other cuckolded killers.

It shouldn't be surprising that more and more defense attorneys relied on the loss-of-self-control argument. As *Brutes in Suits* documents, the late nineteenth and early twentieth centuries saw the widespread, cross-institutional development of a naturalist, de-evolutionary-based masculinity. Law contributed its part. Murder trials, appellate decisions, and state penal codes all turned on the putative fact of a natural-born irresistible impulse toward violence. And yet in looking closely at U.S. provocation doctrine and heat-of-passion defense, we see that lawyers, judges, and juries used the concept of involuntary loss of reason more as a tool for achieving a homosocially acceptable result than as a psychoneurological factor truly affecting the defendant's state of mind. Transport of passion and related metaphors became a way to black out the specifics of the killing and attend instead to the victim's moral blameworthiness. In the thirty years after the *Maher* reasonable-man standard, every state in the country would develop parallel heat-of-passion laws. As we'll see in Texas, some jurisdictions moved toward dropping the *in flagrante delicto* requirement and the pretense of uncontrollable impulse. In Texas a wronged husband could avenge himself by killing his wife's lover with little concern of criminal penalty.

It hardly needs saying that post–Civil War Texas, in fact and legend, was an exceptionally violent state. A cornerstone of the gunslinger myth, Texas excelled in a range of violence, including racially motivated homicide. Between 1865 and 1868, white Texans killed more than a thousand former black slaves; from 1880 to 1930 some 492 people were lynched in the state.[70] Violence over heterosexual competition abounded. Late nineteenth- and early twentieth-century Texas criminal court reporters read like so much pulp fiction. Packed full with insults and showdowns, cheating wives and vengeance killings, the pages divulge the history of a formal criminal justice system deliberately fitting itself to a land of frontier vigilantism. The self-help tradition of gun-toting cowboys helps explain Texas's "paramour statute": a clear break with English common law, this legislation made homicide justifiable and therefore not criminal "when committed by the husband upon one taken in the act of adultery with the wife, provided the killing take place before the parties to the act have separated."[71] Before looking at this remarkably transparent concession to a husband's right to protect his marital property, we should first consider the Texas courts' liberal interpretation of the heat-of-passion defense, for this case law also reveals the state's legitimation of violent responses to sexual infidelity.

Turn-of-the-twentieth-century Texas heat-of-passion law not only ignored evidence regarding the defendant's state of mind during the killing but also regularly excused homicides committed well outside the time frame of the adultery—that is to say, *in flagrante delicto* was no longer a factor for manslaughter. Article 597 of Texas's penal code stated "that adultery with defendant's wife shall be a cause of provocation sufficient to reduce homicide from murder to manslaughter, provided the killing occurred as soon as the fact of the illicit intercourse was discovered by the husband." This last clause regarding timing could have been interpreted to reiterate that the husband needed to act before a cooling period, upon finding his wife and her lover in a compromising position. In *Pauline v. State* (1886), though, the Texas Court of Criminal Appeals ruled that the retaliatory killing "is not required to arise at the time" of the sexual infidelity, only close to when the defendant learned of the adultery by word of mouth or other means.[72] The statute's *discover* didn't require actually seeing the provocation, as in Blackstone's "taking another in the act of adultery with his wife"; it meant merely gaining knowledge of the infidelity and then, under *Pauline,* killing shortly after the fact. Texas courts continued to use heat-of-passion language. Trial and appellate courts alike spoke of whether the defendant had regained the power of "cool reason" or if he killed from the "emotions of the mind known as anger, rage, sudden resentment, or terror."[73] But after dropping the ocular evidence requirement—the shock of actually witnessing the adultery had originally been a key basis for the excuse—Texas law turned the heat-of-passion defense into that much more of a fiction.

Texas continued to distance heat-of-passion law from the *in flagrante delicto* scenario by allowing for manslaughter when a husband killed after piecing together a belief that his wife had committed adultery. In *Young v. State* (1908), the husband had heard rumors for a year about his wife's infidelity with a particular man. In response, he told various friends and associates that he would kill the paramour. On the morning of the homicide, the defendant and his wife found him in a farm field where the three discussed the adultery. After the paramour admitted "Yes, I have had her, and if I want her I can get her again," the husband shot him dead. In finding manslaughter, the appellate court spoke approvingly of the defendant "wreaking his vengeance" upon the paramour. When "the deceased's own declarations" confirmed the adultery, the court reasoned, then the defendant's mind could be "incapable of cool reflection" and manslaughter, not murder, ensued. The extent to which the appellate court would go in excusing a husband's violence can be seen in *Cannister v. State* (1904), another case involving rumors that the defendant's wife had been having sexual relations with another man. On the day of the assault, the defendant went looking for his wife after she hadn't returned from church on time. He found her walking home with three people, including the suspected paramour, whose arm she held. The defendant argued, and the appellate court agreed, that coming upon his wife "in such a compromising attitude" with the victim "corroborate[d] his previous information" about her sexual infidelity and he therefore acted without malice in attempting to kill the man. In response to prosecution evidence that adultery had not in fact occurred, the court went on to hold that it didn't matter if the original information causing the defendant's suspicion had been false, but only that "he believed it to be true."[74] The Texas heat-of-passion defense allowed the husband to guard against the appearance of dishonor or impropriety, laying all the more bare the homosocial logic behind the law.

In Texas the heat-of-passion defense and the justifiable-homicide statute worked together in setting an incredibly low standard of sufficient provocation for a man killing his wife's (suspected) seducer. If *Cannister* shows that a husband could kill based on false rumors matched with the sight of his wife holding the other man's arm after church, a sequence of justifiable-homicide cases from the late nineteenth and early twentieth centuries reveals that Texas law *permitted* homicide under circumstances covered in other jurisdictions by manslaughter. As explained in *Dewberry v. State* (1903), the manslaughter statute applied when a husband killed after "having been informed by some one of the fact of adultery"—the Texas courts' definition of "discovering"—whereas the justifiable-homicide statute covered scenarios in which the husband saw or witnessed the adultery itself.[75] As we'll discover, though, even that requirement of *in flagrante delicto* would be liberally construed.

In *Price v. State* (1885) the Texas Court of Criminal Appeals interpreted the state's justifiable-homicide statute within broad historical context, recognizing that it authorizes what other states punish as manslaughter, and deciding that circumstantial evidence could be used to establish the fact of adultery. The defendant in *Price* had come upon his wife at night in his corn crib with another man who lived nearby. The husband shot him once and then, after getting dressed, went back and hit him in the head twice with the stock of his gun. The victim died early the next morning. Both the husband's statement at trial and the appellate decision devote considerable attention to the annoyance the victim had made of himself by giving gifts to the defendant's wife and flirting with her; this is because the defendant never saw his spouse having sex with the victim—"I can't say," he admitted, "that I thought they were having connection with each other at the time"; and therefore the justifiable-homicide statute's requirement of killing when "taken in the act of adultery with his wife" went technically unfulfilled. No matter, the court ruled. In construing the "taken in the act" clause from the husband's perspective and interests, it wrote that "we cannot believe that the law requires or restricts the right of the husband to the fact that he must be an eye-witness to physical coition of his wife with the other party." The court added: "Such positive proofs of the commission of the crime of adultery are not required, and are rarely attainable." Following the defendant's statement that "I supposed that their object was to have connection with each other," the court held that the totality of the circumstances as understood by the husband needed to suggest that adultery had occurred or is about to occur. Accordingly, the court also ruled that the statute's last clause requiring the husband to come upon the couple "before the parties . . . have separated," means only that the paramour and wife need to be "still together in company with each other" and not actually joined in sexual intercourse.

Under the Texas statute, the law of justifiable homicide made little reference to heat of passion or to other supposed changes to the defendant's state of mind during the killing. The *Price* court recognized that the statute's key clause "taken in the act of adultery" went back to Blackstone's *Commentaries,* English provocation doctrine, and the idea that a man's discovery of his wife's infidelity could cause him to lose control of his actions.[76] Justifiable homicide in Texas didn't depend, though, on that guise of irresistible impulse. The law still viewed the husband's discovery of adultery as a crucial moment, a catastrophic happening that automatically lifted the standard responsibilities of peace and civility toward others. But in developing justifiable-homicide law in early twentieth-century Texas, courts envisioned a rather sober-minded, matter-of-fact response by the wronged husband. As the Texas Court of Criminal Appeals simply put it in *Gregory v. State* (1906), the statute "authorized" the husband, upon finding adultery, to "slay the invader of his home." And, following the *Price* decision, the court in *Gregory* set a very low standard for the husband's finding of spousal infidelity: the defendant contested the trial judge's instructions to the jury that the statute's expression "taken in the act of adultery" means "that the husband must see the parties together in such a position as indicates with reasonable certainty to a rational mind that they had just then committed the adulterous act, or were then about to commit it"; the appellate court agreed that "reasonable certainty to a rational mind" placed "on defendant a heavier burden than the law cast upon him" and that instead the killing would be justified "if the circumstances were such as to cause [the defendant] to reasonably believe from his standpoint that his wife and deceased had copulated" or were going to copulate.[77] While the court didn't want to hold the cuckold to a rational state of mind (perhaps a nod to the heat-of-passion defense), *Gregory* and justifiable-homicide case law overall forwarded a transparent model of honor killing when it appeared to the husband that his marital property had been violated.

The straightforward vengeance model of Texas's justifiable-homicide law comes to new light in *Sensobaugh v. State* (1922), an appellate decision that denied a cuckold the right to maim or torture a paramour. In *Sensobaugh* the husband entered his house and found his wife and another man under "circumstances," as the opinion described, "justifying the conclusion that they were about to have criminal relations." After pulling a gun, the husband told the victim that he didn't want to kill him. Instead, he tied the man up and cut off his penis with a razor. At trial and on appeal the husband claimed that his actions had been justified under the state's so-called "paramour statute." The Texas Court of Criminal Appeals recognized that "our statute upon the subject is an innovation," but found "no warrant" for extending it to mutilating the paramour. In dictum, the court said that the case's facts would have justified killing the victim. And, "doubtless," the court continued, "if serious bodily injury had been inflicted by the appellant in an attempt to kill the injured party, his immunity would be secure under the statute." The husband "chose, however, not to kill him, but to maim him, or to inflict serious bodily injury upon him without the intent to kill."[78] This last phrase, "without intent to kill," demonstrates how far Texas's justifiable-homicide statute had come from the common-law heat-of-passion defense: the whole basis for the provocation doctrine had been that the surprise of the adulterous circumstances prevented the husband from forming the intent to kill; *Sensobaugh* reveals that the paramour statute, an outgrowth of heat-of-passion law, permitted homicide when the cuckold had the presence of mind to kill. Otherwise a humane decision, *Sensobaugh* shows the brutal quid-pro-quo logic of the justifiable-homicide law in Texas.

The cold-bloodedness of Texas law also comes through in comparing it to the few other American jurisdictions with statutes justifying the husband's killing of his wife's paramour after finding them together in some suggestion of adultery. For instance, the Georgia courts interpreted its justifiable-homicide law as a category of self-defense. Unlike Texas's licensing of vengeance, Georgia required that the killing happen before imminent adultery. If the homicide followed the infidelity, it could no longer be justified because it hadn't been meant to prevent what Georgia law took to be an assault. And Utah's justifiable-homicide law required some evidence of the husband's heat of passion precipitating the killing.[79] In one of the most interesting cuckold justifiable-homicide decisions outside of Texas, the New Mexico Supreme Court looked closely at the intent behind its state's statute allowing that "Any person who kills another who is in the act of having carnal knowledge of such person's legal wife shall be deemed justifiable." In *State v. Greenlee* (1928), the court explicitly rejected the many Texas precedents "establish[ing] a quite liberal rule" of justifiable homicide: New Mexico's statute, in contrast, is not "designed to authorize an injured spouse to pronounce and execute sentence of death upon the destroyer of his family." The court continued: "The purpose of the law is not vindictive. It is humane. It recognizes the ungovernable passion that possesses a man when immediately confronted with his wife's dishonor. It merely says the man who takes life under those circumstances is not to be punished; not because he has performed a meritorious deed; but because he has acted naturally and humanly." In a decision unlikely to have been made in neighboring Texas, the *Greenlee* court recognized the statute's "narrow" authorization of homicide and ruled against the defendant-husband, even though he had come upon his wife seated on the lap of her confirmed paramour who had his hands under her clothing and on her "vulva" and "private parts." By his own testimony at trial, the court recognized, the husband killed the paramour because he feared for his own life and not because he believed the parties were then committing adultery.[80]

Texas did set limits to the malice aforethought of the cuckold killer, beyond which he clearly committed murder. While justifying intentional homicides, it didn't license long-premeditated killings. The state's justifiable-homicide law still required a narrow time frame between the discovery of the adultery and the homicide, even as it accepted the role of a dishonored husband as clearheaded executioner. So in *Burton v. State* (1935) the Court of Criminal Appeals affirmed a murder verdict of a husband who killed his wife's paramour after having found them in "compromising positions" on at least two former occasions. And in the fantastic case of *Zimmerman v. State* (1932), the appellate court found murder when the husband, at night and in slippers, snuck over to the house to which his wife had moved and placed dynamite in the kitchen stove knowing full well that the alleged paramour would build a fire there the next morning. Scheming, especially highly imaginative scheming, wasn't allowed in Texas's legal code of honor killings. The justifiable-homicide law also limited itself to husbands. In *Reed v. State* (1933), the appellate court disallowed the benefit of the statute to a wife who killed her husband's lover after coming upon them in true *flagrante delicto*. "If the Legislature in their wisdom," the court stated not unreasonably, "has not given equal rights to the wife as they have given to the husband . . . the courts are without power to do so."[81] The marital regime in Texas contributed to masculine domination by making liberal allowances for male violence. Even those husbands convicted for murdering their wife's paramour received astoundingly light sentences. In a state unabashedly committed to the death penalty, the killers in *Burton* and *Zimmerman* received prison sentences of seven and nine years respectively.

The Texas legislature repealed the paramour statute in 1973.[82] By that time the law had become "an anachronism," as a state official later commented, "a frontier idea whose time had gone" and which made "the state a legal laughing stock."[83] From this perspective, anthropologist Burton Pasternak's 1989 testimony in *Chen* that "your average American" didn't expect violence to follow the discovery of adultery seems plausible. If Texans felt the need to eliminate their licensing of honor killing, then the rest of the country must have been at least as far along. And yet the heat-of-passion defense for cuckold killers has lived through the turn-of-the-twenty-first century. As more and more critics call for its abolition, courts across the country still grant light sentences to men who kill adulterous wives and unfaithful girlfriends.

Provocation doctrine's staying power can be explained in part by the unintended consequences of progressive reform. Some twenty states have adopted the Model Penal Code, which dropped the category of adultery as sufficient provocation for reducing a killing from murder to manslaughter. The code substitutes "heat of passion" as the test for manslaughter with whether one killed while suffering "extreme mental or emotional disturbance for which there is a reasonable explanation or excuse." In trying to move away from the patriarchally driven protection of a husband's claim on his wife's sexuality, reform jurisdictions expanded both the type of relationships that produce provocation claims and the range of behavior that can be defined as "infidelity." Under the code, for instance, killers have successfully reduced the charge to manslaughter for killing a fiancée after she danced with another man and for killing a wife when she turned her back on the defendant after sexual intercourse.[84]

The larger problem with the Model Penal Code and other reform efforts, as Victoria Nourse has incisively shown, is that they still empower courts to make normative judgments about emotional responses when the judges and juries responsible for such determinations have internalized the patriarchal biases informing the traditional heat-of-passion defense. The criminal justice system continues to produce shockingly light sentences for wife killers, oftentimes accompanied by a judge's statement exposing, among other things, the emotional investment heterosexual men make in their sexual property. Thus we have the 1994 Maryland case of Kenneth Peacock, the long-distance trucker who killed his wife with a hunting rifle four hours after finding her naked with another man in the married couple's bed. Peacock pleaded guilty to voluntary manslaughter. At his sentencing, Judge Robert E. Cahill of the Baltimore County Circuit Court stated that he didn't want to send Peacock to prison at all, but he knew he had to keep "the system honest."

After giving Peacock only eighteen months in prison, Judge Cahill added: "I seriously wonder how many men married five, four years would have the strength to walk away without inflicting some corporal punishment, I shudder to think what I would do." Embedded in the judge's comments is the "troubling" approval of "a male paradigm that anger and violence are mixed," legal scholar Donna Coker commented, "as though they can't be separated." Five years after *Chen* found a Chinese-American man's homicidal response to his spouse's adultery to be an idiosyncratic remnant from a foreign culture, Judge Cahill declared that homosocial dictates within modern American culture all but forced Peacock to kill his wife.[85]

The examples roll on, with Texas characteristically providing one of the more violent and telling cases. In December 1998, Jimmy Watkins's wife kicked him out of the house because he had sexually assaulted a relative. The wife's boyfriend moved in the same day. After making several phone calls threatening to take her life, Watkins burst into the house and shot her once in the head while their ten-year-old son looked on. He then shot her boyfriend twice. When his gun jammed, Watkins left, fixed it, and then returned and fired five more bullets into his wife's head, killing her as she called 911. Watkins couldn't plead for manslaughter because in 1994 the Texas legislature eliminated the heat-of-passion defense as a partial excuse to homicide. Under the new law the defendant's state of mind could only be considered at the penalty phase of the trial. So in a late twentieth-century version of the unwritten law, the jury convicted Watkins of murder but then recommended that he serve no jail time and be sentenced only to probation because he killed in sudden heat of passion. In following the jury's will, the judge perpetuated the long-standing social approval of honor killing, even as the state's most democratic branch of government had tried to distance Texans from that bloody tradition. (How hard the legislature tried is a legitimate question, because it did let provocation doctrine in at sentencing.) Traditions die hard, especially when they are coupled with normative dispositions of a dominant sex and when they are dispersed through emotion and long reinforced by positivist law. Watkins had hardly become "inured" to the idea of his wife's infidelity.[86] And, like China for Chen, a certain part of turn-of-the-century Texas expected Watkins to act as he did.

Burton Pasternak had it partially right in explaining the cause of Chen's wife killing. Cultural anthropology best gets at a man's motivation to respond violently to spousal infidelity. "It's a terrible shame if he lets it slide. What kind of man is that?" The problem is that Pasternak ignored the modern American pressure to act in the same way. The omission is understandable since it was more the prosecutor's job to show that the United States had laws against spousal homicide, even though sexual jealousy, hardly peculiar to China, was alive and well in American society. Pasternak may have also missed the homegrown tradition of honor killing because Anglo-American law had long disguised it as an involuntary emotional response rather than recognizing it as a value-laden cultural defense. With this in mind, we can almost come to respect the straightforwardness of Texas's prere-form heat-of-passion and justifiable-homicide law. By dropping the pretense of un-controllable passion, it basically allowed a husband to protect his sexual property with deadly force. Of course, we must also recognize the affective aspect of law. Like literature, like post-Reconstruction lynching, heat-of-passion law configured masculine emotion. It prescribed behavior. And in this regard, legally sanctioned folk justice went a long way toward making twentieth-century Texas an extremely brutal place. Think of the defendant in *Sensobaugh* who felt that his wife's adultery gave him free reign to torture her paramour. We must also guard against seeing contemporary cases granting probation to convicted wife killers as aberrations, as exceptions that prove a gender-equal rule of law. Despite well-meaning reform, provocation doctrine and the heat-of-passion defense continue to support a het-erosexual-marital regime that privileges the social needs and sexual security of husbands.

Heat-of-passion law also supports the pathological composition of de-evolutionary masculinity. Beginning in early modern English law and crystallizing in the mid-nineteenth-century "reasonable man" standard of provocation over spousal infi-delity, the heat-of-passion defense fosters the idea that masculine psychology has a built in "cracking factor," an insanity function triggered by evidence of a wife's adultery. Insanity, in other words, is promoted as an instinct. As with other strands of the brutes-in-suits complex, the heat-of-passion defense's explanation of violent sexual jealousy locates socially determined conventions of male aggression in self-serving computations of biology.

Compulsory Heterosexuality, the Charles Atlas Muscle-Beach Fable, and Sexual Dimorphism Unbound

Finally, in examining man-made laws of sexual selection, we need to consider compulsory heterosexuality, what Adrienne Rich has defined as the violent and par-tially successful effort to bond women's sexuality to the material interests of men "despite profound emotional impulses and complimentarities drawing women to-wards women." Rich sees a primary "falseness" in compulsory heterosexuality. It's a "political institution" devoted to transforming "the means of impregnation" for "species survival" into what is sold and enforced as a natural feminine trait: "a mystical/biological heterosexual inclination, a 'preference' or 'choice' which draws women toward men."[87] While serving masculine dominance, compulsory hetero-sexuality also covers men, both empowering them and limiting their emotional and behavioral options toward women and other men. Compulsory heterosexuality can be read as a dictate of masculine normativity, one that achieved particular power in the United States at the turn of the twentieth century. "[A]s queer men began to define their difference from other men on the basis of their homosexuality," the historian George Chauncey has written, "'normal' men began to define their difference from queers on the basis of their renunciation of any sentiments or behavior that might be marked as homosexual."[88] Simultaneous with this enterprise, "real men" renewed the effort to distance the ideal male form from what they considered to be its female counterpart. Muscularity, phallic potency, and other signs of physical prowess took on unusual power amid a culture defining heterosexuality as a preexistent instinctive force.

To understand the compulsory workings of heterosexuality we first need to recognize the relatively recent emergence of *heterosexual* and *homosexual* as separate and binary identities for U.S. men. As Michel Foucault and others have argued, late nineteenth-century medical, legal, literary, and psychological discourses constructed a new and rigid sexual taxonomy that categorized all adult humans as either homosexual or heterosexual. Instead of law and society simply marking certain same-sex acts as wrong and illegal—as, for instance, Anglo-American sodomy law had done for centuries—this new epistemological regime looked to sexual desire and behavior in defining individual subjects as essentially deviant or normal.[89] More than the means to reproduction, more than a primary source for pleasure, sexuality became, as Chauncey has stated, a distinct definitional field of one's "personhood."[90] To emphasize, among turn-of-the-century American men who wanted to place themselves on the normative side of the equation, compulsory heterosexuality mandated the renouncement of same-sex attraction and desire even as the same men depended on close homosocial bonds for enjoying masculine dominance over women and achieving high social status overall. "[T]he normal condition of male heterosexual entitlement," as literary critic Eve Kosofsky Sedgwick has described this fundamental dissonance, embraced a highly charged and potentially violent strain of "male homosexual panic." Fear of being identified as "homosexual" led to the frantic and forceful denigration of that condition in oneself and in others.[91]

Working from the assumption that homosexuality is "a crime against nature," as many state sodomy statutes have read, U.S. law has made heterosexuality compulsory in a myriad of ways: from bars on same-sex marriage, to criminalizing sodomy between consenting adults, to bans on gays and lesbians in the military. Worth considering here is what we might call "the gay-panic defense," a modern innovation in American manslaughter law that partially excuses the killing of one who made a homosexual advance because of the affront to the defendant and, ultimately, to the repugnance of the victim's behavior.[92] In the Samuel Andrews murder trial of 1868, the first case that accepted this new category of provocation doctrine, the defense successfully argued that the killer became "so intoxicated by passion" as to lose "his reason" after the deceased threw him down and pulled down his pants. In response, Andrews killed his assailant by smashing him in the head several times with a rock. With the deceased's actions constituting a crime "nearly as great in the law as the crime of murder," as the defense attorney put it, the jury convicted Andrews of voluntary manslaughter.[93]

Twentieth-century development of the gay-panic defense would continue to cast the killer as victim, even when the homosexual advances were far less violent than in *Andrews* or not violent or physical at all. Amid the 1920s rise of American psychoanalysis, psychiatrists and lawyers explicitly coined the term "homosexual panic" to describe the violent psychotic response of a "latent homosexual" to an anxiety-producing same-sex advance. Under this conceptualization, the "mental disorder" of repressed homosexuality caused the defendant to kill. In the mid- to late twentieth century, though, the law buried the notion of the defendant's panic over his own homosexual disposition and categorized an unwanted, nonviolent homosexual advance as an adequate provocation for heat-of-passion killing. This defense asks whether the reasonable man would lose self-control and kill after an unsolicited homosexual advance. By the turn of the twenty-first century, few juries followed the defense by mitigating such killings to manslaughter. But, at the same time, most trial court judges still ask juries to decide as a matter of fact whether the homosexual advance made up an adequate provocation rather than ruling as a matter of law that no jury could rationally find that such an advance would be sufficient provocation to kill.[94] In general, the gay-panic defense extends compulsory heterosexuality by focusing on the victim's putative transgression rather than the defendant's violent insecurities; and, almost needless to say, it is blind to the aggression and force that drives heterosexual relations: unwanted heterosexual advance cannot be used to mitigate murder to manslaughter.

In combination with positivist law, late nineteenth- and early twentieth-century medicine, psychology, and the emergent popular discourse of sexology contributed to compulsory heterosexuality by defining different-sex eroticism as a human instinct originating in the propagation of the species. While Freud's libidinal drive theory (coupled as it was with Darwinian sexual selection) had the most lasting effect on the idea of sex instinct, the British sexologists Havelock Ellis and Edward Carpenter and their "new morality" of full sexual expression also helped overthrow the U.S. middle-class's commitment to control and repression. Overall, this enterprise highlighted the male sex drive. Carpenter's widely read book *Love's Coming of Age* (1900, 1911), though unusually expansive in outlining female sexuality, stresses the primary potency of male sexual instinct: "For the sex-passion in man is undoubtedly a force—huge and fateful—which has to be reckoned with." And Ellis's popular study, *Man and Woman: A Study in Human Secondary Characters* (1894), contrasts the "elusive" and "diffuse" nature of female sexuality with the "predominantly open and aggressive" male sex drive, "focused to a single point . . . the ejaculation of semen into the vagina."[95] When it comes to sex, Carpenter and Ellis suggested, all men are brutes.

At the same time that sexual science naturalized brutish masculine heterosexuality, U.S. culture made a considerable investment in the spectacle of male bodies—their size, muscle mass, and capacity for force and violence. This "cult of muscularity," as Elliott Gorn has called it, grew alongside the rise of modern sport, the leading American medium for bodily development and performance.[96] The turn of the twentieth century also brought the phenomenon of the professional body builder. With his origins in vaudeville more than sport, the body builder became, sui generis, a model to boys and men of real manliness. Eugene Sandow, Bernarr MacFadden, and Charles Atlas, among a host of others, combined inventive display of their sculpted bodies (primarily through photojournalism in their own promotional publications) with impressive business acumen to create by midcentury a multimillion dollar commercial industry devoted to enlarging the male form.[97] They sold their bodies as well as their stylized workouts, together guaranteeing, in the words of Atlas's famous advertisement, to "make a man out of 'Mac.'"

A primary effect of body building on U.S. gender relations has been the augmentation of sexual dimorphism, the anthropological term given to what are considered to be fundamental skeletomuscular differences between men and women. Coming at a time of unusual social and ideological tumult between the sexes, turn-of-the-twentieth-century body building urged men to increase their superiority over women in physical strength and size. As George Chauncey describes: "[M]en sought to root their difference from women in the supposedly immutable differences of the body at a time when other kinds of difference no longer seemed so certain."[98] As we'll see, body building did appeal to women. Its regimen and exercise equipment advertisements explicitly addressed women (although usually as a secondary class of potential converts to physical fitness). It made good business sense. And thousands of twentieth-century American women actually took up body building. Female body building has certainly been in keeping with twentieth-century athletic feminism by blurring separate sexual spheres and developing individual women's strength and autonomy. Simultaneously, though, and to greater effect, body building in the United States has separated the sexes from each other. Far more men have tried to increase their muscular bulk, as women have followed other, more traditionally feminine models of physical perfection.

Another dynamic of body building and sexual dimorphism has been the inten-sification of invidious physical comparison *between* men. Because size, strength, and bulk are relative terms, body building restarted homosocial scrutiny and rank-ing of men by physical capacity, which also established one's attractiveness to het-erosexual women, or at least masculine understanding of that quality. While it's uncertain to what extent U.S. women have followed muscularity in selecting men, we do know that the turn-of-the-twentieth-century scientific and popular privileg-ing of men's brutish heterosexual nature fully supported public display of physical prowess. Like Darwin's plot of sexual selection, modern American heterosexual competition turned on measurement of a man's potential for physical force and violence. In so closely attending to the shape, size, and power of the male body, heterosexuality heightened homoeroticism between men, while also increasing the chances of an individual man being shamed by unfortunate comparison.

"The Insult That Made a Man Out of Mac" (1929): created by Charles Roman as a mail-order advertisement for the Charles Atlas Dynamic Tension fitness pro-gram, this comic-strip fable is one of the most formative commercial texts on normative American masculinity ever seen—more than the Marlboro Man, more than beer and truck television spots during football games, even more than early twenty-first-century Viagra, Levitra, and Cialis commercials combined. The ad popularized body building. It bridged the first physical culture programs of Eu-gene Sandow and Bernarr MacFadden into the mid-twentieth century by revealing just what's at stake within the homosocial-heterosexual world of male bodily dis-play. The seven-box, muscle-beach drama tells the story of a young man of slight build who loses the woman he's sitting with after a larger, muscle-bound man kicks sand on him and threatens to beat him up. But through strenuous body building, Mac wins her back by punching out his antagonist before admiring on-lookers. In closely examining this seemingly simple story line, we'll notice that the bully's provocation—or, more exactly, his unanswered provocation—produces the anxiety that pushes Mac into pumping up and retaliating against the bully. "The Insult That Made a Man Out of Mac" underlines the easy masculine associations between underperformance and shame and the violent impulses accompanying that emotion.

Telling precursors to the muscle-beach ad appeared in the late nineteenth-cen-tury publication the *National Police Gazette*, a popular tabloid featuring lurid crime stories, sports results, and, as historian Kevin J. Mumford has examined, pages and pages of notices promising to cure male sexual impotence. These ads—com-positionally crude in comparison to the Roman-Atlas texts—prefigured the com-mercial interpellation of masculine anxieties over physical capacity. Size clearly mattered: with Dr. Sanden's electric belt guaranteeing to "enlarge shrunken or undeveloped organs," and with other ads urging men to improve themselves by way of "giant strength and power" and "develop[ed] parts," the *Gazette*'s readership came to appreciate the relational and physical determination of manhood (fig. 5.1). In keeping with this comparative dynamic, many notices, like the Modern Appliance Company's ad for its "practical vacuum appliance," counted on the specter of "lost manhood" to impel "weak men" to buy their product without "delay." With normative masculinity itself as a type of epistemology of potential loss and shame, expectations of male heterosexual capacity would be most effectively stated in the negative—that is, in prescriptions against the abnormalcies of homosexuality, underdeveloped organs, and impotency. By the early twentieth century the American medical establishment addressed male sexuality in the same terms of potential shame through debility and underperformance.[99] The prominent physician William J. Robinson, for instance, who described heterosexuality as "man's most dynamic urge," wrote in his book *Sexual Impotence* (1912) that "an impotent man is a more pitiable man than a venereally infected one." Citing a range of causes of impotence—from masturbation to "overcivilization" and "sexual neuresthania"—Robinson approved an equally wide range of treatments, including the "undoubtedly beneficial" rub of crushed garlic and lard.[100]

A more contemporary context for "The Insult That Made a Man Out of Mac" advertisement was Bernarr MacFadden's *Physical Culture* magazine (founded in 1899), a publication read by Atlas as a boy, and one that by 1940 reached 400,000 monthly paid subscribers. With the imperative "Weakness Is a Crime—Don't Be a Criminal" heading every issue's cover, *Physical Culture* concentrated on body building in combination with diet, medicine, sex, aerobic exercise, and a host of other roads to healthful living. Highly stylized photographs of Eugene Sandow—the first internationally renowned body builder—appeared throughout the magazine in its first years. Perusal of *Physical Culture*'s articles from 1899 to 1900 show it to be a clearinghouse for all things masculinist. Turn-of-the century articles include "The Advantages of Football"; "Theodore Roosevelt, Rough Rider and Athlete"; "Muscular Heroes in Fiction"; "A Study in Muscles"; "A Gladiator's Romance"; "The Strength and Symmetry of Man Compared with Animals"; and "The Elimination of the Weaklings—Shall We Kill Them or Cure Them?" The magazine also published pages and pages of advertisements for foods, elixirs, and equipment promising a strong body; *Physical Culture* editors sold its space by declaring that most advertisers there received more than forty replies per day.

One of the most frequently run turn-of-the-century advertisements in *Physical Culture* was for "Sandow's Own Combined Developer" (fig. 5.2), an exercise "apparatus" replete with dumb bells, chest expander, and, per the ad's top illustration, the promise of female adoration and presumably sexual selection. Demonstrating the sexually dimorphic workings of body building, this ad favors men through its two illustrations: with the lower photographic image of Sandow brandishing the ideal male form—evidence of what the developer could do for a man if used correctly—the top image depicts the machine's final payoff, heterosexual success through large muscles. Within this context, the ad's line "particularly recommended to ladies" seems little more than a business-minded supplement. Sandow certainly wanted women to buy his product, but he and his advertising agency knew that among *Physical Culture*'s largely male readership exaggerated physical difference between the sexes would hook the largest number of customers. To whit, the fully and properly dressed woman swooning over the at least topless man's biceps created a heterosexually charged attention of men to the merits of Sandow's machine. A cartoon appearing in the August 1900 issue of *Physical Culture* also evinces the heterosexual benefits of body building (fig. 5.3). Notice within this before-and-after story line the role of sexual dimorphism. The hapless supplicant Algernon Clerkly is smaller in size and stature than his love interest. Rejected, the frail, overcivilized, white-collar Clerkly saves himself from suicide through six months of body building. In the last frame he has shed his business attire for what looks vaguely like a turn-of-the-century football sweater. More importantly, Clerkly clearly outsizes the now-amorous woman who admires how "big and strong" he has become. The fabulous success that Clerkly realized through a five-cent and six-month investment bears a striking resemblance to Atlas's muscle-beach fable. Although, as we can see, appearing almost thirty years later, "The Insult That Made a Man Out of Mac" is far more accomplished aesthetically and complete in its masculinist address.

Charles Atlas was born Angelo Siciliano (1893–1972) in southern Italy and then settled at age ten in Brooklyn, New York. From this point forward, his biography becomes difficult to verify, because most written material on his life seems assembled for selling the story of the self-made perfect body, although that construction itself is instructive when coming to terms with the appeal and meaning of Atlas's muscle-beach fable. As a young teenager, Siciliano apparently suffered a terrible beating from an older and bigger boy; he also said that he had sand kicked in his face while sitting with a girl on the beach at Coney Island. The ninety-seven-pound weakling vowed to build himself up. On a school trip to the Brooklyn Museum, as the story goes, Siciliano looked up from tying his shoes to see a giant statue of Hercules, bulging with stone muscles, and imploring him to become strong. After his teacher told him that muscles come from exercise, Siciliano pasted a picture of Eugene Sandow onto the mirror of his dresser and started lifting a broomstick with two 25-pound stones on each end. It didn't work. His epiphany came during a Sunday visit to Brooklyn's Prospect Park Zoo. "I was standing there in front of a lion's cage, and the old gentleman was lying down asleep, and all of a sudden he gets up and gives a stretch," as Atlas told the story: "Well, he stretched himself all over—you know how they do, first one leg and then another—and the muscles ran around like rabbits under a rug. I says to myself, 'Does this old gentleman have any barbells, any exercisers? No, sir. Then what's he been doing?' And it came over me. I said to myself, 'He's been pitting one muscle against another!'" Thus was born Atlas's "Dynamic-Tension" technique for "build[ing] muscles fast." Using isometric exercise, Siciliano became Charles Atlas, winning Bernarr MacFadden's "The Worlds' Most Perfectly Developed Man" contest in 1921 and 1922, after which MacFadden shut the competition down because Atlas would win it every time.[101]

As Atlas became one of the most sought after male models in New York City, he tried to turn his body-building program into a successful mail-order business. Early 1920s advertisements like "Are You a Red Blooded Man?" and "Do You Want to Be a Tiger?" drew moderate sales of his fitness course. Then Atlas met Charles Roman, a young advertising copywriter who quickly coined the term "dynamic tension" and who—inspired by Siciliano's Coney Island story—created the seven-block sand-in-face comic-strip advertisement, what has been called "the single greatest mail order ad of all time."[102] On the basis of the before-and-after story line—varied slightly over the decades—Atlas and Roman built a business empire. Charles Atlas Ltd. sold 3,000 courses at $30 each in 1929, its first year of business; sales increased through the 1930s, as Atlas and Roman marketed the program throughout the world; in 1941 more than 10,000 Americans bought the course; in 1942 the *New Yorker* magazine reported that Atlas had "250,000 alumni of his course"; and, in 1971, a year before Atlas's death, the company sold over 23,000 courses worldwide.[103] And Charles Atlas lives on. In 1997 Roman sold the company to Jeffrey Hogue, who advertises the course on the Web at www.charlesatlas.com. As historians Elizabeth Toon and Janet Golden have pointed out, "the metaphoric vigor" of Atlas's heroic transformation continues to inspire; during the First Gulf War, President George Herbert Walker Bush urged American troops to battle by calling Saddam Hussein "a classic bully, kicking sand in the face of the world."[104]

In examining the "Insult That Made a Man Out of 'Mac'" advertisement (circa 1950), what stands out is its biological literalness, the explicitness with which it plays out Darwin's view of sexual selection (fig. 5.4). Muscles mean everything at Mac's beach. They distinguish male from female and separate the "real men" from the "little boys." While the superimposed image of the bronzed, leopard-skin-suited Charles Atlas embodies the ideal heterosexual competitor, the alpha male beyond challenge by other men, the muscle-beach fable itself depicts the relational dynamic of masculine fitness, with the woman validating the inter-male "law of battle," as Darwin described sexual selection, by embracing Mac after he "drove away" his "rival." Is the woman in frames three and seven actively select-ing her mate or passively enforcing the male-determined physical competition for her affections? Darwin recognized little female selective agency. He did notice that among some bird species the males "endeavor to charm or excite their mates by love-notes, songs, and antics"; it's improbable, then, "that the females are indiffer-ent to the charms of the opposite sex, or that they are invariably compelled to yield to the victorious males." But Darwin virtually dropped the notion of "deliberate" female choice, especially among the greatly sexually dimorphic species of human beings.[105] The lead woman in Atlas's advertisement seems impressed with noth-ing but physical prowess. If, before frame one, Mac was regaling her with his wit, humor, storytelling, or love songs, it clearly didn't work. The woman is finally both subject and party to selection by inter-male physical competition.

In other words, the woman is crucial to enforcing the law of battle. Frame three may very well be the most momentous part of the Atlas ad. More damaging than frame two's "you're so skinny" insult by the bully, frame three's "Oh don't let if *bother* you, little boy!" comment by the woman is insulting and dismissive. Her kiss-off affirms physical prowess as *the* factor of sexual selection. And it points to the social basis of the law of battle. The woman needn't have left Mac after the bul-ly's insult. Indeed, outside of Atlas's muscle-beach world, women would respond to the scene in a range of ways, from sitting back down with "Mac" to kissing him off. Within "The Insult That Made a Man Out of 'Mac,'" though, only one rule applies: a fact confirmed in frames six and seven, the "after" scene in which the woman rewards Mac for his size and aggression.

Atlas's advertisement also underscores the role of provocation and shame within human laws of sexual selection. Note in frame two that the bully doesn't hit Mac. Grabbing him by the arm, calling him skinny, and threatening to "smash" his "face," along with the original sand kicking, are provocation enough, espe-cially since they all happen in front of the woman. As in the nonhuman animal world, the law of battle doesn't always lead to actual violence. Posturing and siz-ing up—the essence of frame two—are oftentimes enough in sexually selecting the fittest male. Most telling is that the bully's provocation first goes unanswered. The homosocial shame from Mac's failure to retaliate—more than his desire for the woman—fuels his decision to buy Atlas's program and pump himself up. The emotion of shame drives "The Insult That Made a Man Out of 'Mac'" advertise-ment. In the written text below the comic strip, Atlas assumes that the reader is "soft, frail, skinny, or flabby" and used to "seeing the huskies walk off with the best of everything." Comparing his earlier, pretransformation self to the reader, Atlas says "I know just how you feel." He continues: "I was so ashamed of my scrawny frame that I dreaded being seen in a swimming suit." The only question, Atlas concludes, is whether that shame will make you do something about it. He thus uses shame avoidance to push the reader into body building.

Overcoming shame explains the culminating scene in frame six, where Mac punches out the beach bully, exclaiming "Here's something I owe you!" In one sense, the bully did *not* have that coming, because he only kicked sand at Mac and insulted him in front of his woman friend. (Another, less common, version of the Atlas ad has the bully punching Mac in frame two.) But that's still plenty within the homosocial context of honor, provocation, and retaliation. Publicly shamed and humiliated, Mac is well within his "rights" in socking the bully's jaw. And that attack, of course, supplies the payoff for the whole muscle-beach story line. It galvanizes the law of battle into one frame of performative violence. Those witnessing Mac's revenge proclaim him "hero of the beach," while the woman attaches herself to him in sensual approval and desire. Homosocial attention and status also come with Mac's bodily prowess. Again, the ad's written text emphasizes the point. "If you're like I was," Atlas continues his address to the reader, "you want a powerful muscular well-proportioned build you can be proud of any time anywhere. You want the 'Greek God' type of physique that women rave about at the beach—the kind that makes other fellows green with envy." Fellow-male admiration and (do we dare say?) desire are Mac's final and perhaps primary payoffs for buying Atlas's program and building his body.

The issue of same-sex desire in the Atlas ad takes us back to Eve Kosofsky Sedgwick and the idea of a homoerotic continuum in male homosocial relations. To be sure, "The Insult That Made a Man Out of 'Mac'" underscores female heterosexual attraction to muscularity and aggression. The woman's absolute elation in Mac's attack on the bully, along with the two other women's sudden enraptured attention to him in the last frame, perfectly encapsulate the spectatorial-performative binary in normative American femininity and masculinity that I have discussed throughout *Brutes in Suits*: "Gosh! What a build." But at the same time consider the comic strip's very last figure and utterance: a man of less-than-full build (like Mac and the woman in frame three, he's no bigger than his female companion) affirming Mac's newfound homosocial status—"He's already famous for it!"—and looking on at Mac with admiration and desire. A dimension of this same-sex attraction is explicit homosexual desire. (One of the many fascinating phenomena of late twentieth- and early twenty-first-century American body-building subculture is the common practice of "hustling"—a builder getting paid to have another man perform oral sex on him.) Homosocial desire also entails envy and emulation, the type of attraction Atlas counted on in his own beef-cake poses. To categorize one type of desire as sexual and the other nonsexual is to miss Sedgwick's point: "For a man to be a man's man is separated only by an invisible, carefully blurred, always-already-crossed line from being 'interested in men.'"[106] Wanting to be a "real he-man," in Atlas's term, necessarily involves attraction to big and hard male bodies. While informing female heterosexual selection, the same-sex desire for size, strength, and prowess has continually charged the widest range of relations between men.

In sum, the "Insult That Made a Man Out of 'Mac'" composed a pure environment of bodily display and desire, a sexually dimorphic text of big muscles and the sexual, social, and psychic rewards that go with them. The real-place Muscle Beach came together in southern California, first at Santa Monica in the 1930s and then in the 1950s at Venice, where body builders made up their own performative environments of body pyramids and hand walking, carnivalesques of ever bigger and harder bodies and the polymorphic sexualities that accompany them. Historians of American body building tend to see the mid-twentieth century as a golden age, before anabolic steroids and the fantastic hypertrophy of the human male form. *Muscle* (1991), Sam Fussell's discerning confessional of his complete submersion in late 1980s southern Californian body building, testifies to that culture's commitment to pain, pharmacology, caricature, and camp. It also substantiates body building's breakneck evolution in size. After four years of single-minded effort, Fussell looked in the mirror and found himself to be only "a bodybuilder from the 1950s. I was light-years beyond Sandow at the turn of the century." But his eighteen-inch arms put him only "halfway between Charles Atlas and Arnold" of the 1970s.[107] The unboundedness of late twentieth-century sexual dimorphism comes through in the fanciful muscle growth in male action figures. In 1964, when Hasbro Industries first released GI Joe, the toy's bicep circumference extrapolated to a six-foot man measured 12.2 inches; in 1974, along with a new kung-fu grip, its arms had grown to 15.2 inches; by 1994, Gung Ho, the ultimate Marine GI Joe, had 16.4 inch arms; and by 1998 GI Joe Extreme's arms had blown up to 26.8 inches! In impressive fashion, Charles Atlas's arms would have actually held up quite nicely against GI Joe, at least through 1994. In 1942 his biceps measured 17 inches; that same year, heavyweight boxing champion Joe Louis's arms came in at a puny 14 inches.[108]

In their book *The Adonis Complex: The Secret Crisis of Male Body Obsession* (2000), Harrison G. Pope, Katherine A. Phillips, and Roberto Olivardia coin the term *muscle dysmorphia*—"a new syndrome in which boys and men believe that they aren't muscular enough." They link this "obsessive preoccupation with muscularity" to an equally "new emotional problem," one "we call 'threatened masculinity,'" which "arises from the long-standing desire of boys and men to establish their 'maleness' within their societal group."[109] If the authors are off by more than one hundred years in dating these phenomena, they do contribute to our understanding of the extent to which turn-of-the-twentieth-first century American men went in securing their masculinity: synthetic testosterone and anabolic steroid use by a rapidly widening demographic of men; $2 billion spent in 1996 by men on commercial gym memberships, and $2 billion more on home exercise equipment; some 690,361 cosmetic surgical procedures on men in 1996, including hair transplants, liposuctions, and operations to augment, among other things, pectoral muscles, buttocks, calves, and, finally replacing the pump and electric belt, penises.[110] After Pfizer Corporation released Viagra in 1998 a host of other drugs for sexual impotency quickly followed. Doctors and therapists now report that many sexually healthy men take impotence drugs as psychological palliatives against an ultimate male performance anxiety. "In this city there's a lot of pressure to look good, to make money and to perform well," explained one New York City Viagra user: "It's just one more added thing to give you more masculine, virile attributes and to have that insurance."[111] The makers of Cialis, an impotence drug that stays in the bloodstream for thirty-six hours, lure users with the putative warning, "Although a rare occurrence, men who experience an erection for more than 4 hours should seek immediate medical attention." Bigger, harder, stronger, longer: through the continuing felt need to follow the dictates of sexual selection, along with constant advances in medicine and pharmacology, sexual dimorphism and the anxious psychology that goes with it are alive and well in another century.

"If your subject is law, the roads are plain to anthropology," Oliver Wendell Holmes Jr. wrote in 1886: "It is perfectly proper to regard and study the law simply as a great anthropological document."[112] In making this statement Holmes referred to *law* in its first sense. Case law, penal codes, and other statutory law enjoy no inherent link to moral certainty, authority, or truth, Holmes believed; they are nothing more or less than formalized, textual manifestations of social conventions and the majority's will to power; and anthropology opens inroads to the interests, needs, and idiosyncracies giving rise to a people's legal system. This chapter has worked from the premise that Holmes's point might also be applied to *law* in its second sense. So-called natural laws of human behavior do not emanate from any pre-existent or uniform metaphysical force but can be traced back to long-standing, historically determined power relations between groups of people—intermediate causes of human behavior that eternalize themselves, as Pierre Bourdieu put it, by embedding their contingent status within a particular construction of biological nature. Darwin's "law of battle" is an example of such a naturalized construction. Its expectation of violent inter-male competition for reproductive access to women perpetuates both a de-evolutionary masculinist psychology of reflexive, uncontrollable anger and aggressiveness as well as exaggerated physical dimorphism between the sexes. In the early twenty-first-century United States, anorexia nervosa and muscular dysmorphia remain among the most representative body-image problems for middle-class women and men, respectively.

Charles Atlas's "The Insult That Made a Man Out Mac" advertisement demonstrates how culture ingrains certain dispositions and behaviors into putative laws of human nature. Evolutionary psychologists might explain the story line of Mac winning the woman on the beach after he violently overcomes his male competition as only so much superstructure to a biological base of sexual selection. That Darwin's "law of battle," like other biological knowledge, is itself composed through the stuff of culture—through small and relatively neutral units of language as well as plots, values, and biases—turns the nature-nurture equation back around again. In epistemological terms, biology depends on culture for its expression. Ontologically, following Dewey, biologically rooted instincts have no content or direction without culture. "In human beings," Clifford Geertz wrote, "sexuality is not, like the opposable thumb, a biological fact with some cultural implications, but, like speech, a cultural activity sustaining a biological process."[113] And the variable, meaning-giving quality of human sexuality only grows with that activity's continuing separation from the goal of propagating the species.

The "ultimate cause" of reproduction tells us very little about de-evolutionary masculinity's emotional economy and its calibration with sexuality. Apparent psychological reflexes of sexually jealous rage and violence stem from such intermediate causes as social constructions of race—as seen in the above discussion of white lynching of black men in the post-Reconstruction South—and patriarchy, including its support of men protecting their marital property rights through the legal fiction of uncontrollable heat of passion—a fiction that nevertheless has a real, affective function within homosocial standards of honor and comportment. Often stated as an imperative, as a law, masculine brutishness is a self-perpetuating expectation, one that prescribes a specific zoomorphic psychological state and works to advance the male domination that gave it birth.

Irony, Instinct, and War

"Thinking," as political theorist Harvey Mansfield has written, "is by itself a challenge to the superiority of manliness."[1] That masculinity is undone by mindfulness has been a first principle of this study. And yet thought and masculinity are hardly antithetical. As detailed in the preceding chapters, normative U.S. masculinity, with all of its brutish content, has been an elaborate intellectual enterprise, mediated by literature and language and ideas, and manifested in culturally constructed mental habits and disposition. De-evolutionary masculinity betrays a certain self-consciousness, I have argued, an intentionality that belies the complex's assumptive naturalist psychology and tends to prove its collaboration in male power taking over women and other men.

My intellectual history of modern American masculinity has worked from an epistemological formulation best summarized by William James:

I, for, my part, cannot escape the consideration, forced upon me at every turn, that the knower is not simply a mirror floating with no foot-hold anywhere, and passively reflecting an order that he comes upon and finds simply existing. The knower is an actor and coefficient of the truth on one side, whilst on the other he registers the truth which he helps to create. Mental interests, hypotheses, postulates, so far as they are bases for human action—action which to a great extent transforms the world—help to *make* the truth which they declare. In other words, there belongs to mind . . . a spontaneity, a vote. It is in the game, and not a mere looker-on; and its judgments of the *should-be,* its ideals, cannot be peeled off from the body of the *cogitandum* as if they were excrescences.[2]

Committed as he was to a Darwinist psychology of instinct, James still insisted on a wedge of mindfulness inserting itself between any preexistent motivational force and the particularities of human thought and behavior.

The mind—even the masculinist mind—"is in the game": that idea has guided my research and analysis in the preceding chapters. Normative U.S. masculinity's obsession with rugged individualism can be better explained by Frederick Jackson

Turner's frontier thesis and other historical and social scientific thought as well as by the elaborate culture of mimicking the autonomous figure of the Old West than by the biological dynamic of a person's neurological response to vast, open, and unpopulated physical space. Affective states of aggressiveness—while hardly inconsistent with man's primordial past—have been cultivated through a narrative formula of savagery and killing found in popular masculinist novels, short stories, and hunting stories. Masculinist emotion has been further structured over the past 130 years or so through modern sport, including college football, which has stylized player and fan alike as a bloodthirsty brute loyal to a larger corporate whole. Killing a fellow human being in martial combat also has deep roots in human history, although the drives to do so can be traced to such intervening causes as nationalism and deriving culturally privileged pleasure in taking another life. And, similarly, the so-called natural law of sexual selection and its attendant reflex of sexual jealousy and violent rage have immediate origins in both male homosocial relations and Anglo-American common law—a contingent legal tradition that has underwritten a man's interest in protecting his marital property.

My goal in every chapter has been to isolate the institutional arrangement of a de-evolutionary psychological turn back to man's imagined animalistic past. This historical exercise has called for no small amount of irony. Locating and coming to terms with the masculinist mind's decision making—its "vote"—requires simultaneous immersion in and distancing oneself from meaning-making formulations that are all too alive and well today, even as they have become subject to satire, caricature, historicizing, and increasing rejection.

Irony, Sam Fussell's *Muscle,* and Masculinity as a "Parodic Tableau Vivant"

Just how far does presence of mind go in undermining hypermasculinity? Certainly irony has a corrosive effect on masculinity and its reliance on what it takes to be instinct. Irony can approximate James's wedge of knowingness, a self-conscious breach between biologically or culturally inherited impulse and behavior. And in focusing on the late twentieth and early twenty-first centuries, it's impossible to ignore the diffusion of irony into virtually every effort to maintain normative U.S. masculinity. From the parodic *Real Men Don't Eat Quiche* (1982) by Bruce Ferstein and Lee Lorenz; to the instantaneous satire and criticism of the mythopoetic men's movement lead by poet Robert Bly and his call for a "Wild Man" in *Iron John: A Book about Men* (1990); and to the constant flow of wry journalistic accounts of overanxious middle-class American manhood such as John Tierney's 1998 *New York Times Sunday Magazine* article "Going Where a Lot of Other Dudes with Really Great Equipment Have Gone Before: The Call of the Pseudo-Wild": in many circles the very words "masculinity" and "manliness" are almost obsolete—they can hardly be uttered without a smirk or knowing inflection.[3] Some late twentieth-century parodies reached the level of rank comedy, as in Matt Groening's television character Homer Simpson and his 1991 *Life in Hell* cartoon "Akbar and Jeff's Wild-man Weekend" (fig. E.1). For at least twenty years now, masculinity has been stuck in a high postmodernist moment. Just as a core characteristic of postmodernism is supreme irony coupled with pure obsession over the object of that irony, masculin-ist psychology is structured by the paradox of not taking seriously that which still has enormous constitutive and practical power. Irony is often built into the subject position of masculinity itself.

Sam Fussell's book *Muscle: Confessions of an Unlikely Bodybuilder* (1991) is an accomplished rendering of both de-evolutionary masculinity and the complicity between that pathology and irony. Amid his story of total immersion in the ste-roid-filled subculture of New York City body building and then the "Iron Mecca" of southern California, Oxford-educated Fussell sets down a consistent line of his-torical perspective and personal skepticism. "I would give my life for a man who is looking for the truth," reads a quote from Spanish film maker Luis Buñuel that Fussell cites in a chapter epigraph. "But I would gladly kill a man who thinks he has found the truth." Jamesian knowing in the Shangri-La Fitness and Training Center makes for keen cultural observation and potent self-reflexivity, an ironic en-ergy the author fixes on his Oedipal struggle with Paul Fussell, the notable Univer-sity of Pennsylvania literary critic who expects his son to earn an Ivy League Ph.D. and follow in his academic footsteps. Having raised Sam to be an "English gentle-man," father finds his son's muscle-bound rebellion to be an "atavistic nightmare." Sam tellingly uses the same word in his 1994 essay on fin-de-siècle American body building. "The longing" for supersized muscles "is atavistic," Fussell writes in per-fect evolutionary psychological fashion: "It's a primordial return to the time when strength and sex were synonymous for survival of the species." Fussell also likens the body builder to "American Adam": he epitomizes "the romantic idealization of pre-lapsarian, natural man, untrammeled by thought, by knowledge of good and evil, by, in fact, knowledge. Intellect is held to be effete, essentially feminine and suspect. Better a blank slate, clean and unpolluted, than a mind, filled as it is with vacillation and moral quandary." Given the thoughtfulness of this "Bodybuilding Americanus" article and of *Muscle* itself, the why and how of Fussell diving head-first into iron pumping makes his experience paradigmatic of de-evolutionary U.S. masculinity.[4]

That is to say that Fussell's story embodies devolution. As a supposed-to-be Eng-lish gentleman turned primordial gym rat, Edgar Rice Burroughs's Tarzan comes to mind with Fussell. But he's closer geographically to Frederick Jackson Turner's rugged individualist: after growing up in Princeton, New Jersey, going to prep school at Lawrenceville and university at Oxford, Fussell classically sets off on Turner's East to West, right to left de-evolutionary arc; passing through New York City, where he begins his cultural unbuilding, he lands in Los Angeles, where his self-described "metamorphosis" completed itself, as he shed street clothes for tank top and bikini briefs, and intellectual ambition for the gym. Finally, he writes, "I didn't have to think. I didn't have to care. I didn't have to feel. I simply had to lift." Fussell appreciates the well-wornness of his course. In sizing up his alternatives to New York City and graduate school, he considers the wilderness. "Relocation was another possible solution," Fussell imagines: "heading off in a silver camper with an untainted water supply to the mountain peaks of the West, proclaiming myself a 'survivalist.'" And in "Bodybuilding Americanus," Fussell explicitly connects the phenomenon to Turner's thesis: "So today's yuppies flock to the gym, one and all seeking the myth of the frontier." For Fussell, the gym, like Turner's frontier, combines a safety valve with the promise of atomization: "I loved iron not for its offering of a community, but for its promise of solitude, for the chance to escape from everyone and everything."[5]

What exactly pushes Fussell to the body-building borderline between savagery and civilization is answered in the alternative in *Muscle*. Escape from Father and the expectations of intellectual accomplishment is one reflexive drive; Sam achieved the first stage of his physical metamorphosis the same year that his father pushed him to start Yale's Ph.D. program in American Studies. And in close keeping with the rugged individualist theme, Fussell latches onto the closed spaces of the metropolis. "The problem, you see, was New York," he explains: "I felt trapped by the teeming populace, dwarfed by skyscrapers, suffocated by the fumes from factories and expressways." Sam is a latter-day neurasthenic, linking his deterioration in health to the City. "Urban dissonance," he and his friends call it: "the inevitable result of the great flux of cultures and tribes, languages and races that make up the city. Too many people, too little space." So, as the postmodernist dude that he is, Fussell lights out for the territories. Once he has reached the frontier of southern Californian body building, though, Fussell comes to realize that the problem really lay within. "The attempt at physical perfection grew from seeds of self-disgust," Fussell admits summarily: "The fright I'd felt on the streets of New York I also felt deep within myself."[6] It's what Fussell does or doesn't do with this nugget of self-understanding that implicates *Muscle* in the complex it succeeds in exposing.

At an early point in the story the book's ironic air crystallizes into sharp-edged skepticism over the affected nature of body building. "That's when it hit me,"

Fussell remembers of his first weeks of serious body building in New York. "Bad theater. Every word they uttered," he says of his two lifting companions and teachers, "every move they made seemed rehearsed—as rehearsed, in fact, as any performance I'd ever seen on stage." The very "essence of the sport," Fussell continues, "meant playing at being a body builder." Some of Fussell's most effective writing comes in close yet ironic participant observation of self-display. "Every afternoon," he says of the living room practice sessions with his Los Angeles roommates, "we resembled a parodic tableau vivant, mechanically moving in and out of our poses." And with such description comes strong criticism. "But while my friends delighted in their posing, I couldn't quite stomach it. It was no problem for me to make myself a living statue. It was a problem to believe in it," Fussell acknowledges in calling to mind James's wedge of knowingness. "No matter how I figured it," he adds, "the fundamental purpose of a posing routine seemed to be to encapsulate and reduce life to 90 ticking seconds. Somehow, it rankled me; it seemed *wrong*." And finally: "No matter how hard I tried, I couldn't eradicate my skepticism." But if *Muscle* proves anything, it's the great difference between seeing through something and rejecting it. Fussell understands early on that "bodybuilding involved premeditated reinvention"—a type of *faux* self-transformation.[7] And yet reinvent he does, with abandon, and with sustained acceptance of its brutish consequences.

With Fussell's physical metamorphosis comes a sea change in his disposition: an oversized hard body "brought with it a completely different way of perceiving that world and my place within it." He elaborates: "Top and bottom, black and white, good and evil, positive and negative, big and small, I retreated into the narrow world of dichotomy." And within his strong-weak binary, might makes right or, more accurately, physical size and strength presents a myriad of opportunities for intimidation and dominance and, with that, muscle creates a juice all of its own. Fussell becomes a bully. "In the beginning I planned to use bodybuilding purely as a system of self-defense," he explains. "It wasn't until later, 80 muscle-crammed pounds later, that I learned to use it as my principal method of assault." Early on, while Fussell is still working for a New York City publishing firm, a co-worker makes the mistake of holding the door open for him. "Not in a million years, my friend," Fussell responds smartly. Locked in "a test of wills," with each refusing to go through the door first, Fussell wraps his arms around his counterpart, lifts him off the ground, and throws him through the door and "on to his ass." After moving to southern California and starting the inevitable injection of steroids, Fussell occasionally speaks of his drugged-up yearning for violence as something beyond him: "I watched as almost a spectator as my body operated beyond my control. I wasn't just aching for a fist fight, I was begging for it. I longed for the release." Overall, though, *Muscle* documents Fussell's willful embrace of the "ocean of violence raging beneath my taut T-shirt." He "needed to rule."[8] Setting this will to power next to Fussell's skepticism over the theatrics of body building is very telling indeed. Despite his keen and everlasting irony, hypermasculinity's violent aggressiveness reproduces itself within Fussell. Body *is* destiny, apparently, and there is little that knowingness can do about it.

Fussell's "attitude adjustment" through body building involved a slide toward war in the head and its attendant parts of sacrifice, combat, and the search for greater meaning. With his New York apartment called "the bunker," and his southern Californian gym a former munitions factory, Fussell, like many body builders, immerses himself in military metaphor and symbolism. "In this sublimation of war, arms are called guns," he writes in his post-*Muscle* essay on body building: "Your own body is the battleground, your deltoids a victorious campaign against indolence, your abs a tribute to discipline and strain." But the connection between body building and war goes beyond metaphor. "There are no more wars," one of Fussell's Los Angeles roommates explains: "That's why we have [lifting]." Fussell acknowledges that his friend's "search for war wasn't too different from my own entry into the gym. As long as we created for ourselves a rite of passage, we could instill our lives with meaning."[9] And, finally, it is this idea of body building as a man-making rite of passage that merges Fussell's story with that of his father. Famous Ivy League professor and literary critic Paul Fussell came of age as a U.S. Army lieutenant fighting and getting wounded on battlefields in World War II Europe. That combat experience opened the door to his most important book, *The Great War and Modern Memory* (1975), a study of how the killing fields of World War I gave rise to "modern understanding"—an ironic Anglo-American literary mind-set marked by a "collision between innocence and awareness" and a shattering of meliorism. The son's story ends on this note of deflated irony. Eighty pounds of muscle later, Sam realizes, as if he didn't know already, that body building did nothing for his self-worth. "[I]f you could somehow find a chink in my armor," Fussell concedes after deciding to give up lifting, "and pry apart a muscular pauldron from a gorget, you'd find nothing within that vast white empty space but a tiny soul about the size of an acorn."[10] A fair comment that on the pathology of de-evolutionary masculinity.

Also edifying is *Muscle*'s breakdown of the dichotomy between mind and body, its fusion of Fussell's brawn and barbell with his father's realm of thought and literature. Sam certainly sets the two against each other—and Paul doesn't disappoint in his constant criticism of body builders as "derelicts" and "poseurs" and "atavistic nightmares"—but, like so many other aspects of hypermasculinity, the son's "pilgrimage into this strange world" of pumping iron is very much a literary undertaking. Sam catches "the disease" of body building after seeking shelter from the streets of New York in the Strand Bookstore, where, after gravitating to the autobiography section, he comes upon *Arnold: The Education of a Bodybuilder* (1978) by Arnold Schwarzenegger. From that point on, gaining muscle for Sam is a highly textual experience. Before setting foot in the gym, he spends the next day at work "educating myself about the lifting world," Fussell writes, "underlining passages from *Arnold*" and, then, immersing himself in the constant flow of muscle magazines: "*Flex, Power, Ironman, Muscular Development, Muscle & Fitness*—I got them all, and passed the afternoon in my cubicle going through the glossy pages."[11] Throughout his own book, Fussell routinely backs up his empirical findings with excerpts from the considerable corpus of body-building literature. "My reading seemed to confirm it" is a constant refrain in *Muscle*.

The textual nature of body building hardly satisfies Fussell's father, one supposes, but then again Sam does publish a well-received novel (for it is fictive) or memoir, a book written in part through his body, not completely unlike the way, say, Swofford, Mailer, Hemingway, Crane, and Paul Fussell used their wartime experience to literary advantage. If Father does remain unsatisfied with Sam's accomplishment, does the fault lay in *Muscle*'s textual shortcomings—compared to, say, an American Studies dissertation and then book on the role of irony in late twentieth-century urban fiction—or the fact that his son tried to make himself a man through a paltry postmodernist substitute for military combat? For our purposes, Sam Fussell's work well illustrates normative U.S. masculinity's continuing dependency on self-conscious performance and obsessive mimicry. "To live without apology, without complaint, without compliance" are the Schwarzeneggerian watchwords that send Fussell into his de-evolutionary tailspin. In *Muscle*'s first pages, Fussell speaks of "a savage force that swallowed me whole from a bookstore in New York City and did not relent until it had chewed me up and spit me out."[12] As both his story and my book make clear, that force comes not from within but from an elaborate cultural apparatus that tends to absorb ironic knowingness and historical critique.

Instinct, Deep Masculinity, and the Decline of Males

Instinct lives! That pretty much sums up the recent outpouring of biologically driven studies of contemporary masculinity.[13] The word *instinct* isn't always used. Innate motivational force, biogram, inherent trait, and predisposition are more common constructions today. But the meaning is the same. Exclamatory in tone and argument, many male sociobiologists and evolutionary psychologists speak of how millennia of sexual selection have built into women and men separate and distinct cognitive and emotional characteristics. "Along the way," the socio-biological anthropologist Lionel Tiger has written, "the sexual and social choices of thousands of generations were genetically established. That result became our human nature for the next hundred thousand years and for now."[14] What emerges from this historical view is "deep masculinity," a concept posited in evolutionary psychology and the mythopoetic men's movement alike: human males share an essence of temperament and energy; one derived from the distant yet living past; and one distinguished by wildness, competition, and aggression. The corollary to deep masculinity is a tragic dislocation between that essence and the vicissitudes of industrial and postindustrial society. Tiger's book *The Decline of Males: The First Look at an Unexpected New World for Men and Women* (1999) may be misnamed; we know from the preceding chapters that his is hardly the "first look" at the supposedly debilitating difference between natural man and modern man; it is nevertheless very representative of the turn-of-the-twenty-first-century academic propagation of masculinist defensiveness, victimhood, and cultural crisis; and it is indicative of the biological conservatism underlying much evolutionary psychology of sexual difference.

Meanwhile, along with intelligent design, human cloning, and perhaps a few other issues, the question of whether there are biologically inherited differences between male and female cognition, intelligence, and emotion remains a flash point of public controversy and misunderstanding over the intersection between evolutionary thought and social policy. In January 2005 Harvard University president Lawrence Summers, in an effort to "provoke" discussion and analysis of the gender gap in high-level science and engineering, said that one likely explanation is that men have more "intrinsic aptitude" for complex mathematics and science. Summers's tentative support of the nature side of the nature-nurture divide sparked international debate and dissension at Harvard, where the arts and sciences faculty's move to censure him for the comment contributed to his resignation in early 2006. Summers's few words did go the heart of the matter: do differences between male and female brain size and structure translate into universal intellectual capacities and behavioral differences between the sexes? Some people just don't want to consider that question. 326Harvard evolutionary psychologist Steven Pinker commented in response to the Summers firestorm: "Human nature in the eyes of many academics is morally tainted and that gets in the way of figuring out what makes us tick."[15]

Pinker has a point. A type of know-nothingness toward biology and human nature can be found among some academics in the social sciences and humanities. As the Brown University biologist Anne Fausto-Sterling explained in 2000, "feminist definitions of sex and gender left open the possibility that male/female differences in cognitive function and behavior could *result* from sex differences, and thus, in some circles . . . there seemed no choice but to ignore many of the findings of contemporary neurobiology."[16] Some historians of women and gender take sociocultural construction as almost a matter of faith, although, contrary to what Pinker and others charge, that belief comes less from a positive commitment to a blank slate theory of mind than from a pragmatic interest in patriarchy and its power structures, including the production of knowledge about gender and sexual difference. At the same time, other academics rather insist that biology and culture be understood to develop within their own linguistic and analytical realms. Over and against entomologist and premier sociobiologist E. O. Wilson's zeal for creating a "unity of knowledge" around biology, his Harvard colleague Richard Lewontin has recently argued that "Darwinian models" for "explaining human social phenomena" be dropped altogether. "We would be much more likely to reach a correct theory of cultural change," Lewontin writes, "if the attempt to understand the history of human institutions on the cheap, by making analogies with organic evolution, were abandoned." Philosopher Richard Rorty has also urged us to let biology and genetics, on the one hand, and humanities and culture, on the other, coexist peacefully, separately, and on their own. Their "vocabularies are irreducible to one another," Rorty insists: "As we pragmatists see it, there can and should be thousands of ways of describing things and people."[17] Incommensurability between biology and culture, under this view, is less a problem than a necessary condition for unencumbered research and interpretation within each enterprise.

In contrast to the separate spheres model advanced by Lewontin and Rorty, many who consider the matter want to break down the "demented dualism," as historian Jackson Lears has called it, between biology and culture.[18] Feminist scientists and intellectuals such as Donna Haraway, Barbara Smuts, Barbara Ehrenreich, and Fausto-Sterling—women who are quite critical of how "nature" has been used to maintain social hierarchies—don't want to reject evolutionary theory as an analytical tool for studying human sexuality and gender. "To set humans apart from even our closest animal relatives as the one species that is exempt from the influences of biology is to suggest that we do indeed possess a defining 'essence,' and that it is defined by our unique and miraculous freedom from biology," Ehrenreich and Janet McIntosh wrote in 1997. "The result is an ideological outlook eerily similar to that of religious creationism," they continued: "Like their fundamentalist Christian counterparts, the most extreme antibiologists suggest that humans occupy a status utterly different from and clearly 'above' that of all other living beings. And, like the religious fundamentalists, the new academic creationists defend their stance as if all of human dignity—and all hope for the future—were at stake." Synthesis between Darwinism and cultural studies won't be easy, they conclude; it will take "courage" and a "nuanced mind to deal with the interface of culture and biology." To do otherwise, though, to follow the "extreme anti-innatism" currently holding sway, will be to extend a "climate of intolerance" among leftist academics supposedly committed to open and free inquiry.[19]

But current Darwinian studies of masculinity lack nuance and anything close to a meaningful interface between biology and culture. Adding greatly to the problem, as Ehrenreich and McIntosh state, in the hands of male academics "evolutionary psychology has become . . . a font of patriarchal social prescriptions."[20] Evolutionary psychology of masculinity can usually be boiled down to so much antifeminist backlash. A beleaguered defensiveness pervades Tiger's *Decline of Males;* masculinity, in a word, is in crisis: "No man or woman could have foretold the swift collapse of male public dominance in symbol and, increasingly, in practice." Over and against the "startling new politics" of feminism, Tiger sets up the life-was-very-different-ten-thousand-years-ago when-humans-were-hunters-and-gatherers argument: because men and women today still carry the mental capacities and structures of that primordial period—as Tiger puts this key idea, "*Homo sapiens* is a species designed to live in a zoo very different from the one on which it is currently the leaseholder"—the drastic social and cultural change wrought by the feminist onslaught is dangerously out of step with human nature.[21] Deep masculinity, then, an instinct for aggression, among other things, is alive but hardly well, Tiger warns in close keeping with his masculinist predecessors of a century before.

To emphasize, Tiger's de-evolutionary return to the Stone Age brings with it a conservative reactionary politics of sex and gender difference. *The Decline of Males* obsesses the late twentieth-century "pattern of growth in the confidence and power of women, and of erosion in the confidence of men." It repeatedly notes a loss of male economic power—"Women as a group are working more and earning more. Men are working less and earning less"—without acknowledging that, if this change is really taking place (women in the United States still make only seventy cents to a man's dollar), it involves slow and incomplete equalization of income rather than a net shortfall for men. Tiger's book suffers from unabashed social nostalgia:

> A fundamental change in the lives of men and women has flowed from a striking new reality. It has overtaken us altogether. Once upon a time many, if not most, women could expect to secure some education, then perhaps work for a few years. Thereafter they would marry and have children. Forever after they would be part of a family supported by a husband who would supply virtually all his earnings until he died. The young men and women in my college classes in the 1950s scarcely questioned

this plan. We expected to follow it, more or less, if we were lucky and we behaved. There was no thought that men were being exploited because they had to work or that women were being deprived because they didn't. It was life's deal. Dwellings, time, resources, and a sense of life's meaning were shared.[22]

Underlying this mythical view of a lost golden age of Tiger's youth is that "just-so story" of the Pleistocene past when men hunted in groups, women had babies and gathered crops, and, presumably, the meanings attached to this division of labor remained perfectly static and "shared." As Ehrenreich told Tiger in a 1999 *Harper's* magazine discussion, "You essentially made up a story and what made it so suspect is that the picture of prehistory you created looks so much like Levittown in 1957."[23] Indeed, Tiger and other sociobiologists conjure up (in E. O. Wilson's term) a "deep history" of the species to argue for a type of essential purposefulness in the sexes.

Underlying deep history of masculinity, in turn, is an unqualified embrace of Darwinism and, more specifically, its theory of sexual selection as nothing less than *the* font of human behavior, experience, and meaning. "Charles's Big Idea" is how Tiger exuberantly introduces sexual selection in *The Decline of Males*. "As Darwin theorized," he writes, "what created our nature today was the sexual behavior in which we engaged over countless yesterdays, and that behavior remains at the behavioral core of the abiding preoccupation with sexual matters people experience throughout their lives." Like many other sociobiologists and evolutionary psychologists, Tiger, the Charles Darwin Professor of Anthropology at Rutgers University, fails to notice how Darwin's own thinking on human sexuality suffered from contemporary gendered stereotypes, especially the Victorian assumption of male physical and intellectual superiority. Just as Darwinism is infallible for Tiger, biology provides "the broadest and most comprehensive answer" for understanding the problems besetting men today. In sanctifying "the elegant unity of nature," Tiger is conservative in the truest sense of that term.[24] There is a pragmatic and political aspect to his backward lookingness. Rejecting that key cultural anthropological measure of making the normal strange—focusing on the fixedness rather than contingency and variability of human nature—Tiger anxiously seizes upon the story of sexual competition as some Ur source of male aggression, violence, and predominance. Tiger seems to want and need this history. My book, in sharp contrast, approaches masculinity, including de-evolutionary thinking such as Tiger's, as learned behavior—a disposition, as much as anything else, that has spread over time and space like a disease.

The Iraq War, Hypermasculinity, and the Metaphor of Disease

Approaching war as a human invention and involving a contingent state of mind helps us to understand masculinity as an infectious disease. As the historian Paul Crook has written, Darwinism doesn't need to fix on sexual competition and other forms of struggle as the most determinative dynamic in human history: in contrast to sociobiological obsession with intraspecies violence, other evolutionary theorists concentrate on how a deep history of human cooperation leads to a type of "peace biology"—an alternative, ecological-based Darwinist tradition that establishes war to be "a biological disaster for humankind." Similarly, the primatologist Frans de Waal's book *Our Inner Ape* (2005) questions the notion of aggressiveness as *the* central feature of human nature. Yes, chimpanzees—human beings' close primate relative—are now known to be territorial, hierarchical, and quite given to war. At the same time, though, bonobo primates—just as close genetically to humans as chimps—are gentle, peaceful, and erotic. "It's plain," de Waal explains in extrapolating human's shared primate heritage, "that our finest qualities run deeper in our DNA than many experts have previously thought."[25] These variations on human biohistory are illuminating because they denaturalize the species' brutality. Human history has been one long bath of blood. Decoupling that history from the biological imperative of sexual selection allows us to see war as a human creation, an increment of culture without any fixed origin except its ideological connection to masculine self-representation. In post-1865 American culture, as chapter 4 documents, U.S. war making has been bound up with a psychology perhaps best described as *hypermasculinity:* de-evolutionary masculinity in exaggerated form; an animalistic mind-set embracing man's putative instinct for violence; a ramped-up disposition, contagious through its excitation, and easily calibrated with a yearning for adventure, combat, and the experience of killing.

While living amid one of the most dynamic and startling moments in the history of U.S. war making, I can only observe in passing here how hypermasculinity spreads like a disease at home while working with devastating effect to kill and brutalize the country's enemies abroad. An epidemic loop has been set down between the streets of Iraq and American culture. "[T]ens of thousands of . . . veterans are bringing the war in Iraq home," Chris Hedges has warned. "War is a plague that can spread outward from the killing fields to tear apart individuals, families, communities, and finally nations," he continues in fully deploying the disease metaphor: "The longer the war goes on in Iraq, the deadlier our infection will be. And unlike most of the soldiers and Marines sent to Vietnam, those in Iraq are often traumatized and then shipped back a few months later to be traumatized again."[26] With Iraqi casualties of nearly genocidal proportions, President Bush's war has produced a new generation of American killers. "Murderous Maniacs" is how Fallujah residents referred in 2003–4 to soldiers of the U.S. Army's 82nd Airborne Division, 1st Battalion, 504th Parachute Infantry Regiment stationed at Forward Operating Base Mercury, where American forces interrogated suspected Iraqi insurgents.[27] Abu Ghraib and Fallujah are far from being wholly representative of young Americans' service in the Iraq War. Sacrifice, courage, and goodwill have intermixed with brutality and killing. But war is about violence. And here we may find that the disease metaphor goes only so far. After recognizing the conscious acceptance of and oftentimes the enthusiasm for violence among U.S. soldiers and marines (in contrast to the increasing rejection of it by others), the notion of an individual unwittingly or involuntarily being infected by war's brutality becomes harder and harder to accept, at least among those of us critics enjoying the safety and comforts of civilian life.

Military service and competitive sport remain closely imbricated in American culture. Since the March 2003 invasion of Iraq, the Pentagon and commercial television have converted the National Football League Superbowls into extravaganzas of patriotism and homage to American firepower and troops. The close institutional correspondence between the military and football comes through in the compelling story of Pat Tillman. Pac-10 Defensive Player of the Year in college and All-Pro safety for the NFL Arizona Cardinals, Tillman turned down a $3.6 million contract to enlist in the U.S. Army after the September 11, 2001, attacks. After completing training for the elite Army Rangers, Tillman served in Operation Iraqi Freedom and then redeployed to Afghanistan where he was killed on patrol. The Pentagon and the prowar press tried to make full use of Tillman's sacrifice; conservative journalist Ann Coulter, for instance, lionized him as "an American original—virtuous, pure and masculine like only an American male can be"; the effort stalled, however, when, despite the Army's efforts to bury the fact, it came out that Tillman had been inadvertently killed by friendly fire. That Tillman opposed President Bush and thought the Iraq War "illegal" further complicated his heroism.[28] In a very different vein, consider this 82nd Airborne sergeant's description of what he saw at Forward Operating Base Mercury. "On their day off people would show up all the time. Everyone in camp knew if you wanted to work out your frustration you show up at the PUC [person under control] tent," the sergeant reported to Human Rights Watch. "In a way it was sport," he continued: "The cooks were all US soldiers. One day a sergeant shows up and tells a PUC to grab a pole. He told him to bend over and broke the guy's leg with a mini Louisville slugger that was a metal bat. He was the fucking cook. He shouldn't be in with no PUCs."[29]

In upholding its "first to fight" tradition in the post–September 11 wars, the U.S. Marine Corps continues to generate abundant examples of the pathological excesses of war in the head. "Actually, it's a lot of fun to fight," Marine General James Mattis told two hundred civilians in San Diego in February 2005. "You know, it's a hell of a hoot. I like brawling," he continued in making quite plain what had already been both implied in the American vernacular overlap between combat and adventure and stated in numerous marine memoirs: "It's a hell of a lot of fun to shoot them [Afghani Taliban]." Boot camp remains the crucial medium for passing along corps "spirit" toward killing from one generation to the next. Chris White, a former marine and now a recent Ph.D. in Latin American history from the University of Kansas, excerpts a letter from a young recruit describing his boot camp experience: "Every response was 'kill,' every chant we had, whether it was in line for the chow hall or PT was somehow involved with killing. And not simply killing the enemy, we had one just standing in line for chow which was '1,2,3, attack the chow hall (repeat) Kill the women, Kill the children, Kill, Kill, Kill em all.'" The marine explained to White: "Constantly using the term 'kill' as though it meant nothing was used to desensitize the recruits to the notion of killing and its implications." And White very tellingly recalls his own first days in the Marines: "boot camp training instilled in me not just the ability to kill, but the lust to kill, and as strange as it sounds, they made it feel natural."[30] Learning to be instinctive: White's comment perfectly encapsulates the brutes-in-suits phenomenon.

That such a brutal psychology would spill into nonmilitary American society is hardly surprising, especially when considering its extensive application in Iraq and Afghanistan and how quickly some marines and soldiers return to civilian life without care, treatment, or decompression. Given this fact, Marine Sergeant Daniel Cotnoir's post-Iraq problems are quite understandable. Named Marine of the Year in 2005 for his service in Iraq, Cotnoir later that year in Lawrence, Massachusetts, fired his shotgun out his apartment window at a noisy crowd leaving a nearby nightclub. "I question whether he was completely reality-based when he made his decisions," a court-appointed psychologist testified.[31]

When the full military history of the Iraq War is written, the November 2004 battle of Fallujah will probably receive a prominent place. U.S. "Operation Phantom Fury" involved some ten thousand marines and soldiers and Iraqi troops fighting to regain control of Fallujah, a largely Sunni city of about 500,000 and insurgent stronghold from which the Marines withdrew earlier that year. The Marines were particularly motivated to take Fallujah. "The enemy has got a face," Marine Colonel Gareth Brandl told his troops before attacking: "He's called Satan. He lives in Fallujah. And we're going to destroy him."[32] The ensuing battle saw American forces use white phosphorous against civilians; it included videotape of a marine shooting a wounded, unarmed Iraqi to death in a mosque. Fallujah undoubtedly brought some of the hardest, house-to-house, room-to-room fighting of the war.

Fallujah's environment of close combat helps contextualize the iconic *Los Angeles Times* photograph of Marine Lance Corporal James Blake Miller smoking a cigarette after more than twelve hours of fighting. "It was kind of crazy out here at first," as the rural-Kentucky-born marine described his time on a roof of a house fending off insurgents trying to take the building. Dubbed the "Marlboro Man" and "The Face of the War," Miller's picture appeared in over one hundred U.S. newspapers. Scores of American civilians, many of them women, emailed the newspapers asking how to contact the marine. Back in his hometown, Miller's high school basketball coach barely recognized him. "That expression, that look," the coach said bewilderedly: "Those are not the eyes I'm used to seeing in his face."[33] With a stunned and removed weariness, it's the "thousand-yard stare" reemergent in the Iraq War, a perspective and visage that has been absorbed to some extent by American society and culture at large.

The eye feeds war in the head. And, more than ever, moving pictures tighten the loop between combat abroad and homegrown interest in experiencing the horror and excitement of fighting and killing in battle. Hollywood's World War II and Vietnam War films still do their work, as recorded in Anthony Swofford's astounding account of him and his fellow marines getting off on supposedly antiwar movies before deployment to the Gulf War. The Iraq War documentary film *Gunner Palace* (2005) includes a scene in which a field artillery unit listens to Wagner's "Ride of the Valkyries," the same music that Robert Duvall's Colonel Kilgore plays for his troops when leveling a Vietnamese village in *Apocalypse Now*. If Francis Ford Coppola used the soundtrack to satirize hypermasculinity, the early-twenty-first-century American soldiers either missed the point or simply chose not to recognize it. Again, irony does little in opposing masculinity. With the post–September 11 wars, we can clearly speak of a war porn genre. Some of it comes from embedded television crews, as in CNN's videotape of the marine executing the Iraqi in a Fallujah mosque. Another source is amateur documentary films produced by marines and soldiers themselves. Armed with lightweight video cameras and digital technology, American infantry shoot footage of their fire fights and the resultant death and destruction. Editing software allows them to piece films together from camp and then circulate them over the Internet. It's a new form of trophy taking, the digital-age equivalent of a dead enemy's ear. This "extreme cinema vérité" is far more accessible than a body part, however.[34] Such war porn inevitably seeps into broader American visual culture, where it helps inform and excite young views of battle.

If the eye is a key to war making, then the advent of sophisticated first-person shooter military videogames will go a long way in training new generations of Americans interested in fighting and killing for their country. *America's Army*, created by the Pentagon at a cost of $6.3 million, is part of the U.S. Army's official Web site. Used for recruitment, the videogame offers "young adults," as the Web site explains, "a first hand look at what it is like to be a Soldier." Medical training and weapon assembly "courses" approximate basic training content, while the patrol missions and fire fights, the game's centerpiece, develop the hand-eye coordination and enemy recognition skills needed for actual combat. The army is presently adding the game's "virtual experience" to the real training of new recruits.[35] The Marines' *Close Combat: First to Fight* involves an elaborately constructed mission of clearing the streets of Beirut in 2006 of radical Islamic insurgents. Minimal in explicit carnage and gore compared to, say, *Grand Theft Auto*, both *Close Combat* and *America's Army* are still remarkably calibrated toward stylizing the eye and its determination of mind and emotion for war.

In closing this book and its discussion of war, I can't help but wonder what will happen to hypermasculinity as more and more fighting becomes automated and computerized. The Pentagon's Future Combat Systems program—said to be the biggest spending contract in American military history—includes plans for not only drone tanks, helicopters, and planes, but also an army of robot soldiers.[36] How will they be programmed? It's hard to imagine artificial intelligence improving on hypermasculinity—if indeed reflexive violence, shooting everything in sight, homosocial cohesion, and shame avoidance could all be placed in a chip. At the same time, would we want to do that to ourselves? It's an increasingly timely question of science fiction, the answer to which gender studies may contribute. The idea of masculinity as a disease should be taken seriously. Great care should therefore be taken to isolate it from any force potentially more powerful than ourselves.

Introduction • The De-Evolutionary Turn in U.S. Masculinity

1. McVeigh's letter quoted by Dan Rather, *CBS Evening News,* 19 August 1995.

2. For a smart critical summary of the field of men's history, see Toby L. Ditz, "The New Men's History and the Peculiar Absence of Gendered Power: Some Remedies from Early American History," *Gender and History* 16 (April 2004): 1–35. For an earlier, more prospective, yet valuable, historiographical essay, see Nancy F. Cott, "On Men's History and Women's History," in *Meanings for Manhood: Construction of Masculinity in Victorian America,* ed. Mark C. Carnes and Clyde Griffen (Chicago: University of Chicago Press, 1990), 205–12.

3. Walter Blair and Franklin J. Meine, *Mike Fink, King of the Mississippi Keelboatmen* (New York, 1933), as cited by Elliott J. Gorn, "'Gouge and Bite, Pull Hair and Scratch': The Social Significance of Fighting in the Southern Backcountry," *American Historical Review* 90 (February 1985): 29.

4. Frank Norris, *The Responsibilities of the Novelist and Other Literary Essays* (New York: Doubleday, Page and Company, 1903), 72–73.

5. Charles Darwin, *The Descent of Man, and Selection in Relation to Sex* (1871; repr., Amherst, N.Y.: Prometheus Books, 1988), 583.

6. Gayle Rubin, "The Traffic in Women: Notes on the 'Political Economy' of Sex," in *Toward an Anthropology of Women,* ed. Rayna R. Reiter (New York: Monthly Review Press, 1975), 157.

7. Stephen Jay Gould, "Biological Potentiality v. Biological Determinism," in *Ever Since Darwin: Reflections in Natural History* (New York: W. W. Norton, 1977), excerpted in *Darwin,* ed. Philip Appleman (New York: W. W. Norton, 1979), 464.

8. Stephen J. Gould, "Darwinian Fundamentalism," *New York Review of Books,* 12 June 1997, 36.

9. Adam Kuper summarized in David T. Courtwright, *Violent Land: Single Men and Social Disorder from the Frontier to the Inner City* (Cambridge, Mass.: Harvard University Press, 1996), 7.

10. William H. Durham, *Coevolution: Genes, Culture, and Human Diversity* (Stanford: Stanford University Press, 1991). My understanding of coevolution has also benefited greatly from Paul Ehrlich, *Human Natures: Genes, Culture, and Human Diversity* (Washington, D.C.:

Island Press, 2000); and Carl N. Degler, *In Search of Human Nature: The Decline and Revival of Darwinism in American Social Thought* (New York: Oxford University Press, 1991).

11. The foundational work of evolutionary psychology is Jerome Barkow, Leda Cosmides, and John Tooby, eds., *The Adapted Mind: Evolutionary Psychology and the Generation of Culture* (New York: Oxford University Press, 1992). For a textbook synthesis of the field, see David M. Buss, *Evolutionary Psychology: The New Science of the Mind* (Needham Heights, Mass.: Allyn & Bacon, 1999).

12. Darwin, *Descent of Man*, 372.

13. "Evolved motivational mechanism" is from Mary Daly and Margo Wilson, *Homicide* (New York: Aldine de Gruyter, 1988), 5.

14. Gilman's concept of "androcentricism" can be found, among her other works, in *The Man-Made World* (1911; repr., Amherst, N.Y.: Humanity Books, 2001).

15. Darwin, *Descent of Man*, 585.

16. Ibid., 584. Darwin added: "We may also infer, from the law of deviation from averages . . . that if men are capable of a decided pre-eminence over women in many subjects, the average of mental power in man must be above that of woman" (584).

17. Ibid., 592.

18. Ibid., 560. Darwin revealed here nearly a complete dependency on animal analogy: "how close is the parallelism between the sexual differences of man and the Quadrumana [gorilla]."

19. Ibid., 583.

20. Karl Marx and Friedrich Engels, *Selected Correspondence*, 2nd ed. (Moscow: Progress, 1965), 302.

21. Steven Pinker, *The Blank Slate: The Modern Denial of Human Nature* (New York: Penguin Books, 2002), 54.

22. Owen D. Jones, "Evolutionary Analysis in Law: An Introduction and Application to Child Abuse," *North Carolina Law Review* 75 (1997): 1128; Owen D. Jones, "Sex, Culture, and the Biology of Rape: Toward Explanation and Prevention," *California Law Review* 87 (1999): 827–909; Owen D. Jones, "Proprioception, Non-law and Biological History," *Florida Law Review* 53 (2001): 831–78.

23. Pinker, *Blank Slate*, 340–41.

24. Buss, *Evolutionary Psychology*, 340.

25. Steven Goldberg, *The Inevitability of Patriarchy* (New York: William Morrow, 1973), 93.

26. Gerda Lerner, *The Creation of Patriarchy* (New York: Oxford University Press, 1986). For intelligent evolution-based complication of Lerner's history of patriarchy, see Barbara B. Smuts, "The Evolutionary Origins of Patriarchy," *Human Nature* 6 (1995): 1–32; Richard Wrangham and Dale Peterson, *Demonic Males: Apes and the Origins of Human Violence* (Boston: Houghton Mifflin, 1996).

27. Heidi Hartmann, "The Unhappy Marriage of Marxism and Feminism: Towards a More Progressive Union," in *Women and Revolution: A Discussion of the Unhappy Marriage of Marxism and Feminism*, ed. Lydia Sargent (Boston: South End Press, 1981), 14.

28. Darwin, *Descent*, 122.

29. Helen Thompson Woolley, "A Review of the Recent Literature on the Psychology of Sex," *Psychology Bulletin* 7 (1910): 340, quoted in Cynthia Eagle Russett, *Sexual Science: The Victorian Construction of Womanhood* (Cambridge, Mass.: Harvard University Press, 1989), 155.

30. Gilman, *Man-Made World,* 125.

31. "Feral fantasies" is from Murray G. Murphey, introduction to John Dewey, *Human Nature and Conduct* (1922; repr., Carbondale: Southern Illinois University, 1988), x.

32. William James, *The Principles of Psychology* (1890; repr., Cambridge, Mass.: Harvard University Press, 1981), 1004.

33. William James, "The Moral Equivalent of War," *McClure's Magazine,* August 1910, reprinted in *The Writing of William James,* ed. John J. McDermott (Chicago: University of Chicago Press, 1967), 380–81.

34. James, quoted in Charlene Haddock Seigfried, *William James's Radical Reconstruction of Philosophy* (Albany: SUNY Press, 1990), 214.

35. Thorstein Veblen, *The Theory of the Leisure Class* (1899; repr., New York: Funk and Wagnalls, 1970).

36. John Dewey, "Interpretation of Savage Mind," *Psychological Review* 9 (May 1902): 217–30; W. I. Thomas, "The Gaming Instinct," *American Journal of Sociology* 6 (May 1901): 750–63.

37. Dewey, "Interpretation of Savage Mind," 226; Dewey, *Human Nature and Conduct,* 32.

38. Dewey, *Human Nature and Conduct,* 104; Robert B. Westbrook, *John Dewey and American Democracy* (Ithaca: Cornell University Press, 1991), 289; Dewey, *Human Nature and Conduct,* 104.

39. Sigmund Freud, "Why War?" (1932), reprinted in Freud, *Character and Culture* (New York: Macmillan Publishing, 1963), 136; Dewey, *Human Nature and Conduct,* 67.

40. Philip Reif, *Freud: The Mind of the Moralist* (New York: Viking Press, 1959), 30–33; my use of Reif here stems from Westbrook, *John Dewey and American Democracy,* 291–92.

41. Dewey, *Human Nature and Conduct,* 54, 75.

42. Ibid., 77.

43. John Dewey, *Individualism Old and New* (New York: Milton, Balch and Company, 1930), 74–100.

44. Dewey, *Human Nature and Conduct,* 75.

45. Pierre Bourdieu, *The Logic of Practice* (Stanford: Stanford University Press, 1980), 55; Loïc Wacquant, "Habitus," in *International Encyclopedia of Economic Sociology,* ed. Milan Zafirovski (London: Routledge, 2004).

46. Pierre Bourdieu, *Masculine Domination* (Stanford: Stanford University Press, 2001), vii-viii, 1.

47. Ibid., 22–23.

48. Ibid., 3.

49. Wacquant, "Habitus."

50. Barbara Ehrenreich's story confirmed in email correspondence, 1 December 2005. Judith Butler, *Gender Trouble: Feminism and the Subversion of Identity* (New York: Routledge, 1990).

51. Sociobiologist E. O. Wilson has written that "genes hold culture on a leash. The leash is very long but inevitably values will be constrained in accordance with their effects on the human gene pool." Wilson, *On Human Nature* (Cambridge, Mass.: Harvard University Press, 1978), 167.

52. The transformation in American manhood from the mid-nineteenth-century middle-class ideal of the Victorian gentleman to the turn-of-the-twentieth-century primitive is a

central theme in U.S. men's history, with Anthony Rotundo's adoption of Warren Susman's paradigm of "personality" being a crystallized formulation of the idea. Rotundo, "Body and Soul: Changing Ideals of Middle Class Manhood, 1770–1920," *Journal of Social History* 16 (1983): 23–38, and *American Manhood: Transformations in Masculinity from the Revolution to the Present Era* (New York: Basic Books, 1993). Michael Kimmel extends this analysis in *Manhood in America: A Cultural History* (New York: Free Press, 1997). Most influential though in developing the middle-class primitivist theme in men's history is John Higham, "The Reorientation of American Culture in the 1890s," in *Writing American History: Essays on Modern Scholarship* (Bloomington: Indiana University Press, 1970), 73–102. A more recent analysis of the white male imbrication with savagery is Gail Bederman's accomplished work, *Manliness and Civilization: A Cultural History of Gender and Race in the United States, 1880–1917* (Chicago: University of Chicago Press, 1995).

53. Darwin explicitly recognized the point in *On the Origin of the Species:* "Every one knows what is meant and is implied by such metaphorical expression, and they are almost necessary for brevity." *On the Origin of the Species* (1859; repr., New York: D. Appleton and Company, 1876), 63.

54. For metaphorical and fictional structures informing Darwinian biology, see Gillian Beer, *Darwin's Plots: Evolutionary Narrative in Darwin, George Eliot and Nineteenth-Century Fiction* (London: Routledge and Kegan Paul, 1983); Daniel P. Todes, *Darwin without Malthus: The Struggle for Existence in Russian Evolutionary Thought* (New York: Oxford University Press, 1989); Marshall Sahlins, *The Use and Abuse of Biology: An Anthropological Critique of Sociobiology* (Ann Arbor: University of Michigan Press, 1976).

55. Roderick Nash, *Wilderness and the American Mind* (New Haven: Yale University Press, 1967), 141–42.

56. F. C. Selous, *Hunting Trips in North America* (New York: Scribner's Sons, 1907), 349.

57. J. Howard Moore, *Savage Survivals* (Chicago: Charles H. Kerr & Company, 1916), 119, 127. Moore easily encapsulated evolutionary psychology's central thesis: "If we take 500,000 years as the length of time man has existed on the earth, then something like 400,000 of these years must be given to the period of Savagery," 98.

58. William J. Fielding, *The Cave Man within Us* (New York: E. P. Dutton & Company, 1922), 15, 43.

59. Moore, *Savage Survivals*, 141, 98; Fielding, *Cave Man within Us*, 47.

60. G. T. W. Patrick, "The Psychology of War," *Popular Science Monthly* 87 (1915): 155, 110–11; William Lee Howard, "The Psychology of War: Why Peoples and Nations Fight," *New York Medical Journal* (2 January 1915): 16; John T. MacCurdy, *The Psychology of War* (New York: E. P. Dutton & Company, 1918), 6; Barbara Ehrenreich, "The Roots of War," *Progressive*, April 2003, 15.

61. Dewey, *Human Nature and Conduct*, 77.

One • Rugged Individualism

1. Richard Slotkin, *Gunfighter Nation: The Myth of the Frontier in Twentieth-Century America* (New York: Atheneum, 1992), 38.

2. Frederick Jackson Turner, "The Significance of the Frontier in American History" (1893). Citations to the essay are from Frederick Jackson Turner, *The Frontier in American*

History (New York: Holt, Rinehart and Winston, 1947; repr., Madison: University of Wisconsin Press, 1986), 37.

3. Linda Kerber, "Can a Woman Be an Individual? The Discourse of Self-Reliance," *Massachusetts Review* 30 (Winter 1989): 589–609, reprinted in *American Chameleon: Individualism in Trans-National Context*, ed. Richard O. Curry and Lawrence B. Goodheart (Kent, Ohio: Kent State University Press, 1991), 152. The point that American character studies are really about men was early and most succinctly expressed by David Potter, "American Women and the American Character" (1962), reprinted in *American Character and Culture in a Changing World: Some Twentieth-Century Perspectives*, ed. John A. Hague (Westport, Conn.: Greenwood Press, 1979), 209–26.

4. For unraveling the relationship between Darwin, Spencer, and Lamarck, see George W. Stocking Jr., *Race, Culture, and Evolution: Essays in the History of Evolution* (New York: Free Press, 1968), 234–69; Robert C. Bannister, *Social Darwinism: Science and Myth in Anglo-American Thought* (Philadelphia: Temple University Press, 1979); Cynthia Eagle Russett, *Darwin in America: The Intellectual Response, 1865–1912* (San Francisco: W. H. Freeman, 1976); Carl Degler, *In Search of Human Nature: The Decline and Revival of Darwinism in American Social Thought* (New York: Oxford University Press, 1991), 85–100.

5. Turner, "Significance of the Frontier in American History," 2–3.

6. Lewis Henry Morgan, *Ancient Society; or, Researches in the Lines of Human Progress from Savagery through Barbarism to Civilization* (1877; repr., New York: Henry Holt & Company, 1907), vi; Lewis H. Morgan, *League of the ho-de-no-sau-nee or Iroquois* (Rochester: Sage & Bros., 1851).

7. Turner, "Significance of the Frontier in American History," 3. For Morgan's influence on Turner, I have been helped by Shari M. Huhndorf, *Going Native: Indians in the American Cultural Imagination* (Ithaca: Cornell University Press, 2001), 55–59.

8. Herbert Spencer, *The Principles of Sociology* (New York: D. Appleton & Company, 1876–97); Herbert Spencer, *The Study of Sociology* (1873; repr., New York: D. Appleton & Company, 1896); Richard Hofstadter, *Social Darwinism in American Thought* (1944; repr., Boston: Beacon Press, 1955); Russett, *Darwin in America;* Bannister, *Social Darwinism.*

9. Turner, "The Significance of History" (1891), in *Rereading Frederick Jackson Turner: "The Significance of the Frontier in American History" and Other Essays*, with commentary by John Mack Faragher (New Haven: Yale University Press, 1998), 22; Turner, "Some Sociological Aspects of History," Lake Forest University Lecture, 1895, Frederick Jackson Turner Papers, Huntington Library, San Marino, California; Turner, "Significance of the Frontier in American History," 2.

10. Stocking, "Lamarckianism in American Social Science, 1890–1915," in Stocking, *Race, Culture, and Evolution,* 234–69; Allan Chase, *The Legacy of Malthus: The Social Costs of the New Scientific Racism* (New York: Alfred A. Knopf, 1977), 105–7.

11. Turner, "Significance of the Frontier in American History," 37; Turner, "Contributions of the West to American Democracy," *Atlantic Monthly* 91 (1903): 92–94.

12. Lee Benson, *Turner and Beard: American Historical Writing Reconsidered* (Glencoe, Ill.: Free Press, 1960), 33–34.

13. Ray Allen Billington, *Frederick Jackson Turner: Historian, Scholar, Teacher* (New York: Oxford University Press, 1973), 124. Cf. Allan G. Bogue, *Frederick Jackson Turner: Strange Roads Going Down* (Norman: University of Oklahoma Press, 1998), 109–10.

14. Turner, "Significance of the Frontier in American History," 11.

15. Ibid., 1–3.

16. Ibid., 3–4. For Turner's substitution of environmental determinism for cultural exchange, see Richard White, "Frederick Jackson Turner," in *Historians of the American Frontier: A Bio-Bibliographical Sourcebook,* ed. John R. Wunder (New York: Greenwood Press, 1988), 665.

17. Turner, "Significance of the Frontier in American History," 4.

18. Ibid., 4–10.

19. Ibid., 11.

20. Brian W. Dippie, *The Vanishing American: White Attitudes and U.S. Indian Policy* (Middletown: Wesleyan University Press, 1982); Roy Harvey Pearce, *Savagism and Civilization: A Study of the Indian and the American Mind* (Berkeley: University of California Press, 1988); Philip J. Deloria, *Playing Indian* (New Haven: Yale University Press, 1998); Robert F. Berkhofer Jr., *The White Man's Indian: Images of the American Indian from Columbus to the Present* (New York: Vintage Books, 1979).

21. Turner, "Significance of the Frontier in American History," 11.

22. Turner, "Contributions of the West to American Democracy," 93.

23. The German embryologist August Weismann had disproved Lamarck's inheritance of acquired characteristics as early as 1889, although many evolutionary thinkers held onto the concept well past that point. Degler, *In Search of Human Nature,* 22–23.

24. Bogue, *Strange Roads Going Down,* 114.

25. Turner, "Contributions of the West to American Democracy," 94; Turner, "Significance of the Frontier in American History," 4, 11. For Turner's use of palimpsest metaphor, see Mary Lawlor, *Recalling the Wild: Naturalism and the Closing of the American West* (New Brunswick: Rutgers University Press, 2000), 43.

26. Student notes from Turner's 1911 Harvard University course "The History of the West," Turner Papers, file drawer 14A (16).

27. Myra Jehlen, *American Incarnation: The Individual, the Nation, and the Continent* (Cambridge, Mass.: Harvard University Press, 1986). Amid all the scholarship on individualism as a historically constructed ideology rather than a preexistent and constant unit of consciousness, the following have been particularly helpful in terms of the gendered meanings of the ideal: Kerber, "Can a Woman Be an Individual?"; Elizabeth Fox-Genovese, *Feminism without Illusions: A Critique of Individualism* (Chapel Hill: University of North Carolina Press, 1991); Mark E. Kann, "Individualism, Civic Virtue, and Gender in America," *Studies in American Political Development* 4 (1990): 46–81; Wilfred M. McClay, *The Masterless: Self and Society in Modern America* (Chapel Hill: University of North Carolina Press, 1994); Nancy F. Cott, "On Men's History and Women's History," in *Meanings for Manhood: Constructions of Masculinity in Victorian America,* ed. Mark C. Carnes and Clyde Griffen (Chicago: University of Chicago Press, 1990), 205–12.

28. Turner, Commonplace Book, vol. II, 1883, Turner Papers; Turner, "Significance of History," 45; Student notes from Turner's "History of Liberty" lecture at Harvard, 1911, Turner Papers, file drawer 14c.

For Turner's biographical detail I have relied primarily on Billington, *Frederick Jackson Turner,* and Bogue, *Strange Roads Going Down.*

29. The two ideals of objectivity and realism and their relative impact on the history

profession are substantially overlapped. Both depend on freedom from subjective bias and the epistemological authority of fact. But they also have their differences in emphasis. While objectivity finally asks the historian to reach a level of truth in interpretation, the ideal of realism is based on comprehensiveness and detail, the ability to describe the way things really were. I think realism had a greater role in connecting professional history to middle-class American culture. What success Turner and other professional historians had in shaping historical understanding was less a matter of people's actually believing historical thought to be true than achieving a comprehension through the details of past experience. John Higham, *History: Professional Scholarship in America* (1965; repr., Baltimore: Johns Hopkins University Press, 1989), 92–96; Dorothy Ross, *The Origins of American Social Science* (New York: Cambridge University Press, 1991), 58–59. Cf. Peter Novick's overemphasis of the objectivity ideal in the history profession in his nevertheless valuable study *That Noble Dream: The "Objectivity Question" and the American Historical Profession* (Cambridge: Cambridge University Press, 1988).

30. Turner, "The Winning of the West," *The Dial* August 1889, 71–73; Turner, "Francis Parkman and His Work," *The Dial*, December 1898, 451–53; Justin Winsor, "The Perils of Historical Narrative," *Atlantic Monthly* 66 (September 1890): 296; Turner, "Francis Parkman," 452.

For the important role of realism in turn-of-the-century American culture, see Miles Orvell, *The Real Thing: Imitation and Authenticity in American Culture, 1880–1940* (Chapel Hill: University of North Carolina Press, 1989); Amy Kaplan, *The Social Construction of American Realism* (Chicago: University of Chicago Press, 1988); David E. Shi, *Facing Facts: Realism in American Thought and Culture, 1850–1920* (New York: Oxford University Press, 1995).

31. Turner, "Contributions of the West to American Democracy," 95.

32. David M. Potter wrote perceptively that in Turner's "quest to discover the traits of the American character, he relied for proof not upon descriptive evidence that given traits actually prevailed, but upon the argument that given conditions in the environment would necessarily cause the development of certain traits." "The Quest for National Character," in *The Reconstruction of American History*, ed. John Higham (New York: Harper and Row, 1962), 202.

33. Turner, "Significance of the Frontier in American History," 37.

34. Turner, "The Significance of History," 19.

35. Franklin quotation is in Turner, Commonplace Book, vol. III, 1886; Turner, Commonplace Book, vol. I, 1881; both in Turner Papers.

36. Ralph Waldo Emerson, "The Young American" (1844) and "History" (1841), in *Selected Writing of Emerson*, ed. Donald McQuade (New York: Modern Library, 1981), 212, 107; Turner, Syllabus for "History of Liberty" course at Harvard University, 1911, Turner Papers, file drawer 10b; Turner; Commonplace Book, vol. I, 1881, Turner Papers.

37. William Cronon, "Landscape and Home: Environmental Traditions in Wisconsin," *Wisconsin Magazine of History* (1990–91): 82–105; Turner to Carl Becker, 23 November 1923, Turner Papers.

38. Alexis de Tocqueville, *Democracy in America* (1835–40; repr., New York: Alfred A. Knopf, 1945), 2:105, 144, 145.

39. Turner, "Significance of the Frontier in American History," 37, 2, 8.

40. Turner to Carl Becker, 23 November 1923, Turner Papers; Turner, "Significance of the Frontier in American History," 9, 4.

41. Hector St. John de Crevecoeur, *Letters from an American Farmer* (1793; repr., New York: E. P. Dutton, 1951), 39–86.

42. Turner, "The Hunter Type" (1890), in *Frederick Jackson Turner's Legacy: Unpublished Writings in American History*, ed. Wilbur R. Jacobs (San Marino, Calif.: Huntington Library, 1965), 153–55.

43. Turner, "Significance of the Frontier in American History," 15; Turner, "The Development of American Society" (1908), in Jacobs, *Frederick Jackson Turner's Legacy*, 173.

44. Turner, "Significance of the Frontier in American History," 15; Turner, "Development of American Society," 173; Turner, "Significance of the Frontier in American History," 4.

45. Turner, "Significance of the Frontier in American History," 37.

46. Ibid., 38.

47. Turner to Mae Sherwood, 21 August 1886, Turner Papers, box A#18.

48. Turner, "Significance of the Frontier in American History," 38, 37; Turner to Max Farrand, 27 September 1908, Turner Papers, box 62.

49. Turner, "Speech at Alumni Banquet, 31 January 1906," Frederick Jackson Turner Papers, University of Wisconsin Archives, Madison, box 2, "Athletics," Wis/Mss/A1.

50. Student notes from Turner's "History of the West" course at Harvard University, 1911, Turner Papers, file drawer 14c; Turner, "Since the Foundation of Clark University," *The Historical Outlook* 15 (November 1924): 340. The art critic Robert Hughes has used Turner's comments on American imagination as an early formulation of the modernist aesthetic. *Nothing If Not Critical: Selected Essays on Art and Artists* (London: Collins Harvill, 1990), 4.

51. Turner, "The Significance of the Section in American History" (1925), reprinted in Faragher, *Rereading Frederick Jackson Turner*, 214.

52. Steiner, "From Frontier to Region," 418.

53. A valuable intellectual history of post–World War II tension between mass society and the individual is McClay, *Masterless*, 226–95.

54. C. Wright Mills, *White Collar: The American Middle Classes* (New York: Oxford University Press, 1953), 3–5.

55. Henry Seidel Canby, "Back to Nature," *Yale Review* 6 (1917): 755–67.

56. Henry Childs Merwin, "On Being Civilized Too Much," *Atlantic Monthly*, June 1897, 838–46; E. S. Martin, "Jostling the Simple Life," *Harper's Monthly*, April 1907, 950–53; G. S. Dickerman, "The Drift to the Cities," *Atlantic Monthly*, September 1913, 349–53; John Muir, "Our National Parks" (1901),reprinted in *Our National Parks* (Boston: Houghton Mifflin Company, 1916), 1.

57. George M. Beard, *American Nervousness: Its Causes and Consequences* (New York: G. P. Putnam's Sons, 1881). Compare this list of causes to Muir's analysis: "Awakening from the stupefying effects of the vice of over-industry and the deadly apathy of luxury, they [turn-of-the-century Americans] are trying as best they can to mix and enrich their own little ongoings with those of Nature, and to get rid of rust and disease. Briskly venturing and roaming, some are washing off sins and cobweb cares of the devil's spinning in all day storms on mountains." *Our National Parks*, 3–4.

58. Tom Lutz, *American Nervousness, 1903: An Anecdotal History* (Ithaca: Cornell University Press, 1991).

59. Georg Simmel, "The Metropolis and Mental Life" (1903), in *The Sociology of Georg Simmel*, ed. Kurt H. Wolf (New York: Free Press, 1950), 409–24. For a valuable discussion

of modernity theory as it relates to the early twentieth-century American metropolis, see Ben Singer, *Melodrama and Modernity: Early Sensational Cinema and Its Contexts* (New York: Columbia University Press, 2001).

60. Small quoted in Philip Rieff's introduction to Charles H. Cooley, *Social Organization: A Study of the Large Mind* (1909; repr., New York: Schocken Books, 1962), vi.

61. Cooley, "Social Consciousness," *American Journal of Sociology* 12 (1907): 676; Cooley, *Social Organization*, 4–5.

62. William McDougall, "The Social Basis of Individuality," *American Journal of Sociology* 18 (1912): 1–2, 4.

63. Howard B. Woolston, "Urban Habit of Mind," *American Journal of Sociology* 17 (March 1912): 602–14.

64. John Dewey, *Individualism, Old and New* (New York: Milton, Balch & Company, 1930), 74–100.

It is worth noting that, while Dewey's naturalist social psychology recognized human instinct, he did not include individualism as one of those impulses. He understood individualism to be a highly variable "local" construction of self and society, a habit of mind and behavior that can be purposefully shaped by intelligence. Much recent sociobiology, in contrast, represents individualism as an innate trait, a first ontological fact of human history. Mary Midgley, *The Ethical Primate: Humans, Freedom and Morality* (London: Routledge, 1994), 124–25.

The Social Cage: Human Nature and the Evolution of Society (Stanford: Stanford University Press, 1992), by sociologists Alexandra Maryanski and Jonathan H. Turner, for instance, goes back some 7.5 million years to the last common ancestor (LCA) between apes and humans—the idea is that by uncovering the social-psychological features of that ancestral population, "inferences" can be made about the content of human "biological propensity," "innate predisposition," or "instinct" (13). The authors' "central finding is that, compared with most Old World monkeys, the reconstructed blueprint of the social structure of the LCA of apes and humans reveals the hominoid lineage as predisposed toward low-density networks, low sociality, and strong individualism" (76). The posited origin of human individualism in *The Social Cage* is not unlike that of American individualism in the frontier thesis: the common inference is that life in sparsely populated space produces intellectual characteristics of self-reliance and independence, mental traits that then take hold through culture and perhaps biology, for Frederick Jackson Turner, or genetic programming, for Maryanski and Jonathan Turner, and end up lasting well past the environmental conditions that gave them birth. In effect, individualist-minded apes—Maryanski and Turner contend in an unparalleled example of social scientists infusing latter-day concepts and values into the (extremely distant) past—have sent human beings on an eternal quest for social conditions that sustain autonomy and mobility.

Having posited a "basic" human "need" for individualism, Maryanski and Turner then measure its satisfaction within the different stages of the species' history: the hunting and gathering stage was idyllic in its provision for freedom and mobility; but with horticultural and agrarian societies and the formation of "cages of kinship" and the state's "cage of power" humans grew disconnected, alienated from their natural state. This trend has been reversed, however, in the industrial and postindustrial periods, when democracy and the loosening of traditions have weakened the social cage, again making way for individualism. Without mentioning early twentieth-century scholarship, the authors portray their reading of the consistency between individualism and modern society as a new "twist" in sociology. What *is* unusual is Maryanski and Turner's use of sociobiology to champion industrial capitalism. "[P]eople are often miserable in early industrial societies," the authors concede while largely ignoring the consciousness of the slave and low-wage laborers that produced these economies, but "they have a certain freedom, autonomy, and capacity for individuality not present in traditional agrarian societies." Modern society provides further for individualism with "the rights of citizenship and the vote," Maryanski and Turner write; and, in the ultimate sociobiological embrace of capitalism, they add that "an ever-expanding number of . . . markets for virtually all goods and services" allows people to "regain some of their lost capacities for choice and individuality." (Ibid., 12, 13, 140.) Rampant consumerism breaks down the social cage, the authors suggest; high-definition television sets and pedicures move humans closer to their primate heritage.

A flawed study, *The Social Cage* is representative in the extreme of sociobiology's scientific faith in individualism as an original fact of human constitution. How do Maryanski and Turner know that what the LCA apes were thinking, feeling, and doing 7.5 million years ago was the stuff of *individualism*? What meaning does that word and concept have outside of its post-sixteenth-century European-American linguistic construction—a construction tied to the rise of liberal economics, the creation of racial and gender differences, and a host of other temporally specific and ideologically driven formulations? Maryanski and Turner stress the apes' free movement through space. But why label that individualism? The requisite high nervous energy for such mobility could just as likely be linked to the traits of territoriality and competitiveness. A more promising application of their methodology would be to trace, as considered in chapter 4, hominoid predisposition toward aggressiveness through to the origins of human violence—a history that has reached a species-threatening peak under industrial capitalism. The point here is that *The Social Cage* betrays the fallibilism inherent in evolutionary science and, more specifically, how subjective values and aspirations take hold of outwardly objective accounts of human history and sociology. (Ibid., esp. 13, 76, 12, 12, 140.)

65. Norman Mailer, "The White Negro: Superficial Reflections on the Hipster" (1957), reprinted in *Partisan Review,* Spring 1959, 276–93.

66. Raymond Williams credited Georg Simmel with distinguishing individuality and uniqueness from individualism and singleness. *Keywords: A Vocabulary of Culture and Society* (New York: Oxford University Press, 1976), 164.

67. The most valuable works for my study of pre–World War I Greenwich Village have been Casey Blake, *Beloved Community: The Cultural Criticism of Randolph Bourne, Van Wyck Brooks, Waldo Frank, and Lewis Mumford* (Chapel Hill: University of North Carolina Press, 1990); Thomas Bender, *New York Intellect: A History of Intellectual Life in New York City* (New York: Random House, 1987); Christine Stansell, *American Moderns: Bohemian New York and the Creation of a New Century* (New York: Metropolitan Books, 2000); Leslie Fishbein, *Rebels in Bohemia: The Radicals of* The Masses (Chapel Hill: University of North Carolina, 1982); Edward Abrahams, *The Lyrical Left: Randolph Bourne, Alfred Stieglitz, and the Origins of Cultural Radicalism in America* (Charlottesville: University Press of Virginia, 1986); Rick Beard and Leslie Cohen, eds., *Greenwich Village: Culture and Counterculture* (New Brunswick: Rutgers University Press, 1993); Adele Heller and Lois Rudnick, eds., *1915: The Cultural Moment*

(New Brunswick: Rutgers University Press, 1991); Christopher Lasch, *The New Radicalism in America, 1889–1963: The Intellectual as a Social Type* (New York: Vintage Books, 1965); Henry F. May, *The End of American Innocence: A Study of the First Years of Our Time, 1912–1917* (London: Jonathan Cape, 1960); Daniel Aaron, *Writers on the Left* (Oxford: Oxford University Press, 1961).

68. "Was Nietzsche a Madman or Genius?" *Current Literature* 44 (June 1908): 641–44. Three years later in the literary journal *The Bookman,* a critic noticed that "today Nietzsche comes trippingly to the tongue; the superman is a platitude of conversation, people can even spell his name and quote what George Bernard Shaw has said about him." George Middleton, "Review of Daniel Halevy's *Life of Nietzsche,*" *The Bookman* 33 (May 1911): 319. By 1915, as an editorial in the *North American Review* explained, Nietzsche had "gained the power to make the world stop and think, to make it consider at least a revision of its most cherished values." Unsigned book review of *The Life of Nietzsche, North American Review* 201 (1915): 763.

69. Perhaps the most sophisticated prewar American account of Nietzsche came from Harvard philosopher Josiah Royce. Published posthumously in *Atlantic Monthly* in 1912, Royce's study casts *Thus Spoke Zarathustra* and its evolutionary figure of the superman as a powerful provocation to individual expression and development. "Man is something that shall be surpassed," Royce quoted Nietzsche: "What have ye done to surpass him?" (Josiah Royce, "Nietzsche," *Atlantic Monthly* 119 [April 1912]: 321, 324). In positively comparing Nietzsche to his colleague William James, Royce highlighted the German philosopher's psychological imperative of constant self-revision. New states of consciousness are sought with a knowingness that all frames of cognition, identity, and social reference are provisional. Self-satisfaction is to be avoided at all costs. "Nietzsche understands," as Royce explained, "the delightfulness of experience which enables the free soul in its best moments to take delight in the very tasks that its skepticism and self-criticism seem to make so endless and in one respect so hopeless. Be dissatisfied with yourself, and yet assert yourself. Believe nothing and yet have courage in the midst of your very suspicions and cultivate your intuitions even while suspecting them" (328). In gleaning freedom from contingency, Royce's Nietzsche is almost a pragmatist, although even in this most generous rendering there is little interest in cultivating "the will to believe" or to act instrumentally for social good.

Another leading academic interpretation of Nietzsche further divulges the privatism inherent in both his world view and the American take on it. From 1913 to 1915, the Chicago literary journal *The Little Review* ran more than a dozen essays on Nietzsche, all written by George Burnham Foster, a liberal theologian and philosopher at the University of Chicago. Foster, like Royce, focused on *Thus Spoke Zarathustra*'s superman and its spur to self-revision. For Nietzsche, Foster declared, "not stationariness but self-changing is the life task of man." One has a responsibility to move past all preexistent forms. "The new loyalty is loyalty to change and becoming rather than to conventions; to freedom rather to authority; to personality rather than to respectability; to our hunger rather than to our satiety" (George Burnham Foster, "The New Loyalty," *The Little Review* 1 [July 1914]: 25, 66). This loyalty to subversion, this affirmation of negation, was Nietzsche's main contribution to prewar American counterculture. "We moderns," Foster wrote in summarizing Nietzsche's project, "all somehow live in a disloyalty which we have committed—imparted to us as transgression, viewed by us as our strength and pride. We have all become unfaithful, as children to our parents, as pupils to our teachers, as disciples to our masters" (30).

70. Van Wyck Brooks, *America's Coming of Age* (1915; repr., Garden City, N.Y.: Doubleday, 1958), 61.

71. Elizabeth Cady Stanton, "Solitude of the Self," reprinted in *Elizabeth Cady Stanton, Susan B. Anthony: Correspondence, Writings, Speeches,* ed. Ellen Carol DuBois (New York: Schocken Books, 1981), 251.

72. The most influential formulation of this view is Carol Gilligan, *In a Different Voice: Psychological Theory and Women's Development* (Cambridge, Mass.: Harvard University Press, 1982).

73. Fox-Genovese, *Feminism without Illusions,* 234; the phrase "life-style feminism" is from Karen Offen, "Response to Nancy Cott," *Signs* 15 (Autumn 1989): 208. For other valuable critiques of individualism by women's historians, see Linda Gordon, *Woman's Body, Woman's Right: A Social History of Birth Control in America* (London: Penguin Books, 1976), 200; Linda Gordon; "Why Nineteenth-Century Feminists Did Not Support Birth Control and Twentieth-Century Feminists Do: Feminism, Reproduction, and the Family," in *Rethinking the Family: Some Feminist Questions,* ed. Barrie Thorne and Marilyn Yalom (New York: Longman, 1982), 46, 50; Gordon, "Individualism and the Critique of Individualism in the History of Feminist Theory" (paper presented at the Simone de Beauvoir Commemorative Conference, New York, 1979); Karen Offen, "Defining Feminism: A Comparative Historical Approach," *Signs* 14 (Autumn 1988): 119–57; Linda Kerber, "Women and Individualism in American History," *Massachusetts Review* 30 (Winter 1989): 589–609.

74. Flynn cited in Kate Witterstein, "The Heterodoxy Club and American Feminism, 1912–1930" (Ph.D. dissertation, Boston University, 1989), 13; Florence Guy Woolston, "Marriage and Custom and Taboo among the Early Heterodites," *Scientific Monthly* 34 (November 1919): 84. For the integral link between early twentieth-century U.S. feminism and Heterodoxy, see Nancy F. Cott, *The Grounding of Modern Feminism* (New Haven: Yale University Press, 1987), 11–51. See also Judith Schwarz, *Radical Feminists of Heterodoxy: Greenwich Village, 1912–1940* (Lebanon, N.H.: New Victoria Publishers, 1982); June Sochen, *The New Woman: Feminism in Greenwich Village, 1910–1920* (New York: Quadrangle Books, 1972); Christine Clare Simmons, "'Marriage in the Modern Manner': Sexual Radicalism and Reform in America, 1914–41" (Ph.D. dissertation, Brown University, 1982); Witterstein, "The Heterodoxy Club and American Feminism, 1912–1930"; Elizabeth Ammons, *Conflicting Stories: American Women Writers at the Turn into the Twentieth Century* (New York: Oxford University Press, 1992).

75. Edna Kenton, "Feminism Will Give—Men More Fun, Women Greater Scope, Children Better Parents, Life More Charm," *Delineator* 85 (July 1914): 17.

76. "Talks on Feminism," *New York Times,* 18 February 1914, 2.

77. Charlotte Perkins Gilman, "Our Androcentric Culture; or, the Man-Made World," *The Forerunner* 1 (March 1910): 18; Charlotte Perkins Gilman, "Our Androcentric Culture; or, the Man-Made World," *The Forerunner* 1 (June 1910): 20.

78. Charlotte Perkins Gilman, "The Humanness of Women," *The Forerunner* 1 (January 1910): 12; Simone de Beauvoir, *The Second Sex* (1949; repr., New York: Vintage Books, 1989), xxvii.

79. "Paradox" comes from Nancy F. Cott, *The Grounding of Modern Feminism* (New Haven: Yale University Press, 1987), 39.

80. Rose Young, "What Is Feminism?" *Good Housekeeping,* April 1914, 679–81; Rose Young, "Men, Women and Sex Antagonism," *Good Housekeeping,* May 1914, 489–90.

81. Cott, *Grounding of Modern Feminism* 38.

For early twentieth-century discussion of Nietzsche's connection to feminism and women, see, e.g., "Did Nietzsche Predict the Superman as Well as the Superwoman?" *Current Literature* 40 (March 1907): 282–84; Mrs. Havelock Ellis, "Nietzsche and Morals," *Forum* 44 (October 1910): 425–38; "Superman v. Superwoman," *Living Age* 267 (November 12, 1910): 433–36; Hubert Bland, "Nietzsche and the Woman," *Living Age* 278 (July 12, 1913): 122–24; "A Feminist Disciple of Nietzsche," *Current Opinion* 54 (February 1913): 47–48.

82. Gilman cited in Ann J. Lane, *To Herland and Beyond: The Life and Work of Charlotte Perkins Gilman* (New York: Meridian, 1990), 285.

83. Bliss Carman, "Physical Freedom for Women," *Harper's Weekly* 58 (September 1913): 12.

84. John Dewey, *Experience and Nature* (1925; repr., New York: Dover, 1958), 243.

85. Van Wyck Brooks, "Towards National Culture," *The Seven Arts* 1 (March 1917): 542–43; Van Wyck Brooks, "Young America," *The Seven Arts* 1 (December 1916): 150.

86. Gilman, "Our Androcentric Culture; or, the Man-Made World," 21; E. A. Randall, "The Artistic Impulse in Man and Woman," *Arena* 24 (October 1910): 415; Peter Minuit, "291 Fifth Avenue," *The Seven Arts* 1 (November 1916): 63.

87. Donald Kuspit, *The Cult of the Avant-Garde Artist* (New York: Cambridge University Press, 1993), 2; Eastman quoted in Aaron, *Writers on the Left*, 54.

88. Randolph Bourne, *History of a Literary Radical* (New York: B. W. Heubsch, 1920), 12; Alfred Booth Kuttner, "The Artist," *The Seven Arts* 1 (February 1917): 412; Eunice Tietjans, "The Revolt of the 'Once Born,'" *The Little Review* 1 (July 1914): 51.

89. "To Our Readers," *The Quill: A Magazine of Greenwich Village* 1 (June 30, 1917): 3; James Oppenheim, *The Seven Arts* 1 (June 1917): 18; Nietzsche quotation from Allan Megill, *Prophets of Extremity: Nietzsche, Heidegger* (Berkeley: University of California Press, 1986), 39.

90. Eastman and Dell quotations from Aaron, *Writers on the Left*, 50–52.

91. James Oppenheim, "Expression," *The Seven Arts* 1 (January 1917): 207.

92. George Burnham Foster, "The Prophet of a New Culture," *The Little Review* 1 (March 1914):14; John Temple Graves Jr., "Radicalism," *The Forum* 49 (1911): 561; Randolph Bourne, *Youth and Life* (Boston: Houghton Mifflin Company, 1913), 155.

93. Bourne, *Youth and Life*, 284, 249.

94. Ibid., 278–79, 250, 252, 286.

95. Ibid., 253–54.

96. Ibid., 271–72; Daniel Bell, *The Cultural Contradictions of Capitalism* (New York: Basic Books, 1976), 71–72.

97. Floyd Dell, *Homecoming: An Autobiography* (New York: Farrar and Rinehart, 1933), 53.

98. Bourne, *Youth and Life*, 287; Floyd Dell, *Intellectual Vagabondage: An Apology for the Intelligentsia* (New York: George H. Doran Company, 1926), 182, 183; F. Scott Fitzgerald, *The Great Gatsby* (1926; repr., New York: Penguin Books, 1956), 187–88.

Late nineteenth- and early twentieth-century works of "vagabond" literature include Bliss Carman and Richard Hovey, *Songs from Vagabondia* (Boston: Copelan and Day, 1894); Josiah Flynt Willard, *The Little Brother: A Story of Tramp Life* (New York: The Century Company, 1902; repr., Upper Saddle River, N.J.: Gregg Press, 1968); Jack London, *The Road* (1907; repr., London: Arco Publications, 1967) and *From Coast to Coast with Jack London* (1917; repr., Grand Rapids, Mich.: Black Letter Press, 1969); Harry Kemp, *Tramping Life: An Autobiographical Narrative* (New York: Boni Publishers, 1922). For an interesting contemporary study of the early twentieth-century vagabond as a social type, see Nels Anderson, *The Hobo: The Sociology of the Homeless Man* (Chicago: University of Chicago Press, 1923).

99. *Dude Ranches: Big Horn Mountains, Wyoming* (1920), 13, brochure is from Dude Ranch collection, American Heritage Center, University of Wyoming, Laramie; Frank Norris, *The Responsibilities of the Novelist and Other Literary Essays* (New York: Doubleday, Page and Company, 1903), 72–73; Mary Roberts Rinehart, *Through Glacier Park: Seeing America First with Howard Eaton* (Boston: Houghton Mifflin Company, 1916), 24, 26. For an incisive discussion of the cultural construction of nature and wilderness, see William Cronon, "The Trouble with Wilderness; or, Getting Back to the Wrong Nature," in *Uncommon Ground: Toward Reinventing Nature*, ed. William Cronon (New York: W. W. Norton, 1995), 69–90.

100. The meaning of the word *dude* changed during the turn of the twentieth century. Originally "a name given in ridicule to a man affecting an exaggerated fastidiousness in dress, speech and deportment," western ranch workers kept that same derisive usage in describing paying visitors from the East. "Dude," *Oxford English Dictionary Online*, http://dictionary.oed.com.

101. *Dude Ranches: Big Horn Mountains, Wyoming* (c. 1925), 7, American Heritage Center collection.

102. Hal Rothman, *Devil's Bargains: Tourism in the Twentieth-Century American West* (Lawrence: University Press of Kansas, 1998). See also Earl Pomeroy, *In Search of the Golden West: The Tourist in Western America* (New York: Alfred A. Knopf, 1957).

103. Laura Jane Moore, "'She's My Hero': Women's History at the Cowgirl Hall of Fame," *Gender and History* 6 (November 1994): 474.

104. A female "hell raiser" type can be found in Wild Western popular literature and culture. See Henry Nash Smith, *Virgin Land: The American West as Symbol and Myth* (Cambridge, Mass.: Harvard University Press, 1950), 112–20; Joan A. Jensen and Darlis A. Miller, "The Gentle Tamers Revisited: New Approaches to the History of Women in the American West," *Pacific Historical Review* 49 (1980): 177. Most of these figures, however, are from male-authored texts. Helpful overviews of women in the west include Glenda Riley, "Western Women's History: A Look at Some of the Issues," *Montana: The Magazine of Western History* 41 (Spring 1991): 66–70; Sarah Deutsch, "Coming Together, Coming Apart—Women's History and the West," *Montana: The Magazine of Western History* 41 (Spring 1991): 58–61.

105. Charlotte Perkins Gilman, *Women and Economics* (1898; repr., New York: Harper and Row, Publishers, 1966), 148–49. For historical accounts of the Gibson Girl, see Martha Banta, *Imaging American Women: Idea and Ideals in Cultural History* (New York: Columbia University Press, 1987), 85–91; Lois W. Banner, *American Beauty* (Chicago: University of Chicago Press, 1983); Allen Guttmann, *Women's Sports: A History* (New York: Columbia University Press, 1991), 113–14, 125–26; Carolyn Kitch, *The Girl on the Magazine Cover: The Origins of Visual Stereotypes in American Mass Media* (Chapel Hill: University of North Carolina Press, 2001), 37–55.

106. From Guttman, *Women's Sports*, 114.

107. Rinehart, *Through Glacier Park*, 151; Caroline Lockhart, *Dude Wrangler* (New York: A. L. Burt Company, 1921), 7.

108. For background on rodeo, see Michael Wallis, *The Real Wild West: The 101 Ranch and the Creation of the American West* (New York: St. Martin's Griffin, 1999), 136–39; Jack Weston, *The Real American Cowboy* (New York: Amsterdam Books, 1985); Mary Lou LeCompte, *Cow-*

girls of the Rodeo: Pioneer Professional Athletes (Urbana: University of Illinois Press, 1993), 1–69.

109. LeCompte, *Cowgirls of the Rodeo*, 3, 1, 9.

110. Beth Day, *America's First Cowgirl: Lucille Mulhall* (New York: Julian Messner, 1955).

111. Vera McGinnis, *Rodeo Road: My Life as a Pioneer Cowgirl* (New York: Hastings House Publishers, 1974), 19, 92, 163, 124.

112. See, for instance, Joyce Gibson Roach, *The Cowgirls* (Denton: University of North Texas Press, 1977), 124.

113. McGinnis, *Rodeo Road*.

114. Elizabeth Cady Stanton, "Man Superior—Intellectually, Morally, and Physically," *The Lily* 2 (April 1, 1850), 31.

115. McGinnis, *Rodeo Road*, 172.

116. LeCompte, *Cowgirls of the Rodeo*, 44–45.

117. Roach, *The Cowgirls*, xviii.

118. Teresa Jordan, *Cowgirls: Women of the American West* (Lincoln: University of Nebraska Press, 1982), xxxvii.

119. Theodore Roosevelt, *Ranch Life and the Hunting Trail* (New York: The Century Company, 1888); *Ranch Life: "Buffalo Bill" Country, Wyoming-Burlington Route* (1923), 2, American Heritage Center collection.

120. For historical background on the development of American dude ranches, see Jerome L. Rodnitzky, "Recapturing the West," *Arizona and the West* 10 (Summer 1968), 111–26; Rothman, *Devil's Bargains;* Bucky Kings, "The First Dudes: The Story of Pittsburgh and Eaton's Ranch," *Western Pennsylvania Historical Magazine* 57 (1974): 233–38; M. Kast, "Dude Ranching in the United States," *Southwestern Social Science Quarterly* 22 (June 1941–March 1942): 33–38; Lawrence R. Borne, "Dude Ranching in the Rockies," *Montana: The Magazine of Western History* 38 (Summer 1998): 14–27; Lawrence R. Borne, *Dude Ranching: A Complete History* (Albuquerque: New Mexico University Press, 1983).

121. Lockhart, *Dude Wrangler*, 171.

122. *The Bar B C Ranches: Ranching, Camping, Fishing, Hunting in the Rocky Mountains* (1927), 17; *Eaton's Ranch: Wolf, Wyoming* (1917), 7; *Go West This Summer: The Bar E D Ranch* (1922), 1; all in American Heritage Center collection.

123. *Eaton's Ranch*, 6; *Ranch Life*, 4.

124. *Dude Ranches: Big Horn Mountains, Wyoming* (1924), 7, American Heritage Center collection; Struthers Burt, *The Diary of a Dude Wrangler* (New York: Charles Scribner's Sons, 1924), 60.

125. Lockhart, *Dude Wrangler*, 141; Struthers Burt, "'Dude Ranch' Calls for an Accent Hard and Flat," *Casper Tribune-Herald*, 6 May 1928, 16; Burt, *Diary of a Dude-Wrangler*, 50, 52, 56.

126. Burt, "'Dude Ranch' Calls for an Accent Hard," 14.

127. *Ranch Life: "Buffalo Bill" Country*, 3.

128. *The Valley Ranch: Horseback Trip in the Rockies for Young Men* (1929), 8, 17, 7, American Heritage Center collection. The brochure also lists extensively the "the type of schools our boys come." They include Andover, Exeter, Groton, and other elite prep schools and Harvard, Swarthmore, Yale and other elite colleges and universities.

129. *Ranch Life: "Buffalo Bill" Country*, 15.

130. Burt, *Diary of a Dude-Wrangler*, 311, 319, 310.

131. For biographical material on Burt, see Raymond C. Phillips Jr., *Struthers Burt* (Boise: Boise State University Western Writer Series, 1983).

132. Ibid., 328. In the beginning of his book, Burt observed: "To bring a young boy up in the city is to make him walk through hell" (*Diary of a Dude-Wrangler*, 11).

133. Burt, *Diary of a Dude-Wrangler*, 313, 311, 312; Burt, "'Dude Ranch' Calls for an Accent Hard," 13.

134. *The Bar E D Ranch*, 2. The New Mexico Tent Rock Ranch's brochure from the early 1920s exclaimed: "The only way to reach the wildest, most interesting and most beautiful sections of the country surrounding the ranch is by pack and saddle." *Tent Rock Ranch: Pena Blanca, New Mexico* (c. 1923), 10, American Heritage Center collection. The point that a dude ranch's distance from civilization only added to its allure is made well by Rothman, *Devil's Bargains*, 118.

135. *Eaton's Ranch*, 15; Turner, "Significance of the Frontier in American History," 4.

136. Burt, *Diary of a Dude-Wrangler*, 111.

137. Ibid.,183; Letter from Billy to Mother, 10 July 1920, American Heritage Center collection.

138. "Roughneck," *Oxford English Dictionary Online*, http://dictionary.oed.com.

139. Theodore Roosevelt, *Theodore Roosevelt: An Autobiography* (New York: Macmillan Company, 1913), 135–36; Greene quoted in Hermann Hagedorn, *Roosevelt in the Badlands* (Boston: Houghton Mifflin Company, 1930), 154.

140. *Minneapolis Journal*, 17 March 1921, from news clippings, Turner Papers.

141. Margaret Deland, "The Change in the Feminine Ideal," *Atlantic Monthly*, March 1910, 293. In 1912 Harvard University athletic director Dudley A. Sargent criticized the masculinization of female athletes: "In nearly every instance, however, it will be found that the women who are able to excel in the rougher and more masculine sports have either inherited or acquired masculine characteristics. This must necessarily be so, since it is only by taking on masculine attributes that success in certain forms of athletics can be won." Sargent, "Are Athletics Making Girls Masculine? A Practical Answer to a Question Every Girl Asks," *Ladies' Home Journal* March 1912, 57.

142. The term *masculine mystique* has been used to describe women's compulsion toward masculinity by Myriam Miedzian, *Boys Will Be Boys: Breaking the Link between Masculinity and Violence* (New York: Doubleday, 1991), 15; Robert S. McElvaine, *Eve's Seed: Biology, the Sexes, and the Course of History* (New York: McGraw-Hill, 2001), 323.

143. Gilman, "Politics and Warfare," *The Forerunner*, October 1910, reprinted in Gilman, *The Man-Made World* (New York: Charlton, 1911), 208–26.

144. D. H. Lawrence, *Studies in Classic American Literature* (1923; repr., New York: Penguin Books, 1977), 68.

Two • Brute Fictions

1. My reading of *Tarzan* as a central imaginative rendering of early twentieth-century masculine primitivism has benefited from Marianna Torgovnick, *Gone Primitive: Savage Intellects, Modern Lives* (Chicago: University of Chicago Press, 1990), 42–74; Gail Bederman, *Manliness and Civilization: A Cultural History of Gender and Race in the United States, 1880–1917* (Chicago: University of Chicago Press, 1995), 218–32.

2. In *Living with Books: The Art of Book Selection* (New York: Columbia University Press, 1935), Helen E. Haines describes the importance of book reviews on the reading public: "[C]urrent book reviewing still makes the most direct personal appeal to readers and still sets the fashions in popular tastes." For the role of book reviewing in popular literary culture, see Nina Baym, *Novels, Readers, and Reviewers: Responses to Fiction in Antebellum America* (Ithaca: Cornell University Press, 1984).

3. "With Anthropoid Apes," *New York Times*, 5 July 1914, 299; *The Nation*, 1 October 1914, 409; Gore Vidal, "Tarzan Revisited," *Esquire*, December 1963, 264.

4. Christopher Wilson, *The Labor of Words: Literary Professionalism in the Progressive Era* (Athens: University of Georgia Press, 1985), xiv.

5. Joan Shelley Rubin, *The Making of Middle Brow Culture* (Chapel Hill: University of North Carolina Press, 1992); Janice Radway, *A Feeling for Books: The Book-of-the-Month Club, Literary Taste, and Middle-Class Desire* (Chapel Hill: University of North Carolina Press, 1997).

6. Edgar Rice Burroughs, *Tarzan of the Apes* (1914; repr., New York: Penguin Books, 1990), 175–76.

7. Ibid., 103.

8. Ibid., 58, 247.

9. Ibid., 108, 77, 82, 175, 136.

10. For the centrality of killing in American literature, see David Brion Davis, *Homicide in American Fiction, 1798–1860* (Ithaca: Cornell University Press, 1957); Richard Slotkin, *Regeneration through Violence: The Mythology of the American Frontier, 1600–1860* (Middletown: Wesleyan University Press, 1973); Richard Slotkin, *The Fatal Environment: The Myth of the Frontier in the Age of Industrialization, 1800–1890* (Middletown: Wesleyan University Press, 1986); Richard Slotkin, *Gunfighter Nation: The Myth of the Frontier in Twentieth-Century America* (New York: Atheneum, 1992).

11. John G. Cawelti, *Adventure, Mystery, and Romance: Formula Stories as Art and Popular Culture* (Chicago: University of Chicago Press, 1976); Tzvetan Todorov, *Genres in Discourse* (Cambridge: Cambridge University Press, 1990); Steven Mailloux, *Interpretive Conventions: The Reader in the Study of American Fiction* (Ithaca: Cornell University Press, 1982).

12. Wilson, *Labor of Words;* Carl F. Kaestle, *Literacy in the United States: Readers and Reading since 1880* (New Haven: Yale University Press, 1991); Richard Ohmann, *Selling Culture: Magazines, Markets and Class at the Turn of the Century* (London: Verso, 1996); Matthew Schneirov, *The Dream of a New Social Order: Popular Magazines in America, 1893–1914* (New York: Columbia University Press, 1994).

13. Stuart P. Sherman, *On Contemporary Literature* (New York: Henry Holt and Company, 1917), 95; Georg Lukacs, *The Theory of the Novel,* trans. Anna Bostock (Cambridge, Mass.: MIT Press, 1971), 125.

My understanding of literary naturalism has benefited from Alfred Kazin, *On Native Grounds: An Interpretation of Modern American Prose Literature* (New York: Harcourt, Brace and Jovanovich, 1942); Lee Clark Mitchell, *Determined Fictions: American Literary Naturalism* (New York: Columbia University Press, 1989); June Howard, *Form and History in American Literary Naturalism* (Chapel Hill: University of North Carolina Press, 1985); *The Cambridge Companion to American Realism and Naturalism,* ed. Donald Pizer (New York: Cambridge University Press, 1995); Walter Benn Michaels, *The Gold Standard and the Logic of Naturalism* (Berkeley: University of California Press, 1987).

14. Theodore Roosevelt, *The Wilderness Hunter,* vol. 1 (1893; repr., New York: G. P. Putnam's Sons, 1907), vii; Thorstein Veblen, *The Theory of the Leisure Class* (1899; repr., New York: Penguin Books, 1994), 257; Roosevelt's comment on killing a Spaniard quoted in Gerald F. Linderman, *The Mirror of War: American Society and the Spanish-American War* (Ann Arbor: University of Michigan Press, 1974), 95.

15. For the development of American sport hunting, including the rise of hunting clubs, I have greatly benefited from Daniel Justin Herman, *Hunting and the American Imagination* (Washington, D.C.: Smithsonian Institution Press, 2001), and Daniel Justin Herman, "The Other Daniel Boone: The Nascence of a Middle-Class Hunter Hero, 1784–1860," *Journal of the Early Republic* 18 (Fall 1998): 429–57. For production of guns in nineteenth-century America, see Michael Bellesiles, "The Origins of Gun Culture in the United States, 1760–1865," *Journal of American History* 83 (1996): 425–55. Helpful for overview of American sport hunting is George Baster Ward III, "Bloodbrothers in the Wilderness: The Sport Hunter and the Buckskin in the Preservation of the American Wilderness Experience" (Ph.D. dissertation, University of Texas at Austin, 1980).

16. This summary of sport hunting literature draws from Herman, *Hunting and the American Imagination,* and Herman, "The Other Daniel Boone." For modern meaning infused into the sport, I have relied on Matt Cartmill, *A View to a Death in the Morning: Hunting and Nature through History* (Cambridge, Mass.: Harvard University Press, 1993); Stuart A. Marks, *Southern Hunting in Black and White: Nature, History, and Ritual in a Carolina Community* (Princeton: Princeton University Press, 1991).

17. Isaac McLellan, "Forest and Stream," *Forest and Stream,* 14 August 1873, 1.

18. Samuel H. Hammond, *Hills, Lakes, and Forest Streams; or, A Tramp in the Chateaugay Woods* (New York, 1854), quoted in Herman, *Hunting and the American Imagination,* 133; A. W. Money et al., *Guns, Ammunition and Tackle* (New York: The Macmillan Company, 1904), 5–6.

19. "Forest and Stream Geography," *Forest and Stream,* 28 September 1876, 120; Money, *Guns, Ammunition, and Tackle,* 5.

20. Benjamin Rush, *Thoughts upon the Amusements and Punishments Which Are Proper for Schools* (Philadelphia, 1790), 2, quoted in Herman, *Hunting and the American Imagination,* 65; Abbot H. Thayer, "Sport and Sportsmen," *Forest and Stream,* 8 August 1903, 23–24; Muir quotation from Robert Underwood Johnson, *Remembered Yesterdays* (Boston, 1923), 388, quoted in Roderick Nash, *Wilderness and the American Mind* (New Haven: Yale University Press, 1967), 139.

21. Cartmill, *View to a Death,* 159; Kent quoted in Nash, *Wilderness,* 153; Charles Paige, "The Things Men Kill," *Forest and Stream,* 4 July 1903, 6.

22. Roosevelt's "war dance" is described in Herman Hagedorn, *Roosevelt in the Badlands* (Boston: Houghton Mifflin Company, 1930), 45. For Roosevelt and the Boone and Crockett Club, see Slotkin, *Gunfighter Nation,* 37–38; Nash, *Wilderness,* 152–53.

23. Roosevelt, *Wilderness Hunter,* 1:7; Roosevelt, *Hunting Trips of a Ranchman* (1885; repr., New York: George Putnam and Sons, 1907), 36, 7; Roosevelt, *Wilderness Hunter,* 1:vii.

24. Theodore Roosevelt, "Hunting the Grisly," *Field and Stream,* January 1899, from *Field and Stream* online, http://www.fieldandstream.com/fieldstream/hunting/biggame /article/0,13199,409852,00.html.

25. Ibid.

26. Ibid.

27. "Elk Hunting in Nebraska," *Forest and Stream,* 14 August 1873, 116.

28. Ibid.

29. Allan Hendricks, "A Turkey of the Wilderness," *Forest and Stream,* 14 September 1897, 25.

30. Ibid.

31. "The Individual and the Crowd," *Forest and Stream,* 28 November 1903, 1; "The President and the Press," *Forest and Stream,* 29 September 1907, 1.

32. Roosevelt quoted in Nash, *American Wilderness,* 150; "The Individual and the Crowd," 1; "The President and the Press," 1; Theodore Roosevelt, *The Wilderness Hunter,* vol. 2 (1893; repr., New York: G. P.. Putnam's Sons, 1907), 267.

33. Statistics of increase in turn-of-the-century publishing of fiction are from James D. Hart, *The Popular Book: A History of America's Literary Taste* (Berkeley: University of California Press, 1961), 183. William S. Gray and Ruth Munroe, *The Reading Interests and Habits of Adults* (New York: Macmillan Company, 1929), also offers a detailed account of the yearly increase in the publishing of new books. The best studies of the development of modern American publishing and readership are Wilson, *Labor of Words;* James L. West III, *American Authors and the Literary Marketplace since 1900* (Philadelphia: University of Pennsylvania Press, 1988); John Tebbel, *Between Covers: The Rise and Transformation of Book Publishing in America* (New York: Oxford University Press, 1987).

34. Hart, *Popular Book,* 191. Wilson, *Labor of Words;* West, *American Authors;* and H. Borus, *Writing Realism: Howells, James, and Norris in the Mass Market* (Chapel Hill: University of North Carolina Press, 1989).

35. Statistics on literary journals cited in West, *American Authors,* 132; Thomas B. Connery, "A Third Way to Tell the Story: American Literary Journalism at the Turn of the Century," in *Literary Journalism in the Twentieth Century,* ed. Norman Sims (New York: Oxford University Press, 1990), 3–20.

36. The best discussion of book advertising at the turn of the century is in Tebbel, *Between Covers,* 173–74. Tebbel (175) also talks about how critical reviews of new fiction became more objective and trusted at the turn of the century.

37. For women's literary culture at the turn of the century, Ann Douglas, *The Feminization of American Culture* (New York: Anchor Press, 1977); Sandra M. Gilbert and Susan Gabor, *No Man's Land: The Place of the Woman Writer in the Twentieth Century* (New Haven: Yale University Press, 1988); Lois Rudnick, "The New Woman," and Elizabeth Ammons, "The New Woman as Cultural Symbol and Social Reality: Six Women Writers' Perspectives," in *1915, the Cultural Moment: The New Politics, the New Woman, the New Psychology, the New Art and the New Theatre in America,* ed. Adelle Heller and Lois Rudnick (New Brunswick: Rutgers University Press, 1991); Elizabeth Ammons, *Conflicting Stories: American Woman Writers at the Turn into the Twentieth Century* (New York: Oxford University Press, 1991).

38. Wolfgang Iser, *The Fictive and the Imaginary: Charting Literary Anthropology* (Baltimore: Johns Hopkins University Press, 1993), xiv–xv; Norman N. Holland, "Unity, Identity, Text, Self," *PMLA: Publications of the Modern Language Association* 90 (1975): 813–22 ; Janice Radway, "Women Read the Romance: The Interaction of Text and Context," *Feminist Studies* 9 (1983): 53–78; Shelley Streeby, "Opening Up the Story Paper: George Lippard and the Construction of Class," *boundary 2* 24 (Spring 1997): 185; Georges Poulet, *The Structuralist Controversy: The Languages of Criticism and the Sciences of Man* (Baltimore: Johns Hopkins University Press, 1977), 56. For a highly influential work on turn-of-the-century masculine

literary culture, see Amy Kaplan, "Romancing the Empire: The Embodiment of American Masculinity in the Popular Historical Novel of the 1890s," *American Literary History* 2 (Winter 1990): 659–90.

39. Frank Norris, *The Responsibilities of the Novelist and Other Literary Essays* (New York: Doubleday, Page and Company, 1903), 8–12.

40. *The Saturday Evening Post*, 12 July 1902, 18. Most reviews of *The Virginian* emphasized the way it connected to contemporary understanding of manhood. Some reviewers described an almost physical hold or power that the book could have on a reader. For instance, in discussing his attraction to the story, a critic for *The Bookman* described Wister's book as a "strong and vigorous novel." *The Bookman*, August 1902, 369.

41. Owen Wister, *The Virginian: A Horseman of the Plains* (1902; repr., New York: Penguin, 1979), x.

42. Fredric Jameson, "Magical Narratives: Romance as Genre," *New Literary History* 7 (1975): 135; Peter Brooks, *Reading for the Plot: Design and Intention in Narrative* (New York: Alfred Knopf, 1984); Mailloux, *Interpretive Conventions*, 132; Cawelti, *Adventure, Mystery, and Romance*, 35.

43. For the power of fictional characters written by *type*, see Jane Tompkins, *Sensational Designs: The Cultural Work of American Fictions, 1790–1860* (New York: Oxford University Press, 1985). Also important to my understanding of how literature works on masculinity is David Leverenz, *Manhood and the American Renaissance* (Ithaca: Cornell University Press, 1989).

44. For background on London's literary career, and the quotations from London, I have relied on Wilson, "The Brainworker: Jack London," in *Labor of Words*, 92–112.

45. Jack London, *Before Adam* (1907; repr., Oakland: Star Rover House, 1982), 21, 32, 26.

46. Jack London, *The Call of the Wild* (1903; repr., Chicago: Nelson-Hall, 1980), 10.

47. My reading of *Call of the Wild*, including this point regarding Buck's presence of mind, has benefited from Jonathan Auerbach, *Male Call: Becoming Jack London* (Durham: Duke University Press, 1996), and Jonathan Auerbach, "'Congested Mails': Buck and Jack's 'Call,'" in *Rereading Jack London*, ed. Leonard Cassuto and Jeanne Campbell Reesman (Stanford: Stanford University Press, 1996), 31.

48. London, *Call of the Wild*, 19, 42, 23.

49. Ibid., 75, 64, 43.

50. Ibid., 36–37.

51. Ibid., 37–38.

52. Ibid., 84.

53. *San Francisco Chronicle*, 2 August 1903, 32; *Reader*, September 1903, 408–9; *Book News Monthly* 22 (September 1903): 7–10.

54. Auerbach, "'Congested Mails,'" 29; London, *Call of the Wild*, 25, 36.

55. Zane Grey, "What the Desert Means to Me," *The American Magazine*, November 1924, 6–8, 72–76.

For the composition and preeminence of the western in turn-of-the-century popular literature and culture, see Jane Tompkins, *West of Everything: The Inner Life of the Westerns* (New York: Oxford University Press, 1992); Lee Clark Mitchell, *Westerns: Making the Man in Fiction and Film* (Chicago: University of Chicago Press, 1996); Richard Slotkin, *Gunfighter Nation: The Myth of the Frontier in Twentieth-Century America* (New York: Atheneum, 1992);

John G. Cawelti, *The Six-Gun Mystique* (Bowling Green: Bowling Green University Popular Press, 1971); John Seeyle, introduction to *Stories of the Old West: Tales of the Mining Camp, Cavalry Troop, and Cattle Ranch,* ed. John Seeyle (New York: Penguin Books, 1994); Will Wright, *Six Guns and Society: A Structural Study of the Western* (Berkeley: University of California Press, 1975).

56. Wister, *Virginian,* 236, 20. For Wister's biographical background, Edward G. White, *The Eastern Establishment and the Western Experience: The West of Frederic Remington, Theodore Roosevelt, and Owen Wister* (New Haven: Yale University Press, 1968).

57. Wister, *Virginian,* 31, 236, 235.

58. *The Saturday Evening Post,* July 12, 1902, 18.

59. The distinction between desire and identification originated in Freudian literary criticism. For its formulation and deconstruction, see Diana Fuss, *Identification Papers* (New York: Routledge, 1995); Eve Kosofsky Sedgwick, *Between Men: English Literature and Male Homosocial Desire* (New York: Columbia University Press, 1985), 105–6.

60. Wister, *Virginian,* 20.

61. Ibid., 1, 3, 2–4.

62. Ibid., 7.

63. Ibid., 9, 18–19.

64. Ibid., 193, 238, 272–74.

65. Ibid., 296–303.

66. Ibid., 298, 284.

67. Frank Norris, "The Frontier Gone at Last," *World's Work,* February 1902, 1728–31.

68. Frank Norris, *McTeague: A Story of San Francisco* (1899; repr., New York: Fawcett Publications, 1960), 304.

69. Stephen Crane, "The Blue Hotel" (1899), in *Maggie and Other Stories* (New York: Washington Square Press, 1960), 169–72.

70. Ibid., 175, 178.

71. Ibid., 179, 181–83, 185.

72. Ibid., 186–87, 191.

73. Ibid., 192–93, 196–98.

74. Ibid., 196.

75. Norris, *McTeague,* 49, 153.

76. Susan Mizruchi asserts that *"McTeague* is probably the most gruesome work in the American literary canon." *The Science of Sacrifice: American Literature and Modern Social Theory* (Princeton: Princeton University Press, 1998), 83.

77. For Norris's intellectual biography, as well as the quotations from LeConte and Zola, see Donald Pizer, *The Novels of Frank Norris* (Bloomington: Indiana University Press, 1966).

For the scientific and medical reception of Lombroso's thought in the United States, see Robert Fletcher, "The New School of Criminal Anthropology," *American Anthropologist* 3 (July 1891): 201–36.

78. Robert Louis Stevenson, *Dr. Jeckyll and Mr. Hyde* (1886; repr., London: Penguin Books, 1979), 81; Pizer, *Novels of Frank Norris,* 36.

79. Frank Norris, "A Case for Lombroso," originally published in *The Wave,* 11 September 1897, reprinted in *The Apprentice Writings of Frank Norris,* vol. 2, ed. Joseph K. McElrath and Douglas K. Burgess (Philadelphia: American Philosophical Society, 1996), 127–32.

80. Frank Norris, "A Reversion to Type," originally published in *The Wave*, 14 August 1897, reprinted in McElrath and Burgess, *Apprentice Writings of Frank Norris*, 2:80–85.

81. Review of *Vandover and the Brute*, *Boston Herald*, 9 May 1914.

82. Frank Norris, *Vandover and the Brute* (posthumously published 1914; repr., Lincoln: University of Nebraska Press, 1978), 120; Pizer, *Novels of Frank Norris*, 36; Norris, *Vandover*, 214–15.

83. "A Novel by Frank Norris," *New York Times*, 12 April 1914.

84. Norris, *McTeague*.

85. Ibid., 10, 9, 10.

86. "He Was Born for the Rope," *San Francisco Examiner*, 14 October 1893, 8. Other accounts of Collins's murder that Norris may very well have read include "Twenty-Nine Fatal Wounds," *San Francisco Examine*, 10 October 1893, 10; "Slashed to Death," *San Francisco Chronicle*, 10 October 1893, 10; "Dark for Collins," *San Francisco Chronicle*, 11 October 1893, 8.

87. "He Was Born for the Rope," 8.

88. Norris, *McTeague*, 24, 26, 29.

89. Ibid., 64, 67, 213, 215.

90. Ibid., 42, 46, 214.

91. Ibid., 161–67.

92. Burroughs, *Tarzan*, 33, 62.

93. Grey, "What the Desert Means to Me," 6–7.

Three • College Football

1. For application of anthropology to American football, see Michael Oriard, *Reading Football: How the Popular Press Created an American Spectacle* (Chapel Hill: University of North Carolina Press, 1993), 10–11; William Arens, "The Great American Football Ritual," *Natural History* 84 (October 1975): 72–81; John Pettegrew, "The Return to Primal Man: The Psychology of Primitivism in Turn-of-the-Century Naturalist Fiction and College Football," *Journal of Men's Studies* 2 (August 1993): 29–52. While more sociological than anthropological, David Riesman and Reuel Denney, "Football in America: A Study in Culture Diffusion," *American Quarterly* 3 (Winter 1951): 309–25, is an invaluable social scientific study of the game.

2. *San Francisco Chronicle*, 27 November 1896, 8.

3. Ibid.

4. Clifford Geertz, "Art as a Cultural System," *Modern Language Notes* 91 (December 1976): 1478; Clifford Geertz, *The Interpretation of Cultures* (New York: Basic Books, 1973), 449.

5. Thorstein Veblen, *The Theory of the Leisure Class* (1899; repr., New York: Penguin Books, 1994), 19.

6. Riesman and Denney, "Football in America," 310.

7. Melissa Dabakis, "Douglas Tilden's Mechanics Fountain: Labor and the 'Crisis of Masculinity' in the 1890s," *American Quarterly* 47 (June 1995): 204–35.

8. *Daily Palo Alto*, 20 November 1894, 1.

9. Veblen, *Theory of the Leisure Class*, 261–62. My understanding of Veblen within turn-

of-the-twentieth-century social thought has benefited from David Riesman, *Thorstein Veblen: A Critical Interpretation* (New York: Charles Scribner's Sons, 1953); John P. Diggins, *The Bard of Savagery: Thorstein Veblen and Modern Social Theory* (New York: Seabury Press, 1978); Cynthia Eagle Russett, *Darwin in America: The Intellectual Response, 1865–1912* (San Francisco: W. H. Freeman, 1976); Joseph Dorfman, *Thorstein Veblen and His America* (New York: Viking Press, 1934).

10. Veblen, *Theory of the Leisure Class*, 275, 19.

11. Ibid., 261, 256.

12. Ibid., 261; *The Sequoia*, 14 November 1900, 1.

13. Riesman and Denney, "Football in America," 318.

14. In addition to Riesman and Denney, "Football in America," see Oriard, *Reading Football*, esp. 35–56; John Stuart Martin, "Walter Camp and His Gridiron Game," *American Heritage*, October 1961, 50–55, 77–81; Ronald Smith, *Sports and Freedom: The Rise of Big-Time College Athletics* (New York: Oxford University Press, 1988), 83–88; Donald J. Mrozek, *Sport and American Mentality, 1880–1910* (Knoxville: University of Tennessee Press, 1983), 166–71; Varda Burstyn, *The Rites of Men: Manhood, Politics, and the Culture of Sport* (Toronto: University of Toronto Press, 1999), 72–75.

15. For the early history of English football presaging the American game, see Walter Camp and Lorin F. Deland, *Football* (Boston: Houghton Mifflin and Company, 1896); Riesman and Denney, "Football in America"; Robert Malcolmson, *Popular Recreations in English Society, 1700–1850* (Cambridge: Cambridge University Press, 1973); Leonard Ellis, "Men among Men: An Exploration of All-Male Relationships in Victorian America" (Ph.D. dissertation, Columbia University, 1982), 495–97; Burstyn, *Rites of Men*, 69–71.

16. Philip Stubbs, "Anatomy of Abuses," quoted in David Starr Jordan, *The Days of a Man: Being Memories of a Naturalist, Teacher and Minor Prophet of Democracy*, vol. 2 (Yonkers-on-Hudson, N.Y.: World Book Company, 1922), 195.

17. Harvard poem quoted in Smith, *Sports and Freedom*, 20–21.

18. For early American football and rush, see Parke H. Davis, *Football: The American Intercollegiate Game* (New York: Charles Scribner's Sons, 1911); Henry D. Sheldon, *Student Life and Customs* (New York: D. Appleton and Company, 1901); Ellis, "Men among Men."

19. My understanding of this critical formative period of American college football and the importance of its rule changes stems from Oriard, "Football as Narrative," *Reading Football*, 25–56; Riesman and Denney, "Football in America"; Davis, *Football*; Smith, *Sports and Freedom*, 83–98.

20. Camp quotation from Davis, *Football*, 82.

21. Oriard, *Reading Football*, 33.

22. Typescript copy of the Intercollegiate Football Association Rules of 1893, Walter Camp Papers, Yale University, New Haven; details of the fighting during the Stanford-Reliance game of 1893, *The Sequoia*, 15 November 1893, 1; comment on the Princeton-Yale game, *New York Times*, 1 December 1894.

23. *New York Times*, 10 October 1905, 1. For discussion of this period of football reform, see John Hammond Moore, "Football's Ugly Decades, 1893–1913," in *The American Sporting Experience: A Historical Anthology of Sport in America*, ed. Steven A. Riess (Champaign: Leisure Press, 1984), 168–89; Smith, *Sports and Freedom*, 191–208.

24. Smith, *Sports and Freedom*, 93.

25. David Starr Jordan, *Spalding's Official Rugby Football Guide, 1911* (New York: American Sports Publishing Company, 1911), 11; "Says Prof. David Starr Jordan of Stanford University. Football Dangerous, Brutalizing and Made Evil by Professionalism," *San Francisco Bulletin*, 9 December 1909.

26. Moore, "Football's Ugly Decades," 181. For the most exact data on this period's football injuries and deaths, see John Sayle Watterson, *College Football: History, Spectacle, Controversy* (Baltimore: Johns Hopkins University Press, 2000), including appendix 1, "Casualties in College Football," although these numbers work from incomplete contemporary record keeping by daily newspapers.

27. A representative reference to football armor is in Camp and Deland, *Football*, 26: "There are also many appliances in the way of shin guards, nose guards, and other parts of armor, but there is a rule that forbids the use of any metal substance on the person of the player, so that such armor as is used is supposed to be of a material that will not injure the opponents." A good pictorial source for the evolution of football uniforms and gear are the advertisements in the published football guides of the period, such as *Spalding's Football Guide*, ed. Walter Camp (New York: American Sports Publishing Company, 1896).

28. Joseph Choynski, "An Opinion from the Prizering," *The New York Journal*, 1 November 1896.

29. *Football Facts and Figures: A Symposium of Expert Opinions on the Game's Place in American Athletics*, ed. Walter Camp (New York: Harper and Brothers Publishers, 1894).

30. Originally published in the *Munchener Nachrichten;* quoted in Davis, *Football*, 99.

31. *Harvard Crimson*, 26 November 1894; *New York Times*, 25 November 1894; *Harvard Crimson*, 26 November 1894.

32. Patrick B. Miller, "The Manly, the Moral, and Proficient: College Sport in the New South," *Journal of Sports History* 24 (Fall 1997): 285–316.

33. Camp and Deland, *Football*, 41.

34. Victor Turner, *The Ritual Process: Structure and Anti-Structure* (Chicago: Aldine Publishing Company, 1969), 96.

35. Ibid., 128–29.

36. Victor Turner, "Liminality and the Performative Genres," in *Rite, Drama, Festival Spectacle: Rehearsals toward a Theory of Cultural Performance*, ed. John J. MacAloon (Philadelphia: Institute for the Study of Human Issues, 1984), 20.

37. In addition to his own writing, my understanding of Turner and his congruencies with the study of sport have benefited from John J. MacAloon, *This Great Symbol: Pierre de Coubertin and the Origins of the Modern Olympic Games* (Chicago: University of Chicago Press, 1981); MacAloon, "Introduction: Cultural Performances, Culture Theory," in *Rite, Drama, Festival, Spectacle*, 5–23; Caroline Walker Bynum, "Women's Stories, Women's Symbols: A Critique of Victor Turner's Theory of Liminality," in *Anthropology and the Study of Religion*, ed. Robert L. Moore and Frank E. Reynolds (Chicago: Center for the Scientific Study of Religion, 1984), 105–25.

38. Victor Turner, *From Ritual to Theatre: The Human Seriousness of Play* (New York: PAJ Publications, 1982), 44, 55–59.

39. *The Sequoia*, 4 November 1899.

40. Turner, *Ritual Process*, 95.

41. Turner, "Liminality and the Performative Genres," 21; Turner, *Ritual Process*, 94–95.

42. Ellis, "Men among Men," 500.

43. *Daily Palo Alto*, 18 September 1896.

44. "Stanford Student Life," *The Sequoia*, 1 March 1904.

45. *San Francisco Examiner*, 27 November 1896.

46. *The Sequoia*, 4 November 1899.

47. *Intercollegiate Football: A Complete Pictorial and Statistical Review, from 1869 to 1934* (New York: Doubleday, Doran & Company, 1934); Robin Lester, *Stagg's University: The Rise, Decline and Fall of Big-Time Football at Chicago* (Urbana: University of Illinois Press, 1999); Watterson, *College Football*; Davis, *Football*; Smith, *Sports and Freedom*.

48. Patrick B. Miller, "The Manly, the Moral, and the Proficient," *Journal of Sport History* 24 (Fall 1997): 285–316.

49. John S. Steckbeck, *Fabulous Redmen: The Carlisle Indians and Their Famous Teams* (Harrisburg, Pa.: J. Horace MacFarland Company, 1951), 95, as quoted in Gerald Gems, "The Construction, Negotiation, and Transformation of Racial Identity in American Football: A Study of Native and African Americans," *American Indian Culture and Research Journal* 22 (1998): 35; for the Carlisle Indian football team, in addition to Gems, see Oriard, *Reading Football*, 233–47.

50. Patrick B. Miller, *The Playing Fields of American Culture: Athletics and Higher Education, 1850–1945* (New York: Oxford University Press, forthcoming); Patrick B. Miller, "To 'Bring the Race Along Rapidly': Sport, Student Culture, and Educational Mission at Historically Black Colleges during the Interwar Years," *History of Education Quarterly* 35 (Summer 1995): 112.

51. Howard University's *Hilltop*, 29 April 1924, as quoted in Miller, "To 'Bring the Race Along Rapidly,'" 111.

52. Wiley College quotation in Miller, "To 'Bring the Race Along Rapidly,'" 118; for southern college teams playing northern teams with African American players, see Miller, "Proving Equality: The Color Line in College Sport and the Meaning of Black Athletic Performance," in *Playing Fields of American Culture*.

53. For historical overviews of Stanford's founding and its first years, see Orrin Leslie Elliott, *Stanford University: The First Twenty-Five Years* (Stanford: Stanford University Press, 1937); Edith R. Mirrielees, *Stanford: The Story of a University* (New York: G. P. Putnam's Sons, 1959). For the Stanford Athletic Association, see Mirrielees, *Stanford*, 67.

54. *The Sequoia*, 9 December 1891.

55. *The Sequoia*, 17 February 1892.

56. *The Sequoia*, 30 March 1892.

57. *The Stanford University Register, 1891–92*, Stanford University Special Collections and Archives, Stanford, Calif.; "The New Gymnasium," *The Sequoia* 16 December 1891.

58. "Mind or Muscle?" *The Sequoia*, 6 January 1892. "A student must have a good physique to succeed," as *The Sequoia* flatly put it in 1897. "Many more students are compelled to leave the University on account of *not* taking gymnasium work than from excess along athletic lines." *The Sequoia*, 3 December 1897.

59. Jordan, *Daily Palo Alto*, 5 December 1893; *Daily Palo Alto*, 20 September 1893; *The Sequoia*, 11 December 1899.

60. *The Sequoia*, 14 November 1900.

61. Carroll Smith-Rosenberg, "The New Woman as Androgyne: Social Disorder and

Gender Crisis, 1870–1936," in *Disorderly Conduct: Visions of Gender in Victorian America* (New York: A. A. Knopf, 1985), 250.

62. Leland Stanford quoted by David Starr Jordan in *The Foundation Ideals of Stanford University* (Stanford: Stanford University Press, 1915), 17.

63. *The Sequoia*, 1 December 1891. For an early overview of Stanford women in athletics, Laura Wells, "With the College Woman," *The Sequoia*, 12 December 1902, 137–42.

64. Riesman and Denney, "Football in America," 325.

65. G. Stanley Hall, "Student Customs," *Proceedings of the American Antiquarian Society* 14 (1902): 119.

66. *The Sequoia*, 7 December 1892.

67. *The Sequoia*, 8 November 1895.

68. *Daily Palo Alto*, 24 November 1893.

69. H. M. Brace, "The Difference," *The Sequoia*, 17 September 1897.

70. Carolus Ager, "A Hero," in *Four-Leaved Clover*, ed. Charles K. Field (San Francisco: C. A. Murdock & Company, 1899).

71. *Daily Palo Alto*, 14 September 1894; 21 September 1892; 9 November 1892; 11 September 1893.

72. *The Sequoia*, 3 February 1892, 20 January 1892.

73. Camp and Deland, *Football*, 41–42.

74. E.g., *Daily Palo Alto*, 9 October 1894.

75. *Daily Palo Alto*, 1 December 1892; 10 November 1892.

76. *The Sequoia*, 30 March 1892; 17 December 1892.

77. Walter Camp, "Western Football," *The Sequoia*, 17 December 1892.

78. *Daily Palo Alto*, 20 September 1893; 11 November 1892.

79. *Daily Palo Alto*, 7 October 1892; 8 November 1892; *The Sequoia*, 7 March 1892; *Daily Palo Alto*, 11 November 1892.

80. *The Sequoia*, 20 September 1893; 1 November 1893.

81. *The Sequoia*, 17 December 1892.

82. *Daily Palo Alto*, 14 November 1895; 28 October 1892; 14 October 1894; *The Sequoia*, 26 November 1897.

83. *Daily Palo Alto*, 13 November 1895.

84. *Daily Palo Alto*, 13 November 1895; *The Sequoia*, 14 November 1895.

85. *Daily Palo Alto*, 27 November 1894; 22 November 1894.

86. Arens, "Great American Football Ritual," 79.

87. *Daily Palo Alto*, 22 November 1894.

88. *Daily Palo Alto*, 12 December 1892.

89. *Daily Palo Alto*, 1 December 1892.

90. *Daily Palo Alto*, 29 November 1893.

91. *The Sequoia*, 26 November 1897.

92. In 1882 the Intercollegiate Football Association decided that the two top teams each season would play their championship game the following year on Thanksgiving Day in New York City. Davis, *Football*, 90. By 1883 as many as 15,000 fans watched the Yale-Princeton championship game, and by the mid-1890s approximately 40,000 people attended the holiday game. Also by the mid-1890s approximately 5,000 football games took place in the United States on Thanksgiving Day. Smith, *Sports and Freedom*, 79–82. For more on Thanksgiving Day college football, see Oriard, *Reading Football*, 89–102.

93. *Daily Palo Alto*, 4 September 1896; 23 September 1896; 4 September 1896; 19 September 1896.

94. *Daily Palo Alto*, 13 November 1896; 20 November 1896.

95. *Daily Palo Alto*, 24 November 1896.

96. "Students Cheer Football Heroes," *San Francisco Chronicle*, 26 November 1896, 8–9.

97. *San Francisco Examiner*, 27 November 1896, 1, 5; *San Francisco Chronicle*, 27 November 1896, 8.

98. *San Francisco Examiner*, 27 November 1896, 2.

99. For the interplay between Geertz's cultural anthropology and historical practice, see Ronald G. Walters, "Signs of the Times: Clifford Geertz and Historians," *Social Research* 47 (1980): 537–56; Jean-Christophe Agnew, "History and Anthropology: Scenes from a Marriage," *Yale Journal of Criticism* 3 (1990): 29–50; William Roseberry, "Balinese Cockfights and the Seduction of Anthropology," *Social Research* (1982): 1013–28; William Roseberry, "The Unbearable Lightness of Anthropology," *Radical History Review* 65 (1996): 5–25; Adam Kuper, "Clifford Geertz: Culture as Religion and as Grand Opera," in *Culture: The Anthropologists' Account* (Cambridge, Mass.: Harvard University Press, 1999), 75–121. Geertz also discussed his work's relationship with history in "History and Anthropology," *New Literary History* 21 (1990): 321–41, and "The State of the Art," in *Available Light: Anthropological Reflections on Philosophical Topics* (Princeton: Princeton University Press, 2000), 89–142.

100. Clifford Geertz, "Deep Play: Notes on the Balinese Cockfight," in *The Interpretation of Cultures*, 449.

101. Ibid., 451.

102. Geertz, "Thick Description: Toward an Interpretive Theory of Culture," in *Interpretation of Cultures*, 5, 14, 9.

103. Walters, "Geertz and Historians," 543.

104. One could argue that Geertz's focus in his best-known essay, a cockfight, isn't exactly a sporting event as people in the West have come to understand the experience; he does suggest that his methodology and reason for such a focus would apply to U.S. sports contests: "As much of America surfaces in a ball park, on a golf links, at a race track, or around a poker table, much of Bali surfaces in a cock ring." Geertz, "Notes on a Balinese Cockfight," 417.

105. Ibid., 444, 450–51.

106. Ibid., 452, 448.

107. Oriard, *Reading Football*, 11; Heywood Broun, *Introduction to Football and How to Watch It* (Boston: Marshall Jones, 1922), quoted in Oriard, *Reading Football*, 11.

108. Geertz, "Notes on a Balinese Cockfight," 449.

109. *Daily Palo Alto*, 8 November 1892.

An 1897 poem by Stanford student Dane Coolidge also illustrates the emotional involvement and determinacy the fans realized through cheering:

The howling banks of rooters rise
And swing their colors while they cheer
The eager players toward the goal.
Then thousand people sway and strain
And play the game from where they stand
Willing the champions down the field;
Cheering their rushes, roaring their names,

Who have no thought, no wish, no goal
Except to cross that white line
And hear the Stanford yell!
("The Game," *The Sequoia*, 26 November 1897.)

110. *San Francisco Examiner*, 27 November 1896, 1–3.
111. *San Francisco Chronicle*, 27 November 1896, 8–10.
112. After this example of the endemic conflation of turkey, football players, and eating, Berkeley's song slipped into martial verse, rehearsing the vengeance of the previous year's loss to Stanford:

Our Golden Bear went forth to war,
A victor's crown to gain,
But lo, his vanquished crown is sore
And eke he suffers pain,
For 'leven horrid Stanfordites
Assailed his ursine ribs
And smote him sundry sinful smites
Upon his golden ribs.
Upon his golden ribs, ah me,
Upon his golden ribs,
We'll take him home to Berkeley
And nurse his ursine ribs,
But when again he rages forth
His foes shall flee afar,
And we'll be joyful in the North
And California!

This song ends with a blow-by-blow account of the assault on Stanford:

We want a man in a card'nal shirt,
With a lot o' card'nal hair,
We want to roll him in the dirt,
We want to make him swear,
We want to twist his card'nal nose,
We want to punch his chin—
In fact, most any darn thing goes,
If only we can win!
If only we can win boys,
If only we can win,
If only we can win boys,
If only we can win,
We'll play the dickens of a game,
We'll howl like very sin,
For though all Stanford up an' shcrame,
It's Berkeley's got to win!
(*The Berkleyean*, 20 November 1896)

Stanford's prize football song "When Stanford Begins to Score" was written to the Civil War tune "When Johnny Comes Marching Home" and includes general martial reference:

Oh there's nothing wrong with the Stanford throng
All right all the Stanford men
And my, what a brick is our "Captain Fick"
With his gallant and husky ten,
He'll drive his line down the good gridiron
For fifty yards or more
And he'll make it hot for the U.C. lot
When Stanford begins to score.
(*Thanksgiving Game Program 1896, California-Stanford*)

Another Stanford cheer for the 1896 Big Game fixes on the classic mix of mind and muscle:

Our players every one are made
Of mind and muscle tough;
The combination always works
For they are up to snuff;
They'll show the Berkeley fellows
That they're diamonds in the rough,
While we are shouting for Stanford.

Though the second verse drops concern with mind:

Then rush! O rush!
We'll rush the ball along,
A kick, a shove,
We'll send it through the throng,
No line can stop our fellows
In their rushes fierce and strong,
While we're shouting for Stanford.
(*San Francisco Chronicle*, 27 November 1896, 9)

As in "A kick, a shove," these cheers often included threats or incitements to aggressive extralegal play. California's ditty "Oh me! Oh my! Won't we black those Stanford's eye?" is one of the clearest albeit least imaginative examples of the genre. *San Francisco Chronicle*, 27 November 1896, 9.

113. *Thanksgiving Game Program 1896, California-Stanford.*

114. The axe saga is detailed in Archie Cloud, *The Stanford Axe* (Palo Alto: Pacific Books, 1952); Elliott, *Stanford University*, 185–86; "History of the Stanford Axe," unpublished manuscript in Stanford University Special Collections and Archives; John T. Sullivan, *Cal-Stanford: The Big Game* (West Point, N.Y.: Leisure Press, 1982), 7–9.

115. Geertz, "Notes on a Balinese Cockfight," 449, 448.

116. Joanne Sloan and Cheryl Watts, *College Nicknames and Other Interesting Sports Traditions* (Northport, Ala.: Vision Press, 1993), 277–78.

117. George Carlin, "Baseball and Football," in *Brain Droppings* (New York: Hyperion, 1997), 50–53.

118. For discussion of catharsis theory, see Richard Sipes, "War, Sports and Aggression: An Empirical Test of Two Rival Theories," *American Anthropologist* 75 (1973): 64–86; Burstyn, *Rites of Men*, 38–44; Oriard, *Reading Football*, 6–7; Gordon A. Bloom and Michael Smith, "Hockey Violence: A Test of Cultural Spillover Theory," *Sociology of Sport Journal* 13 (1996): 65–77; Eric Dunning, "Sociological Reflections on Sport, Violence and Civilization," *International Review for the Sociology of Sport* 25 (1990): 65–82.

119. George Santayana, "Philosophy on the Bleachers," originally published in *The Harvard Monthly*, July 1894, in *George Santayana's America: Essays on Literature and Culture*, ed. James Ballowe (Urbana: University of Illinois Press, 1967), 121–30. Santayana's view of sports as art is similar to that of Geertz and worth quoting at fuller length: "The relation of athletics to war is intimate, but it is not one of means to end, but more intrinsic, like that of drama to life." In sports, as in the arts, "we all participate through the imagination in the delight and meaning of what lies beyond our power of accomplishment. A few moments of enjoyment and intuition, scattered throughout our lives, are what lift the whole of it from vulgarity. They form a background of comparison, a standard of values, and a magnet for the estimation of tendencies, without which all our thought would be perfunctory and dull. Enthroned in those best moments, art, religion, love, and the powers of the imagination, govern our character, and silently direct the current of our common thoughts. Now, in its sphere, athletic sport has a common fiction."

Santayana went on to speak of the specific virtues of football: in the game there is "a great and continuous endeavor, a representation of all the primitive virtues and fundamental gifts of man. The conditions alone are artificial, and when well combined are even better than any natural conditions for the enacting of this sort of physical drama, a drama in which all moral and emotional interests are in a manner involved. For in real life the latter are actually superposed upon physical struggles. . . . Therefore, when some well-conceived contest, like our football, displays the dramatic essence of physical conflict, we watch it with an interest which no gymnastic feat, no vulgar tricks of the circus or of legerdemain, can ever arouse. The whole soul is stirred by a spectacle that represents the basis of its life."

120. Camp's "safety valve" comments appear in "What Are Athletics Good For?" *Outing* 63 (October 1913): 259–72, quoted by Oriard, *Reading Football*, 6; Camp's 1892 Stanford talk is excerpted in *Daily Palo Alto*, 13 December 1892.

121. *Daily Palo Alto*, 13 December 1892.

122. A. A. Brill, "The Why of the Fan," *North American Review* 228 (October 1929): 429–34.

123. Francis Butler Simkins and Charles Roland, *A History of the South* (New York: Knopf, 1972), as cited in Miller, "College Sport in the New South," 316.

124. Miller, "College Sport in the New South," 298.

125. *Intercollegiate Football*, 25.

126. Background material on Camp Randall, "The Story of Camp Randall," August 1953; "The Story of Camp Randall," July 1954; Clarke Smith, "Memorandum to University of Wisconsin President Fred: Ownership and Control of Camp Randall Memorial Park," August 1953; all unpublished manuscripts, Camp Randall collection, University of Wisconsin Archives, Madison.

127. *Dedication of Camp Randall Memorial* (Madison: University of Wisconsin Publications, 1956).

128. For history of the composition and rise in popularity of the song, see Louise Phelps Kellogg, "'On Wisconsin'—The Football Song," *The Wisconsin Magazine of History* 21 (September 1937), 33–38; "'On Wisconsin'-Universal Favorite," *Wisconsin Then and Now*, September 1973, 7–8.

129. "How 'On Wisconsin,' Pride of the State, Was Written," *The Milwaukee Journal*, 5 February 1922.

130. Miller, "College Sport in the New South," 292.

131. *New York Times*, 24 November 1895.

132. *San Francisco Chronicle*, 8 November 1896.

133. *San Francisco Examiner*, 27 November 1896, 1–3.

134. *New York Times*, 25 November 1894, 5.

135. *A Decennial of Stanford Song* (Stanford: Stanford University Publications, 1902).

136. Bristow Adams, "From the Side-Lines," *The Sequoia* 26 November 1897.

137. Garry Wills, *Lincoln at Gettysburg: The Words That Remade America* (New York: Simon and Schuster, 1992), 65.

138. Henry L. Higginson, "The Soldier's Field" (1890), in *Life and Letters of Henry Lee Higginson*, ed. Bliss Perry (Boston: Atlantic Monthly Press, 1921), 529–36.

139. "Stadium Dedicated at Service This Morning," *Daily Palo Alto*, 1 June 1921.

140. "Story of the Stadium," unpublished manuscript, Athletic Department Collections, Bancroft Library, University of California Archives, Berkeley.

141. *New York Times*, 2 December 1894.

142. Bliss Perry, *The Amateur Spirit* (Cambridge, Mass.: Houghton-Mifflin, 1904), 34; N. S. Shaler, "The Athletic Problem in Education," *Atlantic Monthly* 63 (1889): 81.

143. Henry S. Curtis, "A Football Education," *American Physical Education Review* 9 (December 1904): 264; Raymond G. Gettel, "The Value of Football," *American Physical Education Review* 22 (March 1917): 139–42, quoted in Mrozek, *Sport and American Mentality*, 66.

144. Camp and Deland, *Football*, iii.

145. Ibid., iii, 48, 278–81.

146. William James, "The Moral Equivalent of War," *McClure's Magazine* (August 1910), reprinted in *The Writings of William James*, ed. John J. McDermott (Chicago: University of Chicago Press, 1967), 660–71.

147. Ibid., 662.

Four • War in the Head

1. Sigmund Freud, "Why War?" (1932), reprinted in Freud, *Character and Culture*, with an introduction by Philip Rieff (New York: Macmillan Publishing, 1963), 134–47 (emphasis in original). For Freud's earlier views on instinct and war, see "Reflections upon War and Death" (1915), in *Character and Culture*, 107–33.

2. William James, "The Moral Equivalent of War," *McClure's Magazine*, August 1910, reprinted in *The Writings of William James*, ed. John J. McDermott (New York: Random House, 1967), 660–71.

3. Freud, "Why War?" 144.

4. H. H. Powers, *The Things Men Fight For* (New York: Macmillan Company, 1916), 337.

5. Robert Service, "The Volunteer," *Collected Poems of Robert Service* (New York: Dodd, Mead, 1966), 297–98.

6. For a valuable critical analysis of one manifestation of this macrohistorical phenomenon, see John Ellis, *The Social History of the Machine Gun* (Baltimore: Johns Hopkins University Press, 1975).

7. Samuel Hynes, *The Solders' Tale: Bearing Witness to Modern War* (New York: Penguin, 1997), III. On human attraction to war, see, in addition to Hynes, John Glenn Gray, *The Warriors: Reflections on Men in Battle* (New York: Harper and Row, 1967); Joanna Bourke, *An Intimate History of Killing: Face to Face Killing in 20th Century Warfare* (New York: Basic Books, 1999); Niall Ferguson, "The Death Instinct: Why Men Fought," in *The Pity of War* (New York: Basic Books, 1999), 339–66.

8. Anthony Swofford, *Jarhead: A Marine's Chronicle of the Gulf War and Other Battles* (New York: Scribner, 2003), 103.

9. Charles Royster, *The Destructive War: William Tecumseh Sherman, Stonewall Jackson, and the Americans* (New York: Alfred A. Knopf, 1991); Robert Penn Warren, *The Legacy of the Civil War* (Cambridge, Mass.: Harvard University Press, 1961).

10. James M. McPherson, *For Cause and Comrades: Why Men Fought in the Civil War* (New York: Oxford University Press), 30, 45, 150.

11. Statistics on Civil War casualties from Oscar Handlin, "The Civil War as Symbol and Actuality," *Massachusetts Review* 3 (Autumn 1961): 137.

12. Merle Curti, *The Roots of American Loyalty* (New York: Columbia University Press, 1946), 177.

13. For a good summary of inclusive fitness and an intelligent discussion of human biological and cultural evolution, see Paul R. Ehrlich, *Human Natures: Genes, Cultures, and the Human Prospect* (Washington, D.C.: Island Press, 2000).

14. David W. Blight, *Race and Reunion: The Civil War in American Memory* (Cambridge, Mass.: Harvard University Press, 2001); Nina Silber, *The Romance of Reunion: Northerners and Southerners, 1865–1900* (Chapel Hill: University of North Carolina, 1993); Cecilia Elizabeth O'Leary, *To Die For: The Paradox of American Patriotism* (Princeton: Princeton University Press, 1999); Paul Buck, *Road to Reunion, 1865–1900* (Boston: Little, Brown, 1937).

15. Webster's definition of citizenship is from Linda Kerber, "'May All Our Citizens be Soldiers and All Our Soldiers Be Citizens': The Ambiguities of Female Citizenship in the New Nation," in *Arms at Rest: Peacemaking and Peacekeeping in American History*, ed. Joan R. Challinar and Robert Beisner (New York: Greenwood Press, 1987), 5; James Whiteclay Chambers II, *To Raise an Army: The Draft Comes to Modern America* (New York: Free Press, 1987), 65; Selective Draft Law Cases, 245 U.S. 366 (1918), 375. For conceptions of citizenship at the time of the Revolution, see Marcus Cunliffe, *Soldiers and Civilians: The Martial Spirit in America* (Boston: Little, Brown, 1968); Charles Royster, *A Revolutionary People: The Continental Army and American Character, 1775–1783* (Chapel Hill: University of North Carolina Press, 1979); Mark E. Kann, *A Republic of Men: The American Founders, Gendered Language, and Patriarchal Politics* (New York: New York University Press, 1998). In addition to Chambers's book on citizenship and the draft, see Linda Kerber, *No Constitutional Right to Be Ladies: Women and the Obligations of Citizenship* (New York: Hill and Wang, 1998); James Kettner, *The Development of American Citizenship* (Chapel Hill: University of North Carolina Press, 1978).

16. J. Sloat Fassett, *Memorial Day Address on the Battlefield of Gettysburg*, 25; John Sharp Williams, *Address to Company "A," Confederate Veterans* (Memphis: Paul Douglas Company,

1904), 6. Memorial Day addresses, including those without publishing information, are taken from Memorial Days addresses Pamphlet Collection, State Historical Society of Wisconsin, Madison.

Formulations of citizenship in terms of duty run throughout turn-of-the-century Memorial Day addresses. P. C. Knox, for instance, spoke of service at Gettysburg in 1908: "And so there died upon this field of battle many thousand defenders of the Union—many thousand patriots—many thousand heroes, who offered up their lives a military sacrifice that this country might be in fact, as in theory, wholly free." *Memorial Address on the Battlefield of Gettysburg*, 13. As did Harry Bingham in Littletown, New Hampshire, 1880: With memory of the war "the old emotions come back again; your pulses are quickened and your hearts thrilled; you are ready once more to do and dare any and all things that duty requires." *Memorial Day Address*, 12. Thomas Chambers Richmond spoke of service in dramatic terms in Madison, Wisconsin: "Memory carries the soldier back and there in his strong youth, in his stalwart manhood, the old scenes are re-enacted, the drum's long roll is heard, the scurried ranks of blue are formed, the heart-breaking 'good-bye' is uttered, and the soldiers of the Union march away to discharge a citizen's duty, to make the patriot's sacrifice, to do and die for their country." *Memorial Address* (1902), 6–7. Another good example of the republican idea of duty applied to war was made by Union veteran and future president James Garfield, writing in the *North American Review* in 1878: "A republic, however free, requires the service of a certain number of its men whose ambition is higher than mere private gains, whose lives are inseparable from the life of the nation, and whose labors and emoluments depend absolutely upon the honor and prosperity of the Government, and who can advance themselves only by serving their country." *North American Review* 126 (1878): 458. Theo W. Bean also spoke explicitly of "manhood and the republic" in his memory of the Civil War in 1888: "Citizenship, grounded in the traditional and historical love of unity of country, was the last and accepted sacrifice. None more effectively than the soldier of the war has contributed to the nation's moral and religious progress. The true soldier was an exponent of manliness, his moral fabric was strengthened rather than impaired by his devoted service in a holy cause." *Address at Seven Pines National Cemetery*, 4.

17. William Crosby, *Memorial Day Speech*, 8; T. F. Lang, *Oration on Decoration Day* (Baltimore: Union Post Musical Association, 1880), 9. John Williams in Memphis in 1904 developed one of the most explicit descriptions of the link between memory of the Civil War and contemporary manhood: "A country without memories is a country without history, a country without history is a country without traditions, and a country without traditions is a country without ideals and community aspirations, and a country without these is a country without sentiment, and a country without sentiment is a country without capacity for achieving noble purposes, developing right manhood or taking any truly great place in the history of the world." *Address to Company "A,"* 15.

18. John M. Thurston, *Oration at the Arlington National Cemetery* (1898), 5; William Ruffin Cox, *Address Delivered before the Oakwood Memorial Association* (Richmond: F. J. Mitchell Printing Corporation, 1911), 3.

19. T. F. Lang, *Oration on Decoration Day* (Baltimore: Union Post Musical Association, 1880), 9; Joseph Lamar, *Address* (New York: Eagle Press, 1902), 8.

20. Richmond, *Memorial Address*, 8; Theodore Roosevelt, *Address of President Roosevelt at Antietam, September 17, 1903* (n.p., 1903), 14.

21. Oliver Wendell Holmes Jr., "Soldier's Faith," in *The Occasional Speeches of Oliver Wendell Holmes, Jr.,* ed. Mark De Wolfe Howe (Cambridge, Mass.: Harvard University Press, 1962), 81; other Holmes quotations are cited in Marcia Jean Speziale, "Oliver Wendell Holmes, Jr., William James, Theodore Roosevelt, and the Strenuous Life," *Connecticut Law Review* 13 (Summer 1981): 678, 669.

The combination of Holmes's experience in the Civil War and his unqualified acceptance of social Darwinism make him one of the most relativistic figures in American intellectual history. He is somebody to be compared to Nietzsche ("When there is peace, the warlike man attacks himself."); indeed, there are interesting biographical and historical parallels between the two men: birth dates—Holmes 1841, Nietzsche 1844; domineering intellectual fathers; classical education; supplemented formal education with Goethe, Kant, and Emerson; rejection at an early age of the idea of the existence of God; the experience of war at the center of their self understanding; significant portion of their work tried to prove the illusory quality of morality; thought supported twentieth-century nationalism.

A valuable way to understand Holmes's social and legal thought is within the framework of martial heroism and, in particular, the social function of individual physical sacrifice. His "Soldier's Faith" speech did as much as any modern American text to glorify the sacrifice of men in battle. And his conception of human experience as a world in which one group of people makes its view prevail by murdering those who disagree leads to the importance of people giving themselves up for the good of the whole. "Every society rests on the death of man," Holmes wrote, and this idea can be seen in his legal decisions. The best example is *Buck v. Bell,* 274 U.S. 200 (1927), which affirmed the authority of the state of Virginia to sterilize Carrie Bell because of her alleged feeblemindedness. In the majority opinion, Holmes observed that "more than once" had public welfare called upon "the best citizens for their lives" and "it would be strange if [the state] could not call upon those who already sap the strength of the State for lesser sacrifices." Holmes went on to say that "it is better for all the world if instead of waiting to execute degenerate offspring for crime, or let them starve for their imbecility, society can prevent those who are manifestly unfit from continuing their kind." Holmes concluded, "three generations of imbeciles is enough" (204–6).

22. See *The Nation* 61 (19 December 1895): 440–41, and *New York Evening Post,* 17 December 1895, for criticism of "Soldier's Faith" speech; both are cited in Royster, *Destructive War,* 281.

23. Williams, *Address to Company "A,"* 9; William Crosby, *Memorial Day Speech,* 8.

24. Ulysses Grant, *Personal Memoirs of U.S. Grant,* 2 vols. (New York: Charles L. Webster & Company, 1885–86); for *Century's* publication details, see Frank Mott, *A History of American Magazines, 1865–1885* (Cambridge, Mass.: Harvard University Press, 1957), 457–80; Bruce Catton, foreword to *The American Heritage Century Collection of Civil War Art* (New York: American Heritage Publishing, 1974), 10; Johnson and other editor cited in Blight, *Race and Reunion,* 175. Valuable studies of Civil War literature: Edmund Wilson, *Patriotic Gore: Studies in the Literature of the American Civil War* (New York: Oxford University Press, 1966); Daniel Aaron, *The Unwritten War: American Writers and the Civil War* (New York: Alfred A. Knopf, 1973); Alice Fahs, *The Imagined Civil War: Popular Literature of the North and South, 1861–1865* (Chapel Hill: University of North Carolina Press, 2001); Blight, *Race and Reunion;* Thomas C. Leonard, *Above the Battle: War-Making in America from Appomatox to Versailles* (New York: Oxford University Press, 1978).

25. Catton, *Century Collection*, 8.

26. Ibid., 9–11.

27. While it is difficult to estimate the popularity of these memoirs, there is some evidence that the books became an important element of the growing subculture of Civil War veterans. One of the most popular memoirs was John O. Casler's *Four Years in the Stonewall Brigade* (Girard, Kans.: Appeal Publishing Company, 1906; repr., Marietta, Ga.: Continental Book, 1951), which in its second edition, included letters from both northern and southern veterans, from Oklahoma to New York City, saying how much they enjoyed the book. For instance, a former Union sergeant from Massachusetts wrote: "I found it a vivid reminder of the days gone by, and regardless of the fact as to whether one was a 'Johnnie' or 'Yank,' it should be a very large sale with all. . . . I hope to hear from you again, Old Comrade, and should you ever come this way, the latch-string is out, and we will drink from the same canteen."

28. Carlton McCarthy, *Detailed Minutiae of Soldier Life in the Army of Northern Virginia, 1861–1865* (Richmond: Carlton McCarthy and Company, 1882), 95; S. H. M. Byers, *With Fire and Sword* (New York: The Neale Publishing Company, 1911), 77. Among the scholarly studies of Civil War soldiers' experiences in battle, the following have been particularly helpful: James M. MacPherson, *For Cause and Comrades: Why Men Fought in the Civil War* (New York: Oxford University Press, 1997); Gerald Linderman, *Embattled Courage: The Experience of Combat in the American Civil War* (New York: Free Press, 1987); Earl J. Hess, *The Union Soldier in Battle: Enduring the Ordeal of Combat* (Lawrence: University Press of Kansas, 1997); Reid Mitchell, *Civil War Soldiers: Their Expectations and Their Experiences* (New York: Simon and Schuster, 1988).

Veterans did not hesitate to talk about the results of fighting—that is, death and severe injury. In *Battlefield and Prison Pen* (Philadelphia: Hubbard Brothers, 1882), John W. Urban, a former soldier in the Union infantry, described the hand-to-hand combat at Cold Harbor: "The fighting was now of the most terrible description, and would often be at such close quarters that the savage thrust of the bayonet, and the crash of the butt of the musket, as it struck through the head of some poor misfortunate, added to the occasion. The nature of the wounds inflicted proved the close proximity in which the combatants contested for the mastery. Some of the dead had heads broken in my blows from butts of rifles, and others lay dead with bayonets thrust through them, the weapon having been left sticking in their bodies" (120).

29. B. F. Scribner, *How Soldiers Were Made* (Chicago: Donohue and Hennsberry, 1887), 147, 165.

30. Byers, *With Fire and Sword*, 83. In his memoir *Under Five Commanders: A Boy's Experience with the Army of the Potomac* (Paterson, N.J.: News Printing Company, 1906), Jacob R. Cole remembered going to sleep "with the slain and with groans of the wounded ringing in our ears." One night during the Battle of Fair Oaks, Cole set down between two of his comrades, or so he thought, only to find after shaking them the next morning that they were dead Confederates. "It did not take me long to get up," Cole remarked (68).

The veterans' use of the concept of hell can be found throughout the memoirs. In *A Boy at Shiloh*, Joseph Cockerill described what he saw as he marched closer and closer to the battle in quite graphic terms of hell: "the roar and din of battle in all its terror outstripped my most fanciful dreams of Pandemonium. The wounded and butchered men who came out of the blue smoke in front of us, and were dragged and sent hobbling to the rear, seemed like bleeding messengers come to tell us of the fate that awaited us." Cited in Royster, *Destructive War*, 274–75. Other descriptions of the results of violence are worth repeating. For instance, in *How Soldiers Were Made*, Scribner talked about his comrades at Chickamauga: "More than twenty-three have passed away since that distressing night; other horrors have since filled my mind, but the long painful vigil of that night of gloomy forebodings is yet fresh in my memory! As I crouched, brooding over my lonely fire, the incidents of the day passed in review before me, renewing each sad scene. I was surprised and shocked again at the bleeding bodies of much loved comrades. I mourned again over the prostrate form of Col. Maxwell, of the Second Ohio, whom I assisted to an ambulance after the battle of the morning. He was shot through the lungs, the bullet entering his breast and making its exit at his back. He wore a light buff vest which was soaked through with blood, which made him a ghastly spectacle to look upon" (152).

31. Review of *The Red Badge of Courage*, *New York Times*, 19 October 1895, in *Stephen Crane: The Critical Heritage*, ed. Richard M. Weatherford (London: Routledge and Kegan Paul, 1973), 87; negative Union veteran response, Alexander C. McClurg, *Dial* 20 (April 1886): 227; Thomas Wentworth Higginson, *Philistine* 3 (July 1896): 36; positive response by Union veteran cited in Steven Wertheim, *Hawthorne, Melville, Stephen Crane: A Critical Bibliography* (New York: Free Press, 1971), 46.

32. Stephen Crane, *The Red Badge of Courage* (1895; repr., New York: Vintage Books, Library of America, 1990), 51, 37.

33. Ibid., 48.

34. Ibid., 51, 52, 58, 59.

35. Cited in Lee Clark Mitchell, ed., *New Essays on the Red Badge of Courage* (Cambridge: Cambridge University Press, 1986), 4.

36. Crane, *Red Badge of Courage*, 10, 9, 97, 134.

37. Ibid., 25, 35, 36, 105, 23.

38. Ibid., 48, 14.

39. Ibid., 63, 101.

40. McCarthy, *Detailed Minutiae*, 95; Crane, *Red Badge of Courage*, 132.

41. Crane, *Red Badge of Courage*, 95, 105.

42. Ibid., 26, 5, 108.

43. Ibid., 105, 108.

44. Ibid., 65.

45. Ibid., 51, 23.

46. Ibid., 102–3.

47. Very helpful here have been Richard Koenigsberg's applications of psychoanalysis to nationalism and war in the History-and-Theory listserv, H-Net Discussion list, H-HISTORY-AND-THEORY@H-NET.MSU.EDU. I do think, however, that Koenigsberg has an enormous blind spot over the role of *pleasure* in killing and war making.

48. Crane, *Red Badge of Courage*, 124.

49. Ibid., 92, 105, 127, 96–97, 134.

50. Statistics on volunteers cited in Gerald F. Linderman, *The Mirror of War: American Society and the Spanish-American War* (Ann Arbor: University of Michigan Press, 1974), 63–64. Along with *Mirror of War*, the most helpful historical works on the Spanish-Ameri-

can War have been Kristin L. Hoganson, *Fighting for American Manhood: How Gender Politics Provoked the Spanish-American and Philippine-American Wars* (New Haven: Yale University Press, 1998); O'Leary, *To Die For;* Richard Hofstadter, "Cuba, the Philippines, and Manifest Destiny," in *The Paranoid Style in American Politics and Other Essays* (New York: Alfred A. Knopf, 1966).

51. Klaus Theweleit, *Male Fantasies,* 2 vols. (1978; repr., Minneapolis: University of Minnesota Press, 1989).

52. Ibid., 1:x; Brook Adams cited in John P. Mallan, "Roosevelt, Brooks Adams, and Lea: The Warrior Critique of the Business Civilization," *American Quarterly* 8 (1956): 216; Theweleit, *Male Fantasies,* 2:155.

53. Sandburg and Beveridge cited in O'Leary, *To Die For,* 137, 142.

54. Theodore Roosevelt, *The Rough Riders* (1899; repr., New York: Modern Library, 1996), 14.

55. The "everything I can get out of it" and "bullet, butt, and bayonet" quotations are from Linderman, *Mirror of War,* 52, 95; "wolf rising in the heart," killing Spaniard with his own hand, and "bully fight" from Edmund Morris, *The Rise of Theodore Roosevelt* (1979; repr., New York: Modern Library, 2001), 661, 685, 697; and Roosevelt dancing cited in Virgil Carrington Jones, *Roosevelt's Rough Riders* (New York: Doubleday, 1971), 92.

56. The "great day of my life" quotation is from Linderman, *Mirror of War,* 95; for Crane's and others' negative assessments of Roosevelt at Las Guasimas, see Dale L. Walker, *The Boys of '98: Theodore Roosevelt and the Rough Riders* (New York: Tom Doherty Associates, 1998), 170–74; Roosevelt, *Rough Riders,* 79; Tom Hall, *The Fun and Fighting of the Rough Riders* (New York: Frederick A. Stokes Company, 1899), 194; Roosevelt, *Rough Riders,* 79–80; "neatly as a jackrabbit" from Morris, *Rise of Theodore Roosevelt,* 686; post–San Juan Hill battle comment by Bob Ferguson, Morris, *Rise of Theodore Roosevelt,* 687.

57. For example, Thomas W. Handford's, *Theodore Roosevelt: The Pride of the Rough Riders, an American Ideal* (1899); Charles Eugene Banks and Leroy Armstrong, *Theodore Roosevelt: A Typical American* (Chicago: S. Stone, 1901). Jacob Riis, *Theodore Roosevelt: The Citizen* (New York: The Outlook Company, 1903), dedicated to the "Young Men of America"; Charles Morris, "Theodore Roosevelt as America's All-Around Man and Champion," in *Heroes of Progress in America* (Philadelphia: J. B. Lippincott Company, 1906).

58. Theodore Roosevelt, "The Strenuous Life," in *The Strenuous Life: Essays and Addresses* (New York: The Century Company, 1911), 4, 7; *Chicago Daily Tribune,* 11 April 1899, 1. In Chicago, the same day of his "Strenuous Life" speech, Roosevelt also spoke to upperclassmen at the University of Chicago. University president R. W. Harper introduced Roosevelt: "Some men we reverence, some men we admire, some men we love. Some men we reverence, admire and love. We reverence the hero, whether he be young or old. Acts of courage make men's blood run faster. . . . Our guest is one we revere, a hero to whom we do honor, a statesman whom we trust. More than all that, he is one with whom we come into closest contact and sympathy." *Chicago Daily Tribune,* 11 April 1899, 3.

59. Roosevelt, *Rough Riders,* 1–24. In his memoir *Santiago Campaign, the Rough Riders' Experiences* (n.p., 1898), Edwin Tyler wrote: "Of course, Colonel Wood was commander, but everything seemed to revolve around Colonel Roosevelt—even the cable cars in San Antonio were decked out by the people with banners, making a grand display for Colonel Roosevelt and his 'Rough Riders,'" 5.

60. Roosevelt, *Rough Riders*, 9–13.

61. Ibid., 8–9.

62. Ibid., 11, 13, 49; Tyler, *Santiago Campaign*, 8.

63. Stephen Crane, "Vivid Story of the Battle of San Juan," *New York World*, 13 July 1898, reprinted in *Stephen Crane: Prose and Poetry*, ed. J. C. Levenson (New York: Library of America, 1996), 1004. John Seeyle, *War Games: Richard Harding Davis and the New Imperialism* (Amherst: University of Massachusetts Press, 2003).

64. Richard Harding Davis, *The Cuban and Porto Rican Campaigns* (London: William Heinemann, 1899), 202, 205, 159.

65. Stephen Bonsal, *The Fight for Santiago* (New York: Doubleday and McClure, 1899), 98; Edward Marshall, *The Story of the Rough Riders* (New York: G. W. Dillingham Company, 1899), xi.

66. Marshall, *Story of the Rough Riders*, 33, 25, 28,101.

67. Ibid., 19.

68. "Ode to Grigby's Cowboys," *Daily Argus-Leader* (Sioux Falls, S.Dak.), 14 May 1898, copied in Clifford P. Westermeir, *Who Rush to Glory* (Caldwell, Idaho: Caxton Printers, 1958), 164. For background on the song, see http//www.nfo.net/WWW/melodva.html; among the many Spanish-American War memoirs mentioning the singing of "Hot Time," see Hall, *Fun and Fighting of the Rough Riders*, vi.

69. "Cowboy's Battle Song," *Daily-Argus Leader* (Sioux Falls, S.Dak.), 24 May 1898, copied in Westermeier, *Who Rush to Glory*, 164–66.

70. *Reminiscences and Thrilling Stories of the War by Returned Heroes Containing Vivid Accounts of Personal Experiences by Officers and Men* (Philadelphia: Elliott Publishing Company, 1899), 529.

71. Ibid., 512–13.

72. "The New York Volunteer," "Riding a Raid," in *Songs of the Civil War*, ed. Irwin Silber (New York: Dover Publications, 1960), 187, 82.

73. From the song "Longing for Battle" by Calvin Goss in *Spanish-American War Songs*, ed. Sidney A. Witherbee (Detroit: by the author, 1898), 402.

74. *Reminiscences and Thrilling Stories of the War*, 569–70.

75. Ibid., 534.

76. Ibid., 517.

77. Fahs, *Imagined Civil War*, 96; "After the Battle," in *Reminiscences and Thrilling Stories of the War*, 533–34.

78. *Reminiscences and Thrilling Stories of the War*, 537–38.

79. Ibid., 587.

80. Roosevelt, *Rough Riders*, 54; Marshall, *Story of the Rough Riders*, 195, 197. *In Fun and Fighting*, Hall writes of the Rough Riders: "There was no groaning among the wounded. Often there was an exclamation of surprise, and the man would hunt around curiously to see where he had been hit. Then he would grinningly inform his comrades. Their attitude was very similar to that of the irish hod carrier who fell four stories from the window of a house in process of construction and on striking the pavement looked up and remarked, 'I broke me poipe,'" 146.

81. Marshall, *Story of the Rough Riders*, 120–21.

82. "Let Me Like a Soldier Fall," *Reminiscences and Thrilling Stories of the War*, 593.

83. Marshall, *Story of the Rough Riders,* 103.

84. *Reminiscences and Thrilling Stories of the War,* 548, 543, 549, 594, 593.

85. Ibid., 605, 554.

86. Richard Barry, "The Call," *Harper's Weekly,* 20 August 1898, 819. "Fall in Line" follows the same theme of sectional reunion supporting the War of 1898: "Hark the drum and bugle call, / Fall in line. / Sister States both great and small / Fall in line. / On the land and on the sea / Let the ready watchword be, / Fall in line / Veterans of the Gray and Blue, / Fall in line. / Sons of veterans strong and true, / Fall in line. / Soldiers ,sailors, one and all, / hearken to your country's call / Fall in line . . . ," *Reminiscences and Thrilling Stories of the War,* 575.

87. *Reminiscences and Thrilling Stories of the War,* 582, 589.

88. "The Dudes before Santiago" *Chicago Daily Tribune,* 12 July 1898, cited in Westermeier, *Who Rush to Glory,* 151; "Yankee Dude'll Do," *Reminiscences and Thrilling Stories of the War,* 524.

89. Richard Slotkin, *Gunfighter Nation: The Myth of the Frontier in Twentieth-Century America* (New York: Atheneum, 1992), 51–54, 83–86, 101–6; Amy Kaplan, "Romancing the Empire: The Embodiment of American Masculinity in the Popular Historical Novel of the 1890s," *American Literary History* 2 (Winter 1990): 659–90. Hoganson, *Fighting for American Manhood,* 133–55.

90. Walter Hines Page, "The War with Spain, and After," *Atlantic Monthly* 81 (June 1898): 725–27; "Anglo-American" and "The Saxon," *Reminiscences and Thrilling Stories of the War,* 597, 554.

91. Matthew Frye Jacobson, "'War, What Sort of Mistress Are You?' Militarism, Masculinity, and the Polish-American Response to American Intervention in 1898" (paper presented at the Organization of American Historians conference, Chicago, April 1992). Polish-American contribution to the war is discussed in Frye Jacobson's excellent work, *Whiteness of a Different Color: European Immigrants and the Alchemy of Race* (Cambridge, Mass.: Harvard University Press, 1998).

92. "Romance of the Rough Riders—Gathering of the Clans," in Thomas W. Handford, *Theodore Roosevelt: The Pride of the Rough Riders, an Ideal American* (Chicago: Donohue, Henneberry & Company, 1899), 104–6.

93. Frederick Douglass cited in Royster, *The Destructive War,* 271; George Washington Williams, *History of the Negro Troops in the War of Rebellion* (New York: Harper and Brothers, 1888), 23; W. E. B. Du Bois cited in Edward Coffman, *The War to End All Wars: The American Military Experience in World War I* (New York: Oxford University Press, 1968), 69. Blight, *Race and Reunion,* esp. 348–53. For a valuable discussion of African American military service in exchange for rights of citizenship, see Steven A. Reich, "Soldiers of Democracy: Black Texans and the Fight for Citizenship, 1917–1921," *Journal of American History* 82 (March 1996): 1478–1504.

94. "The United States Can Protect Cubans but Not Americans at Home," *Afro-American Sentinel,* 9 July 1898; "White America's Cruelty Equals Spain's," *Iowa State Bystander,* 6 May 1898. Both articles excerpted in *The Black Press Views American Imperialism,* ed. George P. Marks III (1898–1900; repr., New York: Arno Press, 1971), 70, 52.

95. *Washington Colored American,* 30 April 1898, cited in Willard B. Gatewood Jr., "Black Americans and the Quest for Empire, 1893–1903," *Journal of Southern History* 38 (November

1972): 548; sergeant quoted in Willard B. Gatewood Jr., *Black Americans and the White Man's Burden* (1898–1903; repr., Urbana: University of Illinois Press, 1975), 58–59. For African Americans participation in the Spanish-American War, see Gatewood, *Black Americans and the White Man's Burden;* Bernard C. McNalty, *Strength for the Fight: A History of Black Americans in the Military* (New York: Free Press, 1986), 63–77; Gerald Early, "The Negro Soldier in the Spanish-American War" (M.A. thesis, Shippensburg State University, 1970); Marvin Edward Fletcher, "The Negro Soldier and the United States Army, 1891–1917" (Ph.D. dissertation, University of Wisconsin, 1968); Robert B. Edgerton, *Hidden Heroism: Black Soldiers in America's Wars* (Boulder, Colo: Westview Press, 2001), 39–68.

96. Roosevelt cited in E. A. Johnson, *History of the Negro Soldiers in the Spanish-American War* (Raleigh: Capital Printing Company, 1899), 39; Booker T. Washington, *A New Negro for a New Century* (Chicago: American Publishing, 1909), 12, 28.

97. *Washington Post* article cited in Herschel V. Cashin, *Under Fire with the Tenth U.S. Cavalry* (London: F. Tennyson Neely, 1899), 160; Pershing cited in Frank Freidel, *The Splendid Little War* (Boston: Little, Brown, 1958), 173.

98. Davis, *Cuban and Porto Rican Campaigns,* 244; the other two quotations are from Johnson, *History of Negro Soldiers,* 47, 68.

99. *Reminiscences and Thrilling Stories of the War,* 561–62, 540; *Under Fire with the Tenth,* 58–59.

100. Roosevelt, *Rough Riders,* 87–88; "malicious slander" from *Cleveland Gazette,* 6 May 1899, quoted in Gatewood, *Black Americans and the White Man's Burden,* 203. See Gatewood, *Black Americans and White Man's Burden,* 201–4, for full discussion of this controversy.

101. Enoch Herbert Crowder, *The Spirit of Selective Service* (New York: The Century Company, 1920), 296; Roosevelt, *Address at Antietam* (1903), 14.

102. James, "Governor Roosevelt's Oration," in *The Work of William James: Essays, Comments and Reviews,* ed. Frederick Burkhardt (Cambridge, Mass.: Harvard University Press, 1987), 162–64.

103. Hall, *Fun and Fighting of the Rough Riders,* vii.

104. Malcolm Cowley, *Exile's Return: A Literary Odyssey of the 1920s* (1934; repr., New York: Penguin Books, 1996), 41–42; David M. Kennedy, *Over Here: The First World War and American Society* (New York: Oxford University Press, 1980), 215; *Stars and Stripes,* 27 September 1918.

105. *Reminiscences and Thrilling Stories of the War,* 535.

106. Davis, *Cuban and Porto Rican Campaigns,* 140–41.

107. Crane, *Red Badge of Courage,* 104, 108, 104.

108. Keegan quoted by Richard Koenisberg in "Psychology of Warfare," on the History and Theory listserve, H-HISTORY-AND-THEORY@H-NET.MSU.EDU, 5 November 2002; L. B. R. Briggs, "Intercollegiate Athletics and the War," *Atlantic Monthly,* September 1918, 303; for British football during World War I combat, see Paul Fussell, *The Great War and Modern Memory* (Oxford: Oxford University Press, 1975), 27. In a revealing statement regarding the functional relationship between sport and war and the willingness of American college athletes to go and fight in Europe, Briggs glibly commented: "This war has come nearer [to] justifying our methods in intercollegiate athletics than we had thought possible" (303). Also valuable for World War I and sport, Michael C. Adams, *The Great Adventure: Male Desire and the Coming of World War I* (Bloomington: Indiana University Press, 1990).

109. H. G. Wells, "Looking Ahead. The Most Splendid Fighting in the World," *Daily Chronicle*, 9 September 1914, 4, quoted in Samuel Hynes, *The Soldier's Tale: Bearing Witness to Modern War* (New York: Penguin Books, 1997), 81; Cecil Lewis, *Sagittarius Rising* (London: P. Davies, 1936), 45, quoted in Hynes, *Soldier's Tale*, 86–87. Hynes's *Soldier's Tale* has been invaluable to my understanding of air war as well as modern combat overall.

110. Briggs, "Intercollegiate Athletics and the War," 303.

111. "Hobey Baker Makes His Final Flight," *Stars and Stripes*, 3 June 1919; John Davies, *The Legend of Hobie Baker* (Boston: Little, Brown, 1966).

112. Baker quoted in Davies, *Legend of Hobie Baker*, 77, 96.

113. *Stars and Stripes*, 8 February 1918.

114. Editorial memos and comments quoted in Alfred E. Cornebise, *The Stars and Stripes: Doughboy Journalism in World War I* (Westport, Conn.: Greenwood Press, 1984), 8, 7; on constant flow of soldier material, Cornebise, *Stars and Stripes*, 31. Regarding control of the newspaper from above, Cornebise quotes a memo from General Headquarters: "The Commander-in-Chief has noticed recently that The Stars and Stripes is criticizing the A.E.F. Some of these criticisms have appeared in a humorous vein. You will take proper steps to the end that no article containing a criticism of any kind appears in the Stars and Stripes" (10).

115. *Stars and Stripes*, 23 August 1918.

116. *Stars and Stripes*, 15 March 1918; 24 May 1918.

117. *Stars and Stripes*, 10 May 1918. Cornebise, *Doughboy Journalism*, 141–43, discusses the slacker issue.

118. *Stars and Stripes*, 15 March 1918; 10 May 1918.

119. *Stars and Stripes*, 26 July 1918.

120. *Stars and Stripes*, 26 July 1918.

121. *Stars and Stripes*, 11 October 1918.

122. *Stars and Stripes*, 9 August 1918; 15 February 1918.

123. *Stars and Stripes*, 16 August 1918.

124. *Stars and Stripes*, 14 March 1919; 8 March 1918.

125. *Stars and Stripes*, 26 February 1918; 23 August 1918.

126. *Stars and Stripes*, 8 March 1918; 15 February 1918.

127. *Stars and Stripes*, 2 August 1918.

128. *Stars and Stripes*, 15 February 1918; 8 February 1918; 30 August 1918.

129. Ellis, *Machine Gun*, 175.

130. *Stars and Stripes*, 22 November 1918.

131. Albert Jay Cook, "The Machine Gun," in *Yanks A. E. F. Verse* (New York: G. P. Putnam's Sons, 1919), 100–101.

132. Chris Hedges, "War Is Vivid in Gun Sights of the Sniper," *New York Times*, 3 February 1991, 1.

133. Craig M. Cameron, *American Samurai: Myth, Imagination, and the Conduct of Battle in the First Marine Division, 1941–1951* (New York: Cambridge University Press, 1994); 1921 birthday message quoted in Cameron, *American Samurai*, 28; World War II marine quoted in Cameron, *American Samurai*, 144. Also helpful for the history of the U.S. Marine Corps, James A. Donovan, *The United States Marine Corps* (New York: Frederick A. Praeger, 1967); Allan R. Millett, *Semper Fidelis: The History of the United States Marine Corps* (New York: Macmillan, 1980). For American experience of World War II combat, Gerald F. Linderman, *The*

World Within War: America's Combat Experience in World War II (Cambridge, Mass.: Harvard University Press, 1997); Peter S. Kindsvatter, *American Soldiers: Ground Combat in the World War, Korea, and Vietnam* (Lawrence: University Press of Kansas, 2003).

134. E. B. Sledge, *With the Old Breed: At Peleliu and Okinawa* (New York: Oxford University Press, 1981), 5.

135. Ibid., 29, 64.

136. Ibid., 5, 13, 18, 40–41.

137. Ibid., 100.

138. Ibid., 115, 315.

139. Donovan, *Marine Corps*, 72–74; Millett, *Semper Fidelis*, 560–61.

140. Ron Kovic, *Born on the Fourth of July* (New York: Simon and Schuster, 1977), 54, 112.

141. Marine quotation from Cameron, *American Samurai*, 184.

142. Philip Caputo, *A Rumor of War* (New York: Henry Holt, 1977), xvii.

143. Ibid., 6, xiv, 5, 302.

144. Ibid., 14, 306.

145. Ibid., 12, 36. For analysis of Marine boot camp, see Cameron, *American Samurai*, 49–88; and for the logic of military basic training overall, see Bourke, *Intimate History of Killing*, 57–90.

146. For an overview of the scholarly literature on war and sex, see Joshua Goldstein, *War and Gender: How Gender Shapes the War System and Vice Versa* (Cambridge: Cambridge University Press, 2001), 332–79.

147. Caputo, *Rumor of War*, 71, 81, 268; Marine captain quoted in Goldstein, *War and Gender*, 349.

148. Ibid., xviii, 119, 268.

149. Ibid., 304–5, 311.

150. Ibid., 294, 137.

151. James William Gibson, *Warrior Dreams: Violence and Manhood in Post-Vietnam America* (New York: Hill and Wang, 1994); paintball quotation at 135–36; Bush quotation at 292.

152. Swofford, *Jarhead*, 231 (emphasis in original), 255.

153. Ibid., 5, 6–7.

154. Ibid., 43, 14 (emphasis in original), 50, 228.

155. Ibid., 103, 70, 137, 205, 247, 247–48.

156. Ibid., 254, 222 (emphasis in original).

157. Caputo, *Rumor of War*, 229–30.

158. Dexter Filkins, "Either Take a Shot or Take a Chance," *New York Times*, 29 March 2003, 1, 5; Steven Lee Meyers, "Haunting Thoughts after a Fierce Battle," *New York Times*, 29 March 2003, 5. Amid the "post-victory" fighting in the Iraq War, the U.S. Army announced that it would begin to instill a greater degree of fighting spirit among all of its all-volunteer soldiers. Eric Schmitt, "All Soldiers Will Be Fighters in the New Army, Even Cooks," *New York Times*, 7 September 2003, 24.

Five • Laws of Sexual Selection

1. *Oxford English Dictionary Online,* http://dictionary.oed.com (Oxford University Press, 2004).

2. Charles Darwin, *Origin of the Species* (1859; repr., London: Penguin Classics, 1982), 263.

3. Charles Darwin, *The Descent of Man, and Selection in Relation to Sex* (1871; repr., Amherst, N.Y.; Prometheus Books, 1988), 583.

4. Randy Thornhill and Craig T. Palmer, *Rape: A Natural History of Biological Bases of Sexual Coercion* (Cambridge, Mass.: MIT Press, 2000).

5. Martin Daly and Margo Wilson, *Homicide* (New York: Aldine de Gruyter, 1988), 137–49.

6. David M. Buss, *The Dangerous Passion: Why Jealousy Is as Necessary as Love and Sex* (New York: Free Press, 2000).

7. Daly and Wilson, *Homicide,* 5.

8. Gayle Rubin, "The Traffic in Women: Notes on the 'Political Economy' of Sex," in *Toward an Anthropology of Women,* ed. Rayna Reiter (New York: Monthly Review Press, 1975), 174.

9. Joel Williamson, *The Crucible of Race: Black-White Relations in the American South since Emancipation* (New York: Oxford University Press, 1984), 111. For southern lynching of black men, I have relied most on W. Fitzhugh Brundage, *Lynching in the New South: Georgia and Virginia, 1880–1930* (Urbana: University of Illinois Press, 1993); Philip Dray, *At the Hands of Persons Unknown: The Lynching of Black America* (New York: Modern Library, 2003); *Under Sentence of Death: Lynching in the South,* ed. W. Fitzhugh Brundage (Chapel Hill: University of North Carolina Press, 1998); Stewart Tolnay and E. M. Beck, *A Festival of Violence: An Analysis of Southern Lynchings, 1882–1930* (Urbana: University of Illinois Press, 1992); Jacquelyn Dowd Hall, *Revolt against Chivalry: Jessie Daniel Ames and the Women's Campaign against Lynching* (New York: Columbia University Press, 1974); Hazel V. Carby, "On the Threshold of the Women's Era: Lynching, Empire and Sexuality in Black Feminist Theory," in *"Race," Writing and Difference,* ed. Henry Louis Gates (Chicago: University of Chicago Press, 1986), 301–16.

10. Brundage, *Under Sentence of Death,* 4; Trudier Harris, *Exorcising Blackness: Historical and Literary Lynching and Burning Rituals* (Bloomington: Indiana University Press, 1984), 7.

11. *Sunday News* (Charleston, S.C.), 4 June 1882, as cited in Tolnay and Beck, *Festival of Violence,* 64.

12. Richard Wright, *Black Boy: A Record of Childhood and Youth* (New York: Harper and Row, 1966), 190.

13. *DeSoto Democrat* (De Soto, La.), October 25, 1886 as cited in Tolnay and Beck, *Festival of Violence,* 88.

14. Ida B. Wells, *Southern Horrors* (1892; repr., Boston: Bedford Books, 1997), 62; Henry McNeal Turner, "An Emigration Convention" (1893), in *Respect Black: The Writings and Speeches of Henry McNeal Turner,* ed. Edwin S. Redkey (New York: Arno Press and New York Times, 1971), 153; Wells, *Southern Horrors,* 163.

15. Jacquelyn Dowd Hall, "'The Mind That Burns in Each Body': Women, Rape, and Racial Violence," in *Powers of Desire: The Politics of Sexuality,* ed. Ann Snitow, Christine Stansell, and Sharon Thompson (New York: Monthly Review Press, 1983), 334.

16. Stephen Kantrowitz, "'No Middle Ground': Gender Protection and the Wilmington Massacre and Coup of 1898," Graduate Seminar Paper, Princeton University, 1990, in the Wilmington Race Riot collection, Wilmington Public Library, North Carolina.

17. Charles W. Chestnutt, *The Marrow of Tradition* (1901; repr., New York: Penguin Books, 1993), 86.

18. Alfred M Waddell speech printed in *Wilmington Messenger*, 25 October 1898, 2; "We have taken a city" quotation by Reverend Peyton H. Hoge, First Presbyterian Church, reported in *Raleigh News and Observer*, 13 November 1898. For Wilmington massacre and coup, David S. Cecelski and Timothy B. Tyson, eds., *Democracy Betrayed: The Wilmington Race Riot of 1898 and Its Legacy* (Chapel Hill: University of North Carolina Press, 1998); H. Leon Prather Sr., *We Have Taken a City: Wilmington Racial Massacre and Coup of 1898* (Rutherford: Farleigh Dickinson University Press, 1984); Williamson, *Crucible of Race*, 195–200; Glenda Elizabeth Gilmore, *Gender and Jim Crow: Women and the Politics of White Supremacy in North Carolina, 1896–1920* (Chapel Hill: University of North Carolina Press, 1996), 91–118; Kantrowitz, "'No Middle Ground.'"

19. Chestnutt, *Marrow of Tradition*, 89.

20. Jesse C. Duke editorial, *Montgomery (Ala.) Herald*, 13 August 1887, as cited in Martha Hodes, *White Women, Black Men: Illicit Sex in the Nineteenth-Century South* (New Haven: Yale University Press, 1997), 188; for white response to Duke's editorial, see Hodes, *White Women, Black Men*, 188–90.

21. Ida B. Wells editorial, *Memphis Free Speech*, 21 May 1892, reprinted in Wells, *Southern Horrors*, 52; the white paper, *Evening Scimatar*, cited in Wells, *Southern Horrors*, 52.

22. Prather, *We Have Taken a City*, 68–69.

23. Felton speech in *Atlanta Journal*, 12 August 1897.

24. Williamson, *Crucible of Race*, 198.

25. Jack Thorne, *Hanover; or, Persecution of the Lowly* (n.p., 1901; repr., New York, 1969), 68.

26. Manly's *Wilmington Record* editorial reprinted in *Wilmington Messenger*, 4 September 1898, 1.

27. *Wilmington Messenger*, 21 August 1898, 4; Gilmore, *Gender and Jim Crow*, 72; *Wilmington Messenger*, 23 August 1898.

28. *Wilmington Messenger*, 25 August 1898, 1.

29. *Monroe Journal* excerpt in *Wilmington Messenger*, 28 August 1898, 6; *Charlotte News* excerpt in *Wilmington Messenger*, 25 August 1898, 3; *Goldsboro Argus* excerpt in *Wilmington Messenger*, 25 August 1898, 7.

30. *Raleigh Post* excerpt in *Wilmington Messenger*, 26 August 1898, 2; *Goldsboro Argus* excerpt in *Wilmington Messenger*, 26 August 1898, 2; *Wilmington Messenger*, 27 August 1898, 2.

31. *Wilmington Messenger*, 20 October 1898, 1; 22 October 1898, 3.

32. *Wilmington Messenger*, 25 October 1898, 2.

33. Ibid.

34. Ibid.

35. Ibid.; *Wilmington Messenger*, 10 November 1898, 1; 11 November 1898, 1; 12 November 1898, 1; 14 November 1898.

36. Rebecca Cameron to A. M. Waddell, 26 October 1898, A. M. Waddell Papers, Southern Historical Collection, University of North Carolina Library, Chapel Hill, as cited by Kantrowitz, "'No Middle Ground,'" 17.

37. Winthrop D. Jordan, *White over Black: American Attitudes toward the Negro: 1550–1812* (New York: Penguin, 1969), 151–52; Trudier Harris, *Exorcising Blackness: Historical and Literary Lynching and Burning Rituals* (Bloomington: Indiana University Press,1984), 22. Psychoanalytic analyses of lynching abound. Philip Resnikoff recognized in 1933 that "since the assertion that Negroes are lynched because they seduce white women has no basis in reality, it must originate in the minds of the accusers and is a projection of their own phantasies. . . . Even in the days of slavery the whites were imputing to the blacks their own repressed desires." "A Psychoanalytic Study of Lynching," *Psychoanalytic Review* 20 (October1933): 422. And the Georgia writer Lillian Smith wrote that "the lynched negro becomes . . . a receptacle for every man's damned-up hate, and a receptacle for every man's forbidden feelings. Sex and hate . . . pour out their progeny of cruelty on anything that can serve as a symbol of an unnamed relationship that in his heart each man wants to befoul." *Killers of the Dream* (New York: Norton, 1978), 162–63, as cited in Brundage, *Lynching in the New South*, 65. Along with Harris, particularly helpful is Robyn Wiegman, "The Anatomy of Lynching," *Journal of the History of Sexuality* 3 (1993): 445–67.

38. James Baldwin, "Going to Meet the Man" (1964), in *James Baldwin: Early Novels and Stories* (New York: Library of America, 1998), 934.

39. Ibid., 936–38.

40. Ibid., 943–49.

41. Ibid.

42. *Boston Transcript* article reprinted in *Macon Telegraph*, 20 August 1897, as cited in LeeAnn Whites, "Love, Hate, Rape, Lynching: Rebecca Latimer Felton and the Gender Politics of Racial Violence," in Cecelski and Tyson, *Democracy Betrayed*, 150.

43. *Atlanta Constitution*, 1 August 1897, as cited in Whites, "Love, Hate, Rape, Lynching," 147; Georgia Women's Federation spokeswoman quoted in *Dalton (Ga.) Argus*, 24 July 1897, as quoted in Edward L. Ayers, *Vengeance and Justice: Crime and Punishment in the 19th-Century South* (New York: Oxford University Press, 1983), 248; *Newnan Herald and Advertiser*, 28 April 1899, as cited in Dray, *Hands of Persons Unknown*, 72.

44. Nathan Shaler, *The Neighbor: The Natural History of Human Contacts* (Boston: Houghton, Mifflin and Company, 1904), 301, 299–300; Dean Richmond Babbitt, "The Psychology of the Lynching Mob," *Arena* 32 (December 1904): 586.

45. Stephen Kantrowitz, *Ben Tillman and the Reconstruction of White Supremacy* (Chapel Hill: University of North Carolina Press, 2000).

46. Benjamin Tillman, "The Race Problem," speech in the U.S. Senate, 23–24 February 1903, as quoted in Kantrowitz, *Tillman*, 260; Tillman, "The Black Peril," speech in the U.S. Senate, 1907, *Congressional Record*, 59th Cong., 2nd sess., 21 January 1907, as cited in Williamson, *Crucible of Race*, 116.

47. Atticus Haygood, "The Black Shadow across the South," *Forum* 16 (1893): 167–68; Clarence H. Poe, "Lynching: A Southern View," *Atlantic Monthly* 93 (April 1904): 158; Tillman, *Black Peril*, as cited in Williamson, *Crucible of Race*, 116–17.

48. Wells, *Southern Horrors*, 70; Chestnutt, *Marrow of Tradition*, 284.

49. Herbert Shapiro, *White Violence and Black Response: From Reconstruction to Montgomery* (Amherst: University of Massachusetts Press, 1988).

50. *Finch v. State*, 44 Tex. Crim. 204 (1902).

51. Victoria Nourse, "Passion's Progress: Modern Law Reform and the Provocation Defense," *Yale Law Journal* 106 (March 1997): 1331–1448; Donna K. Coker, "Heat of Passion

and Wife Killing: Men Who Batter/Men Who Kill," *Southern California Review of Law and Women's Studies* 2 (Fall 1992): 71–130; Deborah E. Milgate, "The Flame Flickers, but Burns On: Modern Judicial Application of the Ancient Heat of Passion Defense," *Rutgers Law Review* 51 (Fall 1998): 193–227; Elizabeth Rapaport, "Capital Murder and the Domestic Discount: A Study of Capital Domestic Murder in the Post-Furman Era," *SMU Law Review* 49 (July–August 1996): 1507–48.

52. Cynthia Lee, *Murder and the Reasonable Man: Passion and Fear in the Criminal Courtroom* (New York: New York University Press, 2003).

53. William Blackstone, *Commentaries on the Laws of England* 1 (1765; repr., Chicago: University of Chicago Press, 1979), 430; Hendrik Hartog, *Man and Wife in America: A History* (Cambridge, Mass.: Harvard University Press, 2000), 115–22.

54. Nourse, "Passion's Progress," 1331.

55. Ibid., 1382.

56. On definition of cultural defense, Leti Volpp, "(Mis)Identifying Culture: Asian Women and the 'Cultural Defense,'" *Harvard Women's Law Journal* 17 (1994): 57; Alison Dundes Renteln, *The Cultural Defense* (New York: Oxford University Press, 2004).

57. *New York v. Dong Lu Chen*, No. 87–7774 (N.Y. Sup. Ct. Dec. 2, 1988); Celestine Bohlen, "Holtzman May Appeal Probation for Immigrant in Wife's Slaying," *New York Times*, 5 April 1989, B3.

58. James J. Sing, "Culture as Sameness: Toward a Synthetic View of Provocation and Culture in the Criminal Law," *Yale Law Journal* 108 (May 1999): 1845–84; Daina C. Chiu, "The Cultural Defense: Beyond Exclusion, Assimilation, and Guilty Liberalism," *California Law Review* 82 (July 1994): 1053–1125; Volpp, "(Mis)Identifying Culture," 72.

59. *New York v. Chen*, 48–128.

60. Ibid.; Volpp, "(Mis)Identifying Culture," 72.

61. *New York v. Chen*, 76.

62. Volpp, "(Mis)Identifying Culture," 61–62.

63. Jeremy Horder, *Provocation and Responsibility* (Oxford: Clarendon Press, 1992), 1–42.

64. Blackstone, *Commentaries* 4, 191–92.

65. Horder, *Provocation*, 72–109.

66. *Maher v. The People*, 10 Mich. 212 (1862).

67. Robert M. Ireland, "The Libertine Must Die: Sexual Dishonor and the Unwritten Law in the Nineteenth-Century United States," *Journal of Social History* 23 (Fall 1989): 27–44; W. Lewis Roberts, "The Unwritten Law," *Kentucky Law Journal* 10 (January 1922): 45–52.

68. Hartog, *Man and Wife*, 230–31.

69. Felix G. Fontain, reporter, *Trail of the Hon. Daniel E. Sickles: For Shooting Philip Barton Key, Esq. U.S. District Attorney, Washington D.C., February 27, 1859* (New York: R. M. De Witt, 1859). For the importance of the Sickles trial, see Hartog, *Man and Wife*, 218–41.

70. Brundage, *Under Sentence of Death*, 4.

71. Vernon's Ann.P.C. art. 1220.

72. Statute cited in case, *Pauline v. State*, Tex. App. 21 (1886), 453–54.

73. *Finch v. State* (1902).

74. *Young v. State*, 54 Tex. Cr. R. (1908), 277–80; *Cannister v. State*, 46 Tex. Cr. R. (1904), 24–25.

75. *Dewberry v. State*, 74 S.W. (1903), 307–9.

76. *Price v. The State*, 18 Tex. App. (1885), 474–82.

77. *Gregory v. State*, 94 S.W. (1906), 1041–43.

78. *Sensobaugh v. State*, 244 S.W. (1922), 379–80.

79. Jeremy D. Weinstein, "Adultery, Law, and the State: A History," *Hastings Law Journal* (November 1986): 195–238.

80. *State v. Greenlee*, 269 P. (1928), 331–7.

81. *Burton v. State*, 86 S.W. 2d (1935), 768–71; *Zimmerman v. State*, 51 S.W. 2d (1932), 327–31; *Reed v. State*, 59 S.W. 2d (1933), 122–24.

82. Texas Penal Code Ann sec. 19.02(d).

83. Albert Alschuler as cited in Dan M. Kahan and Martha C. Nussbaum, "Two Conceptions of Emotions in Criminal Law," *Columbia Law Review* 96 (March 1996): 349.

84. Nourse, "Passion's Progress."

85. Karl Vick, "Maryland Judge Taking Heat in Cuckolded Killer Case," *Washington Post*, 30 October 1994, A1.

86. Watkins case discussed by Lee, *Murder and the Reasonable Man*, 42–43.

87. Adrienne Rich, "Compulsory Heterosexuality and Lesbian Existence" (1980), in *Blood, Bread, and Poetry: Selected Prose, 1979–1985* (New York: W. W. Norton, 1986), 23.

88. George Chauncey, *Gay New York: Gender, Urban Culture, and the Making of the Gay Male World, 1890–1940* (New York: Basic Books, 1995), 117.

89. Michel Foucault, *The History of Sexuality: An Introduction* (1978; repr., New York: Vintage Books, 1990); Jonathan Ned Katz, *The Invention of Heterosexuality* (New York: Dutton, 1995); Chauncey, *Gay New York*, 111–25.

90. Chauncey, *Gay New York*, 117.

91. Eve Kosofsky Sedgwick, *Between Men: English Literature and Male Homosocial Desire* (New York: Columbia University Press, 1985).

92. See Robert B. Mison, "Homophobia in Manslaughter: The Homosexual Advance as Insufficient Provocation," *California Law Review* 80 (1992): 133–78; Christina Pei-Lin Chen, "Provocation's Privileged Desire: The Provocation Doctrine, 'Homosexual Panic,' and the Non-Violent Unwanted Sexual Advance Defense," *Cornell Journal of Law and Public Policy* 10 (Fall 2000): 195–235; Joshua Dressler, "When 'Heterosexual' Men Kill 'Homosexual' Men: Reflections on Provocation Law, Sexual Advances, and the 'Reasonable Man' Standard," *Journal of Criminal Law and Criminology* 85 (Winter 1995): 726–63.

93. Charles G. Davis, *Report of the Trial of Samuel M. Andrews Indicted for the Murder of Cornelius Holmes, before the Supreme Judicial Court of Massachusetts, December 11, 1868* (New York: Hurd and Houghton, 1869).

94. Chen, "Provocation's Privileged Desire."

95. This summary of sexology relies upon and the Carpenter and Ellis quotes are taken from Mari Jo Buhle, *Feminism and Its Discontents: A Century of Struggle with Psychoanalysis* (Cambridge, Mass.: Harvard University Press, 2000), 36–37.

96. Elliott J. Gorn, *The Manly Art: Bare-Knuckle Prize Fighting in America* (Ithaca: Cornell University Press, 1986), 192.

97. For the rise of body building in the United States, see Harvey Green, *Fit for America: Health, Fitness, Sport, and American Society* (New York: Pantheon Books, 1986); David L. Chapman, *Sandow the Magnificent: Eugen Sandow and the Beginnings of Bodybuilding* (Urbana: University of Illinois Press, 1994); Robert Ernst, *Weakness Is a Crime: The Life of*

Bernarr MacFadden (Syracuse: Syracuse University Press, 1991); John F. Kasson, *Houdini, Tarzan, and the Perfect Man: The White Male Body and the Challenge of Modernity in America* (Hew York: Hill and Wang, 2001).

98. Chauncey, *Gay New York*, 114.

99. Kevin J. Mumford, "'Lost Manhood' Found: Male Sexual Impotence and Victorian Culture in the United States," in *American Sexual Politics: Sex, Gender, and Race since the Civil War*, ed. John C. Fout and Maura Shaw Tantillo (Chicago: University of Chicago Press, 1990), 75–99.

100. William Robinson, *Sexual Impotence* (New York: Critic and Guide Company, 1912).

101. Atlas quoted in Robert Lewis Taylor, "Self-Made Man—and Body," *The New Yorker* (January 3, 1942), 43; Elizabeth Toon and Janet Golden, "Rethinking Charles Atlas," *Rethinking History* 4 (2000): 80–84.

102. R. Schultz, "The Two Faces of DM," *DM News*, 15 November 1988, 44, as cited by Toon and Golden, "Rethinking Charles Atlas," 80.

103. Warren Greene, "A Child of Three Fathers: Physical Culture and the Birth of the Modern Fitness Magazine" (M.A. thesis, Lehigh University, 2003).

104. Toon and Golden, "Rethinking Charles Atlas," 82.

105. Darwin, *Descent of Man*, 379.

106. Kosofsky Sedgwick, *Between Men*, 89.

107. Samuel Wilson Fussell, *Muscle: Confessions of an Unlikely Bodybuilder* (New York: Avon Books, 1991), 186.

108. "As GI Joe Bulks Up, Concern for the 98-Pound Weakling," *New York Times*, 30 May 1999, sec. 4, 2; Harrison G. Pope, Katharine A. Phillips, and Robert Olivardia, *The Adonis Complex: The Secret Crisis of Male Body Obsession* (New York: Free Press, 2000), 430–44.

109. Pope, Phillips, and Olivardia, *The Adonis Complex*, 2, 23.

110. Ibid., 2–4; Lynne Luciano, *Looking Good: Male Body Image in Modern America* (New York: Hill and Wang, 2001), 3–4, 169–82.

111. Warren St. John, "In an Oversexed Age, More Guys Take a Pill," *New York Times*, 14 December 2003, sec. 9, 1–2.

112. Oliver W. Holmes Jr., "The Profession of the Law" (1886), in *Collected Legal Papers*, ed. Harold Joseph Laski (New York: Harcourt, Brace and Company, 1920), 25.

113. Clifford Geertz, "Sociosexology," *New York Review of Books* 26 (January 24, 1980), 41.

Epilogue • Irony, Instinct, and War

1. Harvey Mansfield, "The Partial Eclipse of Manliness," *London Times Literary Supplement*, 17 July 1998, 15.

2. William James, 1876, quoted in *William James: The Essential Writings*, ed. Bruce Wilshire (New York: Harper and Row, 1971), vii.

3. Bruce Feirstein, *Real Men Don't Eat Quiche: A Guidebook to All That Is Truly Masculine* (New York: Pocket Books, 1982); Robert Bly, *Iron John: A Book about Men* (Reading, Mass.: Addison-Wesley, 1990); John Tierney, "Going Where a Lot of Other Dudes with Really Great Equipment Have Gone Before: The Call of the Pseudo-Wild," *New York Times Magazine*, 26 July 26, 18–23, 33–34, 46–48.

4. Samuel Wilson Fussell, *Muscle: Confessions of an Unlikely Bodybuilder* (New York:

Avon Books, 1991); Samuel Wilson Fussell, "Bodybuilding Americanus," in *The Male Body: Features, Destinies, Exposures*, ed. Laurence Goldstone (Ann Arbor: University of Michigan Press, 1994), 56–57.

5. Fussell, *Muscle*, 62, 23–24; Fussell, "Bodybuilding Americanus," 57; Fussell, *Muscle*, 155.

6. Fussell, *Muscle*, 20, 21, 48.

7. Ibid., 48, 133, 48.

8. Ibid., 67, 82, 69, 130.

9. Fussell, "Bodybuilding Americanus," 56; Fussell, *Muscle*, 138.

10. Paul Fussell, *The Great War and Modern Memory* (Oxford: Oxford University Press, 1975); Fussell, *Muscle*, 247.

11. Fussell, *Muscle*, 29.

12. Ibid., 60, 15.

13. Along with Lionel Tiger's book discussed later in this section, see, e.g., David M. Buss, *The Dangerous Passion: Why Jealousy Is as Necessary as Love and Sex* (New York: Free Press, 2000); Randy Thornhill and Craig T. Palmer, *A Natural History of Rape: Biological Bases of Sexual Coercion* (Cambridge, Mass.: MIT Press, 2000); Michael P. Ghiglieri, *The Dark Side of Man: Tracing the Origins of Male Violence* (Reading, Mass.: Helix Books, 1999); Richard Wrangham and Dale Peterson, *Demonic Males: Apes and the Origins of Human Violence* (New York: Houghton Mifflin Company, 1996).

14. Lionel Tiger, *The Decline of Males: The First Look at an Unexpected New World for Men and Women* (New York: St. Martin's Griffin, 1999), 30–31.

15. Pinker quoted in Richard Monastersky, "Women and Science: The Debate Goes On," *Chronicle of Higher Education* 51 (4 March 2005): 1, 12.

16. Anne Fausto-Sterling, *Sexing the Body: Gender Politics and the Construction of Sexuality* (New York: Basic Books, 2000), 4.

17. Richard Lewontin, "The Wars over Evolution," *New York Review of Books* 52 (20 October 2005): 54; Richard Rorty, "Against Unity," *Wilson Quarterly*, Winter 1998, 33.

18. Jackson Lears, "The Iron Cage and Its Alternatives in Twentieth-Century American Thought," in *Perspectives on Modern America: Making Sense of the Twentieth Century*, ed. Harvard Sitkoff (New York: Oxford University Press, 2000), 311.

19. Barbara Ehrenreich and Janet McIntosh, "The New Creationism: Biology under Attack," *The Nation* 264 (9 June 1997): 10–16.

20. Ibid., 12.

21. Tiger, *Decline of Males*, 8, 15.

22. Ibid., 2, 3.

23. Barbara Ehrenreich, Lionel Tiger, "Forum: Who Needs Men?" *Harper's Magazine* 298 (June 1999): 42, 44.

24. Tiger, *Decline of Males*, 15, 14, 15.

25. Paul Crook, *Darwinism, War and History: The Debate over the Biology of War from the "Origin of the Species" to the First World War* (Cambridge: Cambridge University Press, 1994); Frans de Waal, *Our Inner Ape: A Leading Primatologist Explains Why We Are Who We Are* (New York: Riverhead Books, 2005).

26. Chris Hedges, "War Trauma Reaches Deep into America," *Albany Times Union*, 24 September 2005, sec. 1, 11.

27. Report by Human Rights Watch, "Torture in Iraq," excerpted in *New York Review of Books* 52 (3 November 2005): 67–72.

28. "Pat Tillman," *Wikipedia,* http://en.wikipedia.org/wiki/Pat_Tillman.

29. Human Rights Watch, "Torture in Iraq," *New York Review of Books* 52, no. 17 (3 November 2005), 67.

30. "Top U.S. Marine General, It Is 'Fun to Shoot Some People,'" NBCSandiego.com, 2 February 2005; Chris White, "First to Fight Culture," *Counterpunch,* http://www.counterpunch.org, 22 May 2004.

31. Denise Lavoie, "War Took Toll on Decorated Marine Accused of Opening Fire on Noisy Crowd," *Boston Globe,* boston.com, 15 August 2005.

32. Paul Wood, "Fixing the Problem of Falluja," BBC News electronic World Edition, http://news.bbc.co.uk/2/ni/middle_east/3989639.stm, 7 November 2004.

33. Patrick J. McDonnell, "The Conflict in Iraq; Marine Whose Photo Lit Up Imaginations Keeps His Cool," *Los Angeles Times,* 13 November 2004, A.1.

34. Louise Roug, "Extreme Cinema Verite," *Los Angeles Times,* http://www.latimes.com, 14 March 2005.

35. Andrea Lewis, "Virtual Combat," *Progressive,* July 2005, 32–33.

36. George Johnson, "Who Do You Trust: G.I. Joe or A.I. Joe?" Ideas and Trends, *New York Times,* 20 February 2005, 10.

Archival Sources

Camp Randall collection, University of Wisconsin Archives, Madison, Wisconsin

Dude Ranch brochure collection, American Heritage Center, University of Wyoming, Laramie

Frederick Jackson Turner Papers, The Huntington Library, San Marino, California; University of Wisconsin Archives, Madison

Hobart A. Baker Papers, Princeton University Archives, Princeton University, Princeton, New Jersey

Memorial Day Address collection, Pamphlet Collection, State Historical Society of Wisconsin, Madison

Stanford University Athletic Department Papers, Stanford University Special Collections and Archives, Stanford University, Stanford, California

Stanford University student scrapbook collection, Stanford University Special Collections and Archives, Stanford University, Stanford, California

Walter Camp Papers, Sterling Library, Yale University, New Haven, Connecticut

Western Americana, Bancroft Library, University of California, Berkeley

Western Americana, Huntington Library, San Marino California

Wilmington Race Riot collection, Wilmington Public Library, Wilmington, North Carolina

World War I Veterans' Survey, U.S. Army Military History Institute, Carlisle Barracks, Carlisle, Pennsylvania

As I suggest in chapter 1, a formative yet flawed historiographical context for my study of de-evolutionary masculinity begins with Frederick Jackson Turner's frontier thesis and its speculation that the mental trait of rugged individualism would be passed on to Americans living in a modern urban environment. The thesis's *naturalist* assumptions have informed a good part of U.S. cultural history and a greater part of men's history to an extent heretofore unrecognized. So in an effort to appreciate but separate out the frontier thesis from my own understanding of normative masculinity, it's worth tracing here just what an impact Turner had on subsequent historians' examination of late nineteenth- and early twentieth-century middle-class culture. While including in this historiography such key scholars as

John Higham and Michael Kimmel, I do not mean to dismiss their primary contributions to my study.

In the first sustained attempt by a professional historian to study the fate of pioneer traits in modern America, Frederic L. Paxson examined as a type of natural reflex to "the closing of the old frontier" the late nineteenth-century "Rise of Sport," *Mississippi Valley Historical Review* 4 (September 1917): 143–68. Paxson—Turner's replacement at Wisconsin and future winner of the Pulitzer Prize for his book on the nineteenth-century American West—explicitly recognized his debt to the frontier thesis, characterizing it as "the most distinguished feat in American historical scholarship in the last half century." Paxson did not mention the trait of individualism by name, but he did pin his whole argument on the carryover of a "spark of youth and life," a force, an energy that needed release outside of "[c]ity congestion." Turner's prediction that "the expansive character of American life" will find "a wider field for its exercise" led to Paxson's most provocative statement: "When the frontier closed in the eighties the habit of an open life was too strong to be changed offhand." The phrase "habit of an open life" documents the development of Turner's idea in the next generation of academic historians. It points to how cultural historians would interpret not only organized sports but the larger, de-evolutionary masculine turn to primitive and rugged forms.

"Habit of an open life" evokes a mind-set, a temperament, a predisposition toward free movement in unencumbered space. Like the frontier thesis, Paxson's article construes an almost literal equation between environment and intellect. If American attitudes and behavior bear the imprint of the frontier, then, as Paxson reasoned, the generation coming of age in the late 1870s and 1880s (during the closing of the frontier) holds the key to how that predisposition would express itself: "No people has passed through greater changes in a single lifetime." And, indeed, these were the Americans, according to Paxson, most responsible for the rise of sport. But why exactly did this generation feel the need to create, in his words, "a substitute for pioneer life" (143)? What mechanism was at work? While Paxson didn't really address this issue, his use of the word *habit* is instructive: it indicates movement away from a biological explanation of the "open life" compulsion; *habit*, compared to *trait*, suggests a learned rather than an inherited tendency to think and act in a certain way; it most likely meant for him something close to tradition or custom—a cultural accretion. And yet Paxson's essay betrays a naturalist, determinist grain as well: American sport emerged not through human will or decision making but as an automatic reflex to the frontier's demise. It, Paxson wrote, "could not have failed" to develop (167). Paxson, like Turner, may have employed this determinist language for rhetorical effect; it celebrates how a vigorous American sporting life was simply meant to be. But the trope also divulges in Paxson's work and subsequent cultural history an unexamined dependence on biological metaphor if not biology itself. This tendency comes at the expense of a sophisticated understanding of how culture worked to make "the open life" *seem* essential and how it selected sport and other virile activities over other ways late nineteenth-century Americans might have spent their time, energy, and attention.

Jump ahead some forty-eight years to John Higham's essay "The Reorientation of American Culture in the 1890s," originally published in 1965 but expanded in a lengthier, revised piece in *Writing American History: Essays on Modern Scholarship* (Bloomington: Indiana University Press, 1970), 73–102 This essay is a master synthesis of the widespread "rebellion against the constraints of a highly organized society" (88) and the text most responsible, after Turner's work, for extending the frontier thesis into the late twentieth-century study of middle-class American masculinity. Higham's essay includes a profile of the Wisconsin historian: Turner, William James, and Frank Lloyd Wright best represent the intellectual facet of the American "opposition to all closed and static patterns of order" (96). Higham paid little attention, though, to the specifics of the frontier thesis. Moreover, he didn't acknowledge that his own analysis of 1890s culture works within Turner's paradigm of American modernity, that geographically determined epoch in which a people used to the wide-open spaces of the West would have to mediate the interiority of the city. It is as if the frontier thesis had become so basic to American history that Higham couldn't or didn't have to bring it to light.

What Higham did was revivify Turner's thesis through artful historical description of the immediate postfrontier culture. "[I]t was everywhere," Higham wrote, "a hunger to break out of the frustrations, the routine, and the sheer dullness of an urban-industrial culture. It was everywhere an urge to be young, masculine, and adventurous"(79). Making explicit the gendered quality of the cultural reorientation, Higham offered as examples of this turn to virility many of the subjects and figures men's historians would consider in depth: "[a] rage for competitive athletics" and body building through weight lifting and other "rugged exercise"; a passion for hiking, camping, and hunting in the great outdoors, accompanied by intense literary interest in nature and the "wild West"; and a romanticization of the dangers of war, with Teddy Roosevelt—"the outstanding fugleman of the whole gladiatorial spirit"—as the archetype of the hypermasculine "strenuous life" (84). Higham also recognized that middle-class women appreciated the possibility of personal empowerment through masculine forms; in throwing off the Victorian ideal of sentimental femininity, the "New Woman" cultivated traits of boldness, vigor, and individuality.

In addition to the essay's synthetic quality, it displays unusual regard for the theory and methodology of cultural history. Higham was one of the most attentive students of the American history profession. And in this essay he presented a brief on the strength of cultural history, its expertise in "the configurations of attitude and habit that connect [the] different levels of experience at a given point in time" (76). He also discussed cultural history's limitations, including its difficulty in "locating the source of change." In fact, Higham had the presence of mind to ask that crucial question *why* Americans reacted so sharply to "the constrictions of a routinized society"? To which he replied: "Historians have no satisfactory answers to such large problems" (85). Higham may have been suggesting that this matter is best left to psychoanalysts or philosophers of metaphysics; historians don't have the tools to discern how the flux of time and space conspire to produce experience and meaning; all they can do is discover what was done and said and make interpretive observations about patterns of change in preponderances of thought and behavior. With academic historians well ensconced by the 1960s in the explanatory model of sociocultural construction, Higham didn't dare speak explicitly of a biological base to the strenuous life ideal of 1890s America. At the same time, though, if we look closely at the language he used to describe this cultural phenomenon, we can detect that same vague sociobiological metaphor as found in Turner's frontier thesis and Paxson's history of American sport.

After submitting that historians are unable to understand why the reorientation of American culture occurred, Higham risked something of an explanation anyway, writing that the strenuous life of the 1890s "was partly a revival of buried impulses" (86). A strategically indefinite reference to a psychological predisposition, "buried impulse" hints of an inherited mental trait, an instinctive component of national character. It renewed Turner's idea that intellectual traits selected by the frontier would live on in modern America. Admittedly, Higham never explicitly characterized the frame of mind as one of individualism. But he did describe it in terms close to individualism's corollary of restless nervous energy: "an exuberant libertarian aggressiveness, impatient of restraint and tradition." Probably the most influential point of Higham's essay is its repeated emphasis of how the "master impulse that seized American people in the 1890s" had been triggered by, in what would become the stock description of U.S. modernity, the closed space of a new urban environment. Higham's mechanistic dynamic of environmental stimulus and psychological response would take hold in the next generation of cultural history, where his connection between "artificiality and effeteness" of the city and the turn-of-the-century middle-class quest for hardy masculine experience also helped give rise to the subfield of men's history (78).

Several major works in American cultural history incorporated Higham's Turnerian theme of a middle-class reorientation toward ruggedness in the 1890s. Roderick Nash's *Wilderness and the American Mind* (New Haven: Yale University Press, 1967) and its examination of the cult of the primitive; *No Place of Grace: Antimodernism and the Transformation of American Culture, 1880–1920* (New York: Pantheon Books, 1981), Jackson Lears's analysis of the bourgeois drive for authentic experience; Elliott J. Gorn's *The Manly Art: Bare-Knuckle Prize Fighting in America* (Ithaca: Cornell University Press, 1986), including its sections on "The Strenuous Life" and "Fighting Clerks, Boxing Brahmins, Vigorous Victorians": taken together these studies developed the foundation for modern American men's history around the idea of a decisive late nineteenth-century cultural break with the past. In the hands of men's historians, this periodization marked the beginning of the crisis of masculinity.

The clearest early example of the Turner-Higham paradigm of American modernity leading to the historicizing of masculine crisis can be found in Joe L. Dubbert's book *A Man's Place: Masculinity in Transition* (Englewood Cliffs, N.J.: Prentice-Hall, 1979), one of the first full-length scholarly studies of manhood in the United States. While drawing liberally from Higham's "reorientation" essay for his discussion of sport, Dubbert organized the whole book around Turner's thesis and the late nineteenth-century "revolution" in middle-class male "self-perception" triggered by the close of the frontier. "In 1800, a vast, unsettled continent stretched before American men. It was possible for men to move," Dubbert wrote, "from point to point in space. They blazed trails, cleared land, built crude buildings, and likely as not moved again to repeat the process." The legendary frontiersmen Davie Crockett and Daniel Boone epitomized the "adventurous, courageous, strong-willed, autonomous males who survived mostly on the strength of their natural animal instincts" (9). But by 1890, Dubbert explained while citing Turner and the Census Bureau, this way of life had ended: "Here was a crisis for American males as the *space* paradigm was threatened" (80). Another early historical formulation of normative American manhood through a Turnerian conception of space comes from G. J. Barker-Benfield, *The Horrors of the Half-Known Life: Male Attitudes toward Women and Sexuality in Nineteenth Century America* (New York: Harper and Row, 1976), 13: "The possibilities for men who wanted to experience autonomy, to leave home and go not only to a new place for them but a new place for anyone, were enormous in nineteenth-century America: no checks on movement horizontally and formally, and none vertically for white men, together with a typing of life style that strenuously encouraged motion, from country to town, job to job, ambition to ambition, and the most striking area for this motion was the West." Twentieth-century men tried to accommodate the change by, among other strategies, adopting exaggerated forms of what they considered to be historically essential masculinity.

The work of Michael S. Kimmel, a leading scholar of American manhood, depends on an environmental determinist theme in his analysis of the turn-of-the-twentieth-century crisis of masculinity. In "The Contemporary 'Crisis' of Masculinity in Historical Perspective," in *The Making of Masculinities*, ed. Harry Brod (Boston: Allen and Urwin, 1987), he takes the frontier thesis at face value, substituting the concept of manhood for Turner's individual. "The early-nineteenth century provided a fertile environment for an expansive manhood," Kimmel writes literally of the wide-open space of the West. "But that era was over," Kimmel continues, supporting the statement with Turner's pronouncement that the frontier had closed in 1890. He goes on to speak of the "profound" masculine "rejection of the industrial city," quoting Higham's point that the back-to-nature movement provided "'an indispensable remedy for the artificiality and effeteness' of late-nineteenth-century urban life." This same dependence on the Turner-Higham spatial paradigm of American modernity can be found in Kimmel's broadly gauged synthesis *Manhood in America: A Cultural History* (New York: Free Press, 1995). With the crisis of masculinity organizing the book's coverage of the post–Civil War period, Kimmel refers to Higham's reorientation essay as "a classical historical statement of the problem and the variety of responses." But the most crucial text for Kimmel is Turner's thesis itself. He continually draws from it without recognizing its part in constructing the very ideology Kimmel tries to expose and criticize. By the late nineteenth century, Kimmel observes, American men "frett[ed] that the new crowds surrounding them would put them in a straightjacket. And sadly, escape was increasingly difficult" (87). Kimmel romanticizes the past: "In the rush of the new at the turn of the century, the old way of life was passing quickly from view—and with it the possibilities to test and prove manhood in the time-honored ways that American men had historically used" (89). In this instance at least, Kimmel's historical perspective is nearly subsumed by the frontier thesis.

Finally, a certain acceptance of Turner can be found in *Gunfighter Nation: The Myth of the Frontier in Twentieth-Century America* (New York: Atheneum, 1992), the last volume of Richard Slotkin's magisterial trilogy examining European American "regeneration through violence." The myth and symbol school—a line of American cultural history of which Slotkin's work is a leading example—has in many ways moved past Turner: his thesis has been transformed into a complex, interdisciplinary critique of the interlocking ideals of nature, frontier, and pioneer and their ideological hold on U.S. social relations, political culture, and literary imagination; celebration of rugged individualism and westward expansion has been replaced with close attention to the long history of imperialist transgressions over American Indians, the wilderness, and foreign peoples. But for all the modifications, qualifications, and revisions of Turner, this scholarship has remained largely within his framework of understanding American history. "When I imagined I was operating without hypotheses," Henry Nash Smith has commented about his book *Virgin Land: The American West as Symbol and Myth* (Cambridge, Mass.: Harvard University Press, 1950), "I was sometimes unwittingly using those of Turner" (Henry Nash Smith, "Symbol and Idea in *Virgin Land*," in *Ideology and Classic American Literature*, ed. Sacvan Bercovitch and Myra Jehlen [Cambridge: Cambridge University Press, 1986], 27). Slotkin himself has hardly been unwitting of Turner's thesis. *Gunfighter Nation* begins with an explicit comparison between it and Teddy Roosevelt's "frontier thesis" in *Winning of the West* and other writings. This is where Slotkin is too easy on Turner, however. Slotkin believes that Turner's historical vision rejected racialism and the mystique of frontier violence. In comparison to Roosevelt, of course, Turner's attention to racial violence *was* subdued. But, as argued in chapter 1, Turner did build the military defeat of Native Americans into his account of western settlement—just as he included the rugged quality of, in a classic example of compositional indirection, resisting Indian aggression in his reading of national character. To my mind, Turner's unexamined assumptions and understated martial ideals have been, in the long run, as ideologically powerful as Roosevelt's undisguised bloodlust.

Another basic and more critical context for my understanding of sexuality, gender, and masculinity is second-wave feminist scholarship, including key anthropological works Gayle Rubin, "The Traffic in Women: Notes on the 'Political Economy' of Sex," in *Toward an Anthropology of Women*, ed. Rayna R. Reiter (New York: Monthly Review Press, 1970); and Sherry Ortner, "Is Female to Male as Nature Is to Culture?" in *Woman, Culture, and Society*, ed. Michelle Zimbalist Rosaldo and Louise Lamphere. (Stanford: Stanford University Press, 1974). Academic feminist historical scholarship fundamental to my work includes Linda Gordon, *Woman's Body, Woman's Right: A Social History of Birth Control in America* (London: Penguin Books, 1976); Gerda Lerner, *The Creation of Patriarchy* (New York: Oxford University Press, 1986); Carroll Smith-Rosenberg, *Disorderly Conduct: Visions of Gender in Victorian America* (New York: A. A. Knopf, 1985); Rosalind Rosenberg, *Beyond Separate Spheres: Intellectual Roots of Modern Feminism* (New Haven: Yale University Press, 1982); and Nancy F. Cott, *The Grounding of Modern Feminism* (New Haven: Yale University Press, 1987).

My critical perspective on Darwinism and its construction of gender and sexual difference depend upon feminist work Donna Haraway, *Primate Visions: Gender, Race, and Nature in the World of Modern Science* (New York: Routledge, 1989) and *Simians, Cyborgs, and Women: The Reinvention of Nature* (New York: Routledge, 1991); Cynthia Eagle Russett, *Sexual Science: The Victorian Construction of Womanhood* (Cambridge, Mass.: Harvard University Press, 1989); Barbara B. Smuts, "The Evolutionary Origins of Patriarchy," *Human Nature* 6 (1995): 1–32; Simone de Beauvoir, "The Data of Biology," in *The Second Sex* (1949; repr., New York: Vintage Books, 1989); Anne Fausto-Sterling, *Myths of Gender: Biological Theories about Women and Men*, 2nd ed. (New York: Basic Books, 1992) and *Sexing the Body: Gender Politics and the Construction of Sexuality* (New York: Basic Books, 2000); Sandra Harding, *The Science Question in Feminism* (Ithaca: Cornell University Press, 1986); and Evelyn Fox Keller, *Reflections on Gender and Science* (New Haven: Yale University Press, 1985). Further important scholarship on evolutionary theory and the interrelationship between biology and culture includes Ernst Mayr, *One Long Argument: Charles Darwin and the Genesis of Modern Evolutionary Thought* (Cambridge, Mass.: Harvard University Press, 1991); Carl N. Degler, *In Search of Human Nature: The Decline and Revival of Darwinism in American Social Thought* (New York: Oxford University Press, 1991); William H. Durham, *Coevolution: Genes, Culture, and Human Diversity* (Stanford: Stanford University Press, 1991); Paul Ehrlich, *Human Natures: Genes, Culture, and Human Diversity* (Washington, D.C.: Island Press, 2000).

The most immediate historiographical context for my study—the work to which I owe the greatest debt—is the critical scholarship on American manhood that takes its subject to be the product of social construction. I began with Anthony Rotundo, "Body and Soul: Changing Ideals of Middle-Class Manhood, 1770–1920," *Journal of Social History* 16 (1983):

23–38, and *American Manhood: Transformations in Masculinity from the Revolution to the Present Era* (New York: Basic Books, 1993). Also very influential has been the distinctly pro-feminist scholarship of Michael Kimmel: "Men's Responses to Feminism at the Turn of the Century," *Gender and Society* 1 (September 1987): 261–83; "The Contemporary 'Crisis' of Masculinity in Historical Perspective," in *The Making of Masculinities*, ed. Harry Brod (Boston: Allen and Urwin, 1987); *Manhood in America: A Cultural History* (New York: Free Press, 1996); and *The Gendered Society* (New York: Oxford University Press, 2000).

Rotundo and Kimmel have employed an ideal-based model of men's history, an approach which Gail Bederman has improved upon in "'Civilization,' the Decline of Middle-Class Manliness, and Ida B. Wells's Antilynching Campaign (1892–94)," *Radical History Review* 52 (Winter 1992): 5–30; "'The Women Have Had Charge of the Church Work Long Enough': Men and the Religion Forward Movement of 1911–1912 and the Masculinization of Middle-Class Protestantism," *American Quarterly* 41 (September 1989): 432–65; *Manliness and Civilization: A Cultural History of Gender and Race in the United States, 1880–1917* (Chicago: University of Chicago Press, 1995). Bederman's book contributed greatly to my understanding of evolutionary thought and its determination of race, gender, and masculinity; as reflected in my endnotes, I have benefited from her critical interpretations of such key masculinist subjects as Teddy Roosevelt and *Tarzan;* from my perspective, though, her work overemphasizes the importance of recapitulation theory in turn-of-the-twentieth-century social thought while also exhibiting the interpretive strengths and limitations of Foucault for gender historians.

Accomplished works in cultural history have made significant contributions to men's history. The seemingly reflexive late Victorian cognitive turn to the past is examined in monumental fashion in Lears, *No Place of Grace*. Gorn's *The Manly Art* is a model of cultural history and historical writing; it includes a valuable summary and analysis of the middle- and upper-class male fixation on strenuosity and sport in the late nineteenth-century. Literary historian David Leverenz's studies of manhood are particularly incisive: *Manhood and the American Renaissance* (Ithaca: Cornell University Press, 1989); "The Last Real Man in America: From Natty Bumppo to Batman," *American Literary History* 3 (Winter 1991): 753–81. And Slotkin's *Gunfighter Nation* and its analysis of "regeneration through violence" at the turn of the century is a core source for my book.

Other valuable work on American manhood includes Peter Filene, *Him/Her/Self: Sex Roles in Modern America* (New York: Harcourt Brace Jovanovich, 1975); Mark C. Carnes and Clyde Griffen, eds., *Meanings for Manhood: Constructions of Masculinity in Victorian America.* (Chicago: University of Chicago Press, 1990); R. W. Connell, *Masculinities* (Berkeley: University of California Press, 1995); Kevin White, *The First Sexual Revolution: The Emergence of Male Heterosexuality in Modern America* (New York: New York University Press, 1992); Rupert Wilkinson, *American Tough: The Tough-Guy Tradition and American Character* (Westport, Conn.: Greenwood Press, 1984); Kim Townsend, *Manhood at Harvard: William James and Others* (Cambridge, Mass.: Harvard University Press, 1996). For two interesting historical studies that venture into sociobiology, see David Courtwright, *Violent Land: Single Men and Social Disorder from the Frontier to the Inner City* (Cambridge, Mass.: Harvard University Press, 1996); Robert S. McElvaine, *Eve's Seed: Biology, the Sexes, and the Course of History* (New York: McGraw-Hill, 2001). Two recent historiographical essays have placed a finer critical edge on the field of men's history: Bruce Traister, "Academic Viagra: The Rise of

American Masculinity Studies," *American Quarterly* 52 (2000): 274–304; Toby L. Ditz, "The New Men's History and the Peculiar Absence of Gendered Power: Some Remedies from Early American History," *Gender and History* 16 (April 2004): 1–35. Of a very different historiographical moment, yet helpful for relativizing masculinity, are the "male-liberationist," profeminist works by John Charles Cooper, *A New Kind of Man* (Philadelphia: Westminster Press, 1972); and Jack Nichols, *Men's Liberation: A New Definition of Masculinity* (New York: Penguin Books, 1975).

My analysis of the de-evolutionary turn tries to compose a cognitive-emotional-dispositional dispensation of masculinity—a type of intellectual history that relies on anthropology and psychology. Most important for the imbrication of culture and meaning is Clifford Geertz, *Interpretation of Cultures* (New York: Basic Books, 1973); Geertz, *Available Light: Anthropological Reflections on Philosophical Topics* (Princeton: Princeton University Press, 2000). Other helpful works include Nancy J. Chodorow, *The Power of Feelings: Personal Meanings in Psychoanalysis, Gender, and Culture* (New Haven: Yale University Press, 1999); Richard S. Lazarus, *Emotion and Adaptation* (Oxford: Oxford University Press, 2000); Aaron T. Beck, *Prisoners of Hate: The Cognitive Basis of Anger, Hostility, and Violence* (New York: Harper Collins, 1999); Martha C. Nussbaum, *Upheavals of Thought: The Intelligence of Emotions* (Cambridge: Cambridge University Press, 2001); Mari Jo Buhle, *Feminism and Its Discontents: A Century of Struggle with Psychoanalysis* (Cambridge, Mass.: Harvard University Press, 2000); Tom Lutz, *American Nervousness, 1903: An Anecdotal History* (Ithaca: Cornell University Press, 1991); Elizabeth Lunbeck, *The Psychiatric Persuasion: Knowledge, Gender, and Power in Modern America* (Princeton: Princeton University Press, 1994).

For chapter 1 and the gendered nature of individualism I have benefited from Linda Kerber, "Can a Woman Be an Individual? The Discourse of Self-Reliance," *Massachusetts Review* 30 (Winter 1989): 589–609; Elizabeth Fox-Genovese, *Feminism without Illusions: A Critique of Individualism* (Chapel Hill: North Carolina University Press, 1991); Nancy F. Cott, "On Men's History and Women's History," in *Meanings for Manhood: Constructions of Masculinity in Victorian America*, ed. Mark C. Carnes and Clyde Griffen (Chicago: University of Chicago Press, 1990), 205–12. Wilfred M. McClay, *The Masterless: Self and Society in Modern America* (Chapel Hill: University of North Carolina Press, 1994) is an impressive sustained analysis of individualism in American thought. Also valuable is Myra Jehlen, *American Incarnation: The Individual, the Nation, and the Continent* (Cambridge, Mass.: Harvard University Press, 1986).

No American historian has received more scholarly attention than Frederick Jackson Turner. Although it gets Turner wrong, Richard Hofstadter, *The Progressive Historians: Turner, Beard, Parrington* (New York: Alfred Knopf, 1968) is still a landmark historiographical work. Ray Allen Billington, *Frederick Jackson Turner: Historian, Scholar, Teacher* (New York: Oxford University Press, 1973), and Allan G. Bogue, *Frederick Jackson Turner: Strange Roads Going Down* (Norman: University of Oklahoma Press, 1998) are meticulous, authoritative, different, and invaluable to studying Turner. A powerful assessment of Turner's impact on western history is William Cronon, "Revisiting the Vanishing Frontier: The Legacy of Frederick Jackson Turner," *Western Historical Quarterly* 18 (1987): 157–76. A most valuable monograph on academic history, including its incisive account of Turner, is John Higham, *History: Professional Scholarship in America* (1965; repr., Baltimore: Johns Hopkins University Press, 1989). My understanding of Turner was greatly enriched by conversations with his student Merle Curti.

Leading works on American social science include George W. Stocking Jr., *Race, Culture, and Evolution: Essays in the History of Anthropology* (New York: Free Press, 1968); Thomas L. Haskell, *The Emergence of Professional Social Science: The American Social Science Association and the Crisis of Authority* (Urbana: University of Illinois Press, 1977); Mary O. Furner, *Advocacy and Objectivity: A Crisis in the Professionalization of American Social Science, 1865–1905* (Lexington: University of Kentucky Press, 1975); Dorothy Ross, *The Origins of American Social Science* (New York: Cambridge University Press, 1991).

For European American historical understanding of American Indians I have relied on Brian W. Dippie, *The Vanishing American: White Attitudes and U.S. Indian Policy* (Middletown: Wesleyan University Press, 1982); Kevin Klein, *Frontiers of Historical Imagination: Narrating the European Conquest of Native America, 1890–1990* (Berkeley: University of California Press, 1997); Harvey Pearce, *Savagism and Civilization: A Study of the Indian and the American Mind* (Berkeley: University of California Press, 1988); Philip J. Deloria, *Playing Indian* (New Haven: Yale University Press, 1998); Robert F. Berkhofer Jr., *The White Man's Indian: Images of the American Indian from Columbus to the Present* (New York: Vintage Books, 1979); Shari M. Huhndorf, *Going Native: Indians in the American Cultural Imagination* (Ithaca: Cornell University Press, 2001). Studies on primitivism and the American West include Helen Carr, "Reading the Savage Mind," in *Inventing the American Primitive: Politics, Gender and the Representation of Native American Literary Traditions, 1789–1936* (New York: New York University Press, 1996); Mary Lawlor, *Recalling the Wild: Naturalism and the Closing of the American West* (New Brunswick: Rutgers University Press, 2000). A very valuable account of the inauthenticity of the western wilderness is William Cronon, "The Trouble with Wilderness; or, Getting Back to the Wrong Nature," in *Uncommon Ground: Toward Reinventing Nature,* ed. William Cronon (New York: W. W. Norton, 1995).

My discussion of gender and individuality within pre–World War I Greenwich Village has relied upon Cott, *Grounding of Modern Feminism;* Casey Blake, *Beloved Community: The Cultural Criticism of Randolph Bourne, Van Wyck Brooks, Waldo Frank, and Lewis Mumford* (Chapel Hill: University of North Carolina Press, 1990); Thomas Bender, *New York Intellect: A History of Intellectual Life in New York City* (New York: Random House, 1987); Christine Stansell, *American Moderns: Bohemian New York and the Creation of a New Century* (New York: Metropolitan Books, 2000); Leslie Fishbein, *Rebels in Bohemia: The Radicals of The Masses* (Chapel Hill: University of North Carolina Press, 1982); Edward Abrahams, *The Lyrical Left: Randolph Bourne, Alfred Stieglitz, and the Origins of Cultural Radicalism in America* (Charlottesville: University Press of Virginia, 1986); Rick Beard and Leslie Cohen Berlowitz, ed., *Greenwich Village: Culture and Counterculture* (New Brunswick: Rutgers University Press, 1993); Adele Heller and Lois Rudnick, eds., *1915: The Cultural Moment* (New Brunswick: Rutgers University Press, 1991); Christopher Lasch, *The New Radicalism in America, 1889–1963: The Intellectual as a Social Type* (New York: Vintage Books, 1965); Henry F. May, *The End of American Innocence: A Study of the First Years of Our Time, 1912–1917* (London: Jonathan Cape, 1960); Daniel Aaron, *Writers on the Left* (Oxford: Oxford University Press, 1961).

The cultural history of the modern "Old West" is a wide-open field of study. My discussion relies on Hal Rothman, *Devil's Bargains: Tourism in the Twentieth-Century American West* (Lawrence: University of Kansas Press, 1998); Earl Pomeroy, *In Search of the Golden West: The Tourist in Western America* (New York: Alfred A. Knopf, 1957). For women's rodeo, see Mary Lou LeCompte, *Cowgirls of the Rodeo: Pioneer Professional Athletes* (Urbana: University of Illinois Press, 1993); and for dude ranches, Michael Wallis, *The Real Wild West: The 101 Ranch and the Creation of the American West* (New York: St. Martin's Griffin, 1999).

My study in chapter 2 of masculine literary culture benefited from Leverenz, *Manhood and the American Renaissance;* Amy Kaplan, "Romancing the Empire: The Embodiment of American Masculinity in the Popular Historical Novel of the 1890s," *American Literary History* 2 (Winter 1990): 659–90; and Christopher Wilson, *The Labor of Words: Literary Professionalism in the Progressive Era* (Athens: University of Georgia Press, 1985). The work of John G. Cawelti, including *Adventure, Mystery, and Romance: Formula Stories as Art and Popular Culture* (Chicago: University of Chicago Press, 1976), has been very helpful in my examination of popular literary history.

Murder in the American literary imagination is well covered in David Brion Davis, *Homicide in American Fiction, 1798–1860* (Ithaca: Cornell University Press, 1957); Richard Slotkin, *Regeneration through Violence: The Mythology of the American Frontier, 1600–1860* (Middletown: Wesleyan University Press, 1973); Richard Slotkin, *The Fatal Environment: The Myth of the Frontier in the Age of Industrialization, 1800–1890* (Middletown: Wesleyan University Press, 1986); and Slotkin, *Gunfighter Nation.*

For sport hunting in American culture, I have relied on Daniel Justin Herman, *Hunting and the American Imagination* (Washington, D.C.: Smithsonian Institution Press, 2001); Matt Cartmill, *A View to a Death in the Morning: Hunting and Nature through History* (Cambridge, Mass.: Harvard University Press, 1993); Stuart A. Marks, *Southern Hunting in Black and White: Nature, History, and Ritual in a Carolina Community* (Princeton: Princeton University Press, 1991)

The most valuable studies of the Western in turn-of-the-century popular literature and culture include Jane Tompkins, *West of Everything: The Inner Life of the Westerns* (New York: Oxford University Press, 1992); Lee Clark Mitchell, *Westerns: Making the Man in Fiction and Film* (Chicago: University of Chicago Press, 1996); Slotkin, *Gunfighter Nation;* John G. Cawelti, *The Six-Gun Mystique* (Bowling Green: Bowling Green University Popular Press, 1971); John Seeyle, introduction to *Stories of the Old West: Tales of the Mining Camp, Cavalry Troop, and Cattle Ranch,* ed. John Seeyle (New York: Penguin Books, 1994); Will Wright, *Six Guns and Society: A Structural Study of the Western* (Berkeley: University of California Press, 1975); Joy S. Kasson, *Buffalo Bill's Wild West: Celebrity, Memory, and Popular History* (New York: Hill and Wang, 2000)

The anthropological approach to college football in chapter 3 works from a long-standing relationship between that social science and sport, a starting point for which is Johan Huizinga, *Homo Ludens: A Study of the Play Element in Culture* (1950; repr., Boston: Beacon Press, 1995); a very good example of the effectiveness of anthropology in sports history is John J. MacAloon, *This Great Symbol: Pierre de Coubertin and the Origins of the Modern Olympic Games* (Chicago: University of Chicago Press, 1981). Synthesis between anthropology and cultural history is advanced by the prolific anthropologist Adam Kuper, including *Culture: The Anthropologists' Account* (Cambridge, Mass.: Harvard University Press, 1999). Ronald G. Walters, "Signs of the Times: Clifford Geertz and Historians," *Social Research* 47 (1980): 537–56, is a wonderfully practical discussion of the topic; also helpful is Jean-Christophe Agnew, "History and Anthropology: Scenes from a Marriage," *Yale Journal of Criticism* 3 (1990): 29–50.

For the early years of American college football, two studies stand out: Michael Oriard,

Reading Football: How the Popular Press Created an American Spectacle (Chapel Hill: University of North Carolina Press, 1993); and David Reisman and Reuel Denney, "Football in America: A Study in Cultural Diffusion," *American Quarterly* 3 (Winter 1951): 309–25. Parke H. Davis, *Football: The American Intercollegiate Game* (New York: Charles Scribner's Sons, 1911) is very useful for its detailed factual account of the subject. Valuable recent studies include Robin Lester, *Stagg's University: The Rise, Decline and Fall of Big-Time Football at Chicago* (Urbana: University of Illinois Press, 1999); and John Sayle Watterson, *College Football: History, Spectacle, Controversy* (Baltimore: Johns Hopkins University Press, 2000). Broader studies of American sport with good focus on football include Ronald Smith, *Sports and Freedom: The Rise of Big-Time College Athletics* (New York: Oxford University Press, 1988), 83–88; Elliott J. Gorn and Warren Goldstein, *A Brief History of American Sports* (Chicago: Lawrence Hill Press, 1993); and Donald J. Mrozek, *Sport and American Mentality, 1880–1910* (Knoxville: University of Tennessee Press, 1983), 166–71. My understanding of football and American sport is greatly indebted to the work of Patrick B. Miller, including "The Manly, the Moral, and the Proficient," *Journal of Sport History* 24 (Fall 1997): 285–316; "To 'Bring the Race Along Rapidly': Sport, Student Culture, and Educational Mission at Historically Black Colleges during the Interwar Years," *History of Education Quarterly* 35 (Summer 1995); and *The Playing Fields of American Culture: Athletics and Higher Education, 1850–1945* (New York: Oxford University Press, forthcoming). A sharp, critical if flawed study of masculinity and American sport from an explicitly feminist perspective is Varda Burstyn, *The Rites of Men: Manhood, Politics, and the Culture of Sport* (Toronto: University of Toronto Press, 1999).

The history, anthropology, and psychology of war making constitute an expansive field of study, a composite subject area from which chapter 4 on war in the head draws liberally. A number of broadly gauged works have contributed to my understanding of masculinist psychology and war making: John Glenn Gray, *The Warriors: Reflections on Men in Battle* (New York: Harper and Row, 1967); Samuel Hynes, *The Solders' Tale: Bearing Witness to Modern War* (New York: Penguin, 1997); Marcus Cunliffe, *Soldiers and Civilians: The Martial Spirit in America* (Boston: Little, Brown, 1968); Michael S. Sherry, *In the Shadow of War: The United States since the 1930s* (New Haven: Yale University Press, 1995); Gwynne Dyer, *War* (New York: Crown Publishers, 1985); Chris Hedges, *War Is a Force That Gives Us Meaning* (New York: Public Affairs, 2002); Klaus Theweleit, *Male Fantasies*, 2 vols. (1978; repr., Minneapolis: University of Minnesota Press, 1989); Joshua Goldstein, *War and Gender: How Gender Shapes the War System and Vice Versa* (Cambridge: Cambridge University Press, 2001); and Barbara Ehrenreich, *Blood Rites: Origins and History of the Passions of War* (New York: Metropolitan Books, 1997). Extremely helpful works on evolutionary theory and social thought regarding war are Paul Crook, *Darwinism, War and History: The Debate over the Biology of War from the "Origin of the Species" to the First World War* (Cambridge: Cambridge University Press, 1994); and Doyne Dawson, "The Origins of War: Biological and Anthropological Theories," *History and Theory* 35 (February 1996): 1–28

The masculinist warrior mentality is intimately related to nationalism, I argue—a line of analysis stemming from the rich work of George Mosse, including *Nationalism and Sexuality: Respectability and Abnormal Sexuality in Modern Europe* (New York: Howard Fertig, 1985). Other valuable work on nationalism includes Hans Kohn, *The Idea of Nationalism: A Study in Its Origins and Background* (New York: Macmillan Company, 1944); Merle Curti, *The Roots of American Loyalty* (New York: Columbia University Press, 1946); John Higham, "The Nationalist Nineties," in *Strangers in the Land: Patterns of American Nativism, 1860–1925* (New York: Atheneum, 1963); Eric Hobsbawm, *Nations and Nationalism since 1780: Programme, Myth, Reality* (New York: Cambridge University Press, 1990); Kristin L. Hoganson, *Fighting for American Manhood: How Gender Politics Provoked the Spanish-American and Philippine-American Wars* (New Haven: Yale University Press, 1998); Cecilia Elizabeth O'Leary, *To Die For: The Paradox of American Patriotism* (Princeton: Princeton University Press, 1999); Melinda Lawson, *Patriot Fires: Forging a New American Nationalism in the Civil War North* (Lawrence: University Press of Kansas, 2002); and Robert B. Westbrook, *Why We Fought: Forging American Obligations in World War II* (Washington, D.C.: Smithsonian Books, 2004).

The historical literature on the memory and cultural legacy of the Civil War is immense, impressive, and important. I have gained the most from David W. Blight, *Race and Reunion: The Civil War in American Memory* (Cambridge, Mass.: Harvard University Press 2001); Nina Silber, *The Romance of Reunion: Northerners and Southerners, 1865–1900* (Chapel Hill: University of North Carolina, 1993); O'Leary, *To Die For;* Paul Buck, *Road to Reunion, 1865–1900* (Boston: Little, Brown, 1937); Robert Penn Warren, *The Legacy of the Civil War* (Cambridge, Mass.: Harvard University Press, 1961). The most valuable studies of Civil War literature are Edmund Wilson, *Patriotic Gore: Studies in the Literature of the American Civil War* (New York: Oxford University Press, 1966); Daniel Aaron, *The Unwritten War: American Writers and the Civil War* (New York: Alfred A. Knopf, 1973); and Alice Fahs, *The Imagined Civil War: Popular Literature of the North and South, 1861–1865* (Chapel Hill: University of North Carolina Press, 2001).

My treatment of the Spanish-American War relies most on Gerald F. Linderman, *The Mirror of War: American Society and the Spanish-American War* (Ann Arbor: University of Michigan Press, 1974); Hoganson, *Fighting for American Manhood;* O'Leary, *To Die For;* and Richard Hofstadter, "Cuba, the Philippines, and Manifest Destiny," in *The Paranoid Style in American Politics and Other Essays* (New York: Alfred A. Knopf, 1966).

Works essential to my analysis of World War I are David M. Kennedy, *Over Here: The First World War and American Society* (New York: Oxford University Press, 1980); Edward Coffman, *The War to End All Wars: The American Military Experience in World War I* (New York: Oxford University Press, 1968); and Steven A. Reich, "Soldiers of Democracy: Black Texans and the Fight for Citizenship, 1917–1921," *Journal of American History* 82 (March 1996): 1478–1504.

A relatively new subfield of military history might be labeled battle culture studies, leading examples of which include Gerald F. Linderman, *Embattled Courage: The Experience of Combat in the American Civil War* (New York: Free Press, 1987); James M. McPherson, *For Cause and Comrades: Why Men Fought in the Civil War* (New York: Oxford University Press, 1997); Earl J. Hess, *The Union Soldier in Battle: Enduring the Ordeal of Combat* (Lawrence: University Press of Kansas, 1997); Reid Mitchell, *Civil War Soldiers: Their Expectations and Their Experiences* (New York: Simon and Schuster, 1988); Craig M. Cameron, *American Samurai: Myth, Imagination, and the Conduct of Battle in the First Marine Division, 1941–1951* (New York: Cambridge University Press, 1994); Peter S. Kindsvatter, *American Soldiers: Ground Combat in the World War, Korea, and Vietnam* (Lawrence: University Press of Kansas, 2003); and Gerald Linderman, *The World Within: America's Combat Experience in World War II* (Cambridge, Mass.: Harvard University Press, 1997).

As part of battle culture studies, scholarship is focusing on the act of killing itself: Joanna

Bourke, *An Intimate History of Killing: Face to Face Killing in 20th Century Warfare* (New York: Basic Books, 1999); Niall Ferguson, "The Death Instinct: Why Men Fought," in *The Pity of War* (New York: Basic Books, 1999), 336–66; Charles Royster, *The Destructive War: William Tecumseh Sherman, Stonewall Jackson, and the Americans* (New York: Alfred A. Knopf, 1991); and Dave Grossman, *On Killing: The Psychological Cost of Learning to Kill in War and Society* (Boston: Little, Brown, 1995).

Discussion in chapter 5 of sexual violence and the legal regime that has supported it is based on key works in feminist theory and queer studies: Adrienne Rich, "Compulsory Heterosexuality and Lesbian Existence" (1980), in *Blood, Bread, and Poetry: Selected Prose, 1979–1985* (New York: W. W. Norton, 1986); Rubin, "The Traffic in Women"; Gayle Rubin, "Thinking Sex: Notes for a Radical Theory of a Politics of Sexuality" (1984), reprinted in *The Lesbian and Gay Studies Reader*, ed. Henry Abelove, Michlele Aina Barale, and David M. Halperin (New York: Routledge, 1994), 3–44; Eve Kosofsky Sedgwick, *Between Men: English Literature and Male Homosocial Desire* (New York: Columbia University Press, 1985); Michel Foucault, *The History of Sexuality: An Introduction* (1978; repr., New York: Vintage Books, 1990); Jonathan Ned Katz, *The Invention of Heterosexuality* (New York: Dutton, 1995). Feminist jurisprudence is an unusually dynamic and pragmatic line of scholarship, a leading example of which is Jill Hasday, "Contest and Consent: A Legal History of Marital Rape," *California Law Review* 88 (2000): 1373–1505. A landmark work in gender history—and one invaluable to my study—is George Chauncey, *Gay New York: Gender, Urban Culture, and the Making of the Gay Male World, 1890–1940* (New York: Basic Books, 1995).

Most helpful works on post-Reconstruction lynching and its sexual and racial politics include Jacquelyn Dowd Hall, *Revolt against Chivalry: Jessie Daniel Ames and the Women's Campaign against Lynching* (New York: Columbia University Press, 1974); Glenda Elizabeth Gilmore, *Gender and Jim Crow: Women and the Politics of White Supremacy in North Carolina, 1896–1920* (Chapel Hill: University of North Carolina Press, 1996); Hazel V. Carby, "On the Threshold of the Women's Era: Lynching, Empire and Sexuality in Black Feminist Theory," in *"Race," Writing and Difference*, ed. Henry Louis Gates (Chicago: University of Chicago Press, 1986), 301–16. Also important are W. Fitzhugh Brundage, *Lynching in the New South: Georgia and Virginia, 1880–1930* (Urbana: University of Illinois Press, 1993); Philip Dray, *At the Hands of Persons Unknown: The Lynching of Black America* (New York: Modern Library, 2003); W. Fitzhugh Brundage, ed., *Under Sentence of Death: Lynching in the South* (Chapel Hill: University of North Carolina Press, 1998); Stewart Tolnay, *A Festival of Violence: An Analysis of Southern Lynchings, 1882–1930* (Urbana: University of Illinois Press, 1992). For the Wilmington massacre I have relied on David S. Cecelski and Timothy B. Tyson, *Democracy Betrayed: The Wilmington Race Riot of 1898 and Its Legacy* (Chapel Hill: University of North Carolina Press, 1998); H. Leon Prather Sr., *We Have Taken a City: Wilmington Racial Massacre and Coup of 1898* (Rutherford: Farleigh Dickinson University Press, 1984).

For the heat-of-passion defense and sexual violence, Jeremy Horder, *Provocation and Responsibility* (Oxford: Clarendon Press, 1992) is extremely valuable for the early modern English origins of the doctrine. For its modern American manifestations, Victoria Nourse, "Passion's Progress: Modern Law Reform and the Provocation Defense," *Yale Law Journal* 106 (March 1997): 1331–1421; Donna K. Coker, "Heat of Passion and Wife Killing: Men Who Batter/Men Who Kill," *Southern California Review of Law and Women's Studies* 2 (Fall 1992): 71–130; James J. Sing, "Culture as Sameness: Toward a Synthetic View of Provocation and

Culture in the Criminal Law," *Yale Law Journal* 108 (May 1999): 1845–84; Deborah E. Milgate, "The Flame Flickers, but Burns On: Modern Judicial Application of the Ancient Heat of Passion Defense," *Rutgers Law Review* 51 (Fall 1998): 193–227; Elizabeth Rapaport, "Capital Murder and the Domestic Discount: A Study of Capital Domestic Murder in the Post-Furman Era," *SMU Law Review* 49 (July–August 1996): 1507–48; Cynthia Lee, *Murder and the Reasonable Man: Passion and Fear in the Criminal Courtroom* (New York: New York University Press, 2003)

The most helpful studies of the cultural defense include Leti Volpp, "(Mis)Identifying Culture: Asian Women and the 'Cultural Defense,'" *Harvard Women's Law Journal* 17 (1994): 57–80; Daina C. Chiu, "The Cultural Defense: Beyond Exclusion, Assimilation, and Guilty Liberalism," *California Law Review* 82 (July 1994): 1053–1124; and Alison Dundes Renteln, *The Cultural Defense* (New York: Oxford University Press, 2004).

Among the historical works on the institution of marriage in America, I have relied most on Hendrik Hartog, *Man and Wife in America: A History* (Cambridge, Mass.: Harvard University Press, 2000); and Nancy F. Cott, *Public Vows: A History of Marriage and the Nation* (Cambridge, Mass.: Harvard University Press, 2002).

The rise of body building in the United States is covered in S. Harvey Green, *Fit for America: Health, Fitness, Sport, and American Society* (New York: Pantheon Books, 1986); David L. Chapman, *Sandow the Magnificent: Eugen Sandow and the Beginnings of Bodybuilding* (Urbana: University of Illinois Press, 1994); Robert Ernst, *Weakness Is a Crime: The Life of Bernarr MacFadden* (Syracuse: Syracuse University Press, 1991); and John F. Kasson, *Houdini, Tarzan, and the Perfect Man: The White Male Body and the Challenge of Modernity in America* (New York: Hill and Wang, 2001).

More broadly formulated studies that go to male body type and size include Chauncey, *Gay New York;* Susan Bordo, *The Male Body: A New Look at Men in Public and Private* (New York: Farrar, Straus and Giroux, 1999); Kevin J. Mumford, "'Lost Manhood' Found: Male Sexual Impotence and Victorian Culture in the United States," in *American Sexual Politics: Sex, Gender, and Race since the Civil War,* ed. John C. Fout and Maura Shaw Tantillo (Chicago: University of Chicago Press, 1990), 75–99; and Clifford Putney, *Muscular Christianity: Manhood and Sports in Protestant America, 1880–1920* (Cambridge, Mass.: Harvard University Press, 2001).